Progress in Forensic Genetics 10

Progress in Forensic Genetics 10

Proceedings of the 20th International ISFG Congress held in Arcachon, France between 9 and 13 September 2003.

Editors:

Professor Christian Doutremépuich
Laboratoire d'Hématologie
Université Victor Ségalen
U.F.R. des Sciences Pharmaceutiques
Bordeaux
FRANCE

Niels Morling, MD DSc
Associate Professor, Director
Department of Forensic Genetics
Institute of Forensic Medicine
University of Copenhagen
DENMARK

ELSEVIER

2004

ELSEVIER B.V.
Sara Burgerhartstraat 25
P.O. Box 211, 1000 AE Amsterdam
The Netherlands

ELSEVIER Inc.
525 B Street, Suite 1900
San Diego, CA 92101-4495
USA

ELSEVIER Ltd
The Boulevard, Langford Lane
Kidlington, Oxford OX5 1GB
UK

ELSEVIER Ltd
84 Theobalds Road
London WC1X 8RR
UK

First edition 2004

Library of Congress Cataloging in Publication Data
A catalog record from the Library of Congress has been applied for.

British Library Cataloguing in Publication Data
International Society for Forensic Genetics. Conference (20th : 2003 : Arcachon, France)
Progress in forensic genetics 10 : proceedings of the 20th International ISFG Congress held in Arcachon, France between 9 and 13 September 2003. - (International congress series ; 1261)
1. Forensic genetics - Congresses
I. Title II. Doutremepuich, C. (Christian) III. Morling, Niels 614.1

ISBN 0444515054

International Congress Series No. 1261
ISBN: 0-444-51505-4
ISSN: 0531-5131

∞ The paper used in this publication meets the requirements of ANSI/NISO Z39.48-1992 (Permanence of Paper).
Printed in The Netherlands.

To
Françoise Doutremépuich, biologist

ELSEVIER

International Congress Series 1261 (2004) vii

www.ics-elsevier.com

Preface

The 20th International Congress of the International Society for Forensic Genetics was held from the 9th to the 13th of September 2003 in Arcachon, France. The president of the congress was Professor Christian Doutremépuich, Laboratoire d'Hématologie, Université Victor Ségalen, U.F.R. des Sciences Pharmaceutiques, Bordeaux, France.

A pre-congress Forum on DNA Databases was held on the 9th of September 2003 with presentations by invited international speakers. The congress began on 10th September 2003 and had six invited speakers on specialist themes of forensic interest, 52 selected, oral presentations as well as 239 posters.

The board of the ISFG presented a prize for the best oral presentation to Ms. Martina Nilsson for the work M. Nilsson, U. Gyllensten and M. Allen: Sequence analysis of the complete mitochondrial genome. The prize for the best poster was given to Ms. Christine Keyser-Tracqui for the work C. Keyser-Tracqui, P. Blandin, E. Petkovski, F.X. Ricaut, E. Crubezy and B. Ludes: SNP analysis of a 2000-year-old Xiongnu population from Mongolia.

This volume of Progress in Forensic Genetics contains mainly short three-page manuscripts of the oral and poster presentations at the congress. The manuscripts have been through a reviewing and an editing procedure in order to maintain the high quality of the series and in order to keep the total volume of the book at a level that can be afforded by the ISFG. However, priority was given to fast publication of the volume and, therefore, the manuscripts were not edited in details if the message was clear to the reader. We hope that the readers will understand and agree in this decision.

Professor Christian Doutremépuich
President of the ISFG Congress
Niels Morling
Treasurer of the ISFG

doi:10.1016/j.ics.2004.01.008

20th International ISFG Congress
Arcachon, 9th–13th of September 2003

Congress President
Christian Doutremépuich

ISFG Board and Scientific Committee
Angel Carracedo (Spain)
Bjørnar Olaisen (Norway)
Wolfgang Mayr (Austria)
Niels Morling (Denmark)
Peter Schneider (Germany)

Local Congress Arrangement Committee
Marie-Paule Carlotti
Marie-Hélène Cherpin
Françoise Doutremépuich
Oscar Garcia-Fernandez
Bertrand Ludes
Miriam Martinez de Pancorbo
Begona Martinez Jarreta
Jean-Paul Moisan
Philippe Rouger
Myriam Sabatier
Dominique Saint Dizier
Véronique Van Huffel

Congress Organisers
Macs'Organisation
Marianne Pujol
BP-118
F-33313 Arcachon Cedex
France
Tel: +33 5 56 54 32 48
Fax: +33 5 56 66 70 04
e-mail: macsorg@wanadoo.fr

Contents

ELSEVIER

International Congress Series 1261 (2004) 1–8

www.ics-elsevier.com

National DNA databases—practice and practicability. A forum for discussion

Peter D. Martin*

Ex-Metropolitan Police Laboratory, London, La Borderie, 87440 Saint Mathieu, France

Abstract. The success of the established National DNA databases (NDNAD) in linking crimes and nominating possible suspects has prompted many countries to enact legislation for the introduction of their own databases. While the technology used in the production of the DNA profiles remains consistent (there is a core set of STR loci common to all laboratories), there is considerable variation in the regulations which cover the entry of personal profiles. Five invited speakers presented the current situation with NDNADs in Europe and North America. The presentations included: (1) the various categories of crime for which a profile can be entered onto a database; (2) the numbers of profiles held on the databases; (3) whether the DNA samples can be retained for future analysis; (4) the successes of the various databases; (5) the interaction between the operators of the databases and other elements of the criminal justice systems. There were also discussions of the possible future technological developments that may affect the databases and a cautionary note on the quality measures necessary to ensure accuracy of analysis and database management and the potential for the misuse of the data retained.

Keywords: National DNA database; DNA profile; STR multiplexes

1. Introduction

DNA databases for criminal offenders and unsolved crimes have now become established in many countries as an everyday tool for use in the investigation of crime. Also, there is now very little challenge to their use in courts of law. However, the collection and storage of personal data has always been an emotive issue as there is a public perception that either the scientists or the authorities might use the information for something other than the stated purpose.

While it is universally accepted that DNA profiles obtained from all crime scene samples should be automatically entered and retained on a database, the subject of the entry of personal profiles from suspects or convicted persons continues to be debated. Given the robustness and reliability of DNA profiling, it has been suggested that everyone

* Tel.: +33 555003426.

E-mail address: petermartin@wanadoo.fr (P.D. Martin).

doi:10.1016/S0531-5131(03)01844-2

should be placed on a DNA database. While there is no argument with this logic, there are practical concerns for its implementation not least of which is the cost.

It is taken for granted that all DNA profiles which are obtained from scenes of crime should automatically be added as data for future comparison. This cannot infringe any civil rights issues as initially these results are not assigned to any individual.

In general terms, there is now almost no objection to the existence of national DNA databases as they have had considerable success in crime investigation and in the identification of possible perpetrators of very serious offences. There remains, however, considerable discussion about which individuals should have DNA profiles entered onto the databases and which samples should be retained for future analysis.

2. The current situation in the UK

The UK DNA database was first established in 1995 and is now used as a routine step in the investigation of crime. In the initial stages, the need for a National DNA Database (NDNAD) was identified to aid in crime reduction. As past records have shown in the UK, the majority of those who commit serious crime have previous convictions for minor offences. Consequently, in the UK, there was a decision to allow for the retention of personal DNA profiles from offenders convicted of minor as well as serious crime, the objective being to identify the perpetrator of a serious crime before the commission of a series of offences such as sexual assault or murder.

By April 2003 the UK NDNAD held approximately 2.3 million profiles and had achieved more than 280,000 person to crime matches and about 30,000 crime to crime matches. Typically, there are 1250 matches reported per week which include on average 14 murders, 20 sex offences and 137 violent crimes. The current aim is to process the samples within 14 days to allow for rapid elimination or inclusion. As well as providing the names of possible suspects in crime cases, the NDNAD is also able to provide links between different offence types (see Table 1).

Recently, there was a successful initiative to form a partnership with the police to provide a fast-track service designed to identify the perpetrators of burglary before they could commit multiple offences. During this initiative, which lasted for 11 months, nearly four times the previous number of samples were received and the analysis time was reduced from 29 days to 10 days. The analysis of 425 cases was undertaken and 74% resulted in the production of a profile suitable for a database search. Scene of crime to person matches were found in 221 cases (52%) and 48 individuals were convicted. Subsequently, the UK government gave financial assistance for additional scene of crime officers and funding to

Table 1
Matches obtained by the UK NDNAD with crimes other than the arrestable offence

Arrest offence	Autocrime	Burglary	Damage	Drugs	Robbery	Theft	Violence	Homicide	Other sex	Rape
Total matched	1193	1593	1105	1209	307	3687	1521	32	103	39
Percentage matched different offence type	51%	26%	80%	98%	75%	42%	96%	69%	84%	49%
Percentage matched serious offence	4%	2%	4%	8%	17%	5%	10%	50%	24%	69%

the laboratories to continue the initiative to reduce crime. The rapid production of DNA profiles has played a key role in this intelligence-led approach to crime investigation.

3. The current situation in Europe

The majority of European countries now have either operational NDNADs or are in the process of implementation (see Table 2).

In the UK, the law is comparatively liberal and comprehensive by allowing profiles to be obtained and retained from a wide range of individuals who are either suspected or convicted of crimes. There is also the legal right to keep all samples for further analysis if required. This situation does not pertain to all European countries and Table 3 illustrates the wide diversity of criteria which legislate for the operation of the various NDNADs.

The situation is further complicated with reference to the samples which are used for profiling. These can be retained for future testing in England, Austria, Finland, Denmark, Hungary, Slovenia and Croatia but, in the other countries, samples must either be destroyed after the profile is obtained or after the court has reached a decision.

While the 10 SGM Plus loci are most commonly used within Europe, not all 10 loci are always used for databasing. Some countries have opted for different systems but seven agreed loci are always part of all European databases.

At the present time, the European NDNADs have reached different stages of maturity with some showing remarkable success rates in the identification of suspects and also in identifying crime to crime links (see Table 4). The UK National DNA Database is the most effective in Europe in terms of the individuals nominated as suspects in crime investigation and also as a means of determining links between different crime scenes. The major reason for this success comes from the law which allows for the retention of such a large number of personal DNA profiles. The databases that generate most matches are those which contain a very large percentage of personal profiles. Anyone suspected or convicted of an extremely wide variety of crimes could have their DNA profile entered onto the NDNAD and the results could remain on the database indefinitely regardless of whether or not a conviction is obtained.

4. The current situation in France

Although the necessary legislation for the French NDNAD was enacted in 1998, the database is still in its infancy. Originally, it was implemented to hold profiles only from

Table 2
National DNA databases in Europe

1995	England
1996	Northern Ireland, Scotland
1997	The Netherlands, Austria
1998	Germany, Slovenia
1999	Finland, Norway
2000	Denmark, Switzerland, Sweden, Croatia, Bulgaria
2001	France, The Czech Republic
2002	Belgium, Estonia, Lithuania, Slovakia
2003	Hungary, Latvia
In preparation	Poland, Portugal, Spain, Greece, Ireland, Yugoslavia

Table 3
Criteria for retaining DNA profiles in various European countries

Country	Entry criteria for suspects	Entry criteria for convicted offenders	Removal criteria
England	Any recordable offence		Never removed, including suspects
Austria	Any recordable offence		After acquittal
Croatia	Any recordable offence		Never removed
Slovenia	Any recordable offence		Dependent on severity of crime
Switzerland	Any recordable offence		After acquittal or 5–40 years after conviction
Germany	>1 year in prison	After court decision	After acquittal or 5–40 years after conviction
Finland	>1 year in prison		After acquittal but never if convicted
Denmark	>1.5 years in prison		10 years after acquittal or 5–40 years after conviction
Norway	Many serious offences	After court decision	Never removed
Hungary	5 years in prison		After acquittal or 5–40 years after conviction
Sweden	No suspects entered	>2 years in prison	5–40 years after conviction
Belgium	No suspects entered	After court decision	5–40 years after conviction
Netherlands	No suspects entered (except when the suspect's DNA is tested for the case)	>4 years in prison	5–40 years after conviction
France	No suspects entered	Serious offences, voluntary samples only	5–40 years after conviction

Table 4
The composition of National DNA databases for some European countries

	UK	Netherlands	Austria	Germany	Finland	Sweden	Denmark	Switzerland	Slovenia	Belgium	France
Last update	April 03	August 03	March 03	July 03	April 03	July 03	July 03	July 03	September 03	June 03	August 03
Entries	2.31 million	13,100	68,800	285,700	9700	11,200	5300	38,640	6450	3470	6400
Persons	92%	25%	80%	86%	64%	34%	36%	85%	68%	16%	90%
Suspects included	+	–	+	+	+	–	+	+	+	–	–
Stain samples	8%	75%	20%	14%	36%	66%	64%	15%	32%	84%	10%
Hits	313,600	6450	1900	13,200	1480	2620	1040	800	380	210	150

Most other European countries either have or are in the process of developing databases.

those found guilty of sexual assaults and offences against minors. In 2001, the law was changed to include serious offences against persons and property and in 2003 another law was enacted to include almost all categories of serious offences. This new law also allows for a police officer to take a buccal sample, for DNA profiling and database search, without reference to an investigating magistrate or a public prosecutor.

The NDNAD is controlled by a committee under the direction of a high ranking prosecutor and is operated, using the CODIS software, by the technical and scientific police who are responsible to the Minister of the Interior. The scene of crime samples are stored at the National Criminal Research Institute of the Gendarmerie. At the moment there are 28 scientists in 14 different laboratories who are authorised to perform the DNA analyses within the guidelines of well established methodologies. The aim is to gain accreditation for all laboratories given the authority to do work for the NDNAD.

Although the French law does not compel a person to provide a sample for analysis anyone who refuses could face the prospect of a jail sentence or a considerable fine. Following an administrative order, the DNA profile can remain on the database for up to 40 years but there is a system whereby a person can request its removal.

5. The current situation in the USA

The NDNAD in the USA came into existence following the enactment of the DNA Identification Act of 1994. In its initial stages, the database was designed to cope with entries from a number of DNA technologies but its mainstream activity has now settled on a system of entry and search against profiles obtained from 13 STR loci that can be typed for with commercially available kits.

The FBI designed and implemented the system and now has overall responsibility for an operation which includes input from 173 state and local laboratories as well as the US Army Crime Laboratory and Puerto Rico. The CODIS software for running the database has been extremely successful and has been adopted by 18 other countries worldwide.

While the database has expanded rapidly and contains files from a number of activities (see Table 5), there are plans for further expansion.

Under current legislation only personal DNA profiles are entered onto the database from those individuals convicted of certain specified crimes (the categories of crime will vary according to the specific laws of the individual states). However, due to the success in nominating crime suspects and linking crimes, there are now plans to widen the scope of the database to include a variety of further crime categories and to incorporate personal profiles from arrested and indicted individuals. At present, some past cases may come under the Statute of Limitations (a time limit after which no prosecution can take place) and, following so many DNA identifications in old cases, it is considered that there would be advantage in either extending the time or eliminating this statute. Other files including Missing Persons and Relatives of Missing Persons will also accept mtDNA, SNP and Y chromosome STR data to allow for the examination of skeletal remains and also other degraded material.

To address concerns that DNA data and samples will be used inappropriately, access to the data is limited to criminal agencies for law enforcement identification purposes, to

Table 5
File entries in the US National DNA database

Convicted offenders	1,519,584
Forensic samples	67,191
Missing persons	72
Relatives of missing persons	248
Human remains	116
Population statistics	August 2003

judicial proceedings and for criminal defence purposes where a defendant might require information pertinent to analyses performed in his or her case. There are both federal and state laws which protect against the unauthorised disclosure of database information.

6. National DNA databases issues

In the early stages of development of NDNADs, there was considerable challenge to the accuracy and statistical relevance of matches, especially in the adversarial forms of criminal justice practiced in such countries as the UK and USA. Nowadays, there is relatively little challenge to the evidence and this has allowed the scientists more time to concentrate on the quality issues associated with the detailed maintenance of the databases. While all countries have legislation to prevent the unauthorised disclosure of database information, it would be foolhardy to believe that all the databases are error-free. However, NDNADs do allow for vast pairwise comparison experiments and provide a unique opportunity to test the impact of the phenomenon of errors into the process of genetic matching. With the knowledge that these large collections of genetic data will invariably contain errors, it is important to introduce systems which will first of all recognize potential sources of errors and then steps may be taken to assist the process. To this end, expert systems are being developed to recognize the source of errors. However, there is an onus, not only on the operators of the database but also on the laboratories submitting data to the NDNAD for searching, to have quality systems in place to ensure that the profiles being stored and searched have been correctly prepared.

All those involved with the criminal justice systems should be aware that, when a random match is obtained from a database search, it is an aid to the investigation of a crime and not necessarily evidence of guilt. The ‘prosecutor’s fallacy’ (typically where the probability of a random match is transposed into the evidence of guilt) can unfairly bias the decision of a court, and there are instances where a database search has pointed at an individual who could not possibly have committed the crime.

As most of the NDNADs are operated within criminal justice organisations, successful partnerships are emerging in which cooperation between the NDNADs, law enforcement agencies and laboratories is encouraged to identify linked crimes. However, there has been some debate concerning the desirability of using other independent organisations as the guardians of the genetic information. While this might have some cosmetic appeal, it is important not to lose the understanding which has developed within this framework. In the Netherlands the defendant has the right to have the samples reanalysed by an independent, university-based laboratory and this is a simple but effective way of checking that the submitting laboratories and the NDNAD operators are competent.

The STR technology, currently used to form the databases, has no apparent value in giving genetic information other than for individuality. However, it is not only the results of the DNA analysis which are retained. The samples, which are provided for the analyses, can also be stored in case there is a need for re-analysis in a particular case or because there is a change in the technology whereby all accumulated samples can be re-examined. In some countries, the law allows for these samples to be held forever and here lies a potential problem. Molecular biology is advancing at a rapid pace and more and more personal information can be gleaned from genetic studies. In the event of the breakdown of stable sociopolitical systems, there would be the availability of some potentially harmful information from such a comprehensive set of DNA samples. Therefore, it is not surprising that many of the European legislators have insisted that DNA samples should be destroyed following analysis.

7. Future

Without doubt, the evolution of NDNADs has been a success story and the creation of large searchable databases will continue to be an invaluable asset in the investigation of crimes. The very success, however, is in some way, a potential bar to technological progress. The profiling of such large numbers of samples has involved a great deal of work and a substantial cost and embracing a change in the technology would require an overwhelming amount of work. It is generally agreed that, although SNP technology has the potential for a faster and cheaper way of performing the analyses, it is unlikely to supplant the current methodology in the foreseeable future. However, systems using SNPs in forensic science continue to be researched and, in the USA, they have been used in casework to provide indications of biogeographical origin. In The Netherlands, new legislation has already allowed for the future use of physical characteristics, determined from DNA analysis, in crime investigations. The determination and use of genetic disorders and disease associations is specifically prohibited and the methodology will only be used if it is pertinent to the particular investigation, the information obtained is shown to be reliable and the cost is within reason.

One of the most valuable assets of the current technology is that laboratories worldwide have settled on the use of comparable packages of STR loci. This offers the potential for any NDNAD to be interrogated for a match with a result from a crime scene sample. Although this is scientifically possible, the difficulties with the various legal systems remain. In the USA, there is a single database which receives input from all the state law enforcement agencies and entries and searches are carried out according to local state legislation. The advantage of this system is that a crime committed in one state could well be linked to a person living in another state. In Europe, the scientists initially involved with DNA profiling worked towards, and achieved, a harmonised system that would allow for the interchange of results. The introduction of the technology had coincided with a European Union initiative to have open borders and it was realised that there was the potential for an increase in cross-border crimes. The amount and seriousness of cross-border crime is difficult to evaluate, but there are many unsolved crimes within the member states which could well have been perpetrated by persons not domiciled in that particular country. In many cases, the interrogation of all the available databases could prove valuable but, at the present time, there are many legal obstacles to the exchange of DNA information (particularly personal profiles) and, without some harmonisation of the legal systems, this problem will remain. A possible solution to this obstacle could be the creation of a European database which contains only DNA profiles from unsolved crime cases where there is evidence that the offender comes from another country. These DNA profiles could be downloaded individually and compared against the respective NDNAD. Thus, the personal DNA profiles could be used for international database searches but remain within the jurisdiction of the specific national DNA databases.

Acknowledgements

This report has been prepared from the presentations made by Bruce Budowle (FBI, Washington, DC, USA), Peter Gill (Forensic Science Service, Birmingham, UK), Isabelle Goanvic (Ministère de Justice, Paris, France), Vince Pascali (Università Cattolica del S. Cuore, Rome) and Peter Schneider (Johannes Gutenberg University, Mainz, Germany) with additional commentary by Peter Martin.

In the process of setting up the forum, it was appreciated that many countries have well established, successful DNA databases, but time constraints allowed for only a limited number of presentations.

ELSEVIER

International Congress Series 1261 (2004) 9–11

www.ics-elsevier.com

Detection of genetic variation by MALDI-TOF mass spectrometry: rapid SNP genotyping using the GENOLINK system

D. Niemeyer[a], T. Elssner[a], K. Fahr[a], D. Peters[a], T. Wenzel[a], E. Petkovski[b,c], M. Kostrzewa[a,*]

[a] *Bruker Daltonik GmbH, Permoserstrasse 15, D-04318 Leipzig, Germany*
[b] *CODGENE Laboratory, Strasbourg, France*
[c] *Institute of Legal Medicine, Louis Pasteur University, Strasbourg, France*

Abstract. Single nucleotide polymorphisms (SNPs) are the most common form of genetic variation in the human genome. Because of their low mutation rate, SNPs have the potential to be as discriminating as loci of higher polymorphism, e.g. for forensic approaches such as paternity tests or human identification in general. To balance the lack of polymorphic information the number of markers which are tested has to be increased. Here, we introduce a new automated platform for SNP genotyping by matrix-assisted laser desorption/ionisation time-of-flight mass spectrometry (MALDI-TOF MS), easy to use as well for higher DNA sample throughput as also for the analysis of an increased number of SNPs. © 2003 Elsevier B.V. All rights reserved.

Keywords: SNP genotyping; Human identification; MALDI-TOF MS; Automated sample preparation

1. Introduction

In forensic casework, single nucleotide polymorphisms (SNPs) are of considerable interest because of the capability to genotype very short amplified fragments [1]. Therefore, SNPs may get of increasing importance for analysis of strongly degraded samples. In forensic routine casework methods for SNP genotyping have to achieve highest quality requirements. The limited discriminatory nature of biallelic SNPs can be balanced by increasing their number per analysis. A set of about 50 different SNPs is necessary to obtain the discrimination power of existing STR multiplexes. Nowadays SNP databases already contain numerous suitable and validated loci [2].

We present the analysis of nine autosomal SNPs, located in non-coding regions, which might serve as forensic markers. The analysis was performed using GENOLINK, a SNP genotyping platform for functional genomic studies [3]. GENOLINK is the combination of

* Corresponding author. Tel.: +49-341-4912-170; fax: +49-341-4912-179.
E-mail address: km@bdal.de (M. Kostrzewa).

doi:10.1016/S0531-5131(03)01836-3

Table 1
PEX-primer/product sequences and masses

	PEX-primer sequence 5′-3′	PEX-primer	PEX-products
PCI	Rx: bio-ctg ggg gca gcg gLa gcc aag	2194 Da	ddA: 2492/ddG: 2507 Da
C1r	Fx: bio-gtg ctt ccc gLa gca aat	2194 Da	ddC: 2467/ddT: 2481 Da
C8a	Fx: bio-gtt cta caa ctt Ltg taa gg	2240 Da	ddA: 2538/ddC: 2514 Da
DNaseI	Fx: bio-gtt gca ggg atL ctg ctc c	2112 Da	ddA: 2410/ddG: 2426 Da
WI 1126	Rx: bio-caa gaa ata aaa gLc aag tcc	2146 Da	ddA: 2443/ddG: 2459 Da
WI 1306	Rx: bio-aag gta gcc cLc aga agc	2195 Da	ddC: 2468/ddT: 2483 Da
WI 1349	Fx: bio-cag aaa ata tga ttL gaa aaa g	2243 Da	ddA: 2539/ddC: 2515 Da
WI 1888	Rx: bio-gtt gtc ttt tct Ltg taa tg	2216 Da	ddC: 2489/ddT: 2504 Da
WI 867	Fx: bio-tct ttc cct ttL cat ctc c	2096 Da	ddA: 2394/ddG: 2410 Da

a novel method for SNP genotyping, genoSNIP [4], dedicated hardware for automated sample preparation and analysis, and a bioinformatic package.

2. Materials and methods

2.1. DNA amplification

PCR was performed in singleplex and multiplex reactions. Amplicons of 64–194 bp were generated. Residual primers and nucleotides were disabled by incubation with Shrimp Alkaline Phosphatase (SAP) at 37 °C for 45 min. After deactivation of SAP (90 °C, 10 min), this reaction mixture was directly used for the following primer extension reaction (PEX).

2.2. Primer extension reaction

Primers with a biotin label at the 5′ end and a photocleavable building block at position 8 or 9 from the 3′ end were used for single base extension (Table 1). The PEX mixture contained 1 U of PEX-Polymerase and 2 mM of each ddNTP.

The primer extension products were purified using genostrep kits (Bruker Daltonik). The biotin-labelled oligonucleotides were specifically bound to the streptavidin-coated cavities of special microtiter plates. Salts and other impurities were removed by

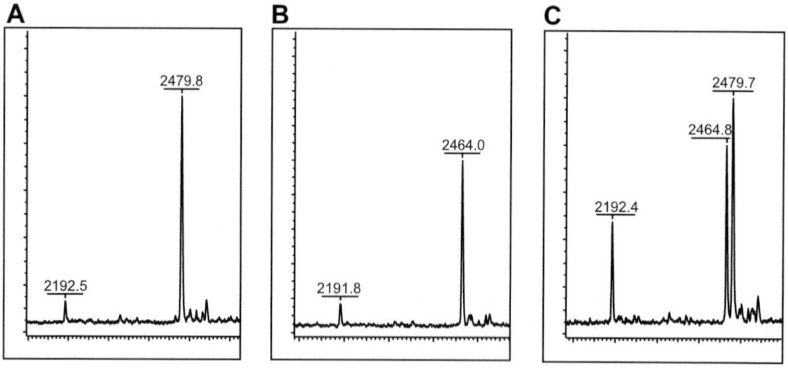

Fig. 1. Three example spectra for SNP WI 1306. *X*-axis—mass/charge ratio; *Y*-axis—relative intensity. (A) Homozygous person + ddC. (B) Homozygous person + ddT. (C) Heterozygous person.

washing. After adding the elution buffer the plate was exposed to UV light (366 nm, UV-unit CL-366, Bruker Daltonik). The primers were cleaved and the specifically extended 3′ end was eluted and directly supplied to matrix-assisted laser desorption/ionisation time-of-flight mass spectrometry (MALDI-TOF MS) analysis. All pipetting steps were performed by the puredisk robot (Bruker Daltonik).

2.3. MALDI-TOF MS

Samples were transferred onto an AnchorChip target 400-384 and measured in linear mode in an autoflex mass spectrometer (Bruker Daltonik). The matrix was 3-hydroxypicolinic acid (20 mg/ml 3-HPA + 1 mg/ml di-ammoniumhydrogen-citrate). The spectra were automatically analysed using the software genotools 2.0 (Bruker Daltonik). The analysis implied the genotype assignment and a quality check of the spectrum/result.

3. Results

All SNPs of interest could be genotyped successfully. Fig. 1 shows the results of the assay for three different anonymous DNA samples, representing the three different genotypes for SNP WI 1306.

To demonstrate multiplex capability, several SNPs were successfully combined in duplex or triplex reactions (Clr/WI1349, WI867/1126, WI867/Clr/WI1348, data not shown). Automated screening runs, using the puredisk for all pipetting were performed for a 96-microtiter plate containing 93 anonymous DNA samples and 3 water controls.

4. Discussion

GenoSNIP delivered reliable genotyping results. The PEX-primers hybridise directly adjacent to the polymorphic sites and are converted into allele specific products by single nucleotide extension. The photo-cleavable building block in their sequence enables the elution after purification. As the released fragments consist of only 8–10 nucleotides, they are measured with high precision and sensitivity, in particular because of a decreased affinity to salt ions. The slightest mass difference between two nucleotides (9 Da between A and T) can steadily be detected in this mass range.

The mass spectra were translated into genotypes by the genotools 2.0 software. The samples were transferred from the 96-raster to the 384-raster and therefore each sample was measured four times. Analysis of four spectra per sample gave equal results and therefore verified the reliability of analysis. Summing up the GENOLINK system comprises a complete solution for automated, highly accurate SNP genotyping by MALDI-TOF MS.

References

[1] P. Gill, An assessment of the utility of single nucleotide polymorphisms (SNPs) for forensic purposes, Int. J. Leg. Med. 114 (4–5) (2001) 204–210.

[2] D. Sachidanandam, et al., A map of human genome sequence variation containing 1.42 million single nucleotide polymorphisms, Nature 409 (2001) 928–933.

[3] W. Pusch, et al., MALDI-TOF mass spectrometry based SNP genotyping, Pharmacogenomics 3 (2002) 537–548.

[4] T. Wenzel, et al., GenoSNIP: SNP genotyping by MALDI-TOF MS using photocleavable oligonucleotides, Nucleosides Nucleotides Nucleic Acids 22 (5–8) (2003) 1579–1581.

International Congress Series 1261 (2004) 12–14
www.ics-elsevier.com

Development of SNP microarray for supplementary paternity testing

P. Ellonen[a,*], M. Levander[a], I. Ulmanen[b], M. Lukka[b]

[a] *Department of Molecular Medicine, National Public Health Institute, Biomedicum PL104, SF-00251 Helsinki, Finland*

[b] *Paternity Testing Laboratory, National Public Health Institute, Helsinki, Finland*

Abstract. We have developed a SNP microarray for paternity testing, which contains 10 SNPs and in addition X and Y chromosome-specific markers. SNPs were selected with an emphasis on their high allele frequency in the Finnish population. Coding regions of known genes were excluded. With this setup of SNPs, we have calculated the average exclusion power in paternity testing to be 86.5%. The array was validated by comparison with the results in 120 paternity trios obtained with microsatellite markers (Profiler™ and SGM+ ™ kits, Applied Biosystems). We conclude that the SNP microarray provides a feasible method to obtain additional genotype information especially in complex paternity cases.

Keywords: SNP; Microarray; Paternity testing

1. Introduction

Microsatellite (STR) marker sets are predominantly used in paternity testing. While genotyping of STR markers is everyday routine in laboratories, reliable and scalable SNP genotyping methods are intensely developed [1]. In complex paternity testing cases such as mutations or deficiency cases, when the DNA profiles of mother or alleged father are not available or father candidates are closely related additional genotype information would be helpful. For such instances, we have applied an alternative approach, a SNP microarray. Due to the mostly biallelic nature of SNPs, their information content is lower than in STR markers and thus larger number of markers are required to produce same information. On the other hand, SNPs have lower mutation rate, are abundant throughout the human genome and are more easily automated for high throughput genotyping.

Abbreviations: STR, short tandem repeat; SNP, single nucleotide polymorphism; PCR, polymerase chain reaction.

* Corresponding author. Tel.: +358-09-47448752; fax: +358-09-47448480.

E-mail address: pekka.ellonen@ktl.fi (P. Ellonen).

doi:10.1016/S0531-5131(03)01824-7

2. Material and methods

SNP genotyping was performed on microarray format with maximum of 80 samples per one microarray. Allele discrimination was performed with allele-specific oligonucleotides in a primer extension reaction (Fig. 1) described by Pastinen et al. [2].

Microarray slides were manufactured with OmniGrid microarrayer, which dispenses nanoliter volumes of allele-specific oligonucleotides on microscopic slides. Oligonucleotides attach to slide surface via aminated 5′ termini by formation of a covalent bond. Each biallelic SNP requires two allele-specific oligonucleotides differing in the 3′ nucleotides defining the alleles. The SNP loci were amplified in a single multiplex PCR reaction. Subsequently PCR products were in vitro transcribed by T7 RNA polymerase utilizing T7 promoter sequence introduced to the amplicons via PCR primers. After transcription, PCR products were enzymatically degraded to yield single-stranded RNA template to facilitate hybridization to allele-specific oligonucleotides on microarray surface. RNA samples were hybridized on a microarray slide in humid chamber at a constant temperature. After hybridization, allele-specific oligonucleotide/RNA hybrids were extended by MMLV-RT enzyme catalyzed reaction using fluorescently labeled deoxynucleotides. Oligonucleotides having complete hybridisation with sample RNA were extended in this reaction whereas incomplete hybridisation showed no or residual primer extension. Microarray slides were scanned with ScanArray4000 laser scanner instrument and fluorescent signals were quantitated by QuantArray software. Raw signals were converted to genotypes with the SNPSnapper software developed by Dr. Juha Saharinen in National Public Health Institute, Helsinki, Finland (ajuha.saharinen@ktl.fi).

The 120 trios for the validation of the SNP array method were selected from the paternity cases analysed in our laboratory with microsatellite markers using Profiler™ kit (Applied Biosystems) and when needed SGM+ ™ kit (Applied Biosystems).The exclu-

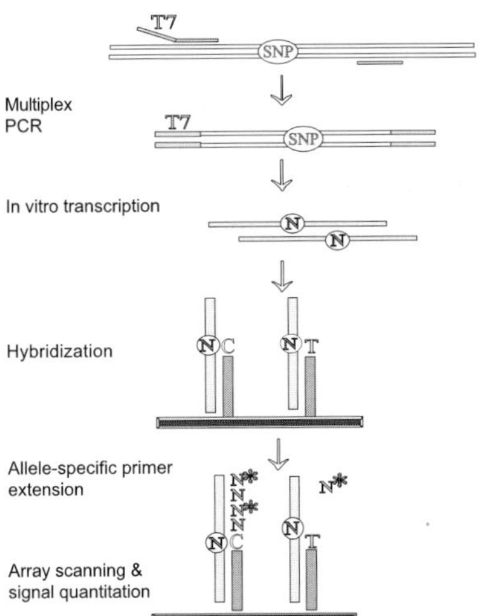

Fig. 1. Principle of the allele-specific primer extension SNP microarray.

Table 1
The SNP loci used for the paternity array

Reference number	Minor allele frequency	Chromosomal location
rs2239393	0.44	22q11
rs324026	0.46	3q13
rs936461	0.42	11p15
rs904952	0.49	15q14
rs726283	0.40	6q25
rs6265	0.25	11p13
rs6279	0.38	11q23
rs6293	0.49	9q34
rs6311	0.43	13q14
rs1014531	0.42	13p14

sions were based at least on three loci and in the non-exclusion cases the power of evidence was at least 99.8%.

3. Results and discussion

The selected 10 SNP loci are shown in Table 1. SNPs were scattered in the genome and in addition X and Y chromosome-specific markers were included. These loci were not located within coding regions of genes. Based on the allele frequencies of the SNPs, the average exclusion power of these markers is 86.5% in the Finnish population. This provides reasonable supplementary genotype information which may be helpful in complex paternity cases such as mutation or in deficiency cases. The exclusion power can be increased by selecting more SNP loci for the array.

A set of 120 trios which were previously genotyped with the Profiler™ and SGM+™ kits were genotyped with allele-specific primer extension microarray. Blinded genotyping experiment produced genotype information to identify 33 out of 34 exclusion cases and no Mendelian errors were found among the 86 non-exclusion cases. SNP microarray produced reliable genotypes in all tested samples and no discrepancies were seen in duplicate genotypes. Validation experiments showed that allele-specific primer extension microarray provided a reliable and feasible method to produce additional information in complex paternity cases. Additional SNPs will be tested to increase the exclusion power of SNP microarray.

Acknowledgements

The expert technical assistance of Lea Näsänen is thankfully acknowledged.

References

[1] A.-C. Syvänen, Assessing genetic variation: genotyping single nucleotide polymorphisms, Nature Reviews Genetics 2 (2001) 930–942.

[2] T. Pastinen, et al., A system for specific, high-throughput genotyping by allele-specific primer extension on microarrays, Genome Res. 10 (2000) 1031–1042.

International Congress Series 1261 (2004) 15–17
ELSEVIER
www.ics-elsevier.com

Multiplex Y chromosome SNP genotyping using MALDI-TOF mass spectrometry

J. Mengel-Jørgensen[a,*], J.J. Sanchez[a], C. Børsting[a], F. Kirpekar[b], N. Morling[a]

[a] *Department of Forensic Genetics, Institute of Forensic Medicine, University of Copenhagen, 11 Frederik V's Vej DK-2100 Copenhagen Ø, Denmark*

[b] *Department of Biochemistry and Molecular Biology, University of Southern Denmark, Odense, Denmark*

Received 8 September 2003; received in revised form 8 September 2003; accepted 15 September 2003

Abstract. Matrix-assisted laser desorption/ionisation time-of-flight (MALDI-TOF) mass spectrometry (MS) offers a reliable, inexpensive and time-saving method for SNP genotyping. The method is based on weight determination of single base extended (SBE) primers. Here, we present a MALDI-TOF protocol for typing 17 Y chromosome SNPs using biotin-labelled ddNTP in the SBE reaction and solid-phase avidin capture purification of extended primers. All 17 fragments were amplified in a multiplex reaction and all 17 primers were extended in a single SBE reaction.

Keywords: Y chromosome; SNP; MALDI-TOF

1. Introduction

One of the most promising techniques for SNP typing is the matrix-assisted laser desorption/ionization time of flight (MALDI-TOF) mass spectrometry (MS). This technique is fast, accurate and easy to automate. The most widely used MALDI-TOF SNP typing strategy is based on single base extension (SBE) [1].

The smallest difference in mass between the four dideoxynucleotides (ddNTPs) is 9 Da between A and T. It is very difficult to distinguish two peaks differing by only 9 Da using primers of usual length (16–25 bases) and mass (5000–8000 Da) [2]. However, by using modified biotin-labelled ddNTPs in the SBE reaction, the smallest difference in mass is 16 Da between G and A, and two peaks differing by 16 Da can be separated by MALDI-TOF using primers of usual mass (5000–8000 Da) [3]. Here, we present a protocol for simultaneous detection of 17 Y chromosome SNPs by SBE and MALDI-TOF MS analysis using biotin-labelled ddNTPs in the SBE reaction.

2. Materials and methods

2.1. PCR and SBE

Seventeen SNPs placed on 17 different PCR fragments were selected from a 35 Y-SNP package [4]. The multiplex SBE primers were designed based on criteria previously

* Corresponding author. Tel.: +45-3532-6266; fax: +45-3532-6120.
E-mail address: jonas.mengel@forensic.ku.dk (J. Mengel-Jørgensen).

0531-5131/
doi:10.1016/S0531-5131(03)01544-9

described [4]. The mass was calculated using Mongo Oligo Mass Calculator v 2.05. (http://www.medlib.med.utah.edu/masspec/mongo.htm by Jef Rozenski, 1999). No mass overlap between extended and un-extended primers was allowed. The minimal difference in mass was 13 Da. The length of the primers varied from 17 to 31 bases.

The multiplex PCR conditions were as previously described [4].

Cycle SBE was performed in an 8-μl reaction volume with 0.4 μl of the purified PCR product (10–20 fmol of each product) or 50 fmol doped template (Fig. 1) using 0.6 μl thermosequenase reaction buffer, 0.4 μl ddNTP or biotin-ddNTP (PerkinElmer and Roche), 0.75 μl 3 units Themosequenase (Amersham Biosciences) and 0.6 μl primers (0.005–0.07 μM). The following programme was used: 35 cycles of 96 °C for 10 s, 50 °C for 5 s and 60 °C for 30 s.

2.2. Purification of SBE products and MALDI-TOF analysis

Drop dialysis was performed as previously described [5].

Solid-phase reverse phase columns were in-house fabricated as described [6] with the exception that we used Poros OligoR3 (Applied Biosystems) column material and eluted the samples with 2 μl 25% acetonitrile/15mM triethyl ammonium acetate.

The solid-phase avidin column was based on a modification of an existing protocol [3] using 5 μl monomeric avidin (Pierce). Washing was done two times with 30 μl 0.1 M NH_4HCO_3 pH 7.0. Rescue of biotin-labelled DNA was done directly on the target by 3 μl 5% triethyl amin pH 12.5. The samples were prepared by the dry droplet method [6]. Samples were analysed on a Voyager DE-PRO (Applied Biosystems) Instrument.

3. Results and discussion

Since very pure DNA is needed for MALDI-TOF MS analysis, we investigated the efficiency of two purification approaches: drop dialysis and in-house fabricated reverse phase microcolumns. Our results showed that the recovery by both purification protocols were approximately 85%. Samples purified by either protocol resulted in high quality MALDI-TOF spectra, demonstrating that the purification protocols were very efficient.

We used a doped template to analyse the separation of the four possible alleles on the MALDI-TOF using conventional ddNTPs and mass-tagged ddNTPs (biotin-labelled ddNTPs) in the SBE reaction. Fig. 1 shows spectres with four peaks, one peak from each alleles. Our results showed insufficient separation between the A and T peaks in the mass area 5000–10,000 *m/z* when conventional ddNTPs were used (Fig. 1a). However, by using modified biotin-labelled ddNTPs (Fig. 1b), it was possible to obtain acceptable separation between all peaks in the mass range 5000–10,000 *m/z*.

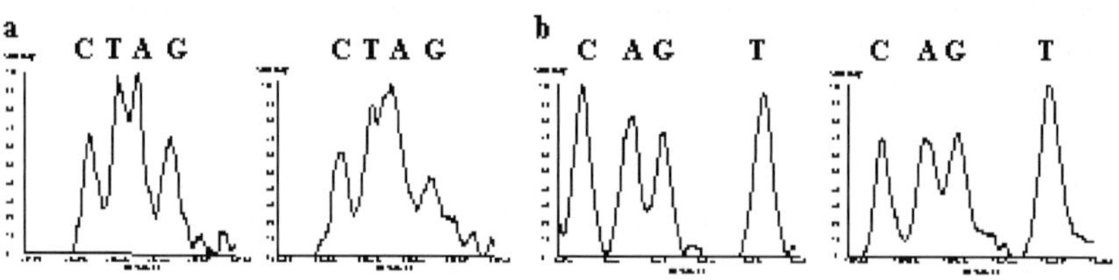

Fig. 1. Separation of peaks by MALDI-TOF. A doped DNA template containing a random nucleotide in the SNP position, and either conventional ddNTPSs (a) or biotin-labelled ddNTPs (b) was used in the SBE reaction.

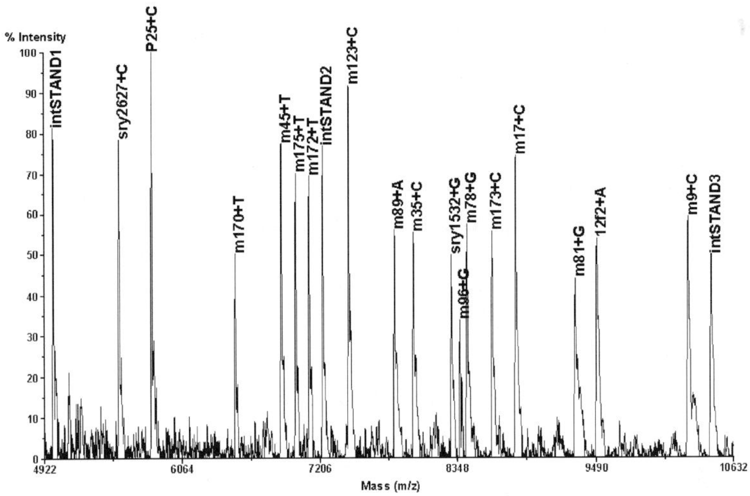

Fig. 2. MALDI-TOF results from a 17 SNP SBE reaction using biotin-labelled ddNTPs.

To avoid problems with separation of the A/T alleles, we continued to use biotin-labelled ddNTPs in the SBE reaction and we combined this approach with our newly developed one-step purification protocol for biotin-labelled DNA. The recovery from the solid-phase avidin capture assay was slightly lower then the recovery from the drop dialysis and the reverse phase purification. Seventeen primers were designed for detection of 17 SNPs selected from a 35 Y-SNP package [4]. Fig. 2 shows the SBE results obtained from a single male sample using the 17 Y-SNP package. The spectrum displays 20 peaks, three internal biotin-labelled standards and 17 extended primers, whereas un-extended primers and one internal standard without biotin label are not displayed, demonstrating the specificity of the solid-phase avidin capture purification assay.

In conclusion, the combined use of biotin-labelled ddNTPs in the SBE reaction and the solid-phase avidin capture purification assay results in better resolution of the peaks and in a much more simple spectrum than the spectrum obtained from conventional SBE.

References

[1] J. Tost, I.G. Gut, Analysis and accurate quantification of CpG methylation by MALDI mass spectrometry. Nucleic Acids Res. (2003) 1;31(9):e50.

[2] M. Shahgholi, et al., Sugar additives for MALDI matrices improve signal allowing the smallest nucleotide change (A:T) in a DNA sequence to be resolved, Nucleic Acids Res. 29 (19) (2003) E91.

[3] S. Kim, et al., Solid phase capturable dideoxynucleotides for multiplex genotyping using mass spectrometry, Nucleic Acids Res. 30 (16) (2002) e85.

[4] J.J. Sanchez, et al., Multiplex PCR and minisequencing of SNPs—a model with 35 Y chromosome SNPs, Forensic Sci. Int. (in press).

[5] Z. Fei, L.M. Smith, Analysis of single nucleotide polymorphisms by primer extension and matrix-assisted laser desorption/ionization time-of-flight mass spectrometry, Rapid Commun. Mass Spectrom. 14 (11) (2000) 950–959.

[6] F. Kirpekar, et al., DNA sequence analysis by MALDI mass spectrometry, Nucleic Acids Res. 26 (1998) 2554–2559.

ELSEVIER

International Congress Series 1261 (2004) 18–20

www.ics-elsevier.com

Selecting single nucleotide polymorphisms for forensic applications

C. Phillips*, M. Lareu, J. Sanchez, M. Brion, B. Sobrino, N. Morling, P. Schneider, D. Syndercombe Court, A. Carracedo

The SNP for ID Consortium, Spain

Abstract. The selection criteria that can be used for choosing a core set of discriminatory SNPs from large scale databases for forensic use are reviewed.

Keywords: SNP; Linkage disequilibrium; LD blocks; Forensic analysis

1. Introduction

With nearly 6 million SNPs in numerous online databases available to choose and develop, it is increasingly important to formulate appropriate criteria for selecting the most useful and robust loci for forensic analysis. We aim to develop a core panel of SNPs for the optimum discrimination of individuals, in addition to developing specialized SNP sets. Studies of binary polymorphisms suggest that between 50 and 80 loci are required to match the discrimination levels of 16 STRs [1]. This makes linkage a critical factor in SNP selection, as several markers will be needed on each chromosome. Furthermore, SNPs rarely have optimum allele frequencies and often show marked differences in frequency distributions between populations, making polymorphic content an important additional characteristic. Lastly, flanking sequence quality needs to be considered in the context of the kind of genotyping assay to be used when selecting candidates.

2. Materials and methods

2.1. Number of candidate loci selected and databases used

We decided to genotype selected markers using SNaPshot minisequencing since this was a simple and reliable technique that most forensic labs can readily perform. SNP typing assays have varying conversion rates (i.e. successful incorporation of loci into the

* Corresponding author. Institute of Legal Medicine, University of Santiago de Compostela, Calle San Fransisco s/n, 15705 Santiago de Compostela, Spain. Tel.: +34-981582327; fax: +34-981580336.

E-mail address: chrisp@usc.es (C. Phillips).

doi:10.1016/j.ics.2003.12.001

assay), averaging between 70% and 80%. Some candidates prove less polymorphic than supposed or difficult to amplify in multiplexes, reducing the conversion rate to 50–60%. Primer design constraints caused by the small amplicon sizes required (60–120 bp) and complex interactions as the primer pool expands further reduce the number. So it was decided to select an initial pool of 400 candidates, taken from the telomeric region of the p-arm and q-arm of each autosome. Four different online SNP databases were used to select candidate markers:

(a) Celera Discovery Systems database (CDS) comprises 4,802,233 SNPs discovered from the private human genome mapping initiative plus the best validated SNPs from public databases (www.celeradiscoverysystem.com).
(b) Applied Biosystems Assays-on-Demand (ABI) database comprises 146,636 SNPs with the best allele information currently available (derived from 46 Africans and Europeans) (http://www.appliedbiosystems.com/products/assays).
(c) NCBI dbSNP database comprises 2,243,761 unique SNPs discovered from centres contributing to the public HGMP (http://www.ncbi.nlm.nih.gov/entrez/).
(d) The SNP Consortium (TSC) database comprises 1,255,326 SNPs taken from dbSNP but with higher levels of validation from three population groups (http://snp.cshl.org/).

2.2. Selection criteria: validation, polymorphic content, flanking sequence and linkage

Validation status is important to ensure each SNP is both real (i.e. not due to a sequencing error) and unique (i.e. mapping once in the genome). Growing numbers of SNPs are validated by genotyping and this provides the allele frequencies necessary to properly assess locus variability. The polymorphic content of a marker is often measured in forensic analysis by the discrimination index (Dp). The Dp values for SNPs change very little between minimum allele frequencies of 0.5–0.3 (dropping from 62.5% to 58%), so this range was used for selecting SNPs with sufficient variability. Polymorphism levels also need to be sufficiently high in at least two of the three population groups quoted in the TSC and ABI databases—many SNPs exhibit high variability in only one population and so are not applicable—these comprised about 10% of the, otherwise good, candidate SNPs found. Sequence features that are of importance in candidate selection include repeat motifs, % GC, polybases, secondary structures and SNP clustering. Good GC balance and an absence of tandem repeats around the SNP are essential to ensure good primer design. Potential secondary structures were not actively detected during selection but 7 of the 46 first SNP candidates failed the primer design process due to this problem. Examples of problem sequence encountered are shown in Fig. 1. SNP clustering is a characteristic that

Repeats	TCAAAATAATAATAATAATAAT**D**ATAATAATAATAATAATAAT	rs379091
%GC	TGGTTGGGGGGTGTGTGTGGG**B**GGGGGGACGGTGTGGAGGGC	rs1574185
	TAATTTTTTTTCTTTTCTTTT**H**TTTTTTNTGCAAAAAGATGTCT	rs727936
Polybases	AAGAATTCAAGATGGTATTT**W**AAAAAAAAACCTCATATCTT	rs113492

Fig. 1. Sequence characteristics of several SNPs that gave assay design problems.

often interferes with primer design: about 15–20% of otherwise good markers were rejected because of additional variable positions in close proximity to the SNP of interest.

Establishing if linkage disequilibrium (LD) is shown by SNPs is important in order to use a cumulative frequency for a multiple SNP profile. Current studies examining LD distribution report that chromosomal blocks exist where markers are in almost complete LD across relatively large distances. Such blocks are not consistent with the established model of genetic distance measured by a uniform recombination rate. Recent analysis of whole chromosomes (6, 21 and 22) using high density SNP maps [2] reveals LD, in certain cases, extending as far as 300 kb between two positions and varying in extent between different populations. However, the average size of these regions, termed LD or haplotype blocks, was only 26 kb in Caucasians (with just 30% of LD blocks longer than 25 kb) and 18 kb in Africans (with just 22% of LD blocks longer than 25 kb). Clearly, an average block size of ~ 20–25 kb means the risk of LD between SNP and gene is extremely low over distances greater than 100 kb making this a realistic window to use around known genes. In addition, LD between two SNP positions though highly variable is also unlikely to regularly extend over greater distances. Association analysis of two SNPs, 1 Mb apart, on chromosome 10 will form part of our initial validation process. Once SNP analysis is established, it is likely that forensic testing will often make use of both STRs and SNPs in parallel. The STR markers in routine forensic use are all mapped and equivalent distances can be used around these loci to avoid linkage issues.

3. Results and discussion

The first set of 23 markers selected using the criteria outlined above have now been successfully combined into a single multiplexed PCR and minisequencing reaction. This assay is currently being used to validate allele frequencies in several populations and to test for robustness and sensitivity in routine forensic analyses. It appears that none of the criteria used and outlined here will need major revision when further sets of loci are selected.

References

[1] P. Gill, Int. J. Leg. Med. 114 (2001) 204–210.
[2] F. De La Vega, et al., (poster 85), Proceedings of the 8th Int. Human Genome Meeting, 2003.

International Congress Series 1261 (2004) 21–23
www.ics-elsevier.com

SNPs: tools for individual identification

E. Petkovski*, C. Keyser-Tracqui, D. Niemeyer, R. Hienne, B. Ludes

Departement Genetique, Institut de Medecine Legale de Strasbourg et Laboratorie CODGENE 11, rue Human, 67085, Strasbourg, Cedex, France

Abstract. SNPs, DNA sequence alterations at a single nucleotide position, present useful advantages over other markers for forensic purposes. The most important advantage is the analysed DNA sequence size, which is much shorter than the one used for STR research. Therefore, SNP profiles could have an application in filiations and individual identification, especially in anthropology where samples are old and often degraded. The aim of this study is the selection of a panel of informative SNPs and the confirmation of their transmission on unrelated French paternity cases. SNPs being biallelic, the analysis of about 50 of them is necessary to obtain the discrimination power of the existing STR multiplexes. We selected a set of informative SNPs and optimised their amplification through multiplex (6–10 fragments) reactions. Pools of two to three loci are analysed simultaneously using MALDI-TOF mass spectrometry. We consider automatic analysis and profile-sample attribution through collaboration with Bruker Daltonique (France). Besides applying these markers to paternity cases, we also evaluate selected SNPs on different populations in order to evaluate population specific frequency data.

Keywords: Forensic genetics; Single nucleotide polymorphism (SNP); Paternity; Individual identification; MALDI-TOF MS

1. Introduction

Despite the fact they are biallelic and therefore of limited discriminatory value, SNPs offer attractive features as genetic markers. For forensic and anthropology applications, the particular advantage of SNPs over other genetic markers is in the length of the studied DNA region. The needed DNA sequence being much shorter, SNP profiles could have an application in studies where only small or degraded samples are available analysis. Furthermore, it has been demonstrated that relatively small arrays of approximately 50 loci are comparable to existing STR multiplexes provided that their alleles range in proportion between 0.2 and 0.8 [1].

The aim of the present study is the selection and validation of a panel of informative biallelic markers, i.e. phenotypically not expressed but conserved and represented at high frequencies, their analysis by matrix assisted laser desorption ionisation time of flight mass

* Corresponding author. Tel.: +33-3-90-24-31-65; fax: +33-3-88-24-00-85.
E-mail address: petkovski@ulp.u-strasbg.fr (E. Petkovski).

0531-5131/
doi:10.1016/S0531-5131(03)01721-7

Table 1
Masses of fragments expected after MALDI-TOF MS analysis

Product	Annotation in Fig. 1	Product mass
Primer AB1T	1	4772 Da
Primer AB2I	2	4858 Da
AB1T-allele A	1a	5085 Da
AB2I-allele A	2a	5171 Da
AB1T-allele G	1b	5406 Da
Primer WI 1732	3	5588 Da
WI 1732-allele A	3a	5901 Da
AB2I-allele G	2b	6159 Da
WI 1732-allele G	3b	6230 Da

In this example, the PEX medium requires dGTP, ddATP and ddTTP to detect the three concerned polymorphisms AB1T [3], AB2I [4] and WI 1732 [5].

spectrometry (MALDI-TOF MS) in order to establish individual specific profiles and evaluate the potential discrimination power.

2. Materials and methods

The SNPs were chosen from published results or the SNP consortium LTD database according to the criteria described in the introduction. Seventy-six individuals belonging to 21 unrelated STR-confirmed and 3 exclusionary paternity cases were genotyped for the 39 selected markers. DNA was extracted from blood samples. Six to 10 SNP containing fragments were co-amplified in multiplex PCR reactions. SNP detection was achieved

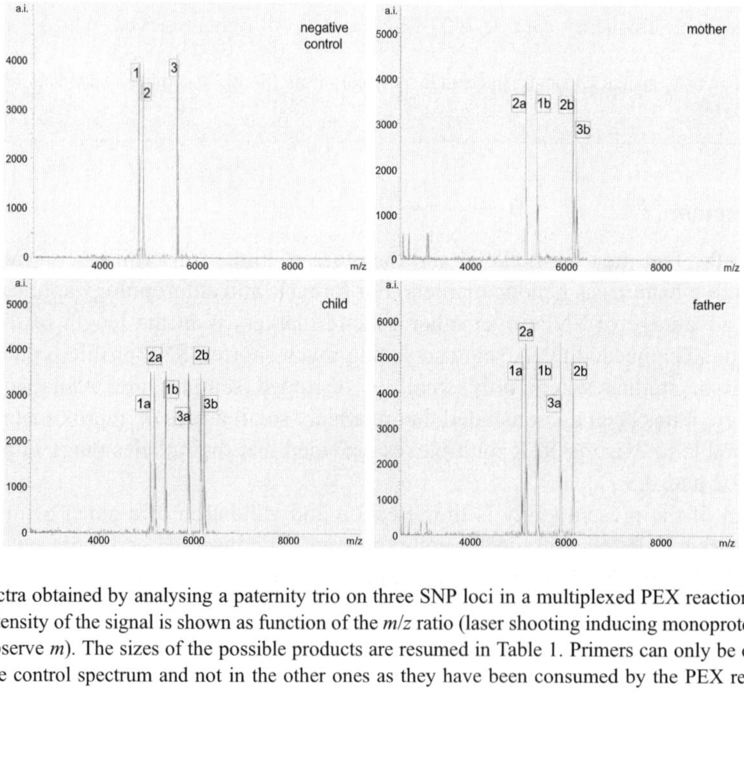

Fig. 1. Spectra obtained by analysing a paternity trio on three SNP loci in a multiplexed PEX reaction. Here, the absolute intensity of the signal is shown as function of the m/z ratio (laser shooting inducing monoprotonation, we virtually observe m). The sizes of the possible products are resumed in Table 1. Primers can only be observed in the negative control spectrum and not in the other ones as they have been consumed by the PEX reaction.

Table 2
Summary of genotypes observed in the example illustrated in Fig. 1 and the thereout calculated paternity indexes for each of the three loci

SNP	Mother	Child	Father	PI
AB1T	G/G	G/A	G/A	2.0243
AB2I	G/A	G/A	G/A	1
WI1732	G/G	G/A	A/A	2

through multiplexed (two to three SNPs) primer extension reactions (PEX) in order to have a minimal 80 Da size difference between the different products. These reactions were designed according to primer compatibility, nucleotides necessary to the PEX and masses of the possible products. An example of fragment masses expected after MALDI-TOF MS analysis are summarised in Table 1. Purification steps were accomplished using Genopure™ technology (Bruker Daltonics). Raw data obtained thanks to an Ultraflex™ MALDI-TOF mass spectrometer (Bruker Daltonics) were interpreted manually. A project of automatic analysis and sample-profile attribution is underway.

3. Results and discussion

An example of the obtained results can be observed in Fig. 1. The MALDI-TOF spectra are easily interpreted by the assessment of the presence or absence of a peak at distinct time-of flight points (corresponding to the mass of the fragment). The genotypes of the paternity trio on these three loci are summarized in Table 2 along with the paternity indexes, which can be calculated thanks to the formulae routinely used in STR analysis [2] and the reported allelic frequencies.

4. Interpretation and discussion

When five loci genotypes inconsistent with paternity were observed, exclusion was concluded, as the probability of the five inconsistencies being linked to mutation is minimal. The obtained results allowed to calculate partial probabilities of paternity by the formula $W = \mathrm{PI}/(1 + \mathrm{PI})$ estimating the probability prior to considering genetic evidence to 50%. These partial W ranged between 99.98% and 99.9999%, which confirms the utility of SNPs as markers for individual identification. Despite the bias due to the presence of persons sharing their genetic material (parents and children), the frequencies we observed on these 76 individuals neighbour the ones reported. This indicates the chosen SNPs are suitable for this application. Furthermore, an SNP profile was obtained from difficult forensic samples such as hairs that did not allow a complete STR profile. This method could allow the achievement of individual specific genetic profiles in short time and at low costs.

References

[1] P. Gill, Int. J. Leg. Med. 114 (4–5) (2001) 204–210.
[2] L.D. White, et al., Oral presentation, Ninth International Symposium on Human Identification, 1998.
[3] P.Y. Kwok, et al., Genomics 31 (1) (1996 Jan 1) 123–126.
[4] H. Haga, et al., J. Hum. Genet. 47 (11) (2002) 605–610.
[5] The SNP Consortium Ltd SC_JCM|AC021163.3_76585.

International Congress Series 1261 (2004) 24–26

www.ics-elsevier.com

Whole genome amplification—the solution for a common problem in forensic casework?

P.M. Schneider[a,*], K. Balogh[a], N. Naveran[b], M. Bogus[a], K. Bender[a], M. Lareu[b], A. Carracedo[b]

[a] *Institute of Legal Medicine, Johannes Gutenberg University, Am Pulverturm 3, 55131 Mainz, Germany*
[b] *Institute of Legal Medicine, University of Santiago de Compostela, Spain*

Abstract. To assess the quality of amplified DNA obtained by whole genome amplification, 17 independent STR loci have been typed using two multiplex kits. Results have been compared for correct genotypes, heterozygous peak balance and allelic dropout.

Keywords: Forensic DNA; STR typing

1. Introduction

A typical problem in forensic stain cases as well as in mass disaster victim identification is the lack of sufficient amounts of genomic DNA in adequate quality. Furthermore, the success of the PCR-based typing methods has led to a dramatic increase in casework samples where only a few nanograms of DNA are available for typing. A possible solution for this "bottleneck" of forensic DNA analysis could be the amplification of the entire genomic DNA prior to locus-specific PCR analysis. Recently, this approach has been improved considerably by using the highly processive Phi29 DNA polymerase which can be used in an isothermal "rolling circle amplification" [1]. Briefly, amplification of genomic DNA is initiated by introducing random hexamer primers. The Phi29 polymerase uses a free 3′ end as starting point, but the replication does not stop when a 5′ end of double-stranded DNA is encountered. Phi29 will displace this strand from the 5′ end and continue with the replication process. New hexamers will bind to the displaced strand and initiate further replication sites leading to an almost exponential amplification reaction. Furthermore, Phi29 polymerase has an approximately 10-fold increased replication fidelity compared to Taq polymerase. Therefore, we have

* Corresponding author. Tel.: +49-6131-3932687; fax: +49-6131-3933183.
E-mail address: pschneid@mail.uni-mainz.de (P.M. Schneider).

doi:10.1016/S0531-5131(03)01846-6

Table 1
Whole genome amplification yields from P118 cell line DNA

DNA input	5 ng	500 pg	50 pg	5 pg
Repli-g 625S	511 ng	530 ng	471 ng	464 ng
GenomiPhi	224 ng	204 ng	184 ng	180 ng

tested whole genome amplification regarding its suitability for multiplex STR typing systems.

2. Material and methods

The two following kits were tested: Repli-g 625S (Molecular Staging) and GenomiPhi (Amersham Biosciences). The two human cell lines HepG2 and P118 were used in dilutions down to 5 pg. The amplification conditions were according to the manufacturers' instructions (16 h at 30 °C). The concentrations of the amplified samples were determined by measuring several independent dilutions by fluorometry. The amplified DNA was subjected to multiplex STR typing using both the PowerPlex 16 (Promega) and the AmpFlSTR SGM Plus kits (Applied Biosystems). Each STR analysis was carried out twice for each cell line and dilution, as well as using both kits. Results were assessed by GeneScan computer analysis and by comparing the relative peak heights of the two alleles of selected heterozygous STR loci.

3. Results and discussion

Whole genome amplification was found to be very efficient. The resulting yield of amplified DNA appeared not to be clearly correlated with the amount of DNA present in the reaction, although the overall yield was about 2-fold higher for Repli-g in comparison to GenomiPhi (Table 1). This may indicate that an amplification plateau was reached in all dilutions tested, even when only 5 pg—the equivalent of a single genome—were used. The presence of high molecular weight DNA was clearly demonstrated in all reactions after agarose gel electrophoresis. However, genetic typing of the amplified DNA is required to assess the specificity and the quality of the reaction products.

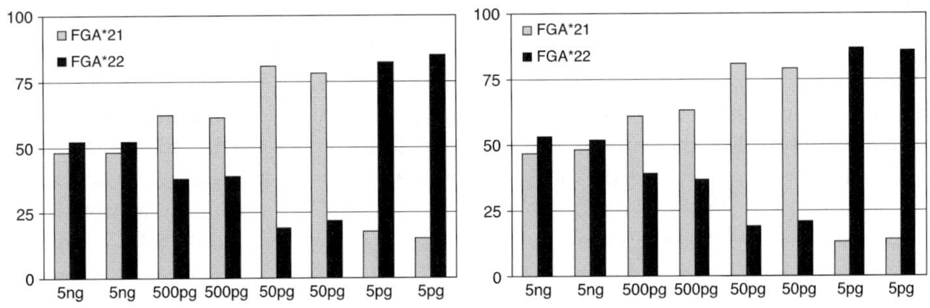

Fig. 1. Repli-g 625S: P118 DNA and FGA peak balance (%) using 5 ng to 5 pg for amplification, left panel: SGM Plus kit; right panel: PowerPlex 16 kit.

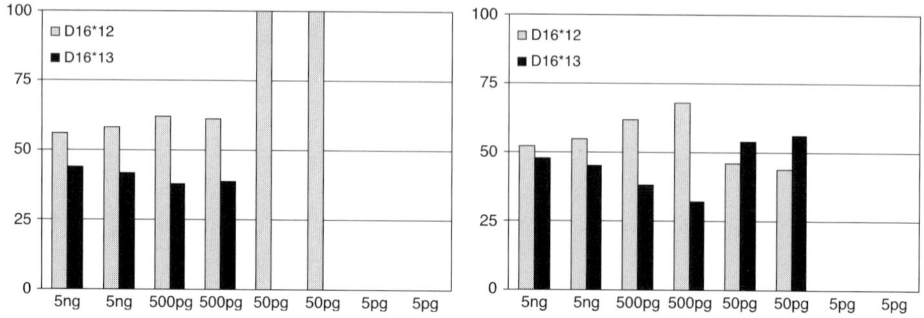

Fig. 2. P118 DNA and SGM Plus D16S539 peak balance (%) using 5 ng to 5 pg for the Repli-g kit (left panel) and the GenomiPhi kit (right panel).

After completion of multiplex STR typing, results from several loci with heterozygous genotypes were further studied to assess peak balance, allelic dropouts and other artefacts. It was found that reliable typing results could be obtained from amplified DNA generated from 500 pg genomic DNA. Dropouts started to occur at 50 pg, and more dramatically at 5 pg. "Drop in" alleles were not observed. In Fig. 1, the results for the two STR multiplex kits for the FGA locus are shown for all DNA concentrations tested in duplicate. It becomes evident that the peak balance is distorted as well as reversed regarding the stronger peak for the 50 and 5 pg reactions, respectively. Also, there is no difference between the two STR kits once the genomic DNA has been amplified. Fig. 2 depicts the occurrence of allelic dropout for the D16S539 locus at 50 pg for the Repli-g kit only, and complete locus dropout at 5 pg for both kits. Obviously, this loss of information occurs due to stochastic effects during genome amplification. Once the amplified DNA has been generated, the stochastic effects lead to genomic regions which may be over- or underrepresented.

It will be important to generate more data on reproducibility to better understand these effects. Whole genome amplification could become a tool for saving precious DNA samples for research purposes, and maybe—once the reliability has been demonstrated—even for limited crime case samples. If stain DNA is sufficient for only two to three direct PCR typings, genome amplification may be used to produce a batch of DNA for further studies without the need to decide about the loci to be analyzed.

Reference

[1] F.B. Dean, et al., Rapid amplification of plasmid and phage DNA using Phi 29 DNA polymerase and multiply-primed rolling circle amplification, Genome Res. 11 (2001) 1095–1099.

ELSEVIER

International Congress Series 1261 (2004) 27–29

www.ics-elsevier.com

Nonbinary single-nucleotide polymorphism markers

Christopher Phillips*, Victoria Lareu, Antonio Salas, Angel Carracedo

Institute of Legal Medicine, University of Santiago de Compostela, Calle San Franscisco s/n 15705 Santiago de Compostela, Galicia, Spain

Abstract. Nonbinary single-nucleotide polymorphism markers (SNPs; i.e., comprising multiple substitutions) may be useful forensic markers as they offer increased discrimination and the possibility of mixture analysis. The NCBI dbSNP database was searched, and, out of the 13 markers selected, nine exhibited nonbinary polymorphism in African and European populations with expected allele distributions.

Keywords: Nonbinary; SNP; Forensic analysis

1. Introduction

Amplification of single-nucleotide polymorphism markers (SNPs) offers the possibility to analyze degraded material with increased success compared to existing techniques. However, the necessary reduction in amplicon size increases the probability of contamination and of encountering mixed DNA patterns [1]. We have examined one possible approach to establish control assays for such events using nonbinary SNPs. These markers amplify with equivalent efficiency to binary SNPs but could indicate the presence of extraneous DNA through the detection of a third or fourth allele. A search of the principal public database: NCBI dbSNP [2] revealed ~ 7000 markers exhibiting one of four types of three-allele polymorphism. From this set, the 13 most informative loci were regenotyped using African and European samples. The initial results of the detection and analysis of simple (two-donor) artificial mixtures are presented.

2. Material and methods

2.1. Bioinformatics

The NCBI dbSNP database was searched using the term: [ALLELE] prefixed with each type of three-allele variation (type V: A/C/G; type D: A/T/G; type B: C/T/G; and type H:

* Corresponding author. Tel: +34-981582327; fax: +34-981580336.
E-mail address: chrisp@usc.es (C. Phillips).

0531-5131/
doi:10.1016/j.ics.2003.12.008

C/T/A) yielding 1885, 1852, 1753 and 1896 SNPs respectively. Each group was reduced using [HETEROZYGOSITY] with “25:65” setting a range 25–65%.

2.2. SNP genotyping

Forty Galician (N.W. Spain) and 40 Mozambican samples were used. PCR primers were designed to give a product size range of 65–120 bp. Multiplex amplifications comprised 400 μM dNTPs, 2 mM MgCl2, 0.4 U Taq Gold polymerase and 2 ng DNA. Cycling conditions were 95 °C for 10 min, 32 cycles of 94 °C for 30 s, 58 °C for 30 s and 70 °C for 30 s, with a final extension of 65 °C for 15 min. Primer concentrations ranged from 0.5 to 1.0 μM. SNaPshot Minisequencing used 1 μl of PCR product cleaned with 0.5 μl of ExoSAP-IT (Amersham Biosciences) with conditions: 96 °C for 10 s, 50 °C for 5 s and 60 °C for 30 s, for 25 cycles. Extension primers were designed with an average t_m of 60 °C.

Table 1
Allele frequency distributions of nine nonbinary SNP loci in European and African samples (n=40) ranked in approximate order of information content

refSNP ID	Population[a]	dbSNP frequencies			Observed frequencies			%Dp	Probability 3rd
		C	A	T	C	A	T		
rs2839675	European	0.46	0.08	0.46	0.54	0.26	0.20	77	33.3
	African				0.38	0.24	0.38	81	41.7
		G	C	T	G	C	T		
rs5030240	European	0.50	0.35	0.15	0.58	0.27	0.15	75	28.5
	African				0.16	0.28	0.56	75	29.6
		A	G	C	A	G	C		
rs385780	European	0.42	0.30	0.28	0.46	0.36	0.18	78	35.6
	African	0.25	0.42	0.33	0.64	0.31	0.05	66	11.4
		C	T	A	C	T	A		
rs3091244	European	0.62	0.33	0.05	0.54	0.34	0.13	75	27.3
	African	0.26	0.41	0.33	0.39	0.49	0.13	75	28.4
		C	G	A	C	G	A		
rs865577	European	0.59	0.41	–	0.54	0.40	0.06	70	16.4
	African	0.35	0.54	0.09	0.39	0.52	0.09	73	22.0
		G	C	A	G	C	A		
rs2069945	European	0.57	0.43	–	0.51	0.40	0.09	72	21.2
	African	0.76	0.24	–	0.86	0.11	0.03	40	2.6
		A	T	C	A	T	C		
rs140676	European	0.57	0.33	0.10	0.58	0.34	0.08	71	18.8
	African				0.67	0.31	0.02	61	4.0
		T	A	G	T	A	G		
rs4540055	European	0.83	0.17	–	0.77	0.20	0.03	54	4.6
	African	0.13	0.47	0.40	0.06	0.45	0.49	70	15.2
		C	G	A	C	G	A		
rs228958	European	0.68	0.32	–	0.65	0.35	–		–
	African	0.45	0.48	0.07	0.53	0.43	0.04	68	12.2

%Dp and probability of observing a third allele in a simple mixture are listed.

2.3. DNA mixture experiments

DNA samples were mixed at ratios ranging from 1:4 to 4:1 and then amplified and minisequenced using a simple but robust three-SNP assay combination.

3. Results and discussion

Out of the 13 SNPs analyzed, nine gave nonbinary polymorphisms, and in both populations studied, eight gave nonbinary polymorphisms as well. Table 1 shows a list of the allele frequencies obtained. Observed alleles were as expected from dbSNP data, and frequencies were in good agreement with those reported elsewhere. One of the other four loci displaying only binary variation shows a third allele that appears to be confined exclusively to diabetic probands. The combined discrimination index of the nonbinary SNPs found is 99.996% in Europeans (8 loci) and 99.995% in Africans (9 loci) equivalent to 11 perfect (0.5:0.5) binary SNPs. In addition, the probability of encountering a third allele in simple mixtures is relatively high when these loci are used in combination. Mixture experiments detected minor component peaks between 1:1 to 1:3 ratios, suggesting that SNaPshot assays can detect extraneous DNA when present at high enough proportions.

References

[1] P. Gill, Int. J. Leg. Med. 114 (2001) 204–210.
[2] http://www.ncbi.nlm.nih.gov/entrez/.

International Congress Series 1261 (2004) 30–32

www.ics-elsevier.com

Population studies using single nucleotide polymorphisms—how important is detailed sample origin information?

C. Thacker[a,*], C. Harrison[a], M. Brion[b], C. Phillips[b], P. Sanchez-Diz[b], D. Ballard[a], A. Carracedo[b], D. Syndercombe Court[a]

[a] *Haematology Department, Barts and The London, Queen Mary's School of Medicine and Dentistry, Turner Street, London E1 2AD, UK*

[b] *Institute of Legal Medicine, Faculty of Medicine, University of Santiago de Compostela, Galicia, Spain*

Abstract. Within the UK there is an increase in the request for information about an individual's ancestory. UK population databases are not uncommon but the detailed origin of samples has not traditionally been collected. Typically samples are classified using very general identifiers such as 'black British'. We have conducted a study to establish whether this lack of detailed information proves to be a major problem when considering population studies relying on SNP data. A panel of Y-chromosome and autosomal SNPs have been used to genotype individuals from a 'black British' population and from six Mozambique population groups. The resulting population data sets were contrasted and differences between a well-defined and a broadly characterized population set were used to illustrate the importance of good sample information. A comparison of the different SNP typing methodologies used throughout this study was conducted and all methods were found to work well.

Keywords: Single nucleotide polymorphism; SNP typing methodologies; Sample information

1. Introduction

An early study used the UK national DNA database to infer the ethnic origin of individuals [1]. Since then, marked population differences in allelic distributions of Y chromosome STRs have been exploited to predict ethnic origin, although the relatively high mutation rates necessitate proceeding with care. With mutation rates of only 2.5×10^{-8} per base per generation [2], SNPs look a more promising marker for this purpose. The study of SNPs is increasing rapidly and consequently there is a large amount of population data available. The majority of studies have concentrated on well-defined populations and as the

* Corresponding author. Tel.: +44-2073-777076; fax: +44-2073-777629.
E-mail address: c.r.thacker@qmul.ac.uk (C. Thacker).

doi:10.1016/j.ics.2003.12.090

significance of forensic analysis often depends upon the population frequency of a finding [3], the question arises as to how valuable this resource is to the UK population.

The possible uses of SNPs are well published but the selection of an appropriate detection platform is something that needs careful consideration.

2. Materials and methods

2.1. DNA samples and DNA extraction

Two databases composed of unrelated, consenting individuals were used for this study. The first database was broadly defined as 'black British'. It was composed of individuals resident within the UK who were identified as belonging to this racial group either by photograph or personal description. The second database was a well-characterized population and was composed of samples donated by indigenous Bantu speakers of Mozambique. The geographical origin of each individual's four grandparents was known. DNA was extracted using Chelex® 100 chelating resin [4].

2.2. SNP selection and primer design

SNPs were not selected for the populations studied. Ten Y-chromosome SNPs and three autosomal SNPs were used. Primers were designed using Primer Express™ 1.5 software (Applied Biosystems). Design constraints were applied to enable the same primers to be used for all the SNP typing methodologies utilised in this study. All primers were HPLC-purified.

2.3. DNA amplification, minisequencing and silver staining

The extracted DNA (10 μl) was amplified in a total PCR reaction volume of 50 μl. For each reaction, 8 μl of PCR product was subjected to a restriction digest. Digested products were run on 9% polyacrylamide gels and visualised following silver staining [5]. The remaining PCR products were pooled and cleaned-up using either ExoSAP-IT® (USB) or MinElute PCR purification columns (Qiagen). Minisequencing was performed using SNaPshot™ (Applied Biosystems) and this was followed by SAP purification (Roche Diagnostics). The purified minisequencing products were analysed using the ABI Prism™ 310 Genetic Analyser (Applied Biosystems).

2.4. TaqMan® detection

TaqMan® detection was performed using the ABI Prism™ 7700 Sequence Detector (Applied Biosystems). As many of the sequences were AT- or GC-rich, MGB probes (Applied Biosystems) were designed for the real-time analysis. Chelex® extract (7 μl) was used in a 25 μl total reaction volume.

3. Results

All technologies worked well however some discrepancies were noted between the manual and SNaPshot™ results. There was no difference in the quality of purification obtained using either ExoSAP-IT® or the MinElute PCR purification columns.

There were noticeable differences between the two populations studied. The well-defined Mozambique samples showed very little intra-group variation. In contrast, the UK black population exhibited a substantial amount of variation between samples. M40 can help define the largely African haplogroup E [6]. The G to A transition characterizes this SNP with all the Mozambique samples exhibiting an A allele. Almost 40% of the UK population tested possessed the G allele. P25 can be used to help define haplogroup R, a European haplogroup [6]. No polymorphism was seen in the Mozambique population (all exhibited the ancestral state, a C allele) whereas 15.4% of the UK black population showed P25 in the derived state (an A allele).

4. Discussion

4.1. Typing techniques

Smaller amplicons were sometimes difficult to accurately size using manual techniques. The discrepancies seen between this method and SNaPshot™ were attributed to this interpretation difficulty. Financial restraints, access to instrumentation and availability of consumables and reagents means that some laboratories have a very limited choice when determining their method of SNP detection. This study has shown that this need not prohibit these laboratories making a significant contribution to the progression of SNP research.

4.2. The black British population

The black British population shows a high level of admixture and as a consequence requires a great deal of caution when assigning a sample to an ethnic group. The UK has strong links with the African Commonwealth countries and its black population will have been influenced in part by the slave trades of the Caribbean and, to a lesser extent, the Atlantic. Although it has been shown that haplotypes can be used to provide useful information on ancestry, it is not possible to use them to reliably predict how an individual from the UK black population would describe themselves. This study has shown that detailed sample information is essential if compiling a population database to be used as a reference source. In the case of populations exhibiting a high level of diversity, published data is not always applicable.

References

[1] A.L. Lowe, et al., Inferring ethnic origin by means of an STR profile, Forensic Science International 119 (2001) 17–22.

[2] R. Thomson, et al., Recent common ancestry of human Y-chromosomes: evidence from DNA sequence data, Proceedings of the National Academy of Sciences of the United States of America 97 (13) (2000) 7360–7365.

[3] M.A. Jobling, C. Tyler-Smith, The human Y-chromosome: an evolutionary marker comes of age, Nature Reviews. Genetics 4 (2003) 598–612.

[4] P.S. Walsh, et al., Chelex 100 as a medium for simple extraction of DNA for PCR-based typing from forensic material, BioTechniques 10 (4) (1991) 506–513.

[5] C.P. Phillips, et al., Manual electrophoretic methods for genotyping amplified STR loci, in: P.J. Lincoln, J. Thomson (Eds.), Methods in Molecular Biology, Forensic DNA Profiling Protocols, vol. 98, Humana Press, Totowa, NY, 1998, pp. 181–192.

[6] Y Chromosome Consortium, A nomenclature system for the tree of human Y-chromosomal binary haplogroups, Genome Research 12 (2002) 339–348.

International Congress Series 1261 (2004) 33–35

www.ics-elsevier.com

Characteristics of D5S818 mutations revealed through study of a flanking marker

Michael Edwards[a], Robert W. Allen[b,c,*]

[a] *Orchid-GeneScreen, Dayton, OH, USA*

[b] *Forensic Sciences, Center for Health Sciences, Oklahoma State University, 1111 W. 17th Street, Tulsa, OK 74107, USA*

[c] *H.A. Chapman Institute of Medical Genetics, 4502 E. 41st, Tulsa, OK 74135, USA*

Abstract. A cytosine/thymosine (C/T) polymorphism was discovered 13 nucleotides upstream from the 5′ end of the tandem array of the D5S818 locus (− 13 SNP). The − 13 SNP coincidently creates a restriction site polymorphism for the restriction endonuclease SnaB1 that is tightly linked to the D5S818 tandem array. RFLP mapping of the − 13 SNP was used to characterize 40 D5S818 addition/deletion mutations encountered in routine parentage testing. Most mutations showed paternal bias and single repeat changes to the tandem array. In 19 instances, it was possible to identify the parental allele that underwent the mutation. Alleles 13 and 14 were especially prone to mutation whereas allele #11 was unexpectedly resistant.

Keywords: D5S818 STR locus; Mutations; Parentage testing

1. Introduction

Occasionally, in parentage investigations using DNA typing, results inconsistent with parentage are encountered with the true parent of a child. The explanation for such inconsistencies are mutations that either add or delete repeats from the tandem array [1, 2].

The D5S818 locus represents a typical VNTR consisting of a 4-basepair repeat element of homogeneous AGAT sequence [4]. In preliminary studies, an RFLP for the enzyme SnaB1 was discovered upstream from the tandem array due to a C/T polymorphism (hereafter called the − 13 SNP). The existence of a flanking SNP marker provided an opportunity to examine the molecular details of 40 D5S818 mutations.

2. Materials and methods

Mutations used for this study were identified from routine parentage testing performed by Orchid-GeneScreen (Dayton, OH) or the H.A. Chapman Institute of Medical Genetics

* Corresponding author. H.A. Chapman Institute of Medical Genetics, 4502 E. 41st, Tulsa, OK 74135, USA. Tel.: +1-918-660-3827; fax: +1-918-660-3840.

E-mail address: rallen@genetictechnologies.com (R.W. Allen).

0531-5131/
doi:10.1016/S0531-5131(03)01777-1

Table 1
Observed versus expected mutations at the D5S818 locus

Progenitor allele	Observed	Expected[a]
<11	0	2.57
11	2	6.71
12	7	6.384
13	6	3.192
14	4	0.247
>14	0	0.076

$p \leq 0.001$[b].

[a] Predicted from allele frequency (or combined allele frequency) averaged over the Caucasian, Black and Hispanic population.

[b] Chi-square statistic considering significance of deviation from expectations. Calculated with 5 degrees of freedom.

(Tulsa, OK). DNA was extracted from buccal swabs or blood samples using standard inorganic extraction methods and amplified using a monoplex kit for the D5S818 locus (Promega Madison, WI). Amplicons were digested with SnaB1 and visualized using a fluorescent scanner (FMBIO, Hitachi) following electrophoresis in 6% polyacrylamide gels.

3. Results

The − 13 SNP exhibits two genotypes in the population. When the C allele is present at the SNP site (~ 80% frequency), D5S818 allele size is reduced by SnaB1 digestion by 27 basepairs from the 5′ end of the amplicon. Amplified alleles of the T genotype (~ 20% frequency) are unaffected by SnaB1 digestion.

The RFLP analysis was applied to 40 D5S818 mutations accumulated from approximately 20,000 paternity cases representing almost 40,000 meioses. The majority of mutations occurred within the paternal lineage (97%) and involved changes of a single repeat (92%), consistent with published data for the D5S818 locus [5]. The number of additions was roughly equal to the number of deletions of repeats from the tandem array (54% versus 46%, respectively). Finally, the C/T genotype at the − 13 SNP site among mutations was consistent with their population frequency, suggesting no correlation of − 13 SNP genotype with susceptibility of a D5S818 allele to undergo mutation.

For 19 mutations, it was possible to determine progenitor alleles in the parent producing the mutant allele in the child. The results of this analysis are shown in Table 1. Allele 14 was identified as the progenitor in 4 of 19 mutations (~ 21%), yet this allele has an average population frequency of only slightly above 1%. In contrast, allele 11 was the progenitor for 2 of 19 mutations (~ 11%), but exhibits a population frequency of about 35%.

4. Discussion

Mutations in our panel were analyzed assuming all trios represent true families, an assumption strongly supported by the extended testing performed in each case. It was also assumed that the addition or deletion to the tandem array did not also alter the genotype of the flanking − 13 SNP. Although "null alleles" are known to exist for STR loci due to single nucleotide variations in the primer binding regions (5, 6), they generally do not affect the integrity of the tandem array [6].

A direct relationship between the number of repeats in the tandem array and the instability of the allele was suggested [2,3,7]. All 40 of our mutations involved progenitor alleles belonging to the 11, 12, 13 or 14 allele classes. Allele 14 (one of the larger alleles at the locus), which accounts for only about 1% of D5S818 alleles, was the progenitor in over 20% of informative mutations. Two additional alleles at the D5S818 locus, 15 and 16 were not involved in any of the mutations in our panel and yet exhibit a combined population frequency somewhat similar to allele 14. If allele instability is directly proportional to the number of repeats, the involvement of either allele 15 or 16 in at least one mutation might have been expected. In contrast, allele 11 (about 35% frequency) was the progenitor in only about 11% of the mutations suggesting an enhanced stability. Taken together, these results suggest that allele length alone is not responsible for instability and that a more complex relationship exists between the allele length and stability from additions and deletions.

The results also suggest that accurate weighting of evidence inconsistent with parentage at the D5S818 locus should incorporate the mutation rate for the particular D5S818 allele rather than an average mutation rate for the locus.

Acknowledgements

Support in part by funds from the H.A. Chapman Charitable Trust.

References

[1] J.L. Weber, C. Wong, Mutation of human short tandem repeats, Hum. Mol. Genet. 2 (1993) 1123–1128.

[2] B. Brinkmann, M. Klintschar, F. Neuhuber, J. Huhne, B. Rolf, Mutation rate in human microsatellites: influence of the structure and length of the tandem repeat, Am. J. Hum. Genet. 62 (1998) 1408–1415.

[3] M. Wierdl, M. Dominska, T.D. Petes, Microsatellite instability in yeast: dependence on the length of the microsatellite, Genetics 146 (1997) 769–779.

[4] H.A. Hammond, L. Jin, Y. Zhong, C.T. Caskey, R. Chakraborty, Evaluation of 13 short tandem repeat loci for use in personal identification applications, Am. J. Hum. Genet. 55 (1994) 175–189.

[5] Annual Report Summary for Parentage Testing Laboratories for 2001, American Association of Blood Banks, Bethesda, MD, 2002.

[6] R.W. Allen, J. Pritchard, J. Harman, S. Chandler, Phenotypic differences at the HUMvWA locus amplified with different STR kits, J. Forensic Sci. 5 (2000) 1166–1167.

[7] C.R. Primmer, N. Saino, A.P. Moller, H. Ellegren, Unravelling the processes of microsatellite evolution through analysis of germ line mutations in barn swallows *Hirundo rustica*, Mol. Biol. Evol. 15 (1998) 1047–1054.

International Congress Series 1261 (2004) 36–38

www.ics-elsevier.com

Cytochrome *P*450 2D6 genotyping of fatal intoxications using Pyrosequencing

A.L. Zackrisson[a,*], P. Holmgren[b], A.B. Gladh[a], J. Ahlner[b], B. Lindblom[a]

[a] *National Board of Forensic Medicine, Department of Forensic Genetics, University Hospital, SE-581 85 Linköping, Sweden*

[b] *National Board of Forensic Medicine, Department of Forensic Chemistry, University Hospital, Linköping, Sweden*

Abstract. Many commonly used pharmaceuticals such as antidepressants and neuroleptics as well as some illegal drugs are metabolised by the Cytochrome *P*450 enzyme debrisoquine 4-hydroxylase (CYP2D6). Seven to ten percent of Caucasians lack this enzyme which can lead to adverse reactions and in some cases to unexpected intoxication even with fatal outcome, upon administration of drugs in normal therapeutic doses. 236 individuals who had died due to intoxication of pharmaceuticals were genotyped for CYP2D6 and compared to a reference group of 281 blood donors. A single nucleotide polymorphism (SNP) method was used to identify five CYP2D6 alleles: *1 (wt), *2, *3, *4 and *6. Allele *5, a complete gene deletion, was identified by a multiplex amplification of long DNA fragments. The prevalence of the CYP2D6 PM genotype in the fatal intoxications was lower (4.7%) compared to the blood donors (8.5%). A significant decrease ($p < 0.005$) was found in the CYP2D6*4 allele frequency among the fatal intoxications.

Keywords: Genotyping; CYP2D6; SNP; Pyrosequencing; Post-mortem

1. Introduction

The Cytochrome *P*450 (CYP) debrisoquine 4-hydroxylase is a liver enzyme coded from the CYP2D6 gene in the Cytochrome *P*450 gene cluster, CYP2D6-D8P, on chromosome 22 in humans. The CYP2D6 enzyme metabolises a variety of toxic plant substances and many drugs, such as antidepressants, neuroleptics, opiates, antiarrythmics and antihypertensive agents [1]. Seven to ten percent of Caucasians lack this enzyme and will have an increased risk for adverse reactions sometimes with fatal intoxication. More than 80 different alleles have been reported for CYP2D6 [2]. The majority of these alleles are rare and associated with a decreased or none CYP2D6 activity known as a poor metabolism phenotype (PM). The most frequent PM alleles are *4, *5, *3 and *6, in decreasing order. These four alleles can predict 93–98% of the PM phenotypes in Caucasians [3–5]. In contrast, 1–7% of the Caucasian population have increased CYP2D6 activity (ultrarapid metabolisers) [3,6]. In previous studies on CYP2D6 in forensic materials [7,8], we found a lower frequency of PMs.

* Corresponding author. Tel.: +46-13-223025; fax: +46-13-136005.
E-mail address: annza@imv.liu.se (A.L. Zackrisson).

0531-5131/
doi:10.1016/S0531-5131(03)01645-5

Table 1
Number of individuals with 0, 1 or 2 functional alleles in intoxications and blood donors

	Number of functional alleles			Total number of individuals
	0	1	2	
	q/q	p/q	p/p	
Intoxications	11 (4.7%)	87 (37%)	138 (58%)	236
Blood donors	24 (8.5%)	127 (45%)	130 (46%)	281

Our aim in this work was to study different Cytochrome *P*450 systems such as CYP2D6, CYP2C9 and CYP2C19 in a larger group of deaths caused by intoxication of pharmaceuticals or illegal drugs. This is a report from a part of the work that comprises CYP2D6.

2. Materials and methods

Samples were taken from 242 consecutive cases when the causes of death were considered by the forensic pathologist to be fatal intoxication with a pharmaceutical. Samples from 281 blood donors were also collected.

At the autopsy, femoral blood was collected and potassium fluoride was added as a preservative. Genomic DNA was extracted with GenoM48™ robotic workstation (GenoVision, Vienna, Austria). Genomic DNA from the blood donors was extracted according to the DTAB/CTAB method [9]. The Regional Ethics Committee (Faculty of Health Sciences, Linköping University, Sweden) gave permission for analysis.

Four alleles associated with the PM phenotype were studied, CYP2D6*3 (2549A>del), *4 (1846G>A), *5 (deleted sequence) and CYP2D6*6 (1707T>del). Additionally the polymorphism 2850C>T in allele *2 was identified. That polymorphism is also present in the alleles *4K, *8, *11–12, *14, *17, *20, *28–32 and *34–35 some of which are associated with a normal or increased enzyme activity and others with low or no activity [4]. The allele *1 (wt) also can include other polymorphisms. The allele CYP2D6*5 was identified using a multiplex long PCR method [10]. The other alleles were identified by single nucleotide polymorphism (SNP) analysis using Pyrosequencing [11–13].

3. Results

The CYP2D6 genotype was established in 236 of the 242 samples. In 11 of the 236 fatal intoxications (4.7%), a PM genotype was found compared to 8.5% in the blood donors. Considering the number of functional alleles (0, 1 and 2) a significant difference

Table 2
Allele frequencies

Alleles	Frequencies	
	Intoxications	Blood donors
*1	0.428	0.367
*2	0.341	0.324
*3	0.015	0.014
*4	0.169	0.244
*5	0.038	0.043
*6	0.008	0.009

($p < 0.0005$) was found (Table 1). The total number of nonfunctional alleles (*3, *4, *5 and *6) was also found significantly decreased ($p < 0.005$) among the fatal intoxications. The allele *4 was found less frequent ($p \approx 0.001$) among the intoxications (Table 2).

4. Discussion

Earlier we have shown a lower frequency of poor metabolisers [7,8] in forensic intoxication cases. However, the number of cases in those studies was small. We wanted to investigate a larger material of forensic cases of intoxications to confirm or discharge those results. The result presented here shows that there is a lower frequency of PM alleles in the forensic cases compared to the blood donors. The decrease of the CYP2D6*4 allele in the fatal intoxications is statistically significant. To our knowledge this has not been shown earlier. The reasons for these findings are so far not known, but further studies are in progress.

Acknowledgements

This work was supported by grants from the National Board of Forensic Medicine (Rättsmedicinalverket), Sweden.

References

[1] K. Brosen, Drug-metabolizing enzymes and therapeutic drug monitoring in psychiatry, Ther. Drug Monit. 18 (4) (1996) 393–396.

[2] M. Ingelman-Sundberg, A.K. Daly, D.W. Nebert, Human Cytochrome *P*450 (CYP) Allele Nomenclature Comittee (www.imm.ki.se/CYPalleles/cyp2d6.htm) eds.

[3] C. Sachse, J. Brockmoller, S. Bauer, I. Roots, Cytochrome *P*450 2D6 variants in a Caucasian population: allele frequencies and phenotypic consequences, Am. J. Hum. Genet. 60 (2) (1997) 284–295.

[4] D. Marez, et al., Polymorphism of the cytochrome *P*450 CYP2D6 gene in a European population: characterization of 48 mutations and 53 alleles, their frequencies and evolution, Pharmacogenetics 7 (3) (1997) 193–202.

[5] C. Sachse, et al., Correctness of prediction of the CYP2D6 phenotype confirmed by genotyping 47 intermediate and poor metabolizers of debrisoquine, Pharmacogenetics 8 (1998) 181–185.

[6] J.A. Agundez, et al., Prevalence of CYP2D6 gene duplication and its repercussion on the oxidative phenotype in a white population, Clin. Pharmacol. Ther. 57 (1995) 265–269.

[7] H. Druid, et al., Cytochrome *P*450 2D6 (CYP2D6) genotyping on postmortem blood as a supplementary tool for interpretation of forensic toxicological results, Forensic Sci. Int. 99 (1999) 25–34.

[8] P. Holmgren, et al., Enantioselective analysis of citalopram and its metabolites in postmortem blood and genotyping for CYP2D6 and CYP2C19, JAT (2003) (in press).

[9] S. Gustincich, et al., A fast method for high-quality genomic DNA extraction from whole human blood. Biotechniques 11 (3) (1991) 298–300, 302.

[10] M. Hersberger, et al., Rapid detection of the CYP2D6*3, CYP2D6*4, and CYP2D6*6 alleles by tetra-primer PCR and of the CYP2D6*5 allele by multiplex long PCR, Clin. Chem. 46 (8 Pt 1) (2000) 1072–1077.

[11] A.L. Zackrisson, B. Lindblom, Identification of CYP2D6 alleles by single nucleotide polymorphism analysis using pyrosequencing, Eur. J. Clin. Pharmacol. 59 (2003) 521–526.

[12] M. Ronaghi, et al., Real-time DNA sequencing using detection of pyrophosphate release, Anal. Biochem. 242 (1) (1996) 84–89.

[13] A. Ahmadian, et al., Single-nucleotide polymorphism analysis by pyrosequencing, Anal. Biochem. 280 (1) (2000) 103–110.

International Congress Series 1261 (2004) 39–41

www.ics-elsevier.com

The identification of the victims of the Linate air crash by DNA analysis

A. Piccinini[a,*], F. Betti[a], M. Capra[a], C. Cattaneo[b]

[a] Forensic Genetics Laboratory, Institute of Legal Medicine, University of Milan, Via L. Mangiagalli, 37-20133 Milan, Italy

[b] Forensic Anthropology and Odontology Laboratory, Institute of Legal Medicine, University of Milan, Via Mangiagalli, 37-20133 Milan, Italy

Abstract. One hundred eighteen people were killed at Milan's Linate airport on October 8th, 2001 in a runway collision between a SAS airliner preparing for take-off and a private Cessna plane. The identification of the victims was carried out with visual, anthropological, odontological, and genetic means. The genetic identification was carried out through comparison of the remains with reference samples from personal objects of the victims or blood/saliva samples from their relatives. DNA typing alone led to the identification of 12 victims and 4 body parts, while DNA in combination with odontology allowed to identify 27 victims. The combined work of pathologists, odontologists and geneticists led to the positive identification of all 118 victims in 14 days.

Keywords: Mass disaster; Air crash; Identification; STR

1. Introduction

One hundred eighteen people lost their lives in the worst Italian civil aviation air crash in a collision between two planes on a heavy fog morning of October 18th, 2001.

One of the main concerns of the multidisciplinary identification team regarded the promptness of the identification procedure, in order to give burial to the victims as quickly as possible. The genetic tests allowed us to identify victims and body parts. The DNA team was composed of four forensic geneticists. Their work started upon conveyance of personal objects belonging to the victims or biological samples from their relatives or sibs. Both procedures were accompanied by signing specific forms, which were signed by the relatives/sibs conveying samples.

The DNA profiles obtained from the relatives or from the victims' personal objects were cross compared with those obtained from the victims' samples. DNA analyses allowed the identification of 43 victims, 39 of which were onboard the airliner or inside the baggage hangar hit by the plane, while 4 were onboard the Cessna plane. DNA

* Corresponding author. Tel.: +39-2-50315700; fax: +39-2-50315724.
E-mail address: andreapiccinini@yahoo.com (A. Piccinini).

0531-5131/
doi:10.1016/S0531-5131(03)01538-3

analyses carried out in combination with odontological, visual and anthropological means allowed the identification of all of the 118 victims in 14 days.

2. Materials and methods

A total of 54 personal objects (15 analysed) and 57 saliva samples (32 analysed) had been conveyed to the Institute of Legal Medicine by the relatives of the victims. Two saliva and four blood samples had been conveyed by the Swedish Authorities. In one case, the Danish Authorities transmitted the genetic profiles obtained by the two daughters of a perished Danish couple. A total of 68 muscle samples had been taken from the victims' bodies (62 analysed) and from four body parts. PCI extraction was carried out in each case; standard PCR followed using the commercial kits SGM Plus™ and Powerplex 16™. Fragments were resolved on a ABI 373 with Genotyper automatic allele call. The derived profiles were stored in Excel tables. The profiles were confronted with one another side by side.

Statistical analyses with population-specific frequency data were carried out by calculating the likelihood ratio of paternity/maternity in motherless/fatherless cases, respectively, using a spreadsheet kindly provided by G. Carmody, Ottawa. No statistical calculations were made in case of direct comparison, being the matching probability in Caucasians 1:1.8 exp 17 (Powerplex), 1:3.3 exp 12 (SGM Plus). When low LR were achieved, no extra loci were analysed as no cross-match nor half-match (paternity/maternity relationships) had been observed among all the remaining samples. The likelihood of parenthood was calculated following the method suggested by Ballantyne [1].

3. Results

Muscle DNA: good results were always achieved except for one case. A second DNA extraction step was then necessary.

Reference samples: good results always except for three toothbrushes and one razor. In these cases, allelic drop-out or PCR failure was observed.

At the end of the identification procedure, 12 victims and 4 body parts were identified by DNA analysis only; DNA analysis in combination with forensic anthropology/odontology led to the identification of 27 victims.

Direct identification (victim-personal objects) was achieved in 11 cases, while indirect identification (mother/father–son/daughter or vice versa) led to the identification of 21 victims. Double identification (relatives and personal object) was achieved in several cases.

In four cases, the DNA identification of one victim allowed the identification of a relative or a sib of the identified victim.

4. Discussion

The team work of forensic pathologists, forensic odontologists and forensic geneticists led to a positive and relatively quick conclusion of the identification procedure of the 118 victims of the worst tragedy of the Italian civil aviation. "Traditional" identification methods (e.g. [2–4]) or completely genetic procedures [5–7] have been employed in cases of mass disaster. In fact the best approach has to be selected case by case, being each mass disaster to be regarded as unique [8]. In this case, some victims were still visually identifiable, while others could be easily identified by cross-matching of ante-mortem and post-mortem dental X-rays, others only by DNA analysis due to complete carbonisation. It has been estimated that the odontological approach is not feasible in case of severe body fragmentation in approximately 20% cases [8] and genetic analyses could similarly be useless—even misleading—in case of non-paternity which could be revealed by the identification procedure itself. Therefore, in the present case, all available tools were employed, as suggested elsewhere [9]. DNA analysis was the only identification tool in 12 cases out of 118 (~ 10%). In other 5 cases, DNA tests results were conclusive due to incomplete odontological data, while in 27 cases (23%), genetic analyses reinforced the odontological identification. DNA analysis was then conclusive in 14.4% cases and it allowed the identification of body parts in four cases. Direct identification was achieved by comparing the victims' genetic profiles with their personal objects; indirect identification was obtained by comparing the victims' profiles with their relatives or their sibs in a paternity/maternity testing-like fashion. The good preservation of the victims' bodies along with reasonable/good amounts of DNA from the retrieved personal objects allowed to obtain reliable profiles; the typical artefacts, which can be observed in cases of low amount of DNA [10], have been observed only occasionally. No mutations in the father/mother-sib relationships were detected, although this could happen [11]. Likelihood ratios have been calculated only in case of mother/father-sibs scenarios: the obtained LRs turned out to be highly significant in some cases, while in some other cases, they resulted in lower values. In the latter case, no extra DNA markers have been analysed both because of the purpose of the analysis (identification in a mass disaster case not in a forensic paternity/maternity setting) and because no cross-matches among the samples were observed. In case of direct identification, the identification power of the commercial kits employed was considered sufficiently informative. Following the described procedures, the identification of the victims of the Linate air crash of October 8th, 2001 was carried out in 14 days.

Acknowledgements

We are grateful to the academic, non-academic, secretarial, technical staff, trainees of the Institute of Legal Medicine of Milan; Applied Biosystems; and Promega for their support.

References

[1] J. Ballantyne, Nat. Genet. 15 (4) (1997) 329–331.
[2] A. Valenzuela, et al., Int. J. Leg. Med. 113 (2000) 236–239.
[3] P. Nambiar, et al., Clin. Anat. 12 (1999) 16–19.
[4] T. Kahana, J. Hiss, J. Clin. Forensic Med. 4 (1997) 7–15.
[5] Swissair DNA Typing Task Force, Proc. First Int. Conf. Forensic Hum. Ident, Forensic Science Service, London, (1999 October) 1–5.
[6] B. Olaisen, et al., Nat. Genet. 15 (4) (1997) 402–405.
[7] D. Corach, et al., Electrophoresis 16 (9) (1995) 1617–1623.
[8] R.B. Brannon, H.P. Kessler, J. Forensic Sci. 44 (1) (1999) 123–127.
[9] G.H. Moody, A. Busuttil, Am. J. Forensic Med. Pathol. 15 (1) (1994) 63–69.
[10] J.P. Whitaker, et al., BioTechniques 18 (4) (1995) 670–677.
[11] C.J. Fregeau, et al., Prog. Forensic Genet. 8 (2000) 40–42.

International Congress Series 1261 (2004) 42–44

www.ics-elsevier.com

Large-scale comparative genotyping and kinship analysis: evolution in its use for human identification in mass fatality incidents and missing persons databasing

B. Leclair*

Myriad Genetic Laboratories Incorporated, Product Development, 320 Wakara Way, Salt Lake City, UT, 84108, USA

Abstract. The discovery of mass graves and the advent of the World Trade Center tragedy have underscored the necessity to better harness the information content of large DNA typing data sets with bioinformatic tools. This presentation will review the evolution of a bioinformatic tool originally created to assist with the identification of the victims of the Swissair Air Disaster in 1998. This tool was re-built in 2001 to handle the much more demanding complexities of the WTC tragedy. This second generation included the capability to process very large STR and SNP data sets, to collapse remains data, to build composite profiles from overlapping partial remains profiles, to search for potential kinship associations on a purely genetic basis, to verify the consistency of complete family pedigrees, and to perform likelihood ratio calculations. The next generation of this tool is under construction as a stand-alone application under a new database architecture. It will provide functionalities to meet the needs of very large mass fatality incidents (MFIs), and of missing persons databasing initiatives. The considerable benefits of integrated, systematic "data mining" approaches will be discussed. © 2003 Elsevier B.V. All rights reserved.

Keywords: Mass fatality incidents; Missing persons databasing; Bioinformatics; Software; STR

1. Introduction

In this last decade, as DNA typing evolved and made it possible to process large numbers of samples, the successful use of the technology in the processing of remains recovered from mass fatality incidents (MFIs) has established the technology as a pivotal human identification tool for this type of event. DNA typing is unique in its ability to derive identity information from any type of tissue, which often proves crucial in incidents where body fragmentation is severe. DNA typing has also proven robust in generating genotyping results from remains exposed to severe environmental insult/decay. Despite these undeniable

* Tel.: +1-801-883-3814; fax: +1-801-584-1190.
E-mail address: bleclair@myriad.com (B. Leclair).

doi:10.1016/S0531-5131(03)01661-3

technical advances, large-scale massive fragmentation/decay MFIs still face significant complexities on the DNA data analysis front, as this type of field exercise rarely benefits from the availability of uncompromised remains, personal effects of reliable source attribution for all the victims, of reference samples from mother + father and/or offspring + spouse for all the victims. The necessity to work with very large but yet incomplete data sets renders the task of making accurate kinship associations more difficult. In that context, large-scale comparative genotyping is unavoidable. This manuscript reviews different iterations of a bioinformatic tool created to carry out such a function in large-scale MFIs.

2. The Swissair Flight 111 air disaster

The event took place in 1998, 229 passengers and crew perished, the crash dispersed thousands of severely fragmented human remains. Successful PCR amplification produced genotypes for 97% of the recovered remains [1]. Perfect matches with the genotypes derived from trace biological evidence recovered from personal effects purported to have belonged to the victims was immediately considered. However, as some of the most useful personal effects of the victims had been lost at sea in luggage, this route, although useful, was not perceived as being sufficient. Kinship analysis was considered, but both biological parents and/or offspring and spouse were available for only 26% of all victims. A total of 43 families including both parents with all or nearly all of their children were among the victims and represented another 26% of the victims. For the latter group, the necessity to reconstruct family pedigrees from within the questioned genotype data set was anticipated to be a demanding task. The anticipated encounter of core repeat slip mutations was also perceived as a complicating factor. A pair-wise genotype comparison scheme where a victim genotype is queried against the entire data set comprised of both next-of-kin references and other victims appeared to be a screening/sorting/scoring solution that could be rapidly implemented in an automated fashion for the rapid identification of significant biological relationships. On the basis of Mendelian inheritance rules, suspected parent/offspring relationships could be inferred by computing the number of loci at which at least one allele is shared. The scheme was automated with VBA in Excel. It permitted for all possible (i.e. 180,000) pair-wise genotype comparisons to be examined. As a closed population of victims was reached for this tragedy, the approach also permitted for the systematic exclusion of fortuitous kinship associations. Despite the design simplicity of the scheme, all inferred identification leads for the 218 victims for whom reference samples were available were supported by frequency and likelihood calculations carried out separately. This outcome confirmed the value of this screening approach as a first step in a victim identification strategy.

3. The World Trade Center tragedy

A very different situation was encountered with the WTC tragedy where nearly 3000 victims had perished, approximately 20,000 human remains were recovered, reference samples from 6000 relatives and 5000 personal effects were collected. A quick assessment with simulated data as to the suitability for the WTC situation of the approach used for the Swissair incident proved positive. However, the processing algorithms needed to be completely redesigned to reduce execution time by 150-fold for the 33×10^6 pair-wise genotype comparisons anticipated for the WTC data. This entirely new platform (MDKAP) included a variety of new functionalities, including the capability to: (1) collapse the 20,000 partial/complete genotypes derived from the remains to a reduced number of consensus genotypes; (2) assemble composite "virtual" genotypes from overlapping partial genotypes. A capability to search for a productive parentage trio was built in as well. However, evidence surfaced several months into the operation that for an unknown number of next-of-kin samples, the reported biological relationship to the victim could prove incorrect. In order to compensate for this deficiency, a triangulation approach was abandoned for a systematic testing, for each queried victim's genotype, of all potential trios that could be assembled with combinatorial pairs of relatives. This systematic approach, albeit computationally intensive, provided a matching process insensitive to potential errors in a sample's accessory information. The calculation of likelihood ratios for pair-wise comparisons was introduced, and was found to produce a very similar ranking of score results. The WTC victims' data set not being a closed population, fortuitous kinship associations could not be systematically eliminated. To alleviate this limitation, a feature was built in to provide the data reviewer with: (1) the score of a matching individual; (2) the score for each other member of the matching individual's family. Entries linked to fortuitous kinship associations systematically showed discrepant scores against the victim among their family relatives, and were easily eliminated from consideration by the software. The entire victim's genotype data set was queried in batch mode against the next-of-kin data set, and the results were stored. In order to facilitate and expedite data review, a prioritization scheme would then draft a list of the victim's genotype in decreasing rank for probability of yielding an identification. The batch process ran unattended and could be run as often as new data releases were produced. Inferred identifications were confirmed with additional pedigree analysis tools.

4. The future

The bioinformatic tools described above showcased the value of systematic "data mining" approaches that allow for optimal and efficient extraction of the biological information content of an available genetic data set. The next version of this tool is under construction and will address the processing needs of MFIs involving much larger numbers of victims, and of missing persons databasing initiatives. Built on a new database architecture, it allows parallel processing to keep execution time constant, accommodates over 10^6 samples, and will include a complex pedigree analysis package.

Acknowledgements

The author gratefully acknowledges George Carmody for the use of the KinTest program for likelihood ratio calculations.

Reference

[1] Leclair, B., Frégeau, C.J., Bowen, K.L., Fourney, R.M. Enhanced kinship analysis and STR-based DNA typing for human identification in mass fatality incidents: the Swissair Flight 111 disaster, submitted for publication, 2003.

International Congress Series 1261 (2004) 45–47

www.ics-elsevier.com

Use of laser microdissection greatly improves the recovery of DNA from sperm on microscope slides

K. Elliott*, D.S. Hill, C. Lambert, T.R. Burroughes, P. Gill

Research and Development, The Forensic Science Service, Trident Court, Solihull Parkway, Birmingham Business Park, Solihull B37 7YN, UK

Abstract. Traditionally, sperm are isolated from vaginal cell mixtures by preferential extraction methods. However, this method is problematic when there are limited amounts (c. 250 pg). In particular, the analysis of sperm from microscope slides has proven difficult. Here, we describe the use of Laser Capture Microdissection (LM) for the isolation of spermatozoa from microscope slides containing sperm and vaginal cells.

Keywords: Laser Capture Microdissection; Preferential lysis

1. Introduction

Evidence in sexual assault investigations frequently comprises semen stains and intimate swabs from victims. One of the first steps in the investigative process is to identify the presence of spermatozoa by staining with haematoxylin and eosin (HE) followed by microscopic examination. If there is evidence of spermatozoa, this is followed by DNA profiling of the evidential material, e.g., swab. With the advent of techniques such as low copy number (LCN) [1,2], the sensitivity of DNA profiling has increased significantly. However, there are many cases that have been unsuccessfully profiled in the past, with the consequence that the only remaining evidence is the original slide. At the FSS, such slides are now routinely submitted for DNA profiling using a modified version of preferential lysis [3] and LCN analysis [1,2].

Use of the preferential lysis technique is universal. However, this method is frequently ineffective on slides with low numbers of sperm, because of unavoidable contamination of the profile by victim DNA. The inefficiency with which the sperm are liberated from the swab (following removal from the slide) may also reduce the effectiveness of preferential lysis.

Laser Capture Microdissection (LM) is a relatively new technique that can be used to isolate single cells from complex tissue samples mounted on microscope slides.

* Corresponding author. Tel.: +44-121-329-5462; fax: +44-121-622-2051.
E-mail address: kel@fss.org.uk (K. Elliott).

doi:10.1016/S0531-5131(03)01509-7

The effectiveness of LM in processing old microscope slides containing sperm and vaginal cells was evaluated by comparing LM with preferential lysis.

2. Materials and methods

2.1. Slide preparation and Laser Capture Microdissection

Slides were prepared 6–30 months prior to LM processing. Slides were prepared and sperm were captured using LM as described by Elliott et al. [4].

2.2. Comparative study

Sixteen pairs of slides were used in the comparative study. Each pair consisted of slides prepared concurrently from a single post-coital vaginal swab cell harvest. Slide pairs were only included in the study if both contained similar numbers of sperm, vaginal cells and debris. From each pair of slides, one was processed using preferential lysis and organic extraction as described by Gill et al. [3] and the other using the LM technique.

The numbers of sperm present on each slide were first accurately counted by visual inspection of the entire slide. From each pair of slides, the one with the least sperm was processed using preferential lysis. The same number of sperm was then removed from the other slide using LM. Pairs of preferential lysis and LM samples were processed concurrently from the PCR stage onwards.

In addition to comparing the technique with preferential lysis, 77 slides were analysed using the LM protocol. Sperm numbers per slide ranged from 2 to 326.

2.3. Sperm lysis

Sperm lysis was carried out using Qiagen extraction chemistry modified for LM as described by Elliott et al. [4]. Following LCN PCR as described by Gill et al. [1] and Whitaker et al. [2], electrophoresis, GeneScan software analysis and Genotyper software analysis were carried out and AMPFlSTR® SGM Plus™ DNA profiles were generated as described by Cotton et al. [5].

2.4. Statistical analysis

2.4.1. Likelihood ratio (LR) calculation

Likelihood ratios were calculated for each DNA profile produced, as described by Evett et al. (1991) [6].

2.4.2. Regression analysis

To analyse the associations between three different variables—namely, time since intercourse (TSI), number of sperm recovered on a slide and the quality of a DNA profile, multiple regression analysis, robust regression and stepwise regression were employed to calculate regression coefficients and associated confidence intervals and test statistics [7]. All analyses were carried out using the MATLAB statistics toolbox, The MathWorks, 3 Apple Hill Drive, Natick, MA 01760-2098, USA.

3. Results and discussion

In a comparative study, where LM and preferential extraction were compared, LR analysis demonstrated the former to be markedly superior, with 15 out of the 16 samples producing better results with LM. The relative ineffective performance of preferential lysis may be explained by sperm trapped on the cotton swab, inadequate removal of female DNA or loss of sperm whilst separating the female supernatant. Male/female mixtures were relatively common. Surprisingly, during prolonged exposure to the vaginal environment, it has been demonstrated that female DNA from lysed cells can actually adhere to the sperm head [8]. Whilst female DNA can be removed from the sperm during preferential lysis, the single extraction step used in LM is a physical process and therefore cannot be used to selectively remove female DNA that is attached to the sperm. There are a number of factors likely to affect the quality of post-coital sperm and DNA within these sperm. In particular, Spadafora [8] and Francolini et al. [9] suggest complex interactions between sperm and exogenous female DNA that results in nucleases within the sperm cleaving the sperm DNA and eventually resulting in apoptosis. The longer the period of TSI, the greater the amount of apoptosis that may occur. Sperm that have undergone nuclear cleavage but not the subsequent stages of apoptosis, which involves destruction of the sperm head, may therefore appear morphologically intact or normal during microscopic examination even though the DNA contained is highly degraded. This interpretation is supported by statistical analysis that demonstrated an association between TSI and profile quality that was independent of the number of sperm analysed. Consequently, the presence of relatively high numbers of sperm does not assure good DNA profiles.

References

[1] P. Gill, J. Whitaker, C. Flaxman, N. Brown, J. Buckleton, An investigation of the rigor of interpretation rules for STRs derived from less than 100 pg of DNA, Forensic Sci. Int. 112 (2000) 17–40.

[2] J.P. Whitaker, E.A. Cotton, P. Gill, A comparison of the characteristics of profiles produced with the AMPFlSTR® SGM Plus™ multiplex system for both standard and Low Copy Number (LCN) STR DNA analysis, Forensic Sci. Int. 123 (2001) 215–223.

[3] P. Gill, A.J. Jeffreys, D.J. Werrett, Forensic applications of DNA "fingerprints", Nature 318 (1985) 577–579.

[4] K. Elliott, D.S. Hill, C. Lambert, T.R. Burroughs, P. Gill, Use of laser microdissection greatly improves the recovery of DNA from sperm on microscope slides, Forensic Sci. Int. (in press).

[5] E.A. Cotton, R.F. Allsop, J.L. Guest, R.R.F. Frazier, P. Koumi, I.P. Callow, A. Seager, R.L. Sparkes, Validation of the AMPFlSTR® SGM Plus™ system for use in forensic casework, Forensic Sci. Int. 112 (2000) 151–161.

[6] I.W. Evett, C. Buffery, G. Willott, D.A. Stoney, A guide to interpreting single locus profiles of DNA mixtures in forensic cases, J. Forensic Sci. Soc. 31 (1991) 41–47.

[7] R.R. Sokal, F.J. Rohlf, Biometry, 3rd ed., Freeman, New York, 2000.

[8] C. Spadafora, Sperm cells and foreign DNA: a controversial relation, BioEssays 20 (1998) 955–964.

[9] M. Francolini, M. Lavitrano, C.L. Lamia, D. French, L. Frati, F. Cotelli, C. Spadafora, Evidence for nuclear internalization of exogenous DNA into mammalian sperm cells, Mol. Reprod. Dev. 34 (1993) 133–139.

International Congress Series 1261 (2004) 48–49

www.ics-elsevier.com

Discrepant results of samples taken from different tissues of a single individual

E.M. Dauber[a,*], G. Dorner[a], M. Mitterbauer[b], S. Wenda[a], I. Faé[a], B. Glock[c], W.R. Mayr[a]

[a] *Department of Blood Group Serology and Transfusion Medicine, Division of Blood Group Serology, University of Vienna, Medical School, Austria*

[b] *Department of Internal Medicine, Division of Hematology and Hemostaseology, University of Vienna, Medical School, Austria*

[c] *Austrian Red Cross, Blood Donation Centre for Vienna, Lower Austria and Burgenland, Laboratory for Molecular Biology, Vienna, Austria*

Abstract. Samples taken from different tissues of five bone marrow transplanted patients at least 5 years after successful bone marrow transplantation were investigated by STR-typing in order to find out whether or not donor cells can also be found in tissues other than blood. Donor alleles were detected in blood, buccal swabs and fingernails, but not in hair samples.

Keywords: Blood stem cell; Bone marrow transplantation; Buccal cell; Chimerism; Hair

1. Introduction

In a prior study, different tissues were investigated by STR-analysis in a pair of chimeric twins, who are dizygotic twins sharing blood stem cells, which have been exchanged during pregnancy. These hematopoietic cells can migrate through intrauterine blood vessel anastomoses of confluent placentas into the other fetus and persist for a lifetime producing blood cells with the genetic pattern of the other twin. Therefore a mixture of their DNA profiles was expected in the blood of both twins, but was also observed to a minor extent in their buccal cells and even in the fingernails of one twin, which was not expected. Only their hair roots exhibited their true genetic pattern [1]. As congenital twin chimerism is a very rare phenomenon, a further study has been extended to bone marrow transplanted patients. After successful engraftment, they represent artificial blood chimeras: their hematopoietic tissue and their blood cells derive from the bone marrow donor, who is usually HLA identical, but genetically different in many other loci. In order to find out, whether or not donor cells can also be found in tissues other than blood, samples of different origin have been analysed.

2. Materials and methods

At least 5 years after successful bone marrow transplantation, samples from blood, buccal cells, fingernails and eyebrows were collected from five patients. DNA samples or

* Corresponding author. Klinische Abteilung für Blutgruppenserologie, Waehringer Guertel 18-20, A-1090 Vienna, Austria. Tel.: +43-1-40400-5320; fax: +43-1-40400-5321.

E-mail address: eva.maria.dauber@univie.ac.at (E.M. Dauber).

0531-5131/
doi:10.1016/S0531-5131(03)01621-2

frozen lymphocytes of the patients and the donors (three siblings, two unrelated donors) prior to transplantation were analysed too. DNA was extracted from all samples with the Qiagen DNA Mini Kit (Qiagen) or the Chelex method or had already been extracted from blood prior to transplantation with the salting out method. In two out of five hair samples an alternative extraction method, which was expected to yield more DNA [2], was kindly carried out by Prof. Dr. P.M. Schneider, Institute of Legal Medicine, University of Mainz, Germany. PCR of the highly polymorphic STR-loci SE33 (fluorescein-labelled reverse primer) and D12S391 (Vic-labelled forward primer) [3,4] was carried out on a 9700 thermal cycler, further analysis on an ABI Prism 310 Genetic Analyser (Applied Biosystems). The method of quantification of the two cell populations was based on peak areas [5].

3. Results and discussion

In all patients a difference between donor and recipient was found at least in one of the two loci. After transplantation, the STR alleles found in the blood samples of all patients were identical with the donor. In all buccal swab samples a mixture of recipient and donor was observed. The median of donor cells found was 32.1% of the total cell population, ranging within 16.6% and 76.3%. In the fingernails the median of donor cells was 24%, ranging between 11.4% and 53.3%. The alleles found in the hair samples of all recipients corresponded to their blood sample prior to transplantation and represented their true genotype.

These results confirm the findings in the pair of chimeric twins [1]: donor cells originating from hematopoietic tissue can migrate into other tissues, where they are found in DNA-analysis. Blood stem cells have the ability to transdifferentiate to cells other than blood. Analogous results have been found recently using in-situ hybridization of a Y-chromosomal marker in female recipients transplanted with a male donor [6].

The findings of this study have to be considered in DNA analysis of samples, which are routinely taken for forensic and clinical genetic investigations: mixed DNA profiles can originate from a single individual. DNA profiles obtained from different tissues of the same individual and DNA profiles obtained from samples taken at different times from the same individual can be different. Only the DNA profile obtained from hair samples exhibited the true genotype of the individual.

References

[1] E.M. Dauber, I. Faé, S. Stadlbacher, B. Glock, D.W.M. Schwartz, W.R. Mayr, STR-typing in a pair of chimeric twins, Int. Congr. Ser. 1239 (2003) 569–571.

[2] A. Hellmann, U. Rohleder, H. Schmitter, M. Wittig, STR typing in human telogen hairs—a new approach, Int. J. Legal Med. 114 (2001) 269–273.

[3] P. Wiegand, B. Budowle, S. Rand, B. Brinkmann, Forensic validation of the STR systems SE33 and TC11, Int. J. Legal Med. 105 (1993) 315–320.

[4] M.V. Lareu, C. Pestoni, M. Schürenkamp, S. Rand, B. Brinkmann, A. Carracedo, A highly variable STR at the D12S391 locus, Int. J. Legal Med. 109 (1996) 134–138.

[5] C. Thiede, M. Florek, M. Bornhäuser, M. Ritter, B. Mohr, C. Brendel, G. Ehninger, A. Neubauer, Rapid quantification of mixed chimerism using multiplex amplification of short tandem repeat markers and fluorescence detection: bone marrow transplant 23 (1999) 1055–1060.

[6] S.D. Tran, S.R. Pillemer, A. Dutra, A.J. Barrett, M.J. Brownstein, S. Key, E. Pak, R.A. Leakan, A. Kingman, K.M. Yamada, B.J. Baum, E. Mezey, Differentiation of human bone marrow-derived cells into buccal epithelial cells in vivo: a molecular analytical study, Lancet 361 (2003) 1084–1088.

ELSEVIER

International Congress Series 1261 (2004) 50–52

www.ics-elsevier.com

Genetic investigation of modern burned corpses

N. von Wurmb-Schwark*, E. Simeoni, A. Ringleb, M. Oehmichen

Institute of Legal Medicine, Christian-Albrechts-Universität Kiel, Arnold-Heller-Str. 12, 24105 Kiel, Germany

Abstract. Burning of corpses is a well-known and widely spread funeral procedure that has been performed for a long time in many cultures. Nowadays more and more corpses are burned in cremations and buried in urns, often for practical and financial reasons. Usually cremation takes place as temperatures of over 1000 °C for more than 70 min, destroying the corpse and only leaving severely burned teeth and some fragments of larger bones. In some scientific, criminal or civil cases even after cremation, there is the need of genetic investigations for identification or paternity testing. Here we present a systematic genetic investigation of 10 corpses that were burned in a crematory. After DNA extraction of the remains, the presence of human nuclear and mitochondrial DNA was tested by a highly sensitive Duplex PCR and quantified via real time PCR; genetic typing was done using the AmpFlSTR Identifiler kit. © 2003 Elsevier B.V. All rights reserved.

Keywords: Cremation; Ancient bones; AmpFlSTR identifiler; Mitochondrial DNA

1. Introduction

Typing of short tandem repeats (STR, "genetic fingerprinting") is the method of choice when analyzing DNA extracted from human bones or teeth (modern or ancient), traces with minute amounts of DNA or simply highly degraded tissues for identification purposes [1–3]. In forensic casework, the genetic typing of deceased individuals is routinely done, usually to confirm identity or for posthumous paternity testing. In cases of soil burial, the body can easily be unearthed for investigation, while STR typing after cremation is of questionable value. Due to development of genetic analysis, e.g. typing of short tandem repeats or sequencing of mitochondrial DNA (mtDNA), biological material (i.e. biopsies, blood samples etc.) taken for medical investigation can successfully be analyzed even after long time storage or formalin treatment. Especially popular is the use of commercially available multiplex kits which amplify up to 15 loci plus the sex determining Amelogenin gene in one reaction mix [4,5]. The aim of this work was to systematically investigate whether human remains can be reliably and reproducibly individualized by STR typing after cremation.

* Corresponding author. Tel.: +49-431-5973633; fax: +49-431-5973612.
E-mail address: nvonwurmb@rechtsmedinzin.uni-kiel.de (N. von Wurmb-Schwark).

doi:10.1016/S0531-5131(03)01830-2

2. Materials and methods

Ten cadavers autopsied at the Institute of Legal Medicine were chosen and a buccal swab was taken. After cremation, the remains were routinely ground by crematory staff. DNA was extracted from each swab and the respective minced bones (0.5 g each) using a slightly modified Invisorb Forensic kit (Invitek, Berlin, Germany). Extracted DNA was eluted in 70 μl buffer. Genetic typing of the swabs was done using the AmpFlSTRIdentifiler kit (Applied Biosystems, Weiterstadt, Germany). To test DNA quality and quantity, DNA extracts from cremation remains were first separated on ethidium bromide containing agarose gels. Then 1, 2.5 and 5 μl of each sample were subjected to a real time PCR amplifying a 94-bp fragment of nuclear specific DNA (a part of the telomerase gene) followed by a Duplex PCR simultaneously amplifying a nuclear specific 164-bp fragment and a mitochondrial specific 260-bp fragment. This PCR turned out to be a suitable pretest prior to STR typing [own unpublished results]. Capillary electrophoresis was done on an AbiPrism 310 Genetic Analyzer with 1 μl PCR product, 11.8 μl formamide and 0.2 μl ROX500 or LIZ500 standard per sample (all Applied Biosystems). Afterwards, STR typing of the cremation samples was done using the Identifiler kit which amplifies 15 STR loci plus the Amelogenin specific gender determination fragments simultaneously [6]. Amplification and detection of PCR products was done according to the manufacturer's recommendations with 32 instead of 28 cycles. Every extraction was done twice, every PCR amplification three times independently.

3. Results and discussion

Separation of 10 μl of DNA containing extract on ethidium bromide agarose gels yielded no signals, implying a DNA concentration below 0.1 ng/μl. To test for the presence of any human DNA, every sample was subjected to a real time PCR amplifying a 98-bp nuclear specific fragment. After 40 cycles, 7 out of 10 samples clearly showed specific signals. Comparison with a standard (10-fold dilutions from 10 pg to 100 ng) indicated a DNA concentration of 100 fg to 50 pg/μl (approx. less than 1 to 10 molecules when assuming 6.6 pg DNA/cell). The other three samples showed an even lower DNA concentration making a reliable quantification difficult or impossible. The subsequently employed Duplex PCR yielded reproducible results and very well correlated with the STR typing results in 7 out of 10 samples: Samples which showed strong signals in the Duplex PCR led to the greatest number of detectable STRs. After reproducible STR amplification, the obtained genetic patterns were compared with the alleles from the corresponding persons (=DNA from buccal swabs taken prior to cremation), and to exclude contaminations, with the STR patterns from every person working in the lab. The genetic profiles amplified out of cremation remains neither corresponded to the buccal swabs of the respective cadaver nor did the alleles match the lab personnel. Some samples were clearly contaminated: in two cases, male signals were detected in samples derived from a woman, and in three instances, more than two alleles were amplified per locus.

4. Conclusion

This study shows that even though the extraction and subsequent STR typing of DNA from the ashes of a cremated person is possible and in some cases does yield reproducible results, a reliable post-cremation identification seems to be unlikely. The genetic profiles obtained from the remains after the burning of a corpse did in no case match the alleles from buccal swabs taken prior to cremation and have to be regarded as contaminations. Since the profiles did also not match those of the lab personnel, the remains are probably contaminated during post-cremation processing (i.e. handling of the ashes, grinding of bones, etc.). As a consequence, STR typing of cremation remains has to be considered unreliable and not suitable for forensic purposes (e.g. identification, paternity testing).

References

[1] E. Hagelberg, I.C. Gray, A.J. Jeffreys, Identification of the skeletal remains of a murder victim by DNA analysis, Nature 352 (1991) 427–429.

[2] A.J. Jeffreys, M.J. Allen, E. Hagelberg, A. Sonnberg, Identification of the skeletal remains of Josef Mengele by DNA analysis, Forensic Sci. Int. 56 (1992) 56–76.

[3] N. von Wurmb-Schwark, M. Harbeck, U. Wiesbrock, I. Schroeder, S. Ritz-Timme, M. Oehmichen, Extraction and amplification of nuclear and mitochondrial DNA from ancient and artificially aged bones, Legal Med. 5 (2003) 169–172.

[4] A. Alonso, S. Andelinovic, P. Martin, D. Sutlovic, I. Erceg, E. Huffine, L.F. de Simon, C. Albarran, M. Definis-Gojanovic, A. Fernandez-Rodriquez, P. Garcia, I. Drmic, B. Rezie, S. Kuret, M. Sancho, D. Primorac, DNA typing from skeletal remains: evaluation of multiplex and megaplex STR systems on DNA isolated from bones and teeth samples, Croat. Med. J. 42 (2001) 260–266.

[5] J.A. Thomson, K.L. Ayres, V. Pilotti, M.N. Barett, J.I.H. Walker, P.G. Debenham, Analysis of disputed single-parent/child and sibling relationships using 16 STR loci, Int. J. Leg. Med. 115 (2001) 128–134.

[6] AmpFlSTR Identifiler, PCR Amplification Kit, User's Manual, Applied Biosystems.

ELSEVIER

International Congress Series 1261 (2004) 53–55

www.ics-elsevier.com

Attribution of DNA profiles to body fluid stains

C. Peel*, P. Gill

Research and Development, Forensic Science Service, 2960 Trident Court, Birmingham Business Park, Solihull Parkway, Birmingham B37 7YN, UK

Abstract. Ultra-sensitive DNA profiling techniques, which now enable a profile to be obtained from a single cell, are greatly advantageous to the forensic community where biological material is often limited. However, it is not always possible to infer the cellular origin of any resulting profile. Here, we assess the likelihood of generating a DNA profile by the standard processing of visible stains that originates from extraneous cells on the substrate rather than the body fluid. Stain size and quality, substrate material and an individual's propensity to deposit DNA were all proven to be significant factors. It was demonstrated that an association between DNA profile and body fluid is not implicit, even where a positive presumptive test is obtained.

Keywords: Low copy number; Presumptive test; Profile attribution

1. Introduction

Scientists reporting body fluid cases in court are frequently requested to provide their expert opinion regarding the origin of any DNA profile obtained. It is well documented that, with the recent development of low copy number (LCN) profiling techniques [1,2], DNA profiles can be obtained from minute amounts of biological material [3,4]. Forensic laboratories now routinely analyse samples yielding less than 100 pg DNA [1].

The recovery of genetic profiles from touched objects and the transfer of DNA from one individual to another in the process of shaking hands has been demonstrated [5]. It has also been shown that a full profile can be recovered from secondary transfer of epithelial cells (from one individual to another and subsequently to an object) at 28 cycles [6]. This sensitivity increases the chance of detecting extraneous cells deposited in an event unrelated to a crime by the standard processing of body fluid stains. Precautions taken in the reporting of LCN cases may therefore be applicable to all cases involving low levels of DNA, such as minute blood stains on touched objects, even when amplified using standard 28 cycle profiling techniques.

* Corresponding author. Tel.: +44-121-329-5343; fax: +44-121-622-2051.
E-mail address: Carole.Peel@fss.pnn.police.uk (C. Peel).

0531-5131/
doi:10.1016/S0531-5131(03)01638-8

2. Methodology

Neat blood and saliva stains were prepared in duplicate from five body fluid donors. 1 μl and 15 μl stains were deposited on cotton and glass surfaces (total of 40 samples). Substrates were briefly handled before or after stain deposition by an individual known to have a high tendency to deposit DNA from epithelial cells (a 'good DNA shedder').

Ten dilutions of blood and saliva were prepared, up to 1/10,000. Substrates were each handled by one of six individuals prior to deposition of diluted samples.

Stains degraded for 0, 3, 5, 7 and 10 months were handled by a good shedder.

Leucomalachite green (LMG) was used for identification of bloodstains [7].

Phadebas tablets were used for detection of salivary amylase in cell harvests, with a blue supernatant indicating a positive result.

DNA extractions were carried out using QIAgen® QIAamp® DNA kit or Chelex 100. PicoGreen® quantification of saliva extracts was performed using Fluoroskan Ascent apparatus and associated software, by comparison with known standards of SHP DNA. The QuantiBlot™ kit (Applied Biosystems) was used to quantify blood samples according to the kit protocol. Template DNA was amplified using the AmpFlSTR® SGM Plus™ kit, electrophoresed and analysed using Genescan® 2.1.1 and Genotyper® 1.1.1 software [8].

The relative contribution of the body fluid and epithelial cells to the resulting DNA profile were calculated as Mx, which is explicitly defined by:

$$\mathrm{Mx} = \mathrm{Pa(H)}/[\mathrm{Pa(H)} + \mathrm{Pa(D)}],$$

where Pa(H) is the peak area contributed to the DNA profile by the substrate handler and Pa(D) is the peak area contributed by the body fluid donor.

Mx values were used to calculate the statistical significance of all factors contributing to the resulting profile using Minitab 10.51 Xtra software.

3. Results

A positive presumptive test was obtained from all samples. Processing of large stains produced DNA profiles originating from the body fluid. The substrate handler contributed the major component of profiles recovered from small stains.

In one exception, a large bloodstain on cotton substrate yielded predominantly the substrate handler's profile. This stain had given a positive presumptive test, although the quant value was uncharacteristically low (0.07 ng/μl compared to an average 0.7 ng/μl for this sample type).

Profiles of substrate handlers were only detected from individuals known to have a very high tendency to deposit DNA. These individuals accounted for approximately 13% of the population, according to the study by Lowe et al. [6].

Results from substrates handled by good shedders showed that the more dilute or degraded a stain, the higher the contribution of the substrate handler's DNA to the resulting profile. A positive presumptive test could be obtained from samples when a profile originating from the body fluid was no longer detectable.

Statistical analysis of all contributing factors showed that the most significant were the tendency of an individual to deposit DNA from epithelial cells, substrate type and stain size and quality ($P<0.001$). The body fluid type was also significant ($P=0.042$).

4. Discussion

In this study, DNA profiles from epithelial cells were only recovered from substrates handled by good DNA ‘shedders’. This corresponds to reports that higher levels of DNA can be recovered from objects touched by certain individuals [5,8]. The mechanism for this is uncertain; it may be that a good DNA shedder sloughs a greater number of epithelial cells, or a higher proportion of nucleated cells, than a poor DNA shedder [4].

Where a quant value obtained is lower than expected for the sample size, then the scientist may not be justified in attributing any DNA profile obtained to the stain. It is suggested that low copy number considerations are applied whether amplification of these samples is carried out at 34 or 28 cycles. The ‘hierarchy of propositions’ described by Evett et al. [9] and Cook et al. [10] explains levels at which prosecution and defence propositions should be examined. Results from this study suggest that, where samples give unexpectedly low quant values, then the evidence may be best evaluated at ‘sub-source level’, consistent with LCN guidelines. This addresses whether a DNA profile obtained matches the suspect. Further information, such as the suspect’s previous legitimate access to a scene, would be required in order for the scientist to infer the source of a profile. All DNA and non-DNA evidence must be considered and may be analysed using Bayesian networks [9]. These models may be used to calculate a likelihood ratio relating to higher level propositions, defined as ‘activity’ or ‘offence’ level, which the scientist can use to advise the courts on the probability that a suspect or an unrelated person has been involved in an activity or committed a crime.

References

[1] P. Gill, et al, An investigation of the rigor of interpretation rules for STRs derived from less then 100 pg of DNA, Forensic Sci. Int. 112 (2000) 17–40.

[2] J.P. Whitaker, E.A. Cotton, P. Gill, A comparison of the characteristics of profiles produced with the AMPFlSTR® SGM Plus™ multiplex system for both standard and low copy number (LCN) STR DNA analysis, Forensic Sci. Int. 123 (2001) 215–223.

[3] R.A.H. Van Oorschot, M.K. Jones, DNA fingerprints from fingerprints, Nature 387 (1997) 787.

[4] R.A. Wickenheiser, Trace DNA: a review, discussion of theory and application of the transfer of trace quantities of DNA through skin contact, J. Forensic Sci. 47 (2002) 442–450.

[5] R.A.H Van Oorschot, M.K. Jones, DNA fingerprints from fingerprints, Nature 387 (1997 June) 6635–6767.

[6] A. Lowe, C. Murray, J. Whitaker, G. Tully, P. Gill, The propensity of individuals to deposit DNA and secondary transfer of low level DNA from individuals to inert surfaces, Forensic Sci. Int. 129 (2002) 25–34.

[7] M. Cox, A study of the sensitivity and specificity of four presumptive tests for blood, J. Forensic Sci. 36 (1991) 1503–1511.

[8] E.A. Cotton, et al, Validation of the AMPFlSTR® SGM Plus™ system for use in forensic casework, Forensic Sci. Int. 112 (2000) 151–161.

[9] I.W. Evett, P.D. Gill, G. Jackson, J. Whitaker, C. Champod, Interpreting samm quantities of DNA: the hierarchy of propositions and the use of Bayesian networks, J. Forensic Sci. 47 (2002) 520–530.

[10] R. Cook, et al, A hierarchy of propositions: deciding which level to address in casework, Sci. Justice 38 (1998) 231–239.

ELSEVIER

International Congress Series 1261 (2004) 56–58

www.ics-elsevier.com

Genetic considerations for interpreting molecular microbial forensic evidence

B. Budowle[a,*], R. Chakraborty[b]

[a] *FBI Laboratory, 2501 Investigation Parkway, Quantico, VA 22135, USA*
[b] *Center for Genome Information, Department of Environmental Health, University of Cincinnati, Cincinnati, OH 45267, USA*

Abstract. Genetic analyses of microbial evidence will be employed to assist in attribution of perpetrators of bioterrorism and biocrimes. There are some similarities and differences between human forensic and microbial forensic DNA analysis practices to consider. These population genetic and statistical interpretation issues center on the different genetic make-up, different inheritance mechanisms, different regulation mechanisms, and lineage-based analyses. In some cases, a quantitative assessment of the results of analysis may be possible; in other cases, it may be more appropriate to provide only a qualitative statement. Published by Elsevier B.V.

Keywords: Microbial forensics; Population genetics; Statistics; Bioterrorism; Biocrime

1. Introduction

Microbial forensic identity testing is used to determine the source of microbial samples or their toxins that have been used in acts of bioterrorism or in the commission of biocrimes. One approach to obtain microbial signatures is by assaying genetic polymorphisms between microbial strains or substrains to infer the origin, relationship, or transmission route of a particular isolate.

2. Interpretation

When the interpretation is "inclusion or match or same lineage," it is desirable to place some significance or weight on these results. There are similarities between human forensic and microbial forensic DNA analysis practices, which include the use of population databases, the use of qualitative conclusions of test results, and the application of QA/QC practices. However, there are several major differences, particularly in the context of data interpretation. Some obvious differences in approach are: database size and composition, statistical interpretation methods, and confidence in outcome of an interpre-

* Corresponding auhtor. Tel.: +1-703-632-8386; fax: +1-703-632-7817.
E-mail address: bruce.budowle@verizon.net (B. Budowle).

0531-5131/ Published by Elsevier B.V.
doi:10.1016/S0531-5131(03)01833-8

tation. Most bacteria and viruses are haploid, so diploid-based statistical approaches would not be appropriate and do not apply. Moreover, most microbes reproduce predominately asexually and, thus, are clonal in nature, making the identification by genetic means of the sole source of an isolate or a laboratory-prepared pathogen often impossible. Therefore, the majority of microbial forensic genetic evidence may only infer common lineage instead of identity.

Population genetics issues to consider are origin and maintenance of microbial diversity. These are dependent on the mode of reproduction (i.e., asexual, although sexual reproduction also must be considered), inter-genic/site variation of mutation rate, recent natural vs. laboratory origin, experimental and natural stress conditions, and horizontal gene transfer. The effects of natural selection together with mutation and recombination will contribute to variation and need to be considered as well.

Since diversity levels in a number of microbial species will not reach that of human populations, microbial forensics will need lineage-based models in which population structure issues are somewhat different than for human samples. But, approaches for statistical analysis do exist that need to be validated with empirical genomic data from model organisms. The extent of mismatch with comparison to a database of samples may be needed to provide quantitative support of the match/non-match evidence. Analysis will likely be based on coalescence theory incorporating population size fluctuation over generations, inter-site variation of mutation rate, recombination, horizontal gene transfer, and conservation of sites (based on function).

Alternatively, some cases may not require any quantitative assessment and a qualitative statement may suffice [1–4]. In other scenarios, a quantitative evaluation can be made, but the bounds on the estimate may be large, owing to the sparsity of data. To increase confidence in quantitative estimates, a better understanding of microbial genome dynamics is necessary. Data on genetic variation and relatedness within and between species can assist in distinguishing between two strains that appear phenotypically identical. Analysis of pathogenicity domains, virulence genes and antibiotic resistance genes, location of recombination sites, development of effective horizontal gene transfer and vertical gene transfer statistical models, general and specific genome site stability studies, near neighbor analyses, and diversity studies [5–8] will enhance capabilities to quantitatively assess the significance of lineage-based comparisons.

Although we provide a list of further studies, this does not suggest that inferences for attribution cannot be made. Substantial data on genetic markers and population diversity have been accumulated for some potential bioweapon species that include: smallpox, *BA*, *Fancisella tularensis*, *Yersinia pestis*, *Burkholderia pseudomallei*, *Burkholderia mallei*, *Escherichia coli*, *Salmonella* ssp., *Shigella* ssp., *Brucella* ssp., and Foot and Mouth Disease Virus. A unifying statistical framework should be considered based on using lineage-based models where the extent of match/non-match evidence is assessed under the hypotheses of a particular sample(s) belonging to one group (or lineage) of putative samples or not. Such statistical models, based on recent developments in phylogenetic analyses of molecular evolution, are under development.

Another important distinction of the human DNA forensic practices from that of microbial forensics is worth noting. In the human forensic context, DNA markers generally chosen for forensic analyses are devoid of functions. In contrast, terrorism-related microbes generally will contain virulence factors. Hence, a reliable and quick method of detecting signatures of virulence could be an important aspect of genomic work in microbial forensics. Molecular tools for detection of signatures of functionally active sites of the genome are now available to apply them to the emerging genomic data on biothreat agents (see, e.g., Ref. [9]).

3. Conclusion

In conclusion, comparative genome sequencing already is providing details of genome organization and genetic variation [10,11]. The number of markers is increasing and the distribution of polymorphisms is being established in representative sets of strains. Model organisms are being studied for estimating inter-site variation of mutation rate, recombination, horizontal gene transfer, and conservation of sites (based on function) [6]. Analyses of these data, based on comparative genomic principles, should improve the capabilities and confidence in providing quantitative assessments of microbial forensic genetic evidence.

Acknowledgements

This is publication number 03-20 of the Laboratory Division of the Federal Bureau of Investigation. Names of commercial manufacturers are provided for identification only, and inclusion does not imply endorsement by the Federal Bureau of Investigation.

References

[1] P. Keim, L.B. Price, A.M. Klevytska, K.L. Smith, J.M. Schupp, R. Okinaka, P.J. Jackson, M.E. Hugh-Jones, Multiple-locus variable-number tandem repeat analysis reveals genetic relationships within *Bacillus anthracis*, J. Bacteriol. 182 (2000) 2928–2936.

[2] P. Keim, K.L. Smith, C. Keys, H. Takahashi, T. Kurata, A. Kaufmann, Molecular investigation of the Aum Shinrikyo anthrax release in Kameido, Japan. J. Clin. Microbiol. 39 (2001) 4566–4567.

[3] C.A. Cummings, D.A. Relman, Microbial forensics—cross-examining pathogens, Science 296 (2002) 1976–1978.

[4] R.S. Lanciotti, et al., Origin of the West Nile virus responsible for an outbreak of encephalitis in the northeastern United States, Science 286 (1999) 2333–2337.

[5] J.W. Drake, B. Charlesworth, D. Charlesworth, J.F. Crow, Rates of spontaneous mutation, Genetics 148 (1998) 1667–1686.

[6] J.E. LeClerc, B.G. Li, W.L. Payne, T.A. Cebula, High mutation frequencies among *Escherichia coli* and *Salmonella pathogens*, Science 274 (1996) 1208–1211.

[7] E.R. Moxon, P.B. Rainey, M.A. Nowak, R.E. Lenski, Adaptive evolution of highly mutable loci in pathogenic bacteria, Curr. Biol. 4 (1994) 24–33.

[8] P.D. Sniegowski, P.J. Gerrish, R.E. Lenski, Evolution of high mutation rates in experimental populations of *Escherichia coli*, Nature 387 (1997) 703–705.

[9] W.H. Li, M. Tanimura, C.C. Luo, S. Datta, L. Chan, The apolipoprotein multigene family: biosynthesis, structure, structure–function relationships, and evolution, J. Lipid Res. 29 (1988) 245–271.

[10] T.D. Read, et al., Comparative genome sequencing for discovery of novel polymorphisms in *Bacillus anthracis*, Science 296 (2002) 2028–2033.

[11] T.D. Read, et al., The genome sequence of *Bacillus anthracis* Ames and comparison to closely related bacteria, Nature 423 (2003) 81–86.

International Congress Series 1261 (2004) 59–61

www.ics-elsevier.com

Assigning individuals to ethnic groups based on 13 STR loci

Xenia Fosella[a], Fabio Marroni[a], Samuele Manzoni[b], Andrea Verzeletti[b], Francesco De Ferrari[b], Nicoletta Cerri[b], Silvano Presciuttini[a,*]

[a] *Center of Statistical Genetics, University of Pisa, Pisa, Italy*
[b] *Institute of Legal Medicine, University of Brescia, Brescia, Italy*

Abstract. Inferring the ethnic origin of individuals by means of short tandem repeat (STR) profiles has received considerable attention recently. Gene frequency variation among human populations has been extensively documented, and it has been suggested that the differences in allele proportions between ethnic groups could form the basis of an inferential system. We report the use of DNA profiles from 13 STR loci for inferring the ethnic origin of samples of unknown provenance using five populations of immigrants. This preliminary work shows that a population assignment test can be already used in real casework studies. © 2003 Published by Elsevier B.V.

Keywords: Ethnicity; Assignment test; STR; Population data

1. Introduction

The town of Brescia (northern Italy) ranks among the highest in Italy for the proportion of censused immigrants from non-EU countries, amounting to about 10% of the local resident population. Most blood crimes in this area happen within ethnically defined groups, and a test that could assign a biological stain to a subject of a particular population would be highly welcomed. We selected several groups of ethnically defined immigrants in this area and assessed the power of 13 STR loci of tracing back their ethnic origin.

2. Materials and methods

The loci included in the AmpFlSTR Profiler Plus™ and SGM Plus™ commercial kits were typed in the following population samples (not all individuals were typed for all loci): (1) Italians, born in Brescia: $N=120$; Indians: $N=38$; Maghrebians: $N=69$; Mongolians: $N=21$; Blacks, from sub-Saharan countries: $N=122$; Slavonians, including Albanians: $N=66$. We first applied the assignment test of the package Arlequin

* Corresponding author. Tel.: +39-50-2213797; fax: +39-50-2213524.
E-mail address: sprex@biomed.unipi.it (S. Presciuttini).

0531-5131/ © 2003 Published by Elsevier B.V.
doi:10.1016/S0531-5131(03)01699-6

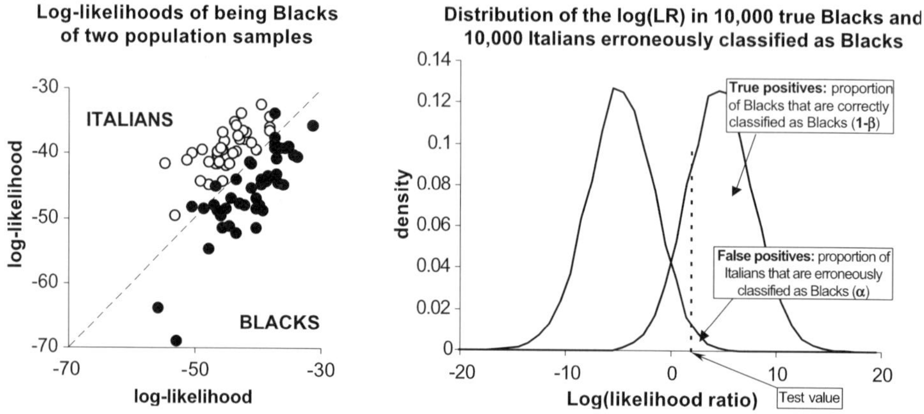

Fig. 1.

http://lgb.unige.ch/arlequin/ to all our data; however, since the assumption made by this program about the frequency of the alleles missing from a sample is not clear, we re-analyzed in more detail the comparison Blacks/Italians using an explicit and conservative assumption.

3. Results

In Arlequin's analysis, the log-likelihoods of each individual from four samples of immigrants (the Mongolians were excluded due to small sample size) were plotted against the log-likelihood of the Italians being falsely attributed to each of these samples. A fair level of discrimination power was evident in all population comparisons (data not shown). Not surprisingly, the sample of Blacks showed the highest level of differentiation; the likelihood of being Italian was higher than being Black in one Black subject only, whereas no Italian was attributed to the Black sample.

The analysis was repeated with our algorithm for the Black sample only, using the allele frequencies estimated from the samples (about 100 subjects typed for each locus in both samples), and assigning a value of 1/200 (= 0.005) to the frequency of the alleles missing from either sample (Fig. 1A). In order to estimate the statistical power of this assignment test with higher accuracy, we simulated 10 000 individuals for both the Italian and the

Table 1

Test value of ln(LR)	α (ratio of false positives)	$1-\beta$ (ratio of true positives)
0.0	6.6%	93.7%
1.0	3.1%	88.4%
2.0	1.5%	80.3%
3.0	0.6%	70.3%
4.0	0.3%	57.9%
5.0	0.1%	45.3%
6.0	0.01%	32.9%

Black samples using the same allele frequencies, and computed the log-likelihood distributions of the true Blacks assigned to the Black sample and the Italians falsely attributed to the Black sample (Fig. 1B).

From this analysis, we obtained the values of α and $1-\beta$ shown in Table 1.

4. Conclusions

The 13 STR loci included in two commercial kits provided a limited but significant power to infer the ethnicity of non-EU individuals immigrating to an Italian town. Contrasting Blacks with resident Whites achieved the highest level of discrimination. When two alternative hypotheses about the ethnic origin of a sample can be formulated with sufficient confidence, a population assignment test can already be applied to real cases. The present work suggests that a sequential test can be highly efficient in assigning individuals to their ethnic group; given a fixed predefined significance level, investigators can start typing a small number of markers, and typing additional marker sets only for the subjects that failed to be classified at the previous step.

International Congress Series 1261 (2004) 62–64

www.ics-elsevier.com

Between country comparison of a large Caucasian STR database collected as part of the Standardisation in DNA Profiling project

D. Syndercombe Court[a,*]
European DNA Profiling group (EDNAP)[b]

[a] *Haematology Department, Barts and The London, Queen Mary's School of Medicine and Dentistry, Turner Street, London E1 2AD, UK*
[b] *EDNAP, UK*

Abstract. *Background:* Standardisation in DNA Profiling (STADNAP) was a project funded by the European Union between 1998 and 2000. One aim was to collect a large amount of frequency data for all the loci being used at the time. The purpose was to provide frequency information and to examine if there was any between country variability. *Methods:* A request for short tandem repeat (STR) genotype information was sent to 165 laboratories known to be working in the field, either as criminal or paternity practitioners. A detailed questionnaire was included so that information about the laboratory's quality practices and the typing methodology they used could be examined with the data. An exact test was used to examine the frequency data set each locus and anomalous patterns examined. *Results:* Thirty-four laboratories provided genotype data from over 20,000 Caucasian individuals, with 95% of the information originating from within Europe. Twenty-nine different STRs were reported, but larger amounts of data were generally seen amongst those loci available in available commercial multiplexes. Rare intermediates were reported in all systems except VWA, TPOX and D16S539. The exact test revealed significant differences in those loci related to the use of older technologies, where difficulties can be experienced in distinguishing alleles that differ by one base pair.

Keywords: Short tandem repeat (STR); Caucasian frequencies; STADNAP

1. Introduction

Standardisation in DNA Profiling (STADNAP) was a project funded by the European Union between 1998 and 2000. A group of forensic scientists from European countries, currently also members of EDNAP, initiated the collection of short tandem repeat (STR)

* Corresponding author. Tel.: +44-2073-777076; fax: +44-2073-777629.
E-mail address: y.d.syndercombe-court@qmul.ac.uk (D. Syndercombe Court).
URL: http://www.isfg.org/ednap/ednap.htm.

doi:10.1016/j.ics.2003.12.085

frequency data from scientists working in the field, in order to provide a large amount of frequency data for all the loci being used at the time. The purpose was to provide frequency information and to examine if there was any between country variability.

2. Materials and methods

Letters were sent to 165 laboratories, throughout Europe and outside, seeking collaboration. In addition, a questionnaire was sent, requesting information on the laboratory's methodologies at the time. We wanted, in particular, to know what technology had been used to produce the database and how the alleles had been defined, including information on how the allelic ladders were produced. We also asked whether the laboratory participated in proficiency testing.

Submitted genotype data was screened for typographical errors and other discrepancies and individual STR genotypes that were in doubt deleted. Formatting differences were standardised before analysis of the data. The exact test was used to look at allele distribution on sets of STR data where more than 3000 genotypes had been collected.

3. Results

Caucasian genotype data was received from 34 laboratories, representing 12 European and 4 non-European countries. Laboratories provided a range of genotype information from between 100 and 6000 individuals resulting in a total of 21,544 profiles, of which 95% were from a European source. Data from 29 different STRs was provided, 16 of which were in common usage because of their availability in commercially available multiplexes, plus SE33, a locus commonly employed in German laboratories. These common loci each provided between 3000 and 15,000 genotypes.

Most samples were typed using automated technology. Applied Biosystems 310 and 377 instruments were the most popular instruments at the time, but a large amount of data was typed using older instrumentation, including ABI 373, Alf and AlfExpress. In addition, a substantial minority of laboratories used silver staining to provide manual types.

Virtually, all the laboratories participated in proficiency testing and all used allelic ladders run concurrently to type the samples. Many allelic ladders were of commercial origin, but homemade ladders were also extensively used. Virtually, all ladders had also been sequenced.

Rare intermediates were reported at around a 0.2% frequency, although none were seen in the VWA (24,000 alleles), TPOX (11,000 alleles) and D16S539 (6000 alleles) loci. The exact test revealed nothing of significance on examination of the D2S1338, D3S1358, D5S818, D13S317, D16S539, D21S11 and TPOX loci.

Significant differences were seen on the exact test in relation to the D18S51 ($p=0.035$), CSF1PO ($p=0.007$), D19S433, FGA, TH01, VWA and SE33 (all $p<0.00001$). Multiple testing could have resulted in the D18S51 locus significance and this was not considered further. The observation of a slight excess of 9 and 14 homozygotes in the CSF1PO locus could also have been due to chance, but other loci differences were likely to be real effects. Examination of the D19S433 locus revealed one laboratory typing data two repeats less than the others. Removal of this data resulted in the exact test becoming nonsignificant. In the FGA locus, there was a tendency to underreport the 0.2 intermediates and, at the TH01 locus, an excess of 10/10 homozygotes reported. Examination of the VWA data revealed nothing obvious other than a slight excess of homozygotes, and more variability comparing observed and expected where genotypes differed by only one repeat. In SE33, there appeared to be less 24 alleles than expected.

4. Conclusions

The only significant difference observed between allele distributions was associated with a difference in nomenclature.

It was notable that the only other differences observed in the exact test were within those loci popular in the early days of STR testing (TH01, FGA, VWA and SE33 all fall into that category). The reduced ability of the early genotyping instruments or manual methods to reliably detect the 0.2 intermediates seen in FGA, and distinguish 9.3 and 10 alleles in TH01, is likely to be the explanation for the observed differences. SE33 is also a complex locus that may have resulted in typing difficulties, although the reason for a particular allele to be underrepresented is not clear. VWA has been the subject of several reports of significant differences over time, but this too is an 'old' locus and examination of data typed only with newer technology may clarify this and the other issues.

Collection of a large amount of data from across Europe has provided a set of reliable STR frequencies for the majority of loci commonly used across the region. It has also revealed the importance of technology that can reliably distinguish single base pair differences.

Acknowledgements

The group would like to acknowledge the European Union for their funding of the STADNAP project, and also to thank the following organisations for their generous contribution of data for this project: University of Buenos Aires, Argentina; Universities of Innsbruck and Vienna, Austria; Universities of Antwerp and Leuven, Belgium; DNA Reference Laboratory, Brazil; University of Copenhagen, Denmark; Scientific Inter-Regional Police Laboratory, Toulouse, France; Institutes of Blood Grouping, Legal Medicine, Forensic Medicine and Human Genetics of Berlin, Cologne, Dresden, Geestacht, Heidelberg, Homburg, Leipzig, Mainz, Marburg, Rostock, LKA Berlin and LKA Nordrhein Westfalen, Germany; Ireland Forensic Science Laboratory; Rome Catholic University, Italy; University of Okinawa, Japan; University of Oslo, Norway; Institutes of Legal Medicine, Coimbra, Lisbon and Porto, Portugal; University of Cape Town, South Africa; Centre for Genetic Analysis (CAGT) and Institutes of Legal Medicine, Madrid and Seville, Spain; Northern Ireland Forensic Science Laboratory and Haematology at Barts and The London, UK.

International Congress Series 1261 (2004) 65–66

www.ics-elsevier.com

FINEX, FAMILIAS: two different approaches for the analysis of defective paternity cases

M. Dobosz[a,*], P. Mostad[b], R.G. Cowell[c], V.L. Pascali[a]

[a] *Istituto di Medicina Legale e delle Assicurazioni, Università Cattolica del S. Cuore, Largo F. Vito, 1, 0168 Rome, RM, Italy*

[b] *Chalmers Technical University, Gothenburg, Sweden*

[c] *City University, London, UK*

Abstract. We provide an overview of the main features of two computer programs enabling to calculate Bayesian probabilities in defective paternity cases: FINEX and FAMILIAS. These packages turn out very useful when computation complexities exceed the ordinary pencil-and-paper approach powers. FAMILIAS is especially suited for all cases in which there is a basic uncertainty on the most likely pedigree. FINEX is an Expert System-based program enabling to tackle very complex cases with plenty of data.

Keywords: Paternity cases; Bayesian analysis; Incomplete data

Paternity tests can be carried out even in the absence of the putative father, by the analysis of some of his relatives [1]. The evaluation of such cases (that are often defined as 'defective paternity cases') is one of the most interesting topics of today's genetic identification.

In more general terms, these cases are part of a larger category of defective identification cases, whose most universal example can be synthesized in the following questions: 'Are two individuals relatives? And what is their most plausible relationship, if there is any?'

The production of probabilistic evidence in these cases will depend on genetic data available and on its combination with all prior information that is actually known to the analyst.

Some very basic prior information—for example, the age and sex of persons involved—will usually help to limit the ways in which two people can exchange family ties.

In the same way, more detailed information on other individuals and their relation to either propositus (or both) (axiomatically regarded as true) can be extremely useful to restrict the parental hypotheses to just one or very few.

* Corresponding author. Tel.: +39-635507031; fax: +39-635507033.

E-mail address: m.dobosz@rm.unicatt.it (M. Dobosz).

0531-5131/
doi:10.1016/S0531-5131(03)01537-1

The Bayesian analysis will always focus on the frequencies of the genetic data available and on the segregational probabilities to be assigned according to the a priory assumptions. Also, the inherent computations may range from plain simplicity to the highest complexity, depending on how big the genealogic tree is.

Two classical computer packages have been devised to tackle these cases: FINEX [2] and FAMILIAS) [3]. Both programs rely on the Bayesian theory but they address the problem from different viewpoints.

FINEX was originally written to automate the process of constructing Bayesian networks (or probabilistic expert systems, PES) and give them a friendly interface (by reproducing the usual genetic tree in the computer screen). In turn, the basic idea underlying Bayesian networks is restructuring a very define genetic problem (in our case, a disputed relationship) in terms of a graphical model (with elementary deterministic relations, probabilistic computational nodes and a query node). What is of interest for our purposes is the fact that FINEX ends up to address the problem as a 'one query problem', according to the prior evidence.

In contrast, FAMILIAS is an open-frame program that, in spite of all prior evidence, tends to examine all possible pedigrees according to the available data and can tell us which is the most plausible.

Our recent casework experience with defective cases showed that these cases tend to be worked out according to a definite a priori opinion on the most plausible family relationship. However, more often that is currently thought, the prior opinion does not exactly comply with the genetic evidence available. Therefore, some of these cases are dismissed under the assumption that the family tie under scrutiny does not sufficiently fit with the genetic evidence proven, whereas the hypothesis of just another family relation would fit much better with this latter. In a recent case, we happen to observe, a judge asked us to verify whether two persons were or not first cousin—a hypothesis that did not actually comply with the genetic data. At a closer scrutiny, the half brother case would fit much better than the judicial query.

The combined use of the two computer programs offers different perspectives of insight into a typical defective case and it will ensure coverage of a broad pattern of hypotheses along with computational counter-check.

References

[1] A.P. Dawid, D. van Boxel, J. Mortera, V.L. Pascali, Inference about disputed paternity from an incomplete pedigree using a probabilistic expert system, Bull. Int. Stat. Inst. Contrib. Pap., Book 1, vol. 58, 1999, pp. 241–242.

[2] T. Egeland, P.F. Mostad, B. Mevag, M. Stenersen, Beyond traditional paternity and identification cases selecting the most probable pedigree, Forensic Science International 110 (2000) 47–59.

[3] R.G. Cowell, FINEX: a probabilistic expert system for forensic identification, Forensic Science International 134 (2003) 196–206.

International Congress Series 1261 (2004) 67–69

www.ics-elsevier.com

Germline mutations at 15 STR loci in the Chinese population

Wai-man Tang, Man-yee Law*

Parentage Testing Section, Forensic Science Division, Hongkong Government Laboratory, 9/F Lai Chi Kok Government Offices, 19 Lai Wan Road Kowloon, Hongkong SAR, China

Abstract. Germline mutation of 15 short tandem repeat (STR) loci was studied for over 52,000 parent–offspring allelic transfers in the Chinese population. Mutation rates varied from < 0.056% to 0.507% (FGA, paternal) and the overall paternal to maternal mutation ratio approximately 5% to 1.94% of the mutations could be explained by losses or gains of one repeat unit and there was no evidence for selection between insertion or deletion changes. Possible silent alleles were detected in three of the paternal exclusions. Mutation data accumulated for the Chinese population was compared with those of the American and European populations.

Keywords: Short tandem repeat (STR); Mutation; Chinese

1. Introduction

DNA markers currently used for forensic investigation are all highly polymorphic loci with high discrimination power. On the other hand, they are not controlled by selection pressure and are hence more susceptible to mutation [1]. Germline mutations are particularly critical for parentage investigation because links made between a child and the alleged parent could result in a false exclusion. With the rapid increase in the application of PCR short tandem repeat (STR) technology for parentage analysis and mass disaster identification, the study and understanding of germline mutations at STR loci has become increasingly important. We report an analysis of mutations in the Chinese population basing on data obtained from over 1800 cases of parentage testing.

2. Materials and methods

Blood samples and buccal swabs were extracted for their DNA using either Chelex [2] or the QIAamp® DNA Blood Mini Kit. The extracted DNA was quantified with either the QuantiBlot® Human DNA Quantitation Kit or the PicoGreen® dsDNA Quantitation Kit.

* Corresponding author. Tel.: +852-2242-6760; fax: +852-2242-6820.
E-mail address: mylaw@govtlab.gov.hk (M. Law).

doi:10.1016/S0531-5131(03)01827-2

PCR amplification was performed using the GenePrint®PowerPlex™ 16 Kit and subsequent genotyping was performed with either the ABI Prism®377 or ABI Prism®310 sequencers and the automatic fragment sizing software provided.

We assumed a mutation when there was an isolated non-Mendelian inheritance parent(s)/child mismatch provided the likelihood of parentage exceeded 10,000 to 1, not taking the isolated mismatch into consideration. Also, in accordance with literature [3], we have assigned the 'new' allele to the shortest mutational step. If both parents exhibited the same change in allelic size, the origin was classified uncertain.

3. Results and discussion

In a total of 52,377 parent/child allele transfers we observed 67 mutations at 14 of the 15 STR loci of the PowerPlex™ 16 system. All allele transfers at only the THO1 locus were consistent with Mendelian inheritance. Table 1 summarizes the mutations observed. The overall paternal to maternal mutation ratio is approximately 5 to 1 which is close to that estimated for an American population [3] and a Caucasian population in Europe [4]. Nine mutations were classified as uncertain.

Consistent with previous findings [4,5], most of the mutations (63 out of 67, 94%) could be explained by losses or gains of one repeat unit. This observation would support the strict stepwise replication slippage mutation model [6]. Of the remaining four cases, three involved two-step changes and the fourth, a possible three-step change. Our data does not seem to suggest selection between insertion or deletion changes overall, as observed by Sajantila et al. [7]. Interestingly, for the possible three-step change, the phenotypes of the family trio suggest the possible presence of a silent allele. Silent alleles could also have explained for the non-Mendelian inheritance observed in two other cases.

Table 1
Characteristics of observed mutations in the Chinese population

Locus	Paternal			Maternal		
	No. of meiosis	No. of mutations	Mutation rate (%)	No. of meiosis	No. of mutations	Mutation rate (%)
D3S1358	1787	0	<0.056	1745	0	<0.057
THO1	1795	0	<0.056	1765	0	<0.057
D21S11	1762	2	0.114	1715	1	0.058
D18S51	1757	6	0.341	1710	3	0.175
Penta E	1798	4	0.222	1763	3	0.170
D5S818	1794	1	0.056	1764	0	<0.057
D13S317	1798	2	0.111	1769	0	<0.057
D7S820	1798	2	0.111	1766	1	<0.057
D16S539	1803	2	0.111	1773	0	<0.056
CSF1PO	1795	2	0.111	1767	0	<0.057
Penta D	1800	3	0.167	1770	0	<0.056
vWA	1639	8	0.488	1525	0	<0.066
D8S1179	1795	7	0.390	1763	1	0.057
TPOX	1794	1	0.056	1756	0	<0.057
FGA	1578	8	0.507	1533	1	0.065
Total	26,493	48		25,884	10	

Table 2
Comparison of mutation rates from Chinese and Western populations

Locus	Paternal mutation rate (%)		Maternal mutation rate (%)	
	AABB	Chinese	AABB	Chinese
D3S1358	0.131	<0.056	0.015	<0.057
THO1	0.010	<0.056	0.009	<0.057
D21S11	0.154	0.114	0.105	0.058
D18S51	0.207	0.341	0.054	0.175
Penta E	0.138	0.222	0.050	0.170
D5S818	0.139	0.056	0.024	<0.057
D13S317	0.138	0.111	0.041	<0.057
D7S820	0.125	0.111	0.015	0.057
D16S539	0.113	0.111	0.022	<0.056
CSF1PO	0.145	0.111	0.024	<0.057
Penta D	0.074	0.167	0.218	<0.056
vWA	0.305	0.488	0.030	<0.066
D8S1179	0.162	0.390	0.019	0.057
TPOX	0.014	0.056	0.004	<0.057
FGA	0.299	0.507	0.059	0.065

The mutation data obtained for the Chinese population by this laboratory is compared with those published by the American Association of Blood Banks [8] on data accumulated from European and American laboratories in Table 2.

Where mutations are observed in the Chinese population, there seemed a good correlation between the two sets of data, in particular on paternal mutation rates. The mutation rates were generally of the same order of magnitude with variations ranging from 1 to 4 fold.

Acknowledgements

The authors would like to express their gratitude to the staff of the Parentage Testing Section of the Government Laboratory, Hong Kong SAR, and the Forensic Science Center of the Guangdong Provincial Public Security Bureau for their technical assistance. Special thanks also to Dr. D.G. Clarke, Government Chemist of the Government Laboratory, Hong Kong SAR and Mr. S.C. Leung, Assistant Government Chemist, for their administrative support and for proofreading the draft.

References

[1] J.M. Butler, Biology of STRs, Forensic DNA Typing: Biology and Technology behind STR Markers, Academic Press, San Diego, CA, 2001, p. 81.

[2] P.S. Walsh, et al., Chelex 100 as a medium for simple extraction of DNA for PCR-based typing from forensic material, Biotechniques 10 (4) (1991) 506–513.

[3] J.L. Weber, C. Wong, Mutation of human short tandem repeats, Human Molecular Genetics 2 (8) (1993) 1123–1128.

[4] B. Brinkmann, et al., Mutation rate in human microsatellites: influence of the structure and length of the tandem repeat, American Journal of Human Genetics 62 (1998) 1408–1415.

[5] E.M. Dauber, et al., Mutational events at human micro- and minisatellite loci: mutation rates and new STR-alleles, Progress in Forensic Genetics 8 (2000) 21–23.

[6] G. Levinson, G.A. Gutman, Slipped-strand mispairing: a major mechanism for DNA sequence evolution, Molecular Biology and Evolution 4 (3) (1987) 203–221.

International Congress Series 1261 (2004) 70–72

www.ics-elsevier.com

The distribution of Y-chromosomal haplotypes: forensic implications

Mark A. Jobling*, Turi E. King

Department of Genetics, University of Leicester, University Road, Leicester LE1 7RH, UK

Abstract. Over 200 single nucleotide polymorphisms (SNPs) and ~40 short tandem repeats (STRs) make the Y chromosome the most informative haplotyping system in the genome. The SNPs define haplogroups forming a unique phylogeny, and with high geographical differentiation, leading to interest in predicting population-of-origin. Data on admixed populations suggest that such predictions may often be misleading. Studies of relationships between surnames and Y haplotypes suggest that surname prediction from DNA will not be reliable. © 2003 Elsevier B.V. All rights reserved.

Keywords: Admixture; Haplogroup; Population genetics; Surnames; Y chromosome

1. Introduction

The human Y chromosome is sex-determining, and therefore male-specific. The non-recombining region thus represents a useful source of polymorphisms for the forensic analysis of male DNA. Since most criminals are men, Y markers are potentially widely applicable. In fact, powerful autosomal short tandem repeat (STR) multiplexes deal effectively with most situations, and Y-STRs find use in specialized applications, including the analysis of mixed samples in rape cases. Here, we address the issues of haplotype distribution, prediction of population-of-origin, and the relationship between Y haplotypes and surnames.

2. Y-SNPs and haplogroups

In evolutionary studies, the most useful Y polymorphisms are binary markers, mostly single nucleotide polymorphisms (SNPs), of which over 200 are currently well characterized. Because mutation rates are low ($\sim 10^{-8}$ per SNP per generation), the haplotypes these SNPs define ('haplogroups'), form a unique bifurcating phylogeny. In an important advance, haplogroup nomenclature has recently been standardized [1].

Abbreviations: SNP, single nucleotide polymorphism; STR, short tandem repeat.

* Corresponding author. Tel.: +44-1162-523377; fax: +44-1162-523378.
E-mail address: maj4@leicester.ac.uk (M.A. Jobling).

doi:10.1016/S0531-5131(03)01787-4

Though this tree represents the best-resolved phylogeny of any human locus, problems remain. Many of the markers have been discovered in a limited sample set, then are typed more widely. This can elevate the apparent diversity in the populations used for discovery—ascertainment bias. Many branches in the phylogeny bear multiple markers, but usually a single marker is typed, so intermediate haplogroups, important for refining tree resolution, will not be found. Typing methods are nonstandardized and control DNAs from particular haplogroups are usually unavailable. Finally, there is no centralized database of haplogroup data—researchers must trawl the literature and often decipher nonstandard nomenclature.

More SNPs are required to resolve parts of the tree and it is tempting to seek these in existing SNP databases. However, ascertainment bias is serious here, since a small number of populations are represented in screening sets, and there is also the problem of validation: many apparent Y-SNPs are actually sequence differences between highly similar duplicated sequences (paralogs) that have been misassembled.

3. Haplogroup distributions

Global surveys reveal a striking picture of geographical haplogroup differentiation [2], and many haplogroups are continent-specific. This specificity is greater that that seen with autosomal or mitochondrial DNA (mtDNA) markers and is explained by the prevalence of patrilocality, a marriage practice where men stay closer to their birthplaces upon marriage than do women [3]. Can we therefore use the Y chromosome to predict population-of-origin of a DNA sample? Studies of admixed populations caution against a simplistic approach. In a sample of British Afro-Caribbeans, all but ~ 1% of individuals carry African mtDNAs, but >25% of Y chromosomes are of European origin (unpublished observations). This reflects sex-biased admixture, where European men, but not women, contributed genes to the ancestors of these people during the period of slavery. Admixture is often sex-biased, and therefore the Y is relatively sensitive to introgression, which could mislead if Y haplogroup were used to guide an investigation. If good population data were available, a likelihood could be presented of population-of-origin of a DNA sample, and this might still constitute useful information ; however, useful markers are probably best found elsewhere in the genome.

4. Y-STRs present and future

Around 30 Y-STRs are in current use and 9 are employed in excellent quality-controlled databases [4]; haplotype diversity is high (virtual heterozygosity = 0.9976 in the European database). Each haplogroup originates as a new SNP mutation in a single man and he carries a single Y-STR haplotype. As time passes, STR mutations accumulate in his descendants and haplotype diversity increases. Eventual diversity depends on time and demography, but is reduced compared to that of Y chromosomes as a whole. So, just as haplogroups show geographical specificity, so do Y-STR haplotypes, though rarely in such a clear way. High-frequency Y-STR haplotypes are not usually encountered, but can be where a single man and his descendants have been particularly successful in reproducing. A good example is the presence of a frequent (8% of sample) 16-locus haplotype over an enormous geographical area stretching from the Pacific to the Caspian Sea and attributed to the activities of Genghis Khan [5].

Known STRs are a mixed bag of different markers with different properties. Availability of the Y chromosome sequence, and the program Tandem Repeats Finder [6], allows systematic searches for further useful STRs. These have yielded well over 100 markers (Kayser et al., in preparation), which will allow STRs with particular properties to be used in the future.

5. Y chromosomes and surnames

The fact that many societies employ patrilineal surnames has stimulated interest in the relationship between surname and Y haplotype. In a perfect world, a detailed Y haplotype would automatically provide the surname of the bearer. However, in reality, there are a several perturbing influences: some names had more than one founder (about 25 generations ago in England); non-paternities and adoptions have introduced other lineages; and people sometimes change their surnames [7]. The only published study, of the surname Sykes [8], suggested either multiple founders or a high non-paternity rate. Even with a rate as low as 1%, the cumulative rate over the $\sim$ 50 generations separating two contemporary men from a shared surname founder is $\sim$ 40%, so we expect to see multiple lineages in most surnames. In our current studies, most of a set of 40 different surnames show multiple Y-STR clusters, each of which represents either an independent surname founder, or, more probably, an independent non-paternity event. Simulation studies are being used to choose between different explanations, but it seems that surname prediction from Y haplotype is likely to remain a fantasy.

Acknowledgements

MAJ was supported by a Wellcome Trust Senior Fellowship (grant no. 057559) and TEK by the Wellcome Trust.

References

[1] Y Chromosome Consortium. A nomenclature system for the tree of human Y-chromosomal binary haplogroups, Genome Res. 12 (2002) 339–348.
[2] M.A. Jobling, C. Tyler-Smith, The human Y chromosome: an evolutionary marker comes of age, Nat. Rev., Genet. 4 (2003) 598–612.
[3] M.T. Seielstad, et al., Genetic evidence for a higher female migration rate in humans, Nat. Genet. 20 (1998) 278–280.
[4] L. Roewer, et al., Online reference database of Y-chromosomal short tandem repeat (STR) haplotypes, Forensic Sci. Int. 118 (2001) 103–111.
[5] T. Zerjal, et al., The genetic legacy of the Mongols, Am. J. Hum. Genet. 72 (2003) 717–721.
[6] G. Benson, Tandem repeats finder: a program to analyze DNA sequences, Nucleic Acids Res. 27 (1999) 573–580.
[7] M.A. Jobling, In the name of the father: surnames and genetics, Trends Genet. 17 (2001) 353–357.
[8] B. Sykes, C. Irven, Surnames and the Y chromosome, Am. J. Hum. Genet. 66 (2000) 1417–1419.

International Congress Series 1261 (2004) 73–75

www.ics-elsevier.com

29 Y-chromosome SNP analysis in European populations

Maria Brion*, Alejandro Blanco-Verea, Victoria Lareu, Angel Carracedo

Institute of Legal Medicine, University of Santiago de Compostela, San Francisco s/n. 15782 Santiago de Compostela, Spain

Abstract. Single Nucleotide Polymorphisms (SNPs) located on the Y chromosome have a specific interest as forensic tools, and based on these facts, we have designed a strategy, which allows to identify the most frequent haplogroups in Europe. Among the 245 binary polymorphisms described in the Y Chromosome Consortium tree, we have selected 29 markers. The whole set has been grouped into four multiplexes, in order to determine the final haplogroup using only one or two multiplexes. In this way, we avoid typing unnecessarily SNPs to define the final haplogroup saving effort and cost, since we only type in the best case 9 SNPs and in the worst possible combination 17 SNPs. One hundred fifty samples from Galicia (Northwest Spain) have been analysed. Data obtained by using the SNaPshot multiplex kit (Applied Biosystems) will be presented. © 2003 Elsevier B.V. All rights reserved.

Keywords: Y-chromosome; SNP; Multiplex analysis; Europe

1. Introduction

Analysis of binary polymorphisms, and especially Single Nucleotide Polymorphisms (SNPs) is becoming an extensive routine. [1]. In particular, Y-SNPs have a specific interest as forensic tools for several reasons. Firstly, the SNPs are the most frequent kind of polymorphism. Secondly, because of their simplicity, SNPs can be analysed from a very low quantity of DNA in small fragments and are amenable to analysis with high throughput technologies. Thirdly, the low mutation rate allows their use in paternity testing. Nevertheless, the presence of only two alleles in addition to the lack of recombination and the highly population-specific distribution, shown in the Y-chromosome, often needs the analysis of large numbers of SNPs.

Despite slow progress in the discovery of Y-chromosome variation, now a large number of SNPs have been described, defining a highly resolved tree of binary haplogroups [2,3] Checking the literature, an extensive search has been performed looking for the allele

* Corresponding author. Tel.: +34-9815-82327; fax: +34-9815-80336.
E-mail address: brioniml@usc.es (M. Brion).

doi:10.1016/S0531-5131(03)01822-3

frequencies of each SNP in Europeans. As a result of this search, a set of 29 SNPs was selected in order to determine the most frequent haplogroups present in Europe.

A large number of SNP genotyping methods are now available; however, the selected method was the SNaPshot multiplex system (Applied Biosystems).

2. Material and methods

PCR multiplexes were performed in 25 μl of final volume, with 1 × buffer, 300 μM of dNTPs, 2 mM of $MgCl_2$, 2 U of Taq Gold polymerase and 10 ng of genomic DNA, except multiplex 2 which was performed with 200 μM, 1.5 mM of $MgCl_2$ and 0.5 U of Taq Gold. The cycling conditions were 95 °C 10 min, 32 cycles of 94 °C 30 s, 59 °C 30 s and 70 °C 30 s, and a final extension at 65 °C during 15 min. Primer concentrations range between 0.1 and 0.5 (primer sequences and concentrations are available from the authors upon request). After PCR, 1 μl of the product was cleaned with 0.5 μl of ExoSAP-IT (Amersham Biosciences), in order to eliminate the unincorporated primers and dNTPs.

Multiplex SNaPshot reactions were performed in 5 μl final volume, including 2 μl of multiplex SNaPshot kit (Applied Biosystems) and 1.5 μl of cleaned PCR product. The cycling conditions were 96 °C 10 s, 50 °C 5 s and 60 °C 30 s, during 25 cycles. Primer sequences and concentrations are available from the authors upon request. To remove the unincorporated ddNTPs, the final product was incubated with 1 U of SAP (Amersham Biosciences). Snapshot products were run on an ABI 3100 and analysed using Genescan 3.7 software (Applied Biosystems).

3. Results and discussion

The 29 SNPs were divided in four multiplex PCRs, according to their location on the Y-chromosome consortium tree. Multiplex 1 allows for the detection of the major clades more frequent in Europe [2,3], multiplex 2 determines haplogroups G, I and J, multiplex 3 subdivides haplogroup E, and multiplex 4 subdivides haplogroup R1b. The strategy adopted for typing the SNPs includes on one hand the development of four multiplex PCRs, and on the other hand the development of four multiplex SNaPshot reactions (Fig. 1).

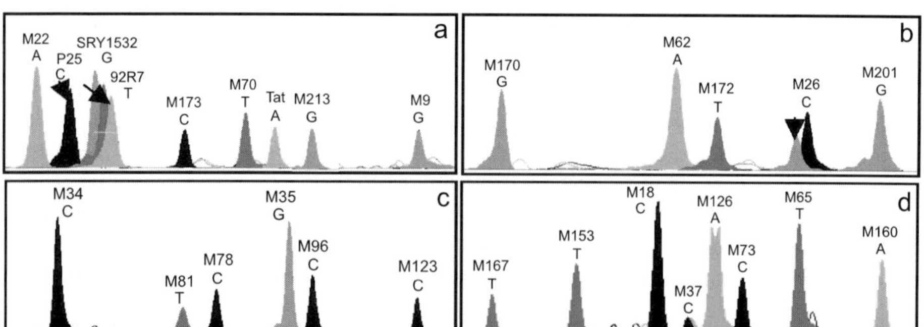

Fig. 1. SNaPshot multiplexes from different samples. (a) Multiplex 1, the P25 shows duplicated pattern; (b) multiplex 2, M26 shows an artefact blue peak; (c) multiplex 3; (d) multiplex 4.

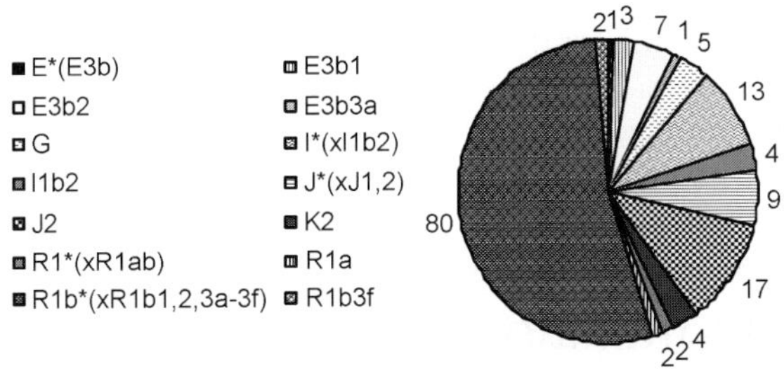

Fig. 2. Haplogroup frequencies in Galicia.

The products of the PCR multiplexes were checked in polyacrylamide gels (data not shown). In the SNaPshot reactions, the products were spatially separated tailing the 5′ end of the minisequencing primers with varying lengths of poly (dC) non-homologous tails.

The reproducibility of these four multiplexes was checked in 150 samples from Galicia. For all the samples, the results agree with the Y-chromosome Consortium tree [2,3]. Only four samples were assigned to the final haplogroup using one multiplex, the remaining samples needed two multiplexes.

The 29 SNPs analysed describe a total of 32 haplogroups; however, in the 150 samples analysed only 14 of these haplogroups were detected (Fig. 2).

With this hierarchical strategy adapted for Europeans the massive typing of SNPs was avoided, and therefore the time and money involved in the study was also reduced. Once more the high degree of population homogeneity present in Europe has been confirmed, since more than half the samples belong to the same paragroup.

Acknowledgements

The technical assistance of M. Rodríguez and R. Calvo is highly appreciated. This work was supported by the grants from the "Xunta de Galicia" (PGIDT01PXI20806PR) and from the "MCYT" (DGCYT.P4.BIO2000-0145-P4-02).

References

[1] Z. Zhao, et al., Investigating single nucleotide polymorphism (SNP) density in the human genome and its implications for molecular evolution, Gene 312 (2003) 207–213.

[2] Y Chromosome Consortium, A nomenclature system for the tree of human Y-chromosomal binary haplogroups, Genome Res. 12 (2002) 339–348.

[3] M.A. Jobling, C. Tyler-Smith, The human Y chromosome: an evolutionary marker comes of age, Nat. Rev., Genet. 4 (8) (2003) 598–612.

ELSEVIER

International Congress Series 1261 (2004) 76–78

www.ics-elsevier.com

Y-chromosomal microsatellite mutation rates: differences in mutation rate between and within loci

B. Myhre Dupuy[a,*], M. Stenersen[a], A.G. Fløneses[a], T. Egeland[b], B. Olaisen[a]

[a] *Institute of Forensic Medicine, University of Oslo, Rikshospitalet, 0027 Oslo, Norway*
[b] *Biostatistics, Rikshospitalet, 0027 Oslo, Norway*

Abstract. We have studied 1766 father–son pairs of confirmed paternity (a total of 15 894 meioses) in nine Y-STR loci. The fathers were also analysed in five biallelic markers defining haplogroups (Hg) 1, 2, 3, 4, 9 and 16. A total of 36 fragment length mutations were observed. Our data demonstrate a significant surplus of gains and a bias towards increase in allele length upon mutational events. Overall, the mutation rate is correlated to STR repeat length, and there is a significant excess of losses in long alleles and gains in short alleles. Significant differences in mutation rate between and within loci are verified as is differences in mutation rates between haplogroups. Our findings clearly demonstrate the necessity of not only locus-specific but even allele-specific mutation rate estimates for forensic and population genetic purposes.

Keywords: Y-STR mutation rate; Microsatellite mutation rate; Father–son pair; Norway

1. Introduction

Precise estimates of mutation rates at Y-chromosomal microsatellite (Short Tandem Repeat) loci make an important basis for paternity diagnostics and dating of Y-chromosome lineage origins. There are indications of considerable locus mutation rate variability between (inter) and within (intra) loci. In light of these observations, we have studied Y-chromosomal microsatellite mutation in a large material of father–son pairs, giving access to direct observation and characterization of the individual mutations, and to individual STR locus mutation rate estimates even at the haplotype level.

2. Material and methods

The material consists of 1766 consecutive father–son pairs from a paternity case material in Norway. Paternity was confirmed at five minisatellite loci. DNA was extracted

* Corresponding author. Rettsmedisinsk Institutt, Rikshospitalet A2-1002, Gaustadalléen 20, 0027 Oslo, Norway. Tel.: +47-23071312; fax: +47-23071278.

E-mail address: b.m.dupuy@labmed.uio.no (B.M. Dupuy).

0531-5131/
doi:10.1016/S0531-5131(03)01791-6

Table 1
Y-STR loci structure and individual STR mutation rates

Locus sorted by increasing mutation rates	Genome database (GDB)	Number of mutations		Locus-specific mutation rate	Average mutation rate
		Simple	Complex compound		
DYS392 (trinucleotide)	456509	0		0	Simple:
DYS388 (trinucleotide)	365729	1		5.70×10^{-4}	3.78×10^{-4}
DYS393	456649	1		5.70×10^{-4}	
DYS19	121409		3	1.70×10^{-3}	
DYS389I (C/D)	366108		4	2.26×10^{-3}	Complex:
DYS389II (A/B)	366108		4	2.26×10^{-3}	3.21×10^{-3}
DYS385	316257		7	3.96×10^{-3}	
DYS391	366118		8	4.53×10^{-3}	
DYS390	366115		8	4.53×10^{-3}	

from venous blood samples by the salting out method [1]. PCR conditions are as described in Ref. [2] and Ref. [3]. The repeat number nomenclature is according to the ISFH guidelines Ref. [4] and Refs. [5,6]. Mutations are identified by electrophoresis as allele length differences between father and son. They are confirmed by reanalysis and DNA sequence analysis.

3. Results

In 1766 father–son pairs (15 894 meioses in total), fragment length analysis demonstrated 36 mutations: 24 gains and 12 losses; thus, there is a surplus of gains [7]. Our data demonstrated significant correlation between STR size and mutation rate. We found relatively more gains in short alleles and more losses in long alleles. We observed one double mutation displaying two mutations at two different loci: DYS389I and DYS389II. These loci are located within 50 base pairs apart, and in addition, changes in both repeat motifs in DYS389II have occurred. Speculations regarding dependency in this particular case might therefore seem appropriate. However, the present data seem to exclude any strong dependency between loci with respect to mutation events. No noteworthy correlation between mutation rate and the father's age at the birth of child is observed. We observed a significant difference between individual STR mutation rate estimates ($p = 0.007$, Fisher's Exact Test) ranging from 0 in DYS392 to 4.53×10^{-3} in DYS390 and DYS391 (Table 1). Differences in mutation rates between the haplogroups (Hg) studied were demonstrated, a phenomenon which is a reflection of the dependence of mutation rate on allele size.

References

[1] S.A. Miller, D.D. Dykes, H.F. Polesky, A simple salting out procedure for extracting DNA from human nucleated cells, Nucleic Acids Res. 16 (3) (1988) 1215.

[2] A.D. Kloosterman, M. Pouwels, P. Daselaar, H.J.T. Janssen, Population genetic study of Y-chromosome specific STR-loci in Dutch Caucasians, 17th Congress of the International Society for Forensic Haemogenetics, Springer, Oslo, 1997, pp. 491–493.

[3] B.M. Dupuy, et al., Y-chromosome variation in a Norwegian population sample, Forensic Sci. Int. 117 (3) (2001) 163–173.

[4] P. Gill, et al., DNA commission of the International Society of Forensic Genetics: recommendations on forensic analysis using Y-chromosome STRs, Int. J. Leg. Med. 114 (6) (2001) 305–309.
[5] P.M. Schneider, et al., Tandem repeat structure of the duplicated Y-chromosomal STR locus DYS385 and frequency studies in the German and three Asian populations, Forensic Sci. Int. 97 (1) (1998) 61–70.
[6] M. Kayser, et al., Evaluation of Y-chromosomal STRs: a multicenter study, Int. J. Leg. Med. 110 (3) (1997) 125–133.
[7] B.M. Dupuy, et al., Y-chromosomal microsatellite mutation rates: differences in mutation rate between and within loci, Human Mutation, 2003, in press.

International Congress Series 1261 (2004) 79–81

www.ics-elsevier.com

Y-SNPs analysis in Japanese using liquid bead array technology

Masaki Hashiyada[a,*], Masayuki Nata[a,1], Toshio Nagashima[b,2]

[a] *Division of Forensic Medicine, Department of Public Health and Forensic Medicine, Tohoku University Graduate School of Medicine, 2-1 Seiryo-Machi, Aoba, Sendai, Miyagi, Japan*

[b] *NTT Data Technology Corporation, 2-2-12 Akasaka Minato, Tokyo, Japan*

Abstract. Forty-two Y chromosome single nucleotide polymorphism (Y-SNP) loci were investigated in 142 unrelated Japanese males by liquid bead array technology, which is a detection method using microspheres and a flow cytometer. Six haplogroups were found in this study. About two-thirds of Japanese were classified into 'Haplogroup O,' which is widely distributed over East Eurasia, and one-third were 'Haplogroup D,' which is different from the haplogroup distribution for other East Asian races. © 2003 Elsevier B.V. All rights reserved.

Keywords: Single nucleotide polymorphism (SNP); Y chromosome; Haplogroup; Japanese population

1. Introduction

Analysis of single nucleotide polymorphism markers on the Y chromosome (Y-SNPs) could provide useful information in some forensic cases or paternal genetic relationships. However, comparing with STR, analyses of many SNPs loci are required to get information of individual identification because SNPs are biallelic loci. There are several different methods for analyzing SNPs. One of them is a liquid bead array system, which is a rapid, cost-effective, high-throughput readout system performed on a flow cytometer, LuminexTM 100 (Luminex, Austin, USA).

2. Materials and methods

Genomic DNA samples were extracted from buccal swabs using Chelex 100 method. A Signet Y-SNP Identification System (Marligen Biosciences, USA) provides the PCR mixture, 43 SNPs primers and specific oligonucleotide complementarily bind the beads.

* Corresponding author. Tel.: +81-22-717-8110; fax: +81-22-717-8112.

E-mail addresses: hashiyad@forensic.med.tohoku.ac.jp (M. Hashiyada), nata@forensic.med.tohoku.ac.jp (M. Nata), Toshio.Nagashima@nttdtec.co.jp (T. Nagashima).

[1] Tel.: +81-22-717-8110; fax: +81-22-717-8112.

[2] Tel.: +81-3-5575-7326; fax: +81-3-5575-7329.

doi:10.1016/S0531-5131(03)01527-9

Table 1
Polymorphic loci included in the Y-SNP identification system and their multiplex assignments

Multiplex	1	2	3	4	5
Markers	M42	M2	M11	M3	M18
	M45	M31	M52	M5	M37
	M60	M32	M130	M95	M87
	M89	M33	M170	M119	M153
	M94	M35	M172	M124	M157
	M168	DYS391	M174	SRY+465	P25
	M175	M75	M201	SRY9138	SRY10831
	M207	M150		Tat	
	Amelogenin	M146			
		M182			
		P3			
		P4			

Forty-three loci cannot be amplified by one tube, but the template DNA is amplified by dividing into five tubes, taking advantage of the characteristic of a marker. Analyzed markers were listed in Table 1. The flow of experiment is as follows: first, the 5-ng template DNA is amplified, then the primers are removed by Exonuclease I enzyme digestion, the PCR products are labeled and the beads hybridized in accordance with manufacturer's

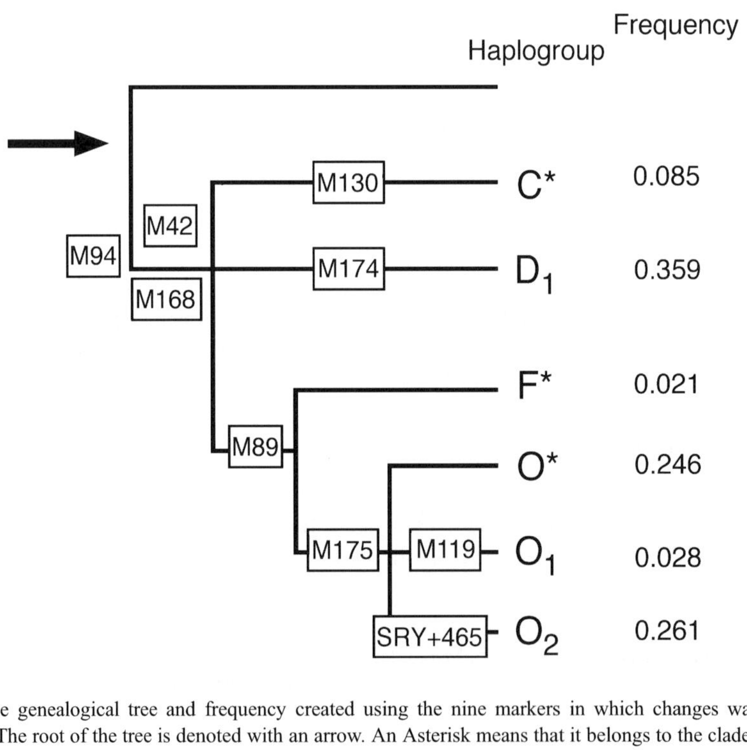

Fig. 1. The genealogical tree and frequency created using the nine markers in which changes was found in Japanese. The root of the tree is denoted with an arrow. An Asterisk means that it belongs to the clade, but not to subclade [1].

protocols. Finally, collected LuminexTM data were analyzed by MasterPlex GT software (MiraiBaio, Alameda, USA).

3. Results and discussion

This Y-SNPs kit is said to determine the ethnic groups using the tree of human Y-chromosomal binary haplogroups, which was made by the Y Chromosome Consortium [1]. Of the 42 Y-SNP markers (without amelogenin), the changes were observed in nine markers in which six haplogroups in 142 subjects analyzed can be classified (Fig. 1). All Japanese samples have changes in the M42, M94 and M168 markers. Haplogroup D and haplogroup O were classified to the major clades defined by M175 and M174 markers in addition to above markers, respectively. Further, 41 samples classified into haplogroup O fell into the subclade O1 and O2 by M119 and SRY+465 markers, respectively. This haplogroup O is widely distributed over East Eurasia, but is hardly found in Africa and Europe [2]. Otherwise, the other major haplogroup D is close to African clade according to genealogical tree [1] and different from the haplogroup distribution for other East Asian races [2]. It might be thought that D lines spread in Japan influenced by random genetic drift. The other two small clades are haplogroups C and F, defined by M130 and M89 markers, respectively.

This system was very effective in SNP genotyping; however, for individual identification, appropriate SNP loci would have to be chosen.

Acknowledgements

A part of this research was supported by Telecommunications Advancement Organization of Japan (TAO), and special thanks to Professor Shigeo Tujii (Chuo University), Ms. Junko Tanoue and Seiitiro Ito (Hitachi Software Engineering) and Steven B. Lee (MiraiBio).

References

[1] The Y Chromosome Consortium, A nomenclature system for the tree of human Y-chromosomal binary haplogroups, Genome Res. 12 (2002) 339–348.

[2] T. Karafet, L. Xu, R. Du, et al., Paternal population history of East Asia: sources, patterns, and microevolutionary processes, Am. J. Hum. Genet. 69 (2001) 615–628.

International Congress Series 1261 (2004) 82–84

www.ics-elsevier.com

The highly discriminating Y-STR DYS464: a reasonable extension of the minimal Y-STR haplotype?

Burkhard Berger, Harald Niederstätter, Anita Brandstätter, Walther Parson *

Institute of Legal Medicine, University of Innsbruck, Müllerstrasse 44, A-6020, Innsbruck, Austria

Abstract. DYS464 is a multi-copy STR system with four positions on the Y chromosome (DYS464a, b, c, and d) which was recently identified and characterized. The aims of our study were to perform a population study, to estimate the mutation-rate and an extensive sequence analysis in order to confirm the nomenclature. Fourteen different alleles were found with allele lengths varying from 9 to 19 repeats. All alleles were cloned and sequenced. A total of 54 different genotypes were identified in 135 men corresponding to a gene diversity (GD) of 0.97. This value is much higher than those of other Y-STRs. DYS464 has the same discrimination capacity as the combination of the five Y-STR loci with the lowest gene diversity of the Y-STR core set. The mutation-rate estimate based on the 70 meioses analyzed amounts to 2.86×10^{-2}.

Keywords: Y chromosome; Y-STR; DYS464; Minimal haplotype; Mutation-rate

1. Introduction

A number of new Y-STRs have been characterized and studied in different populations during the last years. As a small set of the most informative Y-STRs can distinguish Y-chromosomal lineages more efficiently than a large set of less informative loci, it is advantageous to focus on the most diverse group of Y-STR loci. Recently, Redd et al. [1] identified and characterized the multi-copy marker DYS464, showing four copies on the Y-chromosome. A comparison of up to 36 Y-STR loci proofed DYS464 to be the most polymorphic Y-STR yet described.

Abbreviations: STR, short tandem repeat; minHT, minimal haplotype; GD, gene diversity; HD, haplotype diversity.

* Corresponding author. Tel.: +43-512-507-3303; fax: +43-512-507-2764.

E-mail address: Walther.Parson@uibk.ac.at (W. Parson).

0531-5131/

doi:10.1016/S0531-5131(03)01656-X

2. Materials and methods

Blood samples were obtained from 205 male Caucasians from Tirol (Austria). This population sample comprises 135 unrelated men (fathers) as well as 70 sons (paternity index>1000). The DNA was isolated using the QIAmp DNA Blood miniKit (Qiagen, Hilden, Germany).

The primer sequences and the PCR conditions used for the amplification of DYS464 can be found in Ref. [1]. The Y-STRs of the minHT were amplified as in Ref. [2]. Separation of the PCR products was carried out on an ABI 3100.

Selected DNA samples were amplified with unlabeled primers as described above. The PCR products were cloned in the pCR®4-TOPO® vector and sequenced (for details, see Ref. [3]).

Following the ISFG guidelines on the nomenclature of duplicated Y-STRs [4], the alleles are listed in ascending order and are separated by a hyphen. The gene diversity (GD) and the haplotype diversity (HD) are computed as described in Ref. [5].

3. Results and discussion

DYS464 shows a variable repeat block, namely $(CCTT)_n$ as well as five additional non-variant (CCTT) repeat motifs. The general repeat structure is: $(CCTT)_n$...$(CCTT)_2$...$(CCTT)_3$...$(CCTT)_4$...$(CCTT)_2$...$(CCTT)_2$.

In the variant alleles, the tetramer repeat is interrupted by a CTT motif. Two subtypes of allele 14.3 (A and B), differing in the position of the CTT motif within the variable repeat block, were found. Subtype A has the structure $(CCTT)_3CTT(CCTT)_{11}$ and subtype B $(CCTT)_7CTT(CCTT)_7$. According to this classification, all sequenced 15.3 alleles can be designated as subtype B with the structure $(CCTT)_7CTT(CCTT)_8$. Fifty-four different DYS464 genotypes were identified in 135 men, 57% of these being unique. The three most frequent genotypes were 15–17 (8.2%), 12–15–16 (7.4%) and 15–16–17 (7.4%). The most common genotype containing a variant allele (14–15.3–16–17) was found with a frequency of 3.7%. The Y-STR core set enabled us to differentiate 110 paternal lineages. By adding DYS464, it was possible to distinguish 122 haplotypes, 114 (85.7%) of these being unique. The cumulative haplotype diversity of all nine STR loci (minHT + DYS464) was 0.9983. This is a similar value as found for a 19- and a 14-locus Y-STR haplotype [5,6]. DYS464 has the same discrimination capacity as the combination of the five Y-STR loci of the core set with the lowest gene diversity. On the other hand, a combination of the three most diverse loci (DYS464, DYS385 and DYS390) has the same capacity to distinguish paternal lineages compared with the complete minimal haplotype (eight loci).

We analyzed DYS464 in 70 meioses from confirmed father/son pairs and identified two mutations. The mutation-rate estimate amounts to 2.86×10^{-2} (95% CI 3.5×10^{-3}–9.95×10^{-2}). This value is approximately 10 times higher than the average mutation-rate estimate for Y-STRs and 3 to 4 times higher than the mutation-rate of DYS390, which is the locus with the highest mutation-rate known so far [7]. Because of the limited number of observed male germ line transmissions, stochastic sampling effects cannot be excluded.

4. Conclusions

Our results confirm that DYS464 is the most polymorphic Y-STR described (GD = 0.97). The cloning and sequencing of the alleles shows that the variability is

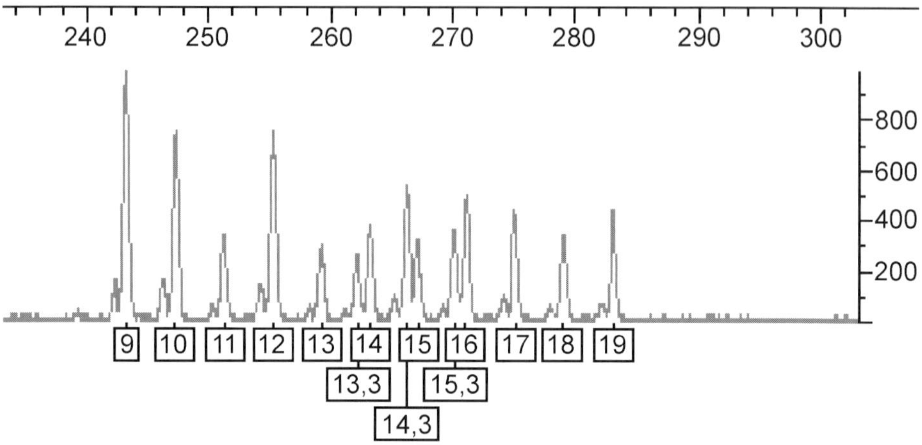

Fig. 1. Electropherogram for the DYS464 allelic ladder. All alleles were cloned and sequenced.

attributed to the first repeat block only and allows for the creation of an allelic ladder in order to meet the ISFG recommendations on forensic analysis using Y-STRs [4] (Fig. 1). We believe that DYS464 is mostly practical for high-throughput screenings and could be successfully applied for mass screenings, e.g. in connection with rape cases or mass disasters.

Acknowledgements

We thank Alexandra Lindinger for her excellent technical assistance and Herbert Oberacher for his valuable discussion.

References

[1] A.J. Redd, A.B. Agellon, V.A. Kearney, V.A. Contreras, T. Karafet, H. Park, et al. Forensic value of 14 novel STRs on the human Y chromosome, Forensic Sci. Int. 130 (2–3) (2002) 97–111.

[2] W. Parson, H. Niederstätter, S. Köchl, M. Steinlechner, B. Berger, When autosomal short tandem repeats fail: optimized primer and reaction design for Y-chromosome short tandem repeat analysis in forensic casework, Croat. Med. J. 42 (3) (2001) 285–287.

[3] B. Berger, H. Niederstätter, A. Brandstätter, W. Parson, Molecular characterization and Austrian Caucasian population data of the multi-copy Y-chromosomal STR DYS464, Forensic Sci. Int. (2003), (in press).

[4] P. Gill, C. Brenner, B. Brinkmann, B. Budowle, A. Carracedo, M.A. Jobling, et al. DNA commission of the International Society of Forensic Genetics: recommendations on forensic analysis using Y-chromosome STRs, Int. J. Legal Med. 114 (6) (2001) 305–309.

[5] E. Bosch, A.C. Lee, F. Calafell, E. Arroyo, P. Henneman, P. de Knijff, et al. High resolution Y chromosome typing: 19 STRs amplified in three multiplex reactions, Forensic Sci. Int. 125 (1) (2002) 42–51.

[6] R. Uchihi, T. Yamamoto, K. Usuda, T. Yoshimoto, M. Tanaka, S. Tokunaga, et al. Haplotype analysis with 14 Y-STR loci using 2 multiplex amplification and typing systems in 2 regional populations in Japan, Int. J. Legal Med. 117 (1) (2003) 34–38.

[7] M. Kayser, A. Sajantila, Mutations at Y-STR loci: implications for paternity testing and forensic analysis, Forensic Sci. Int. 118 (2–3) (2001) 116–121.

International Congress Series 1261 (2004) 85–87

www.ics-elsevier.com

Multiplexed assays for evaluation of Y-SNP markers in US populations

Peter M. Vallone*, John M. Butler

Biotechnology Division, National Institute of Standards and Technology, 100 Bureau Drive Mail Stop 8311, Gaithersburg, MD 20899-8311, USA

Abstract. Genetic markers located on the Y chromosome are of increasing importance in human identity testing. In an effort to evaluate the forensic utility of Y chromosome single nucleotide polymorphism (SNP) markers, we constructed several novel multiplex allele-specific primer extension (ASPE) assays and utilized a new commercial allele-specific hybridization (ASH) multiplex kit to examine 50 Y-SNP markers in 229 males from two US Caucasian and African American populations. The novel ASPE assays covered 18 Y-SNP markers in three multiplex reactions while a commercial ASH kit was used to type 42 Y-SNPs plus amelogenin for sex-typing purposes. There were 10 overlapping loci between the ASPE and ASH methods permitting an evaluation of concordance on over 2000 allele calls. The 50 Y-SNP markers examined in this study define 45 of the 159 possible Y Chromosome Consortium (YCC) haplogroups. Only 18 different haplogroups were observed in our samples. © 2003 Published by Elsevier B.V.

Keywords: Forensic science; Y chromosome; Single nucleotide polymorphism; SNP typing; Y-SNPs; Primer extension; Allele-specific hybridization

1. Introduction

In recent years, single nucleotide polymorphisms (SNPs) have become more widely used in a variety of applications including medical diagnostics, population genetics, and human identity testing [1,2]. Over 250 single nucleotide polymorphisms (SNPs) have been characterized on the non-recombining region of the Y chromosome [3,4]. Two SNP detection formats capable of multiplex analysis are allele-specific primer extension (ASPE) and allele-specific hybridization (ASH), which we use here to examine variation along the Y chromosome.

2. Materials and methods

2.1. DNA samples

Anonymous liquid blood samples with self-identified ethnicities were purchased from Interstate Blood Bank (Memphis, TN) and Millennium Biotech (Ft. Lauderdale, FL).

* Corresponding author. Tel.: +1-301-975-4872; fax: +1-301-975-8505.
E-mail address: peter.vallone@nist.gov (P.M. Vallone).

0531-5131/ © 2003 Published by Elsevier B.V.
doi:10.1016/j.ics.2003.11.023

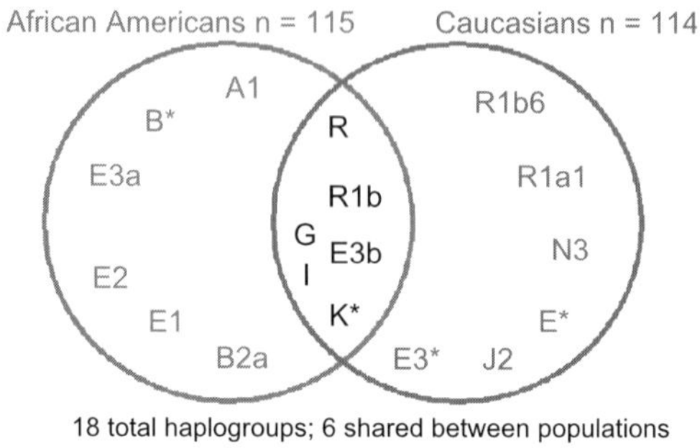

Fig. 1. Summary of YCC haplogroups observed in our sample set.

2.2. Y-SNP markers

The 50 Y-SNPs examined in this study were SRY+465, $SRY_{10831a,b}$, SRY_{9138}, M130 (RPS4Y), M2, DYS391, M168, M170, M182, Tat, M174, M172, M201, M198, M175, M207, M3, M5, P3, M153, M9, M11, M18, M31, M32, M33, M35, M37, M52, M119, M137, M124, M123, M122, M166, M112, M146, M42, M45, M157, M150, M60, M75, M69, M87, M89, M94, M95, P4, and P25. These loci cover the range of known Y-SNP haplogroups. ASPE typing was conducted with SNaPshot reagents (Applied Biosystems, Foster City, CA) and three in-house 6plex assays [5]. ASH typing was performed with the Signet™ Y-SNP Identification System (Marligen Biosciences, Ijamsville, MD), which enables analysis of 42 Y-SNPs in five different multiplex reactions using xMAP™ suspension array technology on the Luminex® 100 flow cytometer (MiraiBio, Alameda, CA). Testing was performed according to the kit protocols using 2 ng of genomic DNA for each multiplex reaction.

2.3. Allele specific primer extension assays

The extension primers were 5′ -tailed with poly-T sets to enable electrophoretic mobility differences between the various loci examined in the multiplex. Primer sequences, reaction conditions, and electrophoretic parameters for the in-house assays are described elsewhere [5].

3. Results and discussion

The 50 markers examined here define 45 of the 159 possible Y Chromosome Consortium (YCC) haplogroups [4]. We examined 114 US Caucasians and 115 African American samples across these 50 Y-SNPs and found 18 different haplogroups (Fig. 1). It is interesting to note that simple analysis of only two Y-SNPs, M2 and P25, would have accurately reflected over 60% of the 229 samples in these population data sets. Additional information from the other 48 markers typed did not further refine the position of these samples on the YCC haplogroup tree.

We observed full concordance between allele calls made with the primer extension and hybridization methods across more than 2000 allele calls. With the ASH method, allele calls are made based on the highest signal observed when both alleles are examined for an

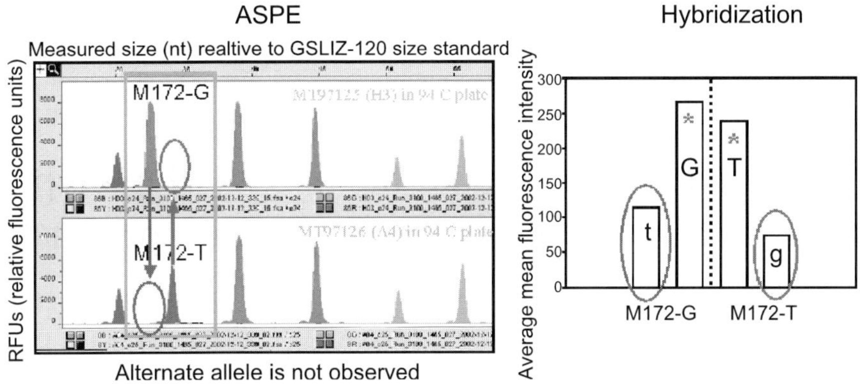

Fig. 2. Comparison of signal-to-noise observed with primer extension vs. hybridization measurements on the same samples with the Y-SNP M172 (G or T). The background signal for the alternate allele is circled. The S/N ratio for the M172 hybridization assay is 2.3 and 3.2 for the G and T alleles, respectively.

SNP marker. The primer extension technique provided a cleaner background than allele-specific hybridization (Fig. 2).

Acknowledgements

This work was supported by research funds from the U.S. National Institute of Justice through Interagency Agreement 1999-IJ-R-094 with the NIST Office of Law Enforcement Standards. Points of view are those of the authors and do not necessarily represent the position of the U.S. Departments of Justice or Defense. The technical assistance and suggestions of Margaret Kline and Jan Redman from our group at NIST and Alan Redd from the University of Arizona are gratefully acknowledged.

Certain commercial equipment, instruments and materials are identified in order to specify experimental procedures as completely as possible. In no case does such identification imply a recommendation or endorsement by the National Institute of Standards and Technology nor does it imply that any of the materials, instruments or equipment identified are necessarily the best available for the purpose.

References

[1] M.A. Jobling, Y-chromosomal SNP haplotype diversity in forensic analysis, Forensic Sci. Int. 118 (2001) 158–162.

[2] A.J. Brookes, The essence of SNPs, Gene 234 (1999) 177–186.

[3] A.J. Y Chromosome Consortium, A nomenclature system for the tree of human Y-chromosomal binary haplogroups, Genome Res. 12 (2002) 339–348.

[4] M.A. Jobling, C. Tyler-Smith, The human Y chromosome: an evolutionary marker comes of age, Nat. Rev., Genet. 4 (2003) 598–612.

[5] P.M. Vallone, J.M. Butler, Y-SNP typing of two U.S. populations using allele-specific hybridization and primer extension, J. Forensic Sci. (2003) (in press).

International Congress Series 1261 (2004) 88–90

www.ics-elsevier.com

How much more should the Y-STR Haplotype Reference Database increase to reach a pragmatic saturation level?

Luisa Pereira[a,*], António Amorim[a,b]

[a] IPATIMUP (Instituto de Patologia e Imunologia Molecular da Universidade do Porto), Rua Dr. Roberto Frias s/n 4200-465, Oporto, Portugal

[b] Faculdade de Ciências da Universidade do Porto, Portugal

Abstract. Empirical saturation curves can be a valuable tool for estimation of sampling effort required to detect an adequate number of Y-STR haplotypes, since they are independent of theoretical models. Nevertheless, they were shown to be highly dependent on current sample size, as detected when applied to the study of the Y-STR Haplotype Reference Database, at a European scale. The influence of geography on sampling saturation was difficult to evaluate due to high heterogeneity of the sample sizes in the database, but at the European level, it is probably very slight. Concerning the present status of the database, it is expected that a fivefold increase in the sample size of the database (up to 60,000 individuals) will reveal twice the current number of haplotypes (11,308 haplotypes), reaching a pragmatic saturation level of 5% (that is, when along with a sample increment of M individuals, no more than $0.05 \times M$ "new" haplotypes are added).

Keywords: Y-STR haplotypes; Saturation curves; Saturation levels; Database

1. Introduction

Statistical problems, namely sampling strategic, when dealing with hypervariable loci such as mtDNA sequences or Y-chromosome STR haplotypes are particularly acute. Among these problems of notorious practical interest are those related to frequency estimations (for instance in evaluating genetic relationships between populations) and to the so-called sampling saturation (i.e., the sample size required for detecting essentially all the distinct items under study in the population). It has been shown, extrapolating from actual European mtDNA HVRI sequence data, that current sample sizes are clearly insufficient for adequate population comparisons, requiring a three- to fourfold increase of the sampling effort per population [1]. In accordance, when analysing the same type of data in an unusually large ($n = 1200$) German sample registered that although haplotype diversity values reached a plateau around $n = 400$, the number of different haplotypes continued to steadily increase [2].

* Corresponding author. Tel.: +351-22-557-0700; fax: +351-22-557-0799.
E-mail address: lpereira@ipatimup.pt (L. Pereira).

0531-5131/
doi:10.1016/S0531-5131(03)01653-4

In this work, we propose to estimate the saturation levels for the number of Y-STR haplotypes in Europe, as currently reported in the Y-STR Haplotype Reference Database, by using empirical saturation curves, which are independent of theoretical models.

2. Material and methods

The Y-STR Haplotype Reference Database was downloaded on 05/04/2003, and from the 12,802 minimal haplotypes present there, we have used the ones for populations in Europe (excluding the ethnic group Romani), summing up 11,692 individuals corresponding to 5524 haplotypes; Y-STR loci of the minimal core (DYS19, DYS389I, DYS389II, DYS390, DYS391, DYS392, DYS393 and DYS385) were considered for analysis. The strategy used consists in performing simulations, which generate sets of random subsamples (four independent assays, by using the function RAND( ) of dBase III+ program) of variable size in sufficient numbers for a direct curve fitting approach. Saturation curves were obtained in the CurveExpert version 1.37 package (http://www.curveexpert.webhop.biz/), under the saturation growth-rate model ($y=(ax)/(b+x)$). Pragmatic saturation levels were set at: 5%, when along with an increment of M individuals, no more than $0.05 \times M$ "new" haplotypes are added; and 1%, when along with an increment of M individuals, no more than $0.01 \times M$ "new" haplotypes are added.

3. Results

The saturation curves obtained for the number of Y-STR haplotypes in each population showed a high heterogeneity inside each geographic area (e.g., central–eastern European populations represented in Fig. 1).

Interestingly, curves with the highest saturation values were observed for populations in which the current sample size is bigger. This indicates that current sample size is a main factor for empirical sampling saturation evaluation.

We then evaluated whether geography had any influence on the sample saturation estimates. We compared the saturation curves obtained in the two ways: (a) each point corresponding to the observed values for each country (and one for the total European

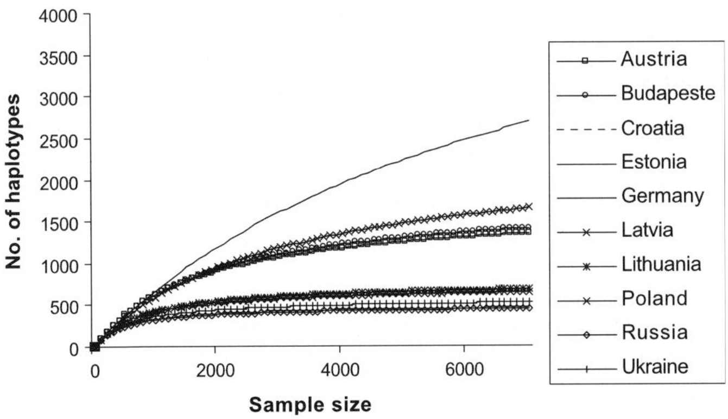

Fig. 1. Saturation curves for the number of Y-STR haplotypes in some European populations.

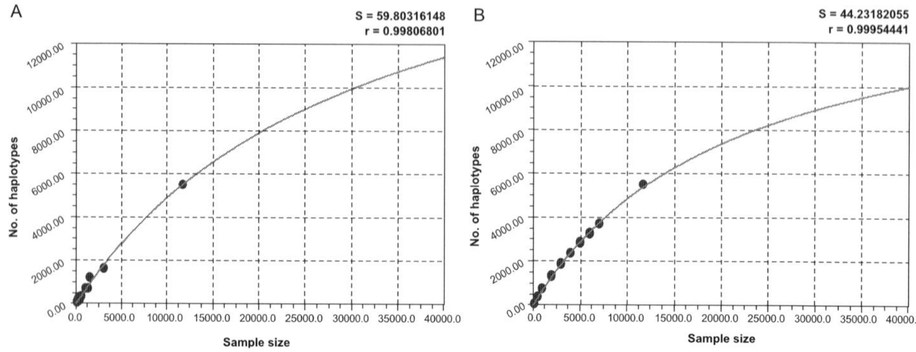

Fig. 2. Saturation curves for the number of Y-STR haplotypes without (A) and with (B) geographic randomisation, as described in the text.

sample; Fig. 2a); (b) using the European sample for simulating points of various sample sizes in four randomised assays (Fig. 2b). There was no significant increase in the correlation coefficient ($r = 0.99806801$ and $r = 0.99954441$, respectively) with geographic randomisation, suggesting a minor geographic influence on the saturation values for the number of Y-STR haplotypes at the European level.

The saturation values obtained with the Y-STR Haplotype Reference Database were: (a) 60,000 individuals corresponding to 11,308 haplotypes, at the 5% level; and (b) 157,000 individuals corresponding to 13,538 haplotypes, at the 1% level.

4. Conclusions

By avoiding the assumptions of theoretical models, the empirical method presented here for the estimation of saturation levels of the number of Y-STR haplotypes is only dependent on the observed variables of sample size and number of haplotypes. Geography was shown to be a minor factor at the European level, supporting the use of large international databases for match searching. Anyway, under our approach, it is predictable that a fivefold increase (up to 60,000 individuals) of the European Y-STR database will reveal about double (11,308) the already sampled haplotypes.

Acknowledgements

This work was partially supported by a research grant to LP (SFRH/BPD/7121/2001) from Fundação para a Ciência e a Tecnologia and IPATIMUP by Programa Operacional Ciência, Tecnologia e Inovação (POCTI), Quadro Comunitário de Apoio III.

References

[1] A. Helgason, S. Sigurðardóttir, J. Gulcher, K. Stefánsson, R.R. Ward, Sampling saturation and the European mtDNA pool: implications for detecting genetic relationships among populations, in: C. Renfrew, K. Boyle (Eds.), Archaeogenetics: DNA and the Population Prehistory of Europe, 2000, pp. 285–294, Cambridge.

[2] H. Pfeiffer, P. Forster, C. Ortmann, B. Brinkmann, The results of an mtDNA study of 1200 inhabitants of a German village in comparison to other Caucasian databases and its relevance for forensic casework, Int. J. Legal Med. 114 (2001) 169–172.

International Congress Series 1261 (2004) 91–93

www.ics-elsevier.com

The mitochondrial DNA tree and forensic science

Martin Richards*

Department of Chemical and Biological Sciences, University of Huddersfield, Queensgate, Huddersfield HD1 3DH, UK

Abstract. Studies of mitochondrial DNA (mtDNA) began with simple restriction assays, moved on to high-resolution restriction analysis and control-region sequencing, and now make use of complete mtDNA sequences. Forensic labs have, by and large, continued to rely on the use of control-region databases, but these databases often contain a disconcertingly large number of sequence errors. A phylogenetic approach to mtDNA data sets can help to uncover such errors, and it is argued that an understanding of both the phylogenetic and phylogeographic context of mtDNA lineages is a valuable tool from which the forensics community can benefit. © 2003 Published by Elsevier B.V.

Keywords: Mitochondrial DNA (mtDNA); Genealogy; Phylogenetic; Phylogeography

1. The mtDNA tree and phylogeography

Phylogenetic analysis is key to the evolutionary analysis of mtDNA. Tree-building methods perform poorly when faced with data sets from control-region sequencing, or even high-resolution RFLP analysis, because of the high levels of recurrent mutation. The introduction of the reduced-median (RM) algorithm for constructing phylogenetic networks has provided a simple means of phylogenetic analysis on such data sets, which performs well in simulation studies [1]. Network approaches portray ambiguities in the data, so that regions of uncertainty are picked out, and they present the phylogenetic estimate complete with uncertainties in a single diagram. The RM algorithm, furthermore, allows the more plausible pathways to be pinpointed using population-genetics criteria not normally employed in tree-building algorithms. By displaying the data in this compact form, networks are also extremely useful for exploratory data analysis. An example is phylogeographic analysis, which provides an additional encoding for the region of origin of each sample, showing how the lineages are distributed in space.

The picture that has emerged of the global mtDNA tree is one of clades of lineages, known as haplogroups, which are more or less geographically restricted at the continental level. The root of the tree lies within eastern and southern African lineages, and is about 200,000 years old [2]. If we trace our way through the tree towards the present, we reach

* Tel.: +44-1484-472428; fax +44-1484-472182.
E-mail address: m.b.richards@hud.ac.uk (M. Richards).

0531-5131/ © 2003 Published by Elsevier B.V.
doi:10.1016/S0531-5131(03)01704-7

the node at the base of haplogroup L3 which gave rise to both African and non-African descendants [3], including just two non-African branches, haplogroups M and N. Although not clearly distinguishable with either control-region sequencing or standard high-resolution RFLP analysis, M and N can be separated by typing a few additional positions in the coding region of the molecule [4]. The two non-African haplogroups are almost exactly the same age—about 65,000 years—and may well have dispersed from Africa together in a single, small group at about this time.

Haplogroups M and N themselves break down into smaller haplogroups that are more restricted geographically [5]. For example, south Asians mainly have lineages within one set of haplogroups within M and N, east Asians another set, and Australasians another. Most Europeans and Near Easterners, and many Central Asians, share a different set of haplogroups again, all within haplogroup N. Haplogroup M was perhaps lost as a result of founder effects as the early groups splintered and some made their way towards Europe.

2. Identifying errors in databases

Evidence is mounting that mtDNA databases are far from error-free [6]. These errors can arise in all sorts of ways: sample mix-up or cross-contamination in the lab; base misscoring due to sequencing artefacts; simple misreading of the output; and—perhaps most commonly—mistakes in transferring data into databases and tables. The impact of these errors on both evolutionary and forensic analyses may not be very great, but it seems risky to assume that it is negligible. In forensics, database errors would depress estimates of the population frequency of genuine mtDNA types, giving a match between a crime scene sample and a suspect more credibility than it deserved.

Fortunately, our knowledge of natural mtDNA variation makes it possible to identify many of these errors. The trick is to locate the new sequence to its approximate position in the mtDNA tree and to carry out a network analysis of it alongside closely related types from the database. To do this, if the typing is normally restricted to HVS-I and HVS-II, it may be necessary to type a few additional coding-region positions (since not all branches in the tree are resolved by control-region mutations—although HVS-I motifs are often sufficient). The new sequence will either match a known type, occur at a previously unsampled internal node in the tree, or generate a new tip with a private polymorphism. The latter are particular candidates for rechecking, since previously unseen variants may be the result of sequencing errors. Errors are particularly obvious when they affect a motif position for a particular mtDNA haplogroup. Bandelt et al. [7] have compiled a taxonomy of errors which can be checked quite systematically using network diagrams, assisted by a knowledge of the mutation rate of each position indicating bases likely to have undergone genuine recurrent mutation [8].

3. Phylogeography and ethnic affiliation

It may also be useful when carrying out forensic analyses to take into account the phylogeography of the mtDNAs one is interested in. The pitfalls of not doing so are illustrated by a recent BBC Television documentary, entitled ‘Motherland: A Genetic Journey’. This film showed several British African–Caribbeans undergoing mtDNA analysis and tracing their lineages back to a particular African ‘homeland’ before the slave trade. However, there are major gaps in the African mtDNA database, and subsequent research has shown that one of the types, localised in the film to the small island of Bioko in tropical west-central Africa, also occurs as far afield as Mozambique, with close relatives in Tanzania. This surprisingly wide distribution is most likely a result of the Bantu dispersals out of west-central Africa 4000 years ago [3]. Similarly, knowledge of the phylogeography and inferred demographic history may usefully inform forensic analyses estimating ethnic affiliation, especially in the absence of databases with perfect geographic coverage.

Acknowledgements

Thanks to Vincent Macaulay and Han-Jürgen Bandelt for critically reading the manuscript.

References

[1] H.-J. Bandelt, et al., Median networks: speedy construction and greedy reduction, one simulation, and two case studies from human mtDNA, Mol. Phylogenet. Evol. 16 (2000) 8–28.
[2] D. Mishmar, et al., Natural selection shaped regional mtDNA variation in humans, Proc. Natl. Acad. Sci. U. S. A. 100 (2003) 171–176.
[3] A. Salas, et al., The making of the African mtDNA landscape, Am. J. Hum. Genet. 71 (2002) 1082–1111.
[4] L. Quintana-Murci, et al., Genetic evidence for an early exit of *Homo sapiens sapiens* from Africa through eastern Africa, Nat. Genet. 23 (1999) 437–441.
[5] M. Richards, V. Macaulay, Genetic data and the colonization of Europe: genealogies and founders, in: C. Renfrew, K. Boyle (Eds.), Archaeogenetics: DNA and the Population Prehistory of Europe, McDonald Institute for Archaeological Research, Cambridge, 2000, pp. 139–151.
[6] P. Forster, To err is human, Ann. Hum. Genet. 67 (2003) 2–4.
[7] H.-J. Bandelt, et al., Detecting errors in mtDNA data by phylogenetic analysis, Int. J. Leg. Med. 115 (2001) 64–69.
[8] H.-J. Bandelt, et al., The fingerprint of phantom mutations in mitochondrial DNA data, Am. J. Hum. Genet. 71 (2002) 1150–1160.

ELSEVIER

International Congress Series 1261 (2004) 94–96

www.ics-elsevier.com

Evaluation and validation of quality assessment of mitochondrial control region sequence data by Phred

E. Sørensen*, E.M. Rasmussen, B. Eriksen, H.J. Larsen, N. Morling

Department of Forensic Genetics, Institute of Forensic Medicine, University of Copenhagen, 11 Frederik V's Vej, DK-2100 Copenhagen, Denmark

Abstract. This study presents the evaluation and validation of the computer programme Phred for semi-automated quality assessment of sequence data from the mitochondrial hypervariable regions HV1 and HV2. We conclude that Phred is a valuable aid in the quality control of mtDNA sequence data. However, Phred is not well suited for identification of base caller induced deletions. This can be compensated for by repeated sequencing. In addition, Phred does not accurately detect base heteroplasmy. Other types of software can be used to supplement Phred in the identification of heteroplasmy.

Keywords: DNA sequencing; Quality assessment; Phred; mtDNA; Forensic genetics

1. Introduction

Sequencing of the mitochondrial control region for forensic purposes generates a large amount of data and, therefore, a thorough quality control of each sequenced base pair is very time consuming. The computer programme Phred (CodonCode) provides quality values (q-values) for each base call in a sequence. The q-values are logarithmically correlated to error probabilities. The relation between a q-value and the error probability (p) is defined as $q = -10 \times \log_{10}(p)$. Thus, a q-value of 20 corresponds to an error probability of 0.01 for the base call, while a q-value of 30 corresponds to an error probability of 0.001 [1,2]. The alignment program Sequencher (GeneCodes) provides a graphical interface, which presents the q-values above and below a chosen threshold (e.g. q-value 20) as various background colours to the nucleotide sequence. In this way, attention is directed to problematic areas in the sequencing results. Thus, the combination of the Phred and the Sequencher programmes is potentially a powerful tool to ensure that base pairs in a sequence are of sufficient quality. Furthermore, the q-values from Phred

* Corresponding author. Tel.: +45-3532-6110; fax: +45-3532-6120.
E-mail address: erik.soerensen@forensic.ku.dk (E. Sørensen).

0531-5131/
doi:10.1016/S0531-5131(03)01507-3

also make it possible to compare the quality of two or more sets of sequencing results. The subject of the current study is to evaluate and validate the accuracy of Phred's error prediction in a forensic genetic venue.

2. Materials and methods

Data from a project involving sequencing of the hypervariable regions HV1 and HV2 from 32 hair shafts (120,419 base pairs) were used for the evaluation. All data originated from electrophoresis on the ABI 310 instrument. Base calling was done by the ABI Sequencing Analysis programme and the data were further analysed by Phred (version 0.000925.c) and then aligned by the Sequencher programme. The true sequences were established by typing each region with both BigDye-primer and -terminator chemistry in both forward and reverse directions. The consensus of at least four typing reactions was considered the correct sequence. The aligned sequences was exported from Sequencher and analysed/grouped by a computer programme (CAF2Table) developed in cooperation with the manufacturers of Phred. After analysis with CAF2Table, the data were imported to MS Excel for the final analysis. The number of actually erroneous base calls, i.e. discrepancies between the actual base call and the consensus of base calls from at least four sequences, was compared to the error rate predicted by Phred.

The data (or segments thereof) were analysed in three different set-ups. In the first set-up, all base pairs were included. When base caller induced deletions occurred (such deletions were revealed by the repeated sequencing), they were given the same q-value as the neighbouring base of least quality. In the second set-up, all bases were included as well, but base caller induced deletions were given a q-value of zero (equal to an error probability of 1). In the third set-up, all sequences with length heteroplasmy were excluded from analysis, and base caller induced deletions were given a q-value of zero.

3. Results

In the first analysis, the correlation between Phred's predictions and the number of observed errors was not satisfactory; e.g. among the 12,379 bases with q-values between 31 and 35, Phred only predicted 5.1 errors while 39 errors were observed (data not shown). In the second analysis, Phred's predictions were better, but still not satisfactory. Here, Phred still predicted 5.1 errors among the 12,361 bases with q-values between 31 and 35, while the observed number of errors was 21 (data not shown). However, in the third analysis, Phred's predictions were in better correlation with the number of observed errors. Table 1 shows a comparison between observed and expected errors grouped according to q-values. In addition, the number of observed errors for each of the sequencing-chemistries and -directions is presented. The table shows that while only a few base caller errors occurred for bases with q-values above 20 sequenced with terminator chemistry, this was not the case for bases of the same quality level sequenced with primer chemistry. This was especially the case for bases sequenced with primer chemistry in the forward direction. A comparison between Phred's predictions and the observed number of base caller errors for each base position in HV1 and HV2 revealed that a highly reproducibly base compression at position 16,053–16,054 was the reason for Phred's inadequate predictions. This compression was seen in sequences that originated from sequencing with primer chemistry

Table 1
Comparison between observed and expected errors grouped according to q-values

q-value	Total			Obs err with different sequencing chemistries			
	N	Obs err	Exp err	PrimFwd	PrimRev	TermFwd	TermRev
0–5	588	587	586.2	288	229	23	47
6–10	1939	243	302.8	139	73	14	17
11–15	1189	66	66.1	11	22	14	19
16–20	2250	56	37.8	21	26	3	6
21–25	1763	17	9.1	12	2	1	2
26–30	2686	6	4.1	4	1	0	1
31–35	7749	2	3.1	2	0	0	0
36–40	15,651	7	2.1	6	1	0	0
41–45	12,474	18	0.5	18	0	0	0
46–50	5337	3	0.1	2	1	0	0
51–65	32,460	0	0.1	0	0	0	0
Total	84,086	1005	1012.0	503	355	55	92

N: number of bases, obs err: observed errors, Exp err: expected errors, PrimFwd: primer chemistry forward, PrimRev: primer chemistry reverse, TermFwd: terminator chemistry forward, TermRev: terminator chemistry reverse.

in the forward direction. In all other positions, with both sequencing chemistries and directions, the q-values were highly accurate (data not shown).

4. Discussion

In the first analysis, base caller induced deletions were given the same q-value as the neighboring base of the lowest quality, while in the second analysis, deletions were given a q-value of zero. This improved Phred's predictions considerably. This indicates that Phred is not accurate when it comes to detecting base caller induced deletions. However, repeated sequencing can compensate for this inaccuracy as it in our experience is unlikely that a base caller induced deletion occurs at the same position using different sequencing chemistries and directions.

In the third analysis, all sequences with length heteroplasmy were removed from the data-set. This also improved Phred's predictions considerable. This result indicate that Phred is not well suited for identification of heteroplasmic bases. This insufficiency could be compensated for by other types of software, e.g. the secondary peak finder in Sequencher.

References

[1] B. Ewing, L. Hillier, M. Wendl, P. Green, BaseCalling of automated sequencher traces using Phred: I. Accuracy assessment, Genome Research 8 (1998) 175–185.

[2] B. Ewing, P. Green, BaseCalling of automated sequencher traces using Phred: II. Error probabilities, Genome Research 8 (1998) 186–194.

International Congress Series 1261 (2004) 97–99

www.ics-elsevier.com

Analysis of SNP-variation in the coding region of mitochondrial DNA

A. Coene, N. Vanderheyden, A. Gilissen, J.-J. Cassiman, R. Decorte*

Laboratory for Forensic Genetics and Molecular Archaeology, Department of Human Genetics, K.U. Leuven, Campus Gasthuisberg ON, Herestraat 49, Louvain B-3000, Belgium

Abstract. A multiplex-PCR procedure was developed for the analysis of single nucleotide polymorphism (SNP) variation defining the European mtDNA-haplotypes in the coding part of the mitochondrial genome. The obtained PCR-products were genotyped for 26 SNPs in four mini-sequencing (SNaPshot™) reactions and analyzed on the ABI PRISM® 3100 Genetic Analyzer. A population study of 157 individuals of Belgian descent revealed 25 different haplotypes belonging to 5 major haplogroups.

Keywords: mtDNA; Single nucleotide polymorphism; Mini-sequencing; Phylogenetics

1. Introduction

Mitochondrial DNA (mtDNA) has been used extensively in the study of the origin and dispersal of modern humans. The geographical distribution of the lineages obtained from SNPs in the coding region of mtDNA and/or control region sequences (HV1) can detect prehistoric movements from one region to another [1]. SNP-typing in the coding region has been based on digestion of PCR products with a battery of 14 different restriction enzymes (RE), which is a tedious method when a large number of samples must be typed. In contrast, primer-extension or mini-sequencing with analysis on automated DNA sequencers provides the possibility for rapid and automated typing of several SNPs in one reaction [2]. In this study, a SnaPshot™ assay was developed for the analysis of mtDNA SNPs characteristic for the West-Eurasian lineages.

2. Materials and methods

The regions containing the SNPs were amplified in four multiplex PCR-reactions, each with four to six amplicons (between 233 and 611 bp; Table 1). The amplification was done in a 25-μl reaction containing 1.5 mM $MgCl_2$, 200 μM dNTPs, 2.5 U AmpliTaq Gold DNA-polymerase, 1 × PCR-Gold-buffer, primers (Table 1) and 1 ng DNA, with denaturation for

* Corresponding author. Tel.: +32-16-345860; fax: +32-16-345997.
E-mail address: ronny.decorte@med.kuleuven.ac.be (R. Decorte).

0531-5131/
doi:10.1016/j.ics.2003.11.010

Table 1
Haplogroup motifs and SNPs defining the most important West-Eurasian clusters

Haplogroup	Subgroup	RFLP motif[a]	SNP	SNapShot	PCR fragment[b]
H		− 7025*Alu*I	T7028C	4	H6764/L7228
		− 14766*Mse*I	T14766C	2	H14293/L14905
V		− 4577*Nla*III	G4580A	1	H4147/L4719
		− 14766*Mse*I	T14766C	2	H14293/L14905
U		+ 12308*Hin*fI	A12308G	3	H12270/L12765
	K	− 9052*Hae*II/ − 9053*Hha*I	G9055A[c]	2	H8726/L9163
		+ 10394*Dde*I	A10398G	3	H9952/L10504
	U1	− 4990*Alu*I	G4991A[c]	3	H4752/L5201
		−	A13104G	1	H13049/L13434
		13103*Hin*fI/ + 13104*Mbo*I + 14068*Taq*I	A14070G	4	H13595/L14102
	U2	+ 15907*Rsa*I	A15907G	2	H15511/L15972
	U4	+ 4643*Rsa*I	T4646C	1	H4147/L4719
		+ 11329*Alu*I	C11332T	3	H11175/L11409
J		+ 4216*Nla*III	T4216C	1	H4147/L4719
		+ 10394*Dde*I	A10398G	3	H9952/L10504
		− 13704*Bst*OI	G13708A	4	H13595/L14102
T		+ 4216*Nla*III	T4216C	1	H4147/L4719
		+ 4914*Bfa*I	A4917G	3	H4752/L5201
		+ 13366*Bam*HI	G13368A	1	H13049/L13434
		+ 15606*Alu*I	A15607G	2	H15511/L15972
		− 15925*Msp*I	G15928A	3	H15511/L15972
	T1	− 12629*Ava*II	C12633A[c]	3	H12270/L12765
I		− 4529*Hae*II	A4529T	2	H4147/L4719
		+ 8249*Ava*II/ − 8250*Hae*III	G8251A	1	H8102/L8575
		+ 10032*Alu*I	T10034C	2	H9952/L10504
W		+ 8249*Ava*II/ − 8250*Hae*III	G8251A	1	H8102/L8575
		− 8994*Hae*III	G8994A[c]	2	H8726/L9163
X		+ 14465*Acc*I	T14470C	4	H14293/L14905
M		+ 10394*Dde*I	A10398G	3	H9952/L10504
		+ 10397*Alu*I	C10400T	1	H9952/L10504
C		+ 10394*Dde*I	A10398G	3	H9952/L10504
		+ 10397*Alu*I	C10400T	1	H9952/L10504
		− 13259*Hinc*II/ + 13262*Alu*I	A13263G	4	H13049/L13434

[a] Macaulay et al. [3].
[b] Position of the primers refer to the 5′ end (H = heavy chain, L = light chain); PCR and SNapShot™ primer sequences are available upon request.
[c] SNPs defined in this study.

10 min at 94 °C, 25 cycles of 1 min at 94 °C, 1 min at 55 °C and 1 min at 72 °C, and final extension of 10 min at 72 °C in a GeneAmp® PCR System 9700.

The primers for genotyping the 26 SNPs were selected with the READIT® Interrogation Probe Design software from Promega (http://www.promega.com/readit/probedesign/default.asp). The manual of the ABI PRISM® SNapShot™ Multiplex Kit (Applied Biosystems) was followed for primer-extension. Sizing of the extension products was done in POP-6™ on an ABI PRISM® 3100 Genetic Analyzer and the results were analyzed with GeneScan® v3.7 and GenoTyper™ v3.7. A reduced median network (Fig. 1) was computed with the program NETWORK 3.1 (http://www.fluxus-engineering.com/sharenet.htm) after star contraction [4].

3. Results and discussion

The mutated position could be identified for 22 SNPs (Table 1) by comparing the RFLP motifs with the "Cambridge Reference Sequence" (CRS). The positions of the

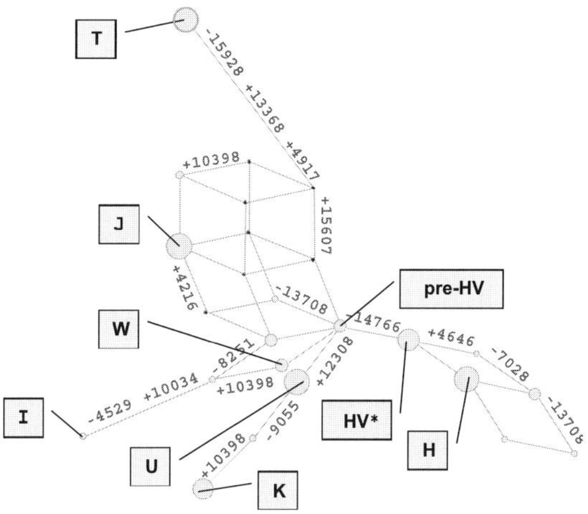

Fig. 1. Reduced median network of a Belgian population typed for 26 SNPs in the coding region of mtDNA. The position of the SNPs according to the CRS are indicated on the branches, while " + " and " – " correspond to the presence or the absence of the RE site.

remaining SNPs were determined by sequence analysis of DNA samples from individuals with a corresponding HV1 motif [3]. Validation of the developed methods in a population sample of 199 individuals revealed a result for all SNPs in 157 individuals. The remaining samples showed for at least one SNP no result indicating the need for further optimisation. In total, 25 haplotypes were identified resulting in a gene diversity of 0.81. The most common lineage present in this population was haplogroup H (42%), while the other common haplogroups were HV* (5.1%), U (including subgroup K and U4; 20.4%), J (18%) and T (8.9%). Pre-HV is identical to the CRS and is present at a frequency of 1.9%. A reduced median network of 18 different haplotypes revealed that pre-HV is the central haplogroup from which 5 clusters radiate—HV, J, T, U and IW—which is in accordance to other studies about European populations [1,3].

Acknowledgements

This work was supported by a grant (no. G.0460.00) from the Fund for Scientific Research Flanders. J.-J. Cassiman is a holder of the "Arthur Bax and Anna Vanluffelen chair of Human Genetics".

References

[1] M.B. Richards, et al., Phylogeography of mitochondrial DNA in Western Europe, Ann. Hum. Genet. 62 (1998) 241–260.
[2] N.M. Makridakis, K.V. Reichardt, Multiplex automated primer extension analysis: simultaneous genotyping of several polymorphisms, BioTechniques 31 (2001) 1374–1380.
[3] V. Macaulay, et al., The emerging tree of west Eurasian mtDNAs: a synthesis of control-region sequences and RFLPs, Am. J. Hum. Genet. 64 (1999) 232–249.
[4] P. Forster, et al., Phylogenetic star contraction applied to Asian and Papuan mtDNA evolution, Mol. Biol. Evol. 18 (2001) 1864–1881.

ELSEVIER

International Congress Series 1261 (2004) 100–102

www.ics-elsevier.com

Beyond HV1 and HV2—identification of valuable mitochondrial DNA single nucleotide polymorphisms

Wojciech Branicki*, Tomasz Kupiec, Paulina Wolańska-Nowak, Agnieszka Parys-Proszek, Grażyna Ba

Institute of Forensic Research, Westerplatte st. 9, 31-033 Cracow, Poland

Abstract. The degree of polymorphism characteristic for hypervariable segments of mitochondrial DNA (mtDNA) is sometimes too low to enable differentiation between individuals revealing most frequent HV1 and HV2 haplotypes. An acceptable solution in such a situation seems to be analysis of additional variation present outside the control region. For practical and ethical reasons, analysis of variation present in the coding part of mitochondrial DNA should be limited to selected single nucleotide polymorphisms. Before selective SNP analysis is possible, those particular valuable mutations, which occur appropriately frequently in a population and are free of medical information, must be determined.

Keywords: Mitochondrial DNA; Single nucleotide polymorphism; Population study; Snapshot

1. Introduction

Sequence analysis of the HV1 and HV2 fragments of mitochondrial DNA (mtDNA) is today a routine method applied to forensic identification in cases where evidence specimens are not suitable for STR analysis. The main limitation of the identification process based on mtDNA analysis is the relatively low power of discrimination associated with HV1 and HV2 sequencing. The most frequent haplotype of mtDNA in the Caucasian population (263G, 315.1C) is characteristic for about 4% of individuals [1]. In order to limit this drawback, analysis of variation associated with the remaining sequence of mtDNA has been proposed [2]. There is known association between genetic diseases and particular mutations in mtDNA [3]. This sort of data must not be obtained in a forensic laboratory. Particular positions revealing appropriate variation and no links with genetic diseases (suitable for forensic identification) must be first determined by nucleotide

* Corresponding author. Tel.: +48-124228755; fax: +48-124223850.
E-mail address: wbranic@ies.krakow.pl (W. Branicki).

0531-5131/
doi:10.1016/S0531-5131(03)01826-0

sequencing. In the routine identification analyses, the identified SNPs can be selectively analysed with one of the currently available methods, e.g., SNaPshot Multiplex Kit. The aim of the present work was to sequence the portion of the coding region of mtDNA for a population sample from Poland in order to find SNPs that could be further subjected to selective analysis in the identification process.

2. Materials and methods

The study was performed on blood or saliva samples collected from 58 unrelated individuals from Poland. DNA was isolated using the standard organic method and the concentration of DNA extract was measured fluorymetricaly.

The 550-bp fragment (amplicon I) of the coding region, encompassing positions 8368–8917 was amplified in an optimised triplex reaction, using the following primers: (1) GCCCCAACTAAATACTACCG; and (2) GTGGTAAGAAGTGGGCTAGG. Two additional amplicons included in the reaction were:

(II) 403 bp, nucleotide positions 10253–10655, covering SNP positions: A10398G, T10463C, A10550G. Primer sequences: (1) TGATCTAGAAATTGCCCTCC; and (2) GGCAATAGGCACAATATTGGC.

(III) 212 bp, nucleotide positions 16344–16555, covering SNP position: T16519C. Primer sequences: (1) CAGTCAAATCCCTTCTCGTCCC; and (2) ATTTAAGGGGAACGTGTGGGC.

The PCR reaction mixture consisted of 1 U Taq DNA polymerase, 2.0 mM $MgCl_2$, 200 μM dNTP, 0.2 μM of each primer; 0.4 μl BSA, 2.0 μl 10 × concentrated PCR buffer and usually 5 ng of template DNA. PCR conditions were as follows: 95 °C/1 min; (94 °C/10 s, 58 °C/30 s, 72 °C/40 s) × 32; 72 °C/10 min; 4 °C. PCR products were purified and subjected to cycle sequencing of the amplicon I. Genetic diversity for the analysed DNA fragment I was calculated according to the formula: $D=1-\Sigma p_i^2$, where p indicates frequency of the observed haplotypes [4].

Amplification products were subjected to a SNaPshot reaction, which was performed according to manufacturers' directions with the following extension primers: SNP-A10398G: GGCCTATGAGTGACTACAAAAAGGATTAGACTGA; SNP-T10463C: AATATTTATGTAAATGAGGGGCATTTGGTA; SNP-T16519C: GACATCTGGTTCCTACTTCAGGG; SNP-A10550G: AGTATATCGCTCACACCTCAT.

3. Results and discussion

The study revealed 12 different haplotypes and 13 polymorphic nucleotide positions among the analysed 58 unrelated individuals. The most frequent variant differed in the single position A8860G, according to the CRS sequence [5]. Table 1 presents information concerning haplotypes, their frequencies and polymorphic sites determined during our study. The genetic diversity equals 0.53. Most of the identified variable positions were discovered in single samples. The only one position—synonymous change G8697A—is characterised by a reasonable degree of polymorphism (86.2% G versus 13.8% A) and can be recommended as a good SNP candidate. Comparative analysis of our results with

Table 1
Haplotypes determined during the study (H1–H12), their frequencies and characteristics of variable positions

	8414	8455	8460	8563	8610	**8697**	8701	8715	8730	8749	8818	8860	8869	Number of individuals
CRS	C	C	A	A	T	**G**	A	T	A	T	C	A	A	
H1		.	.	.	.	.	.	.	.	.	.	G	.	39
H2		.	.	.	.	**A**	.	.	.	.	.	G	.	7
H3	T	.	.	.	.	.	G	.	.	.	.	G	.	1
H4	.	T	.	.	.	**A**	.	.	.	.	.	G	.	1
H5	.	.	.	T	.	.	.	.	.	.	.	G	.	1
H6	.	.	.	.	.	.	.	.	.	.	T	G	.	3
H7	.	.	.	.	.	.	.	.	.	.	.	G	G	1
H8	.	.	.	.	.	.	.	.	G	.	.	G	.	1
H9	.	.	.	.	.	.	.	.	.	C	.	G	.	1
H10	.	.	.	.	C	.	.	.	.	.	.	G	.	1
H11	.	.	.	.	.	.	.	C	.	.	.	G	.	1
H12	.	.	G	.	.	.	.	.	.	.	.	G	.	1
	nonsyn	syn	nonsyn	syn/ nonsyn	syn	**syn**	nonsyn	syn	syn	syn	syn	nonsyn	nonsyn	Total = 58

SNP position G8697A marked in bold. CRS—Cambridge Reference Sequence; syn—synonymous change; nonsyn—nonsynonymous change; syn/nonsyn—nucleotide position placed in overlapping fragment of two genes causing amino acid change in one of them.

previously published Chinese data revealed significant differences in variation patterns [6]. This observation supports the thesis that different SNP-type polymorphisms can be strongly associated with a given population. We optimised a SNaPshot reaction enabling selective analysis of the SNPs found during our previous search (A10398G, T10463C, A10550G) and known polymorphic position T16519C. These hot spots, which are amplified in a multiplex reaction and subjected to SNaPshot reaction, give results concordant with sequencing data. The triplex PCR also includes position G8697A, which, together with other mtDNA SNPs described in scientific publications (e.g., Ref. [7]), will be added to the set of SNPs analysed with SNaPshot kit and the method will be validated for casework analysis.

References

[1] B. Budowle, M.R. Wilson, J.A. diZinno, et al., Mitochondrial DNA regions HVI and HVII population data, Forensic Sci. Int. 103 (1999) 23–35.

[2] T.J. Parsons, M. Coble, Increasing the forensic discrimination of mitochondrial DNA testing through analysis of entire mitochondrial genome, Croat. Med. J. 42 (2001) 304–309.

[3] D.C. Wallace, Mitochondrial diseases in man and mouse, Science 283 (1999) 1482–1488.

[4] D.A. Jones, Blood samples: probability of discrimination, J. Forensic Sci. Soc. 12 (1972) 355–358.

[5] S. Anderson, A.T. Bankier, B.G. Barrel, et al., Sequence and organization of the human mitochondrial genome, Nature 290 (1981) 457–465.

[6] C. Tzen, T. Wu, H. Liu, Sequence polymorphism in the coding region of mitochondrial genome encompassing position 8389–8865, Forensic Sci. Int. 120 (2001) 204–209.

[7] S. Lutz-Bonengel, U. Schmidt, T. Schmitt, S. Pollak, Sequence polymorphisms within the human mitochondrial genes MTATP6, MTATP8 and MTND4, Int. J. Leg. Med. 117 (2003) 133–142.

ELSEVIER

International Congress Series 1261 (2004) 103–105

www.ics-elsevier.com

Measuring by fragment analysis the proportion of length variants in samples carrying length heteroplasmy at the homopolymeric C-stretch in mitochondrial HVII region

L. Prieto[a,*], M. Montesino[a], A. Rodríguez-Monge[a], C. García[a], E. García[a], E. Rivas[a], A. Salas[b]

[a] *Comisaría General de Policía Científica, Servicio de Analisis Cientificos, Laboratorio AND, Julián González Segador s/no., 28043 Madrid, Spain*

[b] *Instituto de Medicina Legal, San Francisco s/no, 15786 Santiago de Compostela, Spain*

Abstract. We describe a method to estimate the proportion of length variants in samples carrying mtDNA homopolymeric C-stretch (303 to 315) originated by a T310C transition. Sequencing analysis of these samples produces blurred electropherograms and the exact number of C-residues remains ambiguous. This has important consequences in forensic casework, since one of the aims in the interpretation of mtDNA profiles is the determination of the existence of a match or a mismatch between two or more sequences under study. HV-2B region (positions 172 to 408) was amplified with two sets of labelled primers. Electrophoresis of fluorescently labelled amplicons was performed on an ABI310 or ABI377. Results were reproducible in repeated PCR experiments, using the two sets of primers and using either capillary or slab-gel electrophoresis. © 2003 Elsevier B.V. All rights reserved.

Keywords: mtDNA; Length heteroplasmy; DNA fragment analysis

1. Introduction

MtDNA control region contains three C-homopolymeric tracts frequently associated with length heteroplasmy. This length variability should not be taken into account when comparing mtDNA profiles, whilst point heteroplasmy is regarded as strength of the evidence [1]. However, in particular cases, it would be desirable to characterize these length variants in order to gain an additional support for the identification by mtDNA analysis.

* Corresponding author. Tel.: +34-91-5822321; fax: +34-91-5822541.
E-mail addresses: biologia.adn@policia.es (L. Prieto), erivas@dgp.mir.es (E. Rivas).

doi:10.1016/j.ics.2003.11.016

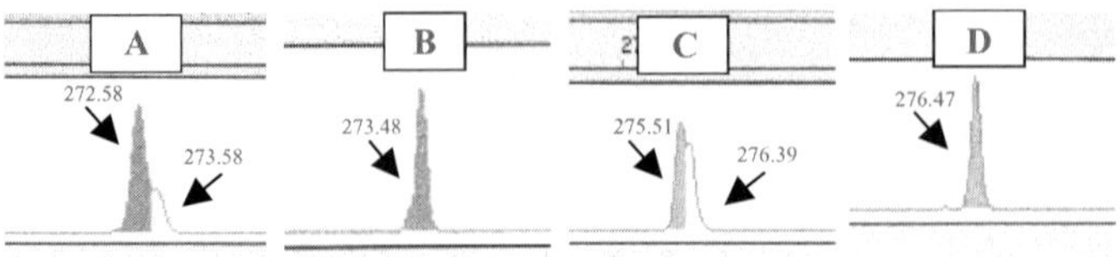

Fig. 1. Sizes of L amplicons (263G 315.1C haplotype) on ABI 310 (A and B) and ABI 377 (C and D) with final extension step (B and D) and without final extension step (A and C).

2. Materials and methods

2.1. Samples

Blood from a female and her daughter (individuals 1 and 2, respectively); two hairs from the daughter; and saliva samples from three maternally related donors (a female and two sons; individuals 3, 4 and 5, respectively). All samples exhibited a partial haplotype 195T 263G 310C. A sample with haplotype 263G 315.1C was used as reference.

2.2. PCR

Two PCRs, using primer pairs 6′ FAM-L 172/H 408 and L 172/ NED-H 408, were carried out to generate fluorescent labelled L and H amplicons. After routine protocol, an additional extension step (72 °C for 45 min) was performed to promote the addition of an extranucleotide by Taq polymerase at the 3′ end of the PCR product.

2.3. Electrophoresis

ABI377 and ABI310 equipments. ROX-500 was used as size standard. The data were analysed using GeneScan software.

3. Results

As expected, PCR fragments with the same length showed differences in size due to different electrophoretic mobility of attached fluorochromes and different nucleotide com-

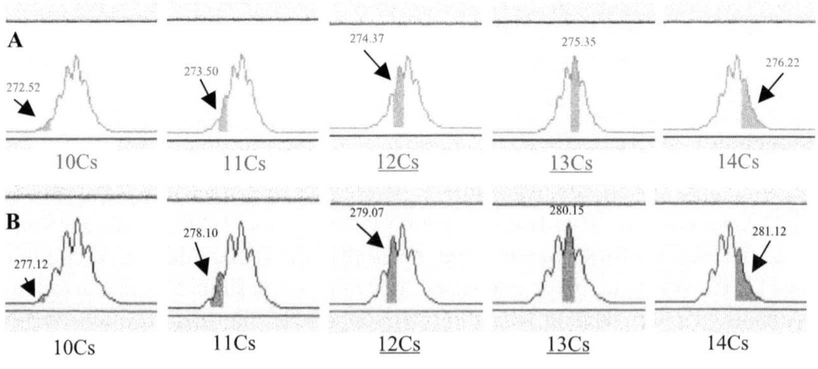

Fig. 2. ABI 377 electrophoretic profiles from individual 1: (A) L strand, and (B) H strand. A low level of 15Cs variant can be observed. Predominant length variants are underlined. Similar patterns were obtained in ABI 310 platform and also from individual 2.

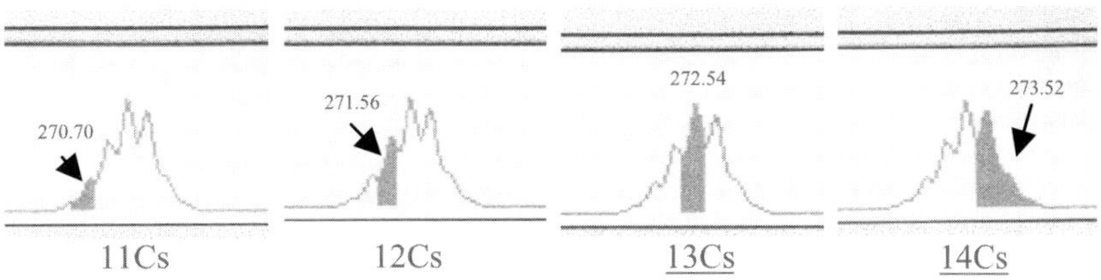

Fig. 3. ABI 310 electrophoretic profile from hair sample of individual 2. Probably 10 and 15Cs variants (first and last shoulder peaks) are present. Predominant length variants are underlined.

position of L and H strands. The differences found between the two platforms may be attributed to the influence of physical electrophoresis conditions [2] (Fig. 1). Sizes of the reference PCR products (14 residues in the C-stretch) were approximately 273.5 bp (L strand) and 278 bp (H strand) on ABI 310 and 276.5 bp (L strand) and 281 bp (H strand) on ABI 377.

Samples with T–C transition rendered electropherograms with multiple peaks differing in size by a single nucleotide (heteroplasmic pattern). The relative proportions of the various length variants were estimated by peak heights. The predominant variants from individual 2 contained 12 and 13C residues in blood sample (Fig. 2) whereas in hair sample contained 13 and 14 (Fig. 3). This is in accordance with intra-individual heteroplasmic variability previously described [3]. A slight difference in the proportion of length variants could be observed between individuals within a single maternal lineage (data not shown).

4. Discussion

The measurement of length variant proportions by fragment analysis showed a great reproducibility since the same pattern was obtained with both strands and on 310 or 377 sequencers. Repeated PCR experiments from the same sample provided similar heteroplasmic patterns, giving further support to the fact that the heteroplasmic state is present in the sample and does not arise during the in vitro replication process. In the forensic practise, the estimation of proportion of length variants could increase the usefulness of this region in order to support or refuse an identification (e.g. when the evidence and known samples come from the same tissue).

Acknowledgements

We are thankful to David Alvarez, Pepa Farfán and Elies Hernandis for their extremely valuable contributions.

References

[1] A. Carracedo, et al., DNA commission of the ISFG: guidelines for mtDNA typing, For. Sci. Int. 110 (2000) 79–85.

[2] K. Lazaruk, et al., Genotyping of forensic STR systems based on sizing precision in a capillary electrophoresis instrument, Electrophoresis 19 (1998) 86–93.

[3] A. Salas, et al., Heteroplasmy in mtDNA and the weight of evidence in forensic mtDNA analysis: a case report, Int. J. Leg. Med. 114 (2000) 186–190.

International Congress Series 1261 (2004) 106–108

www.ics-elsevier.com

EMPOP—the EDNAP mtDNA population database concept for a new generation, high-quality mtDNA database

Walther Parson*, Anita Brandstätter, Martin Pircher, Martin Steinlechner, Richard Scheithauer

Institute of Legal Medicine, University of Innsbruck, Muellerstrasse 44, 6020 Innsbruck, Austria

Abstract. The European DNA Profiling Group (EDNAP) MtDNA Population Database (EMPOP) is an international collaborative project between DNA laboratories performing mtDNA analysis and the DNA laboratory of the Institute of Legal Medicine (GMI) in Innsbruck, Austria. The goal is to set up a directly accessible mtDNA population database, which can be used in routine forensic casework for frequency investigations. Most forensic laboratories do not have the capacity to rapidly generate massive amounts of sequence data. Altogether, however, they dispose of a respectable body of data. Apart from a mutual, non-competitive exchange of molecular genetic techniques, every forensic institute can contribute to the EMPOP project with its familiarity with the individual technology and with the polymorphisms typical for the population inhabiting its surroundings. The EMPOP core laboratory in Innsbruck provides the bioinformatic infrastructure with which to analyze, transcribe, store, and share the data.

Keywords: Forensic mtDNA profiling; Control region sequences; Frequency estimations; Internet database

1. Introduction

The analysis of the control region (CR) of the human mitochondrial genome (mtDNA), in particular, the hypervariable segments of the CR, HV1 and HV2, has proven to be a useful tool for forensic identifications and human evolution studies [1,2]. The lack of mitochondrial recombination urges forensic DNA analysts to compare the HV1/HV2 profile in question to a database of mitochondrial CR profiles for biostatistical frequency estimations. At this very moment, mtDNA databases in general, and forensic mtDNA databases in particular, are at the centre of a scientific controversy relating to the detection of large numbers of errors in published databases. Using phylogenetic investigations and

Abbreviations: CR, Control region; mtDNA, mitochondrial DNA.

* Corresponding author. Tel.: +43-512-507-3303; fax: +43-512-507-2764.
E-mail address: Walther.Parson@uibk.ac.at (W. Parson).

doi:10.1016/S0531-5131(03)01629-7

referring to known patterns of mutations in mtDNA, rampant errors have recently been reported [3–6]. The combination of biochemical, technical, and informatical difficulties made mtDNA databases extraordinarily prone to error. The actual "crisis of quality" in published forensic mtDNA databases requires forensics to achieve a new, higher level of database quality control and supervision.

2. Structure

The European DNA Profiling Group (EDNAP) MtDNA Population Database (EMPOP) is a Web-based SQL database designed for the management of mtDNA sequence data from various populations worldwide, and in general for the assessment of the rarity of a forensic mtDNA haplotype in a given population. In order to address the high error rate connected with mtDNA typing and databasing, logistical features were installed after assessing potential sources of error by performing collaborative exercises (CEs, see below). As a consequence of the CE results, full electronic transfer of the polymorphisms from the raw data (electropherograms) onto the database without further need of manual interaction (transcription) was identified as the most important feature, as clerical errors proved to be the dominant source of errors. Furthermore, sequence raw data of the haplotypes are directly linked to the entries in the database, which enables immediate control of the sequences if necessary. Before loading population data onto the database, these will undergo phylogenetic analysis in order to test for errors caused by mixing up of samples during the process of assessing a HV1/HV2 haplotype, a phenomenon that was observed in the course of the CE. The program of EMPOP allows for searching any fragment in the CR, independent of length and position in the human CR. Example: If only a 150-bp fragment of HV1 brought successful sequencing results (e.g. from a hair shaft), this particular fragment of the CR is searched in the database. The result, i.e., the number of sequences matching the fragment, will then be given according to the total number of sequences that include this 150-bp fragment. Thus, diverse amplification strategies and different primer pairs developed in the laboratories can be used for searching the result in EMPOP.

3. Collaborative exercises

CEs, which have been proven to be a valuable tool for inter-laboratory quality assurance [7], were conducted to ensure analytical reliability and revealed a high correspondence rate of the analytical results obtained by the individual member institutes. A detailed description of the organization and the results of the collaborative exercises will be published soon (Parson et al. submitted). In the EMPOP CE, the mtDNA sequencing results were evaluated by means of inspecting both the raw data and the tabular results submitted by each participating laboratory. Consequently, two different types of results were obtained from the study. First, a measure of the quality of the sequence data reflecting the entire laboratory process involving DNA extraction, PCR setup, and sequence analysis was obtained. Second, the quality of data interpretation and transcription, the latter being a crucial step when reporting mtDNA evidence, was assessed. Since the major portions of all discrepancies observed were clerical errors (the raw data were in agreement with the expected results), the data would meet the requirements in terms of the raw data but at the same time, the data would be considered erroneous with respect to the tabular result. Consequently, such data would display the errors when regarded as results listed in a report. In the context of the laboratory process, however, the samples were typed correctly. Considering the EMPOP CE as means of monitoring the quality of the mtDNA typing process for database purposes (the raw data would be transferred electronically omitting the occurrence of clerical errors), the results demonstrated that the laboratories had accomplished all necessary requirements in order to arrive at the correct result (furthermore, the individual laboratories immediately discovered the clerical errors when being contacted). Following this, a laboratory demonstrating good laboratory practice would still meet the necessary requirements for submitting population to EMPOP even when a clerical error was introduced in the tabular report.

Clerical errors were the major source of error in our collaborative exercises (62.5% of all errors). The errors were introduced in the course of transcription of the variant positions that differed from the CRS sequence from the raw data to the result tables. In two instances, mix-up of the sequenced regions of two samples was observed: This phenomenon, which can be described as a common source of error [3,6], caused 12.5% of all observed errors. Whereas this kind of error can easily be identified in a collaborative exercise, it is difficult to reveal this error in a set of population data. It has been described that phylogenetic methods as prefigured by Bandelt et al. [3] could help to identify erroneous haplotypes, although the methods may be more focussed on the identification of a wrong combination of mtDNA regions from different individuals. In conclusion, clerical errors and sample mix-up errors made up 75% of all errors observed in the EMPOP CEs. This fact strongly emphasizes the need for appropriate safety regulations when mtDNA profiles are compiled for database purposes in order to accomplish the high standard required for forensic mtDNA databases that are used for forensic purposes.

References

[1] W. Parson, T.J. Parsons, R. Scheithauer, M.M. Holland, Population data for 101 Austrian Caucasian mitochondrial DNA d-loop sequences: application of mtDNA sequence analysis to a forensic case, Int. J. Legal. Med. 111 (3) (1998) 124–132.

[2] E. Watson, P. Forster, M. Richards, H.J. Bandelt, Mitochondrial footprints of human expansions in Africa, Am. J. Hum. Genet. 61 (3) (1997) 691–704.

[3] H.J. Bandelt, P. Lahermo, M. Richards, V. Macaulay, Detecting errors in mtDNA data by phylogenetic analysis, Int. J. Legal Med. 115 (2) (2001) 64–69.

[4] H.J. Bandelt, L. Quintana-Murci, A. Salas, V. Macaulay, The fingerprint of phantom mutations in mitochondrial DNA data, Am. J. Hum. Genet. 71 (5) (2002) 1150–1160.

[5] P. Forster, To err is human, Ann. Hum. Genet. 67 (Pt. 1) (2003) 2–4.

[6] A. Rohl, B. Brinkmann, L. Forster, P. Forster, An annotated mtDNA database, Int. J. Legal Med. 115 (1) (2001) 29–39.

[7] S. Rand, M. Schurenkamp, B. Brinkmann, The GEDNAP (German DNA profiling group) blind trial concept, Int. J. Legal Med. 116 (4) (2002) 199–206.

International Congress Series 1261 (2004) 109–111

www.ics-elsevier.com

Is selection at mtDNA really a major concern?

L. Pereira[a,*], A. Amorim[a,b]

[a] IPATIMUP (Instituto de Patologia e Imunologia Molecular da Universidade do Porto), Population Genetics, Rua Dr. Roberto Frias s/n 4200-465 Porto, Portugal

[b] Faculdade de Ciências da Universidade do Porto, Portugal

Abstract. Evidence for selection on human mtDNA has been obtained from the results of some widely used tests: (a) higher replacement (R) to synonymous (S) substitution ratios in human genes ND2, CO1, ATP6, CO3 and CytB (and overall) than expected by human/chimpanzee comparisons; (b) distributions of absolute ($K/(K+S)$) and corrected (for coding degeneracy; $Ka/(Ka+Ks)$) frequencies for R are heterogeneous for human mtDNA genes (higher for ATP6, ATP8 and CytB); and (c) no correlation between gene length-R (in opposition to gene length-S). However, a mere 8.3% of sequences show $R/(R+S) \geq 0.5$ and, furthermore, R/S ratio is strongly correlated with haplogroup classification based on HVR variability. Demographic history seems therefore enough to explain the observed diversity in human mtDNA coding region, with older haplogroups showing lower R/S ratios than younger ones.

Keywords: mtDNA; Selection; Replacement substitution (R); Synonymous substitution (S)

1. Introduction

Some mtDNA genetic features have caused major general concerns: mutation rates, heteroplasmy, recombination and selection. Concerning the last one, the finding of an excess R inside human mtDNA genes [1], the association of certain mtDNA lineages with human longevity [2] or with male fertility [3], seemed to support the inference that natural selection (such as driven by climatic conditions [4]) has shaped regional mtDNA variation in humans. In most of these works, the ratios R/S within haplogroups were analysed. Since haplogroups are just collections of sequences that can vary profoundly but are assumed to share a common origin, we thought that, since individual sequences are indeed the true units of selection, the R/S analysis should be therefore performed using the individual sequences' information. Then, if selection forces had really played a major role in shaping human mtDNA diversity, we should expect that R/S values would be uncorrelated with haplogroup classification (mainly based upon control region variation). The aim of this paper was just to test this expectation.

* Corresponding author. Tel.: +351-22-5570700; fax: +351-22-5570799.
E-mail address: lpereira@ipatimup.pt (L. Pereira).

doi:10.1016/S0531-5131(03)01838-7

2. Materials and methods

We analysed the complete mtDNA sequences of 613 humans [5,6] and 3 chimpanzees (GeneBank accession numbers: D38113, NC_001643, X93335). Hand made alignment of sequences allowed the counting of *R* and *S*. Chi-squared tests and Bonferroni's correction were calculated for *R* vs. *S* contents in each gene, in humans. DnaSP [7] program was used to measure the statistical significance (*G*-test with Williams correction for continuity) of the contingence tables of McDonald–Kreitman test [8], and to calculate the total possible *R* and *S* per gene.

3. Results

McDonald–Kreitman test results showed that the ratio *R*/*S* is significantly higher in humans than what would be expected by human/chimpanzee comparisons, for the following genes: ND2 (G=9.994, P=0.00157**), CO1 (G=16.800, P=0.00004***), ATP6 (G=9.944, P=0.00161**), CO3 (G=8.389, P=0.00378**) and CytB (G=10.146, P=0.00145**). Considering the mtDNA coding region as a whole, the value was also significantly (G=57.461, P=0.00000***), the ratio of *R*/*S* being 1:5 (or 17% of *R*).

The frequency distribution of *R* ($R/(R+S)$) by gene in humans is significantly heterogeneous (χ^2=52.7202, P=0.00000***), and the major genes responsible for this were (decreasingly): ATP6, ATP8 and CytB. We further assayed the influence of two parameters in this measure: length and degeneracy content between genes. For the first, there was a good correlation between gene length-total number of substitutions (Y=7.9298X, R^2=0.8717) and gene length-*S* (Y=11.551X, R^2=0.9241), but almost no correlation was observed for gene length-*R* (Y=23.168X, R^2=0.4079). Since the

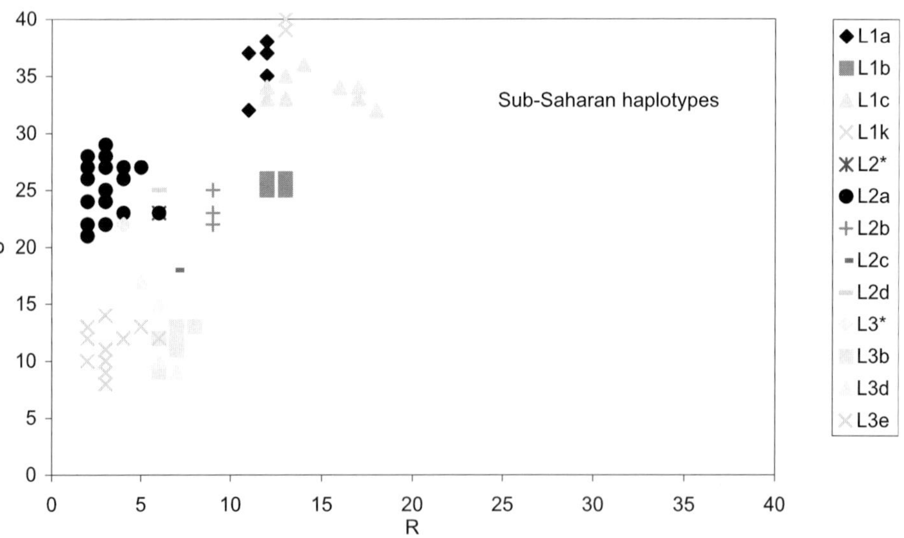

Fig. 1. Distribution of *R* vs. *S* in individual sequences from sub-Saharan haplogroups.

proportion of *S* vs. *R* sites is highly conserved between mtDNA genes, the frequency of *R* corrected for coding degeneracy (Ka/(Ka + Ks), where Ka is the number of *R* per total possible non-synonymous sites and Ks the number of *S* per total possible synonymous sites) is parallel to the absolute frequency distribution of *R*.

Despite these signs for differential accumulation of *R* between human mtDNA genes, when analysing *R* vs. *S* at individual sequences, a mere 8.3% of the sample present a frequency $R/(R+S)$ equal or higher than 0.5. The distribution of $R/(R+S)$ by haplotype is very heterogeneous, but when haplogroup classification is added (e.g. sub-Saharans in Fig. 1), we can observe that there is a high correlation between them. The proportion inside each haplogroup of sequences that showed frequencies Ka/(Ka + Ks) equal or higher than 0.5 by haplogroup were: 19% for haplogroup A1 ($n=26$), 4% for H ($n=217$), 12.5% for HV ($n=8$), 11% for V ($n=9$), 20% for U5 ($n=25$), 67% for J2b ($n=3$) and 93% for J1 ($n=28$). And the distribution of $K/(K+S)$ by gene inside haplogroup *J* was highly heterogeneous.

4. Conclusions

Selection (as detected through *R*/*S* ratios) does not seem to play a major role in shaping human mtDNA diversity since the observed variation of these ratios reflects control region (HVR) defined haplogroups. Selection on coding region would necessarily act in a different way (if any) of that in the control region, and necessarily haplogroup classification should be erased/confounded when considering *R*/*S* ratios. Thus, demographic history seems enough to explain diversity in human mtDNA coding region. With time, haplogroups seem to accumulate more *S* comparatively to *R*, as it is already happening with L haplogroups. Even for haplogroup *J* (relatively young and showing no-star like phylogeny), the one with highest ratios, no specific coding region associated pattern could be discerned.

Acknowledgements

LP has a research grant (SFRH/BPD/7121/2001) from Fundação para a Ciência e a Tecnologia (FCT). IPATIMUP is supported by POCTI (QCA III). This study is included in the Project POCTI/ANT/45139/2002 financed by FCT (Eixo 2, Medida 2.3 do POCTI, QCA III).

References

[1] M.W. Nachman, et al., Genetics 142 (1996) 953–963.
[2] G. Rose, et al., Eur. J. Hum. Genet. 9 (2001) 701–707.
[3] E. Ruiz-Pesini, et al., Am. J. Hum. Genet. 67 (2000) 682–696.
[4] D. Mishmar, et al., Proc. Natl. Acad. Sci. U. S. A. 100 (2003) 171–176.
[5] M. Ingman, et al., Nature 408 (2000) 708–713.
[6] C. Herrnstadt, et al., Am. J. Hum. Genet. 70 (2002) 1152–1171.
[7] J. Rozas, R. Rozas, Bioinformatics 15 (1999) 174–175.
[8] J.H. McDonald, M. Kreitman, Nature 351 (1991) 652–654.

ELSEVIER

International Congress Series 1261 (2004) 112–114

www.ics-elsevier.com

Multiple mutations, covert mutations and false exclusions in paternity casework

C.H. Brenner*

DNA VIEW, Consulting in Forensic Mathematics, 6568 Sobrante Road, Oakland, CA, USA

Abstract. The universal practice, up to now, is to make the judgement "paternity excluded" whenever there are more than some established number—such as two—of loci in which the genetic pattern, barring mutation, is inconsistent with paternity. Such a rule is founded on the implicit assumption that the probability of two mutations is vanishingly small. However, the ideal procedure would of course be to evaluate the paternity index (PI) over all loci, taking possible mutation into account. With STRs, unlike with RFLPs, a reasonably accurate mathematical model of mutation exists and hence the ideal procedure is finally possible. What happens when it is applied is somewhat surprising. Notwithstanding two or even three inconsistent loci, the posterior probability of paternity (assuming 50% prior probability) can easily be 20%. Unless the inconsistencies are particularly implausible as mutations (i.e. multiple repeat units), the posterior probability is not vanishingly small. The old rule causes bad decisions; it excludes fathers. Instead, we should compute the proper paternity index across all loci, considering the possibility of multiple mutations, and evaluate the result. The computing part is easy. The evaluation part brings a new difficulty, for it forces us to confront a question that the inaccurate policy of the past hid from view: How unlikely must paternity be in order to justify the decision "paternity excluded"? An incidental discovery is the heretofore overlooked implication that the existence of "covert mutations" imply that most STR mutation estimates from paternity studies are wrong.

Keywords: Mutation; Covert mutation; Stepwise; Paternity index; Exclusion

1. Introduction

Dealing with possible mutations in paternity casework has always been awkward. In recent years, the use of STR systems have nearly supplanted RFLPs. It is time to reconsider the outmoded policies as well. The mutation rate among STR markers appears to average about 1/400 [1–3 and unpublished data]. Assuming a 13-marker paternity test and binomial model, the expectations are shown in Table 1. Clearly, two inconsistencies is the critical case. Prima facie it supports non-paternity by a likelihood

* Tel.: +1-510-3391911; fax: +1-510-3391181.
E-mail address: cbrenner@uclink.berkeley.edu (C.H. Brenner).

0531-5131/
doi:10.1016/S0531-5131(03)01843-0

Table 1
Paternity inference based on counting inconsistencies

Inconsistencies	Rate among false trios	Rate among true trios	LR supporting paternity
0	1/210,000	1/1	200,000
1	1/10,000	1/49	210
2	1/1100	1/5100	1/4.7
3	1/190	1/860,000	1/4600

ratio of 4.7, which is inconclusive. This paper examines more closely the case of two inconsistencies.

2. Materials and methods

Four hundred paternity trios, half true and half false trios but all with two inconsistent loci, were generated by an accelerated Monte Carlo method. For the true trios, mutations are generated according to a modified stepwise mutation model [4], that most mutations (μ = locus-specific rate of one-step paternal mutations) are by plus or minus one repeat unit (factor by which $|s+1|$ step mutations are rarer than $|s|$ step mutations $\approxeq$ 20) and are paternal (factor by which maternal mutations are rarer than paternal ones $\approxeq$ 3.5). The PI was then computed for each of the 400 cases using the model.

3. Results

3.1. Covert mutations

Analyzing the results of the true-trio simulations revealed an obvious phenomenon which we might call "covert mutations" (Fig. 1) whose significance has not been previously noted. The fraction of mutations that are covert can be quite large–over 25% at some loci.

3.2. Two inconsistencies

As Table 1 shows, two inconsistencies is modest prima facie favoring non-paternity. Table 2 shows that taking into account the rarity of shared alleles and the plausibility as

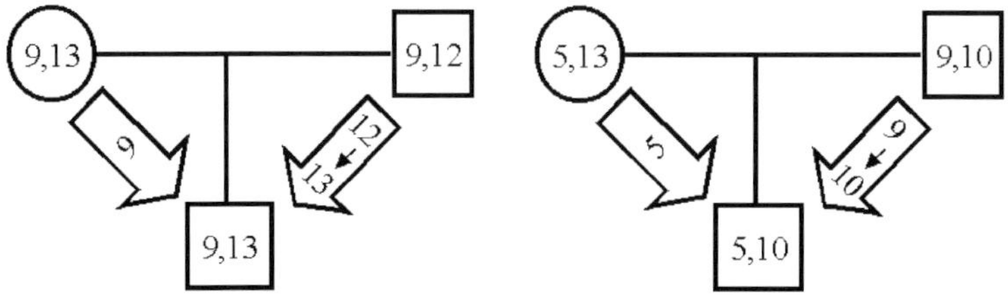

Fig. 1. Ways that a mutation can be covert.

Table 2
Distribution of PIs among simulated two inconsistency cases

x	% false trios with PI>*x*	% true trios with PI>*x*
1000	0	4.5
100	0	19
10	0.5	43
1	3	78
1/10	20	95.5
1/100	47	99.5

mutations of inconsistencies—i.e. computing the PI—somewhat distinguishes true from false trios.

4. Discussion

The significance of covert mutations is that since mutation rates are estimated from paternity studies, all published mutation rates for autosomal loci are too low by a possibly significant amount. The rate of apparent mutations is the right number to use to calculate Table 1, but for case calculations—Table 2—the covert-adjusted μ must be used. For example, in CSF1PO apparent $\mu = 3/1000$ but the true $\mu = 4/1000$. Failure to account for covert mutations thus inflates paternity indices, so is anti-conservative. There may also be an implication in evolutionary studies when a mutational clock is considered.

Taking into account the predominance of true over false trios in paternity laboratories, cases with two inconsistencies are false trios by a margin of only 2:1. Routinely excluding paternity based on two inconsistencies is thus a very poor policy. Computing a likelihood ratio is the proper course. Interpreting it, though, can be problematic when it is small.

Once the untenable policy of the past—pretending in effect that PI = 0 whenever some target number of inconsistencies are observed—is abandoned, one is confronted with making a policy based on interpreting the true PI. For example, if PI = 1/10 000, reporting "paternity excluded" may be acceptable, notwithstanding the paradox that in the symmetrically opposite case that PI = 10 000, no one would report "paternity certain". But what of less extreme cases, such as $1/100 < \text{PI} < 1/10$? Science and judicial custom collide; there is no obvious and acceptable answer. Fortunately, the situation is infrequent (Table 1).

References

[1] AABB, Apparent Mutations Observed at the 13 CODIS STR Loci in the Course of Paternity Testing, http://www.cstl.nist.gov/biotech/strbase/mutation.htm. 1999.

[2] B. Brinkmann, M. Klintschar, F. Neuhuber, J. Huhne, B. Rolf, Mutation rate in human microsatellites: influence of the structure and length of the tandem repeat, Am. J. Hum. Genet. 64 (5) (1999 May) 1473–1474.

[3] M. Kayser, A. Sajantila, Mutations at Y-STR loci: implications for paternity testing and forensic analysis, Forensic Sci. Int. 118 (2001) 116–121.

[4] C.H. Brenner, http://dna-view.com/mudisc.htm, http://dna-view.com/mufeatur.htm.

International Congress Series 1261 (2004) 115–117

www.ics-elsevier.com

Results of the 2003 paternity testing workshop of the English Speaking Working Group of the International Society of Forensic Genetics

B.T. Simonsen*, N. Morling

Department of Forensic Genetics, Institute of Forensic Medicine, University of Copenhagen, 11 Frederik V's Vej, DK-2100 Copenhagen, Denmark

Abstract. We present the results of the 2003 paternity testing workshop of the English Speaking Working Group (ESWG) of the International Society of Forensic Genetics (ISFG). The scenario was an alleged father, one child and the mother. All 51 participating laboratories drew the correct conclusion. The laboratories used a total of 30 autosomal and 17 Y-chromosomal PCR-based STR systems and 7 RFLP-based VNTR systems. The percentage of typing errors was 0.12% for the autosomal systems and 2% for the Y-chromosomal systems. The results from a paper challenge showed that occurrences of rare events such as mutations and possible silent alleles were treated differently among the participating laboratories. Participating laboratories reported mutational events observed in STR systems. Considerable differences between mutation rates in STR loci were reported. There were marked differences between paternal and maternal mutation rates as well as between single-step and multiple-step mutation rates.

Keywords: Paternity testing; DNA profiling; Collaborative exercise; Proficiency testing

1. Introduction

Since 1991, The English Speaking Working Group (ESWG) of the International Society of Forensic Genetics (ISFG) has offered an annual exercise involving genetic analysis of a paternity case [1–4]. The collated results of the exercises include typing results and information about laboratory routines, systems and kits used for paternity testing as well as information about statistical calculations. Since the year 2000, the laboratories have been invited to calculate a paper challenge in addition to the paternity testing.

* Corresponding author. Tel.: +45-35-32-61-10; fax: +45-35-32-61-20.
E-mail address: bo.simonsen@forensic.ku.dk (B.T. Simonsen).

doi:10.1016/S0531-5131(03)01529-2

2. Materials and methods

Blood samples from a mother, a child and an alleged father were sent to the laboratories together with the information needed to treat the case as a paternity case. A questionnaire concerning the techniques, routines and genetic systems used by the laboratories was distributed. Fifty-one laboratories submitted their results.

3. Results

All laboratories concluded that their results were in favour of paternity. Results from a total of 30 autosomal PCR-based systems, 17 Y-chromosomal PCR-based systems and 7 RFLP-based systems were submitted. Of these, results from 26 autosomal PCR-based systems, 12 Y-chromosomal PCR-based systems and 6 RFLP-based systems were submitted by more than one laboratory.

The results showed that most laboratories used the same nomenclature. Among the somatic PCR-based systems, no inconsistencies were due to different nomenclature. Among the Y-chromosomal PCR-based systems, results with inconsistent nomenclature were submitted in two systems (DYS389I and DYS389II).

The typing error rate of the submitted results was 0.12% for the autosomal systems and 2% for the Y-chromosomal systems. All laboratories used one or more commercially available PCR-based STR-typing kits for typing of autosomal systems. In contrast, less than 50% of the labs used commercially available kits for Y-STR typing.

The exercise included a paper challenge with calculation of paternity indices of rare events such as mutations and possible silent alleles and with Y-chromosomal haplotypes. Information was given on the number of observations of the relevant alleles in the database and all calculations were left to the laboratories. Thirty-one laboratories reported PI-values (or other statistical values) for each autosomal system and 23 laboratories included PI-values (or other statistical values) for the Y-chromosomal haplotype. Twenty-six different cumulative PI-values were obtained. Most discrepancies were due to different calculations of the systems with inconsistencies or possible silent alleles. Most laboratories (92%) concluded in the paper challenge that results were inconclusive and recommended further testing, 5% concluded that results were in favour of paternity and 3% that results were against paternity.

Laboratories were asked to report mutation events of STR systems. The overall mutation rate of the autosomal STR systems was 0.114% (range $<0.001-0.780\%$). The overall paternal mutation rate was 0.153% and the overall maternal mutation rate was 0.043%. The overall mutation rate for single-step mutations was 0.109% and the overall mutation rate for multiple-step mutations was 0.005%.

4. Discussion

The use of commercially available STR kits seems to have facilitated a high level of standardisation of methods and nomenclature among the participating laboratories in the paternity testing workshop. The typing error rate of the submitted results was 0.12% for the autosomal systems and 2% for the Y-chromosomal systems. All participating laboratories used one or more commercially available kits for autosomal STR systems but less than half of the reporting laboratories used commercially available kits for Y-STR typing.

While methods and nomenclature have reached a high degree of standardisation, the results of the paper challenge showed that statistical calculations of paternity indices varied when seldom events such as rare alleles, mutations and possible silent alleles were present. The results also showed that there is no consensus on statistical calculations of Y-chromosomal haplotypes.

References

[1] D. Syndercombe Court, P. Lincoln, in: A. Carracedo, B. Brinkmann, W. Bär (Eds.), A review of the 1991–1994 Paternity Testing Workshops of the English Speaking Working Group, Adv. Forensic Haemogenet, vol. 6. Springer-Verlag, Berlin, 1996, pp. 683–685.

[2] A. Bjerre, D. Syndercombe Court, P. Lincoln, N. Morling, A report of the 1995 and 1996 Paternity Testing Workshops of the English Speaking Working Group of the International Society of Forensic Haemogenetics, Forensic Sci. Int. 90 (1–2) (1997) 41–55.

[3] C. Hallenberg, N. Morling, A report of the 1997, 1998 and 1999 paternity testing workshops of the english speaking working group of the international society of forensic genetics, Forensic Sci. Int. 116 (1) (2001) 23–33.

[4] C. Hallenberg, N. Morling, A report of the 2000 and 2001 paternity testing workshops of the english speaking working group of the international society of forensic genetics, Forensic Sci. Int. 129 (1) (2002) 43–50.

International Congress Series 1261 (2004) 118–120

www.ics-elsevier.com

eDNA: networking software tailored for identity testing laboratories

Robert W. Allen[a,b,*], Kent Harman[c], Allan Sieker[c]

[a] *Center for Health Sciences, Oklahoma State University, Forensic Sciences, 1111 W. 17th Street, Tulsa, OK 74107, USA*

[b] *H.A. Chapman Institute of Medical Genetics, 4502 E. 41st, Tulsa, OK 74135, USA*

[c] *Genetic Technologies, Inc., Glencoe, MO, USA*

Abstract

Software (known as eDNA 2.0) has been developed for information management for identity testing labs. The software operates in a browser-based, multiuser environment compatible with intranet or internet accessibility. eDNA 2.0 manages accessioning through reporting in a user-friendly, intuitive manner. Parentage testing and forensic applications are incorporated into eDNA, and a kinship module is under development. Highlights of eDNA 2.0 include (1) accessioning templates that record information in a flexible, annotated way that can be easily tracked, (2) phenotype entry for any number of user-defined STR test batteries, (3) questioned relationships defined using dropdown menus, (4) entry of screening results for body fluids, (5) user-defined methods for dealing with mixed DNA profiles, and (6) capability to examine exclusions for possible sample errors.

Keywords: Identity testing; Information management; DNA typing

1. Introduction

Often, identity testing laboratories rely on multiple software applications to manage the information associated with casework processing. This is especially true in small laboratories where one software application may manage accessioning information while another performs statistical calculations and still a third is used to prepare final reports. Operating a lab in such an environment is less than optimally efficient and is especially prone to the introduction of transcription errors.

Several software packages have been created for calculations and reporting of DNA typing results. Often, however, such products do not manage information generated by an identity testing lab in a comprehensive way. A software product known as eDNA is described here that provides virtually complete information management for the laboratory

* Corresponding author. H.A. Chapman Institute of Medical Genetics, 4502 E. 41st, Tulsa, OK 74135, USA. Tel.: +1-918-660-3827; fax: +1-918-660 3840.

E-mail address: rallen@genetictechnologies.com (R.W. Allen).

doi:10.1016/S0531-5131(03)01835-1

providing parentage testing and/or forensic DNA typing. eDNA software is based upon Microsoft ".net" technology compatible with networking and simultaneous multitasking. Maneuvering in eDNA is accomplished through hyperlinks embedded in program.

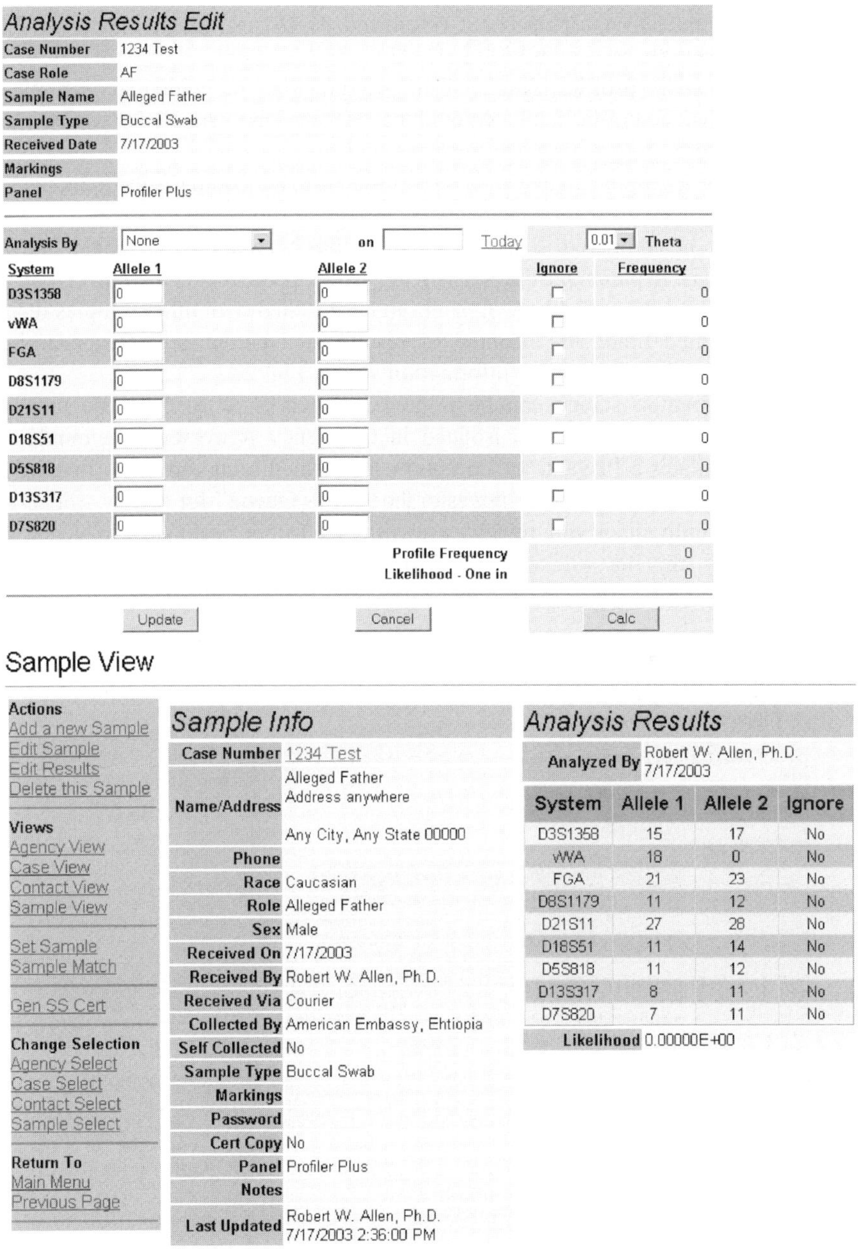

Fig. 1. DNA profile screens for an alleged father before and after completion.

Cases are accessioned using templates for identities and relationships of specimens. If a lab performs work for a client repeatedly, a database of clients is listed in a dropdown list to easily designate names and addresses to receive a report. A database of sample types can also be created in eDNA to track the numbers of samples received. Once a case has been accessioned and DNA typing results produced, DNA profiles are entered for each sample using the templates shown in Fig. 1.

In addition to DNA profiles, results from pre-screening of evidentiary samples for blood, semen, saliva, and urine can be entered into eDNA. Up to six alleles can be entered for each STR system to accommodate mixtures.

Once DNA profile results have been entered for a case, the comparisons to be made are defined by the user from dropdown lists. Each comparison comprises a "test result" for the samples that are to be compared. After a comparison has been defined, a "Calculate" link executes the analysis. In parentage cases involving an excluded alleged parent, eDNA has a feature allowing the child and/or known parent to be matched with other samples received during a user-defined time. An example of results in a parentage test appear in the "Summary Matrix" area in the Test Information screen Fig. 2.

The Test Information screen can be printed and serves as a useful document for Supervisory or Director review. An isolated inconsistency is treated as a mutation by eDNA which calculates a PI value based upon user-defined mutation rates (Fig. 2).

Once a case has been analyzed, it moves to the "Work Queue" for review. Supervisors, directors, or other individuals who review casework data can be designated to have a Work Queue. Ultimately, the file will enter the Work Queue of the Director. After Director review, the case moves to the "Print Queue" for final report printing.

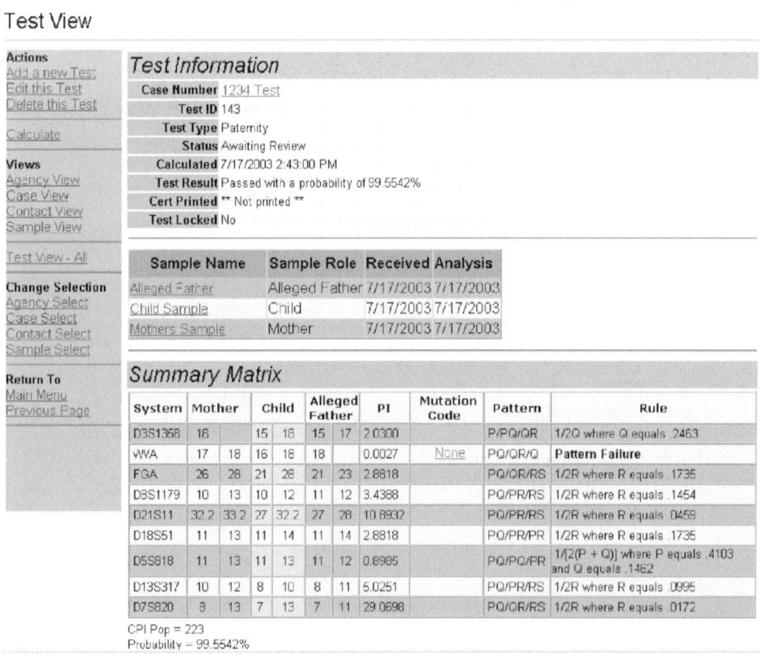

Test View

Actions
Add a new Test
Edit this Test
Delete this Test
Calculate
Views
Agency View
Case View
Contact View
Sample View
Test View - All
Change Selection
Agency Select
Case Select
Contact Select
Sample Select
Return To
Main Menu
Previous Page

Test Information

Case Number	1234 Test
Test ID	143
Test Type	Paternity
Status	Awaiting Review
Calculated	7/17/2003 2:43:00 PM
Test Result	Passed with a probability of 99.5542%
Cert Printed	** Not printed **
Test Locked	No

Sample Name	Sample Role	Received	Analysis
Alleged Father	Alleged Father	7/17/2003	7/17/2003
Child Sample	Child	7/17/2003	7/17/2003
Mothers Sample	Mother	7/17/2003	7/17/2003

Summary Matrix

System	Mother		Child		Alleged Father		PI	Mutation Code	Pattern	Rule
D3S1358	16		15	16	15	17	2.0300		P/PQ/QR	1/2Q where Q equals .2463
vWA	17	18	16	18	18		0.0027	None	PQ/QR/Q	**Pattern Failure**
FGA	26	28	21	28	21	23	2.8818		PQ/QR/RS	1/2R where R equals .1735
D8S1179	10	13	10	12	11	12	3.4388		PQ/PR/RS	1/2R where R equals .1454
D21S11	32.2	33.2	27	32.2	27	28	10.8932		PQ/PR/RS	1/2R where R equals .0459
D18S51	11	13	11	14	11	14	2.8818		PQ/PR/PR	1/2R where R equals .1735
D5S818	11	13	11	13	11	12	0.8985		PQ/PQ/PR	1/[2(P + Q)] where P equals .4103 and Q equals .1462
D13S317	10	12	8	10	8	11	5.0251		PQ/PR/RS	1/2R where R equals .0995
D7S820	8	13	7	13	7	11	29.0698		PQ/QR/RS	1/2R where R equals .0172

CPI Pop = 223
Probability = 99.5542%

Fig. 2. Test information screen.

ELSEVIER

International Congress Series 1261 (2004) 121–123

www.ics-elsevier.com

Proficiency testing programs for DNA typing laboratories offered by the College of American Pathologists

Robert W. Allen*, Rhonda K. Roby, Chantal Harrison, Arthur J. Eisenberg, Herbert F. Polesky

Histocompatibility/Identity Committee, College of American Pathologists, 325 Waukegan Road, Northfield, IL 60093, USA

Received 3 September 2003; received in revised form 4 September 2003; accepted 10 September 2003

Abstract. The College of American Pathologists (CAP) has several proficiency testing programs targeted to laboratories that perform DNA typing of STR loci. Two well-known programs for parentage testing and forensic labs have been available since the early 1990s and are used by labs worldwide. New proficiency surveys introduced by CAP within the last 2 years may also be of interest to DNA typing labs interested in STR typing for new sources of revenue. Recently added surveys include one for labs monitoring engraftment in bone marrow transplant patients, a second survey for labs that perform phenotyping of convicted offenders for databasing programs, and a survey for labs that perform mitochondrial DNA sequencing. Presented here are brief introductions to the proficiency surveys offered by CAP that are of potential interest to DNA typing labs. © 2003 Elsevier B.V. All rights reserved.

Keywords: Proficiency testing; DNA typing; Quality assurance

1. Introduction and discussion

DNA typing of STR loci has application in clinical situations as diverse as identification of suspects in criminal investigations and monitoring engraftment in recipients of bone marrow transplants. Part of any laboratory quality assurance program is participation in proficiency testing, a service provided in most areas of clinical laboratory testing by the College of American Pathologists (CAP). A survey with a long history in the field of identity testing is the parentage testing survey (now known as PAR/PARF), still one of the few formal, graded proficiency tests available worldwide for parentage testing laboratories. The PAR survey provides small aliquots of liquid blood for testing while the PARF

* Corresponding author. H.A. Chapman Institute of Medical Genetics, 4502 E. 41st, Tulsa, OK 74135, USA. Tel.: +1-918-660-3827; fax: +1-918-660-3840.

E-mail address: rallen@genetictechnologies.com (R.W. Allen).

doi:10.1016/S0531-5131(03)01513-9

provides subscribers with the same samples only provided in the form of bloodstains. In both the PAR and PARF surveys, a second alleged father is provided for testing as a buccal swab.

Another survey introduced early in the development of the identity testing field is the forensic identity survey (known as FID). These two programs have been available since the early 1990s, providing typical casework challenges for DNA typing analysts in parentage testing and forensic laboratories. In addition to the laboratory testing component, ungraded paper problems were introduced as part of the parentage testing survey several years to challenge participants with an unusual, yet realistic, case scenario that can be analyzed on paper. These paper challenges have found widespread use among participants as a form of continuing education for staff.

In the past 2 years, CAP has introduced three new surveys of potential interest to DNA typing labs. The DNA/DNAF survey tests proficiency of a lab performing STR typing of samples obtained from convicted felons for entry into an offender database. Similar to the PAR/PARF survey, samples are provided in either liquid form or as bloodstains on filter paper. Subscribers to the DNA/DNAF receive three samples two times a year. Phenotypes are reported to CAP but are not graded. Subscribers can compare their results to those of peers with the Participant Summary which lists the results submitted by all subscribers (Table 1).

Another new survey is known as FIDM and is designed for labs that perform mitochondrial DNA sequencing. The survey consists of samples provided two times annually; reference bloodstains and a hair and/or fingernail representing an evidentiary sample. Subscribers perform their analysis and report polymorphic bases within the mitochondrial DNA recovered from the samples, indicating whether or not any sequences match. The FIDM survey is also not yet graded.

One additional survey of possible interest to forensic DNA typing laboratories is the Engraftment Monitoring survey (ME) which, although designed primarily for labs providing support for bone marrow transplantation programs, can also be useful for forensic labs because challenges consist of blood mixtures from more than one donor. Subscribers report whether or not a sample contains DNA from more than one contributor, moreover subscribers are asked for the relative proportions of DNA from each contributor when mixed samples are provided by CAP. The ME survey is graded by consensus both for the qualitative criteria of whether or not a mixed sample was provided as well as the relative proportion of DNA from each contributor in mixed samples.

Table 1
Number of subscribers for CAP surveys for identity testing laboratories

Survey	Competency	No. of subscribers[a]	Graded	Grading
PAR/PARF	Parentage testing	140	Yes	Mean ± 3S.D.
DNA/DNAF	Convicted offender	103	No	n/a
FID	Forensic STR typing	143	No	n/a
FIDM	Mitochondrial DNA seq.	19	No	n/a
ME	Bone marrow Tx engraftment	49	Yes	Mean ± 3S.D.

[a] Number of subscribers for the most recent mailing for 2003.

As indicated above, some surveys are graded by the College. The PAR/PARF, and ME surveys are graded using a consensus approach which has been described previously [1,2]. Briefly, a mean and standard deviation (S.D.) of all responses for an analyte are calculated. An acceptable range of responses is then defined by the mean response ± 3S.D. Any outliers are removed from the responses (and are identified on individual reports as unacceptable) and a new mean and S.D. are calculated from the remaining responses. A new acceptable range is then produced consisting of the mean ± 3S.D. from remaining responses. Additional outliers, if present, are then identified as unacceptable responses on individual performance reports.

The FID, DNA/DNAF, and FID-M surveys are not yet formally graded. As stated above, performance of a laboratory can be determined by comparing one's answers with those from other subscribers testing the same loci as published in the Participant Summary Report returned to subscribers by the College.

As the field of identification testing evolves, the College of American Pathologists will respond with modifications to the existing surveys as well as offering new surveys when appropriate. The selection of liquid samples versus dry stains is but one example of a CAP response to the needs of the identity testing community.

References

[1] R.W. Allen, C.R. Harrison, A.J. Eisenberg, R.K. Roby, R.H. Walker, R.E. Wenk, H.F. Polesky, Grading of quantitative data in the CAP/AABB parentage testing program, Prog. For. Hemogenet. 8 (2000) 602–605.

[2] R.W. Allen, A.J. Eisenberg, C.R. Harrison, R.H. Walker, C.T. Young, D.L. Zeagler, R. Roby, H.F. Polesky, Grading of qualitative and quantitative responses in the PI proficiency survey of the College of American Pathologists for mailings in 1997–2000, Prog. For. Genet. 9 (2003) 825–829.

International Congress Series 1261 (2004) 124–126

www.ics-elsevier.com

GEP proficiency testing program in forensic genetics: 10 years of experience

Josefina Gómez, Julia García-Hirschfeld, Oscar García, Angel Carracedo*
GEP-ISFG Working group

Institute of Lega Medicine, Forensic Genetics. Calle San Francisco, Facultad de Medicina E-15705 Santiago de Compostela, Galicia, Spain

Abstract. Since 1992 the GEP-ISFG group has been organizing a proficiency testing program open to all the laboratories in the group. The number of participating laboratories increased continuously from 10 in the first exercise (GEP'93) to 89 registered for the last exercise (GEP'02), 86 (95%) having submitted results. Despite the increasing number of laboratories, results remained quite satisfactory. There is a tendency to concentrate errors in a few laboratories and also an association with the use of home made ladders. mtDNA and statistics are the challenges nowadays, and actions have been implemented in the group to solve the difficulties found in the laboratories for this type of expertise. © 2003 Published by Elsevier B.V.

Keywords: Proficiency testing; Quality control

The Spanish and Portuguese Working Group of the International Society for Forensic Genetics (GEP-ISFG) (www.gep-isfg.org) comprises forensic genetics laboratories from Spain, Portugal, France and most of the Portuguese and Spanish speaking countries in America. A total of 324 forensic geneticists from 118 laboratories and 19 countries are members of the group. Spain, Portugal, Brazil, Argentina and Colombia are the countries more represented but the group include most of the laboratories performing forensic genetic casework in the area. Almost all the laboratories are involved in paternity testing but only half (58%) of the laboratories are in criminal casework.

Since 1992 the GEP-ISFG working group has been organizing annual collaborative exercises on DNA profiling with the aim of making progress in standardization and discussing technical and statistical problems in DNA profiling. Since 1995 a proficiency testing program coordinated by Quality Control Unit (National Institute of Toxicology Madrid) was carried out simultaneously with the GEP-ISFG collaborative exercises. The number of participating laboratories increased continuously from 10 in the first exercise

* Corresponding author. Tel.: +34-981582327; fax: +34-981580336.
E-mail address: apimlang@usc.es (A. Carracedo).

0531-5131/ © 2003 Published by Elsevier B.V.
doi:10.1016/S0531-5131(03)01841-7

(GEP'93) to 89 registered for the last exercise (GEP'02), 86 (95%) having submitted results.

The samples included in the proficiency testing are decided by the QC office and include a number (usually five to six) of 100 μl bloodstains (including a paternity testing case), a 2 cm hair shaft (from 2000) and forensic samples, including saliva samples (1997), mixed stains (1998, 2000, 2003), seminal stains (2002) and nonhuman samples (2001). Statistical evaluation of the evidence was required in the last trials, including a theoretical paternity testing case with reported frequencies. Only systems with at least three laboratories having consensus are considered in the PT trial and this number will increase up to five laboratories from 2003. In case of discrepancies in one or more system results are studied by a panel of experts and discussed in the GEP meetings.

All the laboratories used autosomal STRs with an increasing number of markers until recently (now the tendency is for a stabilization in the number of markers used and a policy has been implemented to achieve the goal of a reduction in the number of systems). SLPs were used by a decreasing number of laboratories, and hardly a couple of laboratories have submitted results in the last trial. The same occurs for dot-blot based systems (HLADQA1, Polymarker). On the contrary the mtDNA and Y chromosome are increasingly being used by the laboratories (Fig. 1).

Despite the increasing number of laboratories, results remained quite satisfactory. The total number of errors ranked from 0.6% to 2.3% in the different years (average 1.5%). In general, there is a tendency to concentrate the errors in a few laboratories most of them using manual electrophoretic systems and home made allelic ladders. In the last trial, only five laboratories (10%) are responsible of 50% of errors. In addition if only STRs included in commercially available kits are included the error rate dramatically decreases with an average of 0.65%.

Y STRs have a similar error rate than autosomal STRs and the group have made a great effort towards the standardization of new Y STRs [1], including the compilation of population data [2]. The results of mtDNA are quite variable, depending in the difficulties

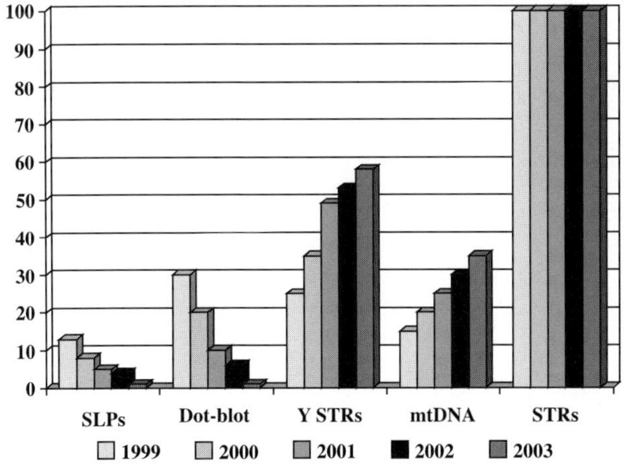

Fig. 1. Percentage of laboratories using the different types of markers.

of the sample. In some case heteroplasmy was detected making more difficult interpretation. The difficulties found in two different years one related with the low/degraded amount of DNA present in the hair shaft samples submitted [3] and other due the variation of heteroplasmy in different hair samples [4] has been recently published.

The group is aware of the need to improve mtDNA results. Similar results were observed in other collaborative exercises or population data compilation. To follow strictly ISFG recommendations regarding contamination, the use of validated software and especially phylogenetical checking of the data are strongly recommended. An important number of statistical errors in statistical programs and calculations were detected in the theoretical paternity testing cases (paper challenges), especially when the difficulties of the case increase. This indicates that a greater effort must be made in this area and the corresponding actions to correct this problem have been implemented, through training courses on basis of statistical evaluation and the use of validated software in various countries of Europe and America.

Acknowledgements

The CYTED program through the network RIGEMAMEF (Subprogram IIIc) supported in part these collaborative exercises.

References

[1] Gusmão, et al., Results of the GEP-ISFG collaborative study on the Y chromosome STRs GATA A10, GATA C4, GATA H4, DYS437, DYS438, DYS439, DYS460 and DYS461: population data, Forensic Sci. Int. 135 (2003) 150–157.

[2] Sánchez-Diz, et al., Results of the GEP-ISFG collaborative study on two Y-STRs tetraplexes: GEPY I (DYS461, GATA C4, DYS437 and DYS438) and GEPY II (DYS460, GATA A10, GATA H4 and DYS439), Forensic Sci. Int. 135 (2003) 158–162.

[3] Alonso, et al., Results of the 1999–2000 collaborative exercise and proficiency testing program on mitochondrial DNA of the GEP-ISFG: an inter-laboratory study of the observed variability in the heteroplasmy level of hair from the same donor, Forensic Sci. Int. 125 (2002) 1–7.

[4] Prieto, et al., The 2000–2001 GEP–ISFG Collaborative Exercise on mtDNA: assessing the cause of unsuccessful mtDNA PCR amplification of hair shaft samples, Forensic Sci. Int. 134 (2003) 46–53.

International Congress Series 1261 (2004) 127–129

www.ics-elsevier.com

Y-SNP typing by SNaPshot™ in the Belgian population and in degraded forensic samples

N. Siebert, B. Hoste*

National Institute of Forensic Sciences, Ch. Vilvorde 98-100, B-1120 Brussels, Belgium

Abstract. Eleven Y-SNPs were typed by minisequencing in a sample of 54 persons of the Belgian population. Seven haplogroups, according to the Y-Consortium nomenclature 2002, were observed with the following frequencies: 7.4% E-M35*, 24.1% F-M89* (× M9), 3.7% K-M9* (× 92R7), 1.8% P-92R7* (× M17, P25), 57.5% R-P25* (× M18, M153, SRY-2627), 3.7% R-SRY-1532b-M17, 1.8% R-SRY2627. In a series of very degraded post-mortem samples from seven victims, four could not be typed for STRs. The Y-SNPs, in 55–87-bp amplicons, were more successful showing full profile for two of these four samples, but no result for the two others. © 2003 Elsevier B.V. All rights reserved.

Keywords: Y chromosome; Single nucleotide polymorphism; Minisequencing; Population; Degraded DNA

1. Introduction

Single nucleotide polymorphisms (SNPs) are a promising tool for very degraded forensic samples, as they can be analysed in very small DNA fragments. We started to test this application with Y-SNPs. After a blind inter-laboratory exercise of the EDNAP group, our SNaPshot technique for 11 Y-SNPs was applied to a Belgian population sample. Seven of the 11 Y-SNPs, in DNA fragments of 55–131 bases, were compared to STR (106–342 bases) in very degraded post-mortem samples.

2. Material and methods

Unrelated male persons of Belgian origin from all over the country. Post-mortem samples from seven male victims, stored at −70 °C, an aliquot thawed twice was left at room temperature for 3 weeks. *DNA isolation*: proteinaseK digestion, phenol–chloroform and Centricon-30 (Millipore) purification. Teeth were first crushed in liquid nitrogen. *DNA quantification*: Quantiblot kit (Applied Biosystems). *STR typing*: in 28 cycles with the ProfilerPlus kit (Applied). *First PCR*: the 11 Y-SNPs were amplified in 3 multiplexes (Table 1). Based on the results of *3-plexI*, either *3plexII* or *4-plexI* was typed to determine

* Corresponding author. Tel.: +32-22434615; fax: +32-22416105.
E-mail address: Bernadette.Hoste@just.fgov.be (B. Hoste).

doi:10.1016/j.ics.2003.12.003

Table 1
PCR and minisequencing (MS) primers for 10 Y-SNPs

Multiplex	Locus	Amplicon size (bp)	MS size (b)	MS strand	Mutation (F-strand)
3-plex-I	SRY-1532	87	36	R	A>G
					G>A
	92R7	55[a]	32	F	G>A
	P25	77	57	R	C>A
3-plex-II	M17 (M18)	70	44	F	+> – G, i.e. G>T
	M153	74	47	F	T>A
	SRY-2627	131[a]	62	F	C>T
4-plex-I	M89	73	24	R	C>T
	M9	341[b]	40	R	C>G
	SRY-8299	218	29	F	G>A
	M35	86	48	R	G>C

bp: base pairs, b: bases, F: forward, R: reverse. M17 and M18 on the same amplicon. All other primers are new, chosen with the Primer3.0 program v.0.2 (www.genome.wi.mit.edu/cgi-bin/primer/primer3), except [a] according to Ref. [2], [b] according to Ref. [1]. The length of the SNaPshot primers was adjusted with tails of non human sequence [3].

the haplogroup. The 2–5-ng DNA template in a 25-μl reaction mix containing 1 × PCR Gold buffer (Applied), 2 mM $MgCl_2$, 0.2 mM of each dNTP, 0.2 μM of each primer except 92R7 (0.1 μM) and 2 units Taq Gold DNA polymerase. For the tetraplex *4-plexI* or for a hexaplex of *3-plexI* and *3-plexII*, the *Multiplex PCR mastermix* (Qiagen) was used. All multiplexes were run with 11 min 95 °C, then 30 cycles of 30 s 94 °C, 90 s 58 °C, 90 s 72 °C. Only for the optimisation, the forward primers were fluorescently 5′ labelled. After Microcon-30 (Millipore) purification, the PCR product sizes (in bp) were analysed on a 377 ABI-Prism sequencer. M18 (± 2 bp) was typed at this step. M17 (± 1 bp) on the same fragment was typed in the next step as the other Y-SNPs. *Minisequencing*: with the SNaPshot kit (Applied). After CentriSep (Applied) cleaning, the sizes of the elongated primers were analysed on the 377 sequencer, with the SNaPshot positive control as external size standard. The PCR primers (Applied) and the minisequencing primers (Qiagen) are listed in Table 1 (sequences available on request).

3. Results

Negative controls, i.e. female DNA (5 ng), blancos (all reagents except DNA) for DNA extraction, first PCR and SNaPshot, as well as PCR products in the SNaPshot mix without the SNaPshot primers, showed no peaks in the Y-SNPs range. In part of the male samples, double peaks were observed for 92R7 G/A or A (Fig. 1, row 1) and P25 C or C/A. They are due to locus duplication [2,4]. The detection threshold was 250 pg, with a 30-cycle PCR.

Y-SNPs haplogroup frequencies are given in the abstract [5]. These frequencies are close to the data in another sample of the Belgian population typed by restriction for a slightly different set of Y-SNPs [6].

Both methods were tested on the same amount (1–2 ng) of very degraded DNA. Victims 1, 3 and 4 showed full STR-profile. Victim 7 (whole canine) only showed a very partial STR-profile (Fig. 1). The STR-profile of drowned victim 2 (testis) was even

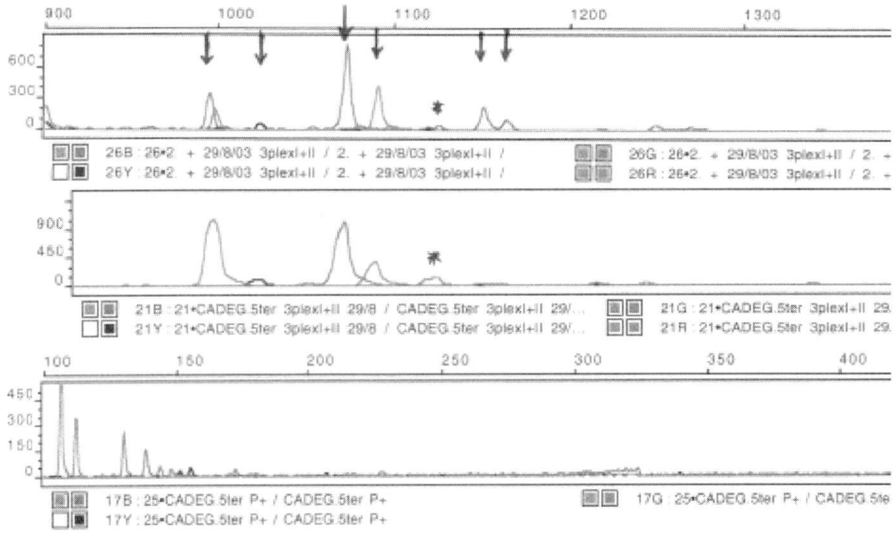

Fig. 1. Y-SNP and STR profile in a very degraded post-mortem sample and in high quality DNA. Row 1: Y-SNPs in high molecular weight DNA. Row 2: Y-SNP in degraded DNA (victim 7). Row 3: STRs (ProfilerPlus) for the same degraded sample. →: The Y-SNPs are 92R7, SRY1532, M17, M153, P25, SRY-2627 in increasing size (P25 lacking in row 2 due to a problem of primer conservation). *: Fluorescent first PCR product 92R7 55 bp.

weaker, as only 0.2 ng were amplified, due to the presence of inhibitors. All samples showed full Y-SNP profiles with fragments up to 87 bp, although the 131-bp fragment could be missing. Victim 5 (a blood sample taken several weeks after death) and victim 6 (whole canine of an old man buried for 7 years) yielded no result by either method. Their DNA amounts were under the detection threshold.

4. Conclusion

We have developed a multiplex of Y-SNPs. Our preliminary results in a small series of seven very degraded post-mortem samples show that, as expected, SNPs in 55–87-bp amplicons are more successful than STRs. Nevertheless, it seems from this limited series that two scenarios often show up: either the degradation is weak allowing the typing of STRs *and* Y-SNPs (if enough DNA is available), or the degradation is so strong that *neither* STR *nor* Y-SNPs can be detected. Further work needs to be done to improve the technique and to refine the results.

References

[1] P.A. Underhill, et al., Genome Res. 7 (1997) 996.
[2] M.E. Hurles, et al., Am. J. Hum. Genet. 65 (1999) 1437.
[3] J.N. Hirschhorn, et al., Proc. Natl. Acad. Sci. 97 (2000) 12164.
[4] J.J. Sanchez, et al., Forensic Sci. Int., (2004) (in press).
[5] The Y-Consortium, Genome Res. 12 (2002) 339.
[6] Z.H. Rosser, et al., Am. J. Hum. Genet. 67 (2000) 1526.

International Congress Series 1261 (2004) 130–132

ELSEVIER

www.ics-elsevier.com

A study of STR loci (D18S51, FGA, TH01, TPOX) in sub-Saharan populations

M. Regueiro[a,*], J.C. Carril[a], B. Caeiro[a], M.L. Pontes[b], D. Abrantes[b], G. Lima[b], M.J. Pereira[b], M.F. Pinheiro[b,c]

[a] *Facultade de Bioloxía (Campus Sur), Dpto. Bioloxía Animal, Área de Antropoloxía, Universidade de Santiago de Compostela, 15782, Santiago de Compostela, Spain*
[b] *Delegação do Porto do Instituto Nacional de Medicina Legal, Porto, Portugal*
[c] *Instituto de Ciências Biomédicas de Abel Salazar, Universidade do Porto, Portugal*

Abstract. As a part of a research project on molecular variation in sub-Saharan Africa, we analyzed four microsatellites (HUMTPOX, HUMTH01, FGA and D18S51) in the Bamileke (Cameroon), the Fon (Benin), the Sidama (Ethiopia), the Tutsi (Rwanda) and the Wairak (Tanzania).

Keywords: Africa; STR; AmpF*l*STR identifiler; Population data; Allele frequencies

1. Introduction

Due to the scarcity of data referring to African populations, and more specifically to the sub-Saharan context, an overview of four STRs in five sub-Saharan African populations is reported.

2. Material and methods

Four autosomal STR markers (TH01, TPOX, D18S51 and FGA) were typed using the Applied Biosystems AmpFLSTR® Identifiler™ kit. Amplification products were analyzed in ABI Prism® 3100 Genetic Analyzer. Allele frequencies were calculated using the gene counting method. Hardy–Weinberg proportions were verified by an exact test and were performed by using GENEPOP 3.1. Correspondence analyses were carried out using the NTSYS-pc version 1.70.

3. Results and discussion

The population database for six sub-Saharan African populations is shown in Table 1. A multivariate analysis, including other populations apart from the sub-Saharan region, is shown in Fig. 1 (Projection I/II). The projection defined by axes I/II explains up to 67.93% of the total cumulative variance. Axis I is basic in the clustering of sub-Saharan populations, which occupy the positive portion of this axis, setting them apart from Caucasian populations.

* Corresponding author. Tel.: +34-981-563100x13348; fax: +34-981-59-69-04.
E-mail address: mpmaria@usc.es (M. Regueiro).

doi:10.1016/S0531-5131(03)01632-7

Table 1
Allele frequencies of the STRs TH01, TPOX, D18S51 and FGA in the populations studied

Locus	Allele	Tutsi	Sidama	Wairak	Fon	Bamileke
TH01	6	0.2016	0.1855	0.2549	0.1250	0.0962
	7	0.4032	0.4355	0.3137	0.4904	0.4423
	8	0.1452	0.1694	0.1373	0.2308	0.2692
	9	0.2016	0.1694	0.2059	0.1154	0.1154
	9.3	0.0161	0.0403	0.0294	0.0289	0.0385
	10	0.0323	0.0000	0.0588	0.0096	0.0385
p-val		0.1221	0.9153	0.5712	0.7759	0.3718
N		124	124	102	104	104
TPOX	6	0.0403	0.0000	0.0192	0.0673	0.0926
	7	0.0242	0.0082	0.0096	0.0289	0.0370
	8	0.2823	0.4180	0.3173	0.2692	0.2315
	9	0.3387	0.2541	0.3269	0.2981	0.2963
	10	0.0726	0.0738	0.0865	0.1058	0.0556
	11	0.1936	0.2131	0.2404	0.1731	0.2778
	12	0.0484	0.0328	0.0000	0.0481	0.0093
	13	0.0000	0.0000	0.0000	0.0096	0.0000
p-val		0.7565	0.3022	0.4051	0.5575	0.3826
N		124	122	104	104	108
D18S51	10.2	0.0185	0.0170	0.0000	0.0000	0.0000
	11	0.0000	0.0424	0.0400	0.0098	0.0000
	12	0.0185	0.0932	0.0800	0.0980	0.0283
	13	0.0556	0.0339	0.0300	0.0196	0.0566
	13.2	0.0185	0.0085	0.0000	0.0294	0.0000
	14	0.0370	0.0593	0.0600	0.0294	0.0283
	14.2	0.0000	0.0000	0.0000	0.0098	0.0377
	15	0.2130	0.1525	0.0900	0.1275	0.1415
	15.2	0.0093	0.0085	0.0400	0.0000	0.0000
	16	0.1482	0.1017	0.2200	0.1667	0.2358
	16.2	0.0000	0.0170	0.0200	0.0000	0.0000
	17	0.1574	0.0848	0.1000	0.1275	0.1604
	17.2	0.0000	0.0085	0.0200	0.0000	0.0000
	18	0.2037	0.1441	0.1100	0.1471	0.1226
	18.2	0.0000	0.0085	0.0100	0.0000	0.0000
	19	0.0926	0.1102	0.0600	0.1078	0.0755
	19.2	0.0000	0.0000	0.0100	0.0098	0.0000
	20	0.0278	0.0848	0.0600	0.0490	0.0472
	20.2	0.0000	0.0000	0.0100	0.0098	0.0000
	21	0.0000	0.0110	0.0100	0.0392	0.0566
	21.1	0.0000	0.0000	0.0200	0.0098	0.0000
	22	0.0000	0.0000	0.0100	0.0000	0.0094
	23	0.0000	0.0170	0.0000	0.0000	0.0000
	25	0.0000	0.0000	0.0000	0.0098	0.0000
p-val		0.0044	0.0640	0.1777	0.5516	0.4834
N		108	118	100	102	106
FGA	13	0.0000	0.0091	0.0000	0.0000	0.0093
	15	0.0088	0.0000	0.0000	0.0000	0.0000
	16.1	0.0000	0.0000	0.0100	0.0000	0.0000
	17	0.0000	0.0000	0.0000	0.0192	0.0000
	18	0.0088	0.0182	0.0300	0.0096	0.0000
	18.2	0.0175	0.0000	0.0000	0.0000	0.0000

(continued on next page)

Table 1 (*continued*)

Locus	Allele	Tutsi	Sidama	Wairak	Fon	Bamileke
	19	0.0351	0.0273	0.0500	0.0577	0.0185
	20	0.0790	0.0727	0.0400	0.0000	0.0833
	20.2	0.0000	0.0000	0.0000	0.0000	0.0093
	21	0.0702	0.1091	0.0400	0.0577	0.0926
	22	0.2281	0.2364	0.1700	0.1923	0.1481
	23	0.0965	0.1273	0.1900	0.1827	0.2037
	24	0.1404	0.1909	0.1600	0.2404	0.2500
	24.2	0.0000	0.0091	0.0000	0.0000	0.0000
	25	0.1140	0.0909	0.0400	0.1346	0.0556
	26	0.1053	0.0273	0.0400	0.0577	0.0556
	27	0.0614	0.0091	0.0400	0.0192	0.0370
	28	0.0000	0.0273	0.0800	0.0192	0.0278
	29	0.0088	0.0182	0.0300	0.0000	0.0000
	30	0.0000	0.0273	0.0600	0.0096	0.0000
	30.2	0.0088	0.0000	0.0200	0.0000	0.0000
	31.2	0.0000	0.0000	0.0000	0.0000	0.0093
	32.2	0.0088	0.0000	0.0000	0.0000	0.0000
	43.2	0.0088	0.0000	0.0000	0.0000	0.0000
p-val		0.0636	0.3142	0.0094	0.3241	0.4834
N		114	110	100	104	108

p-val: Hardy–Weinberg equilibrium, exact test.

Acknowledgements

This work was partially supported by the Xunta de Galicia through Grant XUGA 20011B98. M. R. has been supported by a Xunta de Galicia fellowship.

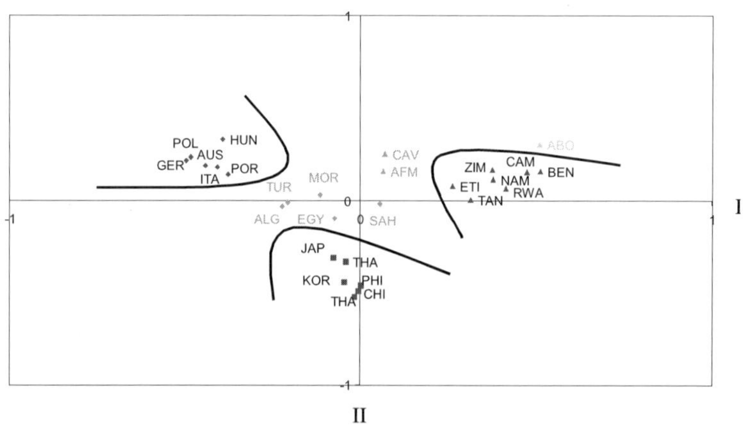

Fig. 1. Correspondence analysis, Projection I/II. Populations analyzed. Caucasian populations: (♦) European: POL (Poland), GER (Germany), HUN (Hungary), AUS (Austria), ITA (Italy), TUR (Turkey), POR (North Portugal); (♦) North African populations: MOR (Morocco), EGY (Egypt), ALG (Algeria), SAH (Western Sahara); (■) Asian populations: JAP (Japan), CHI (China), TAI (Taiwan), THA (Thailand), KOR (Korea), PHI (Philippines); Australian populations: (▲) ABO (Australian aborigines); African populations: (▲) CAV (Cape Verde), AFM (Afroamericans); (▲) sub-Saharan populations: ZIM (Zimbabwe), NAM (Namibia), BEN (Benin), TAN (Tanzania), CAM (Cameroon), ETI (Ethiopia), RWA (Rwanda).

International Congress Series 1261 (2004) 133–135

www.ics-elsevier.com

African STR data based on a newly developed tetraplex fluorescent system (CD4, F13A01, FES and MBPB)

Cíntia Alves[a,*], António Amorim[a,b], Luísa Pereira[a], Leonor Gusmão[a]

[a] IPATIMUP, Rua Roberto Frias, s/n, 4200-465 Oporto, Portugal
[b] Faculty of Sciences, University of Porto, Portugal

Abstract. The development of a fluorescent multiplex system amplifying four STRs (CD4, F13A01, FES and MBPB) was carried out in order to complement commercially available kits (Identifiler from Applied Biosystems and Powerplex 16 from Promega) mainly for application in complex parentage testing. Here, we report African population data from samples of Mozambique and the Cabinda province of Angola. Population differentiation studies were carried out and, in terms of forensic interest, some parameters are reported and compared with available commercial tetraplex kits.

Keywords: Multiplex PCR; STRs; Mozambique; Cabinda; Population data

1. Introduction

A fluorescent multiplex system (CFFM) with the STRs CD4, F13A01, FES and MBPB, was developed to complement, in our laboratory, the routinely used commercial kits AmpFLSTR Identifiler (AB Applied Biosystems) and Powerplex 16 (Promega) which amplify a total of 17 STRs. In some difficult parentage investigations, such as those where the putative father is not accessible, the results obtained with the 17 STR set may not be satisfactory. Therefore, it is important to have other available markers for extending complex investigations (apart from Y chromosome systems or mtDNA), which can be easily and rapidly analysed in order to give an adequate resolution in the shortest period of time.

The choice of these 4 STRs resided basically on the fact that they were well studied and routinely used in singleplex reactions with silver-staining detection, before the introduction of fluorescent equipment and commercial kits in many forensic labs. The kit was

* Corresponding author. Tel.: +351-22-5570700; fax: +351-22-5570799.
E-mail address: calves@ipatimup.pt (C. Alves).

0531-5131/
doi:10.1016/S0531-5131(03)01712-6

developed for ABI fluorescent platforms and sequenced ladders were built based on the most frequent alleles observed in our previously studied Portuguese sample.

Population data for the four mentioned STRs are reported for samples located on opposite sides of the southern African continent: Mozambique on the east (Maputo area) and Angola on the west (Cabinda region). These results are compared between them and with previously published African results where data is available on all four loci [1].

In terms of forensic interest, the overall discrimination powers of this kit are also reported and compared with available data on other kits, namely Promega's FFFL kit.

2. Material and methods

Blood samples of 114 individuals from Mozambique (Maputo area) and 110 from Angola (Cabinda province) were collected. DNA was extracted with the Chelex method [2]. Primers, labels and ladders used for multiplex genotyping were the following:

CD4: 5′-GCCTGAGTGACAGAGTGAGAACC-TET [4] and 5′-TTGGAGTCG-CAAGCTGAACTAG; ladder with alleles 5, 6, 8, 10, 11, 14 and 15.
F13A01: 5-GAGGTTGCACTCCAGCCTTT-TET and 5′-ATGCCATGCAGATTA-GAAA [7]; ladder with alleles 3.2, 4, 5, 6, 7, 13, 14 and 15.
FES: 5′-GCGAAAGAATGAGACTACAT and 5′-GGGATTTCCCTATGGATTGG-FAM [8]; ladder with alleles 8, 10, 11, 12 and 13.
MBPB: 5′-GGACCTCGTGAATTACAATC-Fluorescein [9] and 5′-CTCATGTATC-CATCTATTTACC [10]; ladder with alleles 7, 9, 10, 11 and 12.

For the CD4 locus, the forward primer was modified according to the observation of a C-A substitution at the 3′ end, which would originate allele dropout [3]. The modified primer corresponds to the one described by Edwards et al. [4] without the terminal cytosine.

PCR conditions and fragment analysis procedures can be obtained from the corresponding author on demand.

The Arlequin software ver. 2.000 [5] was used for estimating allele frequencies, for testing Hardy–Weinberg equilibrium and also for population differentiation tests. Heterozygosity was calculated according to Nei [6].

3. Results and discussion

Table 1 reports genetic population data obtained for the four STRs in both African populations under study. Allele frequencies can be obtained from the corresponding author on demand.

The overall power of discrimination (PD) of the CFFM multiplex is 99.992% with a matching probability (MP) of 1/12478 individuals for the Mozambique sample, and slightly superior for the Cabinda sample with 99.995% PD with a MP of 1/19772 individuals. These values are very high when compared with Caucasian populations (e.g., 1/3846 individuals in our previously studied Portuguese sample), mainly due to the high levels of diversity observed for the CD4 locus in African samples. Compared with the commercial FFFL kit (Promega), which, like the CFFM kit, amplifies loci not contained in

Table 1
Parameters of forensic interest for CD4, F13A01, FES and MBPB loci in both African samples

Parameters	Mozambique (Maputo area) $N=114$				Angola (Cabinda province) $N=110$			
	CD4	F13A01	FES	MBPB	CD4	F13A01	FES	MBPB
Het	0.833	0.751	0.729	0.678	0.858	0.803	0.717	0.651
PD	0.951	0.911	0.881	0.846	0.962	0.938	0.878	0.825
PE	0.650	0.536	0.474	0.415	0.689	0.609	0.467	0.391
P	0.052	0.710	0.074	0.540	0.536	0.558	0.526	0.831

Het: Nei's heterozygosity; PD: Power of discrimination; PE: a priori power of exclusion; P: Hardy–Weinberg equilibrium exact test.

the Identifiler or Powerplex systems, in African-Americans, the MP is of 1/16802 individuals (Promega Technical Manual, 1999), higher than the value observed for Mozambique but lower than in Cabinda. This shows that the CFFM system is a useful alternative (as a complement to routinely used STRs) in complex parentage investigations.

Population differentiation tests were undertaken for all four loci comparing our African samples between them and with previously published data from São Tomé and Príncipe islands [1], situated on the west of Africa. There were no significant differences found between the sample from the Cabinda region (Angola) and São Tomé and Príncipe for all loci, which could be expected since both regions lie on the west side of Africa. Our Mozambique sample (on the east) showed significant differences for all loci with São Tomé and Príncipe, but with Cabinda, differences were only found in two loci, F13A01 and MBPB.

Acknowledgements

Financial support was granted by *Fundação para a Ciência e a Tecnologia* (FCT), *Programa Operacional Ciência, Tecnologia e Inovação* (POCTI). Luísa Pereira has a research grant (SFRH/BPD/7121/2001) from FCT. We also thank Dr. Sandra Beleza (IPATIMUP) for the Cabinda samples. Mozambique samples were provided by Dr. Albertino Damasceno and Dr. Benilde Soares from the Eduardo Mondlane University (Maputo).

References

[1] L. Gusmão, et al, Forensic Sci. Int. 116 (2001) 53.
[2] M.V. Lareu, et al, Forensic Sci. Int. 66 (1994) 41.
[3] G. Watanabe, et al, J. Forensic Sci. 43 (1998) 733.
[4] M.C. Edwards, et al, Nucleic Acids Res. 19 (1991) 4791.
[5] S. Schneider et al, University of Geneva, 2000.
[6] M. Nei, Molecular evolutionary genetics, Columbia Univ. Press, New York, 1987.
[7] M.H. Polymeropoulos, et al, Nucleic Acids Res. 19 (1991) 4306.
[8] M.H. Polymeropoulos, et al, Nucleic Acids Res. 19 (1991) 4018.
[9] M.H. Polymeropoulos, et al, Hum. Mol. Genet. 1 (1992) 658.
[10] L. Gusmão, et al, Int. J. Leg. Med. 108 (1996) 313.

ELSEVIER

International Congress Series 1261 (2004) 136–138

www.ics-elsevier.com

Allele frequencies for CODIS loci in a Sicilian population sample

C. Vecchio[a,*], L. Garofano[a], L. Saravo[a], S. Spitaleri[a], G. Iacovacci[a], M. Santacroce[a], V. Manzari[b], B. Budowle[c]

[a] *Raggruppamento Carabinieri Investigazioni Scientifiche, Viale di Tor di Quinto n.151, 00191 Rome, Italy*
[b] *Dipartimento Medicina Università "Tor Vergata"-00100 Rome, Italy*
[c] *FBI Laboratory, 2501 Investigation Pkwy., Quantico, VA 22135, USA*

Abstract. Data from an island population can be useful for understanding effects of forensic evaluations of DNA evidence. In this study, allele frequencies for the thirteen CODIS loci were generated from 220 unrelated volunteer donors from a Sicilian (Italy) population sample, as well as from casework using both the AmpFlSTR™ Profiler and Co-Filer ™ Amplification Kits (PE Applied Biosystems, Foster City, CA). All loci met Hardy–Weinberg expectations. The data were compared with population studies from individuals residing in other Italian geographic locations and found not be substantially different. The combined power of discrimination is high and comparable to other European population groups.

Keywords: DNA; Short tandem repeat (STR); CODIS; Population data; Forensic

1. Introduction

Short tandem repeat (STR) polymorphisms are the genetic markers of choice for human identification and paternity testing. Moreover, STR loci are the genetic markers of national and international DNA databanks, such as CODIS (FBI, USA), based on a core of 13 STRs. In this preliminary study we investigated the 13 STR CODIS loci in a Sicilian sample (220 unrelated Sicilian donors). The results obtained were compared with previous studies on Italian populations and were found not to be substantially different [1,2].

2. Statistical analysis

Allele designations were determined by comparison of the sample fragments with those of the allelic ladders supplied with each kit. At each locus, the frequency of each allele was calculated from the numbers of each genotype in the sample set (i.e., the gene count method). Unbiased estimates of expected heterozygosity were computed as described by

* Corresponding author. Tel.: +39-333-3458105; fax: +39-06-233212993.
E-mail address: cvecchio@carabinieri.it (C. Vecchio).

doi:10.1016/S0531-5131(03)01845-4

Table 1

All	D8		D21		D18S		D3S		FGA		D5S		D13S		D7S		D16S		vWA		TH01		TPOX		CFS	
	Nr.	Freq	Nr.	Freq	Nr.	Freq	Nr.	Freq	N	Freq	Nr.	Freq.	Nr.	Freq.	Nr.	Freq.	Nr.	Freq.	Nr.	Freq.	Nr.	Freq.	Nr.	Freq.	Nr.	Freq.
6																					117	0.266				
7											1	0.002			6	0.014					89	0.202	2	0.005	1	0.002
8	9	0.020									9	0.020	45	0.102	75	0.170	14	0.032			49	0.111	239	0.543	2	0.005
9	3	0.007									20	0.045	27	0.061	41	0.093	50	0.114			82	0.186	57	0.130	17	0.039
9.3																					92	0.209				
10	37	0.084			3	0.007					32	0.073	29	0.066	137	0.311	32	0.073			11	0.025	28	0.064	132	0.300
11	32	0.073			10	0.023					145	0.330	134	0.305	116	0.264	128	0.291					104	0.236	118	0.268
12	48	0.109			77	0.175	1	0.002			139	0.316	146	0.332	52	0.118	100	0.227	2	0.005			9	0.020	143	0.325
13	127	0.289			66	0.150	1	0.002			86	0.195	44	0.100	10	0.023	52	0.118	2	0.005			1	0.002	27	0.061
14	98	0.223			58	0.132	28	0.064			7	0.016	15	0.034	3	0.007	12	0.027	49	0.111						
15	62	0.141			63	0.143	97	0.220									8	0.018	47	0.107						
16	20	0.045			61	0.139	112	0.255			1	0.002					11	0.025	112	0.255						
17	4	0.009			40	0.091	104	0.236	1	0.002							16	0.036	115	0.261						
18					25	0.057	93	0.211	8	0.018							11	0.025	79	0.180						
19					17	0.039	4	0.009	32	0.073							5	0.011	29	0.066						
19.2									2	0.005																
20					6	0.014			52	0.118							1	0.002	5	0.011						
20.2									3	0.007																
21					7	0.016			61	0.139																
21.2									6	0.014																
22					1	0.002			86	0.195																
22.2									2	0.005																
23									74	0.168																
23.2									2	0.005																
24									46	0.105																
24.2									12	0.027																
25									29	0.066																
25.2									1	0.002																
26			1	0.002					18	0.041																
26.2									1	0.002																
27			12	0.027					2	0.005																
28			63	0.143	2	0.005			1	0.002																
29			96	0.218	1	0.002																				
30			112	0.255	2	0.005																				
30.2			18	0.041																						
31			24	0.055	1	0.002																				
31.2			49	0.111					1	0.002																
32			5	0.011																						
32.2			43	0.098																						
33.2			16	0.036																						
35			1	0.002																						

Edwards et al. [3]. Possible divergence from Hardy–Weinberg expectations (HWE) was tested by calculating the unbiased estimate of the expected homozygote/heterozygote frequencies and also by performing an exact test [4]. The probability of discrimination (PD) and probability of exclusion (PE) was calculated according to Fisher [5].

3. Results and discussion

The distribution of observed alleles for all 13 STR loci is shown in Table 1. All loci are highly polymorphic with the loci D18S51 (86.8%), D21S11 (85.5%) and FGA (84.5%) having the highest observed heterozygosities, and the locus TPOX showing the lowest observed heterozygosity (65.5%). The most polymorphic loci are the most discriminating loci: FGA (97%), D18S51 (96.5%) and D21Sll (95.1%). The TPOX locus is the least discriminating (80.3%). For all 13 STR loci the combined power of discrimination is greater than 0.99999999 and the combined probabilities of exclusion are 0.99998. There was no evidence for departures from HWE for any loci based on the exact test. The Sicilian population data for these 13 loci do not differ substantially from other Caucasian data for the loci (data not shown). In conclusion, a database for the 13 STR loci has been established for the Sicilian population. These data can be used for both forensic casework and paternity testing in Sicilian population. These data together with previous studies on Italian populations could be a useful tool to appreciating the diversity of some island populations. Future projects will attempt to increase the number of samples in the Sicilian dataset so that greater confidence can be obtained for statistical estimates of the rarity of a DNA profile.

References

[1] L. Garofano, et al., Italian population data on thirteen short tandem repeat loci: HUMTH01, D21S11, D18S51, HUMVWFA31, HUMFIBRA, D8S1179, HUMTPOX, HUMCSF1PO, D16S539, D7S820. D13S317, D5S818, D3S1358, Forensic Science International 97 (1998) 53–60.

[2] R. Biondo, et al., Regional Italian Allele frequencies at nine short tandem repeat loci, Forensic Science International 115 (1–2) (2001 1 January) 95–98.

[3] R. Edwards, et al., Genetic variation at five trimeric and tetrameric repeat loci in four human population groups, Genomics 12 (1992) 241–253.

[4] S.W. Guo, Ea. Thompson, Performing the exact test of Hardy–Weinberg proportion for multiple alleles, Biometrics 48 (1992) 361–372.

[5] R. Fisher, Standard calculation for evaluating a blood group system, Heredity 5 (1951) 95–102.

International Congress Series 1261 (2004) 139–141

www.ics-elsevier.com

Allele frequencies of 15 STR loci in Argentine population

A.M. Di Lonardo*, M.B. Rodríguez Cardozo, M.V. Cólica, M.A. Abovich, A. Szöcz, C. Echenique, S. Valente, O. Santapá

Immunologia, Banco Nacional de Datos Genéticos, Hospital Dr. C.G. Durand, Juan B. Ambrosetti 743 Planta Baja, Buenos Aires 1405, Argentina

Abstract. Short tandem repeat (STR) loci are the most informative PCR based genetic markers available to date for attempting to individualize biological material. The full use of DNA typing technology in forensic science has grown up by the development of National DNA databases. The aim of this study was to determine allele frequencies and statistical parameters of medico-legal interest, such as heterozygosity value, discrimination power and chances of exclusion in paternity cases for the loci D3S1358, VWA, FGA, D8S1179, D21S11, D18S51, D13S317, D7S820, D16S539, THO1, TPOX and CSF1PO, D2S1338 and D19S433.

Keywords: STRs; PCR; Population genetics; ABI 310; Forensics

1. Introduction

Short tandem repeat (STR) systems are highly polymorphic loci consisting of tandemly repeated sequences 1–6 bp in length. Because of the relatively small size of STR alleles (generally 100–350 nucleotides), amplification by polymerase chain reaction (PCR) is relatively easy, with the additional advantage of making the typing of forensic material successful. In addition, STR loci can be amplified simultaneously in a multiplex PCR. Thus, substantial information can be obtained in a single analysis with the benefits of using less DNA template, reducing labor and contamination. For this reason, short tandem repeat (STR) polymorphism has become a powerful tool for human identification, chromosome mapping and linkage analysis, and the study of molecular evolution and population genetics. These multiplex systems are useful for forensic identification and/or study of biological evidences and parentage testing. The STR loci are ideal candidates for co-amplification and actually we can investigate 16 loci simultaneously, 15 tetranucleotyde loci (13 CODIS loci and the loci D2S1338 Ref. [7] and D19S433 Ref. [8]) and a locus for sex identification: Amelogenin. The fluorescent multicolor dye technology allows these

* Corresponding author. Tel.: +54-11-4982-1716; fax: +54-11-4982-0625.
E-mail address: bndg@infovia.com.ar (A.M. Di Lonardo).

doi:10.1016/S0531-5131(03)01616-9

Table 1
Discrimination power and exclusion power for 15 loci

Locus	PD	PE
D8S1179	0.929	0.634
D21S11	0.941	0.647
D7S820	0.934	0.6
CSF1PO	0.866	0.425
D3S1358	0.922	0.479
TH01	0.905	0.634
D13S317	0.945	0.634
D16S539	0.914	0.647
D2S1338	0.970	0.699
D19S433	0.930	0.536
VWA	0.932	0.490
TPOX	0.775	0.250
D18S51	0.96	0.7
D5S818	0.9	0.48
FGA	0.963	0.713

multiplex loci to be analyzed on an ABI Prism® 310 or 3 100 Genetic Analyzer™ in a single capillary injection. The use of these genetic markers in forensic identification and paternity testing requires the existence of appropriate databases for the populations where the systems are going to be used. To interpret the match significance between genetically typed samples, it is necessary to know the population distribution of alleles at each locus in question.

The aim of this study was to determine allele frequencies and statistical parameters of medico-legal interest, such as heterozygosity value, discrimination power and chances of exclusion in paternity cases for the loci D3S1358, VWA, FGA, D8S1179, D21S11, D18S51, D13S317, D7S820, D16S539, THO1, TPOX and CSF1PO, D2S1338 and D19S433 (Table 1).

2. Materials and methods

Population studies were carried out in 502 unrelated individuals that came from 375 parentage tests. Genomic DNA was isolated from blood samples with salting out Miller's method [9]. The samples were amplified at the loci FGA, VWA, D3S1358, D5S818, D7S820, D8S1179, D13S317, D18S51 and D21S11 using the AmpFISTR® Profiler Plus Kit (PE Biosystems, Foster City, CA) and at the loci CF1PO, TPOX, TH01, D3S1358, D7S820, and D16S539 using the AmpFISTR® Cofiler™ kit (PE Biosystems). The same loci and the D2S1338 and D19S433 were amplified with the AmpFISTR® Identifiler™ Kit (PE Biosystems). Samples were analyzed using the ABI PRISM® 310 Genetic Analyzer (PE Biosystems), according to the manufacturer's recommendations [1] using as separation medium Performance Optimized Polymer (POP) 4™ (PE Biosystems). The data were acquired by ABI PRISM™ 310 Collection 1.0.2 software and analyzed by GeneScan® Analysis 3.1 software and Genotyper® 2.5 according to the manufacturer's recommendations [2,4].

3. Results

All 15 loci were in Hardy–Weinberg equilibrium. Forensic statistical parameters were according to those obtained by other authors.

1. All the loci are highly polymorphics in our population. They showed heterozygosity's percentages from 57% (TPOX) to 85.9% (FGA) [3].
2. TPOX (PD = 0.77) is the less discriminator locus while D2S1338 (PD = 0.97), FGA (PD = 0.963) and D18S51 (PD = 0.96) are greater power discrimination system [3].
3. The Combined Discrimination Power is greater than 0.999999998 [3,5,6].
4. The Match Probability of all loci is 4.58466×10^{-18} [3].
5. The loci with the greatest power of exclusion are FGA and D2S1338 while TPOX has least [7].
6. The Combined Paternity Index is 922295.21 [3].
7. The Combined Exclusion Power is 0.999999 [3].
8. We have absolute concordance in the results obtained for the sample typification with the Identifiler™ Kit and the Profiler-Cofiler™ Kit, except the determination of the 18.2 allele at FGA locus.
9. We find a new allele at D13S317: 6.2 allele, it contains 197.33 bp.

4. Conclusions

This study demonstrates that this multiplex system is a useful and effective tool for forensic identification or individualization of biological evidence and parentage testing in Argentine population.

References

[1] AmpFlSTR®Identifiler™, PCR Amplification Kit User's Manual, Applied Biosystems, Foster City, CA, 2001.

[2] K. Lazaruk, et al., (PE AB): genotyping of forensic short tandem repeat (STR) systems based on sizing precision in a capillary electrophoresis instrument, Electrophoresis 19 (1998) 86–93.

[3] Ch. Brenner, J.W. Morris, Paternity index calculation in single locus hypervariable DNA probes, Proceedings for International Symposium on Human Identification, Promega, Madison, WI, 1998.

[4] O. Henegariu, et al., Multiplex PCR: critical parameters end step-by-step protocol, Biotecniques 23 (3) (1997) 504–511.

[5] W. Bär, B. Brinkmann, B. Budowle, A. Carracedo, P. Gill, et al., DNA recommendations. Further report of the DNA Commission of the ISFH regarding the use of short tandem repeats systems, Intl. J. Leg. Med. 110 (1997) 175–176.

[6] D.A. Jones, Blood samples: probability of discrimination, J. Forensic Sci. 12 (1992) 355–359.

[7] D2S1338, Cooperative Human Linkage Center (CHLC) accession number 41445. GenBank accession number G08202.

[8] D19S433 Cooperative Human Linkage Center (CHLC) accession number 135. GenBank accession number G08036.

[9] S.A. Miller, et al., Nucleic Acid Res. 16 (1988) 1215.

International Congress Series 1261 (2004) 142–144

www.ics-elsevier.com

Allele frequencies of 15 STR loci in a Spanish population

J. C. Carril*, M. A. Ocaña, O. Sierra, A. Molino, R. Cospedal, J. Puente

Department of Human Identification, Genomica S.A.U., Alcarria, 7 28820-Coslada, Madrid, Spain

Abstract. Genetic analysis of 15 STR loci, including the 13 CODIS core STR loci (D3S1358, vWA, FGA, D8S1179, D21S11, D18S51, D5S818, D13S317, D7S820, TH01, TPOX, CSF1PO, and D16S539) and the 2 pentameric STRs (Penta D and Penta E) present in the Powerplex 16™ system (Promega, Madison, WI, USA) were carried out. Blood and/or buccal swab samples were obtained from 341 unrelated Spanish individuals and DNA was extracted using phenol/chloroform and ethanol precipitation.

The 15 STR loci plus de Amelogenin locus were electrophoresed using the ABI Prism 310 Automatic DNA Sequencer and alleles were typed using GeneScan and Genotyper software (Applied Biosystems).

Allele frequencies for each locus were calculated and the exact test and the homozygosity test were performed to evaluate Hardy–Weinberg equilibrium (HWE). The Expected Heterozygosity (He), the Observed Heterozygosity (Ho), the Polymorphic Information Content (PIC), the Power of Discrimination (PD) and the Power of Exclusion (PE) were also calculated.

The results indicate that these 15 loci are useful genetic markers for forensic personal identification and paternity testing in the Spanish population.

Keywords: Short tandem repeat (STR); DNA polymorphism; Spanish population database; Powerplex 16

1. Introduction

STRs are today one of the most effective tools for individual and populational genetic characterization. In routine forensic casework, it is important to establish a populational database for further reliable statistical analyses. Genetic analysis of 15 STR loci, including the 13 CODIS core STR loci (D3S1358, vWA, FGA, D8S1179, D21S11, D18S51, D5S818, D13S317, D7S820, TH01, TPOX, CSF1PO, and D16S539) and the 2 pentameric STRs (Penta D and Penta E) present in the Powerplex 16™ system (Promega) were carried out.

* Corresponding author. Tel.: +34-674-89-90; fax: +34-674-89-91.
E-mail address: jccarril@genomica.es (J.C. Carril).

0531-5131/
doi:10.1016/S0531-5131(03)01659-5

2. Material and methods

Blood and/or buccal swab samples were obtained from 341 unrelated Spanish individuals and DNA was extracted using phenol/chloroform and ethanol precipitation. PCR amplification was performed with Powerplex 16™ System Amplification Kit (Promega) according to the user' s manual provided by the manufacturer [1].

The 15 STR loci plus de Amelogenin locus were electrophoresed using the ABI Prism 310 Automatic DNA Sequencer and alleles were typed using GeneScan v.2.1 and Genotyper v.2.5 Analysis Software (Applied Biosystems).

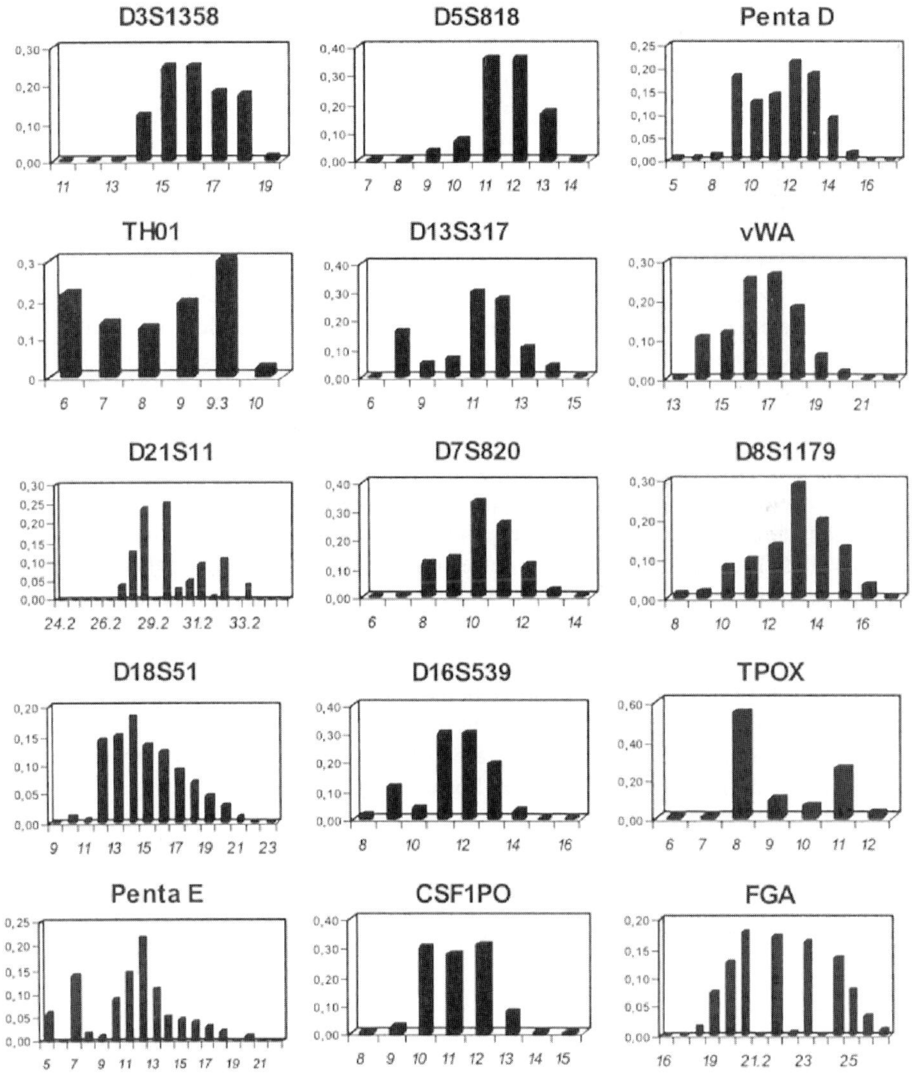

Fig. 1. Allele frequencies of 15 STR loci analyzed.

Table 1
Statistical parameters for the 15 STR loci in Spanish

	N	No. of alleles	He	Ho	PIC	PD	PE
D3S1358	341	8	0.7966	0.7830	0.7600	0.9250	0.5680
vWA	341	9	0.8043	0.7771	0.7700	0.9320	0.5570
FGA	341	16	0.8650	0.8504	0.8500	0.9650	0.6960
D8S1179	341	10	0.8212	0.7947	0.8000	0.9450	0.5890
D21S11	341	17	0.8375	0.8182	0.8200	0.9520	0.6330
D18S51	341	15	0.8740	0.8563	0.8600	0.9690	0.7070
D5S818	341	8	0.7146	0.7390	0.6600	0.8670	0.4910
D13S317	340	9	0.7877	0.7941	0.7600	0.9240	0.5880
D7S820	341	9	0.7765	0.7595	0.7400	0.9170	0.5260
TH01	341	6	0.7914	0.7977	0.7600	0.9220	0.5950
TPOX	341	7	0.6251	0.6276	0.5700	0.8100	0.3250
CSF1PO	341	8	0.7334	0.7361	0.6800	0.8790	0.4860
D16S539	341	9	0.7654	0.7449	0.7300	0.9090	0.5010
Penta D	340	12	0.8404	0.8176	0.8200	0.9520	0.6320
Penta E	341	18	0.8827	0.8944	0.8700	0.9730	0.7840

Allele frequencies for each locus were calculated and the exact test and the homozygosity test were performed to evaluate Hardy–Weinberg equilibrium (HWE) [2,3]. The Expected Heterozygosity (He), the Observed Heterozygosity (Ho), the Polymorphic Information Content (PIC), the Power of Discrimination (PD) and the Power of Exclusion (PE) were also calculated [4].

3. Results and discussion

Fig. 1 shows the allelic classes for every STR and his respective frequencies in the population sample object of study. The allelic range changes among the 6 alleles that presents HUMTH01 and the 18 alleles detected in case of Penta E. Nevertheless (Table 1), the degree of polymorphism of every STR, expressed in Heterozygosity and PIC terms, show HUMTPOX like the fewer polymorphic STR (He = 0.6251; PIC = 0.5700) and Penta E like the more polymorphic STR (He = 0.8827; PIC = 0.8700). Results for the Exact Test for the analysis of deviations of genotype frequencies from Hardy–Weinberg Equilibrium proportions (HWE) do not show significant differences for any STR.

The results indicate that these 15 loci are useful genetic markers for forensic personal identification and paternity testing in the Spanish population.

References

[1] Powerplex 16™ system. Promega, Madison, WI, USA. Part#TMD012.
[2] S.W. Guo, E.A. Thomson, Performing the exact test of Hardy–Weinberg proportions for multiple alleles, Biometrics 48 (1992) 361–372.
[3] GDA v.1.0.
[4] PowerStats v.1.2.

International Congress Series 1261 (2004) 145–147

www.ics-elsevier.com

Allele frequency distribution of two X-chromosomal STR loci in the Han population in China

M. Lv, L. Zhang*, W.B. Liang, B. Zhou, M. Liao, M.Y. Wu

Forensic Biology, College of Forensic Medicine, Sichuan University, No. 17 Section 3, Ren Ming Nan Lu, Chengdu, Sichuan 610041, PR China

Abstract. X-chromosome (ChrX) STR loci have been proven to be a useful tool for paternity testing, especially in some cases. In paternity testing, genetic markers on ChrX are only applicable when the disputed child is female. The author investigated allele frequency distribution of ChrX STR loci DXS6789 and HumSTRX1 in a sample of unrelated individuals (males and females) in Han population living in Chengdu, China, by using PCR and PAGE followed by silver staining. Ten and six different alleles of DXS6789 and HumSTRX1 loci were detected, respectively. The genotype frequencies of DXS6789 and HumSTRX1 loci were in good agreement with the Hardy–Weinberg equilibrium. The observed heterozygosity of DXS6789 and HumSTRX1 loci were 0.795 and 0.748 in females, respectively. It is suggested that these ChrX markers are appropriate for the purposes of forensic analyses.

Keywords: X-chromosome; DXS6789; HumSTRX1; Short tandem repeat; Polymorphism

1. Introduction

DNA typing of X-chromosome (ChrX) STR is underrepresented in paternity testing, and is only applicable in paternity cases when the disputed child is female. The mean exclusion (MEC) of genetic markers on X-chromosome as proposed by Kishida and Tamaki [1] were higher than those on autosomal chromosome as proposed by Krüger et al. [2]. Therefore, they are very useful in some special cases of deficiency paternity testing cases. Such as, in case of whether presumptive half-sisters have the same father when the mother is lacking. For the purpose of solving this problem, only a few ChrX markers are required. To date, the number of ChrX which have been studied in the Chinese population is still very small. The aim of this paper is to investigate the frequency distribution of both DXS6789 and HumSTRX1 in the Han population in Chengdu, China.

2. Survey methodology

Blood Specimens were obtained from 127 unrelated females and 118 unrelated males volunteer donors. DNA were extracted from blood specimens using Chelex-100 [3].

* Corresponding author. Tel.: +86-28-854-60532; fax: +86-28-854-05541.
E-mail address: kjc@scu.edu.cn (L. Zhang).

doi:10.1016/S0531-5131(03)01613-3

Genotyping was carried out by PCR in a PE9600 cycler. The components of a 20 μl reaction mixture were as follows: template DNA 20 ng, primer 0.2 μmol/l each, dNTPs 200 μmol/l each, KCl 50 μmol/l, Tris–HCl (pH8.3) 10 mmol/l, $MgCl_2$ 1.5 mmol/l, Taq polymerase 1 U.

Primer sequences:

DXS6789:

P1:5′-TGT CCT ATT GTA TTA GTC AGG GAT C-3′;

P2:5′-ATG TAA GTT GGT ACT TAA TAA ACC CTC-3′.

HumSTRX1:

P1:5′-GTT TCC TCC TGC AAA ATA CAG C-3′;

P2:5′-TCC AGC ACC CAA GGA AGT C-3′.

PCR conditions: start at 94 °C for 3 min, followed by 30 cycles consisting of 35 s at 94 °C, 40 s at 57 °C, 50 s at 72 °C, followed by a 10 min extension at 72 °C. The amplified products were electrophoresed in 6% polyacrylamide gel by using 100 bp ladder and allelic markers as size markers, followed by silver staining. The amplified products were examined by using an ABI PRISM™ 310 Genetic Analyzer.

The Hardy–Weinberg equilibrium test (HWE) was performed by an exact test [4]. We calculated the polymorphism information content (PIC), average power of discrimination in females (PD^F) and in males (PD^M) [5].

3. Results

Both DXS6789 and HumSTRX1 loci are tetranucleotide [6–8]. DXS6789 exhibited 10 clearly distinguishable alleles ranging from 146 to 182 bp. HumSTRX1 exhibited six clearly distinguishable alleles ranging from 214 to 234 bp. The allele frequency distributions of both ChrX loci, their PD and PIC are shown in Table 1. The parameters of Het, and PIC, in normal family trio testing, as well as the average PD^F and PD^M confirm that both DXS6789 and HumSTRX1 loci are highly polymorphic.

4. Discussion

The genotype frequencies of both loci were shown in Table 2. Genotypes (25 and 12) were found in DXS6789 and HumSTRX1 loci, respectively, and they are in good

Table 1
Allele frequency distributions of DXS6789 and HumSTRX1

DXS6789						HumSTRX1					
Allele	Female number	Female (%)	Male number	Male (%)	Total frequency (%)	Allele	Female number	Female (%)	Male number	Male (%)	Total frequency (%)
14	3	1.2	0	0	0.6	11	0	0	2	0.8	0.4
15	53	20.9	40	16.9	19.0	12	7	2.8	8	3.4	3.1
16	77	30.3	74	31.4	30.8	13	41	16.1	40	16.9	16.5
17	8	3.1	14	5.9	4.5	14	117	46.1	98	41.5	43.9
18	1	0.4	0	0	0.2	15	75	29.5	76	32.2	30.8
19	14	505	2	0.8	3.3	16	14	5.5	12	5.1	5.3
20	51	20.1	46	19.5	19.8		–	–	–	–	–
21	37	14.6	44	18.6	16.5		–	–	–	–	–
22	8	3.1	16	6.8	4.9		–	–	–	–	–
23	2	0.8	0	0	0.4		–	–	–	–	–
Total	127	1	118	1	1		127	1	118	1	1
PD^F: 0.931; PD^M: 0.792; PIC: 0.77						PD^F: 0.837; PD^M: 0.691; PIC: 0.63					

Table 2
Genotypes of DXS6789 and HumSTRX1 found in females

DXS6789				HumSTRX1			
Genotypes	No.	Genotypes	No.	Genotypes	No.	Genotypes	No.
14–16	3	16–20	13	12–13	1	15–16	5
15–15	4	16–21	12	12–14	2	–	–
15–16	11	16–22	4	12–15	4	–	–
15–17	2	16–23	2	13–13	6	–	–
15–18	1	17–20	4	13–14	12	–	–
15–19	4	17–21	2	13–15	15	–	–
15–20	11	19–20	5	13–16	1	–	–
15–21	12	19–21	1	14–14	24	–	–
15–22	4	20–20	6	14–15	47	–	–
16–16	14	20–21	6	14–16	8	–	–
16–19	4	21–21	2	15–15	2	–	–
HWE exact test: $P=0.309>0.05$; Het: 0.795				HWE exact test: $P=0.174>0.05$; Het: 0.748			

agreement with the HWE, and P-values were 0.309 and 0.174, respectively. Investigation in 50 true family trios with female children suggested a codominant X-linked inheritance. No mutations and no mother–child exclusions were found. It is suggested that these ChrX markers are useful for forensic analyses, especially in solving complicated kinship testing and paternity testing of lacking mother.

Acknowledgements

The research was supported by grants from the Chinese Natural Sciences Foundation (No. 30171033) and State Ministry of Education (No. 01143) as well as Trans-Century Training Programme Foundation for the Talents by the Ministry of Education Commission (No. 2001-29).

References

[1] T. Kishida, Y. Tamaki, Japanese population data on X-chromosome STR locus AR, Nippon Hoigaku Zasshi 51 (1997) 376–379.
[2] J. Krüger et al., Zur Verwendung der Erythrozytenphosphatase bei der Vaterschaftsbegutachtung, Dtsch. Z. Gesamte Gerichtl. Med. 64 (1968) 127–146.
[3] J. Singer-Sam et al., Use of Chelex to improve the PCR signal from a small number of cells, Amplification 3 (1989) 11.
[4] S.W. Guo, E.A. Thompson, Performing the exact test of Hardy–Weinberg proportion for multiple alleles, Biometrics 48 (1992) 361–372.
[5] D. Desmarais et al., Development of a highly polymorphic STR marker for identity testing purposes at the human androgen receptor gene (HUMARA), J. Forensic Sci. 43 (1998) 1046–1049.
[6] S. Hering et al., Development of the X-linked tetrameric microsatellite marker HumDXS6789 for forensic purposes, Forensic Sci. Int. 119 (2001) 42–46.
[7] J. Edelmannn et al., 16X-chromosome STR loci frequency data from a German population, Forensic Sci. Int. 124 (2001) 215–218.
[8] Z. Tun et al., Simultaneous detection of multiple STR loci on sex chromosomes for forensic testing of sex and identity, J. Forensic Sci. 44 (4) (1999) 772–777.

International Congress Series 1261 (2004) 148–150
www.ics-elsevier.com

An isolated exclusion in the FGA system

U.-D. Immel[a,*], M. Kleiber[a], M. Neerman-Arbez[b], M. Klintschar[a]

[a] *Institut für Rechtsmedizin, Martin-Luther University Halle-Wittenberg, Franzosenweg 1, 06112 Halle an der Saale, Germany*

[b] *Division of Medical Genetics, CMU, 1 rue Michel-Servet, 1211 Geneva 4, Switzerland*

Abstract. In a paternity test with 35 short tandem repeats (STRs), an isolated exclusion for the FGA system was observed (probability of paternity >99.999%). Different mechanisms suitable to explain this finding like polymerase slippage, primer mismatch, a deletion of the FGA locus or gene conversion after formation of the zygote are discussed.

Keywords: FGA; Deletion; Mutation; Gene conversion

1. Introduction

Short tandem repeat (STR) polymorphisms are prone to germline mutations. The gametic mutability of STR loci routinely used for paternity testing has been closely examined previously [1,2] and single step mutations due to polymerase slippage were identified as most common mutation events. In a paternity test with 35 STRs, an isolated exclusion for the FGA system with a contraction for at least three repeats was observed (Fig. 1). This mutation event cannot easily be explained by simple slippage.

2. Materials and methods

DNA was extracted from Blood and saliva samples twice following standard protocols from Qiagen and amplified for 35 STRs.

3. Results and discussion

In the FGA system, child and mother were homozygous for 21, whereas the alleles of the putative father were 24 and 25 (Fig. 1). Sequencing revealed consensus alleles for FGA. Typing 27 autosomal STRs and eight Y-chromosomal STRs lead to a probability of paternity of >99.999%. There is no evidence of relatives of the putative father as genitors.

The most obvious explanation for a mutation in an STR locus would be a contraction of the repeat stretch due to polymerase slippage. However, these mutations are almost invariably confined to a single repeat [1,2]. Larger contractions or expansions (as observed in disease related triplet sequences) are considered extremely rare, and to be the consequence of recombination rather than slippage. Moreover, the fact that the child is homozygous (the paternally inherited allele has mutated into the same allele as the maternally inherited!)

* Corresponding author. Tel.: +49-345-557-1833; fax: +49-345-557-1587.
E-mail address: uta.immel@medizin.uni-halle.de (U.-D. Immel).

0531-5131/
doi:10.1016/S0531-5131(03)01508-5

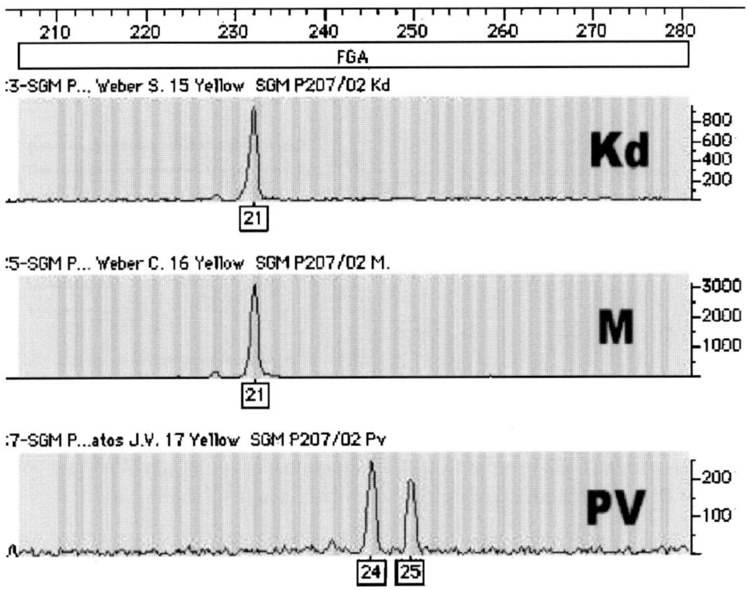

Fig. 1. FGA results with SGM kit.

merits attention: Only by incidence slippage would result in homozygote offspring. Bearing this in mind, we considered alternative mutational mechanisms. One possibility would be a loss of the paternal allele during meiosis, either by introduction of a primer binding mismatch mutation or by deletion of the FGA locus. A primer binding site mutation could be ruled out by amplification with three different primer sets.

Recently, a 11-kb deletion of the fibrinogen alpha-chain gene comprising the FGA polymorphism associated with afibrinogenemia was reported [3]. We succeeded to eliminate this possibility by performing a PCR specific for the 11-kb deletion (Fig. 2). To identify for larger, unknown deletions, we analyzed the chromosomal region surrounding the FGA system. Close polymorphisms of forensic interest are MNSs and FABP. We typed these

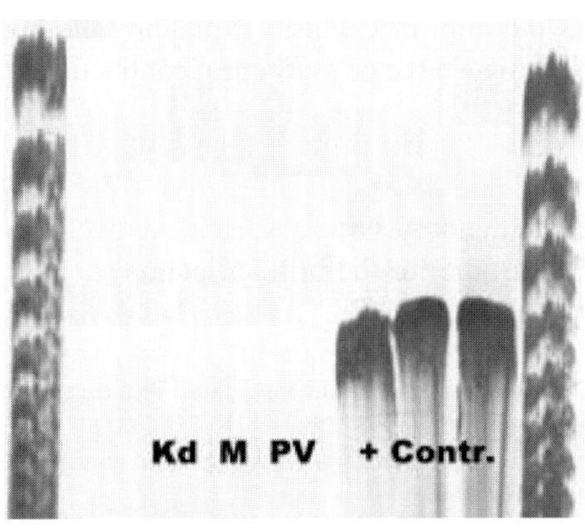

Fig. 2. PCR results from FGA fibrinogen alpha-chain gene comprising the FGA locus.

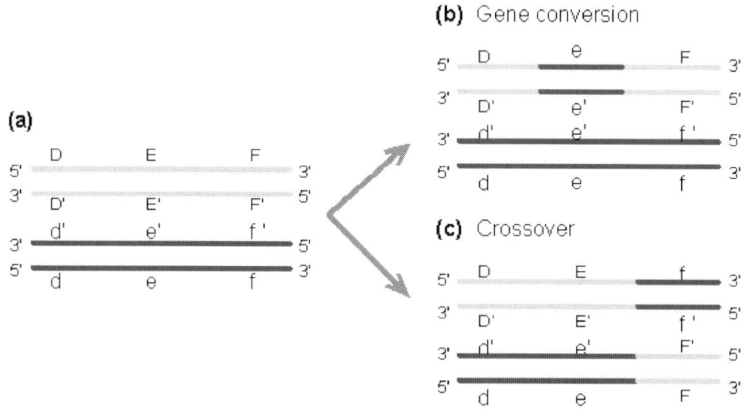

Fig. 3. Comparison between gene conversion and DNA crossover. (a) Two DNA molecules. (b) Gene conversion—the black DNA *donates* part of its genetic information (e–e′ region) to the grey DNA. (c) DNA crossover—the two DNAs *exchange* part of their genetic information (f–f′ and F–F′).

polymorphisms and four further close STRs (D4S1625, D4S1629, D4S2999, and D4S3021) without finding a further exclusion. Moreover, in four of the loci, the child was heterozygous. Finally, we used the relative signal intensities in a multiplex PCR to rule out a deletion of one FGA allele: In the case of a deletion in the child (= only one copy of the locus), the signal of THO1 (relative to the other loci in the multiplex) should be half compared to that for the mother (= two copies). However, in the present case, the mean relative amplification for TH01 in five reactions did not differ between child and mother, allowing us to eliminate a deletion (Fig. 2).

However, gene conversion might be a mechanism that could satisfyingly explain this unusual mutation. Although little is known about gene conversion in mammals, it is well-described in fungi. Basically, it is a nonreciprocal genetic exchange in which the sequence of one DNA-strand (acceptor) is altered to become identical to the sequence of another DNA strand (donor, Fig. 3b) following damage to the acceptor strand. It is thus considered to be part of a mismatch repair mechanism. Gene conversion is usually observed during meiosis, but it is considered to occur during mitosis as well. We thus favor gene conversion after formation of the zygote as the most likely mutational mechanism in this case as (having excluded a deletion) it is the only mechanism explaining the homozygosity of the child which is capable of introducing a three or four repeat contractions. This is the first mutation of that kind reported for FGA.

Acknowledgements

The authors would like to thank A. Graul, A. Heide and S. Salostowitz for the excellent technical assistance and G. Bothe for the brilliant pictures.

References

[1] B. Brinkmann, et al., Mutation rate in human microsatellites: influence of the structure and length of the tandem repeat, Am. J. Hum. Genet. 62 (1998) 1408–1415.

[2] A. Sajantila, et al., Experimentally observed germline mutations at human micro- and minisatellite loci, Eur. J. Hum. Genet. 7 (2) (1999) 263–266.

[3] M. Neerman-Arbez, et al., The 11 kb FGA deletion responsible for congenital afibrinogenemia is mediated by a short direct repeat in the fibrinogen gene cluster, Eur. J. Hum. Genet. 7 (8) (1999) 897–902.

ELSEVIER

International Congress Series 1261 (2004) 151–153

www.ics-elsevier.com

Analysis of 12 STR loci in Antioquia (Colombia) population sample

M.L.J. Bravo[a,*], J.J. Builes[a,b], M.M. de Pancorbo[c], M.A. Moreno[a,b]

[a] *Paternity testing, GENES Ltda. Lab. de Genética Forense y Huellas Digitales del DNA, Carrera 48 No. 10-45, Cons. 612, Medellín 1252, Colombia*

[b] *Instituto de Biología, Universidad de Antioquia, Medellín, Colombia*

[c] *Servicio de Diagnóstico de la Paternidad Biológica e Identificación Genética, Universidad del País Vasco, Spain*

Abstract. In this study, the validation of 12 short tandem repeated (STRs) systems is presented in a sample of the population from Antioquia, central region of Colombia. The DNA for the analyses of PCR was obtained of 244 to 546 unrelated individuals. PCR amplification was performed according to the manufacturer's recommendations, using PowerPlex 1.2 System and FFFL Multiplex (Promega). Amplificated fragments were separated by capillary electrophoresis using the ABI Prism 310 Genetic Analyzer (PE Applied Biosystems). Allele frequencies, Hardy-Weinberg equilibrium, observed and expected heterozygosity and genetic disequilibrium were calculated using GENEPOP ver. 3.3 and GDA ver. 1.1 software. Forensic parameters were calculated using the PowerStat ver. 1.2 software (Promega). The 12 of the loci met Hardy-Weinberg expectations and they reached a combined power discrimination higher than 0.999999999999 and a combined power exclusion similar to 0.9999, showing to be a powerful tool for paternity testing, individual identification and forensic applications in Antioquia population.

Keywords: Antioquia; Population; STR; PowerPlex 1.2 System; FFFL Multiplex; Power of discrimination; Power exclusion

1. Introduction

Antioquia is a central region of Colombia, its population is predominantly Caucasian almost all Spanish descendants with some Basque component [1,2]. In this study, we present validation of 12 short tandem repeated (STR) loci for using in paternity testing and forensic analysis, PowerPlex 1.2 System and FFFL Multiplex kits (Promega). The PowerPlex 1.2 System consists of the STRs loci: CSF1PO, TH01, TPOX, vWA01, D5S818, D7S820, D13S317 and D16S539. The FFFL system consists of the loci FES/FPS, F13A1, F13B and LPL.

* Corresponding author. Tel.: +57-4268-4875; fax: +57-4318-5270.
E-mail address: genforense@epm.net.co (M.L.J. Bravo).

0531-5131/
doi:10.1016/S0531-5131(03)01532-2

Table 1
Observed allele frequencies for PowerPlex® 1.2 System and FFFL® Multiplex loci in Antioquia (Colombia)

Alelles	CSF1PO	TPOX	TH01	vWA	D16S539	D7S820	D13S317	D5S818	F13A01	FESFPS	F13B	LPL
3.2									0.1393			
4									0.1127			
5			0.0003						0.2316			
6		0.0064	0.4042			0.0046	0.0009		0.1783		0.1176	
7	0.0079	0.0046	0.2136			0.0165		0.0211	0.2992	0.0050	0.0336	0.0017
8	0.009	0.5037	0.0938		0.0047	0.1273	0.0422	0.0105	0.0123	0.0182	0.1678	
8.3			0.0030									
9	0.0175	0.0927	0.1328		0.1183	0.0833	0.1135	0.0680	0.0021	0.0182	0.3524	0.0328
9.3			0.1148									
10	0.2408	0.0624	0.0350		0.1654	0.2876	0.0891	0.0565	0.0021	0.2475	0.3289	0.4310
11	0.2426	0.2532		0.0009	0.1904	0.2839	0.1539	0.4042		0.4455		0.2414
12	0.4188	0.0771			0.2385	0.1685	0.2974	0.2663	0.0021	0.2030		0.2345
13	0.0600			0.0093	0.1876	0.0247	0.2130	0.1590	0.0082	0.0611		0.0414
14	0.0037			0.0570	0.0804	0.0028	0.0591	0.0144	0.0041	0.0017		0.0103
15				0.1517	0.0148		0.0300		0.0041			
16				0.3245					0.0041			0.0017
17				0.2335		0.0009						0.0035
18				0.1599								0.0017
19				0.0588			0.0009					
20				0.0046								
Minimum	0.0052	0.0050	0.0059	0.0054	0.0057	0.0055	0.0056	0.0056	0.0121	0.0091	0.0094	0.0096
N	1084	1086	1002	1088	1082	1092	1066	1044	488	606	596	580
Parameters												
Ho	0.7085	0.6330	0.7629	0.7574	0.8169	0.7894	0.79412	0.7471	0.7951	0.6931	0.7215	0.7103
He	0.7043	0.6643	0.7588	0.7856	0.8254	0.7850	0.8180	0.7325	0.7943	0.6958	0.7258	0.6993
HWE-HE	0.1913	0.9967	0.4527	0.9690	0.5331	0.3223	0.6305	0.2908	0.5516	0.6972	0.7343	0.2122
Exact test	0.8565	0.1068	0.1587	0.2625	0.1316	0.4454	0.1666	0.2569	0.0527	0.3559	0.0960	0.0717
PD	0.8628	0.8435	0.9007	0.9222	0.9427	0.9213	0.9437	0.8828	0.9234	0.8510	0.8726	0.8552
PE	0.4415	0.3333	0.5209	0.5224	0.6451	0.5795	0.5882	0.5049	0.5899	0.4176	0.4623	0.4444
MP	0.1372	0.1565	0.0993	0.0778	0.0573	0.0787	0.0563	0.1172	0.0766	0.1490	0.1274	0.1448
PIC	0.6535	0.6197	0.7171	0.7538	0.7993	0.7522	0.7941	0.6923	0.7621	0.6462	0.6769	0.6478
TPI	1.72	1.37	2.05	2.06	2.85	2.37	2.43	1.98	2.44	1.63	1.80	1.73

Ho: Heterozygosity observed, He: Heterozygosity expected, HWE-HE: Hardy-Weinberg Heterozygote Excess test, PD: Power of Discrimination, PE: Power of Exclusion, MP: Matching Probability, PIC: Polymorphism information content, TPI: Typical Paternity Index.

2. Materials and methods

Blood samples were randomly taken from paternity casework of the Laboratory of Human Genetics of the University of Antioquia. DNA was isolated from all samples using a salting out extraction procedure [3]. The amplification was performed by the PowerPlex 1.2 System and FFFL Multiplex kits (Promega), following the manufacturer's recommendations. The amplified products were analyzed by capillary electrophoresis using an ABI Prism™ 310 Genetic Analyzer. The frequency of each allele for each locus tested was calculated from the number of observed genotypes in the sample using GENEPOP software ver. 3.2a [4]. Exact tests for Hardy-Weinberg equilibrium of every locus and linkage disequilibrium between loci were carried out by using GENEPOP ver. 3.2a [4] and GDA ver. 1.0 [5] software. Forensic parameters were performed using POWERSTAS ver. 12 (Promega) and GDA ver. 1.0 [5] software.

3. Results and discussion

Antioquian population data for the 12 STR loci are shown in Table 1. No deviations from Hardy-Weinberg equilibrium were observed for all markers and interclass correlation test analysis demonstrated no evidence for correlation between the alleles for any of the pair-wise comparisons of the loci. The forensic efficiency values suggest that 12 STR loci investigated in this population are highly discriminative. The combined PD of the PowerPlex 1.2 System loci is 0.9999999 and combined for all 12 loci is higher than 0.999999999999. The PE of the PowerPlex 1.2 System in Antioquian population did not provide sufficient discrimination (0.997931) for paternity testing. A combined PE with FFFL Multiplex kit was achieved and the PE value raised to 0.9999. Individuals PE values ranged from 0.3333 (TPOX) to 0.6307 (D16S539). In conclusion, the Antioquian resident population database has been established for the analyzed systems. These 12 STR loci appear to be highly discriminating, thus providing a powerful tool for paternity investigations, individual identification and forensic applications.

Acknowledgements

This work was supported by GENES. Juan José Builes has a PhD fellowship (0058/2001) from COLCIENCIAS.

References

[1] M.L.J. Bravo, Estudio de la Estructura Genética de la Población de Antioquia, Colombia, Antropol Biol. 3 (1995) 15–18.

[2] M.L.J. Bravo, C.Y. Valenzuela, O.M. Arcos, Polymorphisms and phyletic relationships of the paisa community from Antioquia (Colombia), Gene Geogr. 10 (1996) 11–17.

[3] S.A. Miller, D.D. Dykes, H.F. Polesky, A simple salting out procedure for extracting DNA from human nucleated cells, Nucleic Acids Res. 16 (1988) 1215.

[4] M. Raymond, F. Rousset, GENEPOP (version 1.2): population genetics software for exact tests and ecumenicism, J. Heredity 48 (1995) 248–249.

[5] P.O. Lewis, D. Zaykin, Free program distributed by the authors over the internet from http://lewis.eeb.uconn.edu/lewishome/software.html (2001).

ELSEVIER

International Congress Series 1261 (2004) 154–156

www.ics-elsevier.com

Data analysis of D1S1656, D12S391 and D18S535 loci in two Colombian populations: Antioquia and Chocó

Juan-José Builes[a,b,*], Catalina Salazar[a], MLuisa-Judith Bravo[a], Marian Martínez-Pancorbo[c], Manuel-Antonio Moreno[a,b], Claudia-Patricia Gómez[a]

[a] *GENES Ltda., Laboratorio de Genética Forense y Huellas Digitales del DNA, Medellín, Antioquia, Colombia*
[b] *Instituto de Biología, Universidad de Antioquia, Medellín, Colombia*
[c] *Servicio de Diagnóstico de la Paternidad Biológica e Identificación Genética, Universidad del País Vasco, Spain*

Abstract. In the present study, we analyzed allelic and genotypic distribution of three short tandem repeat (STR) loci determined in samples from unrelated individuals from two Colombian populations: Antioquia (314) and Chocó (140). The three loci were found in Hardy-Weinberg equilibrium and they are highly polymorphic in the two populations studied with the locus D18S535 (77.2%) having the lowest observed heterozygosity (Antioquia population), and the locus D1S1656 (89.8%) displaying the highest heterozygosity. The most discriminating locus was D1S1656, Antioquia (PD = 0.976) and Chocó (0.974). The combined probability of exclusion for the three STR loci is 0.964 in Antioquia and 0.967 in Chocó populations. The combined probability of discrimination is 0.9999 in both populations, demonstrating to be a group of excellent markers to be used as complement in the paternity testing, individual identification and other forensic applications in general.

Keywords: Antioquia; Chocó; Colombia; Population; DNA; STR; D1S1656; D12S391; D18S535

1. Introduction

Short tandem repeats (STR) are polymorphic markers widely distributed throughout the human genome [1] that can be amplificated by PCR techniques. Only some of the them have been studied for their use in forensic genetic and paternity testing. The general criteria for selecting STRs include characteristics such as high heterozygosity, low stutter, few and low extra-peaks, robustness, easy multiplexing and a low mutation rate [2]. The aim of this study was to report allele frequency distributions for the D1S1656, D12S391

* Corresponding author. GENES Ltda., Laboratorio de Genética Forense y Huellas Digitales del DNA, Paternity testing, Carrera 48 No. 10-45, Cons. 612, 1252 Medellín, Antioquia, Colombia. Tel.: +57-4-2684875; fax: +57-4-3185270.

E-mail address: genforense@epm.net.co (J.-J. Builes).

0531-5131/
doi:10.1016/S0531-5131(03)01541-3

Table 1
Allele frequencies and statistical parameters

Allele	D1S1656		D12S391		D18S535	
	Antioquia	Chocó	Antioquia	Chocó	Antioquia	Chocó
9					0.04369	0.02878
10	0.00647	0.01095	0.00161		0.00243	0.01079
11	0.04531	0.05839	0.00161		0.01942	0.12590
12	0.10032	0.06204	0.00161		0.22573	0.26259
13	0.06634	0.09854		0.00362	0.33981	0.23381
14	0.11974	0.20438			0.24515	0.25180
15	0.16019	0.17153	0.02412	0.09420	0.10922	0.08273
15.3	0.05178	0.01825				
16	0.16990	0.09489	0.04019	0.06522	0.01214	0.00360
16.3	0.04207	0.09124				
17	0.06634	0.02920	0.09003	0.12319	0.00243	
17.3	0.12621	0.10584				
18	0.00809		0.22990	0.22464		
18.3	0.03398	0.04745				
19			0.27492	0.17754		
19.3	0.00324	0.00730				
20			0.11415	0.18116		
21			0.07878	0.03986		
22			0.05466	0.03623		
23			0.06592	0.03261		
24			0.01286	0.01449		
25			0.00804			
26			0.00161	0.00725		
Minimun	0.0101	0.0226	0.0097	0.0307	0.0092	0.0206
N	314	140	314	140	314	140
Parameters						
Ho	0.883	0.898	0.836	0.804	0.772	0.799
He	0.889	0.883	0.836	0.856	0.761	0.792
HWE-H	0.811	0.878	0.689	0.873	0.379	0.324
Exact test	0.981	0.510	0.177	0.157	0.893	0.634
PD	0.976	0.974	0.949	0.958	0.899	0.915
PE	0.762	0.791	0.667	0.607	0.548	0.596
MP	0.024	0.026	0.051	0.042	0.101	0.085
PIC	0.880	0.870	0.820	0.840	0.720	0.760
TPI	4.290	4.890	3.050	2.560	2.190	2.480

Ho: Heterozygosity observed, He: Heterozygosity expected, HWE-H: Hardy-Weinberg test, PD: Power of Discrimination, PE: Power of Exclusion, MP: Matching Probability, PIC: Polymorphism information content, TPI: Typical Paternity Index.

and D18S535 loci in two Colombian populations: Antioquia [3,5,6] and Chocó [4,7], as well as statistical evaluations, including the possible divergence from Hardy-Weinberg equilibrium and other forensic parameters of interest.

2. Materials and methods

Samples were obtained from 140 unrelated individuals of African descent from the Chocó region and 314 unrelated Caucasian individuals from Antioquia with a similar proportion of male and females. Genomic DNA was extracted by a salting out extraction procedure [8]. The primer sequences of D1S1656, D12S391 and D18S535 loci and cycling conditions were as recommended by Lareu et al. [2]. Briefly, each PCR reaction contained 2–10 ng human genomic DNA, 1 × Taq buffer, 1.5 mM MgC12, 200 μM each dNTP, 1U Taq polymerase (Promega, USA), 0.25 μM each primer in a total volume of 15 μl. A total of 30 cycles were carried out in a PTC-100 (MJ-Research) PCR System with denaturation for 45 s at 95 °C, annealing for 60 s at 6 °C and extension for 60 s at 72 °C.

The PCR products were analyzed using denaturing 4% acrylamide-bis-acrilamide gel electrophoresis and detected by silver staining (Promega). Typing was made by comparison with the sequenced allelic ladders, kindly provided by the Institute of Legal Medicine, University of Santiago de Compostela (Spain). The frequency of each allele for each locus tested was calculated from the number of observed genotypes in the sample using GENEPOP software ver. 3.2a [9]. The exact-test for within-locus (Hardy-Weinberg equilibrium) and between-loci testing (linkage desequilibrium) was carried out by using GENEPOP ver. 3.2a [9] and GDA ver. 1.0 softwares. Forensic parameters were performed using POWERSTATS ver. 12 (Promega) and GDA ver. 1.0 [10] softwares.

3. Results and discussion

Antioquia and Chocó population data for the three STRs are shown in Table 1. No deviations from Hardy-Weinberg equilibrium were observed for all markers in both populations. A comparative study between the two populations showed significant differences for the three loci ($P = 0.000$). On the other hand, Antioquian population showed a similar allelic distribution for the three loci with other Caucasian European populations, confirming findings of previous research showing a high Caucasian component in the Antioquia population [3,5,6]. D1S1656 was the most informative in both populations. The Combined Power of Discrimination (CPD) was of 0.9999 in both populations and the Combined Power of Exclusion (CPE) was 0.964 and 0.967 in the populations of Antioquia and Chocó, respectively.

In conclusion, two population databases have been established for the Caucasian population of Antioquia and for the African descent population of Chocó for STR loci D1S1656, D12S391 and D18S535. The results showed that all three loci are very useful for personal identification and paternity testing in the Colombian populations of Antioquia and Chocó.

Acknowledgements

This work was supported by GENES Ltda. Juan José Builes has a PhD fellowship (0058/2001) from COLCIENCIAS.

References

[1] J.S. Beckman, J.L. Weber, Genomics 12 (1992) 627–631.
[2] M.V. Lareu, et al., in: G.F. Senasabaugh, et al. (Eds.), Progress in Forensic Genetics, vol. 7, Elsevier, Amsterdam, 2000, pp. 198–200.
[3] M.L. Bravo, et al., Gene Geogr. 10 (1996) 11–17.
[4] M.L. Bravo, et al., Homo 51 (2000) 132.
[5] L.G. Carvajal-Carmona, et al., Am. J. Hum. Genet. 67 (2000) 1287–1295.
[6] J.J. Parsons, University of California Press, Berkeley, 1949.
[7] M.L. Bravo, et al., Int. J. Leg. Med. 115 (2001) 102–104.
[8] S.A. Miller, et al., Nucleic Acids Res. 16 (1988) 1215.
[9] M. Raymond, F. Rousset, J. Heredity 86 (1995) 248–249.
[10] P.O. Lewis, D. Zaykin, Free program distributed by the authors over the internet from http://lewis.eeb.uconn.edu/lewishome/software.html, 2001.

International Congress Series 1261 (2004) 157–159

www.ics-elsevier.com

Differences in allele distribution at 15 STR loci among four Japanese regional populations

Toshimichi Yamamoto*, Naohiro Watanabe, Rieko Uchihi, Takashi Yoshimoto, Shi-Lin Li, Rina Kurihara, Yoshinao Katsumata

Department of Legal Medicine and Bioethics, Nagoya University Graduate School of Medicine, 65 Tsurumai-cho, Showa, Nagoya 466-8550, Japan

Abstract. We examined allele frequency distributions at 15 autosomal short tandem repeat (STR) loci including 13 Combined DNA Index System (CODIS) core STRs in four regional Japanese populations (Akita, Nagoya, Oita and Okinawa). Those distributions were compared pairwise and statistically among them. We also analyzed the distributions with published data on a Korean population by genetic distance D_A to construct a tree based on the neighbor-joining method. Consequently, we obtained one that coincides well with their geographical distributions.

Keywords: STR; Japanese; Genetic relationship

1. Introduction

Polymorphic tetranucleotide repeat short tandem repeat (STR) markers have been widely used for personal identification and paternity tests in forensic fields. It has been possible to make a large database for a large number of those loci conveniently and accurately using commercially released multiplex typing kits. Using more than 15 such markers, the allele frequency data in another Japanese population were published previously [1]. Since those STRs have higher mutation rates at meiosis than other DNA markers such as single nucleotide polymorphisms (SNPs), their allelic distributions have a potential to differentiate among geographically close populations. In the present study, the genotypes at 15 STR loci were analyzed using a commercially available multiplex typing kit among four regional populations (Okinawa, Oita, Nagoya and Akita) in Japan. Those allele frequencies at each locus were calculated, and their distributions were compared pairwise and statistically among their populations. Their genetic relationship was also examined by constructing a phylogenetic tree.

* Corresponding author. Tel.: +81-52-744-2119; fax: +81-52-744-2121.
E-mail address: yamachan@med.nagoya-u.ac.jp (T. Yamamoto).

doi:10.1016/j.ics.2003.12.080

2. Materials and methods

2.1. DNA samples

Blood samples were collected from four regions (196 samples in Okinawa, 175 in Oita, 200 in Nagoya and 198 in Akita) in Japan. DNA were extracted from blood samples by a usual organic extraction method or with a QIAamp DNA Blood Mini kit (QIAGEN).

2.2. PCR amplification and typing

Those DNA samples were amplified at 15 STR loci using an AmpFlSTR Identifiler kit according to the manufacturer's instructions except a quarter volume of PCR reaction mixture. The PCR products were analyzed using a Genetic Analyzer 310 and genotyped.

2.3. Statistical analyses

Tests for Hardy–Weinberg equilibrium (HWE) were carried out using a homozygosity test, a likelihood ratio test and an exact test. Some statistical properties for discriminating power were calculated, and the differences in those distributions at 15 STR loci were examined statistically with Genepop software.

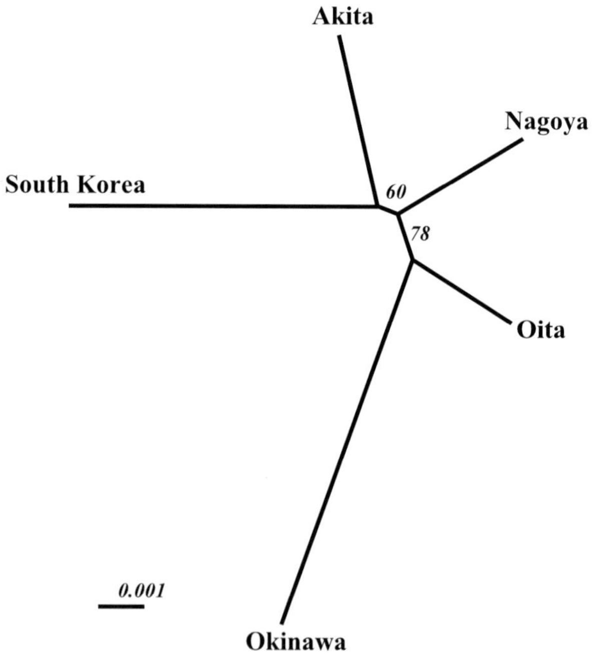

Fig. 1. Neighbor-joining tree based on Nei's D_A genetic distance for 15 STRs in four regional Japanese populations and a Korean population [2].

2.4. Constructing a phylogenetic tree

We calculated a Nei's D_A genetic distance with a Korean population [2] as an outer group, and constructed a tree based on the neighbor-joining method using neighbor-joining tree construction from allele frequency data (NJBAFD) software package.

3. Results and discussion

The allele frequencies at 15 STR loci were calculated in four regional Japanese populations. No significant deviations from HWE were observed using the three tests except a likelihood ratio test at D16S539 ($P=0.0335$) and homozygosity test at TPOX ($P=0.0217$) in Akita, a exact test at D18S51 ($P=0.0412$) in Oita, and homozygosity test at TH01 ($P=0.0117$) in Okinawa. However, these P-values are close to 0.05. The statistical properties for discriminating power in each population were also calculated. The allele frequency distributions were then compared pairwise and statistically, and the number of loci showing significant differences ($P<0.05$) were 5, 8, 4, 3, 1 and 2 between Akita and Okinawa, Nagoya and Okinawa, Oita and Okinawa, Akita and Oita, Nagoya and Oita, and Akita and Nagoya, respectively.

The neighbor-joining tree was constructed based on Nei's D_A genetic distance for 15 STRs in five populations including a Korean population [2] as an outer group (Fig. 1). Consequently, the genetic relationship in these five populations was very consistent with their geographical distribution. The genetic distances between the Okinawa population and the other Japanese populations were slightly farer than those between the Korean population and the other Japanese populations. The present study provides effective information to create a larger database in Japan, and on genetic relationships in/around Japan.

Acknowledgements

This work was supported in part by Grants-in-Aid for Scientific Research from the Ministry of Education, Culture, Sports, Science and Technology of Japan.

References

[1] M. Hashiyada, et al., Polymorphism of 17 STRs by multiplex analysis in Japanese population, Forensic Science International 133 (2003) 250–253.

[2] Y.-L. Kim, et al., Allele frequencies of 15 STR loci using AmpFlSTR Identifiler kit in a Korean population, Forensic Science International 136 (2003) 92–95.

International Congress Series 1261 (2004) 160–162

www.ics-elsevier.com

Extended polymorphism at STR-locus D5S818

M. Dülmer[a], L. Henke[a,*], M. Baur[b], R. Fimmers[b], E. Pick[a], J. Henke[a]

[a] *Institut fuer Blutgruppenforschung, Forensic Genetics, Hohenzollernring 57, 50501 Koeln, Germany*
[b] *Institut fuer Medizinische Biometrie, Informatik und Epidemiologie der Rheinischen Friedrich-Wilhelms-Universität, Bonn, Germany*

Abstract. The locus D8S818 was amplified as a singleplex with two different primer sets as well as part of the multiplexes AmpFlSTR Identifiler (Applied Biosystems (AB), Foster City, USA), AmpFlSTR Profiler Plus (AB), AmpFlSTR Profiler 1 (AB) and PowerPlex 16 (PP16) (Promega, Madison, USA). We observed typing discrepancies between Profiler 1, Identifiler and the singleplexes on the one hand, and PP16 on the other hand. These discrepancies led in two paternity cases to single parental exclusions due to reverse homozygosity. Sequencing results revealed three one base pair substitutions, one of them in the primer binding site of the PP16 primers. All persons who show the substitution in the primer binding site where of German origin and only the allele D5S818 *10var.4 was the carrier of the substitution.

Keywords: PCR; Short tandem repeat; Typing discrepancies; Primer binding site variation

1. Introduction

When employing PP16 in our routine parentage casework, we observed two single parental exclusions at D5S818 due to reverse homozygosity. Using the AB kits, both cases revealed an additional variant allele *10. To explore, if more individuals are false homozygotes, we reanalysed those persons tested homozygous at D5S818 with PP16 only so far.

2. Materials and methods

DNA samples from 2514 unrelated persons and their 1304 children were tested. One thousand and nine hundred seventy-eight out of 2514 person were Germans. Five hundred forty-nine out of 743 unrelated, presumably homozygous individuals typed with Power-Plex 16 could be reanalysed with at least 1 AB kit or D5S818 singleplex 1 amplification.

* Corresponding author. Hohenzollernring 57, d-50672 Koeln, Germany. Tel.: +49-221-253037; fax: +49-221-251247.
E-mail address: bgf.henke@t-online.de (L. Henke).

0531-5131/
doi:10.1016/j.ics.2003.12.091

Table 1
GenBank sequence of the D5S818 locus

Singlep.1	5′-gTgCTTTTTAgCCAAgTgATTCCAATCATAg CCACAgTTTA CAAC**A**TTT
Sequencing	5′-gTgCTTTTTAgCCAAgTgATTCCAATCATAg CCACAgTTTA CAAC**A**TTT
PP16	5′-AgCCACAgTTTACAACATTT
Singlep.1	gT ATCTTTATCT gTATCCTTAT TTATACCT**C**T (ATCT)10 TCAAAATATT
Sequencing	gT ATCTTTATCT gTATCCTTAT TTATACCT**C**T (ATCT)10 TCAAAATATT
PP16	gTATCTTTATCT gTATCCTTAT TTATACCT**C**T (ATCT)10 TCAAAATATT
Singlep.1	AC**A**TAAggAT ACCAAAgAgg AAAATCACCC TTgTCACATA CTTgCTATTA AA
Sequencing	AC**A**TAAggAT ACCAAAgAgg AAAATCACCC TTgTCACATA CTTgCTATTA AA
PP16	AC**A**TAAggAT ACCAAAgAgg AAAATCACC
Singlep.1	ATATACTT TTATTAgTAC AgATTATCTg ggACACCAC TTTAATTAgA AgCTTT
Sequencing	ATATACTT TTATTAgTAC AgATTATC

The primer positions are underlined. Bold bases are the positions of the SNPs.

The chosen primers for singleplex 1 included the DNA stretch of the PP16 kit primers. Primer sequences are shown in Table 1.

Amplifications were performed according to the kit conditions. The analyses were carried out by means of CE. The sequencing reaction was performed with the Big Dye Terminator Cycle Sequencing kit (AB) according to the manufacturers protocol and analysed on an ABI310 (AB).

3. Results

Fifteen out of 549 double tested samples showed an additional allele D5S818 *10. All 15 samples were of German origin. Sequencing results are shown in Table 2. We observed three SNPs at the locus D5S818. Transitions (A⇒G) were observed at positions 79105 and 79153, while a transversion (C⇒A) was found at position 79137. Considering the SNP positions, four different variants of allele D5S818 *10 were observed. *10 variant 4 displays the A⇒G transition in the primer binding site of the PP16 and is responsible for the failure of the amplification under the stringent conditions of the kit's environment.

Table 2
Sequencing results

Allele	Number of samples	Position		
		79105	79137	79153
AC008512	reference	A	C	A
Allele *13 variant 2	$n=1$	A	C	A
Allele *13 variant 3	$n=4$	A	C	G
Allele *12 variant 2	$n=1$	A	C	A
Allele *12 variant 3	$n=4$	A	C	G
Allele *11 variant 3	$n=2$	A	C	G
Allele *10 variant 1	$n=5$	A	A	G
Allele *10 variant 2	$n=1$	A	C	A
Allele *10 variant 3	$n=1$	A	C	G
Allele *10 variant 4	$n=6$	G	C	G
Allele *8 variant 1	$n=3$	A	A	G
Allele *8 variant 3	$n=3$	A	C	G

We calculated the frequency of the D5S818 *10 variant 4 in the German population ($n = 1978$). A proportional reduction of the number of heterozygous genotypes was necessary to reach an appropriate estimation of the frequency of allele *10 variant 4 since only 453 out of 574 German homozygous samples could be retyped. The frequency was calculated as 0.48% with an exact two-sided 95% confidence interval (0.269% and 0.791%).

4. Discussion

It has been shown in many previous reports [1–4] that the heterozygous genotypes were erroneously typed as homozygotes, because of variations (microheterogeneities) at primer binding sites. The striking difference of this report however is that the SNP that is associated with the failure to amplify an STR allele is in relative linkage disequilibrium of 1 with the allele D5S818 *10 variant 4. Moreover, we expect that the estimated frequency of the allele *10 is slightly higher than reported because apparently homozygous D5S818 (10) were not yet subjected to sequencing.

References

[1] C. Thacker, C.P. Phillip, D. Syndercombe Court, Comparison of two commercial multiplexes for use in small volume PCR reactions, Prog. Forensic Genet. 8 (2000) 470–472.

[2] C. Alves, A. Amorin, L. Gusmão, VWA STR genotyping: inconsistency between Perkin Elmers's profiler plus™ kit and promega's geneprint™ CTTV, Prog. Forensic Genet. 8 (2000) 467–469.

[3] S. Hering, J. Edelmann, J. Derßler, Sequence variation in the primer binding regions of the highly polymorphic STR system SE33, Int. J. Leg. Med. 116 (2002) 365–367.

[4] G.-R. Han, E.-S. Song, J.-J. Hwang, Non-amplification of an allele of the D8S1179 locus due to a point mutation, Int. J. Leg. Med. 115 (2001) 45–47.

International Congress Series 1261 (2004) 163–165

www.ics-elsevier.com

Genetic analysis of the short tandem repeat loci FGA, D7S820, D1S355, D9S304, D12S1090, D3S1744 and D18S849 in an Antioquia (Colombia) population sample

J.J. Builes[a,b,*], M.L.J. Bravo[a], J.D. Garcia[b], M.A. Moreno[a,b]

[a] *Paternity Testing, Laboratorio de Genética Forense y Huellas Digitales del DNA, GENES Ltda., Carrera 48 No. 10-45 Cons. 612, Medellín, Antioguia 1252, Colombia*
[b] *Instituto de Biología, Universidad de Antioquia, Medellín, Colombia*

Abstract. In this study, the validation of seven short tandem repeated (STR) systems is presented in a sample of the population from Antioquia, central region of Colombia. The DNA for the analyses of PCR was obtained from 261–450 unrelated individuals (selected using some cases of paternity from the Human Genetics Laboratory, University of Antioquia, and Laboratorio de Genética Forense y Huellas Digitales del DNA, GENES). PCR amplification was performed according to the manufacturer's instructions, using the STR Multiplex I (FGA, D7S820, D1S355 and D9S304) and STR Multiplex II (D12S1090, D3S1744 and D18S849) kits (Lifecodes, Stanford, CT). The seven loci met the Hardy–Weinberg expectations, and they possess a combined power discrimination higher than 0.999999999 and a combined power exclusion similar to 0.9996, showing them to be a group of excellent markers as complement in paternity testing in the identification of individuals and in forensic applications in general.

Keywords: Antioquia; Colombia; Population; DNA; STR

1. Introduction

Short tandem repeats (STR) are polymorphic markers widely distributed throughout the human genome [1], and they can be PCR amplificated, but only some of them have been studied for use in forensic genetic and paternity testing. The general criteria for selecting STRs include characteristics such as high heterozygosity, low stutter, few and low extra-peaks, robustness, easy multiplexing and a low mutation rate [2].

The aim of this study was to report allele frequency distributions for the FGA, D7S820, D1S355, D9S304, D12S1090, D3S1744 and D18S849 loci in a sample of the population from Antioquia, a central region of Colombia [3–5], as well as statistical evaluations,

* Corresponding author. Paternity Testing, Laboratorio de Genética Forense y Huellas Digitales del DNA, GENES Ltda. Carrera 48 No. 10-45 Cons. 612, Medellín, Antioguia 1252, Colombia. Tel.: +57-4-2684875; fax: +57-4-3185270.

E-mail address: genforense@epm.net.co (J.J. Builes).

0531-5131/
doi:10.1016/S0531-5131(03)01534-6

Table 1
Allele frequencies and statistical parameters

Allele	FGA	D7S820	D1S355	D9S304	D12S1090	D3S1744	D18S849
4				0.04441			
5				0.00987	0.00114		
6		0.00299		0.01316			
7		0.01045	0.01724	0.01151			0.00118
8		0.13284	0.07471	0.30757		0.00117	0.00118
9		0.11045	0.08238	0.11349	0.06023		0.00353
10		0.31045	0.05556	0.07566	0.01591	0.00233	0.00118
11		0.28209	0.09387	0.09211	0.05568	0.00233	0.00471
12		0.12687	0.20498	0.22039	0.04659	0.00233	0.00471
13		0.02388	0.26437	0.07895	0.03750	0.00117	0.00471
14	0.00299		0.13027	0.02796	0.03977	0.00117	0.03882
15			0.06897	0.00164	0.01818	0.07925	0.16706
16	0.00149		0.00766	0.00164	0.00227	0.08741	0.45412
17	0.00149			0.00164	0.00455	0.14336	0.23176
18	0.02090				0.01250	0.37646	0.07882
19	0.07313				0.03864	0.14802	0.00824
20	0.09403				0.07955	0.11305	
21	0.15672				0.06477	0.03613	
22	0.10448				0.12614	0.00350	
23	0.12687				0.08977		
24	0.16269				0.05341		
25	0.13433				0.06818	0.00233	
26	0.08806				0.08068		
27	0.02388				0.06705		
28	0.00448				0.01250		
29	0.00488				0.00795		
30					0.00909		
31					0.00682		
32					0.00114		
Minimum	0.0097	0.0088	0.0116	0.0099	0.0080	0.0067	0.0064
n	670	670	522	608	880	896	900
Parameters							
Ho	0.886567	0.785075	0.823755	0.809211	0.938636	0.781250	0.724444
He	0.882230	0.778582	0.843360	0.821696	0.933566	0.787458	0.708671
HWE-H	0.6224	0.7294	0.7336	0.7254	0.2943	0.9968	0.2928
Exact test	0.5252	0.5956	0.3252	0.0635	0.3970	0.0747	0.0968
PD	0.9717	0.9141	0.9578	0.9464	0.9893	0.9261	0.8690
PE	0.7681	0.5716	0.6438	0.6162	0.8748	0.5647	0.4671
MP	0.0283	0.0859	0.0422	0.0536	0.0107	0.0739	0.1310
PIC	0.8689	0.7442	0.8238	0.7997	0.9285	0.7627	0.6669
TPI	4.44079	2.3264	2.8370	2.6207	8.1481	2.2857	1.8145

n: Allele number, Ho: heterozygosity observed, He: heterozygosity expected, HWE-H: Hardy–Weinberg test, PD: power of discrimination, PE: power of exclusion, MP: matching probability, PIC: polymorphism information content, TPI: Typical Paternity Index.

including the possible divergence from Hardy–Weinberg expectations and other forensic parameters of interest.

2. Material and methods

Samples were obtained from 261 to 450 unrelated Caucasian individuals from Antioquia with a similar proportion of male and females. Genomic DNA was extracted by a salt precipitation extraction procedure [6]. PCR amplification was performed according to the manufacturer's directions, using the STR Multiplex I (FGA, D7S820, D1S355 and D9S304) and STR Multiplex II (D12S1090, D3S1744 and D18S849) kits (Lifecodes, Stanford, CT).

The frequency of each allele for each locus tested was calculated from the number of observed genotypes in the sample using GENEPOP software Ver. 3.2a [7]. The exact test for the Hardy–Weinberg equilibrium and linkage disequilibrium between loci was carried out by using the GENEPOP Ver. 3.2a [7] and the GDA Ver. 1.0 software. The forensic parameters were performed using the POWERSTAS software Ver. 12 (Promega) and GDA software Ver. 1.0 [8].

3. Results and discussion

Antioquia population data for the seven STRs are shown in Table 1. No deviations from the Hardy–Weinberg equilibrium were observed for all markers in the studied population. On the other hand, Antioquia population showed a similar allele distribution with other Caucasian European populations. This confirms the findings of past research about high Caucasian component of the Antioquia population [3,5,6].

The seven loci met the Hardy–Weinberg expectations. The combined power discrimination was > 0.999999999 and the combined power exclusion was similar to 0.9996.

In conclusion, a database of Caucasian population from Antioquia has been established for the analyzed systems. The results show that all seven loci are very useful for personal identification and paternity testing in the Antioquia population.

Acknowledgements

This work was supported by GENES Ltda. Juan José Builes has a PhD fellowship (0058/2001) from COLCIENCIAS.

References

[1] J.S. Beckman, J.L. Weber, Genomics 12 (1992) 627–631.
[2] M.V. Lareu, S. Barral, A. Salas, M. Rodríguez, C. Pestoni, A. Carracedo, in: G.F. Senasabaugh, P.J. Lincoln, B. Olaisen (Eds.), Progress in Forensic Genetics, vol. 7, Elsevier, Amsterdam, 2000, pp. 198–200.
[3] M.L. Bravo, C.Y. Valenzuela, O.M. Arcos-Burgos, Gene Geogr. 10 (1996) 11–17.
[4] L.G. Carvajal-Carmona, I.D. Soto, N. Pineda, D. Ortiz-Barrientos, C. Duque, J. Ospina-Duque, M. MacCarthy, P. Montoya, V.M. Alvarez, G. Bedoya, A. Ruiz-Linares, Am. J. Hum. Genet. 67 (2000) 1287–1295.
[5] J.J. Parsons, Berkeley: University of California Press, 1949.
[6] S.A. Miller, D.D. Dykes, H.F. Polesky, Nucleic Acids Res. 16 (1988) 1215.
[7] M. Raymond, F. Rousset, J. Heredity 86 (1995) 248–249.
[8] P.O. Lewis, D. Zaykin, 2001. Free program distributed by the authors over the Internet from http://lewis.eeb.uconn.edu/lewishome/software.html.

International Congress Series 1261 (2004) 166–168

www.ics-elsevier.com

Genetic profile of the Ecuadorian Black population (Ecuador–South America) by using the Power Plex® 16 system kit

Fabricio González-Andrade[a,*], Dora Sánchez de González[a], Begoña Martínez-Jarreta[b]

[a] *Molecular Genetics Department, Metropolitan Hospital, Av. Mariana de Jesus y Occidental, Meditropoli Medical Center, Service of Genetics, Cruz Roja Ecuatoriana, Quito 2119, Ecuador*

[b] *Department of Legal Medicine, University of Zaragoza, Spain*

Abstract. Allele frequency data for the 15 STR systems and Amelogenine were determined in a population sample of healthy Black unrelated individuals. All loci met Hardy–Weinberg expectations and the high discrimination power of combined system showed the forensic efficiency of these genetic markers. There is a lack of information on Ecuadorian population from a genetic point of view and therefore no previous publications on the distribution of STRs on Black population is available. Blackas are descendents of slaves procedentes of Africa. © 2004 Published by Elsevier B.V.

Keywords: Ecuador; STRs; Forensic genetics; Population data; Black population; Power Plex 16

Population sample: Whole blood was obtained in EDTA vacutainers tubes by venipuncture from healthy unrelated Black born and living in Ecuador. Samples came from the Paternity Test Bank of the Cruz Roja Ecuatoriana, Genetics Laboratory [1]. *DNA extraction*: The DNA was extracted using Wizard Genomic DNA Purification Kit System© (Promega, Madison, WI, USA) and the quantity was estimated by UV absorbance (Gene Quant Calculator©, Pharmacia, Uppsala, Sweden). *PCR*: Amplification was performed in a Techne Thermal Cycler, model Genius© following the manufacturer's recommendations [2]. *Typing*: By ABI Prism 310. Fragment size and allele designation of different loci were determined by comparison with allelic ladders distributed into the kit PowerPlex 16 (Promega) [2]. The recommendations of the DNA Commission of the International Society of Forensic Haemogenetics for analysis of STRs systems were followed [3,4]. *Analysis of data*: See Tables 1 and 2. Evaluation of Hardy–Weinberg expectations was

* Corresponding author. Tel./fax: +593-2-2248902.

E-mail address: fabriciogonzalez@usa.net (F. González-Andrade).

0531-5131/ © 2004 Published by Elsevier B.V.
doi:10.1016/S0531-5131(03)01828-4

Table 1
Allele distribution of 15 STR loci and Amelogenine in a population sample of Ecuadorian Black population ($n = 104$)

Allele	PENTA E	D3S1358	FGA	D18S51	D21S11	PENTA D	VWA	D8S1179	D7S820	D13S317	D5S818	D16S539	TH01	CSF1PO	TPOX
2.2	–	–	–	–	–	0.089	–	–	–	–	–	–	–	–	–
3.2	–	–	–	–	–	0.005	–	–	–	–	–	–	–	–	–
5	0.056	–	–	–	–	0.033	–	–	–	–	–	0.009	–	–	–
6	–	–	–	–	–	–	–	–	–	–	–	–	0.257	–	0.037
6.3	–	–	–	–	–	–	–	–	–	–	–	–	0.005	–	–
7	0.093	–	–	–	–	0.047	–	–	–	–	0.014	0.005	0.383	0.037	0.005
8	0.136	–	–	–	–	0.117	–	–	0.145	0.037	0.019	0.009	0.145	0.047	0.421
9	0.037	–	–	–	–	0.136	–	0.005	0.089	0.145	0.061	0.201	0.084	0.042	0.154
9.3	–	–	–	–	–	–	–	–	–	–	–	–	0.117	–	–
10	0.028	–	–	–	–	0.201	0.005	0.023	0.304	0.051	0.051	0.126	0.009	0.266	0.070
11	0.070	–	–	0.005	–	0.145	0.009	0.028	0.238	0.271	0.313	0.327	–	0.257	0.234
12	0.107	0.005	–	0.047	–	0.075	–	0.103	0.192	0.290	0.294	0.168	–	0.299	0.079
13	0.089	0.005	–	0.056	–	0.103	0.019	0.332	0.033	0.159	0.229	0.131	–	0.042	–
13.2				0.009											
14	0.070	0.061	–	0.136	–	0.037	0.033	0.304	0.001	0.047	0.014	0.023	–	0.005	–
15	0.126	0.364	–	0.164	–	0.014	0.173	0.182	–	–	–	–	–	–	–
16	0.061	0.336	–	0.154	–	–	0.271	0.019	–	–	0.005	–	–	–	–
17	0.033	0.168	–	0.178	–	–	0.276	–	–	–	–	–	–	0.005	–
18	0.042	0.051	0.005	0.112	–	–	0.112	–	–	–	–	–	–	–	–
18.2			0.019	–											
19	0.014	0.009	0.070	0.070	–	–	0.084	–	–	–	–	–	–	–	–
19.2	–	–	0.005	–	–	–	–	–	–	–	–	–	–	–	–
20	0.019	–	0.089	0.037	–	–	0.019	–	–	–	–	–	–	–	–
21	0.014	–	0.098	0.014	–	–	–	–	–	–	–	–	–	–	–
22	0.005	–	0.159	–	–	–	–	–	–	–	–	–	–	–	–
23	–	–	0.140	0.014	–	–	–	–	–	–	–	–	–	–	–
24	–	–	0.107	–	–	–	–	0.005	–	–	–	–	–	–	–
24.2	–	–	0.005	–	–	–	–	–	–	–	–	–	–	–	–
25	–	–	0.117	–	–	–	–	–	–	–	–	–	–	–	–
26	–	–	0.107	–	–	–	–	–	–	–	–	–	–	–	–
27	–	–	0.051	–	0.037	–	–	–	–	–	–	–	–	–	–
28	–	–	0.019	–	0.159	–	–	–	–	–	–	–	–	–	–
28.2	–	–	–	–	0.005	–	–	–	–	–	–	–	–	–	–
29	–	–	0.009	–	0.159	–	–	–	–	–	–	–	–	–	–
30	–	–	–	–	0.257	–	–	–	–	–	–	–	–	–	–
30.2	–	–	–	–	0.037	–	–	–	–	–	–	–	–	–	–
31	–	–	–	–	0.098	–	–	–	–	–	–	–	–	–	–
31.2	–	–	–	–	0.107	–	–	–	–	–	–	–	–	–	–
32	–	–	–	–	0.014	–	–	–	–	–	–	–	–	–	–
32.2	–	–	–	–	0.065	–	–	–	–	–	–	–	–	–	–
33	–	–	–	–	0.014	–	–	–	–	–	–	–	–	–	–
33.2	–	–	–	–	0.023	–	–	–	–	–	–	–	–	–	–
34	–	–	–	–	0.009	–	–	–	–	–	–	–	–	–	–
34.2	–	–	–	–	0.005	–	–	–	–	–	–	–	–	–	–
35	–	–	–	–	0.009	–	–	–	–	–	–	–	–	–	–
P (exact-test)	1.0000	0.4798	0.7260	0.6590	0.4532	0.2368	0.9942	0.6914	0.7994	0.2482	0.4308	0.5976	0.2900	0.4780	0.5060
P (chi-square-test)	0.9976	0.6246	0.1506	0.5794	0.3662	0.1282	0.9790	0.1706	0.7551	0.3376	0.2620	0.6930	0.3838	0.2780	0.5408
P (G-test)	0.9998	0.6638	0.7710	0.8184	0.4754	0.2416	0.9800	0.6904	0.9142	0.2728	0.4734	0.5588	0.5026	0.6324	0.3386

Table 2
Forensic value of the analysed systems expressed as various statistical parameters

STR locus	MEC	MEP	PIC	Pm	PD
D3S1358	0.4794	0.4640	0.6716	0.1221	0.8778
HUMTHO1	0.5240	0.5077	0.7070	0.1106	0.8893
D21S11	0.7128	0.7108	0.8386	0.0453	0.9546
D18S51	0.7426	0.7526	0.8620	0.0340	0.9659
PENTA E	0.8280	0.8351	0.9088	0.0186	0.9814
D5S818	0.5333	0.5258	0.7160	0.1026	0.8973
D13S317	0.5923	0.5877	0.7596	0.0800	0.9199
D7S820	0.5779	0.5779	0.7513	0.0820	0.9179
D16S539	0.5942	0.5884	0.7611	0.0783	0.9216
CSF1PO	0.5509	0.5445	0.7292	0.0958	0.9041
PRNTA D	0.7538	0.7584	0.8655	0.0374	0.9625
HUMVWA	0.6094	0.6043	0.7710	0.0717	0.9282
D8S1179	0.5297	0.5195	0.7125	0.1050	0.8949
HUMTPOX	0.5140	0.4853	0.6952	0.1131	0.8868
FGA	0.7815	0.7885	0.8825	0.0275	0.9724

carried out using the exact test and determination of further statistical parameters of forensic interest was carried out by using the computer programme HWE-analysis version 3.3, as previously described [5]. *Other remarks*: Ecuador is a small South American country with almost 12 million inhabitants comprised of three main ethnic groups: (a) Urban populations, usually dihybrid Mestizos or trihybrid and (b) Amerindian natives, more than 100 multiethnic and pluricultural groups, and (c) African-derived populations in fairly isolated communities and descendants of slaves [6,7].

References

[1] F. González-Andrade, et al., Evaluation of 1495 cases of disputed paternity in Ecuador (South America) resolved with STR-PCR polymorphisms, Proceedings of International Association of Forensic Sciences, Monduzzi Ed., 2002, pp. 225–230.

[2] Promega, Gene Print™ STR Systems for Silver Stain Detection, 1998, TMD. No. 004.

[3] International Society for Forensic Haemogenetics, Recommendations of the DNA Commission of the International Society for Forensic Haemogenetics relating to the use of PCR-based polymorphisms, Forensic Sci. Int. 55 (1) (1992 Jul) 1–3.

[4] W. Bär, et al., DNA recommendations. Further report of the DNA commission of the ISFH regarding the use of short tandem repeat systems, Forensic Sci. Int. 87 (3) (1997 Jun 23) 181–184.

[5] B. Martínez-Jarreta, et al., Genetic variation at six STR loci (CTT, FFV) in Aragon (North Spain), Forensic Sci. Int. 100 (1–2) (1999) 87–92.

[6] D. Sánchez, Human identification in Ecuador, in: C. Cerón (Ed.), Memories of 22th Symposium of Biology in Ecuador, Central University of Ecuador, 1998, pp. 79–80.

[7] M. Sáns, Admixture studies in Latin America: from the 20th century to the 21th century, Hum. Biol. 72 (1) (2000) 155–177.

International Congress Series 1261 (2004) 169–172

www.ics-elsevier.com

Genetic study on 10 STR loci in the Romanian population

Ligia Elena Barbarii[a,*], Burkhard Rolf[b], Petre Calistru[c], Dan Dermengiu[c]

[a] *Laboratory of Genetics, National Institute of Legal Medicine "Mina Minovici", 9 Vitan-Barzesti, 75669 Bucharest, Romania*

[b] *Institute of Legal Medicine, Ludwig-Maximilians-University, Munich, Frauenlobstr. 7a, D-80337 Munich, Germany*

[c] *University of Medicine and Pharmacy "Carol Davila", 1 Eroii Sanitari, sector 6, Bucharest, Romania*

Abstract. A population study on 10 tetrameric STR loci (D3S1358, VWA, D8S1179, D21S11, D18S51, D16S539, D2S1338, D19S433, THO1 and FGA) was performed on 104 unrelated individuals from Romania (Bucharest area), by mean of multiplex PCR (AmpFl STR SGM plus) and capillary electrophoresis. The allele frequencies and the usual forensic statistical parameters were defined. A brief comparison of the allele frequency distributions with other available data from European populations is presented. All the analyzed loci met Hardy–Weinberg equilibrium expectations. The high discrimination and exclusion power of the combined system showed the forensic efficiency of these 10 genetic markers. The study is considered to be very useful for paternal lineage testing and identification purposes in current forensic practice with Romanian individuals.

Keywords: Short tandem repeats; Romanian population; Genetic polymorphisms

1. Introduction

Polymorphic STR loci are intensively used as markers for personal identification and paternity testing. The scientific forensic genetic community is interested in compiling STRs data in different populations in order to establish the ethnic and geographic allele frequency distributions needed for the forensic casework. Extensive population studies were carried out on STRs in various European countries [1]. Only limited data on STR markers in Romanian population is available in the literature so far [2,3]. Therefore, the purpose of this study is to deliver population genetic data on 10 STR loci regarding the Romanian population. For this purpose, a population sample of 104 unrelated individuals from Romania was selected to be genotyped in a joint research project.

* Corresponding author. Tel./fax: +40-21-3346260.
E-mail address: genetica@legmed.ro (L.E. Barbarii).

0531-5131/
doi:10.1016/j.ics.2003.12.106

Table 1
The allele frequencies, statistical parameters and the HWE analysis for 10 STR loci in the Romanian population sample (Bucharest area) (N = 104 individuals)

Locus alleles	TH01 (N = 104)	D16S359 (N = 104)	D8S1179 (N = 104)	D18S51 (N = 104)	D19S433 (N = 104)	VWA (N = 104)	D3S1358 (N = 104)	D2S1338 (N = 104)	FGA (N = 104)	D21S11 (N = 104)
5	0.005	–	–	–	–	–	–	–	–	–
6	0.264	–	–	–	–	–	–	–	–	–
7	0.149	–	–	–	–	–	–	–	–	–
8	0.125	0.019	0.024	–	–	–	–	–	–	–
9	0.144	0.139	0.014	–	–	–	–	–	–	–
9.3	0.308	–	–	–	–	–	–	–	–	–
10	0.005	0.077	0.053	0.005	–	–	–	–	–	–
11	–	0.284	0.087	0.010	0.014	–	–	–	–	–
12	–	0.322	0.139	0.135	0.115	–	–	–	–	–
13	–	0.120	0.356	0.159	0.197	0.005	–	–	–	–
13.2	–	–	–	–	0.019	–	–	–	–	–
14	–	0.038	0.197	0.115	0.317	0.144	0.125	–	–	–
14.2	–	–	–	–	0.029	–	–	–	–	–
15	–	–	0.087	0.154	0.120	0.106	0.245	–	–	–
15.2	–	–	–	–	0.058	–	–	–	–	–
16	–	–	0.038	0.163	0.063	0.183	0.231	0.034		–
16.2	–	–	–	–	0.053	–	–	–	–	–
17	–	–	0.005	0.125	–	0.274	0.188	0.245	–	–
17.2	–	–	–	–	0.005	–	–	–	–	–
18	–	–	–	0.053	0.005	0.216	0.192	0.101	0.019	–
18.2	–	–	–	–	0.005	–	–	–	–	–
19	–	–	–	0.019	–	0.053	0.019	0.125	0.082	–
20	–	–	–	0.019	–	0.019	–	0.135	0.091	–
21	–	–	–	0.024	–	–	–	0.034	0.192	–
22	–	–	–	0.010	–	–	–	0.014	0.192	–
22.2	–	–	–	–	–	–	–	–	0.014	–
23	–	–	–	0.010	–	–	–	0.111	0.125	–
23.2	–	–	–	–	–	–	–	–	0.029	–
24	–	–	–	–	–	–	–	0.111	0.149	–
24.2	–	–	–	–	–	–	–	–	0.005	–
25	–	–	–	–	–	–	–	0.063	0.067	–
26	–	–	–	–	–	–	–	0.029	0.019	–
27	–	–	–	–	–	–	–	–	0.014	0.029
28	–	–	–	–	–	–	–	–	–	0.106
29	–	–	–	–	–	–	–	–	–	0.221
30	–	–	–	–	–	–	–	–	–	0.188
30.2	–	–	–	–	–	–	–	–	–	0.072
31	–	–	–	–	–	–	–	–	–	0.038
31.2	–	–	–	–	–	–	–	–	–	0.106
32	–	–	–	–	–	–	–	–	–	0.024
32.2	–	–	–	–	–	–	–	–	–	0.154
33.2	–	–	–	–	–	–	–	–	–	0.063
Hobs	0.807	0.837	0.798	0.865	0.865	0.760	0.865	0.789	0.846	0.875
Hexp	0.781	0.778	0.799	0.877	0.825	0.814	0.802	0.869	0.871	0.862
MEC	0.564	0.568	0.616	0.743	0.659	0.623	0.597	0.731	0.733	0.716
MEP	0.563	0.559	0.597	0.749	0.647	0.624	0.603	0.732	0.736	0.719
PIC	0.742	0.741	0.771	0.859	0.801	0.783	0.767	0.850	0.852	0.842
PM	0.093	0.095	0.071	0.039	0.061	0.064	0.087	0.043	0.040	0.042
D	0.907	0.905	0.929	0.961	0.939	0.936	0.913	0.957	0.960	0.958
HWE test (p-values)										
Exact test	0.700	0.766	0.821	0.251	0.709	0.824	0.630	0.242	0.267	0.940

Hobs (observed heterozygosity), Hexp (expected heterozygosity), (MEC) mean exclusion chance, (MEP) mean paternity exclusion probability, (PIC) polymorphism information content, (PM) match probability, (D) discrimination power, probability values p (Hardy – Weinberg equilibrium exact test based on 5000 shuffling).

2. Material and methods

Whole EDTA blood samples was collected from 104 unrelated Romanian individuals, randomly selected among the patients of a Bucharest hospital. Appropriate informed consent was obtained from the participants. Members of the Romanian minorities (Hungarians, Germans, Gypsies, etc.) were excluded from the study.

DNA was Chelex-extracted from peripheral blood samples as previously described by Ref. [4]. Amplification was carried out using about 1 ng of template DNA in a final volume of 12.5 μl containing 1 μl of Chelex extract. All the samples have been typed for a set of 10 STR autosomal loci loci D3S1358, VWA, D8S1179, D21S11, D18S51, D16S539, D2S1338, D19S433, THO1 using an AmpFlSTR SGM plus system kit (Applied Biosystems), according to the manufacturer's recommendations. The PCR products were separated by capillary electrophoresis on ABI PRISM 310 Genetic Analyzer (Applied Biosystems) and data were analyzed using Genotyper® 2.5 software (Applied Biosystems) with the template included in the kit. The alleles were labeled according to the international nomenclature [5].

The allele frequencies were calculated from each genotype in the sample set. The statistical parameters of forensic importance (observed and expected heterozygosity, mean paternity exclusion chance, mean exclusion probability, polymorphism information content, discrimination power) and the Hardy–Weinberg equilibrium were investigated using a HWE-analysis software package (HWE-Analysis, Version 3.2 developed by Christoph Puers, Institute of Legal Medicine, University of Muenster, Germany).

3. Results and discussion

The allele frequencies and the statistical inferences for each of the investigated STR loci are shown in Table 1. The overall discrimination power was 0.999997 and the combined power of exclusion for the set of 10 STR loci reached 0.99991. Table 1 summarizes the testing results for the correspondence of genotype frequencies with the Hardy–Weinberg equilibrium proportions. No deviations from the Hardy–Weinberg equilibrium were observed (p>0.05 based on 5000 shuffling).

4. Conclusions

A reference database for the Romanian population has been established for a set of 10 STR loci. The results of this population study are very useful in current forensic practice with Romanian individuals in order to estimate the frequency of DNA profiles in casework as well as in paternity testing. The scientific data can also be of great interest for interpopulation comparisons.

Acknowledgements

The samples were obtained with the help of the medical team from the "Victor Babes" Hospital in Bucharest. Ms. Cornelia Iosef who coordinated the sampling procedures is gratefully acknowledged.

References

[1] www.uni-duesseldorf.de/WWW/MedFak/Serology.
[2] W. Huckenbeck, et al., Population genetic studies in the Balkans: II. DNA–STR-systems, Anthropol. Anz. 59 (2001) 213–225.
[3] C. Anghel, et al., Population genetic study of eight short tandem repeat loci CSF1PO, TPOX, TH01, F13A01, FESFPS, vWA, F13B and LPL in the Western Romanian population, Forensic Sci. Int. 131 (2003) 218–219.
[4] P.S. Walsh, et al., Chelex 100 as a medium for simple extraction of DNA for PCR-based typing from forensic material, BioTechniques 10 (1991) 506–513.
[5] W. Bar, et al., DNA recommendations: further report of the DNA Commission of the ISFH regarding the use of short tandem repeat systems, Int. J. Leg. Med. 110 (1997) 175–176.

International Congress Series 1261 (2004) 173–175

www.ics-elsevier.com

Genetic variation at autosomal and Y-chromosome STRs, and HVRI mtDNA in Ibiza population

C. Tomàs, G. Jiménez, A. Picornell, J.A. Castro, M.M. Ramon*

Laboratori de Genètica, Departament de Biología, Universitat de les Illes Balears, Cra Valldemossa, km 7.5, 07122-Palma de Mallorca, Balears, Spain

Abstract. We have analyzed nine autosomal and eight Y-chromosome STR loci, as well as the sequencing of the HVRI mtDNA in a sample from the Ibizan population. Differences between Ibiza and the other islands of the Balearic Archipelago have been detected, especially in the origins of the founder settlements. The mtDNA and autosomal STRs diversities evidence the differentiation, but the Y-chromosome polymorphism did not show clear differences between Ibiza and the other islands.

Keywords: Ibiza population; HVRI mtDNA; Autosomal STRs; Y-chromosome minimal haplotype

1. Introduction

The Balearic Archipelago is located in the western Mediterranean Sea, near the eastern coast of the Iberian Peninsula. It is composed of three major islands, Majorca, Minorca and Ibiza. Due to their geographic position in the Mediterranean Sea, the Balearic Islands have been settled by people of different populations throughout their history. This fact has moulded the genetic structure of the human population of the archipelago. Differences between Ibiza and the other two main islands, Majorca and Minorca, can be found, especially in the origins of the founder settlements [1]. Although there is evidence that Majorca and Minorca were first settled about 4000 B.C. (the "talaiotic"-stone builder-culture), there is no clear proofs of settlements on Ibiza until the arrival of the Carthaginians in 654 B.C. They remained in Ibiza for at least five centuries and were not restricted to coastal areas but also colonized the interior of the island. Ibiza was annexed, but never occupied by Romans. During its history, the human population of Ibiza has been remained isolated and, thus, received little gene flow from outside. This apparent reproductive isolation was disturbed by a 1970s tourist influx that doubled the total population of the island.

The aims of the present study were: to measure the genetic differentiation of the Ibiza population from the other Balearic islands based on the analysis of autosomal and

* Corresponding author. Tel.: +34-971-173152; fax: 34-971-173184.
E-mail address: cori.ramon@uib.es (M.M. Ramon).

0531-5131/ © 2003 Published by Elsevier B.V.
doi:10.1016/S0531-5131(03)01644-3

Y-chromosome microsatellites, and the comparative analyses between Y-specific markers and mtDNA sequence data on the same individuals, that allow us to study possible differences in male versus female contribution patterns.

2. Materials and methods

We have obtained blood samples from 102 individuals of the autochthonous population from Ibiza Island. DNA was organically extracted following a standard protocol. Autosomal STRs: PCR amplification of the tetrameric STR systems D3S1358, vWA, FGA, D8S1179, D21S11, D18S51, D5S818, D13S317 and D7S820 was achieved in a GeneAmp PCR System 2400 (Perkin-Elmer). Y-chromosome markers: Eight microsatellites (DYS19, DYS389I, DYS389II, DYS390, DYS391, DYS392, DYS393, DYS385) and the Y-*Alu* polymorphism at the DYS287 locus were analyzed by means of manual analysis of the poliacrilamide gels and automatic analysis (ABI 310, Perkin Elmer). Mitochondrial DNA data were obtained from a previous work [2]. The statistical analyses were mainly performed using the Arlequin software [3].

3. Results

3.1. Autosomal polymorphism

It was described a total of 71 alleles for the 9 autosomal markers studied: 6 at D3S1358, 7 at vWA, D5S818 and D13S317, 9 at D8S1179, 10 at D211S11, 12 at FGA and 13 at D18S51. As indicated in Table 1, a high level of variability was found (79.9%). No single locus evidenced a departure from HWE. The most significant markers, in terms of genetic differentiation, were D18S51, FGA, D7S820, D21S11, D8S1179 and D13S317.

3.2. Y-chromosome variation

We analysed 45 paternally unrelated male samples from Ibiza for minimal Ychromosome haplotype. We obtained 35 distinct Y-chromosome haplotype configurations. The most frequent haplotype 14-10-17-24–11-13-13-11.14 (DYS19-DYS2389I-DYS2389II-DYS390-DYS391-DYS392-DYS393) was found in four individuals, 27 were observed in unique copies and seven haplotypes were shared by two individuals. Haplotype diversity was estimated at 0.987 ± 0.008 (Table 1).

Table 1
Genetic diversity parameters in Balearic Archipelago

Population	Autosomal STRs			Y-chromosome STRs			mtDNA		
	Number of alleles	Observed heterozigosity	PD[a]	Gene diversity	Haplotype diversity	PD[a]	Haplotype diversity	Haplogroup diversity	PD[a]
Ibiza	8–9	0.797	>0.999	0.415	0.987	0.778	0.938	0.811	0.380
Majorca	9–10	0.800	>0.999	0.459	0.988	0.824	0.957	0.870	0.689
Minorca	8–9	0.822	>0.999	0.473	0.984	0.868	0.987	0.902	0.761

[a] PD = power of discrimination.

3.3. mtDNA variation

With respect to mtDNA [2], Ibiza showed 19 different haplotypes, 26 polymorphic sites and 3.8 pairwise differences. Ten different haplogroups were represented, with a low (0.811) haplogroup diversity. In contrast with the other Balearic populations, haplogroup T (original from the Near East) was well represented in this population. The African haplogroup L was also detected.

It is highly significant the low diversity that shows Ibiza, especially in the case of mtDNA (Table 1). The correlation between the different markers elaborated by means of Mantel test was high significant between mtDNA and STR, but not significant between Y-chromosome and STR and Y-chromosome and mtDNA. The mtDNA and autosomal STRs evidence the differentiation, but Y-chromosome polymorphisms did not show clear differences between Ibiza and the other islands.

References

[1] A. Picornell, A. Miguel, J.A. Castro, M.M. Ramon, R. Arya, M.H. Crawford, Genetic variation in the population of Ibiza (Spain): genetic structure, geography and language, Hum. Biol. 68 (6) (1996) 899–913.

[2] A. Picornell, L. Gómez-Barbeito, C. Tomàs, J.A. Castro, M.M. Ramon, Mitochondrial DNA HVRI Variation in the Balearic Populations, Am. J. Phys. Anthropol. (2003) (in press).

[3] S. Schneider, D. Roessli, L. Scoffier, ARLEQUIN ver. 2000. A Software for Population Genetics Data Analysis, Genetics and Biometry Laboratory, University of Geneva, Switzerland.

International Congress Series 1261 (2004) 176–178

www.ics-elsevier.com

Genotyping inconsistencies and null alleles using AmpFLSTR® Identifiler® and Powerplex® 16 kits

A. Amorim[a,b,*], C. Alves[a], L. Pereira[a], L. Gusmão[a]

[a] *Population Genetics, IPATIMUP (Instituto de Patologia e Imunologia Molecular da Universidade do Porto), R. Roberto Frias s/n, 4200-465, Oporto, Portugal*

[b] *Faculdade de Ciências da Universidade do Porto, Oporto, Portugal*

Abstract. Forensic genetic analyses use more and more commercially available genotyping kits such as AmpFLSTR Identifiler and Powerplex 16. Since they share many STRs, but do not use the same primers, genotyping inconsistencies can arise due to polymorphisms in the primers' annealing sequences. Indeed, if one primer does not match the target sequence, the result will be an allelic dropout and consequently one individual will be classified as homozygous with one kit and heterozygous with the other. Moreover, both can fail to anneal and then null alleles will be only detectable through mother/child or family analyses. We report: (a) the inconsistencies between the above referred kits (a primer concordance study) observed after the extensive genotyping of various population samples (mainly from Portugal and Mozambique) as well as (b) apparent opposite homozygosities in mother/child pairs using both kits. A total of 22 inconsistencies between kits was observed (for D5S818, D8S1179, D16S539, FGA and VWA). Only one mother/child incompatibility was detected out of 769 pairs when using both kits, at D5S818 (12/13), but also attributable to a one-step mutation. It is safe to conclude that the combined use of both kits practically eliminates this source of problem in kinship evaluation and databasing.

Keywords: STR; Primer concordance; Null alleles; PCR

1. Introduction

Forensic genetic analyses, namely kinship and identification, are relying more and more on commercially available genotyping kits such as the AmpFLSTR Identifiler (Applied Biosystems), which includes the STRs CSF1PO, D2S1338, D3S1358, D5S818, D7S820, D8S1179, D13S317, D16S539, D18S51, D19S433, D21S11, FGA, TH01, TPO and VWA; and Powerplex 16 (Promega), with D3S1358, D5S818, D7S820, D8S1179, D13S317, D16S539, D18S51, D21S11, CSF1PO, FGA, Penta D, Penta E, TH01, TPO and VWA.

* Corresponding author. Tel.: +351-225570700; fax: +351-225570799.
E-mail address: aamorim@ipatimup.pt (A. Amorim).

0531-5131/
doi:10.1016/S0531-5131(03)01496-1

Table 1
Observed genotype inconsistencies between AmpFLSTR Identifiler and Powerplex 16 kits

STR	Identifiler	Powerplex	Number of cases	STR	Identifiler	Powerplex	Number of cases
D5S818	11–12	12	1	D16S539	9–11	9	2
	10–12	12	3		10–11	10	2
	10–13	13	1	VWA	16	16–18	2
	12	12–13	1		16	16–19	1
	10–11	11	3		16	16–17	1
	9–11	9	1		18	16–18	1
D8S1179	14	14–16	1		18	17–18	1
FGA	25–26	26	1				

Since these two kits share many of the STRs, but do not use the same primers, it is possible that genotyping inconsistencies do arise due to polymorphisms in the primers' annealing sequences. In fact, if just one of the primers does not match the target sequence, the result will be an allelic dropout and consequently one individual will be classified as homozygous with one kit and heterozygous with the other one. Moreover, it is possible, in case of some degree of overlapping between the primers of the two kits, that both fail to anneal and, in that case, the null allele will be only detectable through mother/child or family analyses.

These issues are a major concern in forensic field, particularly for databasing [1–3]. Moreover, an extra difficulty has arisen from the fact that even different versions of the same kit from the same manufacturer can vary in primer's design [4].

In this work we report: (a) the results of the study of primer concordance between the above referred kits registering the inconsistencies observed after the extensive genotyping of various population samples (mainly from Portugal and Mozambique) as well as (b) the cases of isolated, apparent opposite homozygosity in mother/child pairs with both kits.

2. Materials and methods

Blood samples were obtained during paternity (and other kinship) analyses performed in our institute or from random blood donors. DNA was extracted by the standard Chelex method and amplified according to the manufacturers' instructions (Applied Biosystems for AmpFLSTR Identifiler and Promega for Powerplex 16). Genetic profiles were obtained using ABI 310 with the use of GeneScan software (Applied Biosystems).

Table 2
Number of meioses analyzed per STR

D2S1338	D3S1358	D5S818	D7S820	D8S1179	D13S317	D16S539	D18S51
246	1262	1262	1196	1262	1262	714	1252
D19S433	D21S11	FGA	Penta D	Penta E	TH01	TPO	VWA
248	1258	1268	714	714	1318	1316	1320

3. Results

A total of 22 inconsistencies between kits was observed, as shown in Table 1. One mother/child incompatibility was detected when using both kits, at D5S818 (m. 12/ch. 13). The total number of meioses per analyzed system is shown in Table 2.

4. Discussion

Out of the 13 STRs common to both kits, genotypic discordances have been found in five of them. They were particularly common in D5S818 (10 in 386 unrelated Portuguese) and VWA (6 individuals from the same sample). While most of false D5S818 homozygosities were detected using Identifiler, in VWA all were observed with Powerplex16. The only inconsistency in FGA was also observed in the Portuguese sample. On the contrary, for D8S1179 it was detected in the sample from Mozambique (N = 144). The case of D16S539 is much more interesting since all apparent homozygosities were detected in non-European (one individual of Cape Verdean ancestry and three in the Mozambican sample). It is also interesting to note that while the polymorphisms in the primer binding sequences for D5S818 and VWA (those that were found in Europeans) are associated with various STR alleles, those for D16S539 seem African-specific and are always in linkage with allele 11, undetected with Powerplex16.

These findings confirm the results from previous studies [1–4], showing that a non-negligible proportion of genotypic inconsistencies is expected to occur for any PCR-based system when using different primer pairs. Furthermore, the frequency of many of these sequence variants shows substantial populational diversity. This fact must be kept in mind when designing, loading and analyzing databases, as well as when performing identity or kinship investigations using results that have been obtained by different primer sets.

Concerning the single mother/child incompatibility detected when using both kits, at D5S818 the apparent exclusion can also be attributable to a one-step mutation (12>13), and it is safe to conclude that although both kits show, at least for some systems, a relatively high frequency of null alleles, the combined use of both practically eliminates this source of problem in kinship evaluation such as in paternity cases.

Acknowledgements

This work was partially supported by Programa Operacional Ciência, Tecnologia e Inovação (POCTI), Quadro Comunitário de Apoio III. LP has a research grant (SFRH/BPD/7121/2001) from Fundação para a Ciência e a Tecnologia.

References

[1] B. Budowle, et al., STR primer concordance study, Forensic Sci. Int. 124 (2001) 47–54.

[2] B. Budowle, C.J. Sprecher, Concordance study on population database samples using the PowerPlex 16 kit and AmpFlSTR Profiler Plus kit and AmpFlSTR COfiler kit, J. Forensic Sci. 46 (2001) 637–641.

[3] C. Alves, et al., VWA STR genotyping: further inconsistencies between Perkin-Elmer and Promega kits, Int. J. Leg. Med. 115 (2001) 97–99.

[4] C. Leibelt, et al., Identification of a D8S1179 primer binding site mutation and the validation of a primer designed to recover null alleles, Forensic Sci. Int. 133 (2003) 220–227.

International Congress Series 1261 (2004) 179–181

www.ics-elsevier.com

Hña hñu Amerindian population from La Sierra Otomí-Tepehua (Mexico) characterised by 14 STR–PCR polymorphisms

C. Barrot-Feixat[a,*], A. González-Martín[b], M. Ortega[a], C. Sánchez[a], A. Gorostiza[a], E. Huguet[a], C. Brandt-Casadevall[c], J. Corbella[a], M. Gené[a]

[a] *Unit Legal Medicine and Toxicology, School of Medicine, University of Barcelona, Salut Publica, Catalonia, C/Casanova 143, 3a planta, 08036 Barcelona, Catalonia, Spain*
[b] *Area Acad. Historia y Antropologia, Univ. Autonoma Estado de Hidalgo, Mexico*
[c] *Legal Medicine Institute, Lausanne, Switzerland*

Abstract. The purpose of this study is to report allele frequency data of Hña hñu (Otomí) ethnic Amerindian group population sample from La Sierra Otomí-Tepehua (Estado de Hidalgo-Mexico) for 14 STR–PCR polymorphisms (HumTH01, HumPenta D, HumPenta E, HumvWA, D18S51, D16S539, D13S317, D8S1179, D7S820, D5S818, D3S1358, HumCSF1PO, HumFGA and D21S11).

Keywords: Population genetics; Amerindian; STR polymorphisms; Hña hñu

1. Introduction

The Hña hñu population received the name from its language. It belonged to a group of Otopame language, for which, these people were called Otomí population, too. They were established in different regions of Mexico. The group that was studied in this report lived in La Sierra Otomí-Tepehua from Estado de Hidalgo.

2. Material and methods

DNA was extracted from hair root samples by Chelex® method [1]. PCR were carried out in a 12-μl volume containing 0.5 ng DNA template. PCR amplifications were performed according to the recommendations for the AmpFlSTR® PowerPlex® kit (Promega). Genotypes from DNA-amplified products were analysed in capillary gel electrophoresis using an ABI Prim™ 310 Genetic Analyzer automated laser sequencer [2]. Amplified DNA was mixed with internal fluorescent-labelled size standard and external ladders were also used for adjustment. Allele frequencies were determined. Unbiased estimates of expected

* Corresponding author. Tel.: +34-93-4035289; fax: +34-93-4035290.
E-mail address: cbarrotfeixat@ub.edu (C. Barrot-Feixat).

doi:10.1016/S0531-5131(03)01498-5

Table 1
Allele frequency distribution for HumTH01, HumPenta D, HumPenta E, D16S539, D13S317, D7S820 and D5S818 in the Hña hñu population

	HumTH01	HumPenta D	HumPenta E	D16S539	D13S317	D7S820	D5S818
5			0.0120				
6	0.3373						
7	0.4277		0.0301				0.0915
8	0.0241	0.0063	0.0602		0.0542	0.0783	
9	0.0361	0.2215		0.0915	0.3494	0.0241	0.0488
9.3	0.1747						
10		0.2405	0.0181	0.2012	0.1205	0.2590	0.0732
11		0.1013	0.0361	0.2805	0.1325	0.3132	0.5244
12		0.1772	0.1385	0.3598	0.1506	0.2771	0.1951
13		0.2278	0.1265	0.0609	0.1446	0.0482	0.0771
14		0.0253	0.0843	0.0061	0.0482		
15			0.2108				
16			0.1626				
17			0.0241				
18			0.0361				
18.2							
19			0.0181				
20			0.0241				
21			0.0120				
22			0.0060				

heterozygosity were computed. A standard χ^2 goodness-of-fit was calculated to assess Hardy–Weinberg expectations. From forensic point of view, the power discrimination, heterozygosity value and the a priori chance exclusion value were calculated.

Table 2
Allele frequency distribution for HumvWA, D18S51, D8S1179, D3S1358, HumCSF1PO, HumFGA, D21S11 in the Hña hñu population

	HumvWA	D18S51	D8S1179	D3S1358	HumCSF1PO	HumFGA	D21S11
10			0.0843		0.2073		
11			0.0241		0.2927		
12		0.0988	0.1446		0.4268		
13	0.0241	0.1296	0.3373	0.0181	0.0671		
14	0.0241	0.1852	0.2892	0.0120	0.0061		
15	0.0542	0.1852	0.1084	0.5602			
16	0.3976	0.0802	0.0120	0.2108			
17	0.2349	0.1543		0.1566			
18	0.1928	0.0926		0.0422			
19	0.0723	0.0432				0.0422	
20		0.0123				0.0723	
21		0.0062				0.0723	
22						0.1386	
23						0.1084	
23.2						0.0361	
24		0.0062				0.1205	
25		0.0062				0.2048	
25.2						0.0060	
26						0.1386	
27						0.0602	
28							0.0482
29							0.1506
29.2							0.0120
30							0.2048
31							0.0964
31.2							0.1928
32							0.0060
32.2							0.1747
33.2							0.0663
34.2							0.0482

Table 3
Stadistical parameters of forensic interest (*h*, heterozygosity value, PD, power discrimination, CE, chance of exclusion) and equilibrium Hardy–Weinberg (*p*)

Locus	*n*	*p*	*h*	PD	CE
HumTHO1	83	0.4456	0.699	0.811	0.426
HumPenta D	79	0.8102	0.772	0.924	0.548
HumPenta E	83	0.1496	0.855	0.962	0.706
HumvWA	83	0.2142	0.759	0.882	0.525
D18S51	81	0.1083	0.877	0.950	0.748
D16S539	82	0.5631	0.756	0.878	0.520
D13S317	83	0.6006	0.771	0.928	0.547
D8S1179	83	0.4708	0.723	0.905	0.465
D7S820	83	0.4119	0.771	0.884	0.547
D5S818	82	0.1162	0.720	0.827	0.459
D3S1358	83	0.6873	0.627	0.798	0.324
HumCSF1PO	82	0.4054	0.622	0.850	0.318
HumFGA	83	0.3668	0.904	0.961	0.803
D21S11	83	0.4262	0.880	0.948	0.754

Table 4
Comparison between two Otomí populations; one lives in El Valle de Ixmiquilpan and the other in La Sierra Otomí-Tepehua

Locus	Probability
HumTHO1	0.1702
HumvWA	0.1179
D18S51	0.2521
D16S539	0.0662
D13S317	0.8368
D8S1179	0.3240
D7S820	0.2655
D5S818	0.2481
D3S1358	0.2877
HumCSF1PO	0.2741
HumFGA	0.0804
D21S11	0.0042

3. Results

The allele frequencies observed in each system in the Hña hñu Amerindian population are shown in Tables 1 and 2. In Table 3, we resumed the forensic parameters (*h*, heterozygosity index, CE chance exclusion and PD power discrimination) [3] and the equilibrium Hardy–Weinberg (*p*) [4].

4. Discussion

A great genetic affinity has been obtained in comparison with the previously published Otomí population from El Valle de Ixmiquilpan (Table 4).

Acknowledgements

We are thankful to the Otomí Amerindian population for its generous collaboration in the present study.

References

[1] P.S. Walsh, D.A. Metzger, R. Higuchi, Chelex 100 as a medium for simple extraction of DNA for PCR-based typing from forensic material, BioTechniques 10 (1991) 506–513.

[2] E.S. Mansfield et al., Analysis of multiplexed short tandem repeat (STR) systems using capillary array electrophoresis, Electrophoresis 19 (1) (1998) 101–107.

[3] R. Fisher, Standard calculation for evaluating a blood-group system, Heredity 5 (1951) 95–102.

[4] S.W. Guo, E.A. Thompson, Performing the exact test of Hardy–Weinberg proportion for multiple alleles, Biometrics 48 (1992) 361–372.

International Congress Series 1261 (2004) 182–184
www.ics-elsevier.com

Huastecos Amerindian population (Mexico) characterised by 12 STR-PCR polymorphisms

A. González-Martin[a], C. Sánchez[b,*], C. Barrot[b], M. Ortega[b], C. Brandt-Casadevall[c], A. Gorostiza[b], E. Huguet[b], J. Corbella[b], M. Gené[b]

[a] *Area Acad. Historia y Antropologia, Univ. Autonoma Estado de Hidalgo, Mexico*
[b] *Radioactive Protection, School of Medicine, University of Barcelona, C/ Casanova 143, 5a planta 08036 Barcelona, Spain*
[c] *Legal Medicine Institute, Lausanne, Switzerland*

Abstract. The purpose of this study is to report allele frequency data of a Huastecos ethnic group population sample ($n = 89$) from La Huasteca (Hidalgo, Mexico) for 12 STR-PCR polymorphisms (HumTH01, HumvWA, D18S51, HumTPOX, D19S433, D16S539, D13S317, D8S1179, D7S820, D5S818, HumFGA and D21S11). No significant deviations from Hardy–Weinberg expectation were found for all short-tandem repeats (STR). From forensic point of view, the heterozygosity value, power of discrimination and the a priori chance exclusion value were calculated.

Keywords: Population genetics; Amerindian; STR polymorphisms; Huastecos

An Amerindian population study of 12 short-tandem repeat (STR) loci was performed on 89 unrelated Huastecos.

This ethnic group lives in "La Huasteca", a country northeast of Mexico. The Huasteco, or Nahualt, ethnic group is mainly concentrated in San Luis Potosí, near the Sierra Madre Oriental.

DNA was extracted from hair root samples by Chelex® method [1]. PCR were carried out in a 12-μl volume containing 0.5-ng DNA template. PCR amplifications were performed according to the recommendations for the AmpF*l*STR® Identifiler™ kit (Applied Biosystems). Genotypes from DNA amplified products were analysed in capillary gel electrophoresis using an ABI Prim™ 310 Genetic Analyzer automated laser sequencer [2].

* Corresponding author. Tel.: +34-93-4035736; fax: +34-93-4035290.
E-mail address: cristinasanchez@ub.edu (C. Sánchez).

doi:10.1016/S0531-5131(03)01497-3

Table 1
Allele frequencies distribution for D5S818, D13S317, D7S820, D16S539, HumTPOX and HumTH01 in the Nahualt population

	D5S818	D13S317	D7S820	D16S539	HumTPOX	HumTH01
6						0.4302
7	0.0787					0.4302
8		0.0225	0.0115	0.0063	0.5706	0.0058
9	0.1067	0.3764	0.0387	0.0823	0.0059	0.0058
9.3						0.1279
10	0.0337	0.1910	0.2701	0.2785	0.0353	
11	0.5843	0.1517	0.2989	0.2848	0.1765	
11.2						
12	0.1685	0.1404	0.3448	0.2785	0.2118	
12.2						
13	0.0281	0.0843	0.0402	0.0696		
13.2						
14		0.0337	0.0057			

Amplified DNA was mixed with internal fluorescent labelled size standard and external ladders were also used for adjustment.

Allele and genotype frequencies were determined. Unbiased estimates of expected heterozygosity were computed. A standard χ^2 goodness-of-fit was calculated to asses

Table 2
Allele frequencies distribution for HumvWA, D8S1179, HumFGA, D21S11, D18S51 and D19S433 in the Nahualt population

	HumvWA	D8S1179	HumFGA	D21S11	D18S51	D19S433
10		0.0674			0.0058	0.0057
11		0.0393				0.0115
11.2						0.0057
12		0.1742			0.0698	0.0172
12.2						0.0172
13		0.2584			0.0756	0.0862
13.2						0.1897
14		0.3483			0.2733	0.3046
14.2						0.0402
15	0.0337	0.1011			0.1686	0.1437
15.2						0.1322
16	0.5056	0.0112			0.0872	0.0287
16.2						0.0057
17	0.3258				0.1453	0.0057
17.2						0.0057
18	0.1011		0.0114		0.0523	
19	0.0281		0.1136		0.0523	
20	0.0056		0.0455		0.0174	
21			0.0966		0.0174	
22			0.0852		0.0291	
23			0.0568		0.0058	
23.2			0.0057			
24			0.1420			
25			0.2955			
26			0.0909	0.0056		
27			0.0511			
28			0.0057	0.0225		
29				0.1854		
29.2				0.0056		
30				0.3146		
30.2				0.0056		
31				0.1067		
31.2				0.1461		
32				0.0056		
32.2				0.1067		

Table 3
Stadistical parameters of forensic interest (*h*, heterozygosity value; PD, power discrimination; CE, chance of exclusion) and equilibrium Hardy–Weinberg (*p*)

Locus	*n*	p	*h*	PD	CE
D5S818	89	0.9064	0.607	0.809	0.299
D13S317	89	0.3039	0.236	0.908	0.534
D7S820	87	0.0800	0.264	0.851	0.486
D16S539	79	0.7540	0.316	0.901	0.403
HumvWA	89	0.8398	0.663	0.784	0.373
D8S1179	89	0.6692	0.764	0.912	0.534
HumTPOX	85	0.6417	0.632	0.777	0.331
HumFGA	88	0.9853	0.864	0.953	0.722
HumTH01	86	0.5612	0.605	0.763	0.296
D21S11	89	0.6209	0.775	0.937	0.554
D18S51	86	0.3253	0.756	0.951	0.520
D19S433	87	0.1583	0.799	0.942	0.586

Hardy–Weinberg expectations. From forensic point of view, the power discrimination, heterozygosity value and the "a priori" chance exclusion value were calculated.

The allele frequencies observed in each system in the Nahualt Amerindian population are shown in Tables 1 and 2. In Table 3, we were resumed the forensic parameters (*h*, heterozygosity index, CE chance exclusion and PD power discrimination) [3] and the equilibrium Hardy–Weinberg (p) [4].

The allele frequency data reported were preliminary results of a further study of Amerindian genetic map of Mesoamerica (or Central America).

We are thankful to the Huastecos population for its generous collaboration in the present study.

References

[1] P.S. Walsh, D.A. Metzger, R. Higuchi, Chelex 100 as a medium for simple extraction of DNA for PCR-based typing from forensic material, BioTechniques 10 (1991) 506–513.
[2] E.S. Mansfield, et al., Analysis of multiplexed short tandem repeat (STR) systems using capillary array electrophoresis, Electrophoresis 19 (1) (1998) 101–107.
[3] R. Fisher, Standard calculation for evaluating a blood-group system, Heredity 5 (1951) 95–102.
[4] S.W. Guo, E.A. Thompson, Performing the exact test of Hardy–Weinberg proportion for multiple alleles, Biometrics 48 (1992) 361–372.

International Congress Series 1261 (2004) 185–187

www.ics-elsevier.com

Kurdish (Iraq) and Somalian population data for 15 autosomal and 9 Y-chromosomal STR loci

Margurethe Stenersen*, Dorota Perchla, Ellen Søvik, Anne Grete Flønes, Berit Myhre Dupuy

Department of Family Genetics, Institute of Forensic Medicine, University of Oslo, Rikshospitalet 0027, Oslo, Norway

Abstract. Autosomal STR polymorphisms at 15 loci and Y-chromosomal STR polymorphisms at 9 loci are presented. Samples from current immigration casework including individuals from Somalia ($n \sim 100$) and northern Iraq (Kurds) ($n \sim 100$) were analysed. For the autosomal polymorphisms, the observed heterozygosities ranged from 0.602 (TPOX) to 0.918 (PentaD) in the Iraqi sample and from 0.614 (D13S317) to 0.958 (PentaE) in the Somali sample. One significant deviation from Hardy–Weinberg equilibrium was observed in the Somali sample at D13S317, the expected heterozygosity rate is 0.761 and the observed is 0.614. For the Y-chromosome polymorphisms, 61 and 99 different haplotypes were observed in the samples from Somalia and Iraq, respectively. Combined gene diversity was 0.97 (Somalia) and 0.99 (Iraq). Locus diversity ranged from 0.24 (DYS391) to 0.82 (DYS385) in the population sample from Somalia and from 0.45 (DYS392) to 0.96 (DYS385) in the population sample from Iraq. None of the haplotypes in the two populations were identical. Locus diversity, allele distributions and other relevant forensic genetic parameters will be presented. © 2003 Elsevier B.V. All rights reserved.

Keywords: Forensic population database; PowerPlex 16; Y-STR; Iraqi Kurds; Somali

1. Introduction

In order to establish a database for immigration and paternity casework, two population samples of different ethnic origin were analysed at the fifteen autosomal STR polymorphisms D3S1358, THO1, D21S11, D18S51, Penta E, D5S818, D13S317, D7S820, D16S539, CSF1PO, Penta E, vWA, D8S1179, TPOX and FGA, included in the PowerPLex16® multiplex (Promega, Madison, US). Furthermore, nine Y-chromosomal STR polymorphisms were analysed (DYS19, DYS385, DYS388, DYS389I, DYS389II, DYS390, DYS391, DYS392 and DYS393).

* Corresponding author. Tel.: +47-23071317; fax: +47-23071318.
E-mail address: margurethe.stenersen@labmed.uio.no (M. Stenersen).

doi:10.1016/S0531-5131(03)01823-5

2. Materials and methods

Samples were obtained from current immigration casework—98 unrelated individuals from northern Iraq (Kurds) and 96 unrelated individuals from Somalia. DNA was extracted from venous blood by the method of Ref. [1]. PCR amplification was performed according to the manufacturer's manual (PowerPlex16) and Ref. [3] (Y-chromosome loci). Fragment analysis was done by capillary electrophoresis (ABI PRISM® 3100, AB, Foster City, US). Evaluation of Hardy–Weinberg equilibrium was performed by a modified version of the Markov-chain random walk algorithm (10 000 shuffles) provided by the Arlequin Software (http://anthro.unige.ch/arlequin). Other forensic statistical parameters were obtained by the PowerStats, Promega (http://www.promega.com/geneticidtools/powerstats/Default.htm).

3. Results and discussion

In both population samples, alleles not present in the allelic ladder were observed at several loci. (For details, allele distributions and forensic statistical parameters—see Tables 1 and 2 at http://folk.uio.no/msteners/index.html.htm.) A significant deviation from Hardy–Weinberg equilibrium was observed at the D13S317 locus in the Somalian population (the expected heterozygosity rate was 0.761 and the observed was 0.614, $p=0.002$). To investigate the possibility of "0-alleles" at this locus, families of homozygous individuals (two to six children and the other parent) were analysed. No evidence of 0-alleles was observed. Further experiments, to uncover a possible primer binding site polymorphism, is necessary. No significant deviation from Hardy–Weinberg equilibrium was observed in the Iraqi population sample. The 15 loci possess a combined power of exclusion of 0.9999995 for each population group.

For the Y-chromosome polymorphisms, 61 and 99 different haplotypes were observed in the samples from Somalia and Iraq, respectively. Combined gene diversity (Table 1) was 0.97 (Somalia) and 0.99 (Iraq). Locus diversity [3] ranged from 0.24 (DYS391) to 0.82 (DYS385) in the population sample from Somalia and from 0.45 (DYS392) to 0.96 (DYS385) in the population sample from Iraq. None of the haplotypes in the two populations were identical. The Y-haplotype distributions are presented in Figs. 1 and 2 at http://folk.uio.no/msteners/index.html.htm.

Table 1
Y-chromosome locus diversity and haplotype (HT) diversity

Locus	Somalia	Iraq
DYS19	0.3897	0.6579
DYS389I	0.3172	0.5599
DYS389II	0.6783	0.7247
DYS390	0.3990	0.7168
DYS391	0.2377	0.4996
DYS392	0.3743	0.4521
DYS393	0.3045	0.5918
DYS385[a]	0.8213	0.9586
DYS388	0.3833	0.7240
HT diversity	0.9703	0.9984

[a] Calculated on the basis of recommended nomenclature [2], which may differ from the genomic haplotype.

References

[1] S.A. Miller, D.D. Dykes, H.F. Polesky, A simple salting out procedure for extracting DNA from human nucleated cells, Nucleic Acids Research 16 (3) (1988) 1215.

[2] P. Gill, C. Brenner, B. Brinkmann, B. Budowle, A. Carracedo, M.A. Jobling, P. de Knijff, M. Kayser, M. Krawczak, W.R. Mayr, N. Morling, B. Olaisen, V. Pascali, M. Prinz, L. Roewer, P.M. Schneider, A. Sajantila, C. Tyler-Smith, DNA Commission of the International Society of Forensic Genetics: recommendations on forensic analysis using Y-chromosome STRs, Forensic Science International 124 (1) (2001) 5–10.

[3] B.M. Dupuy, R. Andreassen, A.G. Flønes, K. Tomassen, T. Egeland, M. Brion, A. Carracedo, B. Olaisen, Y-chromosome variation in a Norwegian population sample, Forensic Science International 117 (2001) 163–173.

International Congress Series 1261 (2004) 188–190

www.ics-elsevier.com

Multiplex PCR investigation of the STR loci C1_4_4, C2_4_4 and C3_3_6 in the HLA class I region

S. Wenda[a,*], E.M. Dauber[a], S. Stadlbacher[a], B. Glock[b], G. Dorner[a], W.R. Mayr[a]

[a] *Department of Blood Group Serology and Transfusion Medicine, Division of Blood Group Serology, University of Vienna, Waehringer Guertel 18-20, Vienna, 1160 Austria*

[b] *Laboratory for Molecular Biology, Austrian Red Cross, Blood Donation Center for Vienna, Lower Austria and Burgenland, Vienna, Austria*

Abstract. In this study, we investigated the short tandem repeat loci C1_4_4, C2_4_4 and C3_3_6 situated in the HLA class I region in a sample of 153 unrelated Austrian Caucasoid individuals by multiplex PCR. The sequence structure of C1_4_4 and C3_3_6 alleles is described, as well as the sequence of a new C2_4_4 allele, allele 23.

Keywords: C1_4_4; C2_4_4; C3_3_6; HLA class I region; Multiplex PCR

1. Introduction

Sequence and population data of the short tandem repeat loci C1_4_4, C2_4_4 and C3_3_6, situated in the HLA class I region (6p21.3) near the HLA-B and HLA-C locus, were investigated in this study in order to find out, if they are suitable for identity and paternity testing.

2. Materials and methods

DNA was extracted from peripheral blood lymphocytes (Qiagen) of 153 unrelated Austrian Caucasoid individuals. The forward primers were labelled with fluorescein and the reverse primers were modified to so-called "PIGtail" primers to achieve complete 3′ A addition [1,2]. PCR conditions were chosen as follows (reaction volume 10 μl): 1–2 ng template DNA, 0.8 μM (C1_4_4), 0.2 μM (C2_4_4) and 0.4 μM (C3_3_6) of each primer, 200 μM of each nucleotide, 0.33 U Amplitaq Gold DNA polymerase, 1 × GeneAmp PCR Buffer; 95 °C 11 min for 1 cycle; 94 °C 1 min, 60 °C 1 min, 72 °C 2 min for 30 cycles; 72 °C for 45 min and 4 °C hold (GeneAmp 9700 PCR System, Applied Biosystems).

* Corresponding author. Klinische Abteilung für Blutgruppenserologie, A-1090 Wien, Waehringer Guertel 18-20, Austria. Tel.: +43-1-40400-5320; fax: +43-1-40400-5321.

E-mail address: sabine.wenda@univie.ac.at (S. Wenda).

0531-5131/
doi:10.1016/S0531-5131(03)01625-X

Table 1
Allele frequencies and further statistic parameters

Allele	C1_4_4	C2_4_4	C3_3_6
7	0.215		
8	0.131		0.003
9	0.042	0.095	0.395
10	0.065	0.490	0.183
11	0.046	0.020	0.036
12	0.036		0.206
13	0.059	0.013	0.056
14	0.059	0.003	0.020
15	0.023	0.003	0.072
16	0.056	0.150	0.026
17	0.065	0.092	0.003
18	0.056	0.075	
19	0.072	0.036	
20	0.069	0.013	
21	0.003	0.007	
22	0.003		
23		0.003	
Rate of heterozygosity	0.856	0.699	0.771
Power of exclusion	0.707	0.427	0.547
Polymorphism information content	0.890	0.690	0.730
Matching probability	0.023	0.109	0.097
Power of discrimination	0.977	0.891	0.903
Typical paternity index	3.480	1.660	2.190

Table 2
C1_4_4 sequence structure

Allele	5′ Flanking region position						Repeat structure	Length in bp	Number of sequenced alleles
	50	94	109	226	227	260–262			
7	G	C	G	G	T	AAA	$(GAAA)_7$	380	1
8	G	C	G	G	C	AAA	$(GAAA)_8$	384	2
9	G	A	G	A	C	AAA	$(GAAA)_9$	388	1
10	G	C	G	G	C	AAA	$(GAAA)_{10}$	392	1
11	G	A	G	A	C	AAA	$(GAAA)_{11}$	396	1
12	G	A	A	G	C	AAA	$(GAAA)_{12}$	400	2
13	G	A	A	G	C	AAA	$(GAAA)_{13}$	404	1
14	G	A	A	G	C	AAA	$(GAAA)_{14}$	408	1
15	G	A	G	A	C	AAA	$(GAAA)_{15}$	412	1
16	G	A	G	A	C	AAA	$(GAAA)_{16}$	416	1
16′	A	A	G	A	C	AAA	$(GAAA)_{16}$	416	1
17	A	A	G	A	C	AAA	$(GAAA)_{17}$	420	1
18	A	A	G	A	C	AAA	$(GAAA)_{18}$	424	1
19	G	A	G	A	C	AAA	$(GAAA)_{19}$	428	1
20	G	A	G	A	C	AAA	$(GAAA)_{20}$	432	1
21	G	A	G	A	C	AAA	$(GAAA)_{20}$ $(TAAA)_1$	436	1
22	G	A	G	A	C	AAA	$(GAAA)_{22}$	440	1

Table 3
C3_3_6 sequence structure

Alleles	5′ Flanking region pos. 53	Repeat structure	3′ Flanking region pos. 47	3′ Flanking region pos. 89	Length in bp	Number of sequenced alleles
8	G	$(TTA)_8$	T	A	287	1
9–10	G	$(TTA)_{9-10}$	T	T	290–293	2
11	G	$(TTA)_{11}$	C	A	296	1
12	G	$(TTA)_{12}$	T	T	299	1
13–14	G	$(TTA)_{13-14}$	C	A	302–305	2
15–16	A	$(TTA)_{15-16}$	C	A	308–311	2
17	G	$(TTA)_{17}$	C	A	314	1

Amplification products were analyzed on an ABI Prism 310 Genetic Analyzer. The alleles were assigned by comparison with a sequenced allelic ladder. A template was worked out with the *Genotyper* software to assign allele designations automatically. Cycle sequencing, on an ABI Prism 310 Genetic Analyzer, was performed.

3. Results and discussion

In our population sample 16 alleles at the C1_4_4 locus (380–440 bp), 13 alleles at the C2_4_4 locus (227–283 bp) and 10 alleles at the C3_3_6 locus (287–314 bp) could be differentiated. Allele frequencies and further statistic parameters are shown in Table 1. No deviation from Hardy-Weinberg equilibrium has been found.

A tetranucleotide repeat structure $(GAAA)_{7-22}$ was observed at the C1_4_4 locus (Table 2). Additionally, five SNPs were found. All alleles sequenced differed from the GenBank sequence (Accession No. AC006048) due to 3 instead of 4 A following the position 259 in the 5′ flanking region. Sequence data of the C2_4_4 locus $(RRAR)_n$ have already been described elsewhere [3,4]. Additionally, a new C2_4_4 allele, allele 23, exhibiting the sequence structure GAAA GAAG $(GAAA)_{17}$ AAAA $(GAAA)_3$ was detected.

At the C3_3_6 locus, a trinucleotide repeat structure $(TTA)_{8-17}$ was observed. The allele 9 sequenced in this study was identical with the GenBank sequence (Accession No. AC004207). Among the other alleles, three polymorphic sites (SNPs) were found (Table 3).

C1_4_4 has been found to be a powerful marker, which can be compared with FGA. C2_4_4 and C3_3_6 are approximately as informative as THO1.

These loci are therefore suitable for identity and paternity testing. The linkage disequilibrium between these alleles and HLA class I alleles is under study, as well as the possibility to use C1_4_4, C2_4_4 and C3_3_6 as HLA haplotype markers.

References

[1] G. Tamiya, et al., Twenty-six new polymorphic microsatellite markers around the HLA-B, -C and -E loci in the human MHC class I region, Tissue Antigens 51 (1998) 337–346.

[2] M.J. Brownstein, et al., Modulation of non-templated nucleotide addition by Taq DNA polymerase: primer modifications that facilitate genotyping, BioTechniques 20 (1996) 1004–1010.

[3] S. Stadlbacher, et al., The tetranucleotide repeat polymorphism C2_4_4: sequence and population data, International Congress Series 1239 (2003) 91–93.

[4] S. Stadlbacher, et al., The tetranucleotide repeat polymorphism C2_4_4: population data and linkage disequilibria with HLA class I, Immunobiology 207 (2003) 137–140.

International Congress Series 1261 (2004) 191–193

www.ics-elsevier.com

New sequence data of allelic variants at the STR loci ACTBP2 (SE33), D21S11, FGA, vWA, CSF1PO, D2S1338, D16S539, D18S51 and D19S433 in Caucasoids

E.M. Dauber[a,*], W. Bär[b], M. Klintschar[c,d], F. Neuhuber[e], W. Parson[f], E. Mueller-van der Spruit[a], W.R. Mayr[a]

[a] *Division of Blood Group Serology, Department of Blood Group Serology and Transfusion Medicine, University of Vienna, Medical School, Vienna, Austria*
[b] *Institute of Legal Medicine, University of Zurich, Switzerland*
[c] *Institute of Legal Medicine, University of Graz, Austria*
[d] *Institute of Legal Medicine, Martin-Luther-University Halle-Wittenberg, Germany*
[e] *Institute of Legal Medicine, University of Salzburg, Salzburg, Austria*
[f] *Institute of Legal Medicine, University of Innsbruck, Innsbruck, Austria*

Abstract. On the occasion of a study on mutation rates of human STR loci, numerous alleles have been sequenced. Several new sequence or length variant alleles were found.

Keywords: Sequence data; Sequence variation; Sequencing; Variant alleles

1. Introduction

This study reports sequence data of rare and new sequence or length variant alleles which have been found in course of a study on mutation rates of human STR loci. These variant alleles are briefly discussed, especially with regard to further investigations.

2. Materials and methods

DNA was extracted from blood or buccal swab samples of Caucasoids living in Austria and Switzerland and from one sample which was derived from a black individual. The same primers were used for PCR and sequencing, which was carried out in both directions (GenBank accession nos. M84567, M64982, G07925, G08036 and G08202).

* Corresponding author. Klinische Abteilung für Blutgruppenserologie, Waehringer Guertel 18-20, A-1090 Wien, Austria. Tel.: +43-1-40400-5320; fax: +43-1-40400-5321.
E-mail address: eva.maria.dauber@univie.ac.at (E.M. Dauber).

0531-5131/
doi:10.1016/S0531-5131(03)01700-X

SE33 alleles were designated according to the ACTBP2 nomenclature recommendations of GEDNAP [1].

3. Results and discussion

While the SE33 alleles 7.3, 12.1, 13, 19.2, 20, 25.2, 26.2, 27.2, 29.2, 30.2, 31.2, 33, 33.2 and 34.2 represent the same type of variation already known for this locus [2,3], the alleles 11.2, 12.2, 13.2, 16.2, 16.3 and 18.3 represent a new type of allelic sequence structure lacking the $(AAAG)_3$ AG structure in the 5′ flanking region (Table 1). Additionally, the alleles 16.3 and 18.3 exhibited a doubled G-$(AAAG)_3$ structure in the 3′ flanking region, which is unique so far.

The sequence structure of three variant D21S11 alleles 29, 29.2 and 30 found in this study (Table 2) has not been reported so far, the other variant alleles have already been observed in Asian populations [4], but not in Caucasoid individuals until now. Further sequence or length variant alleles at the FGA and the vWA locus are given in Table 2, including another rare variant vWA allele 15 [5] and a new variant vWA allele 16; it exhibited a C → T transition at position 3 in the 3′ flanking region leading to 13 instead of 11 consecutive TCTA repeats. This type of variation has only been reported for black populations so far in alleles 12–14 [6].

At the CSF1PO locus a rare length variant allele 10.3 was found: $(AGAT)_5$ GAT $(AGAT)_5$. A D16S539 allele 9 and an allele 10 exhibited an A → C transversion at position 16 in the 3′ flanking region, a D18S51 allele 14 showed a G → A transition at position 18 in 5′ flanking region (TTCT strand).

Table 1
Sequence structure of new HumACTBP2 (SE33) alleles

Allele name	Sequence structure	Length in bp	No. of alleles
7.3[a]	$(AAAG)_{11}$	216	1
11.2[b]	$(AAAG)_{15}$	231	2
12.1[c]	$(AAAG)_{12}$	234	1
12.2[b]	$(AAAG)_{16}$	235	2
13	$(AAAG)_{13}$	237	1
13.2[bd]	$(AAAG)_{17}$	239	1
16.2[b]	$(AAAG)_{20}$	251	1
16.3[b]	$(AAAG)_{17}$	252	1
18.3[b]	$(AAAG)_{19}$	260	1
19.2[e]	$(AAAG)_9$ AAAAAG $(AAAG)_9$	263	1
20[e]	$(AAAG)_{20}$	265	1
25.2	$(AAAG)_8$ AAAAAG $(AAAG)_{16}$	287	2
26.2	$(AAAG)_{12}$ AAAAAG $(AAAG)_{13}$	291	1
27.2	$(AAAG)_{14}$ AAAAAG $(AAAG)_{12}$	295	1
29.2	$(AAAG)_{10}$ AAAAAG $(AAAG)_{18}$	303	1
30.2	$(AAAG)_{10}$ AAAAAG $(AAAG)_{20}$	307	1
30.2	$(AAAG)_8$ AAAAAG $(AAAG)_{21}$	307	1
31.2	$(AAAG)_8$ AAAAAG $(AAAG)_{22}$	311	1
33	$(AAAG)_8$ AAAAAG $(AAAG)_{13}$ AAAAAG $(AAAG)_9$	317	1
33.2	$(AAAG)_{12}$ AAAAAG $(AAAG)_{20}$	319	1
34.2	$(AAAG)_{13}$ AAAAAG $(AAAG)_{20}$	323	1

[a] Loss of G $(AAAG)_3$ in the 3′ flanking region. [b] Loss of $(AAAG)_3$ AG in the 5′ flanking region. [c] Insertion of a single A after the first of 12 AAAG repeats. [d] Black individual. [e] A → T transversion at position 17 in the 5′ flanking region.

Table 2
Sequence structure of new and rare variant Caucasoid D21S11, FGA and vWA alleles

Locus	Allele name	Sequence structure	Length in bp	No. of alleles
D21S11	29[a]	$(TCTA)_6$ $(TCTG)_5$ [...] $(TCTA)_{10}$	221	1
	29	$(TCTA)_4$ $(TCTG)_7$ [...] $(TCTA)_{10}$	221	1
	29.2	$(TCTA)_5$ $(TCTG)_6$ [...]$(TCTA)_9$ TA TCTA	223	1
	30[a]	$(TCTA)_5$ $(TCTG)_6$ [...]$(TCTA)_{11}$	225	1
	30	$(TCTA)_4$ $(TCTG)_6$ [...]$(TCTA)_{12}$	225	1
	31[a]	$(TCTA)_4$ $(TCTG)_6$ [...]$(TCTA)_{13}$	229	2
	32[a]	$(TCTA)_5$ $(TCTG)_6$ [...]$(TCTA)_{13}$	233	2
	35.2[a]	$(TCTA)_5$ $(TCTG)_6$ [...]$(TCTA)_{15}$ TA TCTA	247	1
FGA	22[b]	$(TTTC)_3$ TTTTTTCT $(CTTT)_{14}$ CTCC $(TTCC)_2$	196	1
	24.1[c]	$(TTTC)_3$ TTTTTTCT $(CTTT)_{16}$ CTCC $(TTCC)_2$	205	1
	26	$(TTTC)_3$ TTTTTTCT $(CTTT)_{16}$ GTTT CTTT CTCC $(TTCC)_2$	212	1
	27	$(TTTC)_3$ TTTTTTCT $(CTTT)_{17}$ GTTT CTTT CTCC $(TTCC)_2$	216	1
vWA	14	TCTA $(TCTG)_3$ $(TCTA)_{10}$	138	2
	15[d]	TCTA TCTG TCTA $(TCTG)_4$ $(TCTA)_3$ TCCA $(TCTA)_3$TCCA	142	1
	16[e]	TCTA $(TCTG)_4$ $(TCTA)_{11}$	146	1

[a] Already observed in Asian individuals. [b] T→C at position 3 in the 3′ flanking region. [c] Insertion of T following the position 35 in the 5′ flanking region. [d] T→C transition at position 7 in the 3′ flanking region (leading to 3 consecutive TCCA repeats). [e] C→T transition at position 3 in the 3′ flanking region (leading to 13 consecutive TCTA repeats).

All out of four D19S433 alleles sequenced differed from the GenBank sequence (accession no. G08036) by a T→A transversion at position 8 of the 3′ flanking region. Eleven out of fourteen D2S1338 alleles sequenced revealed a T→G transition at position 35 in the 3′ flanking region, which is in contrast to the GenBank sequence (accession no. G08202).

The new SE33 alleles observed in this study might give a further hint how the complex sequence structure at this locus might have evolved. Other allelic variants might have implications on mutation analysis of STR loci, in order define the maternal or paternal origin of a mutation.

References

[1] H.R. Schneider, et al., ACTBP2 nomenclature recommendations of GEDNAP, Int. J. Legal Med. 111 (1998) 97–100.

[2] B. Rolf, et al., Sequence polymorphism at the tetranucleotide repeat of the human beta-actin related pseudogene H-beta-Ac-psi-2 (ACTBP2) locus, Int. J. Legal Med. 110 (1997) 69–72.

[3] B. Brinkmann, et al., Mutation rate in human microsatellites: influence of the structure and length of the tandem repeat, Am. J. Hum. Genet. 62 (1998) 1408–1415.

[4] H.G. Zhou, et al., The HumD21S11 system of short tandem repeat DNA polymorphisms in Japanese and Chinese, Forensic Sci. Int. 86 (1997) 109–118.

[5] E.M. Dauber, et al., Further sequence and length variation at the STR loci HumFES/FPS, HumvWA, HumFGA and D12S391, Int. J. Legal Med. 113 (2000) 76–80.

[6] M.D. Barber, et al., Structural variation of novel alleles at the HumVWA and HumFES/FPS short tandem repeat loci, Int. J. Legal Med. 108 (1995) 31–35.

ELSEVIER

International Congress Series 1261 (2004) 194–196

www.ics-elsevier.com

Polymorphism at three STR loci on chromosome 21 (D21S1411, D21S1414, and D21S1435) in Croatia

Zorana Grubic[a,*], Kristina Crkvenac[b], Katarina Stingl[a], Vesna Brkljacic-Kerhin[a]

[a] *National Referral Organ Transplantation and Tissue Typing Center, Croatia*
[b] *Department for Cytogenetics, University Hospital Zagreb, HR 10000 Zagreb, Croatia*

Abstract. In order to increase the number of STR loci for forensic DNA analysis as well as for prenatal diagnosis of Down syndrom in the Croatian population, we have studied three tetranucleotide STR loci on chromosome 21 (D21S1411, D21S1414, and D21S1435). One hundred and fifty-six unrelated healthy individuals were tested in this study. The results clearly demonstrated that the most polymorphic locus (20 different alleles) was D21S1414 with PIC value of 0.9279, while at D21S1435 locus seven different alleles were observed with PIC value of 0.7706. The third locus, D21S1411, also showed great polymorphism with 15 distinct alleles, PIC value 0.8920.

Keywords: STR; Prenatal diagnostics; Down syndrome

1. Introduction

Short tandem repeat loci have been used as routine genetic markers for population genetics, forensics and paternity testing and for following chimerism after bone marrow transplantation. Recently, many laboratories are developing protocols for prenatal diagnosis of trisomies such are Down's (chromosome 21), Edward's (chromosome 18), or Pataouv's syndrome (chromosome 13) [1]. Namely, classical cytogenetic methods consume 3–4 weeks to obtain results, while application of STR loci in prenatal diagnosis would be helpful because the results can be available after 3–4 days [2]. However, in order to be useful in prenatal diagnosis, any of the STR loci have to display a significant degree of polymorphism within population. For that reason, we examined the allele distribution of three STR loci (D21S1411, D21S1414, and D21S1435) on chromosome 21 in our population.

2. Materials and methods

Blood samples were collected from 156 unrelated healthy individuals living in Zagreb. DNA was isolated using NucleoSpin kit (Macherey-Nagel, Duren, Germany);

* Corresponding author. Tel.: +385-1-23-88-689; fax: +385-1-23-12-684.
E-mail address: zgrubic@kbc-zagreb.hr (Z. Grubic).

0531-5131/
doi:10.1016/S0531-5131(03)01655-8

D21S1411 locus

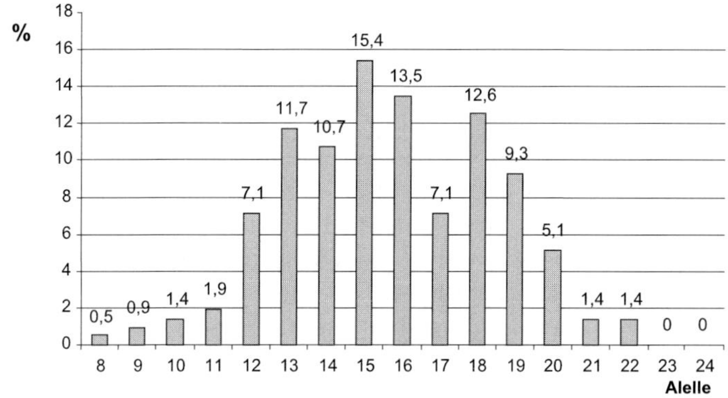

*Legende: Alelles **8**-208bp; **9**-212bp; **10**-216bp; **11**-220bp; **12**-224bp; **13**-228bp; **14**-232bp; **15**-236bp; **16**-240bp; **17**-244bp; **18**-248bp; **19**-252bp; **20**-256bp; **21**-260bp; **22**-264bp; **23**-268bp; **24**-272bp.*

D21S1435 locus

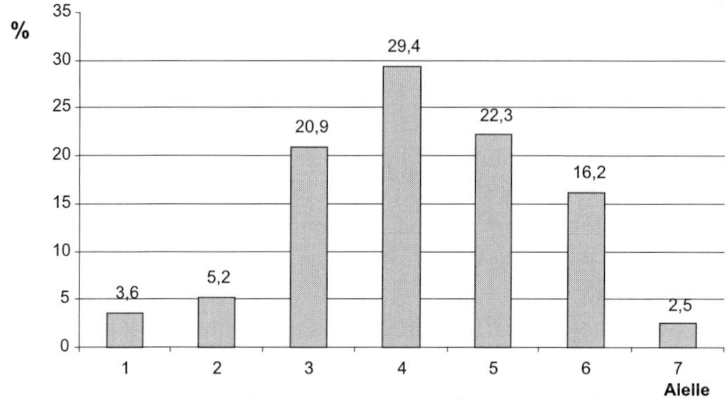

*Legende: Alelles **1**-163bp; **2**-167bp; **3**-171bp; **4**-175bp; **5**-179bp; **6**-183bp; **7**-187bp.*

D21S1414 locus

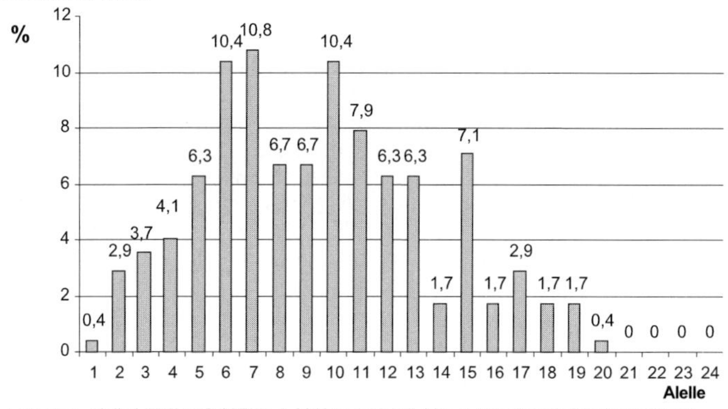

*Legende: Alelle**1**-325bp; **2**-327bp; **3**-329bp; **4**-331; **5**-333; **6**-335; **7**-337; **8**-339; **9**-341; **10**-343; **11**-345; **12**-347; **13**-349; **14**-351; **15**-353; **16**-355; **17**-357; **18**-359; **19**-361; **20**-363; **21**-365; **22**-367; **23**-369; **24**-371.*

Fig. 1. Distribution of alleles at D21S1411, D21S1435 and D21S1414 loci in the Croatian population ($N = 156$).

Table 1
Statistical parameters for D21S1411, D21S1435 and D21S1414 loci

LOCUS	HET_{obs}	HET_{exp}	PIC
D21S1411	0.850467	0.992463	0.891951
D21S1435	0.758242	0.964932	0.770623
D21S1414	0.766666	0.928681	0.927856

HET_{obs}—observed heterozygosity; HET_{exp}—expected heterozygosity; PIC—polymorphism information content.

after isolation DNA samples were amplified in three separate PCR reactions [3]. Electrophoresis was run on 6% polyacrylamide gel in automated laser fluorescence sequencer (ALFexpress, Pharmacia Biotech, Uppsala, Sweden). Allele size determination was performed using Allele Locator program and for standard we used two internal size markers and one commercial. Statistical analysis included the estimation of allele and genotype frequencies, observed (OH) and expected (EH) heterozygosity and polymorphic information content (PIC). The Hardy–Wienberg equilibrium was verified using the χ^2-test.

3. Results and discussion

In this study we present data concerning three STR loci on chromosome 21. The observed allele frequencies are presented in Fig. 1. Alleles at D21S1414 locus have a simple dinucleotide repeat structure, while alleles at the D21S1411 and D21S1435 loci consisted of tetranucleotide repeat units. At D21S1411 and D21S1435 loci we did not observe intermediate alleles. Some statistical parameters are summarised in Table 1. No deviation from Hardy–Weinberg equilibrium was observed. The highest PIC value was observed for D21S1414 locus (0.9278). Our results show that the observed heterozygosity of three STR loci is higher than 75%. It means that these three STR loci have a sufficiently high level of informativeness in the Croatian population and, for that reason, can be applied as genetic markers in prenatal diagnostics as well as in forensics.

References

[1] M. Adinolfi, B. Perti, J. Sherlock, Rapid detection of aneuploidies by microsatellites and the quantitative fluorescent polymerase chain reaction, Prenat. Diagn. 17 (1997) 1299–1311.

[2] R.M. Frederickson, H. Wang, L.C. Surh, Some caveats in PCR-based prenatal diagnosis on direct amniotic fluid versus cultured amniocytes, Prenat. Diagn. 19 (1999) 113–117.

[3] B. Pertl, U. Weitgasser, S. Kopp, P.M. Kroisel, J. Sherlock, M. Adinolfi, Rapid detection of trisomies 21 and 18 and sexing by quantitative fluorescent multiplex PCR, Hum. Genet. 98 (1996) 55–59.

ELSEVIER

International Congress Series 1261 (2004) 197–200

www.ics-elsevier.com

Polymorphism of AmpFlSTR Identifiler of the North Poland population

E. Kapińska, J. Wysocka*, L. Cybulska, Z. Szczerkowska

Department of Forensic Medicine, Medical University of Gdańsk, Gdańsk, Poland

Abstract. This paper presents the results of a population study of 15 STR loci included in AmpFlSTR® Identifiler™ (Applied Biosystems): D8S1179, D21S11, D7S820, CSF1PO, D3S1358, TH01, D13S317, D16S539, D2S1338, D19S433, VWA, TPOX, D18S51, D5S818 and FGA. Blood samples were obtained from adult unrelated individuals living in the north part of Poland. DNA was extracted from blood using a non-enzymatic method and QIAamp® DNA Mini Kit (Qiagen). The loci were amplified together in one multiplex reaction. Products of PCR were separated on an ABI 310 sequencer and genotyped. The allele distribution was in accordance with Hardy–Weinberg equilibrium. High values of heterozygosity, polymorphic information of content, power of discrimination, power of exclusion and paternity index demonstrate that the AmpFlSTR® Identifiler™ system is a valuable tool for both paternity testing and routine forensic casework.

Keywords: AmpFISTR Identifiler; PCR; Short tandem repeats (STRs); Population genetics; North Poland

1. Introduction

Multiplex PCR systems, which allow simultaneous amplification of several STR loci, are a rapid and powerful method for personal identification.

Allele frequency data were investigated in the North Poland population using AmpFISTR® Identifiler™ kit (Applied Biosystems) [1,2]. For all loci, the Hardy–Weinberg equilibrium was tested, and several statistical parameters of forensic interest were calculated.

2. Materials and methods

Blood samples were obtained from 145 adult unrelated individuals. Genomic DNA was extracted using a non-enzymatic method and QIAamp® DNA Mini Kit (Qiagen) [3]. The amplification of the AmpFISTR Identifiler was carried out using 0.1 ng of template

* Corresponding author. Tel.: +48-583-49-1258; fax: +48-583-41-0485.
E-mail address: wysocka@amg.gda.pl (J. Wysocka).

doi:10.1016/S0531-5131(03)01639-X

Table 1
Allele frequencies for AmpFISTR® Identifiler™ in North Polish population ($n = 145$)

Locus allele	D8S1179	D21S11	D7S820	CSF1PO	D3S1358	THO1	D13S317	D16S539	D2S1338	D19S433	VWA	TPOX	D18S51	D5S818	FGA
5	–	–	–	–	–	0.007	–	–	–	–	–	–	–	–	–
6	–	–	–	–	–	0.238	–	–	–	–	–	–	–	–	–
7	–	–	0.014	–	–	0.138	–	–	–	–	–	–	–	–	–
8	0.014	–	0.148	–	–	0.097	0.141	0.007	–	–	–	0.576	–	0.003	–
9	0.014	–	0.128	0.034	–	0.228	0.093	0.103	–	–	–	0.117	–	0.055	–
9.3	–	–	–	–	–	0.290	–	–	–	–	–	–	–	–	–
10	0.072	–	0.328	0.348	–	0.003	0.052	0.041	–	–	–	0.045	–	0.093	–
10.2	–	–	–	–	–	–	–	–	–	–	–	–	0.003	–	–
11	0.086	–	0.224	0.245	–	–	0.359	0.307	–	–	–	0.234	0.041	0.310	–
12	0.016	–	0.131	0.283	0.010	–	0.214	0.341	–	0.072	–	0.028	0.110	0.388	–
12.2	–	–	–	–	–	–	–	–	–	0.007	–	–	–	–	–
13	0.352	–	0.024	0.086	–	–	0.093	0.172	–	0.193	–	–	0.066	0.172	–
13.2	–	–	–	–	0.007	–	–	–	–	0.014	–	–	–	–	–
14	0.200	–	0.003	0.003	0.138	–	0.045	0.028	–	0.379	0.107	–	0.176	0.021	–
14.2	–	–	–	–	–	–	–	–	–	0.038	–	–	–	–	–
15	0.093	–	–	–	0.255	–	0.003	–	–	0.176	0.103	–	0.145	0.007	–
15.2	–	–	–	–	–	–	–	–	–	0.034	–	–	–	–	–
16	0.003	–	–	–	0.248	–	–	–	0.045	0.034	0.217	–	0.121	–	–
16.2	–	–	–	–	–	–	–	–	–	0.024	–	–	–	–	–
17	0.003	–	–	–	0.214	–	–	–	0.275	0.007	0.266	–	0.152	–	–
17.2	–	–	–	–	–	–	–	–	–	0.010	–	–	–	–	–
18	–	–	–	–	0.124	–	–	–	0.090	0.003	0.224	–	0.110	–	0.021

18.2	–	–	–	–	–	–	–	–	–	0.007	–	–	–	–	–
19	–	–	–	–	0.003	–	–	–	0.076	–	0.076	–	0.028	–	0.059
20	–	–	–	–	–	–	–	–	0.155	–	0.007	–	0.028	–	0.159
20.2	–	–	–	–	–	–	–	–	–	–	–	–	–	–	0.100
21	–	–	–	–	–	–	–	–	0.052	–	–	–	0.014	–	0.207
21.2	–	–	–	–	–	–	–	–	–	–	–	–	–	–	0.007
22	–	–	–	–	–	–	–	–	0.014	–	–	–	0.007	–	0.183
22.2	–	–	–	–	–	–	–	–	–	–	–	–	–	–	0.017
23	–	–	–	–	–	–	–	–	0.079	–	–	–	–	–	0.128
24	–	–	–	–	–	–	–	–	0.083	–	–	–	–	–	0.110
25	–	–	–	–	–	–	–	–	0.117	–	–	–	–	–	0.090
26	–	0.003	–	–	–	–	–	–	0.014	–	–	–	–	–	0.007
27	–	0.038	–	–	–	–	–	–	–	–	–	–	–	–	0.003
28	–	0.231	–	–	–	–	–	–	–	–	–	–	–	–	–
29	–	0.179	–	–	–	–	–	–	–	–	–	–	–	–	–
29.2	–	0.007	–	–	–	–	–	–	–	–	–	–	–	–	–
30	–	0.217	–	–	–	–	–	–	–	–	–	–	–	–	–
30.2	–	0.031	–	–	–	–	–	–	–	–	–	–	–	–	–
31	–	0.048	–	–	–	–	–	–	–	–	–	–	–	–	–
31.2	–	0.079	–	–	–	–	–	–	–	–	–	–	–	–	–
32	–	0.007	–	–	–	–	–	–	–	–	–	–	–	–	–
32.2	–	0.131	–	–	–	–	–	–	–	–	–	–	–	–	–
33	–	0.007	–	–	–	–	–	–	–	–	–	–	–	–	–
33.2	–	0.021	–	–	–	–	–	–	–	–	–	–	–	–	–
H_{ob}	0.710	0.876	0.697	0.724	0.745	0.710	0.766	0.772	0.876	0.848	0.800	0.621	0.862	0.745	0.821
H_{ex}	0.790	0.842	0.789	0.733	0.796	0.780	0.786	0.749	0.857	0.781	0.807	0.599	0.881	0.750	0.860
P	0.744	0.752	0.055	0.968	0.586	0.585	0.917	0.242	0.455	0.157	0.508	0.294	0.076	0.749	0.411

Table 2
Statistical parameters of the usefulness of AmpFlSTR® Identifiler™ in forensic medicine

Statistical parameters locus	Power of discrimination (PD)	Polymorphism information of content (PIC)	Power of exclusion (PE)	Matching probability (pM)	Paternity index (PI)
D8S1179	0.926	0.760	0.444	0.074	1.730
D21S11	0.952	0.820	0.746	0.048	4.030
D7S820	0.923	0.760	0.423	0.077	1.650
CSF1PO	0.880	0.680	0.467	0.120	1.810
D3S1358	0.924	0.760	0.501	0.076	1.960
TH01	0.917	0.740	0.444	0.083	1.730
D13S317	0.923	0.760	0.537	0.077	2.130
D16S539	0.885	0.710	0.549	0.115	2.200
D2S1338	0.956	0.840	0.746	0.044	4.030
D19S433	0.918	0.750	0.691	0.082	3.290
VWA	0.928	0.780	0.599	0.072	2.500
TPOX	0.791	0.550	0.316	0.209	1.320
D18S51	0.963	0.870	0.719	0.037	3.630
D5S818	0.887	0.710	0.501	0.113	1.960
FGA	0.958	0.840	0.638	0.042	2.790

DNA, according to the manufacturer's instruction. Products of PCR were analyzed on an ABI Prism 310 sequencer and genotyped.

3. Results and discussion

The distribution of observed allele frequencies for the 15 loci in North Poland is shown Table 1. All loci were highly polymorphic. The observed (H_{ob}) and expected (H_{ex}) heterozygosity rates showed similar values (Table 1). The population data revealed no significant deviation from the Hardy–Weinberg equilibrium (P values shown in Table 1).

The statistical parameters are presented in Table 2 [4,5]. The cumulative power of exclusion for the 15 loci was calculated as 0.99999.

References

[1] Applied Biosystems. AmpFlSTR® Identifiler™ PCR Amplification Kit User's Manual, Foster City, CA, P/N 4322288, 2001.

[2] J.M. Butler, R. Schoske, P.M. Peter, J.W. Redman, M.C. Kline, Allele frequencies for 15 autosomal STR loci on U.S. Caucasian, African American, and Hispanic populations, J. Forensic Sci. 48 (2003) 4.

[3] D.K. Lahiri, S. Bye, J.L. Nurberger, M.E. Hodes, M. Crisp, A non-organic and non-enzymatic extraction method gives higher yields of genomic DNA from whole-blood samples than do nine other methods tested, J. Biochem. Biophys. Methods 25 (1992) 193–205.

[4] T. Sueblinvong, U. Kongsrisook, Population data of 8 short tandem repeat loci in the Thai population, Forensic Sci. Int. 103 (1999) 199–205.

[5] B. Brinkmann, E. Meyer, Discrimination between populations using STRs, Proceedings from the First European Symposium on Human Identification, Promega, 1995, pp. 45–53.

International Congress Series 1261 (2004) 201–203

www.ics-elsevier.com

POP-Gene TIMOR: first forensic DNA marker study of East-Timor people

L. Souto[a,*], L. Gusmão[b], A. Amorim[b,c], E. Ferreira[a], F. Côrte-Real[d,e], D.N. Vieira[d,e], E.F. da Cruz e Silva[a]

[a] *Centro de Biologia Celular, Departamento de Biologia, Universidade de Aveiro, Aveiro, Portugal*
[b] *Instituto de Patologia e Imunologia Molecular da Universidade do Porto, Portugal*
[c] *Faculdade de Ciências, Universidade do Porto, Portugal*
[d] *Delegação de Coimbra, Instituto Nacional de Medicina Legal, Coimbra, Portugal*
[e] *Faculdade de Medicina da Universidade de Coimbra, Portugal*

Abstract. The first population-genetics study for the world newest independent country, East Timor, is presented. In this preliminary work, part of a major ongoing study on East-Timor genetic diversity, the allele frequencies and some statistical parameters of forensic interest were determined for the 15 loci included in AmpFLSTR Identifiler™ genotyping kit. A total of 107 samples, collected from East Timorese of several linguistic groups, was typed. All markers are in Hardy-Weinberg equilibrium (except for D2S1338 and D5S818, but the deviations do not reach significance after Bonferroni correction). Observed heterozigosities varied between 72% (D5S818) and 92% (D8S1179).

Keywords: STR; East Timor; Identifiler; Population genetics

1. Introduction

East Timor, a Portuguese colony from the 16th century until Indonesian occupation in 1975, gained finally its independence, after a tragic and complex political process on May 20th, 2002. East Timor is indeed a complex multilingual mosaic and its ethnic and linguistic heterogeneity has long attracted scientific interest in areas such as anthropology, linguistics and archaeology and constitutes a challenge to human genetics.

The AmpFLSTR® Identifiler™ PCR Amplification Kit (*Applied Biosystems*) is being widely used in forensics (as well as in paternity studies), as it complies with international standards and recommendations such as those from the *Combined DNA Index System* (CODIS), the *European Network of Forensic Science Institutes* (ENFSI) and Interpol. We present preliminary data from the first (to our knowledge) DNA study concerning East-Timorese populations, as part of a broad ongoing study of East-Timor

* Corresponding author. Tel.: +351-234-370783; fax: +351-234-426408.
E-mail address: lsouto@bio.ua.pt (L. Souto).

doi:10.1016/S0531-5131(03)01533-4

Table 1
Allele frequencies and statistical parameters of forensic relevance, for the 15 Identifiler™ STRs in East-Timor population

	D8S1179	D21S11	D7S820	CSF1PO	D3S1358	HUMTH01	D13S317	D16S539	D2S1338	D19S433	HUMVWA	TPOX	D18S51	D5S818	FGA
6						0.098						0.005			
7			0.009			0.159									
8	0.005		0.257	0.005		0.350	0.299	0.028				0.332			
9			0.028	0.061		0.341	0.075	0.154				0.308		0.023	
9.3						0.009									
10	0.042		0.229	0.210		0.042	0.112	0.210				0.028		0.318	
11	0.126		0.285	0.332			0.248	0.318				0.299	0.005	0.229	
12	0.112		0.168	0.290	0.005		0.201	0.182		0.047		0.028	0.037	0.290	
13	0.201		0.019	0.093	0.005		0.051	0.093		0.308			0.079	0.136	
13.2										0.023					
14	0.234		0.005	0.009	0.009		0.014	0.009		0.243	0.117		0.196	0.005	
14.2										0.075			0.005		
15	0.112				0.336			0.005		0.056	0.084		0.145		
15.2										0.182					
16	0.098				0.322					0.033	0.173		0.150		
16.2										0.028					
17	0.065				0.266				0.089	0.005	0.243		0.178		
18	0.005				0.051				0.042		0.257		0.070		0.005
19					0.005				0.215		0.117		0.056		0.089
20									0.042		0.009		0.019		0.051
21									0.028				0.028		0.117
22									0.107				0.019		0.206
23									0.206				0.005		0.206
24									0.192						0.154
25									0.070				0.005		0.093
26									0.005				0.005		0.047
27		0.005							0.005						0.028
28		0.112													0.005
29		0.262													
30		0.196													
30.2		0.005													
31		0.103													
31.2		0.103													
32		0.019													
32.2		0.154													
33		0.005													
33.2		0.028													
35.2		0.005													
37.2		0.005													
H obs.	0.91589	0.84112	0.80374	0.76636	0.74766	0.74766	0.82243	0.79439	0.76636	0.85981	0.84112	0.77570	0.86916	0.71963	0.90654
H exp.	0.85222	0.83818	0.77434	0.75275	0.71541	0.72748	0.79154	0.79356	0.85007	0.80628	0.81436	0.70708	0.87333	0.74722	0.85977
P	0.25516	0.53635	0.20094	0.69158	0.36875	0.26378	0.79872	0.75580	0.02591	0.80129	0.14264	0.20487	0.46464	0.01221	0.36966

H obs.: Observed Heterozygosity; H exp.: Expected Heterozygosity.
P: Hardy-Weinberg equilibrium *P* value, exact test based on more than 2000 shuffling, for standard error <0.01.

Genetics (*POP-Gene TIMOR*), which involves the cooperative efforts of the Ministry of Health of the *República Democrática de Timor-Leste* (RDTL) and Portuguese institutions.

2. Materials and methods

Blood/saliva samples, in FTA™ cards, were collected from 107 unrelated donors (with informed consent), belonging to different geographic (and linguistic) origins in East Timor. The DNA was extracted using the Chelex procedure [1] over a 3-mm^2 cut of the *FTA*™ card.

Amplification of the 15 STR Identifiler™ loci (CSF1P0, D2S1338, D3S1358, D5S818, D7S820, D8S1179, D13S317, D16S539, D18S51, D19S433, D21S11, FGA, TH01, TPOX, VWA), plus the gender marker Amelogenin, was performed following the manufacturer's recommendations.

Amplified fragments were separated using an ABI 310 Automated Sequencer and analysed with GeneScan Software. All "off-ladder" fragments were typed at least twice. The population-genetics analyses were performed using the Arlequin software package [2].

3. Results and discussion

Allele frequencies (and relevant forensic statistical parameters) for the East-Timor subjects studied are shown in Table 1 for the 15 Identifiler™ STRs. No deviations from H–W equilibrium were observed with the exception of D2S1338 and D5S818 loci, but the deviations do not reach significance after Bonnferroni correction. The observed heterozigosities varied between 72% (D5S818) and 92% (D8S1179) and the observed average heterozygosity (81%) is not significantly different from the expected value (79%).

Acknowledgements

The authors would like to thank the former CATTL, *Comissariado para a Transição em Timor-Leste*, the Social Services of the University of Aveiro, Portugal, and the Health Services of the former Portuguese Mission in East Timor for their support. A special thanks to the East-Timorese volunteers for their contribution and empathy.

This work was partially supported by Programa Operacional Ciência, Tecnologia e Inovação (POCTI), Quadro Comunitário de Apoio III.

References

[1] P.S. Walsh, D.A. Metzer, R. Higuchi, Chelex-100 as a medium for simple extraction of DNA for PCR-based typing from forensic material, BioTechniques 10 (1991) 506–513.

[2] S. Schneider, D. Roessli, L. Excoffier, Arlequin: A Software for Population Genetics Data Analysis. Ver 2.000, Genetics and Biometry Lab., Dept. of Anthropology, University of Geneva, Geneva, 2000.

International Congress Series 1261 (2004) 204–206

www.ics-elsevier.com

Population data for 15 STR loci D3S1358, TH01, D21S11, D18S51, Penta E, D5S818, D13S317, D7S820, D16S539, CSF1PO, Penat D, vWA, D8S1179, TPOX and FGA in Japanese

Masaaki Hara[a,*], Yasuhisa Yamamoto[b], Aya Takada[a], Kazuyuki Saito[a], Akira Kido[c], Masakazu Oya[c], Hiroshi Kameyama[b]

[a] *Department of Forensic Medicine, Saitama Medical School, Morohongo 38, Moroyama, Iruma, Saitama 350-0451, Japan*

[b] *Criminal Investigation Laboratory, Saitama Prefectural Police Headquarters, Saitama 330-0036, Japan*

[c] *Department of Legal Medicine, Faculty of Medicine, University of Yamanashi, Yamanashi-ken 409-3898, Japan*

Abstract. Fifteen short tandem repeat (STR) loci D3S1358, TH01, D21S11, D18S51, Penta E, D5S818, D13S317, D7S820, D16S539, CSF1PO, Penta D, vWA, D8S1179, TPOX and FGA were analyzed in 164 unrelated Japanese using the PowerPlex® 16 System kit. The genotype frequency distribution of each locus did not deviate from the Hardy–Weinberg equilibrium. Penta E was the best STR for forensic purpose. The combined power of discrimination (PD) was 0.99999999999999978.

Keywords: Short tandem repeats; Multiplex PCR; Population data; Japanese

1. Introduction

The development of multiplex PCR techniques has made it possible to analyze a number of short tandem repeat (STR) loci simultaneously. In this paper, we report population data for the allele frequency distributions and statistical parameters of the 15 STR loci (D3S1358, TH01, D21S11, D18S51, Penta E, D5S818, D13S317, D7S820, D16S539, CSF1PO, Penta D, vWA, D8S1179, TPOX and FGA) in Japanese.

2. Materials and methods

Blood samples were obtained from 164 unrelated healthy Japanese individuals living in a central region of Japan. DNA was extracted by the phenol–chloroform method and quantified by UV spectroscopy. PCR amplification of the 15 loci was performed using the

* Corresponding author. Tel.: +81-492-76-1178; fax: +81-492-94-9713.
E-mail address: haramasa@saitama-med.ac.jp (M. Hara).

0531-5131/
doi:10.1016/S0531-5131(03)01491-2

Table 1
Allele frequencies and forensic parameters for 15 STR loci in Japanese

Allele	D3S1358	TH01	D21S11	D18S51	Penta E	D5S818	D13S317	D7S820	D16S539	CSF1PO	Penta D	vWA	D8S179	TPOX	FGA
5					0.1098										
6		0.2225									0.0031			0.0031	
7		0.2439				0.0061	0.0091			0.0031	0.0031				
8		0.0396			0.0092	0.0031	0.2957	0.1281		0.0031	0.0213			0.4329	
9		0.4543			0.0031	0.0762	0.1220	0.0427	0.3445	0.0305	0.3293		0.0031	0.1189	
9.3		0.0305													
10		0.0092			0.0396	0.2073	0.0945	0.2012	0.2043	0.2531	0.2317		0.1372	0.0152	
11				0.0031	0.1372	0.2348	0.2073	0.3323	0.1860	0.1890	0.1860		0.1281	0.3933	
12	0.0031			0.0396	0.1463	0.2409	0.1982	0.2470	0.1829	0.3933	0.1189		0.1067	0.0335	
13				0.2134	0.0274	0.1646	0.0640	0.0457	0.0671	0.1128	0.0793		0.2226		
14	0.0335			0.1951	0.0457	0.0671	0.0091	0.0031	0.0122	0.0122	0.0274	0.2378	0.2195	0.0031	
15	0.3476			0.2195	0.1250				0.0031	0.0031		0.0183	0.1067		
16	0.3110			0.1098	0.0579							0.2043	0.0701		
17	0.2287			0.0732	0.0976							0.2713	0.0061		
18	0.0671			0.0610	0.0793							0.2012			0.0396
19	0.0091			0.0305	0.0518							0.0488			0.0518
20				0.0244	0.0335							0.0152			0.1128
21				0.0183	0.0092							0.0031			0.1494
22				0.0031	0.0183										0.2043
22.2															0.0031
23				0.0031	0.0061										0.1921
23.2															0.0061
24				0.0061	0.0031										0.1159
24.2															0.0061
25															0.0610
26															0.0427
27															0.0091
28			0.0366												0.0061
28.2			0.0092												
29			0.2287												
29.2			0.0031												
30			0.3476												
31			0.1006												
31.2			0.0640												
32			0.0183												
32.2			0.1494												
33.2			0.0396												
34.2			0.0031												
ET	0.5637	0.0710	0.5047	0.8050	0.1890	0.9677	0.7927	0.0623	0.0687	0.3860	0.1430	0.8173	0.5177	0.4243	0.3837
H-obs	0.6951	0.7805	0.7988	0.8476	0.8659	0.8293	0.7683	0.6890	0.7805	0.7134	0.7683	0.8232	0.8415	0.6402	0.8659
H-exp	0.7301	0.6820	0.7870	0.8436	0.9042	0.8064	0.8022	0.7678	0.7647	0.7317	0.7817	0.7847	0.8407	0.6424	0.8629
PD	0.8760	0.8273	0.9209	0.9521	0.9782	0.9331	0.9328	0.9110	0.8993	0.8842	0.9195	0.9112	0.9506	0.8099	0.9629
PIC	0.6753	0.6295	0.7596	0.8252	0.8632	0.7780	0.7745	0.7317	0.7290	0.6892	0.7501	0.7503	0.8462	0.5738	0.8481
MEC	0.4788	0.4300	0.5980	0.6903	0.8063	0.6148	0.6124	0.5528	0.5503	0.5006	0.5797	0.5745	0.6778	0.3714	0.7240

PowerPlex® 16 System kit (Promega) according to the manufacturer's recommended protocol [1]. Amplified products were separated by denaturing capillary electrophoresis in an ABI PRISM 310 Genetic Analyzer (Applied Biosystems). The results were analyzed using GeneScan Analysis 3.1 software (Applied Biosystems) and genotyping was performed using Genotyper 2.5 software (Applied Biosystems). Possible divergence from the Hardy–Weinberg equilibrium was determined using the exact test (ET) [2]. Some statistical parameters of forensic interest such as observed and expected heterozygosities (H-obs and H-exp) [3], power of discrimination (PD) [4], polymorphic information content (PIC) [5] and mean exclusion chance (MEC) [6] were calculated.

3. Results and discussion

Allele frequencies and forensic parameters for the 15 STR loci in Japanese are shown in Table 1. The genotype frequency distribution of each locus did not deviate from the Hardy–Weinberg equilibrium expectations based on the exact test (the data were shuffled 3000 times). Penta E gave the highest power of discrimination (0.9782), the highest polymorphic information content (0.8632) and the highest mean exclusion chance (0.8063). The combined power of discrimination was 0.999999999999999978 and the combined mean exclusion chance was 0.9999989.

References

[1] PowerPlex® 16 System kit, Promega, Technical Manual.

[2] S.W. Guo, E.A. Thompson, Performing the exact test of Hardy–Weinberg proportion for multiple alleles, Biometrics 48 (1992) 361–372.

[3] M. Nei, A.K. Roychoudhury, Sampling variances of heterozygosity and genetic distance, Genetics 76 (1974) 379–390.

[4] R.A. Fisher, Standard calculations for evaluating a blood group system, Heredity 5 (1951) 95–102.

[5] D. Botstein, R.L. White, M. Skolnick, R.W. Davis, Construction of a genetic linkage map in man using restriction fragment length polymorphisms, Am. J. Hum. Genet. 32 (1980) 314–331.

[6] Y. Ohno, I.M. Sebetan, S. Akaishi, A simple method for calculating the probability of excluding paternity with any number of codominant alleles, Forensic Sci. Int. 19 (1982) 93–98.

International Congress Series 1261 (2004) 207–209

www.ics-elsevier.com

Population analysis from 12 microsatellite loci reveled by silver stain and assisted by computer software

Alfonso Benítez-Páez*, Sonia Laverde

Genetic and Molecular Biology Laboratory, Forensic Genetic, Carrera 16 # 82 29, 11001, Bogotá D.C., Colombia

Abstract. A Colombian population was typed for 12 STRs by silver stain method. Initial routine was extended from 9 to 12 STR loci for increasing forensic values in paternity testing, new multiplex developed decreased significantly Probability of Match (PM) and increased power of exclusion. Kodak 1D Image Analysis Software was used for assigning allele out-ladders with analysis of their correct molecular sizes.

Keywords: Short tandem repeats; Kodak 1D image analysis software; Silver stain

1. Introduction

Since STRs markers are used for forensic proposes, several studies have published population data reports in worldwide [1,2]. Actually, almost all forensic laboratories do DNA typing with STRs markers by automated methods using fluorescent platforms as ABI310, ABI377 and FMBIO I–II. Proficiency testing has shown error rates higher in silver nitrate method than high throughput methods as ABI and HITACHI but lower than other methodologies (GEP-ISFG, personal communication, 2002). In spite of high precision and great processing sample of fluorescent methods, some laboratories cannot acquire this automated routines. Some tools have been created and enhanced for pattern bands analysis [3,4]. Aim of this study was increased STR profile set and work with a useful tool for DNA profiling by silver stain method that can help to decrease error rates in this typing analysis.

2. Materials and methods

A total of 336 EDTA–blood samples from mestizo unrelated born in Colombia involve in paternity testing were analyzed. A simple salting out method was made for DNA isolating [5].

One hundred samples were typed by triplex CTT , FFv and SilverSTR III distributed by Promega. DNA typing was in agree with technical recommendations. Samples were retyped with primers described by Masibay et al. [6]. The added 226 samples were typed this way. HPRTB, D8S1179 and D5S818 were analyzed in a multiplex reaction agree with primers published in STR database (NIST). D8S1179 region was expanded in order to

* Corresponding author. Tel.: +57-1-2550024; fax: +57-1-6164172.
E-mail address: alfbenpa@hotmail.com (A. Benítez-Páez).

0531-5131/
doi:10.1016/S0531-5131(03)01495-X

eliminate cross size with D5S818 amplicons, forward primer D8S1179 (5′ tctttct-gcccacacggcctgg3′) was derived of AF216671 Genbank sequence. Cycling for HPRTB, D8S1179 and D5S818 triplex was 95 °C by 5 min, 35 cycles of 94 °C by 1 min, 57 °C by 1 min, 72 °C by 75 s and incubation at 70 °C by 30 min. Into denaturing gels, PCR products were separated. Electrophoresis was done during 60 min at 40 W and 55 °C follows by Silver Stain detection. CTT, FFv and SilverSTR III Triplex allelic ladders, K562 cell line and M1 M2 GEP-ISFG 2002 reference samples were used for allelic assignation. Genetic Data Analysis v1.0 (d16c) [7] was used and other references for forensic values [8,9].

3. Results

Allelic frequencies and HW equilibrium values were found. Analyzed population was in HW equilibrium for all markers, however, significant disequilibrium was detected in F13A01 when exact test with Fisher measure was applied but not with Chi-squared measure ($p<0.04$ and $p<0.2172$, respectively). Linkage disequilibrium (LD) between TPOX/D7S820 and TH01/vWA was found with significant values $p<0.0194$ and $p<0.0084$, respectively. Probability of Match (PM), Power of Discrimination (PD), Polymorphic Information Content (PIC) and Typical Paternity Index (TPI) for individual markers, triplex reactions and 12 STR loci were found. Lowest PM values were at increasing order for D13S317, F13A01 and D8S1179 (0.0614, 0.0659, 0.0703, respectively). Triplex information showed lower PM in HPRTB, D8S1179 and D5S818 than CTT triplex (9.66×10^{-4} and 2.12×10^{-3}, respectively). D16S539, D7S820 and D13S317 triplex showed highest PE with 0.9448. TPI increased from 792.2 (9 loci) to 5 050.3 (12 loci).

Some alleles could not be assigned by direct visualization because they were not in commercial allelic ladder, alleles 18 and 17 from F13A01, allele 4 from TH01, alleles 12, 21 and 23 from vWA, all them with allelic frequency 0.0015 (one allele). 1D Image Analysis Soft-

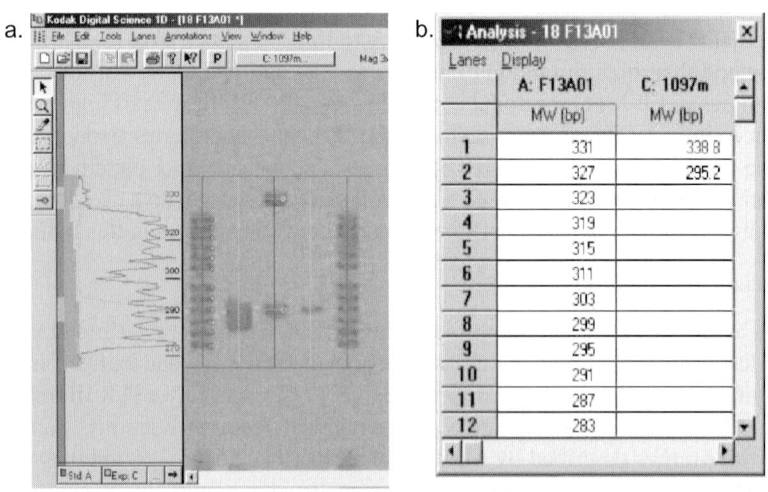

Fig. 1. Allele 18 from F13A01 analysis by 1D Image Analysis Software. (a) Band patterns are shown graphically, probably allele 18 is compared with commercial allelic ladder F13A01 (alleles 4–16) and clearly it is out-ladder range. (b) The software compared and analyzed ladder molecular sizes and determined its weight at 338.8 bp that is in agreement with the consecutive scale at base pairs (339 bp for allele 18).

ware was used for assigning corrected alleles to these samples. Fig. 1 shows allele 18 analysis by this software where molecular sizes from ladder was included into software and it did respective band pattern analysis. This allelic assignation was confirmed by ABI310 analysis in the Institute of Legal Medicine, University of Santiago of Compostela (data not shown).

4. Discussion

Population showed HW equilibrium. However LD was found between TPOX/D7S820 and TH01/vWA loci with significant p values, this fact was gotten because permutations number in exact tests. LD has been reported between FGA/D21S11, D21S11/D18S51 and D7S820/D16S539 loci with significant p values [1]. Thus, is possible to determine LD between so far genome regions. In some laboratories, STR typing silver stain method consists in nine STR profiling; however, new multiplexes can be design for increasing this routine. Additional triplex reaction showed a lower PD than CTT multiplex 0.000966 and 0.00212, respectively. Actually, polymorphic markers as D8S1179 and D5S818 cannot be found in any STR kit for silver stain detection. Enhanced silver stain routine can work 12 or more STR markers provided that laboratory decided to implement new PCR reactions. New triplex reaction increased 6.39-fold TPI. Care should be taken when a laboratory decided to increase STR profile with polymorphic markers and without many microvariants because its assignation is difficult especially when PCR products are long (FGA, D21S11 and D18S51).

Kodak 1D Image Analysis Software v 2.0.1 was useful on the assignation of alleles outladder, allele 18 from F13A01 assigned was confirmed by high throughput analysis (data not shown). Molecular size 338.8 bp was in agreement with its expected size 339 bp. Additional strategies here shown can help quality and performance either DNA typing routine and proficiency testing for laboratories working with silver stain detection.

Acknowledgements

Thanks are given to Institute of Legal Medicine of University of Santiago of Compostela for the technical help.

References

[1] M.C. Miozzo, et al., STRs data for the loci D3S1385, vWA, FGA, D8S1179, D21S11, D18S51, D5S818, D13S317 and D7S820 from Córdoba (Argentina), Forensic Sci. Int. 131 (2003) 214–217.

[2] J. Czarny, Population genetic of the STRs D3S1358, FGA, D2S1338, D8S1179, D21S11, D18S51 and D19S433 in the Pomerania–Kujawy region of Poland, Forensic Sci. Int. 125 (2002) 90–92.

[3] E. Kodak, Kodak Electrophoresis Documentation and Analysis System 120 (EDAS 120). Kodak 1D Image Analysis Software v 2.0.1.

[4] J. Pizzonia, Electrophoresis gel image processing and analysis using the KODAK 1D software, BioTechniques 30 (6) (2001) 1316–1320.

[5] S.A. Miller, et al., A salting out procedure for extracting DNA from human nucleated cells, Nucl. Acids Res. 16 (1988) 1215.

[6] A. Masibay, et al., Promega reveals primer sequences in its testing kits [letter], J. Forensic Sci. 45 (2000) 1360–1362.

[7] Lewis, P.O., Zaykin, D., 2001. Genetic Data Analysis: Computer program for the analysis of allelic data. Version 1.0 (d16c). Free program distributed: http://lewis.eeb.uconn.edu/lewishome/software.html.

[8] C. Li, A. Chakravarti, An expository review of two methods of calculating the paternity probability, Am. J. Hum. Genet. 43 (1988) 197–205.

[9] K. Huston, Statistical analysis of STR data, Profiles in DNA 1 (3) (1998) 14–15.

International Congress Series 1261 (2004) 210–212

www.ics-elsevier.com

Population data on D16S539, D2S1338 and D19S433 loci in a population sample from Brescia (Italy)

N. Cerri*, S. Manzoni, A. Verzeletti, F. De Ferrari

Institute of Legal Medicine, University of Brescia, Piazzale Spedali Civili 1, 25123 Brescia, Italy

Abstract. To establish databases for D16S539, D2S1338 and D19S433 loci for an Italian population sample from Brescia (Northern Italy), 77 unrelated persons were typed. DNA samples were amplified in a multiplex reaction with subsequent automatic detection using capillary electrophoresis. The obtained data are very useful in our practice and they give a contribution to the definition of Italian population short tandem repeat (STR) allelic and genotypic frequencies for the three analysed.

Keywords: STRs loci; Population data; Italy

1. Introduction

Short tandem repeat (STR) markers are widely used in forensics as well as in paternity testing [1]. However, before a new system can be introduced into forensic casework, a database for the relevant population must be established for statistical evaluation of the evidence. Indeed, it is well known that different ethnic group have different allelic frequencies and therefore different kind of genotypes [2–5]. In Italy, there are already data regarding a lot of STRs loci, but no data about D16S539, D2S1338 and D19S433 loci. To have allelic frequencies data regarding the population living in Brescia province (Northern Italy) and so have our own database for these three loci, it has been studied a sample of people from Brescia (Italy).

2. Materials and methods

It was considered 77 unrelated individuals from Brescia province. For each case, DNA was obtained from whole blood or oral swabs. Genomic DNA was extracted using Chelex®-100 method [6]. Amplification was carried out applying AmpFlSTR SGM plus PCR Amplification Kit (PE-AB) in a Perkin Elmer 2400 thermal cycler, according to

* Corresponding author. Tel.: +39-030-3995480; fax: +39-030-3995839.
E-mail address: deferrar@med.unibs.it (N. Cerri).

0531-5131/
doi:10.1016/S0531-5131(03)01551-6

manufacturer's recommendations. Products were loaded on the ABI Prism 310 Genetic Analyser and analysed with the GeneScan analysis software V.3.2.1.

3. Results and discussion

This work gives a relatively detailed picture of allelic and genotypic frequencies in people from Brescia province regarding three STRs loci widely used in forensics (Tables 1, 2).

The preliminary results in the distribution of allelic and genotypic frequencies are similar to that regarding Caucasian population. Among the three loci considered, D2S1338 presents the most relevant polymorphic information contents (0.8276), power of exclusion (0.8253) and power of distribution (0.9571). In no samples were found mutations that were not described in literature yet. These data are very useful in our practice and they give a contribution in the definition of Italian population STRs allelic and genotypic frequencies for the three analysed loci.

Table 1
Genotypes

D19S433		D16S539		D2S1338	
12–13	0.026667	8–11	0.012987013	16–17	0.013333
12–14	0.066667	8–12	0.012987013	16–19	0.013333
12–15	0.026667	9–9	0.012987013	16–20	0.013333
12–15.2	0.013333	9–11	0.12987013	17–17	0.053333
12–16	0.013333	9–12	0.12987013	17–18	0.04
13–13	0.133333	9–13	0.051948052	17–19	0.053333
13–14	0.186667	10–11	0.038961039	17–20	0.08
13–14.2	0.013333	10–12	0.051948052	17–21	0.026667
13–15	0.066667	10–13	0.025974026	17–22	0.04
13–15.2	0.026667	11–11	0.038961039	17–23	0.053333
13–16	0.08	11–12	0.168831169	17–24	0.053333
13–16.2	0.013333	11–13	0.103896104	17–25	0.04
13.2–14	0.013333	12–12	0.051948052	17–26	0.013333
13.2–16	0.013333	12–13	0.090909091	17–27	0.013333
14–14	0.133333	12–14	0.012987013	18–20	0.053333
14–14.2	0.013333	13–13	0.064935065	18–22	0.013333
14–15	0.053333			18–23	0.013333
14–15.2	0.026667			19–20	0.04
14.2–14.2	0.026667			19–23	0.026667
14.2–16	0.013333			19–24	0.026667
15–15.2	0.013333			20–21	0.026667
15–16	0.013333			20–23	0.04
16–16	0.013333			20–24	0.053333
				20–25	0.04
				21–23	0.013333
				22–24	0.04
				22–25	0.013333
				23–23	0.013333
				23–25	0.053333
				25–25	0.026667

Table 2
Allelic frequencies and statistical evaluation

Allele	D16S539	D2S1338	D196433
8	0.012987	–	–
9	0.168831	–	–
10	0.058442	–	–
11	0.266234	–	–
12	0.285714	–	0.08
13	0.201299	–	0.346667
13.2	–	–	0.013333
14	0.006494	–	0.32
14.2	–	–	0.026667
15	–	–	0.086667
15.2	–	–	0.04
16	–	0.02	0.08
16.2	–	–	0.006667
17	–	0.266667	–
18	–	0.06	–
19	–	0.08	–
20	–	0.173333	–
21	–	0.033333	–
22	–	0.053333	–
23	–	0.113333	–
24	–	0.086667	–
25	–	0.1	–
26	–	0.006667	–
27	–	0.006667	–
n	77	75	75
Observed H	0.831169	0.92	0.733334
Expected H	0.770661	0.854044	0.754656
PIC	0.732337	0.827679	0.719416
E	0.61343	0.82531	0.545997
D	0.902007	0.957156	0.905956

H—rate of heterozygosity, PIC—polymorphic information contents, E—power of exclusion, D—power of discrimination.

References

[1] B. Brinkmann, The STR approach, in: A. Carracedo, B. Brinkmann, W. Bar (Eds.), Advances in Forensic Haemogenetics, vol. 6, Springer, Berlin, 1996, pp. 41–51.

[2] B. Budowle, Population studies on 17 STR loci routinely used in forensic analysis, in: A. Carracedo, B. Brinkmann (Eds.), Progress in Forensic Genetics, vol. 9, Elsevier, Amsterdam, 2003, pp. 71–74.

[3] R. Decorte et al., Allele frequency data for 15 STR loci (AmpFlSTR SGM Plus and AmpFlSTR Profiler) in the Belgian population, in: A. Carracedo, B. Brinkmann (Eds.), Progress in Forensic Genetics, vol. 9, Elsevier, Amsterdam, 2003, pp. 219–222.

[4] M. Steinlechner et al., Gabon black population data on the ten short tandem repeat loci D3S1358, vWA, D16S539, D2S1338, D8S1179, D21S11, D18S51, D19S433, TH01 and FGA, Int. J. Leg. Med. 116 (2002) 176–178.

[5] S. Presciuttini et al., Allele sharing in first-degree and unrelated pairs of individuals in the Ge F I AmpFlSTR Profiler Plus database, Forensic Sci. Int. 131 (2–3) (2003) 85–89.

[6] P.S. Walsh et al., Chelex™ 100 as a medium for simple extraction of DNA for PCR based typing from forensic material, BioTechniques 4 (1991) 506–513.

International Congress Series 1261 (2004) 213–215

ELSEVIER

www.ics-elsevier.com

Development and forensic applications of multiplex PCR of autosomal biallele polymorphisms

C. Turchi[a], M. Pesaresi[a], S. Presciuttini[b], F. Alessandrini[a], C. Sassaroli[a], A. Tagliabracci[a,*]

[a] *Policlinico Torrette Institute of Legal Medicine, University of Ancona, via Conca, I-60020 Ancona, Italy*
[b] *Center of Statistical Genetics, c/o C. Retrovirus, University of Pisa Italy*

Abstract. The aim of this study was to set up a multiplex PCR of eight autosomal single nucleotide polymorphisms (SNPs) suitable for forensic purposes. © 2003 Published by Elsevier B.V.

Keywords: SNPs; Multiplex-PCR; Minisequencing; Degraded DNA

1. Introduction

The sequence of the human genome, within the framework of the Genoma Project, has revealed the existence of a new class of DNA polymorphisms involving one single base pair, called single nucleotide polymorphisms (SNPs), constituting an abundant form of genome variation [1,2]. On one hand, this new class of markers offers interesting perspectives in forensic casework, despite a considerable limitation: As they are biallele markers, there are only two different alleles in the population for each SNP, so that a large number of SNPs is required to achieve significant discrimination power [3,4]. On the other hand, SNPs may be used when DNA is highly degraded. SNPs allow us to analyze DNA regions not much longer than amplification primer pairs flanking the polymorphic site. The aims of this study were to set up a multiplex PCR of eight autosomal SNPs suitable for forensic purposes, to assay their discrimination power in a population sample and to compare it with the already known power of STRs commonly used in forensic work, and then to test them on degraded material. The multiplex PCR was constructed with eight primer pairs designed to produce amplicons in a range between 56 and 116 bp. One nanogram of DNA template extracted from 50 healthy Italian subjects and from 7 skeletal remains going back to the Second World War was submitted to amplification reaction. SNP typing was performed by minisequencing with the SnaPshot™ Multiplex Kit (AB). The extension products were electrophoresed in an automated five-colour capillary sequencer.

2. Materials and methods

Eight SNPs (Table 1), with an allele frequency of 0.5 in at least two different samples in a Caucasian population, were extrapolated from the database of "The SNP Consortium"

* Corresponding author. Tel.: +39-71-596-4727; fax: +39-71-596-4723.
E-mail address: medleg@mta01.univpm.it (A. Tagliabracci).

0531-5131/ © 2003 Published by Elsevier B.V.
doi:10.1016/S0531-5131(03)01530-9

Table 1
SNPs selected, PCR primers, length of the relative amplicons and the type of polymorphism analyzed in our study

SNPs	Chromosome	PCR Primers 5′ → 3′	Amplicon length	Ambiguity codes
TSC 127227	Chr 12	GAGAGAATGCCAGTGTGGCTCA TGATTGGCCAGGTGGAGAACTC	56 bp	C/T
TSC 4055	Chr 22	TCCCATGCCCACTCACTTTACTA TGCACATGCCCAGTGTACTCA	76 bp	C/T
TSC 258676	Chr 20	ACTTCTCTGAGTCCACCAGACCTC TGCAAGAGAACAGATTGACCCA	81 bp	C/T
TSC 143414	Chr 16	CTATTTTCTGCATCTCCAAACCCC TGGTGGCAGAGGAGCTTCATA	82 bp	A/G
TSC 9926	Chr 15	AGATTCATCCCCAGGCTCTCA AAGGCTAGCTACCAGTGTCCACCA	85 bp	C/T
TSC 20329	Chr 19	CCCCTTCTGAAAAATGGTTTCACC TTCCGGAGAAAACAGTTCCCC	94 bp	G/T
TSC 21271	Chr 1	TTTCTTGTGGTAGGTGTCTGCCTC GCAAAGCAGCCCATCAGACAT	95 bp	A/G
TSC 249022	Chr 5	GCAGTGAGGCTGTGTTTGACAA GTCCAGAGATAGCTGAATTCCTCC	116 bp	A/G

(http://snp.cshl.org). DNA was extracted from the whole blood of 50 healthy subjects and from bones going back to the Second World War by phenol chloroform [5] and quantified by 1% agarose gel electrophoresis. Multiplex PCR primer sequences were designed by Primer Express™ 1.0 (AB). Table 1 shows the primers obtained and the length of the relative amplicons. One nanogram of genomic DNA was submitted to multiplex amplification in a final volume of 50 μl (PCR Buffer 1 ×, dNTPs mix 800 μM, $MgCl_2$ 2.5 mM, 2.5 U HotStarTaq DNA polimerase (Qiagen), primers 0.05 μM) in a GeneAmp®PCR System9 700 (AB) following these conditions: 95 °C for 15 min; 35 cycles at 94 °C for 1 min, 56 °C for 1 min, 72 °C for 1 min; final extension at 72 °C for 10 min.

Polymorphic sites were detected by multiplex primer single-base extension reactions or minisequencing using the ABI PRISM® SnaPshot™ Multiplex Kit (AB) in the conditions recommended by the manufacturer. Primer extension products were separated by capillary electrophoresis on an ABI PRISM™ 310 Genetic Analyzer.

3. Results

All 50 subjects submitted to analysis showed 50 different genotypes, and this result supports the high polymorphisms of the selected markers. To investigate the discrimination power of SNPs, we calculated the match probability (Table 2) of each locus

Table 2
Probability that any two random individuals share the same genotype at each locus and at all loci

Locus	Match probability
TSC 21271	0.37868
TSC 9926	0.39361
TSC 249022	0.38560
TSC 20329	0.40891
TSC 258676	0.37754
TSC 4055	0.38004
TSC 127227	0.37590
TSC 143414	0.40891
Cumulative	0.00052

Table 3
Match probabilities of three commonly used markers and their cumulative match probability

Locus	Heterozygosity	Match probability
D7S820	0.793	0.07391
D13S317	0.767	0.08518
D5S818	0.723	0.12269
Cumulative		0.00077

(expressing the chance that two randomly chosen subjects have the same genotype). The product of these values is the cumulative match probability, or the probability of finding the same multilocus profile in any two random subjects. By comparison, Table 3 shows the match probabilities of three commonly used STRs. Positive results were obtained typing all the skeletal remains, where amplification of 15 common STRs used in forensic genetic (AmpFlSTR Identifiler PCR Amplification kit, AB) failed.

4. Discussion

This work shows that our multiplex PCR of autosomal biallele polymorphisms is robust and potentially valuable tools for forensic casework analysis. As SNPs are biallele markers, there are only two different alleles in the population for each one, so that a large number of SNPs is required to achieve significant discrimination power. Chakraborty et al. [3] and, later, Gill [4] have suggested that 30–60 SNP loci are necessary to match the power of the CODIS STR set, 13 STRs. This was confirmed by our study, which shows that three loci (D7S820, D13S317, D5S818) produce a cumulative match probability higher than that of the eight SNPs considered (i.e., they have less discriminatory power). A lower value can be obtained using four loci or, alternatively, three loci with higher heterozygosity.

In conclusion, the eight SNPs examined here provide a cumulative match probability similar to that obtained with three average STRs. Experiments on ancient DNA demonstrated that our markers seem to be useful in forensic casework when working with scarce and/or highly degraded material, in which common STRs fail.

References

[1] The International Snp Map Working Group, A map of human genome sequence variation containing 1.42 million single nucleotide polymorphisms, Nature 409 (2000) 928;
Forensic purposes, Int. J. Leg. Med. 114 (2001) 204.
[2] A.J. Brookes, The essence of SNPs, Gene 234 (1999) 177.
[3] R. Chakraborty, et al., The utility of short tandem repeat loci beyond human identification: implications for development of new DNA typing systems, Electrophoresis 20 (1999) 1682.
[4] P. Gill, An assessment of the utility of single nucleotide polymorphisms (SNPs) for forensic purposes, Int. J. Leg. Med. 114 (2001) 204.
[5] B. Budowle, Fs. Baechtel, Modifications to improve the effectiveness of restriction fragment length polymorphism typing, Appl. Theor. Electrophor. 1 (1990) 181–187.

International Congress Series 1261 (2004) 216–218

www.ics-elsevier.com

Population genetic analysis in a German population from Saxony-Anhalt using the Powerplex™ 16 system

U.-D. Immel*, M. Kleiber, M. Klintschar

Institut für Rechtsmedizin, Martin-Luther University Halle-Wittenberg, Franzosenweg 1, 06112 Halle an der Saale, Germany

Received 20 August 2003; received in revised form 20 August 2003; accepted 8 September 2003

Abstract. The use of polymorphic short tandem repeats (STRs) has become important in genetics applications, such as gene mapping, identification and paternity. In forensics, STRs are mainly used for paternity testing and personal identification. In this study, we present the results of a survey aimed at investigating the allele and genotype frequency distribution of 15 loci amplified by the GenePrint® PowerPlex™ 16 system (Promega) in Saxony-Anhalt. DNA was isolated from blood and saliva samples, randomly selected from routine casework. More than 200 unrelated individuals were included in the database. Amplification products were analyzed by capillary electrophoresis using the ABI 310® Genetic Analyzer (Applied Biosystems). Statistical analysis was carried out using various statistical methods (Hardy-Weinberg-Equilibrium, Mean Exclusion Power, Discrimination Power, etc.) to determine allele frequencies and other population parameters of interest.

Keywords: Population study; PowerPlex™ 16; German; STRs

1. Introduction

The use of polymorphic short tandem repeats (STRs) has become important in genetics applications, such as gene mapping, identification and paternity. In forensics, STRs are mainly used for paternity testing and personal identification.

In this study, we present the results of a survey aimed at investigating the allele and genotype frequency distribution of 15 loci amplified by the GenePrint® PowerPlex™ 16 system (Promega) in Saxony-Anhalt.

2. Material and methods

Either blood samples or buccal swabs were taken from 207 Germans in Saxony-Anhalt (Fig. 1) involved in criminal and paternity cases. DNA was isolated using an alkaline lysis extraction protocol [1].

* Corresponding author. Tel.: +49-345-557-1833; fax: +49-345-557-1587.
E-mail address: uta.immel@medizin.uni-halle.de (U.-D. Immel).

doi:10.1016/S0531-5131(03)01484-5

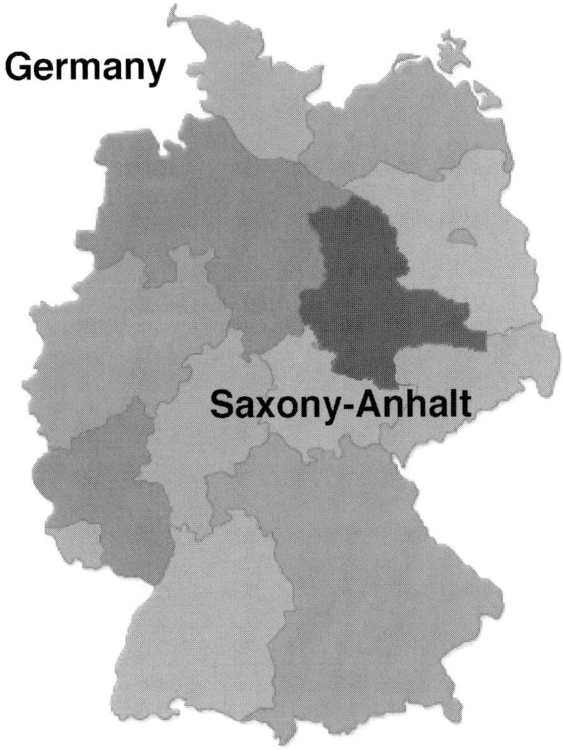

Fig. 1. German population sample from Saxony-Anhalt.

Two milliliters of the extracts was amplified following the protocols described in the GenePrint® PowerPlex™ kit 16 manual with two modifications: No quantification of the DNA in the extracts was performed and the PCR volume was 12.5 μl.

Amplification products were analyzed by capillary electrophoresis using the ABI 310® Genetic Analyzer according to the manufacturer's recommendations (Applied Biosystems).

Forensically relevant statistical analysis like Power of Discrimination or Power of Exclusion were calculated using the Powerstats 1.2 worksheet (Promega). Exact tests for checking the Hardy–Weinberg expectations were performed using the GENEPOP software version 1.2 [2].

3. Results and discussion

All loci met Hardy–Weinberg expectations. A part of the samples was typed using the AmpFLSTR® SGM Plus® Kit, which shares eight loci with the GenePrint® PowerPlex™ kit. The loci typed in both kits did not reveal any discrepancies. The results for these loci have been reported earlier [3]. The results for the remaining seven loci and parameters of forensic interest are given in Table 1.

Table 1
Allelic frequencies and forensic efficiency parameters of 7 STR loci in 207 unrelated Germans

	Penta D	TPOX	Penta E	D5S818	D13S317	D7S820	CSF1P0
Forensic							
Matching probability	0.064	0.201	0.025	0.124	0.083	0.068	0.117
Expressed as 1 in.	15.68	4.98	40.16	8.07	12.00	14.79	8.54
Power of discrimination	0.936	0.799	0.975	0.876	0.917	0.932	0.883
PIC	0.788	0.575	0.880	0.667	0.738	0.787	0.695
Paternity							
Power of exclusion	0.603	0.307	0.714	0.430	0.501	0.752	0.517
Typical paternity index	2.524	1.293	3.569	1.674	1.959	4.121	2.035
Allele frequencies							
Homozygotes	0.198	0.387	0.140	0.299	0.255	0.121	0.246
Heterozygotes	0.802	0.613	0.860	0.701	0.745	0.879	0.754
	Allele	Frequency					
	5	–	–	0.101	–	–	–
	6	–	–	–	–	–	–
	7	0.007	–	0.169	–	–	0.027
	8	0.014	0.523	0.010	0.002	0.142	0.161
	9	0.213	0.084	0.007	0.050	0.082	0.176
	10	0.089	0.059	0.104	0.068	0.044	0.251
	11	0.155	0.290	0.109	0.384	0.347	0.215
	12	0.263	0.044	0.179	0.315	0.270	0.134
	13	0.188	–	0.080	0.174	0.079	0.033
	14	0.060	–	0.051	0.004	0.031	0.002
	15	0.010	–	0.051	0.002	0.004	–
	16	–	–	0.056	–	–	–
	17	–	–	0.034	–	–	–
	18	–	–	0.029	–	–	–
	19	–	–	0.010	–	–	–
	20	–	–	0.007	–	–	–
	21	–	–	–	–	–	–
	22	–	–	0.002	–	–	–
	23	–	–	–	–	–	–
	24	–	–	0.002	–	–	–
	26	–	–	–	–	–	–

Acknowledgements

The authors would like to thank A. Graul, A. Heide and S. Salostowitz for their excellent technical assistance and G. Bothe for the brilliant pictures.

References

[1] M. Klintschar, F. Neuhuber, Evaluation of an alkaline lysis method for the extraction of DNA from whole blood and forensic stains for STR analysis, J. Forensic Sci. 45 (2000) 669–673.

[2] M. Raymond, F. Rousset, GENEPOP on the web (v3.3), Available at: http://wbiomed.curtin.edu.au/genepop/.

[3] B. Reichenpfaader, U. Immel, M. Klintschar, Population data on the short tandem repeat loci D19S433, D16S539 and D2S1338 in Germans and Austrians, Forensic Sci. Int. 123 (2003) 84–86.

International Congress Series 1261 (2004) 219–222

www.ics-elsevier.com

Population genetic data for the STR loci using the AmpFlSTR® Identifiler™ Kit in Bahia, Brazil

M.V. Santos[a,*], M.J. Anjos[b], L. Andrade[b], M.C. Vide[b], F. Corte-Real[c], D.N. Vieira[c]

[a] *Faculty of Medicine, University of Coimbra, CNPq, Brazil*
[b] *Service of Forensic Genetics, Delegation of Coimbra, National Institute of Legal Medicine, Portugal*
[c] *National Institute of Legal Medicine and Faculty of Medicine, University of Coimbra, Portugal*

Abstract. The AmpFlSTR® Identifiler™ is a multiplex kit which coamplifies 16 STR loci, including the segment of the X–Y homologus gene Amelogenin. The study of these STR loci is important for the formation of local human identification databases in order to statistically evaluate the evidence. This report presents allele frequency data for 15 STR loci in 150 unrelated individuals from Bahia, Brazil. The genotype frequencies of the 15 STR loci showed no deviations from HWE expectations. The combined power of exclusion is estimated as 99.99996% and the combined power of discrimination is 99.9999999999999999%.

Keywords: Bahia, Brazil population; STR loci; Population genetic data

1. Introduction

The Brazilian culture and origin has been diversified with the arrival of immigrants, namely the European (mainly the Portuguese) and African groups.

The purpose of this study was to determine the distribution of 15 loci: D19S433, D3S1358, D5S8118, D8S1179, vWA, TH01, D13S317, D21S11, TPOX, FGA, D7S820, D16S539, D18S51, CSF1PO and D2S1338, in the Bahian population.

2. Materials and methods

The bloodstains of 150 unrelated (in three generations) voluntary healthy donors from Bahia, Brazil were collected and extracted using Chelex procedures [1] and, if necessary, purified by the modified salt-chloroform method.

Amplification was done according to the AmpFlSTR® Identifiler™ kit [2] protocol using a 9600 thermal cycler. Amplified products were analysed by capillary electropho-

* Corresponding author. Delegação de Coimbra, Instituto Nacional de Medicina Legal, Largo da Sé Nova, 3000-213 Coimbra, Portugal. Tel.+351-239-85-4230.
E-mail address: diederiche@clix.pt (M.V. Santos).

doi:10.1016/S0531-5131(03)01628-5

Table 1
Allele frequencies and statistical analysis in the Bahian population ($n = 150$)

Allele	D3S1358	VWA	FGA	TH01	TPOX	CSF1PO	D5S818	D13S317	D7S820	D8S1179	D21S11	D18S51	D16S539	D2S1338	D19S433
6				0.220	0.023										
7				0.283	0.013	0.013	0.017		0.007						
8				0.150	0.460	0.020	0.023	0.057	0.136	0.007			0.033		
9				0.127	0.147	0.020	0.010	0.087	0.117	0.010			0.140		0.003
9.3				0.207											
10				0.013	0.077	0.313	0.063	0.047	0.320	0.060		0.013	0.100		
11		0.010			0.250	0.284	0.347	0.336	0.260	0.057		0.017	0.287		0.017
12					0.030	0.277	0.360	0.296	0.120	0.107		0.137	0.277		0.090
12.2															0.013
13	0.007	0.010				0.063	0.160	0.127	0.040	0.286		0.114	0.150		0.304
13.2															0.037
14	0.103	0.066				0.010	0.017	0.040		0.257		0.120	0.010	0.003	0.240
14.2								0.003							0.033
15	0.330	0.147					0.003			0.173		0.170	0.003		0.130
15.2												0.003			0.07
16	0.270	0.240								0.033		0.150		0.040	0.047
16.2															0.013
17	0.197	0.270						0.007		0.010		0.103		0.200	
17.2															0.003
18	0.090	0.133	0.017									0.057		0.053	
18.2															
19	0.003	0.100	0.087									0.047		0.107	
20		0.017	0.090									0.053		0.123	
20.2															
21		0.007	0.177									0.013		0.063	
21.2															

22			0.177									0.003		0.087	
22.2			0.003											0.087	
23			0.123											0.113	
23.2			0.003												
24			0.157											0.093	
25			0.090											0.027	
26			0.033											0.003	
27			0.033								0.037				
28			0.007								0.140				
29											0.250				
30											0.207				
30.2											0.033				
31											0.060				
31.2											0.107				
32											0.013				
32.2											0.087				
33.2											0.047				
34											0.003				
34.2											0.003				
35											0.010				
36											0.003				
42.2			0.003												
Minimum frequency	0.003	0.007	0.003	0.013	0.013	0.010	0.003	0.003	0.007	0.007	0.003	0.003	0.003	0.003	0.003
X^2 test	0.207	0.738	0.706	0.450	0.253	0.114	0.319	1.850	0.165	0.300	0.775	0.734	0.186	0.919	0.703
Exp. H	0.763	0.818	0.874	0.792	0.699	0.742	0.722	0.771	0.784	0.805	0.851	0.886	0.791	0.891	0.818
Obs. H	0.833	0.740	0.880	0.793	0.687	0.773	0.720	0.747	0.760	0.787	0.847	0.887	0.787	0.860	0.773
PE	0.539	0.637	0.741	0.583	0.466	0.502	0.482	0.564	0.579	0.617	0.700	0.763	0.587	0.774	0.646
PD	0.904	0.941	0.970	0.923	0.865	0.887	0.874	0.913	0.920	0.934	0.960	0.975	0.924	0.977	0.944

Exp. H, expected heterozygosity; Obs. H, observed heterozygosity; PE, power of exclusion and PD, power of discrimination.

resis on the ABI PRISM® 310 Genetic Analyzer using Liz 500 as Internal Lane DNA Standard and employing ABI software [3].

Statistical analysis was done using Genepop version 3.1a software package [4] and Microsoft Excel, respectively, in accordance with Refs. [5 and 6].

3. Results and discussion

The observed allele frequencies and results of the statistical tests are shown in Table 1. The genotype frequencies of the 15 STR loci showed no deviations from HWE expectations. The combined power of exclusion is estimated as 99.99996% and the combined power of discrimination is 99.9999999999999999%.

The allele frequencies did not show significant differences in comparison with the other Brazilian populations [7–13].

In conclusion, these systems have been shown to be a useful tool for personal identification, justifying their use for the Bahian population.

Acknowledgements

Special thanks go to the donors of the samples. We would like to thank CNPq/Brazil for financial support and "Universidade Estadual de Santa Cruz" and "Departamento de Polícia Técnica-SSP/BA".

References

[1] P.S. Walsh, D.A. Metzger, R. Higuchi, Chelex 100 as a medium for simple extraction of DNA for PCR-based typing from forensic material, Biotechniques 10 (1991) 506–513.

[2] Applied Biosystems, AmpFlSTR® Identifiler™ PCR Amplification Kit. User's Manual, Applera, 2001.

[3] Applied Biosystems, ABI Prism 310 Genetic Analyzer. User's Manual, Applera, 2001.

[4] M. Raymond, F. Rousset, Genepop (version 1.2): population genetics software for exact tests and ecumenicism, J. Hered. 86 (1995) 248–249.

[5] Y. Ohno, I.M. Sebetan, S. Akaishi, A simple method for calculating the probability of excluding paternity with any number of codominant alleles, Forensic Sci. Int. 19 (1982) 93–98.

[6] R.A. Fisher, Standard calculations for evaluating a blood group system, Heredity 5 (1951) 95–102.

[7] L. Caine, F. Corte-Real, M.J. Anjos, M. Carvalho, A. Serra, H. Antunes, M.C. Vide, D.N. Vieira, Allele frequencies of 13 loci in the Santa Catarina population of Southern Brazil, J. Forensic Sci. 48 (4) (2003) 901–902.

[8] J.A. Soares-Vieira, A.E. Billerbeck, E.M. Pinto, E.S.M. Iwamura, B.B. de Mendonça, P.A. Otto, Population genetics of nine short tandem repeat loci, Am. J. Forensic Med. Pathol. 23 (2) (2002) 182–190.

[9] Population Genetics of STRs in Amazonas-Brazil population, Personal Communication, 2003.

[10] F. Corte-Real, L. Andrade, M.J. Anjos, M. Carvalho, D.N. Vieira, A. Carracedo, M.C. Vide, Population genetics of nine STR loci in two populations from Brazil, J. Forensic Sci. 45 (2) (2000) 432–435.

[11] I.A. Barros de Castro, C.M.C. Rinzler, F.D. Rumjanek, Allele frequency distributions for twelve STR loci in a Brazilian population, J. Forensic Sci. 45 (4) (2000) 941.

[12] L.F. Jobim, M.R. Jobim, F. Gamio, G. Ewald, M. Jobim, L. Fernandes, Paternity testing analysis-allelic distribution, heterozygosity and power of exclusion of commonly used SLTs and STRs in the Brazillian Caucaoid population, Int. Congr. Ser. 1239 (2003) 213–218.

[13] L.A.F. da Silva, B.J. Pimentel, D.A. Azevedo, E.N.P. da Silva, S.S. dos Santos, Allele frequencies of none STR loci-D16S539, D7S820, D13S317, CSF1PO, TPOX, THO1, F13A01, FESFPS AND vWA-in the population from Alagoas, northeastern Brazil, Forensic Sci. Int. 130 (2002) 187–188.

International Congress Series 1261 (2004) 223–225
www.ics-elsevier.com

Population genetic data from El Salvador (Central America) using AmpFlSTR® Identifiler® PCR Amplification Kit

J.A. Morales[a], J.C. Monterrosa[a,*], J. Puente[b]

[a] *Laboratory of Forensic Genetics, Institute of Legal Medicine Dr. Roberto Masferrer, Supreme Court, San Salvador, El Salvador*

[b] *Department of Human Identification, Genomica S.A.U., Madrid, Spain*

Abstract. This study presents allele distribution data of the 13 core short tandem repeat (STR) loci standardized under the Combined DNA Index System (CODIS): CSF1PO, D3S1358, D5S818, D7S820, D8S1179, D13S317, D16S539, D18S51, D21S11, vWA, FGA, TH01, TPOX, and two additional tetranucleotide loci, D2S1338 and D19S433, using AmpFlSTR® Identifiler® PCR Amplification Kit, in an El Salvadoran sample population, consisting of 228 unrelated individuals. All PCR product separations were performed by capillary electrophoresis using an ABI PRISM® 310 Genetic Analyzer. GeneScan® v 3.7. and Genotyper® Software v 3.7 was used for automated STR analysis and allele designation. Allele frequencies for each locus, observed (Ho) and expected (He) heterozygosities, *p* values of chi square test (*p*-Chi) and Fisher test (*p*-Fish) for departures from Hardy–Weinberg expectations (HWE), power of discrimination (PD), probability of exclusion (PE) and Polymorphism Information Content (PIC) were calculated. The results demonstrate that the AmpFlSTR® Identifiler® PCR Amplification Kit is a highly discriminating test suitable for paternity and identity testing in El Salvadoran population.

Keywords: STR; DNA polymorphism; El Salvadoran population database; Identifiler®

1. Introduction

Short tandem repeat (STR) polymorphisms are the standard genetic markers mainly used for paternity testing and human identification. In routine forensic casework, it is important to establish a population genetic database for further reliable statistical analyses. This study presents allele distribution data of the 13 core STR loci standardized under the Combined DNA Index System (CODIS): CSF1PO, D3S1358, D5S818, D7S820, D8S1179, D13S317,

* Corresponding author. Tel.: +503-262-0247; fax: +503-257-7899.
E-mail address: jcmonterrosa@telesal.net (J.C. Monterrosa).

doi:10.1016/S0531-5131(03)01663-7

D16S539, D18S51, D21S11, vWA, FGA, TH01, TPOX, and two additional tetranucleotide loci, D2S1338 and D19S433, in an El Salvadoran sample population.

2. Materials and methods

Blood and/or buccal swab samples were obtained from 228 unrelated El Salvadoran individuals and DNA was extracted using the organic phenol–chloroform–isoamyl alcohol method.

Amplification was performed using the AmpFlSTR® Identifiler® PCR Amplification Kit in a 96-well GeneAmp® PCR System 9700, according to the manufacturer's recommendations, in a 12.5-μl reaction volume.

Table 1
Observed allele frequencies in an El Salvadoran population sample (228 individuals)

	D8S1179	D21S11	D7S820	CSF1PO	D3S1358	TH01	D13S317	D16S539	D2S1338	D19S433	VWA	TPOX	D18S51	D5S818	FGA	
6						0,364	0,0023					0,0088				6
7			0,0044	0,0132		0,3114	0,0023					0,0022		0,0373		7
8	0,0044		0,0855	0,0066		0,068	0,0658	0,0066				0,4846		0,0132		8
9	0,0066		0,0504	0,0307		0,1031	0,2083	0,0987				0,0373		0,0526		9
9,3						0,1447										9,3
10	0,0899		0,2478	0,2149		0,0088	0,114	0,2039				0,057	0,0021	0,0592		10
10,2													0,0021			10,2
11	0,0526		0,3136	0,2763			0,1776	0,3136		0,0023		0,2478	0,0088	0,4627		11
12	0,1513		0,2566	0,3662			0,239	0,261		0,0767		0,1579	0,0987	0,2631		12
12,2										0,0109			0,0022			12,2
13	0,2961		0,0395	0,0877			0,1096	0,1009		0,1886	0,0066	0,0044	0,0987	0,0987		13
13,2										0,1557						13,2
14	0,2588		0,0022		0,0614		0,0789	0,0153		0,2961	0,0724		0,1557	0,0088		14
14,2										0,0439						14,2
15	0,1096			0,0044	0,4825		0,0022			0,1535	0,0833		0,1601	0,0044		15
15,2										0,0373						15,2
16	0,0263				0,2303				0,0373	0,0197	0,3662		0,1382			16
16,2										0,0153						16,2
17	0,0044				0,1403				0,1009		0,307		0,1689			17
18					0,0811				0,0679		0,1228		0,068		0,0044	18
19					0,0044				0,1952		0,0373		0,0373		0,0987	19
20									0,1557		0,0022		0,0285		0,0504	20
21									0,0439		0,0022		0,0066		0,1031	21
22									0,0811				0,0153		0,1118	22
23									0,1908				0,0066		0,1623	23
24									0,0811				0,0022		0,1689	24
25									0,0351						0,1491	25
26		0,0022							0,0088						0,1096	26
27		0,0219							0,0022						0,0329	27
28		0,0833													0,0088	28
29		0,2237														29
30		0,2741														30
30,2		0,0109														30,2
31		0,0329														31
31,2		0,1294														31,2
32		0,0132														32
32,2		0,1491														32,2
33		0,0044														33
33,2		0,0373														33,2
34,2		0,0132														34,2
35		0,0022														35
35,2		0,0022														35,2
Min Freq	0,0126	0,0131	0,0121	0,0125	0,0116	0,0121	0,0129	0,0122	0,0136	0,0132	0,0122	0,0118	0,0136	0,012	0,0136	Min Freq

All PCR product separations were performed by capillary electrophoresis using an ABI PRISM® 310 Genetic Analyzer. GeneScan® v 3.7 and Genotyper® Software v 3.7 was used for automated STR analysis and allele designation.

Statistical analyses were performed using GDA Version 1.0 (d16c) (Lewis, P.O., and Zaykin, D. 2001) and PowerStats v1.2 (Allan Tereba, Promega) programs.

3. Results and discussion

The observed allele frequencies in the El Salvadoran population sample for the 15 STR loci are shown in Table 1. Minimum allele frequencies were also estimated using sample size and the observed heterozygosity at each locus.

The observed (Ho) and expected (He) heterozygosities, p values of chi square test (p-Chi) and Fisher test (p-Fish) for departures from Hardy–Weinberg expectations (HWE), power of discrimination (PD), probability of exclusion (PE) and Polymorphism Information Content (PIC) are displayed in Table 2.

All loci are highly polymorphic with the locus D3S1358 having the lowest observed heterozygosity (Ho) (64.9%) and loci D18S51 and FGA both displaying the highest heterozygosity (86.4%).

The genotype distribution for the 15 loci showed no deviations (p>0.01) from Hardy–Weinberg Equilibrium expectation and an inter-class correlation test analysis showed no evidence for association of alleles between the 15 loci. The combined power of discrimination (PD) for the 15 loci was>0.9999999999999999 and the combined probability of exclusion (PE) was 0.99999544.

In conclusion, these results demonstrate that the AmpFlSTR® Identifiler® PCR Amplification Kit is a highly discriminating test suitable for paternity and identity testing in El Salvadoran population.

Table 2
Statistical parameters of forensic value for AmpFlSTR® Identifiler® Kit

Loci STR	Alleles	He	Ho	p-Chi	p-Fisher	PD	PE	PIC
D8S1179	10	0.801	0.772	0.325	0.241	0.930	0.548	0.77
D21S11	15	0.827	0.816	0.789	0.473	0.945	0.629	0.80
D7S820	8	0.765	0.719	0.313	0.299	0.910	0.459	0.72
CSF1PO	8	0.736	0.759	0.574	0.668	0.878	0.525	0.69
D3S1358	6	0.686	0.649	0.850	0.797	0.861	0.354	0.64
TH01	6	0.736	0.719	0.079	0.091	0.881	0.459	0.69
D13S317	10	0.834	0.798	0.627	0.590	0.950	0.596	0.81
D16S539	7	0.773	0.724	0.500	0.404	0.916	0.466	0.74
D2S1338	12	0.871	0.860	0.436	0.242	0.966	0.714	0.86
D19S433	11	0.821	0.833	0.039	0.219	0.940	0.662	0.80
VWA	9	0.744	0.724	0.906	0.786	0.901	0.466	0.70
TPOX	8	0.675	0.671	0.233	0.605	0.852	0.385	0.63
D18S51	17	0.878	0.864	0.929	0.824	0.970	0.723	0.86
D5S818	9	0.700	0.697	0.378	0.522	0.870	0.424	0.66
FGA	11	0.876	0.864	0.294	0.176	0.967	0.723	0.86

International Congress Series 1261 (2004) 226–228

ELSEVIER

www.ics-elsevier.com

Genetic data on 10 STRs in a population sample of Old Believers living in the northeastern Poland

Witold Pepinski[a,*], Anna Niemcunowicz-Janica[a], Malgorzata Skawronska[a], Jerzy Janica[a], Ewa Koc-Zorawska[a], Ireneusz Soltyszewski[b]

[a] *Department of Forensic Medicine, Medical University of Bialystok, ul. Waszyngtona 13, 15-269 Bialystok, Poland*

[b] *Central Forensic Laboratory of Police, Al. Ujazdowskie 7, 00-583 Warsaw, Poland*

Abstract. This study provides a 10-STR database for a population sample of Old Believers ($n = 116$) living in the northeastern Poland. For the FGA and TH01 loci, a departure from HWE was observed. The combined values of the Matching Probability and of the Power of Exclusion are 3.48×10^{-12} and 0.9949, respectively. Significant differences were found for FGA and D21S11 between the Old Believers and the autochthonous Polish population by using R × C test.

Keywords: Short tandem repeats; AmpFlSTR SGM Plus; Population genetics; Old Believers; Poland

1. Introduction

Old Believers are a fraction of the Russian Orthodox Church who split in opposition to the Russian Church Reform, adopting the liturgy and practices of the Greek Church. The Reform was opposed by a group of Muscovite priests who were persecuted and whose leaders were executed. The harassed people sought shelter in many countries, including Lithuania and Poland. Presently, no more than 600 Old Believers inhabit mostly two villages in Suwalki Landscape Park [1,2]. The objective of this study was to provide a 10-STR database for a population sample of Old Believers living in NE Poland and to discuss its relationship with the reference population of autochthonous Polish Caucasians.

2. Materials and methods

DNA was extracted with the use of Chelex-100 and proteinase K method [3] from the buccal swabs of 116 unrelated Old Believers. AmpFlSTR SGM Plus and ABI 310 (Applera, USA) were used for typing.

* Corresponding author. Tel.: +48-85-7485948; fax: +48-85-7485985.
E-mail address: pepinski@amb.edu.pl (W. Pepinski).

doi:10.1016/S0531-5131(03)01506-1

Table 1
Observed allele frequencies and forensic efficiency parameters for the 10-STR loci in the population of Old Believers (NE Poland), $n = 116$

Allele	D3S1358	VWA	FGA[a]	TH01[a]	D16S539	D2S1338	D21S11	D18S51	D8S1179	D19S433
6	–	–	–	0.271	–	–	–	–	–	–
7	–	–	–	0.079	–	–	–	–	–	–
8	–	–	–	0.079	0.007	–	–	–	–	–
9	–	–	–	0.229	0.107	–	–	–	0.007	–
9.3	–	–	–	0.336	–	–	–	–	–	–
10	–	–	–	0.007	0.007	0.007	–	0.037	0.057	–
11	–	–	–	–	0.279	–	–	0.015	0.064	–
12	–	–	–	–	0.386	–	–	0.074	0.150	0.100
12.2	–	–	–	–	–	–	–	–	–	–
13	–	–	–	–	0.186	–	–	0.118	0.364	0.200
13.2	–	–	–	–	–	–	–	–	–	0.029
14	0.143	0.121	–	–	0.014	–	–	0.154	0.271	0.421
14.2	–	–	–	–	–	–	–	–	–	0.029
15	0.229	0.093	–	–	–	–	–	0.132	0.064	0.136
15.2	–	–	–	–	–	–	–	–	–	0.043
16	0.293	0.179	0.004	–	0.007	0.088	–	0.140	0.021	0.021
16.2	–	–	–	–	0.007	–	–	–	–	0.007
17	0.214	0.321	0.004	–	–	0.213	–	0.169	–	0.007
18	0.107	0.221	0.004	–	–	0.051	–	0.044	–	–
18.2	–	–	–	–	–	–	–	–	–	0.007
19	0.014	0.050	0.095	–	–	0.096	–	0.088	–	–
20	–	0.014	0.153	–	–	0.184	–	0.007	–	–
20.2	–	–	0.004	–	–	–	–	–	–	–
21	–	–	0.207	–	–	0.059	–	0.022	–	–
21.2	–	–	–	–	–	–	–	–	–	–
22	–	–	0.182	–	–	0.037	–	–	–	–
22.2	–	–	0.004	–	–	–	–	–	–	
23	–	–	0.083	–	–	0.081	–	–	–	–
23.2	–	–	0.004	–	–	–	–	–	–	–
24	–	–	0.140	–	–	0.096	–	–	–	–
25	–	–	0.066	–	–	0.081	–	–	–	–
25.2	–	–	0.004	–	–	–	–	–	–	–
26	–	–	0.045	–	–	0.007	0.020	–	–	–
27	–	–	–	–	–	–	0.004	–	–	–
28	–	–	–	–	–	–	0.168	–	–	–
29	–	–	–	–	–	–	0.172	–	–	–
30	–	–	–	–	–	–	0.320	–	–	–
30.2	–	–	–	–	–	–	0.074	–	–	–
31	–	–	–	–	–	–	0.070	–	–	–
31.2	–	–	–	–	–	–	0.078	–	–	–
32	–	–	–	–	–	–	–	–	–	–
32.2	–	–	–	–	–	–	0.066	–	–	–
33.2	–	–	–	–	–	–	0.025	–	–	–
34.2	–	–	–	–	–	–	0.004	–	–	–
Ho	0.829	0.829	0.829	0.671	0.743	0.800	0.843	0.771	0.708	0.829
He	0.790	0.795	0.861	0.753	0.727	0.875	0.816	0.760	0.888	0.756
P	0.430	0.667	0.017	0.028	0.687	0.062	0.462	0.816	0.792	0.981
PIC	0.75	0.76	0.84	0.71	0.68	0.86	0.80	0.87	0.72	0.72
DP	0.902	0.919	0.958	0.892	0.869	0.960	0.943	0.967	0.904	0.898
MP	0.098	0.081	0.042	0.108	0.131	0.040	0.057	0.033	0.096	0.102
TPI	2.92	2.92	3.56	1.52	1.94	4.43	2.65	3.09	2.19	2.92
PE	0.653	0.653	0.714	0.385	0.498	0.588	0.621	0.672	0.547	0.653

Ho: heterozygosity observed, He: heterozygosity expected, P: fisher exact test probability, PIC: polymorphism information content, DP: discrimination power, MP: matching probability, TPI: typical paternity index, PE: power of exclusion.

[a] Departure from HWE.

HWE was tested by the exact test [4] using the GDA software [5]. Comparison of allele frequency distributions was performed by means of R × C test. For the calculations of the forensic efficiency parameters, PowerStats software was used [6].

Table 2
A pairwise comparison (R × C) between the population of Old Believers and the autochthonous Poles

Locus	χ^2	P	G	P
D3S1358	4.2415	0.50100 ± 0.0158	4.5066	0.5220 ± 0.0158
VWA	2.8028	0.9170 ± 0.0087	3.5446	0.8860 ± 0.0101
FGA[a]	45.8666	0.0000 ± 0.0000	26.6576	0.0130 ± 0.0036
TH01	3.7633	0.5740 ± 0.0156	4.0713	0.5790 ± 0.0156
D16S539	7.9641	0.3180 ± 0.0147	8.5249	0.3030 ± 0.0145
D2S1338	10.8335	0.3710 ± 0.0153	10.3364	0.4680 ± 0.0158
D21S11[a]	29.8799	0.0050 ± 0.0022	23.7198	0.0180 ± 0.0042
D18S51	22.0503	0.0980 ± 0.0094	20.5669	0.1170 ± 0.0102
D8S1179	5.0646	0.6340 ± 0.0152	5.4914	0.6220 ± 0.0153
D19S433	21.2792	0.0540 ± 0.0071	18.3280	0.0730 ± 0.0082

χ^2: Chi-square test, G: G statistics, P: probability.

[a] Difference is statistically significant.

3. Results and discussion

FGA and TH01 loci showed a significant departure from HWE in the examined population sample ($p < 0.05$) (Table 1). An average observed value of heterozygosity was 0.799, which is slightly lower than the average calculated for Polish Caucasians (0.826) [7]. The combined forensic efficiency values calculated for the population of Old Believers (MP = 3.48×10^{-12}, PE = 0.9949) were somewhat different from those reported for the population of the northeastern Poland (MP = 4.18×10^{-13}, PE = 0.9914) [7]. A pairwise testing for heterogeneity revealed statistically significant differences between the Old Believers and autochthonous Poles for FGA and D21S11 ($p < 0.05$) (Table 2).

4. Conclusion

A population database for the ethnic group of the Old Believers has been established for 10-STR systems included in AmpFlSTR SGM Plus kit.

References

[1] A. Rochowicz, National minorities in Poland, in: J. Packer, K. Myntti (Eds.), The Protection of Ethnic and Linguistic Minorities in Europe, Abo Akademii University, Turku/Abo, 1993, p. 105.

[2] G. Simoncini, National Minorities in Poland at the End of the Twentieth Century, The Polish Review, New York, 1998, pp. 173–193.

[3] P. Wiegand, T. Bajanowski, B. Brinkmann, PCR typing of debris from fingernails, Int. J. Leg. Med. 106 (1993) 81–84.

[4] S.W. Guo, E.A. Thompson, Performing the exact test of Hardy–Weinberg proportion for multiple alleles, Biometrics 48 (1992) 361–372.

[5] P.O. Lewis, D. Zaykin, Genetic data analysis, Computer Program for the Analysis of Allelic Data, Version 1.0, 1997, http://chee.unm.edu/gda.

[6] A. Tereba, Tools for Analysis of Population Statistics, Profiles in DNA, 3 Promega, 1999, http://www.promega.com/geneticidtools/powerstats/.

[7] W. Pepinski, J. Janica, M. Skawronska, A. Niemcunowicz-Janica, I. Soltyszewski, Population genetics of 15 STR loci in the population of Podlasie (NE Poland), Forensic Sci. Int. 124 (2001) 226–227.

ELSEVIER

International Congress Series 1261 (2004) 229–232

www.ics-elsevier.com

Population genetics of the Identifiler system in Poland

R. Jacewicz[a,*], J. Berent[a], A. Prosniak[a], P. Galecki[b], A. Florkowski[b], S. Szram[a]

[a] *Department of Forensic Medicine, Medical University of Lodz, Lodz, Poland*
[b] *Department of Psychiatry and Neurosis Disorders with Crisis Intervention Word, Medical University of Lodz, Lodz, Poland*

Abstract. Allele frequency data and forensic efficiency parameters for 15 Identifiler STR loci: D8S1179, D21S11, D7S820, CSF1PO, D3S1358, TH01, D13S317, D16S539, D2S1338, D19S433, vWA, TPOX, D18S51, D5S818, FGA, were estimated from a sample of 125 unrelated individuals in central Poland. The accordance with the Hardy and Weinberg equilibrium (HWE) for all analyzed loci was proven. The combined power of discrimination (PD) and probability of identity (DI) were greater than 0.999999999999999 and 6.7×10^{-18}, respectively, which proves that this multiplex system is an excellent tool for forensic casework.

Keywords: Multiplex STR; Identifiler; Population data; HWE; Forensic usefulness; Poland

1. Introduction

One of the two commercially available multiplex systems enabling a simultaneous variability analysis of the 15 different autosomal loci and AMG on the basis of the five-color detection is the Identifiler system [1,2]. The purpose of this work was to establish the allele frequencies for the 15 STR-loci included in this system, i.e., D3S1358, vWA, D16S539, D2S1338, D8S1179, D21S11, D18S51, D19S433, TH01 and FGA in a Polish population sample. The evaluation of Hardy–Weinberg equilibrium (HWE) and the calculation of statistical parameters were another aim of this study.

2. Materials and methods

The database was obtained from blood samples taken from 125 unrelated healthy individuals at the Department of Forensic Medicine, Medical University of Lodz, Poland. Genomic DNA was isolated by the salt extraction procedure as described by Lahiri and Nurnberger [3]. Amplification was carried out using the Identifiler kit according to the User's Manual (Applied Biosystems). PCR products were detected in 5-dye florescent system and genotyped using GeneScan version 3.7 on the ABI Prism 377 sequencer with

* Corresponding author. Tel.: +48-42-6544536; fax: +48-42-6544293.
E-mail address: r.jacewicz@post.pl (R. Jacewicz).

doi:10.1016/S0531-5131(03)01543-7

Table 1
The allele frequencies for the 15 STR loci included in the Identifiler system in the population of central Poland

Allele	D8S1179	D21S11	D7S820	CSF1PO	D3S1358	TH01	D13S317	D16S539	D2S1338	D19S433	vWA	TPOX	D18S51	D5S818	FGA
6						0.22400									
7			0.02000			0.12400									
8	0.00400		0.12400			0.11200	0.11600	0.00400				0.56800		0.00400	
9	0.01600		0.16000	0.04800		0.20800	0.08800	0.05600				0.08800		0.07200	
9.3						0.32400									
10	0.05200		0.30000	0.33600		0.00800	0.07200	0.04000				0.06000	0.00400	0.08400	
11	0.06000		0.20000	0.22800			0.35600	0.32800				0.25200	0.01600	0.32800	
12	0.18400		0.16000	0.31600	0.00400		0.25600	0.32400		0.06000		0.03200	0.13600	0.37600	
13	0.32400		0.02400	0.06400			0.08000	0.20400		0.20400			0.10400	0.12400	
13.2										0.01600					
14	0.20800		0.01200	0.00800	0.18000		0.02800	0.04400		0.40000	0.09600		0.16800	0.00400	
14.2										0.01600					
15	0.12400				0.27600		0.00400			0.16000	0.09200		0.16000	0.00800	
15.2										0.06400					
16	0.02000				0.23600				0.06000	0.04000	0.18000		0.15600		
16.2										0.02800					
17	0.00800				0.15600				0.18000		0.28800		0.12800		
17.2										0.00800					
18					0.13600				0.06800		0.25200		0.07600		0.01200
18.2										0.00400					
19					0.00800				0.11600		0.07600		0.02000		0.06800
20					0.00400				0.15200		0.01600		0.02000		0.13200
21									0.04800				0.00800		0.17600
21.2															0.00400
22									0.00800						0.19600
22.2															0.02400
23									0.10000				0.00400		0.12400
23.2															0.00400
24									0.13200						0.13600
24.2															0.01600
25									0.12400						0.09600
26									0.01200						0.00800
27		0.05200													0.00400
28		0.18800													
29		0.17600													
30		0.21600													
30.2		0.04400													
31		0.06800													
31.2		0.08400													
32		0.00800													
32.2		0.11600													
33		0.00400													
33.2		0.04000													
34.2		0.00400													

Table 2
The HWE evaluation and the forensic efficiency parameters for the 15 STR loci included in the Identifiler system in the population of central Poland

Locus	D8S1179	D21S11	D7S820	CSF1PO	D3S1358	TH01	D13S317	D16S539	D2S1338	D19S433	vWA	TPOX	D18S51	D5S818	FGA
HWE	0.08156	0.47375	0.38188	0.35000	0.96938	0.21688	0.41250	0.85938	0.72500	0.51750	0.53750	0.15063	0.85500	0.82750	0.19625
H_{obs}	0.80500	0.83200	0.78400	0.74400	0.81600	0.72800	0.78400	0.76800	0.86400	0.76000	0.81600	0.61600	0.85600	0.76000	0.84800
H_{exp}	0.79868	0.85899	0.80553	0.73173	0.79598	0.77671	0.77725	0.74210	0.88103	0.76517	0.80064	0.60392	0.87271	0.72623	0.86786
PIC	0.76796	0.83934	0.77447	0.68069	0.76076	0.73815	0.74380	0.69543	0.86494	0.73354	0.76856	0.55090	0.85492	0.67866	0.84942
PD	0.93065	0.96292	0.93308	0.87834	0.92503	0.91329	0.91865	0.88824	0.97243	0.91484	0.93009	0.79056	0.96860	0.87878	0.96664
DI	0.02707	0.05171	0.08323	0.11430	0.06148	0.12784	0.08323	0.09516	0.03448	0.10138	0.06148	0.23829	0.03849	0.10138	0.04270

HWE (Hardy and Weiberg equilibrium)—probability values of exact test based on 2300 shufflings, PIC polymorphism information content, H_{obs}—observed heterozygosity, H_{exp}—expected heterozygosity, PD—power of discrimination, DI—discrimination index. The combined values for the 10 loci of: PD>0.999999999999999, $DI = 6.729 \times 10^{-18}$.

GeneScan-500 LIZ as internal lane standard. Allele frequencies were calculated from the number of each genotype obtained in the sample set. Pairwise interclass correlation tests were performed for all possible two-locus combination. The evaluation of HWE was tested by the exact test with the computer programme GDA [4]. The evaluation of forensic efficiency parameters was estimated according to the appropriate designs: heterozygosity observed (H_{obs}), heterozygosity expected (H_{exp}) [5], polymorphism information content [6], power of discrimination [7], discrimination index [8].

3. Results and discussion

The data on the allele frequencies of the ten STR loci in the sample of population from central Poland are collected in Table 1. No pairwise correlation (not shown) was observed between the alleles of the 15 loci. Based on the results of the exact test, no deviation from the HWE was observed at any of the 15 loci. The 10 investigated loci proved to be highly polymorphic, but the most informative seems to be the following loci: D2S1338, D18S51, D21S11 and FGA (Table 2). All of the 15 loci posses the combined power of discrimination greater than 0.999999999999999 and a combined probability that two randomly selected individuals share the same 10-locus profile is 6.7×10^{-18}. The observed heterozygosities ranged from 0.616 (TH01) to 0.864 (D2S1338) are close to those expected.

4. Conclusion

The 15 DNA STR loci included in the Identifiler multiplex possess a highly discriminating power in forensic casework in the population of central Poland. The allele frequency data will be applied for statistical evaluation of the DNA evidence in human identification as well as healthy population database for clinical studies.

Acknowledgements

This project was supported by the Medical University of Lodz grant no. 502-11-107.

References

[1] Paternity testing workshop of the English Speaking Working Group of the ISFG, 2003 (draft report).

[2] A. Barbaro, P. Cormaci, G. Falcone, A. La Marca, A. Barbaro, Population genetic study of 15 STRs loci using AmpF/STR Identifiler™ kit, Prog. Forensic Genet. 9 (2003) 259–266.

[3] D.K. Lahiri Jr., J.I. Nurnberger, A rapid non enzymatic method for RFLP studies, Nucleic Acids Res. 19 (1991) 5444.

[4] P.O. Lewis, D. Zaykin, Genetic Data Analysis, Version 1.1, 2003, available at: http://lewis.eeb.unconn.edu/lewishome/sofwtware.html.

[5] M. Nei, A.K. Roychoudhury, Sampling variances of heterozygosity and genetic distance, Genetics 76 (1974) 379–390.

[6] D. Botstein, R.L. White, M. Skolnick, R.W. Davis, Construction of genetic linkage map in man using restriction fragment length polymorphism, Am. J. Hum. Genet. 32 (1980) 314–331.

[7] The Evaluation of Forensic DNA Evidence, National Research Council Report, vol. II, National Academy Press, Washingtonm, DC, 1996, pp. 96–97.

[8] Z. Wong, V. Wilson, I. Patel, S. Povey, A.J. Jeffreys, Characterization of a panel of highly variable minisatellites cloned from human DNA, Ann. Hum. Genet. 51 (1987) 269–288.

International Congress Series 1261 (2004) 233–235

ELSEVIER

www.ics-elsevier.com

Population specific single nucleotide polymorphisms

C. Phillips[a,*], M. Lareu[a], A. Salas[a], M. Fondevila[a], G. Berniell Lee[a], A. Carracedo[a], N. Morling[b], P. Schneider[b], D. Syndercombe Court[b]

[a] *Institute of Legal Medicine, University of Santiago de Compostela, Calle San Francisco S/N, Galicia, 15705 Santiago de Compostela, Spain*

[b] *The SNP for ID Consortium, Spain*

Abstract. A search has been made of the Celera SNP database for markers exhibiting population specific polymorphism, where variation is only shown by one of the two populations used for validation. Using the SNPs found, assays are being developed for population-of-origin tests. © 2004 Elsevier B.V. All rights reserved.

Keywords: Population specific; SNP; African; European; SNaPshot; Forensic analysis

1. Introduction

Using polymorphic markers to ascertain the population-of-origin of an unknown sample has long been an area of interest in forensic analysis. Unfortunately, most markers have alleles which are shared between each population, or have population specific alleles at frequencies too low to be useful. SNPs display more differentiated variation between populations owing to the age and stability of nucleotide substitutions. This study aimed to find population specific SNPs, validated to a sufficiently high level, and to develop genotyping assays for these markers. SNP loci exhibiting variation exclusively in one of two population groups (described as African-Americans and Caucasians) were collected from the Celera CDS database comprising 4.8 million SNPs [1]. All the selected markers had allele frequencies estimated to two decimal places using 45 individuals from each population. Initial genotyping of a small set of loci indicates the expected population linked polymorphism in each case.

2. Materials and methods

Suitable autosomal SNPs were selected from the Celera human RefSNP database. For African linked SNPs, allele frequency was set to 0.4–0.5 and combined using intersection [AND] with Caucasians set to 0. This was reversed for European linked SNPs and

* Corresponding author. Tel.: +34-981582327; fax: +34-981580336.
E-mail address: chrisp@usc.es (C. Phillips).

doi:10.1016/j.ics.2003.12.041

extended, in both populations, to lower allele frequency ranges. An additional subset of nonspecific SNPs (exhibiting shared alleles with minimal variability in Africans) was found using the following frequency ranges: Caucasian, 0.4–0.5; African, 0–0.05. Genotyping was performed on 50 Galician (N.W. Spain) and 50 Mozambican samples. PCR primers were designed to give products in the size range 70–110 bp. Amplification and mini-sequencing reactions were as previously described (in this volume, in: "Non-Binary Single Nucleotide Polymorphisms").

3. Results and discussion

A total of 4712 SNPs were found with complete population linked variation. Four African linked SNPs taken from the above set have been genotyped and allele frequency estimates indicate complete population linkage in each case. Eighty-two SNPs exhibited polymorphism with minor allele frequencies 0.4–0.5 (average Dp 62.2%): of these, 81 were African linked and 1 European linked. A further 219 exhibited polymorphism with minor allele frequencies 0.3–0.4 (average Dp 60.2%); of these, 218 were African linked and 1 European linked. Such figures reflect the differing demographic histories and levels of variability that characterize each population. To increase the pool of SNPs with European linked polymorphism, markers were collected showing maximum variability in Europeans (0.4–0.5 minor allele frequency) and minimum variability in Africans (0.01–0.05 minor allele frequency). Including these markers in an assay can provide a

Table 1
Allele frequency distributions and information content of 10 European linked SNP loci

CDS no.	Population	Minor allele	Major Allele	% Informative	% Non-informative	Cumulative non-informative	Cumulative individuals with same genotypes
hCV1140336	Eur.	0.42	0.58	66.36	33.64	33.6400	1 in 3
	Afr.	0	1				
hCV16237183	Eur.	0.33	0.67	55.11	44.89	15.1010	1 in 7
	Afr.	0	1				
hCV2177452	Eur.	0.28	0.72	48.16	51.84	7.8284	1 in 13
	Afr.	0	1				
hCV11250782	Eur.	0.28	0.72	48.16	51.84	4.0582	1 in 25
	Afr.	0	1				
hCV3135019	Eur.	0.28	0.72	48.16	51.84	2.1038	1 in 48
	Afr.	0	1				
hCV151291	Eur.	0.27	0.73	46.71	53.29	1.1211	1 in 89
	Afr.	0	1				
hCV11857041	Eur.	0.27	0.73	46.71	53.29	0.5974	1 in 167
	Afr.	0	1				
hCV2677956	Eur.	0.27	0.73	46.71	53.29	0.3184	1 in 314
	Afr.	0	1				
hCV2039416	Eur.	0.26	0.74	45.24	54.76	0.1743	1 in 574
	Afr.	0	1				
hCV1048567	Eur.	0.25	0.75	43.75	56.25	0.0981	1 in 1020
	Afr.	0	1				

Table 2
Allele frequency distributions and information content of 13 African linked SNP loci

CDS no.	Population	Minor allele	Major Allele	% Informative	% Non-informative	Cumulative non-informative	Cumulative individuals with same genotypes
hCV3095460	Afr.	0.5	0.5	75	25	25.000000	1 in 4
	Eur.	0	1				
hCV1969450	Afr.	0.5	0.5	75	25	6.250000	1 in 16
	Eur.	0	1				
hCV971171	Afr.	0.5	0.5	75	25	1.562500	1 in 64
	Eur.	0	1				
hCV958204	Afr.	0.5	0.5	75	25	0.390625	1 in 256
	Eur.	0	1				
hCV608420	Afr.	0.5	0.5	75	25	0.097656	1 in 1024
	Eur.	0	1				
hCV608417	Afr.	0.5	0.5	75	25	0.024414	1 in 4096
	Eur.	0	1				
hCV2460535	Afr.	0.5	0.5	75	25	0.006104	1 in 16,384
	Eur.	0	1				
hCV11377586	Afr.	0.49	0.51	74	26	0.001588	1 in 62,991
	Eur.	0	1				
hCV15905778	Afr.	0.49	0.51	74	26	0.000413	1 in 242,181
	Eur.	0	1				
hCV12003211	Afr.	0.49	0.51	74	26	0.000107	1 in 931,105
	Eur.	0	1				
hCV3111622	Afr.	0.49	0.51	74	26	0.000028	1 in 3.6 million
	Eur.	0	1				
hCV2960082	Afr.	0.49	0.51	74	26	0.000007	1 in 13.8 million
	Eur.	0	1				
hCV3270591	Afr.	0.49	0.51	74	26	0.000002	1 in 53 million
	Eur.	0	1				
	Afr.	0	1				

likelihood ratio indicating population of origin in a similar way to STR loci [2]. Tables 1 and 2 list the most informative loci that could form a population of origin test: the best African linked and the best European linked. The predictive power of these loci in combination is given by the cumulative "non-informative" result probability: the probability of not finding the population specific allele in an individual originating from that population. Clearly, combining ~ 8 SNPs from each group could provide a powerful predictive test for distinguishing Africans and Europeans.

References

[1] http://www.celeradiscoverysystem.com/.
[2] D. Syndercombe Court, et al., Advances in Forensic Genetics 9 (2003) 67–69.

International Congress Series 1261 (2004) 236–238

ELSEVIER

www.ics-elsevier.com

Short tandem repeat polymorphisms across the HLA-complex: sequence and population data of D6S389 and D6S1051

R.B.K. Reisacher[a], B. Glock[a,*], S.O. Rennhofer[a], E.M. Dauber[b], S. Wenda[b], D. Tröscher[a], C. Hüttler[a], A.M. Dillinger[a], G. Dorner[b], W.R. Mayr[a,b]

[a] *Austrian Red Cross, Blood Donation Centre for Vienna, Lower Austria and Burgenland, Laboratory for Molecular Biology, Nordportalstrasse 248, A-1020, Vienna, Austria*

[b] *Department of Blood Group Serology and Transfusion Medicine, Division of Blood Group Serology, University of Vienna, Medical School, Währinger Gürtel 18-20, A-1090, Vienna, Austria*

Abstract. The tetranucleotide repeat loci D6S389 and D6S1051 situated nearby the HLA class II region (6p) were investigated in an Austrian Caucasoid population sample. Typing of the amplification products and cycle sequencing were carried out using denaturing capillary electrophoresis. For D6S389 and D6S1051, 19 and 7 different alleles were observed. Sequencing of D6S389 revealed a $(GAAA)_n$ repeat pattern in the common alleles. Additionally, infrequent ".1" alleles were seen. Alleles of D6S1051 showed a simple $(GATA)_n$ repeat structure and an A/G-SNP next to the repeat region as well as a T/C-SNP in the 3′ -flanking region. D6S389 proved to be a highly polymorphic marker. D6S1051 is less polymorphic, but interesting because of the existing SNPs. © 2003 Published by Elsevier B.V.

Keywords: D6S389; D6S1051; SNP

1. Introduction

The tetranucleotide repeat loci D6S389 (GenBank L16321, [1]) and D6S1051 (GenBank G08553) situated nearby the HLA class II region (6p) were investigated in an Austrian Caucasoid population sample ($n = 153$) in order to get information about their usefulness in identity and paternity testing or as HLA haplotype markers.

2. Materials and methods

DNA was extracted from peripheral blood lymphocytes (DNA Blood Mini Kit, Qiagen). PCR was carried out in a reaction volume of 15 μl using 0.4 μM of each primer,

* Corresponding author. Tel.: +43-7280199-600; fax: +43-7280199-609.
E-mail address: glock@redcross.or.at (B. Glock).

doi:10.1016/S0531-5131(03)01719-9

Table 1
D6S389 and D6S1051-allele frequencies and statistic parameters ($n = 153$)

Allele designation	Allele frequencies		Number of sequenced alleles	
	D6S389	D6S1051	D6S389	D6S1051
8	0.056		6	
9	0.026	0.003	6	1
10	0.042	0.065	7	9
11	0.082	0.248	6	10
12	0.163	0.386	6	11
13	0.141	0.243	9	12
13.1	0.010		4	
14	0.150	0.052	12	10
14.1	0.003		1	
15	0.121	0.003	11	1
16	0.098		9	
16.1	0.010		1	
17	0.042		7	
18	0.029		5	
18.1	0.003		1	
19	0.010		4	
21	0.007		1	
22	0.003		1	
24	0.003		1	
Rate of heterozygosity	0.915	0.647		
Power of exclusion	0.826	0.351		
Polymorphism information content	0.880	0.680		
Power of discrimination	0.972	0.883		
Typical paternity index	5.880	1.420		

Table 2
Sequence structure of STR locus D6S389

Allele						Length (bp)
8–24	CAAGAAA	$[(GAAA)\ GGAAA]_3$	$(GAAA)_{8-22;24}$	GAA	GAAAAA	287–351
13.1	CAAGAAA	$[(GAAA)\ GGAAA]_4$	$(GAAA)_{11}$	GAA	GAAAAA	308
14.1	CAAGAAA	$[(GAAA)\ GGAAA]_3$	$(GAAA)_{14}$	GAAA	GAAAAA	312
15.1	CAAGAAA	$[(GAAA)\ GGAAA]_4$	$(GAAA)_{13}$	GAA	GAAAAA	316
16.1	CAAGAAA	$[(GAAA)\ GGAAA]_3$	$(GAAA)_{16}$	GAAA	GAAAAA	320
18.1	CAAGAAA	$[(GAAA)\ GGAAA]_3$	$(GAAA)_{18}$	GAAA	GAAAAA	328

Table 3
Sequence structure of STR locus D6S1051

Allele							Length (bp)
9–13	$(GATA)_2$ TAGA	**C**ATA	GATAGAT	$(GATA)_{9-13}$	... AAAAAAA	T**T**AT	218–234
11–15	$(GATA)_2$ TAGA	**C**GTA	GATAGAT	$(GATA)_{11-15}$	... AAAAAAA	T**C**AT	226–242
13	$(GATA)_2$ TAGA	**T**GTA	GATAGAT	$(GATA)_{13}$	... AAAAAAA	T**C**AT	234

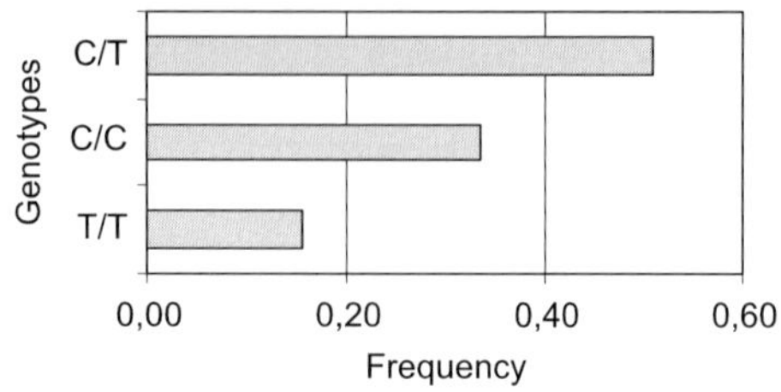

Fig. 1. Distribution of T/C-SNP genotypes in the 3′ flanking region of STR D6S1051.

200 μM dNTPs, 1 × Buffer II, 1.5 mM $MgCl_2$ and 0.5 units AmpliTaq Gold® DNA polymerase for 11 min at 95 °C, 28 cycles of 20 s 94 °C, 1 min 61 °C, 1 min 72 °C and a final extension of 45 min 60 °C (9700 thermal cycler).

Typing of the amplification products in comparison with locus-specific sequenced allelic ladders was carried out using denaturing capillary electrophoresis on an ABI Prism 310® Genetic Analyzer.

SNP analysis in the 3′ flanking region of D6S1051 (ss6492059) employing an "Assay-by-Design" (Applied Biosystems) was performed according to the manufacturer's instructions on an ABI 7700 Sequence Detection System.

3. Results and discussion

Typing for D6S389 and D6S1051 revealed 19 and 7 different alleles. The allele frequencies observed as well as further statistic data are shown in Table 1. No deviation from Hardy–Weinberg equilibrium has been detected.

Sequencing of D6S389 alleles from the current study population and another series of samples showed a $(GAAA)_n$ in the common alleles. Additionally, infrequent ".1" alleles were observed. The different sequence structures are shown in Table 2.

Alleles of D6S1051 showed a simple $(GATA)_n$ repeat structure and an A/G-SNP next to the repeat region as well as a T/C-SNP in the 3′ flanking region. In addition, one sample had a C>T transition on the 66th position of the 5′ flanking region (Table 3).

Analysis of the SNP in the 3′ flanking region of D6S1051 with alleles T and C revealed frequencies of 0.4 and 0.6, respectively. The distribution of genotypes is shown in Fig. 1.

4. Conclusion

D6S389 turned out to be a highly polymorphic marker, which can be used for identity analysis as well as for paternity testing. D6S1051 is less polymorphic, but nevertheless interesting because of the existing SNPs.

Reference

[1] A. Foissac, et al., Microsatellite markers in the HLA region, Tissue Antigens 55 (6) (2000) 477–509.

International Congress Series 1261 (2004) 239–241
www.ics-elsevier.com

The development of two new STR multiplex systems

U. Ricci*, L. Giunti, M.L. Giovannucci Uzielli

Genetics and Molecular Medicine Unit, University of Florence-Azienda Ospedaliera «A. Meyer», Via Luca Giordano 13, 50132 Florence, Italy

Abstract. Here we show two new amplification systems, which were realised for the amplification of 80 highly polymorphic loci, in combination with an Infrared Automated DNA Sequencer LI-COR 4200 (LI-COR, Nebraska, USA). The two amplification systems were indicated as MU5 and MU6. The amplification system MU5 contained D12S391, F13A01, SE33 and Penta D loci, the amplification system MU6 the loci D2S1338, D19S433, F13B and Penta E. Both systems were performed using forward IRDye™ 800 labelled and reverse unlabelled primers, in combination with the QIAGEN Multiplex PCR kit (Qiagen, Germany). The extension of the set of STRs in our laboratory is useful to further improve our ability to resolve complex kinship cases (e.g. deficiency cases, incest, paternity tests with mutations). Moreover, these new multiplex systems can also be used for manual typing, because the STRs do not overlap in size.

Keywords: Short tandem repeat; Multiplex systems; Infrared sequencer

1. Introduction

In our laboratory, we extensively use an Infrared Automatic DNA Sequencer LI-COR 4200 (LICOR, Nebraska, USA) for forensic analyses (paternity tests and stains analysis). The Infrared technology is efficient and robust, although it has become less frequent in forensic genetic laboratories. Amplification of the STR loci for forensic purposes is routinely performed using UV, automated DNA sequencers and commercially available kits. Validation studies, publications and the experience of many laboratories are now available and in our opinion there is no reason for changing the technology. Moreover, we verified that the results obtained using the Infrared technology are comparable with the use of Ultraviolet technology and commercially available kits [1]. Our protocol is based on the loci of the FBI CODIS system (LI-COR 4200) [2]. However, new STRs loci introduced by commercial kits are becoming important in the forensic community. Penta D and Penta E are included in PowerPlex ® 16 System (Promega). D2S1338 and D19S433 are included in AmpFlSTR SGM Plus ™ and AmpFlSTR Identifiler™ (Applied Biosystems). Moreover, SE33 (ACPB22) is used in the German DNA database. We performed two new amplifications systems to analyse all these STR markers, in combination with D12S391, F13B and F13A01 markers.

* Correspondence author. Tel.: +39-555662942; fax: +39-555662931.
E-mail address: ricciugo@tin.it (U. Ricci).

0531-5131/ © 2003 Elsevier B.V. All rights reserved.
doi:10.1016/S0531-5131(03)01643-1

2. Materials and methods

DNA samples from donors and K562 cell lines DNA were used to test the efficiency of these multiplex systems. Then, we used the two amplification systems to analyse three paraffin-embedded tissues, in comparison with blood of the donors.

Both amplification systems were performed using forward IRDye™ 800 labelled and reverse unlabelled primers, in combination with the QIAGEN Multiplex PCR Kit (Qiagen, Germany) [3]. PCR was performed in 12.5 μl, using 5.8 μl of 2 × QIAGEN Multiplex PCR Master Mix and 5.8 μl of a mix of primers. Final concentration for D12S391, Penta D, D2S1338, D19S433, F13B and Penta E was 0.2 μM. For F13A01 it was 0.3 μM and for SE33 0.1 μM. In each PCR mix we used 0.9 μl of undosed DNA. For both systems, the amplification condition was the following: 95 °C for 15 min, then 94 °C for 30 s, 60 °C for 90 s, 72 °C for 90 s. 30 cycles of PCR were performed, with a final extension period of 10 min a 72 °C. Gel electrophoresis was performed in a LI-COR® model 4200 monolaser automated fluorescent DNA sequencer, like described [2].

3. Results

The two amplifications systems produced defined autoradiogram-like patterns in the virtual image of the computer. The QIAGEN Multiplex PCR kit is specifically developed for multiplex PCR and provides an easy-to-use master-mix format. We verified that this eliminates the need for optimisation, making the development of multiplex PCR assays both simple and fast. However, we found that it is possible to obtain a balanced intensity between the microsatellites, using different concentration of the primers. We used a previously published sequence for all primers, except for F13A01 and F13B (Table 1). Efficient primer annealing and extension, irrespective of the primer sequence, is achieved by Factor MP in QIAGEN Multiplex PCR Master Mix. Factor MP increases the local

Table 1
Characteristics of the loci include in MU5 and MU6 amplification systems

	Locus	Chromosomal location	Primer sequence	Allele size (bp)	GenBank accession
MU5	D12S391	12	A-AACAGGATCAATGGATGCAT B-AGCCTCCATATCACTTGAGC	129–173	G08921
	F13A01	6p24–p25	A-GAGGTTGCACTCCAGCCTTT B-AGCCCCAAGGAAGATGAGAAAC	179–235	This work
	SE33	6	A-AATCTGGGCGACAAGAGTGA B-ACATCTCCCCTACCGCTATA	233–333	V00481
	Penta D	21q	A-GAAGGTCGAAGCTGAAGTG B-ATTAGAATTCTTTAATCTGGACACAAG	376–449	AP001752
MU6	D2S1338	2q35–37.1	A-CCAGTGGATTTGGAAACAGA B-ACCTAGCATGGTACCTGCAG	160–212	G08202
	D19S433	19q12–13.1	A-CCTGGGCAACAGAATAAGAT B-TAGGTTTTTAAGGAACAGGTGG	178–212	G08036
	F13B	1q31–q32.1	A-TGAGGTGGTGTACTACCATA B-GTGGTACACGCCTGTAATC	265–289	This work
	Penta E	15q	A-ATTACCAACATGAAAGGGTACCAATA B-TGGGTTATTAATTGAGAAAACTCCTTACAATTT	379–474	AC027004

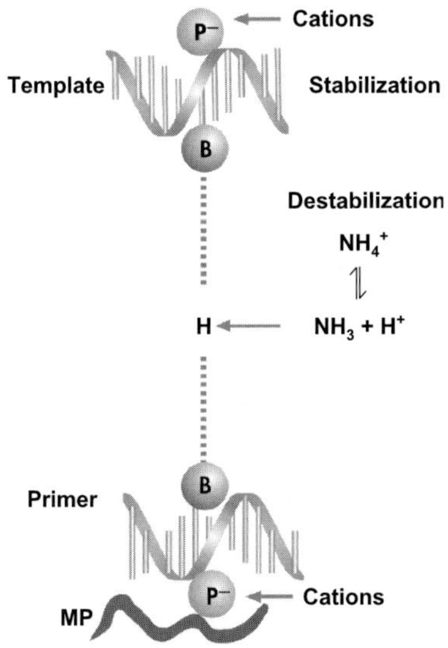

Fig. 1. Mg^{2+} and other salts bind to phosphate groups (P^-) on the DNA backbone, which stabilizes the annealing of the primers to the template. NH_4^+ can interact with the hydrogen bonds between the bases, destabilizing principally the weak hydrogen bonds at mismatched bases (B) of non specifically bound primers. Factor MP (MP) enabling efficient extension of all primers in the reaction (kindly admitted from QIAGEN®).

concentration of primers at the template DNA and stabilises specifically bound primers (Fig. 1). The analysis of paraffin-embedded tissue gave comparable results in comparison with blood of donors. Moreover, we used the QIAGEN Multiplex PCR Master Mix for the amplification of the four amplification systems for CODIS [1]. Preliminary results suggest the usefulness of this new amplification format also for these amplification systems.

The use of these systems, together with the previously described multiplex systems (MU1:AME, vWA, FGA and D16S359; MU2:D3S1358, TPOX, TH01 and CSF1PO; MU3:D8S1179, D21S11 and D18S51; MU4: D7S820, D5S818 and D13S317), enable us to analyse 21 polymorphic loci and amelogenin for gender determination. The extension of the set of STRs is useful to further improve our ability to resolve complex kinship cases (e.g. deficiency cases, incest, paternity tests with mutations). Moreover, these new multiplex systems can also be used for manual typing and for the automatic sequencers that employ just one fluorochrome, because the STRs do not overlap in size.

References

[1] U. Ricci, et al., Identification of forensic samples by using an infrared-based automatic DNA sequencer, Croatian Medical Journal 44 (2003) 299–305.
[2] U. Ricci, et al., Infrared fluorescent automated detection of thirteen short tandem repeat polymorphisms and one gender-determining system of the CODIS core system, Electrophoresis 21 (2000) 3564–3570.
[3] QIAGEN Multiplex PCR Handbook, Qiagen, Germany, 2003.

International Congress Series 1261 (2004) 242–244

www.ics-elsevier.com

Towards Russian reference population data on STR loci

A.G. Smolyanitsky[a,*], P.L. Ivanov[b,c], I.V. Kornienko[d], V.S. Zamaraev[e], I.O. Perepechina[b], Yu. A. Komarovsky[f], V.P. Pushkarev[g], N.N. Khromov-Borisov[a]

[a] *Forensic Medicine Bureau of Leningrad District, Saint Petersburg, Russia*
[b] *Russian Forensic Science Centre of Ministry of Health, Moscow, Russia*
[c] *Engelhardt Institute of Molecular Biology, Russian Academy of Sciences, Moscow, Russia*
[d] *124 Central Laboratory for Medical Forensic Identification of Ministry of Defence, Rostov-on-Don, Russia*
[e] *Volgograd Antiplague Research Institute, Volgograd, Russia*
[f] *Saint Petersburg Forensic Medicine Bureau, Saint Petersburg, Russia*
[g] *Chelyabinsk Regional Forensic Medicine Bureau, Chelyabinsk, Russia*

Abstract. Summary of allele counts for 10 STR loci: CSF1PO, D7S820, D13S317, F13A01, F13B, FESFPS, LPL, TH01, TPOX and vWA obtained by the seven laboratories in a countrywide Russian Caucasians is proposed as a reference population data set.

Keywords: Reference population data; Russia; Caucasians; STR; CSF1PO; D7S820; D13S317; F13A01; F13B; FESFPS; LPL; TH01; TPOX; vWA

1. Introduction

At least three Ministries (Ministry of Health, Ministry of Defense and Ministry of Internal Affairs) in Russia have specialized forensic genetics laboratories in several Federal districts. Moreover, some forensic DNA markers are used in several academic institutes for the studies in ethnogenomics or genogeography, human molecular medicine and genetics [1]. Data accumulated by these laboratories seem to be suitable for creating Russian reference population data bank (see, e.g., [2–5].

2. Population

Several hundred unrelated Caucasians living in about 60 cities and regions (federal cities Saint Petersburg and Moscow, and main federal districts: Northwestern, Central, Northern Caucasus, Volga, Ural, Siberia and Far East) were examined.

3. Extraction

Chelex® 100, phenol-chloroform and/or Expert 1 [6] extraction protocols adapted for, and widely used in forensic studies.

* Corresponding author. Tel.: +7-812-2514000; fax: +7-812-252-4933.
E-mail address: SAG@cards.lanck.net (A.G. Smolyanitsky).

doi:10.1016/S0531-5131(03)01610-8

4. PCR and typing

GenePrint® STR Systems, GenePrint® Fluorescent STR Systems (Promega) and AmpF*l*STR Profiler Plus amplification kit (PE Applied Biosystems) according to the manufacturer's instructions.

5. Data analysis

To test Hardy–Weinberg equilibrium and homogeneity between samples the PC programs which provide exact randomization procedures based on different statistics (probability, chi-square, F_{IS}—fixation indices, etc.) were used (see, e.g., lists in Refs. [3,5]). To construct 95% credible (Bayesian) limits for coancestry coefficient F_{ST} (the correlation of two genes sampled from distinct individuals within the same subpopulation, relative to the total population), the FSTMET routine was applied (http://www.rdg.ac.uk/statistics/genetics/software.html, http://www.reading.ac.uk/~snsbalng/) (see Refs. [7–10]).

6. Access to the data

Detailed results as well as original individual genotype data in form of input files suitable for the use with different software for the population genetic analysis (Arlequin, FSTAT, FSTMET, GDA, GENEPOP, GENETIX, HWE, HWMET, POPGENE, Popula-

Table 1
Allele counts for 10 STR loci in combined samples of unrelated Russian Caucasians

Allele	Locus									
	CSF1PO	D7S820	D13S317	F13A01	F13B	FESFPS	LPL	TH01	TPOX	vWA
3.2				15						
4				35						
5				67				1		
6		1		132	59			286	4	
7	1	12	1	137	11		2	246	3	
8	0	256	195	4	180	24	2	158	520	
9	41	191	121	0	147	7	32	287	70	
9.3	–	–	–	–	–	–	–	413	–	
10	194	349	84	0	292	333	327	37	49	
11	201	280	504	0	6	581	175	2	195	
12	210	219	284	1	3	228	127		23	
13	59	44	109	0		68	19			2
14	9	6	60	5		3				136
15	1			14						177
16				2						322
17										501
18										366
19										140
20										31
21										1
Total allele count	716	1358	1358	412	698	1244	684	1430	864	1676
Lab No.[a]	1,2,5	3,4,5,7	3,4,5,7	1,2	1,6	1,2,5,6	1,3,4	1,3,4, 5,6	1,2,5	1,2,3, 4,5
P^b	0.048	0.313	0.427	0.065	0.350	0.463	0.537	0.117	0.069	0.775
95% CL	0.0006	0.0002	0.002	0.004	0.0003	0.0003	0.0003	0.0004	0.0005	0.0002
for F_{ST}[c]	0.019	0.0077	0.012	0.017	0.019	0.0056	0.022	0.020	0.014	0.004

[a] Number of the lab as shown in the authors' affiliation above.

[b] *P*-value for the inter-laboratory homogeneity.

[c] Credible (Bayesian) limits for the posterior distribution of coancestry coefficient.

tion, PowerMarker, PowerStats, TFPGA, etc.) are available to interested users upon request from the authors SAG@cards.lanck.net or Nikita@NH8333.spb.edu).

7. Results

In each data set presented by the participated laboratories, no significant deviation from Hardy–Weinberg equilibrium was detected. Genotype and allele distributions obtained by the laboratories appeared to be in good agreement (statistically homogeneous) and so could be combined into single reference sample as shown below (Table 1). Evaluated values for coancestry coefficient with the upper 95% credible limit about 0.02 are compatible with those reported for other Caucasians over the world [7,8,10].

8. Other remarks

We insist positively on publication of the absolute allele frequencies so that any user could to calculate relative values with a precision preferred.

Russian Federation consists of seven federal districts that are divided into 89 "subjects" which are: 21 autonomous republics, 1 autonomous oblast, 10 autonomous districts, six regions and 49 oblasts and two federal cities where about 130 different nations are living (see, e.g., http://www.wikipedia.org/wiki/Districts_in_Russia). So further comprehensive study involving samples from different nationalities and ethnic groups is required.

Acknowledgements

We express our sincere thanks to Dr. Karen Ayres for her help to implement the FSTMET and HWMET routines and to Prof. Dr. Grigory I. Zaslavsky for his friendly guidance and support.

References

[1] S.A. Limborska, et al., Ethnogenomics and Gene Geography of Peoples from Eastern Europe, Nauka, Moscow, 2002, 261 pp.
[2] V.P. Pushkarev, P.I. Novikov, The use of capillary electrophoresis for the study of D13S317 and D7S820 microsatellites in Caucasian population of the Ural region of Russia, Forensic Med. Expert. 45 (6) (2002) 31–35 (in Russia).
[3] A.G. Smolyanitsky, et al., Statistical pattern analysis of D1S80 alleles in Northwestern Russians and worldwide database using COLLAPSE software, in: B. Brinkman, A. Carracedo (Eds.), Progress in Forensic Genetics, vol. 9, Elsevier, Amsterdam, 2003, pp. 665–671.
[4] I.V. Kornienko, et al., Genetic variation of the nine Profiler Plus loci in Russians, Int. J. Leg. Med. 116 (2002) 309–311.
[5] A.G. Smolyanitsky, et al., Polymorphism of LDLR, GYPA, HBGG, D7S8, GC, HLA-DQA1, Ig-JH, D17S30, ApoB and D1S80 loci in northwestern Russians, Forensic Sci. Int. (2003) 100–103.
[6] A. Smolyanitsky, et al., Applications of Expert 1 kit for genomic DNA isolation from forensic biological samples: muscle, blood stains, sperm stains and single hairs, Med. Leg. Baltica 7 (1996) 58–61.
[7] D.J. Balding, et al., Population genetics of STR loci in Caucasians, Int. J. Leg. Med. 108 (1996) 300–305.
[8] D.J. Balding, R.A. Nichols, Significant genetic correlations among Caucasians at forensic DNA loci, Heredity 78 (1997) 583–589.
[9] W. Lee, et al., Statistical analysis for estimating heterogeneity of the Korean population in DNA typing using STR loci, Int. J. Leg. Med. 116 (2002) 153–160.
[10] B.S. Weir, W.G. Hill, Estimating F-statistics, Annu. Rev. Genet. 36 (2002) 721–750.

ELSEVIER

International Congress Series 1261 (2004) 245–247

ICS

www.ics-elsevier.com

Validation of STR system FXIIIB for forensic investigation in a population of Central Italy

I. Sani, U. Ricci*, M.L. Giovannucci Uzielli

Genetics and Molecular Medicine Unit, University of Florence, Azienda Ospedaliera «A. Meyer», Via Luca Giordano 13, 50132 Florence, Italy

Abstract. The principle purpose of this study was to investigate the frequency distribution of the short tandem repeat system FXIIIB in a sample of individuals from Tuscany (Central Italy). Samples (204), taken from donors residing in the area of Florence, Prato and Pistoia, were analysed by PCR and vertical denaturing polyacrylamide gel electrophoresis. A sensitivity study was also undertaken and the method was optimised for the study of forensic samples.

The research resulted in the identification of 5 alleles and 11 genotypes. The system was tested for Hardy–Weinberg equilibrium and the Central Italian population was compared with populations from Northern Italy and Austria. Moreover, we introduced the use of this microsatellite in an automatic platform, in combination with other STRs in a new multiplex amplification system. An infrared automatic DNA sequencer was used to analyse this marker. The introduction of this marker in our protocol could be useful to resolve particular intriguing cases of forensic interest, as for example incest or deficitary paternity/maternity tests, in which additional loci must be investigated.

Keywords: Short tandem repeat; FXIIIB; Population studies; Central Italy

1. Introduction

The STR FXIIIB is a tetranucleotide tandem repeat system (TTTA), mapped in the region 1q31–q32.1 [1], which codifies for the coagulation factor XIIIB.

Using techniques of DNA amplification, this polymorphism can be employed in various types of analyses: loss of heterozygosity in tumours, anthropological studies of populations, linkage analysis, paternity studies and the forensic identification of various types of biological samples. A significant number of studies on FXIIIB [2–4] already exist, but no such study has ever been conducted on a population from our geographical area, so we extended the analysis to a population sample of 204 individuals residing in Florence, Prato, Pistoia area (Central Italy). The accumulated data were then compared

* Corresponding author. Tel.: +39-555662942; fax: +39-555662931.
E-mail address: ricciugo@tin.it (U. Ricci).

doi:10.1016/S0531-5131(03)01451-1

with the published data regarding Caucasian population samples from Northern Italy [3] and Austria [4].

2. Materials and methods

2.1. DNA extraction and amplification

DNA was extracted using a modified saline procedure [5] or with the QIAamp Blood kit® (QIAGEN®, Germany) method, for samples from infants (blood and fragments of nail). For the forensic samples, the Chelex extraction method was used [6].

The amplifications were performed as suggested [1].

2.2. DNA detection

Exact identification of the alleles was done through comparison with a mixture of alleles included in the GenePrint™ STR System (Promega, USA), in accordance with ISFG guidelines [7], as previously described [8].

We studied the sensitivity of this polymorphic system, using K562 cell line DNA dilution (Promega).

Moreover, we introduced the use of this microsatellite in an automatic platform, in combination with other STRs in a new multiplex amplification system, as shown in another article in this book. An infrared automatic DNA sequencer (LICOR-4200, Nebraska, USA) [9] was used to analyse this marker. A new pair of oligonucleotide primers was used that produce larger fragments (252–276 bp) than original primers (169–193 bp). The amplicons were labelled using a forward oligonucleotide primer, covalently linked to a new infrared fluorescent molecule (IRDye™ 800). The alleles are displayed as familiar autoradiogram-like images with real-time detection.

3. Statistics

The statistical analysis was performed using a simple BASIC program [10]. Hardy–Weinberg formulation was calculated by comparison of observed with expected phenotypes.

The three populations were compared using two-way contingency tables.

4. Results and discussion

The study of STR FXIIIB was initially conducted on genomic DNA, using a reduced number of cycles which we routinely apply for paternity testing; later, this method was optimised for forensic studies, increasing the number of cycles of amplification to 34. In the sensitivity studies, the analysis of samples of K562 cell line DNA in various dilutions, permitted the identification of up to 0.2 ng/μl of DNA. In our laboratory, this STR was used, together with other markers, to analyse 39 forensic samples (blood, saliva, sperm and hair). Family studies confirmed Mendelian inheritance of alleles. No mutation was observed in the 41 families studied. In the population study, we observed 5 alleles, for a total of 13 genotypes. The distribution of the phenotypes is in Hardy–Weinberg equilibrium (chi-square = 5.28, *d.f.* 12; $0.90 > P > 0.95$). Polymorphic informa-

Table 1
Allele frequencies for FXIIIB in Central Italy (408 alleles), Northern Italy (238 alleles) and Austria (402 alleles)

Allele	Central Italy	Northern Italy	Austria
6	0.105	0.0378	0.114
7	0.009	0.0081	0.022
8	0.257	0.2311	0.241
9	0.225	0.2227	0.276
10	0.401	0.5000	0.341
11	0.000	0.0000	0.005

tion content was 0.688. The observed heterozygosity was 0.68, while the expected value, on the base of the genotypes observed was 0.711 ± 0.032. The chance of exclusion (CE) was 0.44 and the power of discrimination (PD) was 0.866. A statistical analysis was conducted to compare the populations from the area of Milan (Norther Italy) and from Graz (Austria), using a two-way $R \times C$ contingency table and comparing allele frequency. Allele frequency distributions in comparison with these other populations were shown in Table 1. No significant differences were observed in comparison to the Northern Italian population (chi-square = 4.52, *d.f.* 4; $0.50 > P > 0.30$) and to the Austrian population (chi-square = 4.49, *d.f.* 5; $0.50 > P > 0.30$).

In conclusion, this study confirms Hardy–Weinberg equilibrium for the STR FXIIIB. The population data can be used, therefore, for forensic studies and paternity testing.

References

[1] D.Y. Nishimura, J.C. Murray, A tetranucleotide repeat for the F13B locus, Nucleic Acids Res. 20 (1992) 1167.

[2] M. Pablo, A. Alonso, B. Budowle, C. Albarran, O. Garcia, M. Sancho, Spanish population data on 7 tetrameric short tandem repeat loci, Int. J. Leg. Med. 108 (1995) 145–149.

[3] A. Piccinini, K. Moller, P. Wiegand, HumFES/FPS and HumF13B: population genetic data from north Italy, Int. J. Leg. Med. 108 (1996) 283–284.

[4] M. Klintschar, R. Crevenna, Validation of the STR system FXIIIB for forensic purposes in an Austrian population sample, Forensic Sci. Int. 81 (1996) 35–42.

[5] S.A. Miller, D.D. Dykes, H.F. Polesky, A simple salting out procedure for extracting DNA from human nucleated cells, Nucleic Acids Res. 16 (1988) 1215.

[6] P.S. Walsh, D.A. Metzger, R. Higuchi, CHELEX 100 as a medium for simple extraction of DNA for PCR based typing from forensic material, BioTechniques 10 (1991) 506–511.

[7] DNA Commission of the International Society of Forensic Haemogenetics, DNA recommendations—1994 report concerning further recommendations of the DNA Commission of the ISFH regarding PCR-based polymorphisms in STR (short tandem repeat) systems, Int. J. Leg. Med. 107 (1994) 159–160.

[8] U. Ricci, M.L. Giovannucci, M. Klintschar, Modified primers for D12S391 and a modified silver staining technique, Int. J. Leg. Med. 112 (1999) 342–344.

[9] L.R. Middendorf, J.C. Bruce, R.C. Bruce, R.D. Eckles, D.L. Grone, S.C. Roemer, G.D. Sloniker, D.L. Steffens, S.L. Sutter, J.A. Brumbaugh, G. Patonay, Continuos, on-line DNA sequencing using a versatile infrared laser scanner/electrophoresis apparatus, Electrophoresis 13 (1992) 487–494.

[10] U. Ricci, Programma per il calcolo di parametri forensi per sistemi polimorfici codominanti, Riv. Ital. Med. Leg. XXIV (2002) 151–165.

International Congress Series 1261 (2004) 248–250

www.ics-elsevier.com

vWA STR locus structure and variability

C. Cruz[a], T. Ribeiro[a], C. Vieira-Silva[a], I. Lucas[a], R. Espinheira[a], H. Geada[b,*]

[a] *Forensic Genetics, National Institute of Legal Medicine, Lisbon, Portugal*
[b] *Department of Legal Medicine, Faculty of Medicine, Lisbon, Portugal*

Abstract. More than 100 vWA alleles were sequenced to detect any possible sequence difference at this locus in Portuguese Caucasian and African populations. Internal variability was detected—the most common structure is TCTA (TCTG)4 (TCTA)n with a TCTA(TCTG)3(TCTA)n structure more frequent in small alleles and a TCTA (TCTG)5–6 (TCTA)n structure predominantly in large ones. Allele 17 has a unique structure in all 20 studied samples and the nonconsensus allele 14 structure has a prevalence of 60% in both populations. Performing more than 3000 paternity investigation cases with multiplex systems, eight vWA mutations were detected with a 0.0024 average mutation rate. Six mutations at the primer-binding site have also been detected when performing ProfilerPlus/SGMPlus versus Powerplex1.2.

Keywords: vWA locus; Sequencing; Mutations; Forensic typing

1. Introduction

Sequence variation of STR alleles is common to encounter specially in compound and complex STR locus [1]. The high primer-binding mutation observed at this locus and the interest in structure analysis of rare alleles observed in certain population groups were the main reasons to perform vWA sequence. In this study, we will present the structure analysis of vWA alleles from allele 11 to allele 22 studied in two main populations—a Portuguese Caucasian population and an African population mainly from Cabo Verde Islands and Angola, to detect any possible sequence difference at vWA locus in both populations.

2. Materials and methods

Blood samples were extracted by the Chelex method and analysed with ProfilerPlus/SGMPlus (Applied Biosystems) and Geneprint PowerPlex1.2 (Promega) according to the

* Corresponding author. Forensic Genetic Service, Delegação de Lisboa do Instituto Nacional de Medicina Legal, R. Manuel Bento de Sousa, 1150-219, Lisbon, Portugal. Tel.: +351-21-8811800; fax: +351-21-8864493.
E-mail address: hgeada@dlinml.mj.pt (H. Geada).

0531-5131/
doi:10.1016/S0531-5131(03)01774-6

Table 1
Allele nomenclature, sequenced structure and number of alleles sequenced at vWA locus in Portuguese (Port) and African (Afric) populations—consensus structure TCTA (TCTG)3–6 (TCTA)n

Alleles	Structure	Port	Afric
11	TCTA (TCTG)3 (TCTA) 7	–	3
13	TCTA (TCTG)3 (TCTA) 9	1	–
	TCTA (TCTG)4 (TCTA)8	2	4
14	TCTA (TCTG)3 (TCTA)10	2	–
	TCTA (TCTG)4 (TCTA) 9	2	2
	Nonconsensus structure[a]	5	4
15	TCTA (TCTG)4 (TCTA)10	1	1
16	TCTA (TCTG)3 (TCTA)12	–	3
	TCTA (TCTG)4 (TCTA)11	10	2
17	TCTA (TCTG)4 (TCTA)12	12	8
18	TCTA (TCTG)4 (TCTA)13	11	4
	TCTA (TCTG)5 (TCTA)12	1	–
19	TCTA (TCTG)4 (TCTA)14	8	3
	TCTA (TCTG)5 (TCTA)13	–	2
20	TCTA (TCTG)3 (TCTA)16	1	–
	TCTA (TCTG)4 (TCTA)15	2	–
21	TCTA (TCTG)4 (TCTA)16	2	–
	TCTA (TCTG)5 (TCTA)15	3	–
	TCTA (TCTG)6 (TCTA)14	1	2
22	TCTA (TCTG)5 (TCTA)16	2	–

[a] TCTA TCTG TCTA (TCTG)4 (TCTA)3 TCCA (TCTA)3 TCCA TCCA TCCA TCCA.

manufacturer's recommendations in an ABI Prism 377 with Genescan (V.3.1.2.) and Genotyper (v.2.0.) or in an ABI 3100 with Genescan and Genotyper (v.3.7). More than 100 vWA alleles have been sequenced with DNA Sequencing Kit Big Dye™ v.3.0 Terminator Cycle Sequencing (Applied Biosystems) with forward and reverse primers [2]. Sequencing was performed in an ABI Prism 377 DNA Sequencer and samples were analysed by Sequencing Analysis v.3.4.1. (Applied Biosystems).

3. Results and discussion

Table 1 shows allele nomenclature, sequence structure and number of alleles sequenced at the vWA locus in two populations. Internal variability was detected at allelic level at this

Table 2
Eight vWA mutations obtained in paternity investigation cases

	W without mutation	A Father	Mother	Child	W with mutation
Case 1	W=99.99998%	16	17–18	17	W=99.993%
Case 2	W=99.998%	14–18	17–18–19	14–17	–
Case 3	W=99.99995%	18–19	16–19	19–20	–
Case 4	W=99.99999998%	17	15–17	15–16	W=99.999997%
Case 5	W=99.99993%	17–18	18–20	18–19	W=99.98%
	W=99.999997%	17–18	18–20	18–20	(brother)
Case 6	W=99.999998%	17–19	15–16	15–18	W=99.9996%
Case 7	W=99.99996%	16–20	17–19	19–21	W=99.994%
Case 8	W=99.999995%	18–20	14–17	17–19	W=99.9996%

Table 3
Six mutations at the primer-binding site obtained with ProfilerPlus/SGMPlus versus Powerplex1.2

	W without mutation	A Father	Mother	Child	Multiplex systems
Case 1	W=99.9991%	15–18	16	18/16–18	Profiler/Powerplex1.2
Case 2	W=99.9991%	16–18	17 /16–17	16–17	SGM/Powerplex1.2
Case 3	W=99.9991%	16/16–17	14–16	14–16	SGM/Powerplex1.2
Case 4	W=99.999999997%	16–19	17 /16–17	17–19	SGM/Powerplex1.2
Case 5	W=99.9999992%	17–18	17/16–17	18/16–18	SGM/Powerplex1.2
Case 6	W=99.999998%	17/17–18	16	16/16–18	SGM/Powerplex1.2

locus. The most common structure seems to be TCTA (TCTG)4 (TCTA)n, with a prevalence of TCTA(TCTG)3(TCTA)n structure in small alleles and the prevalence of TCTA (TCTG)5–6 (TCTA)n in large ones.

The nine observed nonconsensus allele 14 structures were found either in Caucasian or in African samples with a prevalence of 60% in both populations. Although we have analysed 20 allele 17 samples from both populations, the structure observed was always the same. Considering allelic structure, the most stable alleles seem to be alleles 16 and 17 in Caucasian population and alleles 17 and 18 in African population.

Performing more than 3000 paternity investigation cases with multiplex systems, several types of vWA mutations have also been encountered—null alleles, three-allele genotypes and repeat region mutations. A total of eight vWA mutations were detected in paternal investigation cases with a 0.0024 average mutation rate—one maternal mutation, five paternal mutations and two undetermined mutations (Table 2).

Table 3 illustrates six mutations at the primer-binding site obtained when performing ProfilerPlus/SGMPlus versus Powerplex1.2 (mutation rate 0.0018), which means that any vWA homozygous genetic incompatibility observed in paternity investigation needs to be confirmed with two different sets of primers.

References

[1] K. Lazaruk, J. Wallin, C. Holt, T. Nguyen, P.S. Walsh, Sequence variation in humans and other primates at six short tandem repeat loci used in forensic identity testing, Forensic Sci. Int. 119 (2001) 1–10.
[2] C.P. Kimpton, A. Walton, P. Gill, A further tetranucleotide repeat polymorphism in the vWF gene, Hum. Mol. Genet. 1 (1992) 287.

International Congress Series 1261 (2004) 251–253

www.ics-elsevier.com

16 Y-specific STR analysis in human remains identification

C. Vieira Silva[a], C. Cruz[a], T. Ribeiro[a], I. Lucas[a], H. Geada[b], R. Espinheira[a,*]

[a] *Forensic Genetics, National Institute of Legal Medicine, Rua Manuel Bento de Sousa, No. 3, 1159-219, Lisbon, Portugal*

[b] *Department of Legal Medicine, Faculty of Medicine, Lisbon, Portugal*

Abstract. Degraded samples were studied in order to obtain Y-STR haplotype to provide additional data in paternal lineage identification caseworks. Multiplex reactions were used comprising the minimal Y-STR haplotype DYS19, DYS390, DYS391, DYS392, DYS393, DYS19, DYS389I/II and DYS385 belonging to the Y-STR database. The other Y-STR loci—GATA A 7.1, GATA A 7.2, GATA C4, GATA H4, DYS437, DYS438 and DYS439—were included in the Y-Chromosome Quality Control Group of the Spanish and Portuguese Group (GEPY) of the ISFG. Y-STRs results were successful in almost all the samples when applied some modifications in amplification methods.

Keywords: Y-STRs; Paternal lineage; Degraded DNA; Haplotype

1. Introduction

Forensic investigation based on DNA typing often requires the use of degraded biological material, sometimes even highly degraded, especially for determining the identity of human remains. Due to their paternal inheritance Y-STRs offers new perspectives for identification and kinship analysis, especially in forensic deficiency cases as a complement to autosomal STRs. The aim was the study of 16 Y-STR loci to perform human remains identification, including the minimal Y-STR haplotype (DYS19, DYS390, DYS391, DYS392, DYS393, DYS19, DYS389I/II and DYS385) belonging to the Y-STR database and GATA A 7.1, GATA A 7.2, GATA C4, GATA H4, DYS437, DYS438, DYS439 loci that are part of the Y-Chromosome Quality Control Group of the Spanish and Portuguese Group (GEPY) of the ISFG.

* Corresponding author. Tel.: +351-21-8811800; fax: +351-21-8809958.
E-mail address: bio.lisboa.inml@mail.pt (R. Espinheira).

doi:10.1016/S0531-5131(03)01772-2

Table 1
Y-STRs alleles in degraded samples when applied mentioned modifications in amplification methods

	Sample	Pentaplex					GEPY I				GEPY II				Triplex I			Triplex II		
		DYS 393	DYS 390	DYS 19	DYS 389I	DYS 389II	Gata A7.2	DYS 437	DYS 438	Gata C4	Gata A7.1	Gata A10	DYS 439	Gata H4	DYS 391	DYS 437	DYS 439	DYS 438	DYS 392	DYS 385
Autopsy blood stains	1	13	22	16	13	30	12	17	8	23	10	16	11	27	11	17	11	8	11	15–16
	2	13	23	14	14	30	12	15	12	23	*	14	12	29	10	15	12	12	14	11–15
	3	14	23	14	14	29	13	15	13	23	13	15	*	28	11	15	12	13	14	11–14
	4	13	24	14	14	31	12	15	12	23	11	16	13	28	10	15	13	12	9	12–15
	5	13	24	14	12	28	13	15	12	24	11	15	12	28	11	15	12	12	13	11–14
Blood stored at 4° C	6	13	24	13	13	30	12	14	10	23	9	15	12	28	10	14	12	10	11	16–18
more than 1 year	7	13	24	13	14	30	*	14	10	*	11	15	10	28	9	14	10	10	11	13–14
	8	13	*	*	*	*	*	*	*	*	*	*	*	*	11	15	12	12	9	11–14
	9	13	22	16	14	30	*	*	*	*	10	16	*	*	11	15	11	*	*	*
	10	13	24	13	14	30	13	14	10	21	16	14	10	28	9	14	10	10	11	13–14
Muscle	11	13	22	14	12	*	12	16	10	21	11	17	11	27	10	16	*	10	11	13–15
Bone	12	13	24	14	13	*	12	*	12	23	7	14	13	*	*	*	*	*	*	*
	13	14	21	15	12	29	11	16	10	21	10	13	*	27	10	16	11	10	11	13–16
	14	14	24	14	13	29	12	15	*	23	11	14	13	28	11	15	13	*	*	*
	15	*	*	*	*	*	12	*	*	21	*	14	*	*	*	*	*	*	*	*
	16	14	22	15	13	29	*	*	*	*	*	14	11	27	11	16	11	10	11	12–12
	17	14	*	*	*	*	12	*	*	22	*	14	*	*	*	*	*	*	12	*
Teeth	18	14	23	16	12	27	11	16	10	21	10	14	12	28	10	16	12	10	10	14–15
	13	14	21	15	12	29	11	16	10	21	*	*	*	*	10	16	*	*	*	*
	15	*	*	*	*	*	*	*	*	*	*	14	*	28	*	*	*	*	*	*
	19	14	23	15	13	31	12	14	10	22	*	14	12	27	10	14	12	10	12	15–15

* No results.

2. Material and methods

Samples from 19 deceased individuals—bone, teeth, muscle, blood submitted to toxicological analysis kept at 4 °C for more than 1 year, bloodstains collected during autopsy—were studied and compared with bloodstains of relatives. DNA was extracted by phenol:chloroform methods, and for comparative bloodstains chelex method was used. A pentaplex reaction was carried out according to Kayser et al. [1] and de Knijff et al. [2]. GEPY I and II multiplexes (Table 1) were performed according to Gusmão et al. [3]. Triplex I and II were carried out as described by Ballard et al. [4]. For genetic typing, ABI Prism 31OO Sequencer was used.

3. Results and discussion

The Y-STR typing in degraded biological material has major technical challenges since each sample has unique characteristics. Most of the samples required protocol modifications such as different dilution extractions, distinct DNA and Taq polymerase concentrations, to achieve Y-STRs typing. Pentaplex was the multiplex system that seems to give better results with degraded samples. GEPY I and II systems need more technical modifications than Triplex II and I.

The reason that best results were obtained in autopsy bloodstains may be attributed to the fact that autolysis mechanisms are still incipient. Otherwise, liquid blood maintained at 4 °C for more than a year did not provide the same good results as it may contain porfirinic compounds from hemoglobin, which are powerful PCR inhibitors that difficult to eliminate.

In bone and teeth samples, a haplotype with at least 10 loci was obtained. Two of them did not yield results even when we applied AmpliTaqGold® LD, reamplification and 40 cycles PCR program. In these type of samples, which were exposed to adverse environmental and soil conditions, several problems need to be overcome—such as high DNA fragmentation, high amount of DNA from other microorganisms which invade biological materials, or other source of inhibitors.

Most of the results were obtained with dilution of DNA extraction and adding more Taq, sometimes by 2- or 3-fold. Thus the problem with the studied samples seems not to be DNA quantity, but the out-of-control presence of inhibitors that interfere not only with the extraction but also with the amplification process.

Allele typing in almost all Y-STRs enables comparison between these samples and individuals with the same paternal lineage.

References

[1] M. Kayser, et al., Evaluation of Y-chromosomal STRs: a multicenter study, Int. J. Legal Med. 110 (1997) 125–133 (appendix 141–149).

[2] P. Knijff, et al., Chromosome Y microsatellites: population genetics and evolutionary aspects, Int. J. Legal Med. 110 (1997) 134–149 (appendix 141–149).

[3] L. Gusmão, et al., Results of the GEP-ISFG collaborative study on the Y chromosome STRs Gata A10, Gata C4, Gata H4, DYS437, DYS438, DYS439, DYS460 and DYS461: population data, Forensic Sci. Int. 135 (2003) 150–157.

[4] D. Ballard, et al., Haplotype discrimination amongst three UK population groups using three multiplexes to type eleven Y chromosome STRs, Int. Congr. Series 1239 (2003) 435–437.

International Congress Series 1261 (2004) 254–256

www.ics-elsevier.com

A population study of three Y-STR loci by multiplexing in Han population in Chengdu, China

Y. Jia, L. Zhang*, B. Zhou, M. Lv, W.B. Liang, L. Miao, M.Y. Wu

College of Forensic Medicine, Sichuan University, No. 17 Section 3, Ren Ming Nan Lu, Chengdu, Sichuan, 610041, PR China

Abstract. *Background*: it is necessary to enhance the efficiency of amplification of Y-STR in according with the progress in forensic science. Methods: Using a multiplex of Y-STRs and amplify simultaneously three Y-STRs loci. *Results*: A multiplexing system of three Y-STR loci (DYS390, DYS391 and DYS393) is successfully established followed by a population genetic study of Han population in Chengdu, China. *Conclusions*: The diversity of haplotype is 0.8965, the value of discrimination and the chance of exclusion chance is 0.8965 with the standard error 0.0081. This established system is one of the good tools in personal identification and genetic study.

Keywords: Forensic science; Y-STRs; DYS390; DYS391; DYS393; Multiplexing; Population study

1. Introduction

Y-STRs systems have been used in paternity testing of male offspring, personal identification and population genetic study, The non-pseudoautosomal part of the Y chromosome is inherited only along male lineages. A single Y-STR locus can only provide a limited information. There is no doubt that multiplexing of one more STR loci will provide more informations. We have constructed a multiplex system and amplified three Y-STRs loci simultaneously, followed by non-denaturing polyacrylamide gel electrophoresis and silver staining.

2. Survey methodology

EDTA-blood samples were collected from 105 unrelated male of Han population in Chengdu of China. DNA was extracted using Chelex-100 method [1].

* Corresponding author. Tel.: +86-28-85460532; fax: +86-28-85405541.
E-mail address: kjc@scu.edu.cn (L. Zhang).

0531-5131/
doi:10.1016/S0531-5131(03)01615-7

Table 1
The primer sequences of DYS390, DYS391 and DYS393

Loci	Allele	Primer sequences
DYS390	21–26	P1: 5′-TAT ATT TTA CAC ATT TTT GGC CC-3′
		P2: 5′-GAC AGT AAA ATG AAC ACA TTG C-3′
DYS391	9–11	P1: 5′-CTA TTC ATT CAA TCA TAC ACC CA-3′
		P2: 5′-CTG GGA ATA AAA TCT CCC TGG TTG GGA G-3′
DYS393	12–16	P1: 5′-GTG GTC TTC TAC TTG TGT CAA TAC AG-3′
		P2: 5′-AAC TCA AGT CCA AAA AAT GAG G-3′

In order to reduce the unspecific amplification products, the primers of DYS391 and DYS393 were modified respectively by Leonor et al. [2] and Berit et al. [3].The primers of DYS390 were the same as these in the GDB [4] (Table 1).

The PCR amplifications was conducted in a thermal cycler (HEIMA 480) in a 20-μl reaction volume, which included 50–100 ng of DNA template, 2 μl 10 × PCR reaction buffer, 1.25 μl $MgCl_2$ (25 mmol/l), 1.5 μl DYS390 primers (12.5 pmol/μl), 1.0 μl DYS391 primers (12.5 pmol/μl), 1.2 μl DYS393 primers (12.5 pmol/μl), 1.25 U Taq DNA polymerase.

The PCR conditions were 94 °C for 3 min, followed by 35 cycles at 94 °C for 35 sec, 57 °C for 35 s and 72 °C for 55 s, then extension at 72 °C for another 5 min.

A total of 3 μl PCR products was analyzed by non-denaturing polyacrylamide gel electrophoresis (T=6%, C=5%) with discontinuous buffer system and visualized by silver staining [5].

Table 2
Haplotype distribution of DYS391/DYS390/DYS393 of Han population in Chengdu, China (n = 105)

Haplotype	Frequency	Number	Haplotype	Frequency	Number
9/23/12	0.009524	1	10/25/13	0.028571	3
9/25/12	0.009524	1	10/25/14	0.009524	1
9/25/13	0.019048	2	11/23/12	0.028571	3
10/21/15	0.009524	1	11/23/13	0.066667	7
10/22/12	0.019048	2	11/23/14	0.009524	1
10/22/13	0.009524	1	11/23/15	0.019048	2
10/22/14	0.009524	1	11/23/16	0.009524	1
10/23/12	0.171429	18	11/24/12	0.019048	2
10/23/13	0.07619	8	11/24/13	0.047619	5
10/23/14	0.038095	4	11/24/14	0.019048	2
10/23/15	0.028571	3	11/25/12	0.028571	3
10/24/12	0.142857	15	11/25/13	0.019048	2
10/24/13	0.066667	7	11/25/14	0.009524	1
10/24/14	0.028571	3	11/26/14	0.009524	1
10/25/12	0.038095	4			
Discrimination power = 0.8965			Exclusion chance = 0.8965		
Diversity = 0.8965 ± 0.0081					

3. Results

The haplotype diversity and standard error were calculated in accordance with Hou's method [6]. The formula for calculating the gene diversity: $h=n\ (1-\Sigma x^2)/(n-1)$, where n is the number of individuals tested, h is the gene diversity, x is the frequencies of alleles.

The formula calculating standard error (S.E.): S.E.$=\{2\{\Sigma x^3-(\Sigma x^2)^2\}/n\}^{1/2}$.

The Y chromosome haplotypes of 105 unrelated males from Han population in Chengdu, China are presented in Table 2.

4. Discussion

In case of multiplexing STRs, the optimal ratio of primer pairs used in the multiple system is very important. In this study, the best proportion was 1.5/1.0/1.2 (DYS390/DYS391/DYS393). The $MgCl_2$ is an another important factor to affect the results of the PCR reactions. About 1.25 μl $MgCl_2$ (25 mmol/l) in a 20-μl reaction volume was the best. This method is reliable, easy to perform, time saving, less consuming either samples or reagents.

In our population study, the diversity of haplotype was 0.8965, the value of discrimination and the chance of exclusion chance was 0.8965 with the standard error 0.0081. Our results demonstrated that these three Y-STRs can provide more informations in Han population in Chengdu, China. The application of this multiplex system is helpful in resolving some forensic science cases, such as paternity testing only with son, personal identification, especially examination of mixture stain in rape cases and in anthropological investigation cases.

Acknowledgements

The research was supported by grants from the Chinese Natural Sciences Foundation (No. 30171033) and State Ministry of Education (No. 01143) as well as Trans-Century Training Programme Foundation for the Talents by the Ministry of Education Commission (No. 2001-29).

References

[1] B. Wslsh, et al, Chelex-100 as medium for simple extraction of DNA for PCR-based tying from forensic material, Biotechniques 10 (1991) 506–510.

[2] G. Leonor, et al, Alternative primers for DYS391 typing advantages of their application to forensic genetics, Forensic Science International 112 (2000) 49–57.

[3] M. Berit, et al, DXYS267: DYS393 and its X chromosome counterpart, Forensic Science International 112 (2000) 111–121.

[4] Available at: http://www.gdb.org.

[5] C. Allen, et al, Polymerase chain reaction amplification products separated on rehydratable polyacrylamide gels and stained with silver, Biotechniques 7 (1990) 736–744.

[6] Y. Hou, et al, Allele sequences of six new Y-STR loci and haplotypes in the Chinese Han population, Forensic Science International 118 (2001) 147–152.

ELSEVIER

International Congress Series 1261 (2004) 257–259

www.ics-elsevier.com

Advantages of X-chromosomal microsatellites in deficiency paternity testing: presentation of cases

J. Edelmann[a,*], R. Lessig[a], M. Klintschar[b], R. Szibor[c]

[a] *Institut für Rechtsmedizin, Universität Leipzig, Leipzig, Germany*
[b] *Institut für Rechtsmedizin, Universität Halle, Halle, Germany*
[c] *Institut für Rechtsmedizin, Otto-von-Guericke-Universität Magdeburg, Magdeburg, Germany*

Abstract. We present examples of our routine work, which demonstrate the impact of additional ChrX marker typing in special paternity case situations. In each of the seven cases, an extensive testing of autosomal markers failed to yield satisfying results (W>99.9% or 3 exclusions). However, by expanding the analysis to ChrX markers, these criterions were met in five of seven cases.

Keywords: ChrX marker typing; Deficiency paternity cases

1. Introduction

The major advantage of X-chromosomal (ChrX) STRs arises in deficiency paternity cases, i.e. when a putative father is not available and DNA from paternal relatives has to be analysed instead. In such cases, the exclusion power of autosomal STRs is substantially decreased, whereas ChrX markers are (at least in some cases) more efficient [1]. Female individuals fathered by the same man share their paternal ChrX. Males inherit their only ChrX from their mother. Hence, in cases in which the putative grandmother is available for genotyping, the possible ChrX alleles of the putative father can be determined [2]. ChrX marker typing is highly effective in mother–son kinship and in father–daughter testing. However, linkage and possible linkage disequilibrium between the ChrX markers used have to be taken into consideration.

2. Materials and methods

For the following pedigrees, we tested 11–16 autosomal STRs using the SGM or Powerplex 16 Kits and SE33, resulting in differing probabilities of paternity (W_{autos}).

Additionally, we investigated a panel of 9 ChrX STRs (see Fig. 1), but only four of it (the unlinked markers DXS6807, DXS8377 and the DXS101/DXS7424 haplotype frequency [3]) were used for calculation of probability of paternity (W_{ChrX}). The

* Corresponding author. Tel.: +49-3419715111; fax: +49-3419715109.
E-mail address: edej@medizin.uni-leipzig.de (J. Edelmann).

doi:10.1016/S0531-5131(03)01722-9

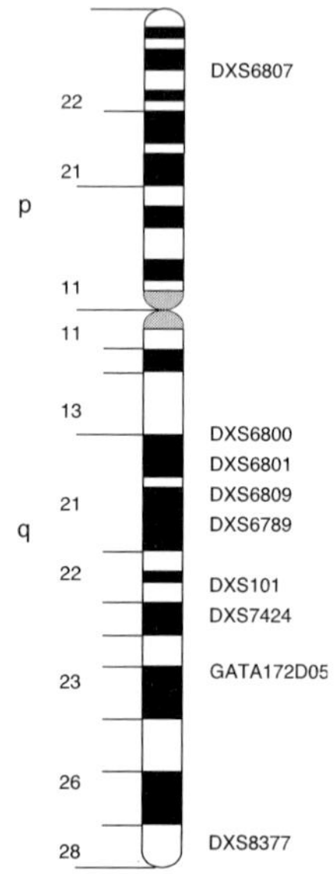

Fig. 1. ChrX ideogram with the investigated markers.

calculations for W_{autos} and W_{ChrX} were performed with the Kinship part of DNA-VIEW (Charles Brenner) considering the ChrX specific inheritance of the markers.

3. Results

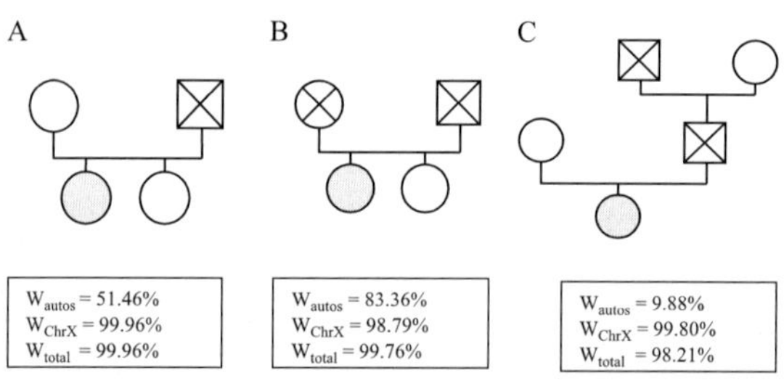

4. Discussion

The presented examples of our routine work demonstrate the impact of information of an additional ChrX marker typing. In each of the cases, an extensive testing of autosomal markers failed to yield satisfying results (i.e. either W>99.9% or at least 3 exclusions). However, by expanding the analysis to ChrX markers, these criterions were met in five of seven cases. Two cases merit special attention: In case C, W_{autos} was 9.88% ("paternity unlikely"). ChrX analysis led to a W_{total} of 98.21%. In case G, W_{autos} was 93.12% when testing the putative grandmother. Including the brother of the putative father reduced the probability to 63.20% (not shown). However, in nine ChrX STRs, four exclusions were found.

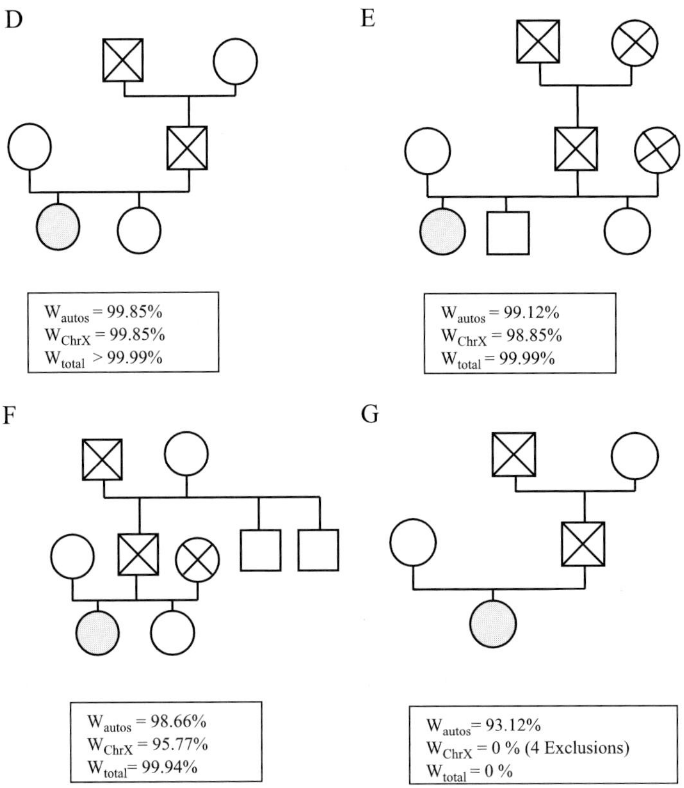

These cases clearly demonstrate that ChrX markers have the potential to solve some paternity cases, which cannot be solved using autosomal markers. Suitable for this analysis are cases with a female child and especially putative grandmother-and putative sister cases. Female individuals with the same father share the same paternal ChrX. The ChrX marker investigation of two sisters or half-sisters can thus exclude paternity, even when none of the parents is available for testing. On the other hand, all ChrX alleles of the putative father can be determined by investigating the putative grandmother. However, ChrX marker genotypes of the putative grandmother can also be reconstructed from her children and if sons (brothers of the putative father) are available, the data are even more informative.

References

[1] R. Szibor, et al., Use of X-linked markers for forensic purposes, Int. J. Legal Med. 117 (2003) 67–74.

[2] R. Szibor, et al., Chromo-some X haplotyping in deficiency paternity testing principles and case report, In: B. Brinkmann, A. Carracedo (Eds.), Progress in Forensic Genetics 9, vol. 1239, Elsevier, ICS, 2003, 815–820.

[3] J. Edelmann, et al., Validation of the STR DXS7424 and the linkage situation on the X-chromosome, Forensic Sci. Int. 125 (2002) 217–222.

ELSEVIER

International Congress Series 1261 (2004) 260–262

www.ics-elsevier.com

Allele distribution of five X-chromosome STR loci in an Italian population sample

G. Peloso[a,*], P. Grignani[b], C. Previderè[a]

[a] Department of Legal Medicine and Public Health, University of Pavia, Pavia, Italy
[b] IRCCS Policlinico S. Matteo, Department of Legal Medicine and Public Health, Pavia, Italy

Abstract. Population genetic data for five X-chromosomal STR loci (DXS7423, DXS6789, DXS6795, DXS9898 and DXS8377) were generated by analysing a population sample from Northwest Italy. Intensive stutter bands were observed for the DXS8377 locus. The analysis of the 40 family trios segregation showed no new mutation.

Keywords: X-Chromosome; STRs; Population data

1. Introduction

The aim of this study was to investigate the distribution of five STR loci (DXS7423, DXS6789, DXS6795, DXS9898 and DXS8377) in a population sample from 120 unrelated individuals (60 females and 60 males) and 40 family trios (20 male and 20 female offspring) living in the Pavia area (Northwest Italy).

2. PCR amplification and allele typing

DXS7423, DXS6789 and DXS6795 loci were amplified in one triplex and DXS9898 and DXS8377 loci in one duplex PCR reaction, using primers sequences already reported [1–5]. Fragment lengths (bp) processed by ABI 310 capillary sequencer were compared to the published data [1–5] and allelic ladders were calibrated by typing K562 and 9947A. Seven alleles of the DXS6795 locus were sequenced in order to identify the repeat motif. The consensus repeat structure of alleles 12 to 15 was the following: $(TAA)_{10-13}$TG(TAA)TTG(-TAA), while allele 10 showed the slightly modified repeat motif $(TAA)_6$(TGA)(TAA)TG(-TAA)TTG(TAA). The alleles were named as recommended by the ISFH [6].

3. Results and discussion

The allele frequencies calculated for females and males independently are shown in Fig. 1. These typing results were consistent with other previously published data

* Corresponding author. Tel.: +39-0382-507810; fax: +39-0382-528025.
E-mail address: gapeloso@unipv.it (G. Peloso).

0531-5131/
doi:10.1016/S0531-5131(03)01814-4

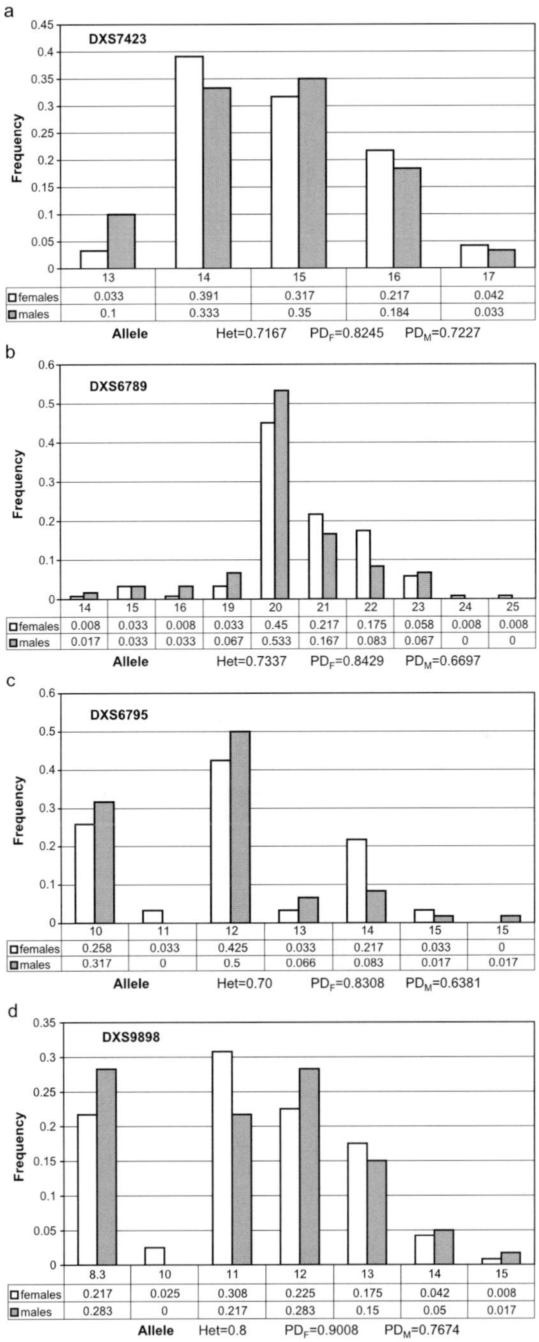

Fig. 1. Allele frequency distribution in females and males.

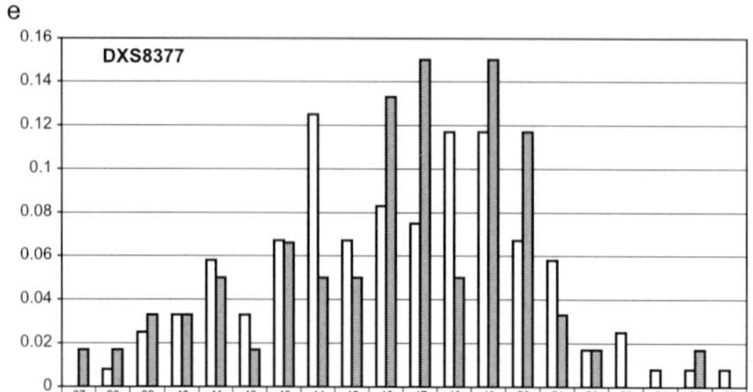

	37	38	39	40	41	42	43	44	45	46	47	48	49	50	51	52	53	54	55	57
females	0	0.008	0.025	0.033	0.058	0.033	0.067	0.125	0.067	0.083	0.075	0.117	0.117	0.067	0.058	0.017	0.025	0.008	0.008	0.008
males	0.017	0.017	0.033	0.033	0.05	0.017	0.066	0.05	0.05	0.133	0.15	0.05	0.15	0.117	0.033	0.017	0	0	0.017	0

Fig. 1 (*continued*).

[2,4,5]. Intensive stutter bands were observed by typing the DXS8377 locus, as already shown [5].

Data compared by Fisher test were similar in males and females for all markers. No deviations from HWE were found in females. Statistical parameters were calculated according to Desmarais et al. [7]. No mutation was found by analysing 40 family trios.

The pooled data for the DXS7423, DXS6798, DXS9898 and DXS8377 loci compared with a population sample from Germany showed very similar distributions.

References

[1] M.T. Zarrabeitia, T. Amigo, C. Sañudo, A. Zarrabeitia, D. Gonzales-Lamuño, J.A. Riancho, A new pentaplex system to study short tandem repeat markers of forensic interest on X chromosome, Forensic Sci. Int. 129 (2002) 85–89.

[2] S. Hering, E. Kuhlisch, R. Szibor, Development of the X-linked tetrameric microsatellite marker HumDXS6789 for forensic purposes, Forensic Sci. Int. 119 (2001) 42–46.

[3] http://www.gdb.org/.

[4] S. Hering, R. Szibor, Development of the X-linked tetrameric microsatellite marker DXS9898 for forensic purposes, J. Forensic Sci. 45 (4) (2000) 929–931.

[5] P. Wiegand, B. Berger, J. Edelmann, W. Parson, Population genetic comparisons of three X-chromosomal STRs, Int. J. Legal Med. 117 (2003) 62–65.

[6] W. Bär, B. Brinkmann, B. Budowle, A. Carracedo, P. Gill, P. Lincoln, W. Mayr, B. Olaisen, DNA recommendations. Further report of the DNA Commission of the ISFH regarding the use of short tandem repeat systems, Int. J. Legal Med. 110 (1997) 175–176.

[7] D. Desmarais, Y. Zhong, R. Chakraborty, C. Perrault, L. Busque, Development of a highly polymorphic STR marker for identity testing purposes at the human androgen receptor gene (Humara), J. Forensic Sci. 43 (1998) 1046–1049.

ELSEVIER

International Congress Series 1261 (2004) 263–265

www.ics-elsevier.com

Allele frequencies for X-chromosomal microsatellites in different populations

J. Edelmann[a,*], R. Lessig[a], S. Hering[b], N. Brundirs[c], E. Kuhlisch[d], R. Szibor[c]

[a] *Institut für Rechtsmedizin, Universität Leipzig, Germany*
[b] *Institut für Rechtsmedizin, Technische Universität Dresden, Germany*
[c] *Institut für Rechtsmedizin, Otto-von-Guericke-Universität Magdeburg, Germany*
[d] *Institut für Medizinische Informatik und Biometrie, Technische Universität Dresden, Germany*

Abstract. We investigated the allele distribution of several X-chromosomal (ChrX) markers in population samples from Peru, Ireland, Germany and Ethiopia. We found no homogeneity between the populations. This could be confirmed by χ^2-test. The most impressive differences were seen between the Peruvian and European population samples.

Keywords: X-chromosome; Allele distribution; Population data

1. Introduction

ChrX markers represent an efficient supplementation of autosomal and Y-chromosomal STR analyses and ChrX haplotyping can elucidate complicated kinship situations [1]. This procedure requires a broad spectrum of well established ChrX markers of well known localisation. Some of them are forensically characterised for few European and Asian population samples [2–4].

2. Materials and methods

We investigated population samples from Peru (118 alleles), Ireland (110 alleles), Germany (900 alleles) and Ethiopia (123 alleles). It has been made sure as possible, that each sample represents the indigenous population. PCR amplifications were performed with a pentaplex reaction for GATA172D05, DXS101, DXS7424, DXS6800, DXS6807, a triplex reaction for DXS6809, DXS6801, DXS6789 and a single PCR for DXS8377. Resulting PCR products were resolved and detected by capillary electrophoresis in the ABI 310 sequencer.

* Corresponding author. Tel.: +49-341-9715111; fax: +49-341-9715109.
E-mail address: edej@medizin.uni-leipzig.de (J. Edelmann).

0531-5131/
doi:10.1016/S0531-5131(03)01837-5

Table 1
Allele frequencies [%] of the population samples: Peru (P), Ireland (I), Germany (G) and Ethiopia (E)

DXS101	P	I	G	E
12	0.0	0.0	0.2	0.8
15	1.7	5.2	4.4	0.8
16	0.0	0.0	0.5	2.4
17	0.0	0.0	0.2	0.8
18	0.8	7.3	8.5	9.8
19	1.7	5.2	4.7	2.4
20	2.5	2.1	1.2	2.4
21	0.0	6.2	3.2	4.9
22	0.8	1.0	2.2	7.3
23	6.8	8.3	6.6	6.5
24	30.5	11.5	21.2	12.2
25	20.3	20.8	15.6	11.4
26	22.0	14.6	11.4	17.1
27	8.5	6.2	7.9	8.9
28	2.5	6.2	7.0	8.1
29	0.8	4.2	2.7	3.2
30	0.8	1.0	2.4	0.8

DXS7424	P	I	G	E
10	1.7	0.0	0.3	2.4
11	0.0	1.0	0.4	3.2
12	0.8	5.1	3.5	4.1
13	4.2	3.1	6.9	2.4
14	22.9	14.3	22.0	26.8
15	29.7	38.8	29.1	25.2
16	29.7	25.5	24.0	29.3
17	8.5	8.2	10.4	4.9
18	1.7	4.1	2.1	1.6
19	0.8	0.0	1.1	0.0

172D05	P	I	G	E
6	14.4	13.4	14.8	33.3
7	0.0	0.0	0.2	2.4
8	6.8	23.7	16.7	15.4
9	3.4	2.1	5.5	5.7
10	35.6	30.9	27.2	24.4
11	24.6	13.4	24.1	8.9
12	15.2	16.5	11.2	9.8
13	0.0	0.0	0.2	0.0

DXS6807	P	I	G	E
10	0.0	0.0	0.0	1.6
11	36.4	57.1	49.2	65.8
12	3.4	1.0	2.1	4.1
13	22.0	1.0	1.1	4.9
14	25.4	26.5	23.5	14.6
15	12.7	13.3	20.2	4.1
16	0.0	1.0	2.9	3.2
17	0.0	0.0	1.0	1.6

DXS6800	P	I	G	E
16	84.0	40.8	36.7	32.5
17	2.5	2.0	5.2	4.9
18	6.8	13.3	8.2	26.0
19	5.1	31.6	33.5	30.1
20	0.8	6.1	4.6	4.1
21	0.0	6.1	9.4	2.4
22	0.8	0.0	2.3	0.0

DXS6809	P	I	G	E
27	0.0	0.0	1.5	1.6
28	0.8	0.0	3.7	2.4
29	0.0	1.0	1.3	8.9
30	2.5	0.0	4.1	5.7
31	16.9	17.0	15.4	14.6
32	23.7	15.0	14.6	16.3
33	32.2	36.0	27.9	26.8
34	15.2	17.0	19.1	17.1
35	5.9	7.0	7.7	5.7
36	2.5	5.0	3.4	0.0
37	0.0	1.0	0.8	0.0
38	0.0	1.0	0.4	0.8

DXS6789	P	I	G	E
15	2.5	7.0	3.6	16.3
16	16.1	1.0	1.4	4.1
17	0.0	1.0	0.1	0.8
18	1.7	0.0	0.2	1.6
19	5.1	0.0	2.9	1.6
20	48.3	31.0	37.9	31.7
21	13.6	34.0	28.6	21.1
22	8.5	19.0	17.3	14.6
23	2.5	7.0	6.3	6.5
24	1.7	0.0	1.6	1.6

DXS6801	P	I	G	E
6	0.0	0.0	0.0	0.8
8	0.0	2.0	1.0	0.0
10	22.0	6.0	3.1	5.7
11	62.7	57.0	55.7	42.3
12	10.2	26.0	26.8	31.7
13	4.2	6.0	11.3	17.1
14	0.8	3.0	2.1	2.4
15	0.0	0.0	0.0	0.0

DXS8377	P	I	G	E
39	0.0	0.0	0.7	0.0
40	0.0	0.0	1.0	0.0
41	0.0	3.3	2.4	0.8
42	0.0	2.2	3.1	1.6
43	9.7	8.8	4.4	3.2
44	19.3	5.5	4.3	8.1
45	15.0	2.2	5.0	5.7
46	0.0	5.5	6.9	8.1
47	16.1	17.6	9.2	7.3
48	8.6	14.3	11.0	10.6
49	14.0	13.2	11.3	16.3
50	3.2	7.7	12.7	7.3
51	5.4	4.4	8.2	7.3
52	3.2	3.3	6.3	10.6
53	2.1	2.2	6.0	7.3
54	2.1	5.5	4.0	3.2
55	0.0	2.2	1.4	0.8
56	0.0	2.2	1.4	0.0
57	1.1	0.0	0.5	0.8
58	0.0	0.0	0.1	0.0
59	0.0	0.0	0.1	0.0
60	0.0	0.0	0.0	0.8

4. Results

Allele frequencies of the population samples are shown in Table 1.

There were significant higher and significant lower observed alleles compared to expected allele numbers after assumption of homogeneity between populations. Detailed data are available by the authors.

4. Discussion

The differences between allele frequencies (Table 1) are indicating that there is no homogeneity between the investigated populations. This could be confirmed by testing homogeneity of allele distribution by χ^2-test. The most impressive differences were seen between the Peruvian and European population samples. In the German population significant linkage disequilibrium was observed between the markers DXS7424 and DXS101 [5]. Hence, for this linkage group haplotype frequencies must be estimated directly from population data. With this study we collected the first haplotype data for other populations, but to check for linkage disequilibrium the number of individuals is insufficient. Apart from the forensic significance of allele distribution and linkage disequilibrium, these results give some interesting information on human world migration history.

References

[1] R. Szibor, M. Krawczak, S. Hering, J. Edelmann, E. Kuhlisch, D. Krause, Use of X-linked markers for forensic purposes, Int. J. Leg. Med. 117 (2003) 67–74.

[2] M.T. Zarrabeitia, T. Amigo, C. Sanudo, M.M. de Pancorbo, J.A. Riancho, Sequence structure and population data of two X-linked markers: DXS7423 and DXS8377, Int. J. Leg. Med. 116 (2002) 368–371.

[3] M.-Y. Chen, F.-C. Wu, L.-M. Meng, S.-M. Cheng, C.-H. Chao, C.-E. Pu, Population data on the X chromosome short tandem repeat loci HPRT and AR in Taiwan, Forensic Sci. Int. 126 (2002) 171–172.

[4] D. Huang, Q. Yang, C. Yu, R. Yang, Development of the X-linked tetrameric microsatellite markers HumDXS6803 and HumDXS9895 for forensic purpose, Forensic Sci. Int. 133 (2003) 246–249.

[5] J. Edelmann, S. Hering, E. Kuhlisch, R. Szibor, Validation of the STR DXS7424 and the linkage situation on the X-chromosome, Forensic Sci. Int. 125 (2002) 217–222.

International Congress Series 1261 (2004) 266–268

www.ics-elsevier.com

A pentaplex PCR assay for the genetic analysis of ChrX short tandem repeat (STR) loci

L. Henke, M. Dülmer, J. Henke*

Forensic Genetics, Institut für Blutgruppenforschung, Hohenzollernring 57, 50501 Cologne, Germany

Abstract. The paper describes the development of a multiplex PCR assay suitable for the simultaneous amplification of 5 X-chromosomal STR loci. © 2003 Published by Elsevier B.V.

Keywords: PCR; Short tandem repeats; Chromosome X; Pentaplex

1. Introduction

So far, X-chromosomal short tandem repeat markers (ChrX-STRs) have played a minor role in forensic genetics. However, under certain circumstances, Chr X typing can complement the analysis of autosomal and Chr Y markers, especially in complicated kinship cases. Thus, this paper aims at introducing the development of a rapid pentaplex PCR assay suitable for fluorescent detection.

2. Methods

Recently, Athanasiadou et al. [1] have described a quadruplex PCR assay, which encompasses X-chromosomal loci STRX1, DXS101, HPRTB, and DXS8377. The recruitment of locus DXS6789 [2] to that multiplex required several modifications, which are outlined below.

2.1. PCR conditions

PCR is performed in a 10-μl volume containing 2 ng target DNA, 2 pmol of primers for loci DXS6789, STRX-1, and HPRTB, 1.7 pmol of DXS8377 primer, 3 pmol of DXS101 primer, 1 μl 10× Accuprime™ Buffer II (Invitrogen, Carlsbad, CA, U.S.A.), 0.25 μl Accuprime™ Taq DNA Polymerase, and 1 μMol dNTPs. Primer sequences and dye-labellings are compiled in Table 1.

* Corresponding author. Tel.: +49-221-253037; fax: +49-221-251247.
E-mail address: bgf.henke@t-online.de (J. Henke).

0531-5131/ © 2003 Published by Elsevier B.V.
doi:10.1016/S0531-5131(03)01723-0

Table 1
Primer sequences of investigated ChrX STR systems

System	Forward primer (5′ → 3′)	Reverse primer (5′ → 3′)
STRX-1	6-FAM-GTTTCCTCCTgCAAAATACAgC	TCCAgCACCCAAggAAgTC
DXS6789	6-FAM-TgTCCTATTgTATTAgTCAgggATC	ATgTAAgTTggTACTTAATAAACCCTC
DXS101	NED-ACTCTAAATCAgTCCAAATATCTCCCTT	CAAATCACTCCATggCACATgTAT
HPRTB	NED-ATgCCACAgATAATACACATCCCC	CTCTCCAgAATAGTTAGATgTAgg
DXS8377	VIC-ACCACTTCATggCTTACCACAg	TATggACCTTTggAAAgCTAg

2.2. Touchdown PCR

Intitial denaturation at 95 °C for 8 min, followed by six cycles for 1 min at 94 °C, 61–58.5 °C for 1 min, respectively, lowering the annealing temperature by 0.5 °C per cycle, followed by 24 cycles at 94, 58, and 72 °C, respectively, for 1 min each, an extension at 72 °C for 1 h and a final extension at 60 °C for 14 h. This last step was undertaken to solve the ± A (adenine) problem (Malik and Bern, personal communication.). Phenotyped DNA samples kindly provided by P. M. Schneider (Mainz) and R. Szibor (Magdeburg) enabled us to construct the respective allelic ladders.

3. Results

The performance of our pentaplex is illustrated by the respective allelic ladders, which are depicted in Fig. 1. The allele designations are based on proposals from previous publications [3–5].

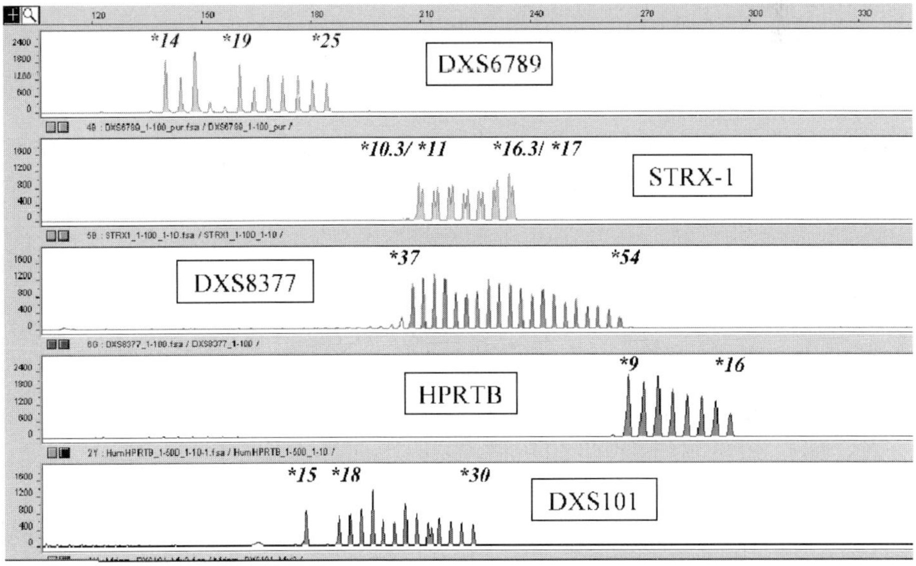

Fig. 1. Allelic ladders of ChrX pentaplex assay.

4. Discussion

After numerous efforts, we were able to adjust the experimental conditions to forensic demands and the above-described pentaplex assay is delivering reproducible typing results. Reviewing the arguments regarding the meaningful application of X-chromosomal STRs to forensic genetics [6], it can be emphasized that their employment is almost exclusively sensible in deficient paternity cases.

References

[1] D. Athanasiadou, B. Stradmann-Bellinghausen, C. Rittner, K.W. Alt, P.M. Schneider, Development of a quadruplex PCR system for the genetic analysis of X-chromosomal STR loci, Int. Congr. Ser. 1239 (2003) 311–314.

[2] S. Hering, E. Kuhlisch, R. Szibor, Development of the X-linked tetrameric microsatellite marker HumDXS6789 for forensic purposes, Forensic Sci. Int. 119 (2001) 42–46.

[3] Z. Tun, K. Honda, M. Nakatome, M. Nakamura, S. Shimada, Y. Ogura, H. Kuroki, M. Yamazaki, M. Terada, R. Matoba, Simultaneous detection of multiple STR loci on sex chromosomes for forensic testing of sex and identity, J. Forensic Sci. 44 (1999) 772–777.

[4] J. Edelmann, R. Szibor, DXS101: a highly polymorphic X-linked STR, Int. J. Leg. Med. 114 (2001) 301–304.

[5] J. Edelmann, D. Deichsel, S. Hering, I. Plate, R. Szibor, Sequence variation and allele nomenclature for the X-linked STR's DXS9895, DXS8378, DXS7132, DXS6800, DXS7133, GATA172D05, DXS7423 and DXS8377, Forensic Sci. Int. 129 (2002) 99–103.

[6] R. Szibor, M. Krawczak, S. Hering, J. Edelmann, E. Kuhlisch, D. Krause, Use of X-linked markers for forensic purposes, Int. J. Leg. Med. 117 (2003) 67–74.

International Congress Series 1261 (2004) 269–271

www.ics-elsevier.com

Analysis of Y-chromosomal haplotypes and haplogroups distribution in a population sample from Portugal (central area)

M. Carvalho[a,*], L. Andrade[a], F. Balsa[a], M.J. Anjos[a], V. Lopes[a], A. Serra[a], J.J. Gamero[b], F. Corte-Real[c], D.N. Vieira[c], M.C. Vide[a]

[a] *Service of Forensic Genetics, Delegation of Coimbra, National Institute of Legal Medicine, Largo da Sé Nova, 3000-213 COI, Coimbra, Portugal*

[b] *Department of Legal Medicine, Faculty of Medicine, University of Cádiz, Spain*

[c] *National Institute of Legal Medicine, Largo da Sé Nova, 3000-213 Coimbra, Portugal*

Abstract. The aim of this study was to analyse the distribution of Y-chromosomal haplotypes and haplogroups found in central Portugal. In this work, we analysed 102 unrelated individuals of central Portugal. Combining the allelic state of 10 biallelic markers (YAP, SRY-8299, 92R7, 12f2, SRY-1532, SRY-2627, Tat, SY81, M9, LLY22g), we defined the haplogroup to which each sample belonged. Y-chromosomal haplotypes were defined by 16 Y-Short Tandem Repeats (STR) (DYS19, DYS385 a/b, DYS389I, DYS389II, DYS390, DYS391, DYS392, DYS393, DYS437, DYS438, DYS439, DYS460, DYS461, GATA A10, GATA C4 and GATA H4). This population study defined 8 different haplogroups and 101 different haplotypes, where 100 haplotypes were unique and 1 was found in two apparently unrelated individuals, both belonging to the same haplogroup.

Keywords: Y chromosome; Haplotypes; Haplogroups; STRs; Biallelic markers

1. Introduction

The comparative analysis of Y-chromosomal biallelic markers and Short Tandem Repeats (STR) in a population may be useful to verify if the distribution of diversity is well balanced [1].

For this purpose, we analysed the distribution of Y-chromosomal haplotypes defined by 16 STRs (Y DYS19, DYS385, DYS389I, DYS389II, DYS390, DYS391, DYS392,

* Corresponding author. Tel.: +351-239854230; fax: +351-239820549.
E-mail address: geneforense@dcinml.mj.pt (M. Carvalho).

doi:10.1016/S0531-5131(03)01526-7

DYS393, DYS437, DYS438, DYS439, DYS460, DYS461, GATA A10, GATA C4 and GATA H4) in the eight different haplogroups defined by 10 biallelic markers (YAP, SRY-8299, 92R7, 12f2, SRY-1532, SRY-2627, Tat, SY81, M9, LLY22g) found in a population sample from Central Portugal.

In the present work, we evaluated the advantage of population analysis based in Y-chromosomal haplotypes and haplogroups (STRs and biallelic markers) in population genetics, evolutionary studies and forensic applications.

2. Materials and methods

DNA was extracted from blood stains collected from 102 unrelated Portuguese males (Central area), by Chelex 100 [3].

Ten biallelic markers (eight Single Nucleotide Polymorphisms (SNP), the Alu insertion YAP-DYS287 and the 12f2 deletion) were studied in a population from central Portugal. Biallelic markers were amplified by PCR and SNPs were also analysed by RFLP through an enzymatic digestion with the respective restriction enzyme. SRY1532, *Dra*III [4]; SRY8299, *Bsr*BI [4]; M9, *Hin*fI [5]; YAP-DYS287 [6]; 92R7, *Hin*dIII [7]; SRY2627, *Bsi*HKAI [8]; TAT, *Nla*III [9]; SY81, *Nla*III [10]; LLY22g, *Hin*dIII (Righetti and Tyler-Smith, Personal communication); 12f2 (Rosser et al., personal communication).

Fragment was detected by electrophoresis in PhastGel™ Gradient 10–15, with PhastGel™ SDS Buffer Strips (PhastSystem™-Amersham Pharmacia Biotech). Fragment length was determined through comparative analysis with 25- or 123-bp DNA ladder (Gibco®).

The Y-STRs DYS19, DYS389I, DYS389II, DYS390 and DYS393 were amplified as described by Gusmão et al. [11]. The DYS385 a/b amplification conditions complied with the methodology described by Schneider et al. [12]. Multiplex amplification of DYS391 DYS392, DYS393 was carried out according to Kloosterman et al. [13].

The Y-STR (DYS437, DYS438, DYS439, DYS460, DYS461, GATA A10, GATA C4 and GATA H4) were described by Ayub et al. [14] and White et al. [15] and were amplified with two PCR tetraplex reactions (GEPY I and GEPY II), using the protocol according to Sanchez-Diz et al. [16].

PCR was performed with Applied Biosystems 9600 and 2700 thermocyclers. Electrophoresis was carried out in ABI377 automated sequencer (4% polyacrylamide denaturing sequencing gels) and in ABI310 genetic analyser. Genotype classification was done using Genescan analysis software with Local Southern Method. Samples were typed by comparison with the allelic ladders obtained using a mixture of previously amplified samples for the most common alleles.

3. Results and discussion

The frequencies of the observed SNP haplogroups (according to Jobling and Tyler-Smith [17]) and STR haplotypes are shown in Table 1.

For the Y-STRs, 101 different haplotypes were observed: 100 haplotypes were unique and 1 was found in two apparently unrelated individuals, both belonging to the same haplogroup (hg 1).

Table 1
Observed haplogroups (HG) and haplotypes among 102 Portuguese males (Central area)

HG	*n*	%	Different STR haplotypes
hg 1	53	51.96	52
hg 2	15	14.71	15
hg 3	1	0.98	1
hg 8	5	4.90	5
hg 9	17	16.67	17
hg 21	2	1.96	2
hg 22	1	0.98	1
hg 26	8	7.84	8

The results of this population analysis based in Y-chromosomal haplotypes and haplogroups are according to the expected. Comparisons with other Iberian samples analysed for the same markers showed a substantial similarity [18].

4. Conclusion

Population surveys based in Y-chromosomal haplotypes and haplogroups (STRs and biallelic markers loci) seem to be the best strategy for the use and validation of Y polymorphisms, for instance, in the haplotype reference databases not only for forensic applications, but also to perform comparative population genetics analysis and evolutionary studies [1,2].

References

[1] K. Bender, B. Stradmann-Bellinghausen, C. Rittner, Int. Congr. Ser. 1239 (2003) 283–286.
[2] B.M. Dupuy, R. Andreassen, A.G. Flones, K. Tomassen, T. Egeland, M. Brion, A. Carrecedo, B. Olaisen, Forensic Sci. Int. 117 (2001) 163–173.
[3] P.S. Walsh, D.A. Metzger, R. Higuchi, BioTechniques 10 (4) (1991) 506–513.
[4] L.S. Whitfield, J.E. Sulston, P.N. Goodfellow, Nature 378 (1995) 379–380.
[5] P.A. Underhill, J. Jin, A.A. Lin, S. Qasim Mehdi, T. Jenkins, D. Vollrath, R.W. Davis, L.L. Cavalli-Sforza, P.J. Oefner, Genome Res. 7 (1997) 996–1005.
[6] M.F. Hammer, S. Horai, Am. J. Hum. Genet. 56 (1995) 951–962.
[7] N. Mathias, M. Bayes, C. Tyler-Smith, Hum. Mol. Genet. 3 (1994) 115–123.
[8] R. Veitia, A. Ion, S. Barbaux, M.A. Jobling, N. Souleyreau, N. Ennis, K. Oster, M. Tosi, T. Meo, J. Chibani, M. Fellous, K. McElreavey, Hum. Genet. 99 (1997) 648–652.
[9] T. Zerjal, B. Dashnyam, A. Pandya, M. Kayser, L. Roewer, F.R. Santos, W. Schiefenhovel, N. Fretwell, M.A. Jobling, S. Harihara, K. Shimizu, D. Semjidmaa, A. Sajantila, P. Salo, M.H. Crawford, E.K. Ginter, O.V. Evgrafov, C. Tyler-Smith, Am. J. Hum. Genet. 60 (1997) 1174–1183.
[10] M.T. Seielstad, et al., Hum. Mol. Genet. 3 (1994) 2159–2161.
[11] L. Gusmão, et al., Forensic Sci. Int. 106 (1999) 163–172.
[12] P.M. Schneider, et al., Forensic Sci. Int. 97 (1998) 61–70.
[13] A.D. Kloosterman, et al., Prog. Forensic Genet. 7 (1998) 491–493.
[14] Q. Ayub, et al., Nucleic Acids Res. 28 (2) (2000) e8.
[15] P. White, et al., Genomics 57 (3) (1999) 433–437.
[16] P. Sánchez-Diz, et al., Forensic Sci. Int. 135 (2003) 158–162.
[17] M.A. Jobling, C. Tyler-Smith, Trends Genet. 11 (1995) 449–456.
[18] M. Brión, et al., Forensic Sci. Int. 106 (1999) 163–172.

ELSEVIER

International Congress Series 1261 (2004) 272–274

www.ics-elsevier.com

Development of a heptaplex PCR system to analyse X-chromosome STR loci from five Italian population samples. A collaborative study

C. Bini[a,*], S. Ceccardi[a], G. Ferri[a], S. Pelotti[a], M. Alù[b], E. Roncaglia[b], G. Beduschi[b], L. Caenazzo[c], E. Ponzano[c], P. Tasinato[c], C. Turchi[d], M. Mazzanti[d], A. Tagliabracci[d], C. Toni[e], I. Spinetti[e], R. Domenici[e], S. Presciuttini[f]

[a] *Department of Medicine and Public Health, Section of Legal Medicine, University of Bologna, via Irnerio 49, 40126 Bologna, Italy*

[b] *Department of Pathological Anatomy and Legal Medicine, Section of Legal Medicine, University of Modena and Reggio Emilia, Italy*

[c] *Department of Environmental Medicine and Public Health, University of Padova, Italy*

[d] *Institute of Legal Medicine, University of Ancona, Italy*

[e] *Unit of Legal Medicine, School of Medicine, University of Pisa, Italy*

[f] *Center of Statistical Genetics, University of Pisa, Italy*

Abstract. A heptaplex PCR has been developed to amplify DXS6789, HUMARA, DXS10011, DXS7423, HPRTB, DXS6807 and DXS101 on Italian samples from Bologna, Modena, Padova, Ancona and Pisa. Statistical analyses were performed for all the loci.

Keywords: Multiplex PCR; Short tandem repeat (STR); X-chromosome; polymorphism

1. Introduction

The aim of this study was to increase the population data for ChrX STRs allele frequencies using a new heptaplex PCR including DXS6789, HUMARA, DXS10011, DXS7423, HPRTB, DXS6807 and DXS101 chosen because of their informativeness and their localization along the ChrX.

2. Materials and methods

DNA was extracted from 556 Italian samples: 101 unrelated native individuals from Bologna, 121 from Modena, 100 from Padova, 74 from Ancona and 160 from Pisa by QIAampDNABlood MiniKits (Qiagen, Germany). PCR was performed in 12.5 μl:10 ng

* Corresponding author. Tel.: +39-51-243250; fax: +39-51-248896.
E-mail address: labemat@medleg.unibo.it (C. Bini).

doi:10.1016/S0531-5131(03)01720-5

Table 1
STR loci with chromosomal locations, fragment sizes, primer concentrations, fluorescent dye labels, and references used in this study

System	Location	Fragment sizes (bp)	Primer concentration (μM)	Dye	Reference
DXS6789	Xq22.3	154–198	0.2	5-FAM	[5]
HUMARA	Xcen-q13	204–273	0.2	5-FAM	[6]
DXS10011	Xq27-28	137–257	1.0	JOE	[7]
HPRTB	Xq26	147–179	0.08	NED	[8]
DXS7423	Xq27-28	185–197	0.16	NED	[9]
DXS6807	Xpter-Xp22.2	251–275	0.24	NED	[10]
DXS101	Xq21.33-Xq22.3	179–233	0.4	ROX	[11]

DNA, 1 × PCR buffer with 1.5 mM $MgCl_2$, 150 μM each dNTP, 1 U AmpliTaq DNA Polymerase (Applied Biosystems, USA). Primer sequence references, concentrations and dye-labeling are listed in Table 1. The temperature profile was 1 min at 94 °C, 1 min at 58 °C and 1 min at 72 °C for 33 cycles and a final extension of 10 min at 72 °C. The samples were detected by using an ABI Prism 310 Genetic Analyzer (Applied Biosystems). Polymorphism information content (PIC) [1], heterozygosity (Het) [2], power of discrimination (PD) in males and females and power of exclusion (PE) [3] were performed; Hardy–Weinberg equilibrium (HWE) was tested following the likelihood ratio test criterion [4].

3. Results

The seven ChrX STRs were conveniently amplified under the above reported conditions (Fig. 1) except for DXS10011 in the Pisa sample. No differences in the allelic distribution patterns for male and female individuals were found. Observed genotype frequencies in females conformed to Hardy–Weinberg expectations, except for DXS7423 ($p = 0.02$). The statistical parameters PIC, Het, PD^F, PD^M and PE for each locus are listed in Table 2.

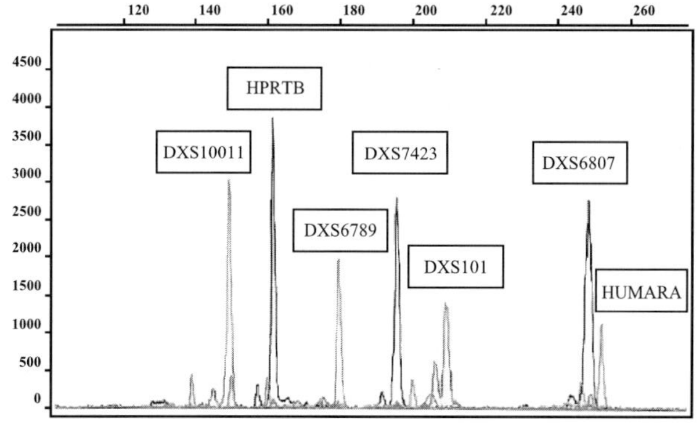

Fig. 1. Electropherogram of K562 heptaplex PCR products.

Table 2
Forensic efficiency of seven ChrX markers in a sample of 268 females and 288 males

	DXS6789	HUMARA	DXS10011[a]	HPRTB	DXS7423	DXS6807	DXS101
PIC	0.69	0.88	0.93	0.73	0.64	0.59	0.87
PD^F	0.891	0.979	0.992	0.91	0.852	0.818	0.973
PD^M	0.744	0.883	0.944	0.787	0.701	0.566	0.885
Het	0.729	0.892	0.937	0.768	0.695	0.645	0.877
PE	0.57	0.782	0.892	0.625	0.501	0.373	0.788
P	0.056	0.999	0.998	0.783	0.02[a]	0.838	0.64

[a] Sample size: 188 females and 208 males.

4. Discussion

Nowadays intense efforts of research are addressed to ChrX to increase the number of markers and to quantify linkage disequilibrium between them. Our heptaplex PCR represents a convenient procedure to type more ChrX STRs in a single reaction. The DXS10011 proved difficult to amplify and needed more primer concentration and DNA template for typeable results. In addition, the HUMARA locus amplification was more difficult than others and frequently showed stutter bands of $n-1$ repeat units high up to 20% the true band. In this study, a new allele for DXS101 (allele 14) in Modena sample and a new inter-allele (allele 19.2) for DXS10011 in the samples of Bologna and Ancona were found. The statistical analysis showed similar allele frequencies in males and females, Het ranging from 0.6451 for DXS6807 to 0.9370 for DXS10011. As expected DXS10011, HUMARA and DXS101 showed a similar very high PIC. Linkage disequilibrium studies are now in progress for a powerful ChrX haplotyping.

References

[1] D. Botstein, et al., Construction of a genetic linkage map in man using restriction fragment length polymorphisms, Am. J. Hum. Genet. 32 (3) (1980) 314–331.
[2] M. Nei, A.K. Roychoudhury, Sampling variances of heterozygosity and genetic distance, Genetics 76 (2) (1974) 379–390.
[3] D. Desmarais, et al., Development of a highly polymorphic STR marker for identity testing purposes at the human androgen receptor gene (HUMARA), J. Forensic Sci. 43 (5) (1998) 1046–1049.
[4] B.S. Weir, Genetic data analysis—II, Sinauer, Sunderland, MA, 1996.
[5] S. Hering, et al., Development of the X-linked tetrameric microsatellite marker HumDXS6789 for forensic purposes, Forensic Sci. Int. 119 (1) (2001) 42–46.
[6] S. Pelotti, et al., Automated fluorescence analysis of CAG repeats at the human androgen receptor gene (HUMARA): evaluation of polymorphism in an Italian sample and report of a new allele, Am. J. Forensic Med. Pathol. 22 (1) (2001) 55–57.
[7] G. Watanabe, et al., DXS10011: a hypervariable tetranucleotide STR polymorphism on the X chromosome, Int. J. Legal Med. 113 (4) (2000) 249–250.
[8] R. Szibor, et al., Population data on the X chromosome short tandem repeat locus HumHPRTB in two regions of Germany, J. Forensic Sci. 45 (1) (2000) 231–233.
[9] M.T. Zarrabeitia, et al., A new pentaplex system to study short tandem repeat markers of forensic interest on X chromosome, Forensic Sci. Int. 129 (2) (2002) 85–89.
[10] J. Edelmann, R. Szibor, Validation of the HumDXS6807 short tandem repeat polymorphism for forensic application, Electrophoresis 20 (14) (1999) 2844–2846.
[11] J. Edelmann, R. Szibor, DXS101: a highly polymorphic X-linked STR, Int. J. Legal Med. 114 (4–5) (2001) 301–304.

ELSEVIER

International Congress Series 1261 (2004) 275–277

www.ics-elsevier.com

Discrimination index of Y-chromosomal haplotypes in an Antioquia (Colombia) population sample

J.J. Builes[a,b,*], M.L.J. Bravo[a], M. Martínez-Pancorbo[c], M.A. Moreno[a,b], C.P. Gómez[a]

[a] *Laboratorio de Genética Forense y Huellas Digitales del DNA, GENES Ltda, Carrera 48 No. 10-45 Cons. 612, Medellín, Colombia*

[b] *Instituto de Biología, Universidad de Antioquia. Medellín, Colombia*

[c] *Servicio de Diagnóstico de la Paternidad Biológica e Identificación Genética, U. del País Vasco, Spain*

Abstract. Y-chromosome STR haplotypes (DYS19, DYS385, DYS389I, DYS389II, DYS390, DYS391, DYS392 and DYS393) in a sample of 507 healthy male blood donors from Antioquia (Colombia) were studied. 323 different haplotypes were found, 256 of them being unique. Gene diversity ranged between 0.3640 at DYS393 and 0.8900 at DYS385. The haplotype diversity value (power of discrimination (PD) and power of exclusion (PE)) calculated from all eight loci combined was 0.9946, which is informative. This study provides further information on the Y-chromosome polymorphisms commonly used in paternity testing, forensic genetics and in the population genetic studies of complex patterns of sex differential racial admixture.

Keywords: Antioquia; Colombia; DNA; Y-chromosome; STR; Population

1. Introduction

The Y-chromosome nonrecombinant portion represents a paternally inherited haploid transmission pattern [1]. Because of that Y-STRs can be used to construct highly discriminative Y haplotypes which are useful in stain analysis [2], paternity testing (lineage cases with male offspring) [1–3], and in discriminating complex differential sex patterns of admixture in population genetic studies as the one described in the population inhabiting the Antioquian State in Colombia, South America [4].

Here we report gene frequencies, gene and haplotype diversity for nine Y-STR loci in the Antioquia (Colombia) population. These will increase the database and the knowledge of polymorphisms on Colombian populations, particularly on the Antioquian communities (Paisa community).

* Corresponding author. Paternity testing, GENES Ltda., Carrera 48 No. 10-45 Cons. 612, Medillin, Colombia. Tel.: +57-4-268-48-75; fax: +57-4-318-52-70.

E-mail address: genforense@epm.net.co (J.J. Builes).

0531-5131/
doi:10.1016/S0531-5131(03)01636-4

2. Materials and methods

Samples of 507 unrelated males were obtained from healthy individuals from Antioquia (Colombia) and from routine paternity cases (fathers). Genomic DNA was extracted by a salt precipitation extraction procedure [5]. The loci DYS389 I/II (0.1 μM) and DYS390 (0.6 μM) were amplified in a triplex PCR reaction, the loci DYS19 (0.2 μM), DYS391 (0.05 μM), DYS392 (0.4 μM) and DYS393 (0.2 μM) in quadruplex PCR reaction and the DYS385 (0.1 μM) as a singleplex.

PCR reactions were carried out in 15 μl and consisted of 20 ng of genomic DNA, 0.5 U Taq DNA Polymerase (Promega), 200 μM dNTPs, 1.5 μl 10 × Buffer, 2.0 mM $MgCl_2$. Samples were amplified with 30 cycles of 95 °C for 30 s, 53 °C for 1 min and 72 °C for 20 s. The primer sequences for DYS389 I/II, DYS390, DYS391, DYS392 and DYS393 are described in Kayser et al. [6], for DYS385 in Schneider et al. [7] and DYS19 modified from Szibor et al. [8].

Detection of the amplified products was conducted by electrophoresis on a 4% denaturing gel containing 8 M urea. Alleles were visualized by silver staining (Promega) and they were identified based on the number of repeats and their attribution was made by comparison with an in-house constructed allelic ladder and following the published nomenclature and ISFG recommendations on forensic analysis using Y-chromosome STRs. The gene frequencies and gene or haplotype diversity

Table 1
Allele frequencies and gene diversity value of seven Y-chromosome STR loci ($n = 507$)

Allele	DYS19	DYS389 I	DYS389 II	DYS390	DYS391	DYS392	DYS393
6					0.002		
8					0.010		
9					0.041		
10		0.002			0.467	0.004	0.002
11		0.002			0.456	0.321	0.006
12		0.122			0.024	0.075	0.105
13	0.170	0.637				0.485	0.787
14	0.594	0.227				0.095	0.083
15	0.152	0.006				0.016	0.018
16	0.061					0.004	
17	0.022	0.004					
18	0.002						
20				0.004			
21				0.083			
22				0.069			
23				0.229			
24				0.479			
25				0.108			
26			0.004	0.026			
27			0.034				
28			0.118	0.002			
29			0.357				
30			0.314				
31			0.130				
32			0.036				
33			0.008				
GD	0.593	0.530	0.744	0.697	0.574	0.649	0.364
SE	0.020	0.020	0.010	0.016	0.010	0.014	0.026

GD: gene diversity. SE: standard error.

Table 2
Allele haplotype frequencies and gene diversity value at the Y-chromosome STR locus DYS385 ($n = 507$)

Genotype	Frequency	Genotype	Frequency	Genotype	Frequency	Genotype	Frequency
9/14	0.012	12/14	0.041	14/14	0.030	51/21	0.004
9/16	0.002	12/15	0.020	14/15	0.034	16/16	0.006
10/14	0.028	12/16	0.004	14/16	0.026	16/17	0.028
11/11	0.006	12/17	0.006	14/17	0.016	16/18	0.016
11/12	0.018	12/19	0.002	14/18	0.012	16/19	0.012
11/13	0.030	13/14	0.039	14/19	0.012	17/17	0.024
11/14	0.304	13/15	0.041	15/15	0.032	17/18	0.020
11/15	0.063	13/16	0.008	15/16	0.018	17/19	0.004
11/16	0.008	13/17	0.020	15/17	0.010	18/18	0.006
11/18	0.012	13/18	0.012	15/18	0.006	18/19	0.002
12/12	0.002	13/19	0.002	15/19	0.006	18/21	0.002

Gene diversity value: 0.890. Standard error: 0.008.

values were calculated using the software ARLEQUIN version 2000 [9] and Nei formulation [10].

3. Results and discussion

Allele frequencies of the systems and gene diversity values are shown in Tables 1 and 2. The highest diversity value in this study was found at the locus DYS385 (0.8900), followed by the DYS389 II (0.744). The gene and haplotype diversity have the same value as the power of discrimination (PD) [11] and chance of exclusion (CE) [12]. The nine STRs described in this study result in informative Y-haplotypes with CE and PD values of 0.9946. We identified 323 different haplotypes and 256 were seen only once. The most frequent haplotype was present in 20 of 507 males. Development of Y-chromosome specific polymorphisms will be of great benefit in analyzing mixed DNA samples, in investigating sexual assaults as well as in paternity testing where the alleged father is not available but other patrilineal relatives are.

Acknowledgements

Supported by GENES. J.J.B. has a PhD fellowship (0058/2001) from COLCIENCIAS.

References

[1] M.A. Jobling, A. Pandya, C. Tyler-Smith, Int. J. Leg. Med. 110 (1997) 118–124.
[2] J. Henke, L. Henke, P. Chatthopadhyay, et al, CMJ 42 (3) (2001) 292–297.
[3] C. Gehrig, M. Hochmeister, B. Budowle, J. Forensic Sci. 45 (2) (2000) 436–439.
[4] L.G. Carvajal-Carmona, I.D. Soto, N. Pineda, et al, Am. J. Hum. Genet. 67 (2000) 1287–1295.
[5] S.A. Miller, D.D. Dykes, H.F. Polesky, Nucleic Acids Res. 16 (1988) 1215.
[6] M. Kayser, A. Caglia, D. Corach, et al, Int. J. Leg. Med. 110 (1997) 125–133(appendix 141–149).
[7] P.M. Schneider, S. Meuser, W. Waiyawuth, Y. Seo, Ch. Rittner, Forensic Sci. Int. 97 (1998) 61–70.
[8] R. Szibor, M. Kayser, L. Roewer, Am. J. Forensic Med. Pathol. 21 (3) (2000) 252–254.
[9] S. Schneider, D. Roessli, L. Excoffier, University of Geneva, 2000.
[10] M. Nei, Molecular Evolutionary Genetics, Columbia Univ. Press, New York, 1987.
[11] G.F. Sensabaugh, Prentice-Hall, Englewood Cliffs (1982).
[12] A. Chakravarti, C.C. Li, American Association of Blood Banks, Arlington, VA (1983).

International Congress Series 1261 (2004) 278–280

www.ics-elsevier.com

Forensic value of the multicopy Y-STR marker DYS464[☆]

John M. Butler*, Richard Schoske[1]

Biotechnology Division, National Institute of Standards and Technology, Gaithersburg, MD, USA

Abstract. The tetranucleotide Y-chromosome short tandem repeat (Y-STR) marker, DYS464, first reported by Redd et al. [Forensic Sci. Int. 130 (2002) 97] appears to be the most polymorphic Y-STR marker discovered to date. A single primer pair can generate up to four distinct peaks over an allele range of 9–20 repeats. Allele calls can be made based on peaks that are present (conservative approach; C-type) or a combination of alleles and peak height ratios (expanded typing method; E-type). We have observed 113 C-types and 179 E-types in 679 males from three US populations.

Keywords: Y-STR; Y-chromosome; DYS464; Multicopy loci; DNA typing

1. Introduction

DYS464 occurs at least four times in the highly palindromic region near the center of the long arm of the Y-chromosome [1–3]. In forensic casework applications where the amount of typable DNA material may be limited, the use of highly polymorphic markers is advantageous in order to limit the number of markers needed to distinguish unrelated individuals.

2. Materials and methods

A total of 679 unique male DNA samples from three different US populations [4] were typed with DYS464 along with 21 additional Y-chromosome short tandem repeat (Y-STR) markers [3]. Only the DYS464 results are described in this report. Two novel DYS464 primer pairs, which differ from those originally described by Redd et al. [2], were used.

☆ Points of view are those of the authors and do not necessarily represent the position of the US Departments of Justice or Defense. Certain commercial equipment, instruments, and materials are identified in order to specify experimental procedures as completely as possible. In no case does such identification imply a recommendation or endorsement by the National Institute of Standards and Technology, nor does it imply that any of the materials, instruments, or equipment identified are necessarily the best available for the purpose.

* Corresponding author. Tel.: +1-301-975-4049; fax: +1-301-975-8505.

E-mail address: john.butler@nist.gov (J.M. Butler).

[1] Current address: Armed Forces Institute of Pathology, Washington, DC, USA.

doi:10.1016/S0531-5131(03)01713-8

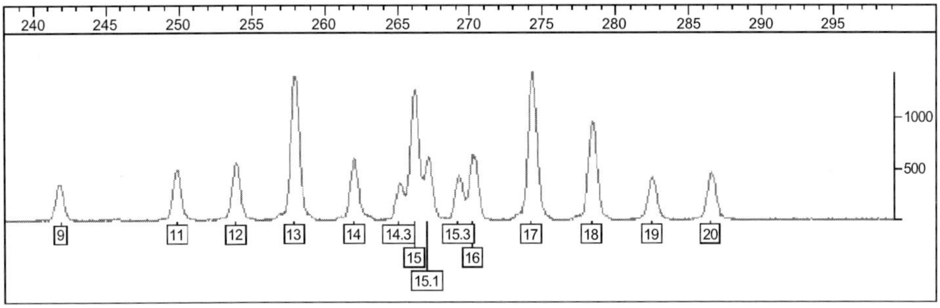

Fig. 1. NIST allelic ladder for DYS464 produced from eight different DNA samples. The variant alleles 14.3, 15.1, and 15.3 are helpful as a tool for measuring single-base resolution in electrophoretic systems.

The primers **VIC**-CTTTGGGCTATGCCTCAGTTT and GCCATACCTGGGTAACAGA-GAGAC produce green-labeled amplicons in the size range of 242–286 bp for DYS464 alleles 9–20, while the primers **6FAM**-AGTTTACGAGCTTTGGGCTATG and GTGGCAAGATCTCATTTCTTCAA generate blue dye-labeled polymerase chain reaction (PCR) products that are 327–367 bp in size. PCR conditions are as previously described for the Y-STR 20plex [5]. An allelic ladder was created for DYS464 (Fig. 1), which contains all of the major alleles as well as single-base variants observed in our population study [3].

3. Results and discussion

We observed 179 expanded types with DYS464 in 679 male samples from three different US population sets: 265 African–Americans, 262 Caucasians, and 152 Hispanics. The addition of peak height information (E-type) to just allele calls (C-type) can result in an expansion in the number of types observed (e.g., Fig. 2). The most common types are 15,15,17,17, which occurs in 10.6% of this data set, and 15,15,16,17, which occurs in 7.5%. All other DYS464 types are found at less than the 5% level, with over half of the observed types occurring only once (92 of 179 observed). If the DYS464 data are collapsed to C-types (conservative typing method), then 113 allele calls are observed in these 679 males. By way of comparison to other DNA typing markers in the same data set, DYS385 exhibited only 56 different types and FGA, the single best autosomal STR examined, had only 78 different genotypes. Furthermore, the four single-copy Y-STRs DYS19, DYS391, DYS392, and DYS393, when combined, only produced 93 different

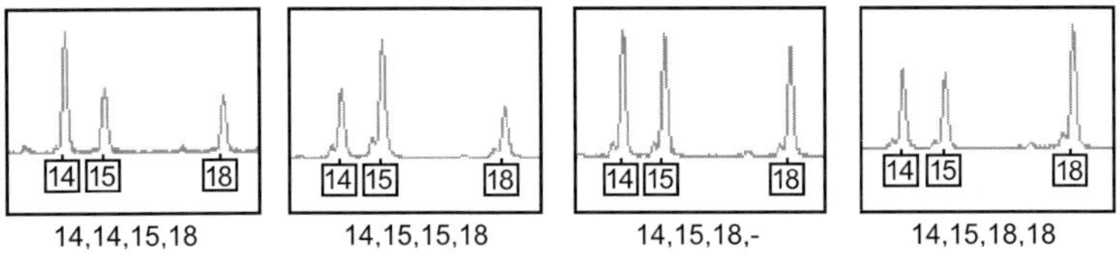

Fig. 2. Example of four samples with the same conservative DYS464 type, 14,15,18, which can be separated from one another by considering their expanded type through peak height variation.

haplotypes. Thus, DYS464 is more polymorphic than DYS385, the previously considered best multicopy Y-STR, and four single-copy Y-STRs in combination. A human Y-chromosome DNA profiling standard, NIST Standard Reference Material (SRM) 2395, is available and contains DYS464 information on its five male samples (see http://www.nist.gov/srm). This SRM will enable laboratories worldwide to accurately calibrate their DYS464 typing results.

Acknowledgements

This work was supported by research funds from the US National Institute of Justice through Interagency Agreement 1999-IJ-R-094 with the NIST Office of Law Enforcement Standards. Much of this work was performed while R.S. was a graduate student at the NIST and the American University through funding from the US Air Force. The technical assistance and suggestions of Peter Vallone, David Duewer, Margaret Kline, and Jan Redman from our group at the NIST and Alan Redd from the University of Arizona are gratefully acknowledged.

References

[1] J.M. Butler, Recent developments in Y-short tandem repeat and Y-single nucleotide polymorphism analysis, Forensic Sci. Rev. 15 (2003) 91–111.

[2] A.J. Redd, A.B. Agellon, V.A. Kearney, T. Karafet, P. de Knijff, H. Park, J.M. Butler, M.F. Hammer, Forensic value of fourteen novel STRs on the human Y chromosome, Forensic Sci. Int. 130 (2002) 97–111.

[3] R. Schoske, P.M. Vallone, M.C. Kline, J.W. Redman, J.M. Butler, High-throughput Y-STR typing of U.S. populations with 27 regions of the Y chromosome using two multiplex PCR assays, Forensic Sci. Int. (In press).

[4] J.M. Butler, R. Schoske, P.M. Vallone, J.W. Redman, M.C. Kline, Allele frequencies for 15 autosomal STR loci on U.S. Caucasian, African American, and Hispanic populations, J. Forensic Sci. 48 (4) (2003) 908–911.

[5] J.M. Butler, R. Schoske, P.M. Vallone, M.C. Kline, A.J. Redd, M.F. Hammer, A novel multiplex for simultaneous amplification of 20 Y chromosome STR markers, Forensic Sci. Int. 129 (2002) 10–24.

International Congress Series 1261 (2004) 281–283

www.ics-elsevier.com

GATA C4 allele 17 as a marker for sub-Saharan origin of Y-chromosome lineages

Leonor Gusmão[a,*], Paula Sánchez-Diz[b], Cíntia Alves[a], Maria Brión[b], Sandra Beleza[a,b], Luísa Pereira[a], Alejandro Blanco[b], Maria João Prata[a,c], Angel Carracedo[b], António Amorim[a,c]

[a] *Population Genetics, IPATIMUP, Institute of Pathology and Immunology of University of Porto, Rua Dr. Roberto Frias, s/n 4200-465 Oporto, Portugal*

[b] *Institute of Legal Medicine, University of Santiago de Compostela, Spain*

[c] *Faculty of Sciences, University of Porto, Portugal*

Received 27 August 2003; received in revised form 27 August 2003; accepted 8 September 2003

Abstract. In 1020 males out of 13 population samples from Argentina, Brazil, Costa Rica, Macao, Mozambique, Portugal and Spain, GATA allele 17 was found exclusively in Mozambique [Forensic Sci. Int. 135 (2003) 158]. In the present work, allele 17 was further observed in samples from Angola (9.33%), Mozambique (10.79%) and S. Tomé e Príncipe (3.53%). This allele differs by at least two repeat units from all reported alleles: no instance of allele 18 was ever found. Allele 17 frequency and distribution, together with the absence of one-step-derived alleles, is compatible with a very low mutation rate and so potentially a good marker for African ancestry and haplogroup identification. We verified this hypothesis in two ways: (a) the sequencing of nine alleles 17 showed that the small number of uninterrupted repeats can explain the low mutation rate and (b) the simultaneous GATA C4 and SNP typing in 75 individuals from Angola, 85 from S. Tomé e Príncipe and 417 from Mozambique proved that, out of 56 samples carrying allele 17, 55 belong to B* paragroup and one to A*, both said to be ancient African lineages. Therefore, GATA C4 allele 17 most probably was originated as a unique event and its extreme association with AB* is compatible with its use as a marker for the assignment to this paragroup. © 2003 Elsevier B.V. All rights reserved.

Keywords: Y chromosome; STR; GATA C4; SNP; Africa; Haplogroup

1. Introduction

The STR GATA C4 is one of the most polymorphic Y chromosome-specific markers currently used in population and forensic genetics. Until now, nine alleles were described in different populations and three different allelic sequence complex structures were

* Corresponding author. Tel.: +351-225570700; fax: +351-225570799.
E-mail address: lgusmao@ipatimup.pt (L. Gusmão).

doi:10.1016/S0531-5131(03)01493-6

identified [1]. The most frequent allele described in African and Asian samples is allele 21, while 23 is the most frequent in European samples [2]. In the same way as for DYS392 and DYS438, GATA C4 presents a bimodal allele frequency distribution in European populations, with allele 21 as the second most frequent. In 1020 males out of 13 population samples from Argentina, Brazil, Costa Rica, Macao, Mozambique, Portugal and Spain, allele 17 was found exclusively in the Mozambique sample [2]. Apart from allele 17, the shortest allele until now described for GATA C4 was allele 19 and no instance of allele 18 was ever found (in Africans, Caucasians or Asians). The allele 17 frequency and distribution, together with the absence of one-step-derived alleles 16 or 18 is compatible with a very low mutation rate in these alleles and, therefore, it seems to be a good marker for African ancestry as well as for haplogroup identification. In order to check our hypothesis (a), we sequenced nine samples with this allele and (b) we studied the GATA C4 alleles association with haplogroups defined by SNPs.

2. Methods and materials

A sample of 75 individuals from Cabinda (Angola, African western coast), 85 from S. Tomé e Príncipe (Gulf of Guinea) and 417 individuals from Mozambique (African eastern coast), were typed for GATA C4 and SNPs. GATA C4 PCR amplification and sequence analysis were performed according to Sánchez-Diz et al. [2]. SRY10831a was typed according to Rosser et al. [3]. The remaining SNPs were typed by sequence analysis using the primers and PCR cycling condition described in Table 1. Sequencing reactions were performed using dRodamine Terminator Cycle Sequencing Ready Reaction Kit (AB, Applied Biosystems) following the manufacturer's instructions. Detection and analysis were undertaken in an ABI 3100 Genetic Analyser (AB, Applied Biosystems).

3. Results and discussion

GATA C4 allele 17 was found in three Sub-Saharan population samples from Angola (9,33%), Mozambique (10,79%) and S. Tomé e Príncipe (3,53%). In the same populations,

Table 1
SNP primer sequences and PCR conditions

SNP	Primers	PCR thermo cycling conditions
M168	5′ AGT TTG AGG TAG AAT ACT GTT TGC T 3′	95 °C–2′
	5′ AAA AAG CCA TGC AAT TAC CTG 3′	
M112	5′ ACT TTT TCC AAC AGT TAT TTT TGA 3′	32 cycles
	5′ TAT ATT TCT TGA TGA TGA GAC CAA T 3′	
M150	5′ GCA GTG GAG ATG AAG TGA GAC 3′	94 °C–30″
	5′ CCT ACT TTC CCC CTC TTC TG 3′	
M108	5′ AGA TGG AGC CAG CAG AAA G 3′	58 °C–30″
	5′ ACA CAG ATG AAT TGA ATG ATG GT 3′	
M109	5′ GGG TAT CAA ATG TCT TCA ACC T 3′	72 °C–45″
	5′ GGG AAT TTC CTG CTA CTT GC 3′	

PCR amplification was carried out using 5 to 50 ng of genomic DNA in a 25 μl reaction volume containing 1.5 mM $MgCl_2$, 200 μM of dNTPs, 1 × Buffer and 0.5 U Taq DNA Polymerase Recombinant (Invitrogen).

Table 2
Haplogroup and GATA C4 alleles distribution inside AB* paragroup

Haplogroup	*N*	M168	SRY10831a	M112	M150	M108	M109	GATA C4
A*	1	C	A	✓	✓	✓	✓	17
B2a1	28	C	G	G	T	T	T	17
B2a* (xB2a1,2)	1	C	G	G	T	T	C	17
B2b	4	C	G	A	C	✓	✓	19
B2b	1	C	G	A	C	✓	✓	20
B2b	6	C	G	A	C	✓	✓	21
B2b	3	C	G	A	C	✓	✓	22
B* (xB2ab)	1	C	G	G	C	✓	✓	21

✓This SNP was not typed in this sample since a phylogenetic strategy was used to determine the paragroup.

this allele differs by at least two repeat units from the remaining alleles (20 to 24 in Angola, 19 to 24 in S. Tomé e Príncipe and 19 to 26 in Mozambique).

The same sequence was found for the nine allele 17 samples analysed, $(TCTA)_2[(TCTA)_2(TGTA)_2]_2(TCTA)_7$. In accordance with previous observations in other STRs, a low mutation rate is expected for allele 17, due to the low number of uninterrupted repeats.

All C4*17 samples ($n = 55$) were classified as belonging to the African AB* paragroup, in fact, just one was of A* paragroup. The GATA C4 allele distribution inside B* paragroup is shown in Table 2. These samples were further characterized using additional SNPs (Table 2). From the results, it was observed that all the samples carrying GATA C4 allele 17 belong to B2a* and no other alleles were found inside this paragroup. Paragroup B2b* was polymorphic for GATA C4, with alleles 19 to 22.

Although associations between STR haplotypes and SNP haplogroups do exist, most of the time STR alleles cannot be used to predict haplogroups, due to their high-STR mutation rates. However, the present results demonstrate that GATA C4 allele 17 most probably was originated as a unique event and, its extreme association with AB* is compatible with the use of GATA C4 as a marker for the assignment to paragroups A* or B2a*.

Acknowledgements

This work was supported by Fundação para a Ciência e a Tecnologia, Programa Operacional Ciência, Tecnologia e Inovação (POCTI).

References

[1] S. Beleza, C. Alves, A. González-Neira, M. Lareu, et al., Int. J. Leg. Med. 117 (2003) 27–33.
[2] P. Sánchez-Diz, L. Gusmão, S. Beleza, et al., Forensic Sci. Int. 135 (2003) 158–162.
[3] Z. Rosser, T. Zerjal, M.H. Hurles, et al., Am. J. Hum. Genet. 67 (2000) 1526–1543.

International Congress Series 1261 (2004) 284–286

www.ics-elsevier.com

Genetic relationships among East and Southeast Asian populations using 14 Y-STR markers

Toshimichi Yamamoto*, Kumiko Tanaka, Takashi Yoshimoto, Rieko Uchihi, Shi-Lin Li, Rina Kurihara, Yoshinao Katsumata

Department of Legal Medicine and Bioethics, Nagoya University Graduate School of Medicine, 65 Tsurumai-cho, Showa, Nagoya 466-8550, Japan

Abstract. We analyzed the genotypes and haplotypes at 14 short tandem repeat (STR) loci on Y-chromosome (Y-STRs) in 10 East and Southeast Asian populations including two regional Japanese populations (Nagoya and Okinawa) using two multiplex typing systems. The allele frequency at each locus was calculated in each population and then compared among the populations. We also estimated the gene diversity at each locus and the haplotype diversity in each population. As a result, Japanese populations seemed to be genetically less diverse than other Asian populations. Furthermore, we constructed a tree based on the neighbor-joining method using a genetic distance D_A. The resultant tree was comprised of three clusters (Japanese, Chinese and Southeast Asian) and coincided well with their geographical distributions. © 2004 Elsevier B.V. All rights reserved.

Keywords: STR; Y-chromosome; Asian; Genetic relationship

1. Introduction

Short tandem repeats on Y-chromosome (Y-STRs) are generally used for male genotyping in sexual assault cases and sibship analyses. We reported previously on the haplotypes of Y-STRs in two regional Japanese populations [1,2]. Such haplotype analyses have also been utilized to examine relationships among various human populations [3]. We analyzed haplotypes at 14 Y-STRs (DYS389I, DYS439, DYS435, DYS19, DYS460, Y-GATA-H4, DYS391, DYS392, DYS438, DYS437, DYS393, DYS389II, DYS390, and DYS385) using two multiplex typing systems from DNA samples in two regional Japanese (Nagoya and Okinawa), six regional Chinese (Beijing, Shaanxi, Jiangsu, Hunan, Fujian, and Guangdong), one Thai (Bangkok), and one Burmese (Yangon) populations. In the present study, the allele frequencies at 14 Y-STR loci were calculated for each population and compared among those populations. Corresponding haplotype analyses

* Corresponding author. Tel.: +81-52-744-2119; fax: +81-52-744-2121.
E-mail address: yamachan@med.nagoya-u.ac.jp (T. Yamamoto).

doi:10.1016/j.ics.2003.12.079

were also performed, and their genetic relationships were examined by constructing a phylogenetic tree based on their allele frequencies at 14 Y-STR loci.

2. Materials and methods

2.1. DNA samples

Male blood samples were collected from two regions (207 in Nagoya and 87 in Okinawa) in Japan, six (77 in Beijing, 41 in Shaanxi, 58 in Hunan, 52 in Guangdong, 55 in Fujian, and 71 in Jiangsu) in China, one (119 in Bangkok) in Thailand, and one (91 in Yangon) in Burma. DNA samples were extracted using a usual organic extraction method or with a QIAamp DNA Blood Mini Kit (QIAGEN).

2.2. PCR amplification and typing

We analyzed a total of 14 Y-STRs with two multiplex PCR-based typing systems. Ten loci, DYS389I, DYS439, DYS435, DYS19, DYS460, Y-GATA-H4, DYS391, DYS392, DYS437, and DYS438 were analyzed with a 10plex system originally devised by Ruitberg and Butler, which we modified to change DYS436 to DYS389I with a newly designed primer set (Y-10plex). Six loci, DYS393, DYS19, DYS389II, DYS390, DYS391, and DYS385, were genotyped with Y-PLEX 6. Since DYS19 and DYS391 were included in both systems, a total of 14 Y-STRs were genotyped. The PCR products were analyzed with a Genetic Analyzer 310, and genotyped semi-automatically using Genotyper 2.5 software with the allelic ladder markers we made for Y-10plex.

2.3. Diversity estimates

The allele frequencies at 14 Y-STRs were calculated, and their haplotypes were aligned. The gene diversity at each locus and the haplotype diversity in each population were also estimated.

2.4. Constructing a phylogenetic tree

We calculated a Nei's D_A genetic distance, and constructed a tree based on the neighbor-joining method using neighbor-joining tree construction from allele frequency data (NJBAFD) software package.

3. Results and discussion

The haplotypes at 14 Y-STRs were analyzed using two multiplex typing systems, and the allele frequencies at 14 Y-STR loci were calculated in each population. Some alleles were apparently distributed differently at some loci between the populations. For example, the frequencies of the alleles 14 at DYS389I, 11 at DYS460 and 11 at DYS392 in the two Japanese populations were apparently higher than those in the other populations. On the other hand, the allele distributions at DYS391 did not seem to be diverse in all populations. The gene diversities were also estimated from these allele frequencies. Although the values at all loci were almost similar, those at DYS391, DYS437 and

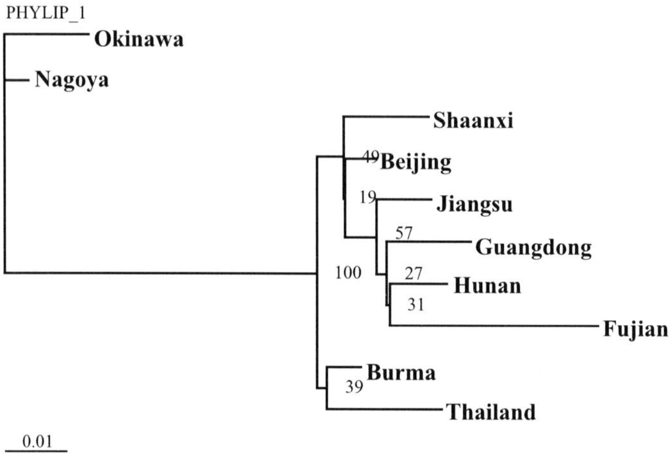

Fig. 1. Neighbor-joining tree based on Nei's D_A genetic distance for the allele frequencies at 14 Y-STRs in 10 East and Southeast Asian populations.

DYS435 in the two Japanese populations seemed to be slightly lower than those in the other populations. Furthermore, when we compared the haplotypes at 14 Y-STRs among all the populations, the haplotypes observed to be more than one in number in the two Japanese populations were not observed in the other Asian populations. Conversely, those in the other populations were not observed in the Japanese populations. The haplotype diversities in the Japanese populations were slightly lower than those in the other populations.

The neighbor-joining tree constructed based on Nei's D_A genetic distance for 14 Y-STRs showed three clusters, each comprised of a Japanese, Chinese and Southeast Asian population, and their genetic relationships coincided well with their geographical distribution as shown in Fig. 1. The genotype and haplotype analyses for Y-STRs such as those in the present study should provide valuable information on human genetic relationships.

Acknowledgements

This work was supported in part by Grants-in-Aid for Scientific Research from the Ministry of Education, Culture, Sports, Science and Technology of Japan.

References

[1] R. Uchihi, et al., Haplotype analysis with 14 Y-STR loci using 2 multiplex amplification and typing systems in 2 regional populations in Japan, International Journal of Legal Medicine 117 (2003) 34–38.

[2] T. Yamamoto, Population database and mutation study for short tandem repeat loci on Y-chromosome (Y-STRs) in Japanese populations, Forensic Science Review 15 (2003) 171–178.

[3] L. Roewer, et al., A new method for the evaluation of the matches in non-recombining genomes: application to Y-chromosomal short tandem repeat (STR) haplotypes in European males, Forensic Science International 114 (2000) 31–43.

International Congress Series 1261 (2004) 287–289

www.ics-elsevier.com

Haplotype distribution of Y-STR loci in Beijing population

Y.C. Liu*, J. Yang, J. Wang, H. Tang, Z.Y. Huo

Forensic Medical Examination and Identification Centre of Beijing Public Security Bureau, 1 Longgang Road, Qinghe District, Beijing 100085, China

Abstract. The use of Y chromosome markers is of special interest because of their male-specificity. Y-STR plays a very important role in forensic science, especially in sexual assault cases when another person masks the DNA of one male and deficiency paternity cases involving male offspring. In our study, we investigated the haplotype distribution of 10 Y-STR loci (DYS393, DYS19, DYS389 II, DYS389 I, DYS390, DYS391, DYS385, DYS439, DYS438, DYS392) in Beijing population.

Keywords: Y-STR; Haplotype; Beijing population

1. Materials and methods

Blood specimens were collected from 123 unrelated males, 100 father–son pairs, 50 male sibling pairs. DNA was extracted using 5% Chelex 100. PCR amplification was performed using Y-Plex™ 6 and Y-Plex™ 5 kit in a 25-μl reaction volume, including 1–5 ng genomic DNA, 5.0 μl primer, 0.5 μl (5 u/μl) AmpliTag Gold™. PCR cycling conditions referred to the kit manual. PCR products ran on ABI 377 DNA sequencer.

2. Results and discussions

Allele frequency distribution, Dp and GD of the 10 Y-STR loci of Beijing population were obtained (see Table 1). Table 2 showed that the more the loci that we used the higher Dp and GD value that we got.

The results of the father–son pairs and sibling pairs proved that the 10 Y-STR loci we studied followed male genetic rules. There were two variances that happened in DYS389 II (29 → 28) and DYS385 (15/17 → 15/18) loci when the father transmitted Y chromosome to the son. So we suggested that more than three different Y-STR typing can lead to exclusion.

* Corresponding author. Tel.: +86-10-62909016; fax: +86-10-62902582.
E-mail address: fyzhx6688@163.com (Y.C. Liu).
URL: www.Fmeicbjpsb.sohu.com.

doi:10.1016/S0531-5131(03)01503-6

Table 1
The frequency of 10 Y-STR loci in unrelated males from Beijing ($n = 123$)

Allele	DYS393	DYS19	DYS389II	DYS390	DYS391	DYS389I	DYS439	DYS438	DYS392	DYS385			
6					0.0053								
7									0.0081	9–18	0.0053	12–19	0.0481
8										10–13	0.0053	12–20	0.0214
9					0.0642		0.0081	0.0163		10–15	0.0053	12–22	0.0107
10	0.0053				0.7701		0.0488	0.6667	0.0081	10–16	0.0107	13–13	0.0481
11	0.0053				0.1444	0.0081	0.3821	0.2520	0.1220	10–17	0.0053	13–14	0.0428
12	0.5294	0.0053			0.0160	0.5203	0.4228	0.0488	0.1060	10–18	0.0214	13–15	0.0160
13	0.2674	0.0374				0.2764	0.1301	0.0163	0.3496	10–19	0.0053	13–16	0.0214
14	0.1551	0.3102				0.1707			0.3659	10–20	0.0053	13–17	0.0267
15	0.0267	0.3743				0.0244	0.0081		0.0325	11–11	0.0214	13–18	0.0642
16	0.0107	0.2193							0.0081	11–12	0.0535	13–19	0.0428
17		0.0481								11–13	0.0214	13–20	0.0374
18		0.0053								11–14	0.0053	14–14	0.0053
19										11–15	0.0053	14–16	0.0053
20										11–16	0.0160	14–17	0.0107
21				0.0160						11–17	0.0214	14–18	0.0267
22				0.0856						11–18	0.0160	14–19	0.0107
23				0.3476						11–19	0.0214	14–21	0.0053
24				0.3743						11–20	0.0053	15–17	0.0053
25				0.1551						11–21	0.0053	15–19	0.0160
26			0.0107	0.0214						12–12	0.0374	15–20	0.0107
27			0.0642							12–13	0.0214	15–21	0.0160
28			0.3262							12–14	0.0428	15–22	0.0053
29			0.3262							12–15	0.0053	16–16	0.0053
30			0.1872							12–16	0.0374	16–17	0.0053
31			0.0802							12–17	0.0428	17–20	0.0053
32										12–18	0.0428		
33			0.0053										
DP	0.6233	0.7118	0.7414	0.7070	0.3817	0.6231	0.6558	0.4891	0.8371		0.9676		
GD	0.6267	0.7156	0.7456	0.7108	0.3838	0.6282	0.6612	0.4931	0.8440		0.972		

Table 2
The relationship between the number of loci and DP, GD

Y-STR loci	Haplotype no.	DP	GD
DYS393 + DYS19	17	0.8792	0.8864
DYS393 + DYS19 + DYS389II	45	0.9527	0.9605
DYS393 + DYS19 + DYS389II + DYS390	76	0.9787	0.9867
DYS393 + DYS19 + DYS389II + DYS390 + DYS391	91	0.9837	0.9917
DYS393 + DYS19 + DYS389II + DYS390 + DYS391 + DYS385	118	0.9912	0.9993
DYS393 + DYS19 + DYS389II + DYS390 + DYS391 + DYS385 + DYS389I	119	0.9913	0.9995
DYS393 + DYS19 + DYS389II + DYS390 + DYS391 + DYS385 + DYS389I + DYS439 + DYS438 + DYS392	121	0.9916	0.9997

Two male DNA were diluted to 0.5 ng/μl, 0.1 ng/μl, 50 pg/μl, 20 pg/μl, 10 pg/μl, 5 pg/μl, 1 pg/μl. Successful Y-STR typing results were obtained when DNA was more than 5 pg.

Female and male DNA were mixed as the following ratio (female/male): 6000:1, 4000:1, 3000:1, 2000:1, 1000:1, 500:1, 100:1, 50:1. Y-STR typing of male was obtained when the ratio was less than 2000:1.

Knowledge about the geographical frequency distribution of Y-STR haplotypes is important for the forensic community. The information of the 10 Y-STR loci in Beijing population provides additional data to autosomal STRs.

ELSEVIER

International Congress Series 1261 (2004) 290–292

www.ics-elsevier.com

Haplotype frequency of the loci DYS437, DYS438, DYS439, DYS460 (Y-GATA A7.1), DYS461 (Y-GATA A7.2), Y-GATA A10, Y-GATA C4 and Y-GATA H4 in the Bahia-Brazil population

M.V. Santos[a,*], M. Carvalho[b], V. Lopes[b], M.C. Vide[b], F. Corte-Real[c], D.N. Vieira[c]

[a] *Faculty of Medicine, University of Coimbra, CNPq/Brazil, Coimbra, Portugal*
[b] *Service of Forensic Genetics, Delegation of Coimbra, National Institute of Legal Medicine, Coimbra, Portugal*
[c] *National Institute of Legal Medicine and Faculty of Medicine, University of Coimbra, Coimbra, Portugal*

Abstract. The study of the Y-chromosome is very important for forensic and population genetics. Although many populations have already been analysed, there is little data about Brazilian populations. The haplotype frequency of eight Y-STRs: DYS437, DYS438, DYS439, DYS460 (Y-GATA-A7.1), DYS461 (Y-GATA-A7.2), Y-GATA-A10, Y-GATA-C4 and Y-GATA-H4 in 72 male individuals from Bahia was established. A total of 67 different haplotypes were observed, of which 63 were unique, three were found in two individuals, and one was found in three individuals. The haplotype diversity and the capacity of discrimination for all eight Y-specific STR loci were calculated to be 98.38% and 93.06%, respectively. A mutational event in both loci DYS437 and DYS439 were found in the same individual.

Keywords: Bahia—Brazil population; Y-STR loci; Population genetic data

1. Introduction

The study of the Y-chromosome is used to identify male profiles in crime samples and to determine male lineage and parentage inclusive in the absence of paternal progenitor. The heterogeneity, intra and inter populations, of the Y-STR loci reveal haplogroups

* Corresponding author. Delegação de Coimbra, Instituto National de Medicina Legal, Lagro da Sé Nova, 3000-213 Coimbra, Portugal. Tel.: +351-239-814381; fax: +351-239-820549 or Tel./fax: +55-73-616-1809 (Post March, 2003).

E-mail address: diederiche@clix.pt (M.V. Santos).

doi:10.1016/S0531-5131(03)01783-7

representing male ancestral lineage and allow the geographical distribution to be evaluated.

The Bahian population has become very diversified due to the inclusion of a wide range of ethnic backgrounds.

In order to create a database representing the Bahian population, the haplotype frequency of the following eight Y-STRs: DYS437, DYS438, DYS439, DYS460, DYS461, Y-GATA-A10, Y-GATA-C4 and Y-GATA-H4 was established.

2. Materials and methods

The bloodstains of 72 males from Bahia, Brazil were collected and extracted using Chelex procedures [1] and, if necessary, purified by the modified salt–chloroform method.

PCR was performed in accordance with recommendations by the The Spanish and Portuguese ISFG Working Group (GEP-ISFG) for the collaborative study of the Y-Chromosome STRs 2001 [2]. We used two tetraplex systems: GEPY I includes the loci DYS461 (Y-GATA-A7.2), DYS437, DYS438 (with a concentration of 0.72 μM) and Y-GATA-C4; and GEPY II includes DYS460 (Y-GATA-A7.1), Y-GATA-A10, DYS439 and Y-GATA-H4. The primers were those described by Ref. [3] and Ref. [4].

PCR products were separated and detected by capillary electrophoresis on the ABI PRISM® 310 Genetic Analyzer using ROX500 (Applied Biosystems) as Internal Lane DNA Standard, employing ABI software [5] and the GEP-ISFG 2001 exercise reference samples [4] to assign the alleles.

Haplotype frequencies were estimated by gene counting, and haplotype diversity was computed according to Ref. [6] and Ref. [7] using haplotype frequency instead of allele frequency. The capacity of discrimination was also calculated. The study intra and inter populations were done using the Arlequin 2000 [8], PHILIP [9] and Treeview [10] softwares packages.

3. Results and discussion

In the Bahian population, a total of 67 different haplotypes were observed, of which 63 were unique, three were found in two individuals, and one was found in three individuals. The most common (DYS437: 15, DYS438: 12, DYS439: 12, DYS460: 11, DYS461: 12, GATA A10: 15, GATA C4: 23 and GATA H4: 27) had a frequency of 4.2%.

The haplotype diversity and the capacity of discrimination for all eight Y-specific STR loci were calculated to be 98.38% and 93.06%, respectively.

A mutational event in both loci DYS437 and DYS439 were found in the same individual. This sample will be sequenced together with the male descendant sample.

The allele with most frequency were 11 to DYS460, 12 to DYS461, 15 to GATA A10, 23 to GATA C4, 28 to GATA H4, 15 to DYS437, 12 to DYS438 and 12 to DYS439. The DYS439 and GATA C4 loci show the largest gene diversity—70.25% and 68.29%, respectively.

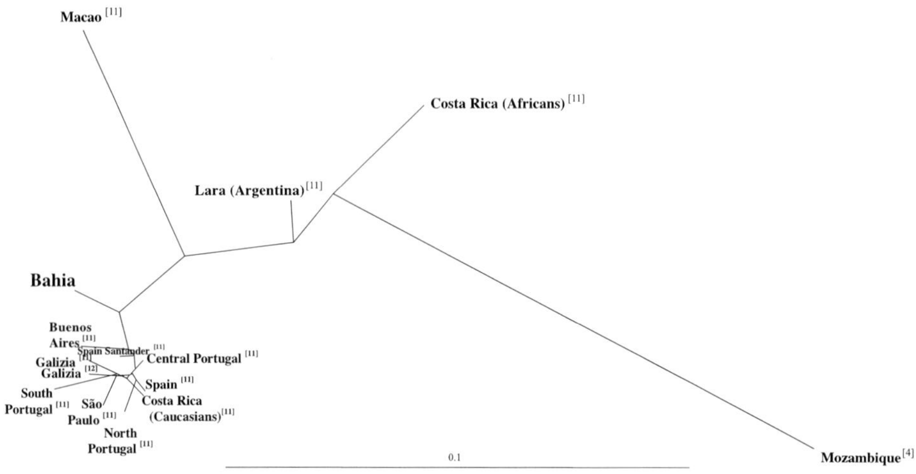

Fig. 1. Genetic tree obtained by method UPGMA using matrix of genetic distances with Φ values. Cited references: [11,12].

A comparison of the results of the pair-wise analysis shown that Bahian population sites in an intermediate position among origin Iberian populations and no Caucasians (Fig. 1).

Acknowledgements

Special thanks go to the donors of the samples. We would like to thank CNPq/Brazil for financial support and "Universidade Estadual de Santa Cruz" and "Departamento de Polícia Técnica—SSP/BA".

References

[1] P.S. Walsh, D.A. Metzger, R. Higuchi, BioTechniques 10 (1991) 506–513.
[2] Available at: http://www.gep-isfg.org.
[3] P. White, et al., Genomics 57 (3) (1999) 433–437.
[4] Q. Ayub, et al., Nucleic Acids Res. 28 (2) (2000) e8.
[5] ABI Prism 310 Genetic Analyzer. User's Manual, Applera, 2001.
[6] M. Nei, Genetics (1978) 583–590.
[7] M. Nei, Molecular Evolutionary Genetics. Columbia University Press, New York.
[8] S. Scheneider, D. Roessli, Excoffier. Arlequin ver. 2000. University of Geneve, Switzerland.
[9] J. Felsenstein, PHYLIP (version 3.2), Cladistics 5 (1989) 164–166.
[10] R.D.M. Page, Treeview, Comput. Appl. Biosci. 12 (1996) 357–358.
[11] L. Gusmão, et al., Forensic Sci. Int. 135 (2003) 150–157.
[12] L. Quintans, et al., Forensic Sci. Int. 131 (2003) 220–224.

ELSEVIER

International Congress Series 1261 (2004) 293–295

www.ics-elsevier.com

Humara X-chromosome inactivation assay for the detection of female minor component in male/female mixed bloodstains

C. Robino*, S. Gino, C. Torre

Laboratory of Criminalistic Sciences, Department of Anatomy, Pharmacology and Legal Medicine, University of Turin, C.so M. D'Azeglio 52, 10126 Turin, Italy

Abstract

Analysis of mixed stains from forensic casework by means of standard PCR-based typing of autosomal short tandem repeats (STRs) becomes difficult when the minor component is present at less than one tenth of the concentration of the major component. The human androgen receptor (HUMARA) X-chromosome inactivation assay allows to detect even a small number of female cells in the presence of a high background of male cells in male/female mixed bloodstains. DNA cleavage by means of methyl-sensitive restriction enzyme (*Hha*I) is followed by typing of the HUMARA locus with the nested PCR technique: methylation of restriction sites on inactivated female X chromosomes allows the efficient amplification of low amounts of endonuclease-resistant female-derived target sequences. In this study, the method attained a 10^{-3} level of sensitivity in the detection of the female minor component.

Keywords: DNA mixture; Human androgen receptor gene (HUMARA); X-chromosome inactivation; DNA methylation; Nested PCR

1. Introduction

Mixtures of body fluids from different individuals are an integral component of forensic casework. It has been shown that, by standard PCR-based typing of autosomal STRs, it is usually difficult to detect the minor component of a mixed stain when it is present at approximately less than one tenth of the major component [1]. For male/female mixtures, identification of the male minor component can be improved through analysis of Y-specific polymorphic STR loci [2].

* Corresponding author. Tel.: +39-116707731; fax: +39-116707732.
E-mail address: carlo.robino@unito.it (C. Robino).

doi:10.1016/S0531-5131(03)01782-5

Here, we report a simple test that allows a highly efficient detection of a small number of female cells in the presence of a high background of male cells. The human androgen receptor (HUMARA) gene contains a polymorphic CAG trinucleotide repeat in its first exon [3]; close to this polymorphism are *Hha*I restriction enzyme sites. The methylation status of the *Hha*I sites corresponds with the inactivation status of the X chromosome and thus allows for the detection between the active and inactive X chromosomes [4]. Methylation (inactivation) of X chromosome prevents *Hha*I from cutting next to the HUMARA polymorphism. Since male HUMARA sequences are always on an active X chromosome, they are prone to digestion by the methyl-sensitive *Hha*I, whereas digestion-resistant HUMARA genes on inactivated X chromosomes are protected from cleavage, allowing the subsequent typing of the female minor component of a mixture [5].

2. Material and methods

Blood samples from male and female donors of known HUMARA genotype were volumetrically mixed in proportions of $1{:}10^{-1}$, $1{:}10^{-2}$, $1{:}10^{-3}$ and $1{:}10^{-4}$, spotted on filter paper and dried. Stains were then extracted by means of spin columns (Macherey-Nagel, Düren, Germany); DNA was quantitated spectrophotometrically and 500 ng of DNA from each stain was digested overnight at 37 °C with 1 U of *Hha*I restriction endonuclease (New England Biolabs, Beverly, MA, USA) in a total volume of 25 μl.

HUMARA polymorphism was analyzed in the digested samples by means of nested PCR. Five microliters of the digested DNA was amplified in a 25-μl PCR reaction volume containing 2 X PCR Master Mix (Promega, Madison, WI, USA) and 0.5 μM of the following outer primers: 5′ -GGT AAG GGA AGT AGG TGG AAG ATT C-3′ ; 5′ -TCT GGG ACG CAA CCT CTC TC-3′ (Sigma-Genosys, Pampisford, UK). The cycle conditions were 94 °C for 7 min; 94 °C for 45 s, 55 °C for 30 s, 72 °C for 45 s, 28 cycles; 72 °C for 15 min final extension. One microliter of the PCR product was then used as template for amplification in a 25-μl PCR reaction volume containing 2 X PCR Master Mix (Promega) and 0.5 μM of the following inner primers: 5′ -(FAM) TCC AGA ATC TGT TCC AGA GCG TGC-3′ ; 5′ -GCT GTG AAG GTT GCT GTT CCT CAT-3′ (Sigma-Genosys). The cycle conditions were 95 °C for 8 min; 95° for 40 s; 63 °C for 40 s; 72 °C for 60 s; 32 cycles; 72 °C for 10 min final extension. Fluorescent PCR products were electrophoresed on ABI Prism 310 Genetic Analyzer (Applied Biosystems, Foster City, CA, USA).

3. Results

Our results showed that, after *Hha*I digestion and nested PCR of the HUMARA locus, female-specific allele peaks could be clearly seen for mixed bloodstains with male/female ratios of $1{:}10^{-1}$, $1{:}10^{-2}$ and $1{:}10^{-3}$. No female-specific PCR products were obtained from mixtures with ratios of $1{:}10^{-4}$. Due to incomplete digestion of active X chromosomes, male-specific allele peaks were present in the electropherograms even at less extreme male/female DNA ratios ($1{:}10^{-1}$). Since the amount of input DNA digested by *Hha*I was 500 ng and one fifth of the digestion volume was subsequently used for nested

PCR, the HUMARA X-chromosome inactivation assay was capable to detect as little as 0.1 ng of female DNA.

4. Discussion

The HUMARA X-chromosome inactivation assay has been recently reported as a highly sensitive method for the detection of microchimerism in sex-mismatched stem cell transplantation from male donors to female recipients [5]. When applied to mock forensic samples (mixed bloodstains), the method displayed a 10^{-3} sensitivity with an observed detection limit—in terms of total female DNA present in the mixture—of 0.1 ng.

Since HUMARA is an extremely polymorphic marker with high power of discrimination, chances of finding a mixture from non-informative individuals (that is, a homozygous woman carrying the same allele of the male contributor) are low [6]. However, the constant presence of male-specific HUMARA allele peaks resulting from partial digestion of active X chromosomes can interfere with the definition of the genotype of the female contributor.

Despite these limitations, HUMARA X-chromosome inactivation assay was shown to be a hundred-fold more efficient than standard autosomal STRs in detecting the female minor component in male/female mixtures and may be applied to forensic case work in selected circumstances. Future characterization of other X-STRs amenable to methylation-specific PCR will also improve the efficacy of this method for identity testing purposes.

References

[1] J.E. Lygo, P.E. Johnson, D.J. Holdaway, S. Woodroffe, J.P. Whitaker, T.M. Clayton, et al., The validation of short tandem repeat (STR) loci for use in forensic casework, Int. J. Leg. Med. 107 (2) (1994) 77–89.

[2] M. Prinz, K. Boll, H. Baum, B. Shaler, Multiplexing of Y chromosome specific STRs and performance for mixed samples, Forensic Sci. Int. 85 (3) (1997) 209–218.

[3] W.D. Tilley, M. Marcelli, J.D. Wilson, M.J. McPhaul, Characterization and expression of a cDNA encoding the human androgen receptor, Proc. Natl. Acad. Sci. U. S. A. 86 (1) (1989) 327–331.

[4] R.C. Allen, H.Y. Zoghbi, A.B. Moseley, H.M. Rosenblatt, J.W. Belmont, Methylation of HpaII and HhaI sites near the polymorphic CAG repeat in the human androgen-receptor gene correlates with X chromosome inactivation, Am. J. Hum. Genet. 51 (6) (1992) 1229–1239.

[5] A. Yamane, M. Karasawa, T. Maehara, N. Tsukamoto, Y. Nojima, X chromosome methylation-based chimerism assay for sex-mismatched hematopoietic stem cell transplantation, Bone Marrow Transplant. 28 (10) (2001) 969–973.

[6] D. Desmarais, Y. Zhong, R. Chakraborty, C. Perreault, L. Busque, Development of a highly polymorphic STR marker for identity testing purposes at the human androgen receptor gene (HUMARA), J. Forensic Sci. 43 (5) (1998) 1046–1049.

International Congress Series 1261 (2004) 296–298

www.ics-elsevier.com

Microgeographic substructure of NW Iberian Y chromosome STR haplotypes

S. Beleza[a,b,*], B. Quintans[b], A. Salas[b], A. Amorim[a,c], A. Carracedo[b], L. Gusmão[a]

[a] *IPATIMUP, Instituto de Patologia e Imunologia da Universidade do Porto, R. Dr. Roberto Frias s/n, 4200 Oporto, Portugal*

[b] *Unidad de Genética Forense, Instituto de Medicina Legal, Universidad de Santiago de Compostela, R. San Francisco s/n, E-15705 Santiago de Compostela, Galicia, Spain*

[c] *Faculdade de Ciências da Universidade do Porto, Praça Gomes Teixeira, 4050 Oporto, Portugal*

Received 1 September 2003; received in revised form 1 September 2003; accepted 9 September 2003

Abstract. In order to assess the microgeographic heterogeneity of Y chromosome lineage's distribution in the north-western part of Iberian Peninsula, 409 male samples from the five districts of Northern Portugal and two districts of Southern Galicia were typed for 15 Y chromosome microsatellite markers. The results suggest that, in NW Iberia, barriers other than political were more important in shaping present Y chromosome lineage substructuring.

Keywords: Y-STRs; NW Iberia; Microgeography; Substructure

1. Introduction

Because of their abundant polymorphism, selective neutrality and ease of assessment, microsatellite loci seem to be ideal markers for population genetic monitoring in short evolutionary time scales, and thus many studies comparing closely related populations have been published [1,2]. The aim of this work was to assess the microgeographic heterogeneity of Y chromosome lineages in the North-Western part of Iberian Peninsula, through the analysis of 15 Y chromosome microsatellite markers in 409 male samples. The region analysed includes the Southern area of Galicia and the neighbouring Northern Portugal. The border between the two countries does not follow in many tracts important geographic barriers, but mountain ranges clearly differentiate interior and coastal parts of both political regions. In the framework of this scenario, the main goal of this research was to assess if geographical barriers present in the NW of Iberia were more important than political and linguistic ones for Y-STR substructuring.

* Corresponding author. Population Genetics, IPATIMUP, Instituto de Patologia e Imunologia da Universidade do Porto, R. Dr. Roberto Frias s/n, 4200 Oporto, Portugal. Tel.: +351-225570700; fax: +351-225570799.

E-mail address: sbeleza@ipatimup.pt (S. Beleza).

doi:10.1016/S0531-5131(03)01501-2

2. Materials and methods

Four-hundred nine blood samples were collected in the five districts of North Portugal (located to the North of Douro River) and two districts of Southern Galicia, from healthy unrelated individuals born in each area, after informed consent. The samples are distributed as follows: 23 from Montes Baixo Miño and 31 from Ourense, 157 from Porto, 54 from Braga, 60 from Viana do Castelo, 45 from Bragança and 39 from Vila Real.

Samples were typed with 15 Y-STRs (DYS19/389I/389II/390/391/392/393/437/438/439/460/461 and GATA A10/C4/H4) in two multiplex reactions as described by Beleza et al. [3].

RST with associated probability values and AMOVA were estimated using the software package ARLEQUIN 2.0 [4].

Microsatellite variance per locus and the average microsatellite variance across loci were calculated according to Goldstein et al. [5] for each population. For the estimation of DYS389II variance, alleles at this locus were considered excluding variation at DYS389I. A variance ratio was also estimated according to Jorde et al. [6], dividing the variance of each microsatellite in each population by the average variance of the microsatellite across the seven populations.

3. Results and discussion

It was possible to identify 378 different haplotypes from the typing of 409 non-related males from the NW of Iberian Peninsula with 15 Y-specific microsatellites, 20 of them being shared by different populations (4 haplotypes were shared by three of them and the remaining 16 by only two).

Analysis of molecular variance (AMOVA) was performed in different ways (Table 1). Considering a political approach, in which the two countries (Portugal and Galicia) were separated in two groups, the percentage of variation explained by differences among groups was slightly smaller than when considering no grouping, reflecting the common ancestry of Northern Portugal and Galicia.

RST pairwise comparison values (data not shown) were low, as it could be predicted from a microgeographic study of neighbouring populations, revealing the homogeneity existent between the samples, but showed a significant difference when comparing the

Table 1
Results from analysis of molecular variance (AMOVA)

Grouping	Source of variation	Variation (%)
No grouping	Among populations	0.29
	Within populations	99.71
Portugal vs. Galicia	Among groups	0.26
	Among populations within groups	0.22
	Within populations	99.52
Bragança vs. others	Among groups	1.07
	Among populations within groups	0.02
	Within populations	98.91

interior Northern Portuguese district Bragança with the coastal Northern Portuguese district Braga. Moreover, the highest pairwise RST values always involved Bragança and the other coastal districts.

In this context, performing AMOVA with Bragança versus all other samples together resulted in a $\approx$ 4-fold increase of the proportion of molecular variation observed between groups (Table 1).

Considerably high haplotype diversities were found in all populations studied (>99%). However, this standard diversity measure does not take variation in microsatellite repeat number (allele size) into consideration. Knowing that microsatellite variance of allele repeat size also offers a good measure of microsatellite diversity [5] a variance ratio was estimated [6] to remove the possible error arising from the contribution of highly mutating microsatellites. The average variance ratios across loci from Vila Real, Bragança and Montes Baixo Miño were significantly lower than the ones from Viana do Castelo, Braga and Ourense. The lower diversity found for Vila Real and Bragança (interior districts) may reflect some genetic drift imposed by important mountains ranges that separate these two districts from the other coastal districts. However, modern demographic migrations may have eroded the genetic substructure that could have existed in the past, and now it is only possible to observe some differentiation of Bragança in comparison to the other populations.

These results suggest anyway that, in NW Iberia, barriers other than political are more important in shaping Y chromosome lineage substructuring.

Acknowledgements

This work was supported by POCTI, Programa Operacional Ciência, Tecnologia e Inovação. Sandra Beleza has a PhD grant (SFRH/BD/860/2000) from FCT.

References

[1] L. Roewer, et al., Hum. Mol. Genet. 5 (1996) 1029–1033.
[2] R. Ploski, et al., Hum. Genet. 110 (2002) 592–600.
[3] S. Beleza, et al., Int. J. Leg. Med. 117 (2003) 27–33.
[4] S. Schneider, et al., Department of Anthropology, University of Geneva, 2000.
[5] D. Goldstein, et al., Mol. Biol. Evol. 13 (1996) 1213–1218.
[6] L. Jorde, et al., Am. J. Hum. Genet. 66 (2000) 979–988.

International Congress Series 1261 (2004) 299–301

ELSEVIER

www.ics-elsevier.com

Multiplex minisequencing strategies for phenotyping M02 haplogroup-derived Y-SNPs in African populations

B. Caeiro[a,*], M. Regueiro[a], D. Abrantes[b], J.C. Carril[a], M.F. Pinheiro[b], J.R. Luis[a]

[a] *Area de Antropoloxía, Facultade de Bioloxía, Campus Sur, Universidade de Santiago de Compostela, 15782 Santiago de Compostela, Galicia, Spain*

[b] *Instituto de Medicina do Porto, Porto, Portugal*

Abstract. A reliable technique for biallelic phenotyping of M02-derived Y-SNPs has been carried out by means of multiplex minisequencing after laser detection of electrophoresed fragments. A tetraplex including PN1, M155, M156 and M191 provides information about the actual status of up to nine SNPs having M02 background. An application of this technique in a population study of four sub-Saharan African populations has been accomplished.

Keywords: Single nucleotide polymorphism; SNP; Y-chromosome; Minisequencing; African populations

1. Introduction

Single nucleotide polymorphisms (SNPs) have been estimated to occur in 1 out of every 1000 nucleotides in humans, and therefore embody the most abundant source of genetic variation so far available [1]. More specifically, Y-SNPs, due to their model of inheritance, offer substantial possibilities in anthropological genetics and forensic studies. Within the YAP insertion, M02-derived lineages represent specific markers in African populations profiling [2]. Biallelic identification by polymerase mediated single-base primer extension by minisequencing, in combination with specific fluorescent targets followed by laser-automated detection, introduces new and relevant opportunities in the population screening of biallelic markers. This work deals with the development of the experimental conditions for the simultaneous screening of four Y-SNPs (PN1, M155,

* Corresponding author. Tel.: +34-981563100; fax: +34-981576904.
E-mail addresses: caeiro@eresmas.com, bajlbc95@usc.es (B. Caeiro).

0531-5131/
doi:10.1016/j.ics.2003.12.105

Table 1
Minisequencing primers of the Y-SNPs under study

SNP	Amplicon (bp)	Sequencing primers	Haplogroup
PN1	179	5′-CAAggg TCTT gAgA gggA gAgC-3′	E3*(xE3a)(C/T)
M155	226	5′-(C)6-gAATggA gAgg AATC CTCA CCTA TC-3′	E3a5(A/G)
M156	116	5′-CGCCGATACTTg CCTC CACg ACTT TCCT-3′	E3a6(A/G)
M191	370	5′-CCTTTTAAATTTAC ATTT TTTT CTTT ACAACTTg ACTA-3′	E3a7(T/G)

M156, M191, all them having the M02 background), by means of minisequencing strategies.

2. Materials and methods

Blood samples were obtained from donors after verbal consent. Only autochthonous individuals going back at least two generations from their respective ethnic groups were considered. The populations studied were: Fon (Benin), Bamileke (Cameroon), Wairak (Tanzania) and Tutsi (Rwanda). DNA was extracted using the standard phenol–chloroform method [3], and stored at -20 °C before use for no longer than 1 year.

PCR multiplex coamplification was carried out at 55 °C in a GeneAmp 9700 (Applied Biosystems). Minisequencing was carried out at an annealing temperature of 60 °C, following the ABI Prism SnaPShot Multiplex kit conditions, using the sequencing primers described in Table 1. An ABI PRISM 3100 Genetic Analyzer was used for capillary electrophoresis, followed by laser detection of fluorescently labelled fragments.

3. Results and discussion

Identification of Y-SNPs phenotypes were made according to molecular size (ranging from 22 bases in PN1, to 39 in M191) (Table 1), and the fluorochrome incorporated into

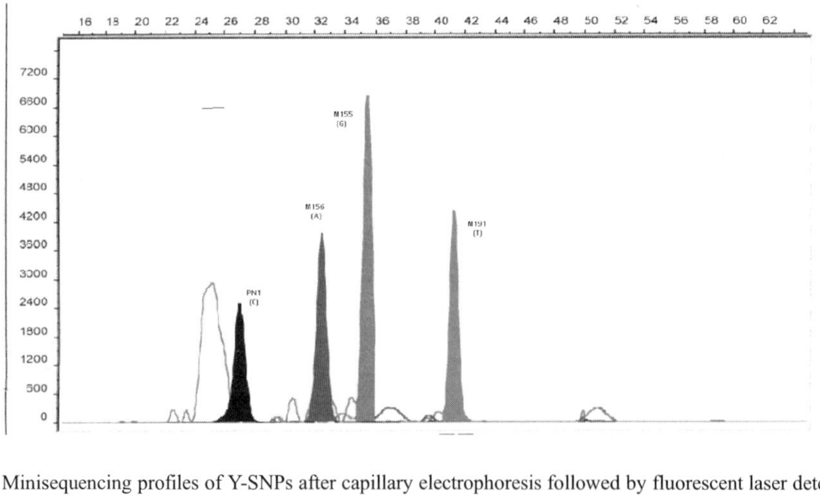

Fig. 1. Minisequencing profiles of Y-SNPs after capillary electrophoresis followed by fluorescent laser detection.

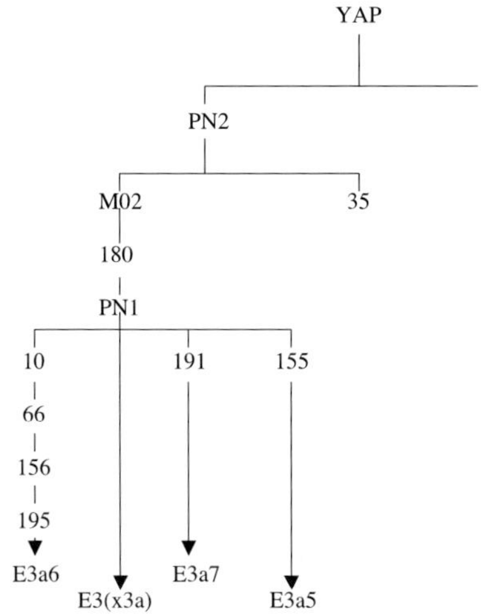

Fig. 2. Y-SNPs tree derived from M02 mutation.

the respective nucleotides. This is significant in the recognition of PN1 transitions (C–T) that may be clearly distinguished from spurious bands that may overlap the reading zone (Fig. 1) [4]. Drawn from YAP insertion, M02 gives rise to lineages that specifically characterise sub-Saharan populations, in which the incidence of PN1 mutation reaches from 0.4 up to 1.0, in contrast to Caucasoid populations in which it is virtually absent. Its presence in northern African populations points to genetic flow as the most important cause.

This multiplex provides information about the actual status up to nine single SNPs with the M02 background (Fig. 2). M02-derived haplogroups give rise to lineages that are well represented in African sub-Saharan populations. However, substantial population differences may be seen, not only in the incidence of the M02 mutation but also in the frequencies of the single derived haplogroups, which are in line with the degree of diversity reported for African populations.

References

[1] L. Kaderali, A. Dasphande, J.P. Nolan, P. Scott White, Nucleic Acids Research 31 (2003) 1796–1802.

[2] P.A. Underhill, P. Shen, A.A. Lin, G. Passarino, W.H. Yang, E. Kauffman, B. Bonne-Tamir, J. Bertranpetit, P. Francalacci, M. Ibrahim, T. Jenkins, J.R. Kidd, S.Q. Mehdi, M.T. Seielstad, R.S. Wells, A. Piazza, R.W. Feldman, M.W. Feldman, L.L. Cavalli-Sforza, P.J. Oefner, Y chromosome sequence variation and the history of human populations, Nature Genetics 26 (2000) 358–361.

[3] T. Maniatis, E.F. Fritsch, J. y Sambrook, Molecular Cloning: A Laboratory Manual, Cold Spring Harbor, New York, 1982.

[4] The Y. Chromosome Consortium, A nomenclature system for the tree of human Y-chromosomal binary haplogroups, Genome Research 12 (2002) 339–348.

International Congress Series 1261 (2004) 302–304

www.ics-elsevier.com

Population genetic comparisons of three X-chromosomal STRs (DXS7132, DXS7133 and GATA172D05) in North and South Italy

S. Turrina, D. De Leo*

Forensic Genetic Laboratory, Department of Medicine and Public Health, Institute of Legal Medicine, University of Verona, Policlinico GB Rossi, Piazzale LA Scuro 10, 37134, Verona VR, Italy

Abstract. Population genetic data of three tetranucleotide X-chromosomal STRs, DXS7132, DXS7133 and GATA172D05, were obtained by analyzing 295 unrelated healthy individuals living in North and South Italy (160 females and 135 males), and 40 family trios with female children. PCR primers for the loci DXS7132 and DXS7133 were redesigned in order to reduce the length of the amplification products compared with conventional design so that improved typing success rate when highly degraded DNA is used as a template. The comparison of the allele frequencies of these three ChrX markers gave similar distributions for North and South Italy although minor variations were found for some alleles. Additionally, some differences were found when comparing the allele frequencies of the male and female samples independently. Based on the investigated meiotic events, mutations were not found.

Keywords: Forensic DNA typing; Paternity testing; Short tandem repeat; X chromosome

1. Introduction

While many autosomal STRs and several Y chromosome markers have been evaluated and widely applied to forensic individual identification and paternity testing, X-linked STRs are scantily studied in forensic sciences. To our knowledge, only 21 X-linked STR markers have been described for forensic applications so far [1].

The analysis of X-chromosomal STRs could help to solve deficiency paternity cases when the disputed child is female or the alleged father cannot be typed. Therefore, as males are hemizygous for the X chromosome, the mean exclusion chance (MEC) of X-chromosomal markers tends to be higher than that of diploid autosomal STR loci with comparable polymorphism information content (PIC) values.

The aim of this work was the study, in two different populations from North and South Italy, of three tetranucleotide STR loci (DXS7132, DXS7133 and GATA172D05) located

* Corresponding author. Policlinico GB Rossi, Istituto di Medicina Legale, Piazzale LA Scuro 10, 37134 Verona, Italy. Tel.: +39-45-8074942; fax: +39-45-505259.

E-mail address: deleodom@tin.it (D. De Leo).

doi:10.1016/S0531-5131(03)01626-1

at the X chromosome in the range from Xq 11 to Xq 24 to validate their potential utility in paternity testing and other forensic cases.

2. Material and methods

DNA was extracted from blood samples of 295 unrelated healthy individuals living in North and South Italy (160 females and 135 males) using GenomicPrep Blood DNA Isolation Kit (APB, Milan, Italy), and 40 family trios including female children were checked for regular X-chromosomal inheritance.

PCR amplification was performed in singleplex using the primers previously published for GATA172D05 and newly designed forward primer sequence for DXS7132 and reverse primer sequence for DXS7133. The newly designed primers were:

DXS7132	5′ -CCCTCTCATCTATCTGACTG-3′
	5′ -GCCAAACTCTATTAGTCAAC-3′
DXS7133	5′ -GCTTCCTTAGATGGCATTCA-3′
	5′ -GCCTGTCGTTCATGCTTA-3′

Primer forward for each locus was Cy5-labelled.

Amplifications were carried out in 25 μl of reaction volume containing 2–5 ng DNA, 0.4 μM of each primer, 200 μM of each dNTP, 1.5 mM $MgCl_2$, 1.5 U AmpliTaq DNA polymerase and 2.5 μl AmpliTaq buffer II (ABI, Foster City, CA). The amplification conditions were the same for the three ChrX markers and consisted of initial denaturation at 94 °C for 5 min, followed by 28 cycles at 94 °C for 60 s, 58 °C for 45 s, 72 °C for 60 s and final extension step at 72 °C for 10 min, in a GeneAmp PCR System 9700 Thermal Cycler (Applied Biosystems, Foster City, CA).

The amplified products were separated on a denaturing polyacrylamide gel by a Automated Laser Fluorescent DNA sequencer (ALF-Express, APB, Uppsala, Sweden), and allelc typing was carried out based on sequenced alleles.

Heterozygosity (HET), polymorphism information content (PIC), power of discrimination (PD) and mean exclusion chance in trios involving daughters (MEC(I)) and in father/daughter duos lacking maternal genotype information (MEC(II)) were determined as proposed by Desmarais [2].

3. Results and discussion

The allele frequencies for each ChrX marker were calculated separately for females and males in both Italian samples and their comparisons did not show any significant statistical difference (Table 1), although rare allelic variants were found.

The allele distribution met the Hardy–Weinberg equilibrium for all three markers studied ($p>0.05$). Furthermore, both populations showed a similar PIC and corresponding values for MEC and HET. Based on the investigated meiotic events, no mutations were detected.

In paternity analysis and especially in deficiency cases, it should be borne in mind that DXS7132, DXS7133 and GATA172D05 are in the same "linkage group" [1]. The new primers were designed to shift closer to the repeat region in order to reduce the length of the amplicons compared with the conventional design.

Table 1
Allele frequencies and forensic efficiency of DXS7132, DXS7133, GATA172D05 markers

Allele	DXS7132				DXS7133				GATA172D05			
	Female		Male		Female		Male		Female		Male	
	North	South	North	South	North	South	North	South	North	South	North	South
5									–	0.007	–	–
6									0.218	0.213	0.180	0.114
7									–	–	–	–
8									0.167	0.167	0.180	0.205
9					0.446	0.467	0.517	0.591	0.034	0.053	0.045	–
10	–	–	–	0.023	0.163	0.147	0.090	0.091	0.316	0.333	0.270	0.455
11	0.006	0.020	–	0.023	0.331	0.333	0.315	0.295	0.178	0.160	0.213	0.159
12	0.128	0.213	0.124	0.182	0.042	0.033	0.056	–	0.086	0.067	0.090	0.068
13	0.291	0.347	0.315	0.341	0.012	0.007	0.022	–				
14	0.343	0.253	0.315	0.341	0.006	0.013	–	0.023				
15	0.192	0.120	0.180	0.091								
16	0.041	0.047	0.045	–								
17	–		0.022	–								
HET	0.692	0.712			0.596	0.578			0.741	0.746		
PIC	0.712	0.725			0.646	0.634			0.774	0.773		
PD	0.845	0.857	0.752	0.726	0.721	0.692	0.622	0.555	0.893	0.890	0.807	0.709
MEC(I)	0.574	0.537			0.414	0.342			0.656	0.626		
MEC(II)	0.700	0.713			0.602	0.585			0.752	0.751		

Furthermore, due to their small size, generally less than 140 bp, DXS7132, DXS7133 and GATA172D05 could be very useful in several specific forensic caseworks when highly degraded DNA samples are involved (e.g., DNA recovered from exhumed skeletons and formalin-fixed, paraffin-embedded tissues).

Like other ChrX markers, these three X-chromosomal STRs are highly informative markers for kinship testing and particularly interesting in deficiency paternity cases.

Acknowledgements

This work was supported by a grant from M.I.U.R. 60% and Donazione Miria Cherubini e Amleto Loro.

References

[1] R. Szibor, M. Krawczak, S. Hering, J. Edelmann, E. Kuhlisch, D. Krause, Use of X-linked markers for forensic purposes, Int. J. Leg. Med. 117 (2003) 67–74.

[2] D. Desmarais, Y. Zhong, R. Chakraborty, C. Perreault, L. Busque, Development of a highly polymorphic STR marker for identity testing purposes at the human androgen receptor gene (HUMARA), J. Forensic Sci. 43 (1998) 1046–1049.

International Congress Series 1261 (2004) 305–306

www.ics-elsevier.com

Population genetic study of y-chromosome haplotypes in the population of El Salvador (San Salvador, Central America)

P. Vásquez, B. Martínez-Jarreta[a,*], B. Budowle[b], E. Abecia[a], I. De Blas I[a]

[a] *Department of Legal Medicine, FacuIdad de Medicina, University of Zaragoza, C/Domingo Miral, sn, 50009 Zaragoza, Spain*

[b] *Laboratory Division, FBI, Washington, DC, USA*

Abstract. Y-chromosomal microsatellites (STRs) are proven to be useful in forensic practice but large and diverse population databases are required in order to facilitate the statistical evaluation of donor-stain matches. Here we present frequencies of a nine-STR loci set (DYS19, DYS388, DYS390, DYS392, DYS393, GATA A71, GATA A10, DYS 439 and GATA H4) in the population of El Salvador (San Salvador, Central America). Blood samples were taken from 120 healthy unrelated male individuals born and living in El Salvador (San Salvador, Central America). DNA was isolated from the samples using standard phenol–chloroform extraction method. Each locus was amplified individually, except for GATA A71, GATA A10, DYS 439 and GATA H4 (PCR-multiplex system). Detection of the amplified products was carried out using the Automatic Laser Fluorescent (ALF) DNA sequencer (Amersham Pharmacia, Uppsala, Sweden). The recommendations of the International Society for Forensic Genetics were followed for typing and interpretation. A total of 119 different haplotypes identified by the nine loci markers were observed. The overall haplotype diversity was 0.9998.

Keywords: Microsatellites; Short tandem repeat; Y-chromosome; Population study; El Salvador

1. Introduction

Y-chromosomal microsatellites (STRs) are proven to be useful in forensic practice but large and diverse population databases are required in order to facilitate the statistical evaluation of donor-stain matches. Here we present frequencies of a nine-STR loci set (DYS19, DYS388, DYS390, DYS392, DYS393, GATA A71, GATA A10, DYS 439 and GATA H4) in the population of El Salvador (San Salvador, Central America). There is a lack of information on the El Salvador population from a genetic point of view and

* Corresponding author. Tel.: +34-976762110; fax: +34-976762070.
E-mail address: mjarreta@unizar.es (B. Martínez-Jarreta).

doi:10.1016/S0531-5131(03)01847-8

therefore no previous publications on the distribution of Y-chromosome STRs are available. The nine-loci set includes new Y-specific STRs that have been recently described (GATA A71, GATA A10, DYS 439 and GATA H4) and characterised for forensic purposes [1].

2. Material and methods

Blood samples were taken from 120 healthy unrelated male individuals born and living in El Salvador (San Salvador, Central America). Genomic DNA extraction: standard phenol–chloroform method and quantification by fluorescence detection with DyNA-Quant 200 (APB). Each locus was amplified individually, except for GATA A71, GATA A10, DYS 439 and GATA H4 (PCR-multiplex system) [1]. Detection of the amplified products was carried out using the Automatic Laser Fluorescent (ALF) DNA sequencer (Amersham Pharmacia). The recommendations of the International Society for Forensic Genetics (ISFG) were followed for typing and interpretation [2].

3. Results and discussion

A total of 119 different Y-chromosome haplotypes were observed in the 120 males from San Salvador (haplotype: 13-12-24-13-13-11-15-12-28 was observed twice). The complete haplotype data are available to any interested researcher upon request. The combined haplotype diversity calculated for this set of Y polymorphisms was 0.9998 and the probability of match: 0.0083. The obtained population data allowed to establish the core of a reference database to be used in forensic casework.

References

[1] L. Gusmao, C. Alves, A. Amorin, Molecular characterisation of four human Y-specific microsatellites for population and forensic studies, Ann. Hum. Genet. 165 (2001) 285–291.

[2] P. Gill, et al., DNA Commission of the International Society for Forensic Genetics: recommendations on forensic analysis using Y-chromosome STRs, Int. J. Leg. Med. 114 (6) (2001) 305–309.

International Congress Series 1261 (2004) 307–309

www.ics-elsevier.com

Population genetics of 10 Y-chromosomal STR loci in Japanese using multiplexed PCR amplification kits, Y-PLEX™ 6 and Y-PLEX™ 5

A. Kido[a,*], M. Hara[b], H. Kameyama[c], Y. Yamamoto[c], R. Susukida[a], A. Takada[b], K. Saito[b], M. Oya[a]

[a] *Department of Legal Medicine, Faculty of Medicine, University of Yamanashi, Yamanashi-ken 409-3898, Japan*

[b] *Department of Forensic Medicine, Saitama Medical School, Saitama 350-0451, Japan*

[c] *Criminal Investigation Laboratory, Saitama Prefectural Police Headquarters, Saitama 330-0036, Japan*

Abstract. Allele and haplotype frequencies of 10 Y-STR loci DYS19, DYS385, DYS389I, DYS389II, DYS390, DYS391, DYS392, DYS393, DYS438 and DYS439 were determined in 115 unrelated Japanese males using the Y-PLEX™ 6 and Y-PLEX™ 5 PCR amplification kits. A total of 105 different haplotypes was observed, 96 of them being unique. The haplotype diversity was 0.9960 and the discrimination capacity was 0.9130.

Keywords: Y-chromosome; Short tandem repeat (STR); Population data; Japanese

1. Introduction

We analyzed allele and haplotype frequencies of 10 Y-chromosomal short tandem repeat (Y-STR) loci DYS19, DYS385, DYS389I, DYS389II, DYS390, DYS391, DYS392, DYS393, DYS438 and DYS439 in a Japanese population using the Y-PLEX™ 6 and Y-PLEX™ 5 PCR amplification kits.

2. Materials and methods

Semen or blood samples were obtained from 115 unrelated Japanese males. DNA was extracted by the phenol-chloroform method. PCR amplification of six loci DYS19, DYS385, DYS389II, DYS390, DYA391 and DYS393 was performed using the Y-PLEX™ 6 kit (ReliaGene Technologies) and the amplification of five loci DYS389I, DYS389II, DYS392, DYS438 and DYS439 was performed using the Y-PLEX™ 5 kit (ReliaGene Technologies) according to the instruction manual. DYS389II was common to the both kits. The amplified products were detected using an ABI PRISM 310 Genetic Analyzer (Applied Biosystems). The results were analyzed using GeneScan Analysis v3.1 software (Applied Biosystems) and the alleles were typed using Genotyper v2.5 software (Applied Biosystems).

* Corresponding author. Tel.: +81-55-273-9548; fax: +81-55-273-6753.
E-mail address: akido@res.yamanashi-med.ac.jp (A. Kido).

0531-5131/
doi:10.1016/S0531-5131(03)01450-X

Table 1
Y-STR haplotypes detected in Japanese

H	DYS19	DYS385	DYS389I	DYS389II	DYS390	DYS391	DYS392	DYS393	DYS438	DYS439	N
1	13	10–14	13	29	24	10	11	14	10	14	1
2	13	11–12	14	31	22	10	14	13	11	11	1
3	13	13–15	13	29	24	10	11	14	10	14	1
4	14	11–12	14	30	23	10	14	13	11	11	1
5	14	11–18	13	29	23	10	14	13	10	11	1
6	14	12–13	13	29	23	10	15	13	10	11	1
7	14	12–19	13	30	25	10	15	12	11	11	1
8	14	13–17	14	32	23	10	12	12	11	12	1
9	14	13–18	12	27	24	10	14	13	11	11	1
10	14	13–18	12	28	24	10	14	12	11	13	1
11	14	13–18	12	28	25	10	14	12	11	11	1
12	14	13–19	12	27	24	10	14	12	11	11	1
13	14	13–19	12	28	23	10	14	12	11	12	1
14	14	13–19	12	28	24	10	14	12	11	11	1
15	15	10–17	12	28	23	10	14	14	10	12	1
16	15	10–18	14	31	22	10	13	13	13	13	1
17	15	10–19	13	28	22	10	13	13	13	12	1
18	15	10–19	13	28	23	10	14	13	13	12	1
19	15	10–19	13	29	23	10	13	13	13	13	1
20	15	10–19	13	30	22	10	11	13	10	12	1
21	15	10–19	14	29	23	10	13	13	13	12	1
22	15	10–19	14	30	22	10	13	13	12	12	1
23	15	10–19	14	30	22	10	13	13	13	12	2
24	15	10–20	13	28	22	10	13	13	14	12	1
25	15	10–20	13	29	21	10	14	13	13	13	1
26	15	10–20	13	29	22	10	13	13	13	11	1
27	15	10–20	13	29	22	10	13	13	13	12	2
28	15	10–20	14	29	22	10	12	13	13	13	1
29	15	10–20	14	29	22	10	13	13	13	12	1
30	15	10–20	14	29	22	10	13	13	13	13	1
31	15	10–20	14	29	22	10	13	14	13	12	1
32	15	10–20	14	30	22	10	13	13	13	11	2
33	15	10–20	15	31	22	10	13	13	13	12	1
34	15	10–21	14	30	22	10	13	13	13	12	1
35	15	10–21	14	30	22	10	13	13	13	12	2
36	15	10–21	14	30	22	10	14	13	13	12	1
37	15	10–22	14	30	23	10	13	13	13	13	1
38	15	11–12	12	29	23	10	12	12	10	14	1
39	15	11–12	13	28	22	10	11	13	10	11	1
40	15	11–12	14	30	22	10	13	13	13	12	1
41	15	11–18	12	28	23	10	12	12	10	11	1
42	15	11–18	13	31	23	10	11	14	10	11	1
43	15	11–19	12	29	23	10	12	12	10	11	1
44	15	12–13	12	29	23	11	14	13	10	12	1
45	15	12–14	14	30	24	11	11	13	10	11	1
46	15	12–16	12	26	24	10	13	13	10	11	1
47	15	12–17	12	29	25	8	11	13	10	13	1
48	15	12–17	13	29	24	11	13	12	10	11	1
49	15	12–17	13	30	23	10	11	14	10	11	1
50	15	12–18	13	31	23	10	11	14	10	11	1
51	15	13–13	12	28	23	10	14	13	10	12	1
52	15	13–17	14	31	24	11	11	13	11	12	1
53	15	13–17	14	31	25	10	11	13	11	13	1
54	15	13–17	14	31	25	11	11	13	11	13	1
55	15	13–17	14	32	23	10	12	12	11	12	1
56	15	14–16	13	30	25	10	11	13	10	11	1
57	15	14–17	13	29	25	10	11	13	10	13	1
58	15	14–17	13	30	24	10	11	13	10	12	1
59	15	14–17	13	30	24	10	11	14	10	12	1
60	15	14–17	13	30	25	10	11	13	10	11	1
61	15	14–17	13	30	25	10	11	13	10	12	1
62	15	14–17	13	30	25	10	11	13	10	13	1
63	15	14–17	14	30	25	10	13	13	13	12	1

Table 1 (*continued*)

H	DYS19	DYS385	DYS389I	DYS389II	DYS390	DYS391	DYS392	DYS393	DYS438	DYS439	N
64	15	15–17	13	30	25	10	11	13	10	12	1
65	15	15–17	14	31	25	10	11	13	10	12	2
66	16	10–12	13	30	25	10	12	13	10	11	1
67	16	10–12	14	29	25	10	11	13	10	12	1
68	16	10–17	13	28	23	10	13	13	13	12	2
69	16	10–19	14	29	23	10	13	12	13	12	1
70	16	10–19	14	29	23	10	13	13	13	13	2
71	16	10–19	14	30	22	10	13	13	13	12	1
72	16	10–20	14	29	23	10	13	13	13	12	1
73	16	10–22	13	29	22	10	13	13	15	13	1
74	16	11–19	14	30	21	10	11	15	10	11	1
75	16	11–21	14	29	23	10	11	15	10	12	1
76	16	12–16	12	29	23	9	12	12	10	12	1
77	16	12–18	12	28	23	10	12	12	10	11	1
78	16	12–18	12	29	25	10	13	12	10	13	1
79	16	12–18	12	31	24	10	13	12	10	11	1
80	16	12–19	12	28	24	10	13	12	10	11	1
81	16	12–19	13	28	25	11	13	12	10	11	1
82	16	13–14	12	28	23	10	13	14	11	11	1
83	16	13–17	14	31	25	10	11	13	10	11	1
84	16	13–17	14	31	25	10	11	13	10	13	2
85	16	13–17	14	31	25	11	11	13	10	12	1
86	16	13–18	13	31	25	11	11	13	10	12	1
87	16	13–18	14	31	26	11	11	13	10	13	1
88	16	14–16	13	30	25	10	11	13	10	12	1
89	16	14–17	14	31	25	11	11	13	10	12	1
90	16	14–17	14	32	23	10	11	13	10	13	1
91	16	16–17	13	30	25	11	11	13	10	12	1
92	17	12–16	11	27	23	11	12	12	10	13	1
93	17	12–17	14	32	24	11	11	13	10	13	1
94	17	12–19	12	28	25	10	13	12	10	12	1
95	17	12–20	12	28	25	10	13	12	10	13	1
96	17	13–13	14	31	24	10	11	13	10	12	1
97	17	13–17	14	31	25	10	11	13	10	12	3
98	17	13–17	14	31	25	12	11	13	10	12	1
99	17	13–17	14	32	25	10	11	13	10	12	1
100	17	13–18	14	31	25	11	11	13	10	13	1
101	17	14–17	11	27	27	10	13	12	10	11	1
102	17	14–17	14	31	25	10	11	13	10	13	1
103	17	14–22	12	28	24	11	13	12	10	11	1
104	17	15–17	12	27	25	11	13	12	10	11	1
105	17	16–20	12	29	25	10	13	12	10	12	1

H: haplotype number.
N: individuals observed for each haplotype.

3. Results and discussion

Gene diversity values of the 10 Y-STR loci in the Japanese population ranged from 0.286 at DYS391 to 0.944 at DYS385. Haplotypes constructed from the 10 Y-STR loci are shown in Table 1. A total of 115 unrelated individuals produced 105 haplotypes, of which, 96 haplotypes were unique, eight were found in two individuals and one was found in three individuals. The haplotype diversity [1] calculated from the 10 Y-STR loci was 0.9960 and the discrimination capacity was 0.9130.

Reference

[1] M. Nei, Molecular Evolutionary Genetic, Columbia University Press, New York, 1987.

International Congress Series 1261 (2004) 310–312

www.ics-elsevier.com

Population genetics of eight new Y-chromosomal STR haplotypes in three Colombian populations: Antioquia, Chocó and Cartagena

J.J. Builes[a,b,*], M.L.J. Bravo[b], A. Montoya[a,b], L. Caraballo[c], B. Martínez[c], M.A. Moreno[a,b]

[a] *GENES Ltda. Laboratorio de Genética Forense y Huellas Digitales del DNA, Medellin, Colombia*
[b] *Instituto de Biología, Universidad de Antioquia, Medellín, Colombia*
[c] *Instituto de Investigaciones Inmunológicas, Universidad de Cartagena, Cartagena, Colombia*

Abstract. In this study, eight new Y-chromosomal (GATA-C4, DYS438, DYS437, DYS461, GATA-H4, DYS439, GATA-A10 and DYS460) short tandem repeat (STR) polymorphic systems were typed by two PCR quadruplex reactions in three Colombian populations: Antioquia, Chocó and Cartagena. GATA-C4 showed the highest gene diversity in the three populations. In the Antioquia population sample, a total of 123 different haplotypes were observed among which 85 were unique and 38 were found at least two times; in the Chocó population sample: 55 different haplotypes, 47 unique and 8 at least two times; in the Cartagena population sample: 82 different haplotypes, 77 unique and 5 at least two times. The highest average gene diversity was found in Cartagena and the lowest was in Chocó. The haplotype diversity for the eight Y-chromosomal STR loci in the Antioquia, Chocó and Cartagena population samples were calculated to be 0.9949, 0.9959 and 0.9940, respectively.

Keywords: Antioquia; Chocó; Cartagena; Y-chromosome; STR; Population; Colombia

1. Introduction

Analysis of short tandem repeat (STR) markers located on the nonrecombining portion of the human Y-chromosome is a powerful tool in male identification, paternity testing and evolutionary studies [1–3].

In this study, eight recently described [4,5] microsatellites (GATA-C4, DYS438, DYS437, DYS461, GATA-H4, DYS439, GATA-A10 and DYS460) have been analysed in three Colombian populations: Antioquia, a population constituted mainly by Caucasian [6]; Chocó, whose inhabitants are mainly of African origin [7]; and Cartagena, which is an admixture of African people and Caucasian named mulattoes [8]. In this work, we analysed some of the parameters that are important for their use in population and forensic studies.

* Corresponding author. Paternity testing, GENES Ltda. Laboratorio de Genética Forense y Huellas Digitales del DNA, Carrera 48 No. 10-45 Cons. 612, Medellin, Antioquia 1252, Colombia. Tel.: +57-4-268-48-75; fax: +57-4-318-52-70.

E-mail address: genforense@epm.net.co (J.J. Builes).

0531-5131/
doi:10.1016/S0531-5131(03)01552-8

2. Materials and methods

Blood samples were obtained from 179 unrelated Caucasian males from Antioquia, 63 unrelated males of African descent from the Chocó region and 92 unrelated mulatto males from Cartagena. Genomic DNA was extracted by a salting out extraction procedure [9]. The primer sequences of loci and cycling conditions were as recommended [4,5,10].

The eight loci were amplified in two multiplexes. Multiplex I includes four STRs: GATA-C4, DYS438, DYS437 and DYS461. Multiplex II includes: GATA-H4, DYS439, GATA-A10 and DYS460. PCR conditions were as follows: 5 ng DNA in 15 μl total reaction volume containing 2 mM $MgCl_2$, 1 × PCR Taq DNA Polimerasa buffer, 0.5 U Taq DNA Polimerasa

Table 1
Gene frequencies and diversities of the eight systems in Antioquia (n = 179), Chocó (n = 63) and Cartagena (n = 92) populations

Locus	Alelles	GF			GD		
		Antioquia	Chocó	Cartagena	Antioquia	Chocó	Cartagena
Y-GATA C4	17			0.011	0.771	0.741	0.735
	19	0.028		0.011			
	20	0.039	0.048	0.054			
	21	0.201	0.302	0.196			
	22	0.156	0.254	0.174			
	23	0.458	0.333	0.435			
	24	0.101	0.032	0.109			
	25	0.017	0.016	0.011			
	26		0.016				
DYS438	7			0.011	0.693	0.665	0.720
	9	0.173	0.016	0.120			
	10	0.190	0.159	0.261			
	11	0.134	0.444	0.185			
	12	0.475	0.349	0.413			
	13	0.028	0.032	0.011			
DYS437	13	0.011	0.032		0.586	0.549	0.596
	14	0.430	0.603	0.413			
	15	0.475	0.302	0.478			
	16	0.084	0.063	0.109			
DYS461	10	0.022		0.011	0.561	0.636	0.617
	11	0.196	0.111	0.207			
	12	0.615	0.476	0.533			
	13	0.162	0.365	0.250			
	14	0.006	0.048				
Y-GATA H4	26	0.034	0.048	0.011	0.564	0.574	0.568
	27	0.385	0.556	0.402			
	28	0.536	0.349	0.522			
	29	0.045	0.048	0.065			
DYS439	9	0.028	0.016	0.022	0.645	0.599	0.655
	10	0.028	0.048	0.065			
	11	0.279	0.317	0.293			
	12	0.508	0.540	0.500			
	13	0.145	0.079	0.109			
	14	0.011		0.011			
Y-GATA A10	11		0.016		0.613	0.671	0.659
	13	0.056	0.190	0.076			
	14	0.251	0.397	0.250			
	15	0.553	0.381	0.500			
	16	0.134	0.016	0.174			
	17	0.006					
DYS460	9	0.022		0.043	0.564	0.462	0.614
	10	0.436	0.317	0.380			
	11	0.497	0.667	0.489			
	12	0.045	0.016	0.087			

GF: Gene frequencies. GD: Gene diversity.

(Promega), 200 μM of each dNTP, 0.53 μM GATA-C4 primers, 1.6 μM DYS438 primers, 0.8 μM DYS437 primers, 1.6 μM DYS461 primers, 0.8 μM GATA-H4 primers, 0.67 μM DYS439 primers, 0.53 μM GATA-A10 primers and 1.06 μM DYS460 primers. The PCR products were analyzed using denaturing 4% acrylamide-bis-acrilamide gel electrophoresis and detected by silver staining (Promega). Alleles were identified based on the number of repeats, and their attribution was made by comparison with an in-house constructed allelic ladder and following the published nomenclature [10] and ISFG guidelines for STR analysis [11]. The gene frequencies and gene or haplotype diversity values were calculated using the software ARLEQUIN version 2000 [12] and Nei formulation [13].

3. Results and discussion

Gene frequencies and diversity values for each STR obtained for the three populations are shown in Table 1. GATA C4 was the most informative loci with gene diversity of 0.771, 0.747 and 0.735 for Antioquia, Chocó and Cartagena, respectively. Cartagena population showed the highest average gene diversity (0.6455); on the other hand, Chocó population showed the lower average gene diversity (0.6121).

The haplotype diversity for the eight Y-chromosomal STR loci in the Antioquia, Chocó and Cartagena population samples were 0.9949, 0.9959 and 0.9940, respectively. This implies that this set of Y-specific STR loci will be valuable additions to our current test panel and will improve the exclusion probabilities in forensic and kinship cases when individuals from Antioquia, Chocó or Cartagena are involved.

Acknowledgements

This work was supported by GENES Ltda.; Vicerrectoría de Investigación (CODI), Universidad de Antioquia and FUNDEMEB (Cartagena). Juan José Builes has a PhD fellowship (0058/2001) from COLCIENCIAS.

References

[1] L. Roewer, J.T. Epplen, Forensic Sci. Int. 53 (1992) 163–171.
[2] M.A. Jobling, et al., Int. J. Leg. Med. 110 (1997) 118–124.
[3] L. Gusmão, et al., Forensic Sci. Int. 106 (3) (1999) 163–172.
[4] Q. Ayub, et al., Nucleic Acids Res. 28 (2) (2000) e8.
[5] P.S. White, et al., Genomics 57 (1999) 433–437.
[6] M.L. Bravo, et al., Gene Geogr. 10 (1996) 11–17.
[7] M.L. Bravo, et al., Homo 51 (2000) 132–140.
[8] L. Caraballo, et al., Tissue Antigens 39 (1992) 128–133.
[9] S.A. Miller, et al., Nucleic Acids Res. 16 (1988) 1215.
[10] L. Gusmão, et al., Forensic Sci. Int. 126 (2002) 129–136.
[11] P. Gill, et al., Int. J. Leg. Med. 114 (2001) 305–309.
[12] S. Schneider, et al., University of Geneva, 2000.
[13] M. Nei, Molecular Evolutionary Genetics, Columbia University Press, New York, 1987.

ELSEVIER

International Congress Series 1261 (2004) 313–315

www.ics-elsevier.com

Population genetics of Y chromosomal STR haplotypes in Japanese population

C. Hashimoto*, S. Nakamura, C. Sasaki, H. Takeshita, T. Nagai, H. Sugie, M. Furukawa, K. Kurihara

Department of Legal Medicine, Kitasato University School of Medicine, Sagamihara 228-8555, Japan

Abstract. Five Y chromosomal short tandem repeat (STR) loci DYS389I, DYS389II, DYS439, DYS438 and DYS392 have been analysed to obtain the allele and haplotype frequencies data in 129 unrelated Japanese male individuals living in Kanagawa by means of multiplex PCR with Y-PLEX™ 5 Primer Mix, followed by capillary electrophoresis using the ABI PRISM 310 Genetic Analyzer. The gene diversity values ranged from 0.555 (DYS439) to 0.737 (DYS389II). A total of 72 haplotypes was detected, of which 51 haplotypes were unique and the others occurred at least two times. The most common haplotype (DYS389I, DYS389II, DYS439, DYS438, DYS392) was 14–30–12–13–13 with a frequency of 10%, and the haplotype diversity was calculated as 0.969. The combined resolutions of the 5 Y STR multiplex system using the Y-PLEX™ 5 was applicable to routine case work.

Keywords: Y chromosome; STR; Gene diversity; Haplotype diversity; Japanese population

1. Introduction

Short tandem repeat (STR) polymorphisms are powerful tools for human identification, paternity analysis and genetic mapping. We have already analysed the AmpFlSTR Profiler Plus STR multiplex system and the 18 STR loci on the X chromosome in the Japanese population [1,2].

Recently, Y chromosomal STRs have been extensively investigated in forensic science for application in male identification and paternity testing. In particular, the Y chromosomal STRs are useful for analysis of stains in forensic investigations when a male suspect is involved, as is the case in most violent crimes, including sexual offenses. A number of Y STR multiplex assays have also been developed [3,4].

* Corresponding author. Tel./fax: +81-42-778-9026.
E-mail address: mm02035r@st.kitasato-u.ac.jp (C. Hashimoto).

doi:10.1016/S0531-5131(03)01703-5

Table 1
Y STR consensus structures and allele ranges

STR marker	Dye label	Repeat motif	Allele size range
DYS389I	FAM	TCTG/TCTA	243–260
DYS389II	FAM	TCTG/TCTA	361–385
DYS439	HEX	GATA	234–254
DYS438	TAMRA	TTTTC	131–158
DYS392	TAMRA	TAT	247–262

In the present investigation, we analysed 5 STR loci DYS389I, DYS389II, DYS439, DYS438 and DYS392 to obtain the allele and haplotype frequencies in a Japanese population living in Kanagawa.

2. Materials and methods

EDTA-treated blood samples were collected from 129 unrelated Japanese male individuals living in Kanagawa, and genomic DNA was isolated by using the DNA IQ™ System (Promega). Five Y chromosomal STRs analysed in the present study were indicated in Table 1. Multiplex PCR amplification of these 5 STR loci was performed using the Y-PLEX™ 5 Primer Mix (Reliagene Technologies, Inc.) according to the user's manual provided by the manufacturer. PCR products of 1 μl were mixed with 0.5 μl of GeneScan-500 [ROX] size standard (PE Applied Biosystems) and 12 μl of Hi-Di formamide. These samples were denatured at 95 °C for 3 min, then chilled on ice. The fluorescently labeled amplified fragments were electrophoresed using the ABI PRISM 310 Genetic Analyzer in a 47 cm, 50 μm i.d. capillary, filled with Performance Optimized Polymer 4 (POP4, PE Applied Biosystems) at 15 kV for 24 min at 60 °C, and analysed

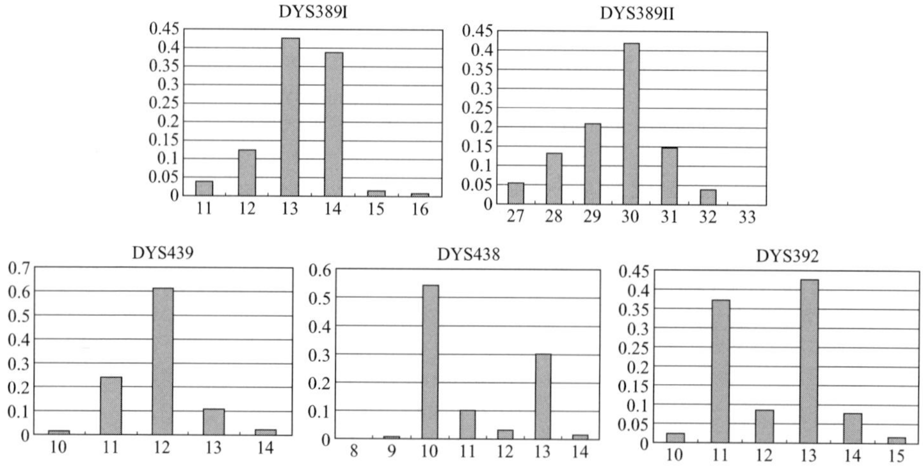

Fig. 1. The distribution of allele frequencies of Y-PLEX™ 5 loci in the Japanese population.

Table 2
Y-PLEX™ 5 gene and haplotype diversities (%) in Japanese population

STR marker	Gene diversity
DYS389I	65.1
DYS389II	73.8
DYS439	55.5
DYS438	60.3
DYS392	66.6
Haplotype diversity	96.9

using GeneScan Analysis Software ver. 3.1.2. The Y-PLEX™ 5 Allelic Ladder was used as a reference for allele designation.

3. Results and discussion

In 129 Japanese male subjects, a total of 6 alleles for DYS389I, 6 alleles for DYS389II, 5 alleles for DYS439, 6 alleles for DYS438, and 6 alleles for DYS392 were observed. The distributions allele frequencies of Y-PLEX™ 5 loci in Japanese population were indicated in Fig. 1. The most common alleles were 13 (42.6%), 30 (41.9%), 12 (61.2%), 10 (54.3%), and 13 (42.6%) for DYS389I, DYS389II, DYS439, DYS438, and DYS392, respectively. The gene diversity values ranged from 0.555 (DYS439) to 0.737 (DYS389II). A total of 72 haplotypes was detected, of which 51 haplotypes were unique and the others occurred at least two times. The most common haplotype (DYS389I, DYS389II, DYS439, DYS438, DYS392) was 14–30–12–13–13 with a frequency of 10%, and the haplotype diversity was calculated as 0.969. Y-PLEX™ 5 gene and haplotype diversities in Japanese population were presented in Table 2. From these results, the five Y STR multiplex system using the Y-PLEX™ 5 was applicable for routine case work.

References

[1] S. Nakamura, T. Nagai, H. Matsui, M. Tabuchi, H. Sugie, M. Furukawa, H. Imai, K. Kurihara, Genetic analysis of AmpFl STR Profiler Plus Loci in Japanese, Prog. Forensic Genet. 8 (2000) 236–238.

[2] H. Matsushita, S. Nakamura, T. Nagai, M. Nakamura, H. Sugie, M. Furukawa, T. Komuro, K. Kurihara, Allele frequencies of dinucleotide repeat marker loci on the X chromosome in the Japanese population, Forensic Sci. Int. 129 (2002) 134–136.

[3] M. Prinz, K. Boll, H. Baum, B. Shaler, Multiplexing of Y chromosome specific STRs and performance for mixed samples, Forensic Sci. Int. 85 (1997) 209–218.

[4] J.M. Butler, R. Schoske, P.M. Vallone, M.C. Kline, A.J. Redd, M.F. Hammer, A novel multiplex for simultaneous amplification of 20 Y chromosome STR markers, Forensic Sci. Int. 129 (2002) 10–24.

International Congress Series 1261 (2004) 316–318

www.ics-elsevier.com

A study of Y-chromosomal microsatellites and biallelic markers in Norway

B. Myhre Dupuy*, M. Stenersen, A.G. Fløbnes, B. Olaisen

Institute of Forensic Medicine, University of Oslo, Rettsmedisinsk Institutt, Rikshospitalet A2-1002, Gaustadalléen 20, 0027 Oslo, Norway

Abstract. Y-chromosomal polymorphisms at nine microsatellite and five biallelic markers in a Norwegian population sample are presented. In 1766 samples, 726 different lineages were encountered. Six known haplogroups were observed (Hg1, 2, 3, 4, 9 and 16). Locus diversity and combined haplotype diversity is given. Signs of regional substructuring of haplogroups are demonstrated.

Keywords: Norway; Y-STR; Microsatellite; Population genetics

1. Introduction, materials and methods

Y-chromosomal polymorphisms at nine microsatellites (DYS19, DYS385, DYS388, DYS389 I, DYS389 II, DYS390, DYS391, DYS392 and DYS393) and five biallelic markers (Tat, YAP, 1–2, SRY1532 and 9–7) were studied in 1766 unrelated Y-chromosomes of Norwegian origin. The males were a pan-Norwegian collection. Methods were as previously described [1,2]. Arlequin was used for calculation of Fst [3]. The repeat number nomenclature follows the ISFH guidelines [4].

2. Results and conclusion

The allele frequencies of the Y-STRs designed by number of repeats are given in Table 1. In 1766 samples, 721 different haplotypes and 726 different lineages were encountered, respectively. Five haplotypes were thus identical by state but not by descent. Six known haplogroups were observed (Hg1, 2, 3, 4, 9 and 16) together with one “new” haplogroup. Three haplogroups (Hg1, 2 and 3) represent about 95% of the population sample. We observed 500 unique lineages as well as 97 pairs and 40 triplets. Locus diversity in regions and total ranged from 0.22 (DYS393, Bergen) to 0.84 (South, Oslo). Signs of regional substructuring of haplogroups are demonstrated particularly in South and West.

* Corresponding author. Tel.: +47-23071312; fax: +47-23071278.
E-mail address: b.m.dupuy@labmed.uio.no (B. Myhre Dupuy).

0531-5131/
doi:10.1016/S0531-5131(03)01840-5

Table 1
Allele frequencies at in regions, cities and in the total population

STR: repeat	South N=76	West N=301	East N=493	Middle N=317	North N=377	Oslo N=109	Bergen N=93	Norway N=1766
DYS19: 13	0.013	0.023	0.026	0.038	0.029	0.018	0.022	0.027
14	0.592	0.571	0.527	0.426	0.544	0.541	0.527	0.524
15	0.289	0.286	0.300	0.366	0.300	0.294	0.258	0.306
16	0.105	0.086	0.118	0.155	0.114	0.101	0.140	0.118
17		0.033	0.028	0.016	0.013	0.046	0.054	0.025
DYS389 I: 8	0.013	0.003			0.005			0.002
9	0.368	0.296	0.373	0.375	0.316	0.339	0.258	0.340
10	0.500	0.538	0.432	0.461	0.456	0.486	0.591	0.475
11	0.118	0.156	0.191	0.164	0.218	0.174	0.151	0.180
12		0.007	0.004		0.005			0.003
DYS389 II: 23	0.013							0.001
24	0.013	0.010	0.012	0.003	0.013			0.009
25	0.329	0.256	0.337	0.297	0.271	0.303	0.247	0.294
26	0.421	0.375	0.282	0.334	0.342	0.321	0.441	0.337
27	0.118	0.216	0.205	0.224	0.236	0.257	0.183	0.215
28	0.105	0.100	0.130	0.120	0.106	0.110	0.108	0.114
29		0.037	0.032	0.016	0.027	0.009	0.022	0.025
30		0.007	0.002	0.003	0.005			0.003
31				0.003				0.001
DYS390: 20					0.003			0.001
21			0.002	0.003	0.003			0.002
22	0.171	0.126	0.178	0.205	0.199	0.211	0.151	0.179
23	0.342	0.302	0.339	0.271	0.292	0.330	0.301	0.308
24	0.355	0.322	0.227	0.237	0.249	0.239	0.290	0.259
25	0.132	0.233	0.229	0.274	0.241	0.193	0.247	0.235
26		0.017	0.024	0.009	0.013	0.028	0.011	0.016
DYD391: 6			0.002		0.003			0.001
8					0.003			0.001
9	0.013	0.003	0.004	0.013	0.003	0.009		0.006
10	0.434	0.498	0.611	0.640	0.546	0.550	0.634	0.573
11	0.539	0.485	0.371	0.334	0.416	0.413	0.344	0.402
12	0.013	0.010	0.012	0.013	0.029	0.028	0.022	0.017
13		0.003						0.001
DYS392: 9					0.003			0.001
11	0.513	0.545	0.669	0.656	0.594	0.541	0.591	0.611
12	0.092	0.060	0.047	0.095	0.040	0.073	0.054	0.060
13	0.395	0.365	0.233	0.211	0.220	0.312	0.301	0.264
14		0.030	0.047	0.038	0.143	0.073	0.054	0.063
15			0.004					0.001
DYS393: 9							0.011	0.001
10				0.006				0.001
11					0.003			0.001
12	0.092	0.020	0.039	0.013	0.016	0.037	0.022	0.027
13	0.829	0.867	0.848	0.874	0.833	0.807	0.882	0.851
14	0.053	0.100	0.091	0.079	0.143	0.128	0.065	0.101
15	0.026	0.013	0.020	0.028	0.005	0.028	0.022	0.018
16			0.002					0.001
DYS382: 8–14			0.002					0.001
9–13							0.011	0.001
10–13			0.002		0.003			0.001
DYS382: 8–14			0.002					0.001
10–14			0.014	0.006	0.019	0.009	0.011	0.010
10–15			0.002		0.005		0.011	0.002
10–19	0.013							0.001
11–11		0.003	0.012	0.006	0.005	0.018	0.022	0.008

Table 1 (*continued*)

STR: repeat	South N=76	West N=301	East N=493	Middle N=317	North N=377	Oslo N=109	Bergen N=93	Norway N=1766
11–12	0.013	0.017	0.004	0.003	0.003		0.043	0.008
11–13	0.105	0.130	0.063	0.038	0.098	0.073	0.086	0.081
11–14	0.355	0.415	0.361	0.413	0.358	0.358	0.376	0.379
11–15	0.079	0.056	0.049	0.063	0.050	0.083	0.032	0.055
11–16		0.023	0.004	0.003	0.016	0.009	0.032	0.011
11–17					0.011			0.002
11–19			0.002					0.001
12–12			0.002					0.001
12–13		0.007	0.004		0.013	0.009	0.011	0.006
12–14	0.013	0.027	0.034	0.025	0.042	0.037	0.011	0.031
12–15			0.004	0.009	0.005			0.004
12–16					0.003		0.011	0.001
12–17			0.002					0.001
13–13	0.013	0.003	0.008	0.009	0.021	0.009	0.011	0.011
13–14	0.053	0.070	0.089	0.120	0.114	0.073	0.054	0.092
13–15	0.039	0.017	0.018	0.019	0.029	0.009	0.011	0.020
13–16		0.007	0.008	0.009	0.003		0.011	0.006
13–17	0.026	0.010	0.006	0.013	0.008	0.009		0.009
13–18			0.002	0.013	0.003	0.009		0.004
13–19					0.003			0.001
13–20			0.002		0.008			0.002
13–21			0.002	0.003	0.005			0.002
14–14	0.118	0.110	0.083	0.091	0.077	0.119	0.065	0.091
14–15	0.105	0.070	0.128	0.082	0.066	0.092	0.140	0.094
14–16	0.013		0.020	0.013	0.013	0.009		0.012
14–17		0.003	0.008	0.003				0.003
14–20			0.002					0.001
15–15	0.026	0.017	0.043	0.041	0.013	0.046	0.022	0.030
15–16	0.026	0.007		0.003	0.003	0.018	0.022	0.006
15–17			0.002	0.003		0.009		0.002
15–18		0.003						0.001
15–20			0.002					0.001
16–16		0.003	0.002	0.006				0.002
16–17				0.003				0.001
16–18			0.004				0.011	0.002
16–19			0.002		0.003			0.001
17–17			0.004					0.001
17–18		0.003	0.002					0.001
DYS388: 10		0.037	0.020	0.019	0.024	0.018	0.054	0.024
11			0.002					0.001
12	0.605	0.651	0.554	0.562	0.594	0.569	0.602	0.586
13	0.079	0.050	0.059	0.088	0.040	0.083	0.054	0.061
14	0.289	0.236	0.341	0.309	0.332	0.294	0.290	0.307
15	0.013	0.017	0.016	0.013	0.011	0.028		0.014
16	0.013	0.010	0.008	0.006				0.006
17				0.003		0.009		0.001

References

[1] B.M. Dupuy, et al., Forensic Sci. Int. 117 (2001) 163–173.

[2] B.M. Dupuy, M. Stenersen, B. Olaisen, in preparation.

[3] S.K.J. Scheneider, D. Roessli, L. Excoffier, Arlequin Ver 1.1: A Software for Population Genetic Data Analysis, 1997.

[4] P. Gill, C. Brenner, B. Brinkmann, et al., Int. J. Legal. Med. 114 (2001) 305–309.

ELSEVIER

International Congress Series 1261 (2004) 319–321

www.ics-elsevier.com

Portuguese population study with 16 Y-STR loci

H. Geada[a,*], J. Baptista[b], M. Felgueiras[b], C. Vieira Silva[b], C. Cruz[b], I. Lucas[b], T. Ribeiro[b], R. Espinheira[b]

[a] *Department of Legal Medicine, Faculty of Medicine, University of Lisbon, Lisbon, Portugal*
[b] *Forensic Genetics, National Institute of Legal Medicine, Lisbon, Portugal*

Abstract. The aim of this study was to present a Portuguese Population Database of 214 Southern Portugal samples studied with 16 Y-STR loci including the eight minimal Y-STR haplotype—DYS19, DYS390, DYS391, DYS392, DYS393, DYS389I/II, DYS385 and other Y-STR loci—GATA A7.1 (DYS460), GATA C4, GATA A7.2 (DYS461), GATA A10, GATA H4, DYS437, DYS438 and DYS439. In this study, 209 different haplotypes could be defined and 205 haplotypes were found just once. This database has a discrimination power of 97.7%, a haplotype diversity of 99.6% and 2.3% of shared haplotypes. Some samples do not match any sample in the Y-STR Haplotype Reference Database which assigned specific region characteristics to these population samples. Forty-three alleged father–child non-exclusion cases were also studied and two possible mutations have been detected in DYS439 and DYS393. Complex paternity investigation cases without alleged father have also been studied. In an autosomal STR exclusion case, the same 16 Y-STR haplotype was obtained between the excluded alleged father and the child.

Keywords: Y-STRs; Population; Paternity; Mutations; Forensic cases

1. Introduction

Although autosomal STRs are commonly used for forensic investigations, Y-chromosome STRs provide very useful information in paternity investigation cases without alleged father and in other investigation cases where paternal lineage identification can be assessed.

In Forensic Genetics, it is necessary to have population databases concerning the main populations which the Forensic Laboratory used to work with. The aim of this study is to present a Portuguese Population Database mainly from Southern Portugal studied with 16 Y-STR loci including the eight minimal Y-STR haplotype—DYS19, DYS390, DYS391, DYS392, DYS393, DYS389I/II, DYS385 and other Y-STR loci—GATA A 7.1 (DYS460), GATA C4, GATA A 7.2 (DYS461), GATA A10, GATA H4, DYS437, DYS438 and

* Corresponding author. Delegação de Lisboa do Instituto Nacional de Medicina Legal, Forensic Genetic Service, R. Manuel Bento de Sousa 1150-219, Lisboa, Portugal. Tel.: +351-21-8811800; fax: +351-21-8864493.
E-mail address: hgeada@dlinml.mj.pt (H. Geada).

doi:10.1016/S0531-5131(03)01773-4

DYS439, included in the Y-Chromosome Quality Control Group of the Spanish and Portuguese Group (GEPY) of the ISFG.

2. Materials and methods

After DNA extraction with the Chelex method, Y-STR amplifications of 214 samples from Southern Portugal population were carried out in a 9600, 9700 or 2400 Perkin-Elmer thermocycler in five multiplex reactions: Pentaplex—DYS393, DYS390, DYS19, DYS389I/II [1]; Triplex I—DYS391, DYS437, DYS439 and Triplex II—DYS392, DYS385, DYS438 [2]; GEPY I—GATA A7.2 (DYS461), GATA C4, DYS437, DYS438 and GEPY II—GATA A7.1 (DYS460), GATA A10, DYS439, GATA H4 [3,4]. Samples were analysed in an ABI Prism 3100 DNA Sequencer with Genescan (v. 3.7).

3. Results and discussion

Table 1 shows some results of the 16 Y-STR Haplotype Portuguese Population Database, mainly haplotypes shared by several individuals. A total of 214 males were analysed for all 16 Y-STR loci—209 different haplotypes could be defined and 205 haplotypes were found just once. This database has a discrimination power of 97.7%, a haplotype diversity of 99.6% and 2.3% of shared haplotypes.

When considering the eight minimal Y-STR haplotype, we can detect haplotypes shared by several individuals making haplotype clusters up to seven non-related individuals. With 16 Y-STR loci, the discrimination power was successfully increased, with haplotype clusters involving only two or three non-related individuals as h15, h82, h169 and h173 in Table 1.

Minimal haplotypes of all samples have been compared with the Y-STR Haplotype Reference Database. When considering the eight minimal Y-STR haplotype, seven individuals shared the most frequent haplotype also detected in different populations in

Table 1
Some 16Y-STR haplotypes detected in a Southern Portuguese population

Haplotype	*N*	DYS 19	DYS 389I	DYS 389II	DYS 390	DYS 391	DYS 392	DYS 393	DYS 385	DYS 437	DYS 438	DYS 439	DYS 460	DYS 461	GATA A10	GATA C4	GATA H4
h1	1	12	13	30	24	10	13	13	11/15	15	12	13	11	12	14	23	27
h2	1	13	12	28	24	10	11	13	17/17	14	10	11	10	13	14	21	27
h15	3	13	14	30	24	9	11	13	13/14	14	10	10	11	13	14	21	28
h16	1	13	14	30	24	9	11	13	13/15	14	10	10	11	13	14	21	28
h82	2	14	13	29	24	11	13	13	11/14	15	12	13	11	12	15	23	27
h83	1	14	13	29	24	11	13	13	11/14	15	12	13	11	12	15	24	27
h99	1	14	13	30	22	9	11	12	13/18	15	9	12	11	13	15	24	27
h133	1	14	14	30	24	11	13	13	11/15	15	12	12	11	13	14	23	28
h134	1	14	14	30	24	11	13	13	11/15	15	12	11	11	12	14	23	28
h169	2	15	13	29	24	11	13	13	11/14	15	12	12	11	12	15	23	28
h173	2	15	13	30	22	11	11	13	14/14	16	10	12	10	12	14	21	27
h201	1	16	15	32	22	10	12	15	16/17	15	10	12	11	12	15	21	27
h208	1	17	13	28	23	10	11	13	12/12	15	10	11	10	11	16	22	28
h209	1	17	13	29	24	11	11	12	14/18	15	9	13	10	13	14	21	27

the Y-STR Haplotype Reference Database (351 matches)—h78 to h83. Only two non-related individuals shared the corresponding extended 16 Y-STR haplotype—h82. Three non-related individuals shared the most frequent haplotype—h15 in the Southern Portuguese population database.

Haplotypes differing by just one or two repeat units such as h15–h16, h82–h83 or h133–h134 can be encountered in this database. Some minimal haplotypes have no matches in the Y-STR Haplotype Reference Database as, for example, h99 and h201.

3.1. Forensic cases

Studying 43 alleged father–child non-exclusion cases with 17 autosomal STRs performed with SGMPlus and Powerplex16, two Y-STR genetic incompatibilities have been detected in DYS439 (12 → 13) and in DYS393 (14 → 13), in cases with W = 99.9999992% and W = 99.999999998%, respectively.

Otherwise, in 14 alleged father–child exclusion cases, 5 to 14 genetic incompatibilities were detected in each case, being DYS385, DYS389II, DYS439 and DYS460 the loci with more exclusions.

The 16-YSTR loci were also used to investigate complex forensic cases without alleged father as in an exclusion paternity case with two alleged half-brothers and a child detecting two different paternal lineage and in an non-exclusion paternity case including an alleged half-brother and a child sharing the same 16 Y-STR haplotype. In an autosomal STR exclusion case with a W = 99.995% (without considering the exclusion systems), the same Y-STR haplotype was obtained between the excluded alleged father and the child, suggesting the same paternal lineage.

The 16 Y-chromosome STR haplotype seems to be extremely helpful in population studies to determine specific region characteristics and in forensic cases to obtain unique paternal lineage profiles.

References

[1] L. Gusmão, A. González-Neira, C. Pestoni, M. Brión, M.V. Lareu, A. Carracedo, Robustness of the Y STRs DYS19, DYS389I and II, DYS390 and DYS 393: optimization of a PCR pentaplex, Forensic Sci. Int. 106 (1999) 163–172.

[2] D. Ballard, C. Phillips, C. Thacker, C. Robson, D. Syndercombe Court, Haplotype discrimination amongst three UK population groups using three multiplexes to type eleven Y chromosome STRs, Int. Congr. Ser. 1239 (2003) 435–437.

[3] L. Gusmão, et al., Results of the GEP-ISFG collaborative study on the Y chromosome STRs GATA A10, GATA C4, GATA H4, DYS437, DYS438, DYS439, DYS460 and DYS461: population data, Forensic Sci. Int. 135 (2003) 150–157.

[4] P. Sánchez-Diz, et al., Results of the GEP-ISFG collaborative study on the Y-STRs tetraplexes: GEPY I (DYS461, GATA C4, DYS437 and DYS438) and GEPY II (DYS460, GATA A10, GATA H4, DYS439), Forensic Sci. Int. 135 (2003) 158–162.

ELSEVIER

International Congress Series 1261 (2004) 322–324

www.ics-elsevier.com

Simultaneous PCR of eight loci for very short Y-STR fragment size

K. Tsukada*, K. Takayanagi, H. Asamura, M. Ota, K. Kobayashi, H. Fukushima

Department of Legal Medicine, Shinshu University School of Medicine, Asahi 3-1-1, Matsumoto, Nagano 390-8621, Japan

Abstract. We selected the DYS19, DYS385, DYS389, DYS390, DYS392, DYS393, DYS483, and amelogenin loci, and designed a new pair of primers to minimize the fragment sizes of these loci as much as possible. As a consequence, these loci were able to detect in the range of 79–259 bp using multiplex PCR amplification. The optimum DNA amount was 100 pg to 10 ng. The haplotype diversity was 0.9979.

Keywords: Y-STR; Degraded DNA; Multiplex PCR; Sexual crime

1. Introduction

Y-STRs are very important tools for identifying perpetrators of sexual crimes, as only males, the most common perpetrators of such crimes, have Y-chromosomes. In a previous paper, we showed the importance of making the STR fragment size small to enable the typing of degraded specimens [1]. In this study, we selected nine loci and designed a new pair of Y-STR primers to minimize the fragment sizes of these loci as much as possible, relative to previously reported fragment sizes. These loci are very popular throughout the world; further, they feature many alleles with little deviation between allele frequencies. In this experiment, we performed multiplex PCR using DNA extracted from mixed stains.

2. Materials and methods

For minimum-sample studies and mixed-sample studies, blood was provided by a healthy male and female. For allele frequency studies, 103 bloodstains from unrelated male individuals were stored at -80 °C. For sex-crime studies, four vaginal stains were stored at -80 °C for 4 years. DNA extraction was performed as described previously [1]. For vaginal stains, the DNA extraction procedure was performed by the one-step method

* Corresponding author. Tel.: +81-263-37-3218; fax: +81-263-37-3084.
E-mail address: tuk-lab@mxl.avis.ne.jp (K. Tsukada).

0531-5131/
doi:10.1016/j.ics.2003.11.015

and the traditional two-step method [2]. Multiplex PCR was carried out using the primers as follows:

DYS19-A VIC-GTGTTTTAGATAGATAGATAGG
DYS19-B GTTTGGGTTAAGGAGAGTGTCAC
DYS385-A 6FAM-TTACATAGTCCTCCTTTCTTTT
DYS385-B GTTTAGAAAGAGGAAAGAGAAAGAAAGGA
DYS389-A PET-CCAACTCTCATCTGTATTATCTATG
DYS389-B GTTTGATGGACTGCTAGATAAATA
DYS390-A 6-FAM-TATATTTACACATTTTTGGGCC
DYS390-B GTTTGCTATGTGTATACTCAGAAAC
DYS392-A NED-CAAATTTTTTCCTTGTATCACCATTT
DYS392-B GTTTAAACCTACCAATCCCATTCCTT
DYS393-A NED-GTGGTCTTCTACTTGTGTCAATAC [3]
DYS393-B GTTTACTCAAGTCCAAAAAATGAGG [3]
DYS439-A VIC-ACATAGGTGGAGACAGATAGATGAT [4]
DYS439-B GTTTGCCTGGCTTCCAATTCTTTT [4]
Amelogenin-A PET-GGGCTCTGTAAAGAATAGTG
Amelogenin-B GTTTGGTAGGAACTGTAAAT

In order to completely induce adenylation, the 5′ end of each reverse primer was modified [1]. PCR reaction was performed with a total volume of 30 μl, containing 1–5 ng of genomic DNA, × 1 PCR reaction buffer, 0.2 mg/ml of BSA, 0.2 mM of dNTPs, 1.0 u of AmpliTaq Gold polymerase, 2 mM of $MgCl_2$, 0.083 μM DYS19, 0.216 μM DYS385, 0.108 μM DYS389, 0.082 μM DYS390, 0.116 μM DYS392, 0.058 μM DYS393, 0.058 μM DYS439, and 0.1 μM Amelogenin. The cycling parameters were pre-PCR-denaturation at 95 °C for 12 min, followed by 32 cycles of 94 ° C for 45 s, 56 °C for 45 s, 72 °C for 30 s using a TP-3000 (Takara Ohtsu, Japan). A final extension was performed at 72 °C for 10 min. The detection of signals was performed using the ABI PRISM 310 Genetic Analyzer. Fragment sizes were determined using the internal standard GeneScan 500 LIZ. AMale-Plex and Male-Plex with/without amelogenin loci, respectively. In order to determine the minimum quantity of DNA required to obtain reliable results, we used male DNA sequentially diluted with distilled water. Mixtures of male and female DNA were prepared in ratios from 1:1 (100 pg/100 pg) to 1:50,000 (100 pg/5000 ng).

3. Results

This multiplex system was not typed, except for amelogenin locus using female DNA. The gene diversity of DYS19, DYS385, DYS389 I, DYS389 II, DYS390, DYS392, DYS393, and DYS439 loci were 0.6471, 0.9532, 0.6832, 0.7868, 0.7860, 0.6762, 0.5469, and 0.5176, respectively. The computed haplotype diversity was 0.9979. When the ratio of the amount of female DNA was increased and PCR amplification was carried out using AMale-Plex, a non-specific peak was observed. Therefore, PCR reaction was performed using Male-Plex. In both cases, the optimum DNA amount in the range was 100 pg to 10 ng (Fig. 1). In the case of Male-Plex, when 100 pg of male DNA was used in

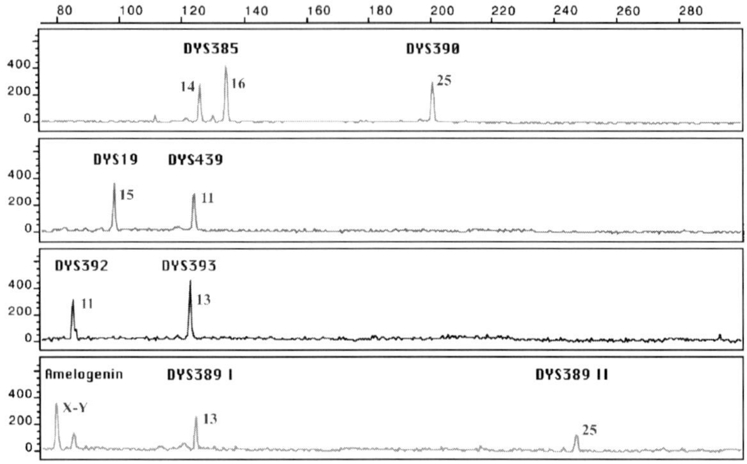

Fig. 1. Electropherogram of AMale-Plex. PCR amplification carried out using 100 pg of male DNA as a template.

1000 ng of female DNA, the allele typing was completely successful. In sex-crime sample studies, all of the vaginal stains were typed as the same alleles by both the one- and two-step extraction procedures.

4. Discussion

It is possible to easily and effectively perform typing using limited samples, as AMale-Plex and Male-Plex were detectable in a DNA amount of 100 pg as a template. In cases in which it is clear that the male DNA is not mixed with female DNA, although the sex of specimens is unknown, PCR reaction can be performed using AMale-Plex. When female DNA amplified by AMale-Plex is used, although all of the Y-loci are not amplified, as the amelogenin locus is amplified by female DNA, the advantage of being able to check whether a PCR reaction is successful is provided. However, in male/female mixed stains, it is necessary to perform a PCR reaction using Male-Plex. In the case of mixed stains, as Male-Plex is able to type a very wide range of mix ratios, we showed that it is not necessary to estimate of amount of DNA extracted by the one-step procedure.

We consider that AMale-Plex and Male-Plex will be effective tools for the allele typing of highly degraded specimens, as a new pair of primers has been designed to minimize the fragment sizes of all loci as much as possible, relative to previously reported fragment sizes.

References

[1] K. Tsukada, et al., Multiplex short tandem repeat typing in degraded samples using newly designed primers for TH01, TPOX, CSF1PO, and vWA loci, Legal Med. 4 (2002) 239–245.

[2] K. Yoshida, et al., The modified method of two-step differential extraction of sperm and vaginal epithelial cell DNA from vaginal fluid mixed with semen, Forensic Sci. Int. 72 (1) (1995) 25–33.

[3] B.M. Dupuy, et al., DXYS267: DYS393 and its X chromosome counterpart, Forensic Sci. Int. 112 (2–3) (2000) 111–121.

[4] C.M. Ruitberg, et al., New primer sets for Y chromosome and CODIS STR loci. (Poster presented at the Eleventh International Symposium on Human Identification, Biloxi, MS), 2000.

International Congress Series 1261 (2004) 325–327

www.ics-elsevier.com

Does the Tat polymorphism originate in northern Mongolia?

C. Keyser-Tracqui[a,*], P. Blandin[a], F.X. Ricaut[b], E. Petkovski[a], E. Crubézy[b], B. Ludes[a,b]

[a] *Laboratoire d'Anthropologie Moléculaire, Institut de Médecine Légale, 11, rue Humann, 67000, Strasbourg, France*

[b] *Anthropobiologie, CNRS, UMR 8555, Université Paul Sabatier, Toulouse, France*

Abstract. It has been suggested that the Y-chromosomal T → C transition arose in Mongolia ~2400–4000 years ago. To test this hypothesis, we screened 2300-year-old Mongolian male specimens and ancient Yakut male specimens for this Y-chromosomal marker. Our results demonstrate that the mutation was present in Asia 2300 years ago. © 2003 Elsevier B.V. All rights reserved.

Keywords: Tat polymorphism; Xiongnu; Yakouts; Ancient DNA

1. Introduction

In the past few years, a large number of polymorphic markers have been identified on the Y chromosome. Among these is the T → C transition (locus RBF5) reported by Zerjal et al. [1] and later called the Tat-polymorphism. The C allele of this biallelic marker has so far been observed only in populations from Asia and northern Europe. It reaches its highest frequency in Yakuts, Buryats, northeastern Siberian populations and Finns (Table 1).

Opinions differ about whether the geographic origin of the T → C mutation lies in Asia or northern Eurasia. Zerjal et al. [1] suggested that this mutation first arose in the populations of Central Asia; they proposed Mongolia as a candidate location for the origin of the T → C polymorphism. In contrast, for Lahermo et al. [2] the wide distribution of the mutation in north Eurasian populations suggests that it arose in northern Eurasia. According to them, the estimated time of the C mutation is ~2400–4440 years ago.

In this study, we screened ancient Mongolian samples from the Egyin Gol necropolis for the Tat marker. The Egyin Gol necropolis, located in northern Mongolia, is ~2300 years old and belongs to the Xiongnu culture [3]. In addition, we genotyped

* Corresponding author. Tel.: +33-390-243347; fax: +33-390-243362.
E-mail address: ckeyser@mageos.com (C. Keyser-Tracqui).

doi:10.1016/S0531-5131(03)01701-1

Table 1
Frequency of the Tat C allele in some Eurasian populations including those tested in this study (references are not exhaustive)

Language family	Population	*n*	Frequency (%)	Reference
Mongolic	Buryats	111, 81	57.7, 28.4	[1,6]
	Mongols	47, 148	2.1, 2.7	[1,6]
?	Xiongnu	22	9.1	This study
Chukchi	Chukchi	24	58.3	[7]
Eskimo-Aleut	Siberian Eskimos	22, 33	50.0, 60.6	[6,7]
Turkic	Yakuts	21–35	85.7	[1,8]
		5	100.0	This study
Finno-Ugric	Finns	41	61.1	[2]

the T→C mutation in ancient Yakut specimens excavated at two sites in the Sakha Republic (Yakutia) [4].

2. Material and methods

The ancient Xiongnu sample was composed of 22 male specimens recovered from the Egyin Gol necropolis (Lake Baïkal region) [3]. The ancient Yakut sample comprised five male specimens from two burial sites (At-Dabaan and Sytygane Syhe) located 30 km from Yakutsk, the capital of the Sakha Republic. Two of these individuals were recovered from a double grave dated from the late 18th century [4]. The three others were exhumed from three graves dated from the 15th century.

The T→C transition was amplified using the procedure reported by Zerjal et al. [1]. The loci DYS19, DYS390, and DYS39 were analysed as previously described [3]. Locus DYS388 was amplified according to Kayser et al. [5].

3. Results

All of the 5 ancient Yakut samples typed contained the C allele, whereas only 2 of the 22 ancient Egyin Gol samples tested (9.1%) showed the mutation (Table 1).

Among the seven ancient samples harbouring the T→C mutation, only four could be typed at the Y-STR loci DYS19, DYS388, DYS390 and DYS391. For all of them, the haplotype obtained was 14-12-23-11 which corresponds to the haplotype 11-11-10-11 reported by Lell et al. [7].

4. Discussion

The frequency of the Tat C allele is high in the Yakut population but the origin(s) of this allele is unclear. The Yakuts are thought to have migrated northwards from the vicinity of Lake Baïkal to the reaches of the Lena River during the 13th and 14th centuries. They were probably driven out by the Buryat and other Mongol conquerors.

All of the seven ancient Yakut individuals tested showed the C allele, confirming that the mutation occurred most probably before their migration from southern regions. Concerning the Xiongnu people, two of them harboured the mutation suggesting that the Tat polymorphism already existed in Mongolia 2300 years ago.

Amplification of four additional polymorphic markers revealed that the Xiongnu and the Yakut individuals belong to the same Tat-C haplotype (11-11-10-11 according to Ref. [7]). This haplotype is not the ancestral one but is the most frequent in native Siberian populations [7].

Since we previously obtained the mitochondrial DNA sequences of the two ancient Egyin Gol specimens bearing the C allele [3] we could also note that the HV1 sequence of one of them perfectly matched two samples from a present-day Yakut population [9].

In conclusion, our study showed that the C allele was present in parent populations to the modern inhabitants of Mongolia or Yakutia, suggesting that the mutation may have arisen in Mongolia more than 2400 years ago [1]. Moreover, our work suggests that the Xiongnu tribe under study may have been composed of some of the ancestors of the present-day Yakut population.

Acknowledgements

This work was made in the framework of the ACI «Espaces et Territoires: le complexe spatial Altaï-Baïkal. Plaque tournante des flux géniques en Haute Asie de la période protohistorique à l'époque moderne».

References

[1] T. Zerjal, B. Dashnyam, A. Pandya, M. Kayser, L. Roewer, F.R. Santos, et al., Genetic relationships of Asians and Northern Europeans, revealed by Y-chromosomal DNA analysis, Am. J. Hum. Genet. 60 (1997) 1174–1183.

[2] P. Lahermo, M.-L. Savontaus, P. Sistonen, J. Béres, P. de Knijff, P. Aula, A. Sajantila, Y-chromosomal polymorphisms reveal founding lineages in the Finns and the Saami, Eur. J. Hum. Genet. 7 (1999) 447–458.

[3] C. Keyser-Tracqui, E. Crubézy, B. Ludes, Nuclear and mitochondrial DNA analysis of a 2000-year-old necropolis in the Egyin Gol valley of Mongolia, Am. J. Hum. Genet. 73 (2003) 247–260.

[4] F.-X. Ricaut, O. Safedoseva, C. Keyser-Tracqui, E. Crubézy, B. Ludes, in press. Genetic analysis of human remains found in two medieval Yakut graves (At-Dabaan site, 18th century), Int. J. Legal. Med.

[5] M. Kayser, A. Caglià, D. Corach, N. Fretwell, C. Gehrig, G. Graziosi, et al., Evaluation of Y-chromosomal STRs: a multicenter study, Int. J. Leg. Med. 110 (1997) 125–133.

[6] T.M. Karafet, S.L. Zegura, O. Posukh, L. Osipova, A. Bergen, J. Long, et al., Ancestral Asian source(s) of New World Y-chromosome founder haplotype, Am. J. Hum. Genet. 64 (1999) 817–831.

[7] J.T. Lell, R.I. Sukernik, Y.B. Starikovskaya, B.L. Su, L. Jin, T.G. Schurr, et al., The dual origin and Siberian affinities of Native American Y chromosomes, Am. J. Hum. Genet. 70 (2002) 192–206.

[8] B. Pakendorf, B. Morar, L.A. Tarskaia, M. Kaiser, L. Jin, T.G. Schurr, et al., The dual origin and Siberian affinities of Native American Y chromosomes, Am. J. Hum. Genet. 70 (2002) 192–206.

[9] B. Pakendorf, V. Wiebe, L.A. Tarskaia, V.A. Spitsyn, H. Soodyal, A. Rodewald, M. Stoneking, Mitochondrial DNA evidence for admixed origins of Central Siberian population, Am. J. Phys. Anthropol. 120 (2003) 211–224.

International Congress Series 1261 (2004) 328–330

www.ics-elsevier.com

SNP and STR Y chromosome markers in the Canary Islands population

J.J. Sanchez[a,*], A. Hernandez[b], C. Børsting[a], A. Zurita[b], I. Mamely[b], N. Morling[a]

[a] *Department of Forensic Genetics, Institute of Forensic Medicine, University of Copenhagen, 11 Frederik V's Vej 11, DK-2100, Copenhagen, Denmark*

[b] *Departamento de Canarias, La Laguna, Instituto Nacional de Toxicología, Tenerife, Spain*

Abstract. Single nucleotide polymorphism (SNP) typing was done with a PCR-based assay with co-amplification of 25 DNA fragments and detection of 35 Y chromosome SNPs by means of minisequencing with Snapshot technique. The Y SNP package can identify 34 Y chromosome haplogroups including the majority of the Y chromosome haplogroups of interest in the Canary Islands population. A total of 348 and 269 unrelated Canary Islands males were typed for 35 Y-SNPs and 8 Y-STRs, respectively. We observed 16 Y chromosome SNP haplogroups with frequencies from 0.3% to 48%. The majority of the individuals carried the Y chromosome haplogroup R1b or I of European origin while ~ 13% and ~ 7% of the Y chromosome haplogroups found indicated African and Middle Eastern heritage. Further diversity was detected when additional typing of Y chromosome STR markers was performed.

Keywords: Y chromosome; Single nucleotide polymorphism; Multiplex PCR; Minisequencing; Canary Islands

1. Introduction

Y chromosome-specific single nucleotide polymorphisms (SNPs) are particularly useful for identification of stable paternal lineages because of their low rate of parallel and back mutations. By testing highly polymorphic Y-STR markers in addition to the Y-SNP markers, an even more detailed DNA profile can be obtained. Here, we have typed 35 Y-SNP and 8 Y-STR markers in a population from the Canary Islands.

2. Materials and methods

DNA samples from unrelated males from Canary Islands were typed for 35 Y chromosome SNPs (348 individuals) and for 8 Y-STRs (269 individuals). SNP typing was done as previously described [1]. The minimal Y-STR haplotype was analyzed

* Corresponding author. Tel.: +45-35326225; fax: +45-35326120.
E-mail address: juan.sanchez@forensic.ku.dk (J.J. Sanchez).

0531-5131/
doi:10.1016/S0531-5131(03)01634-0

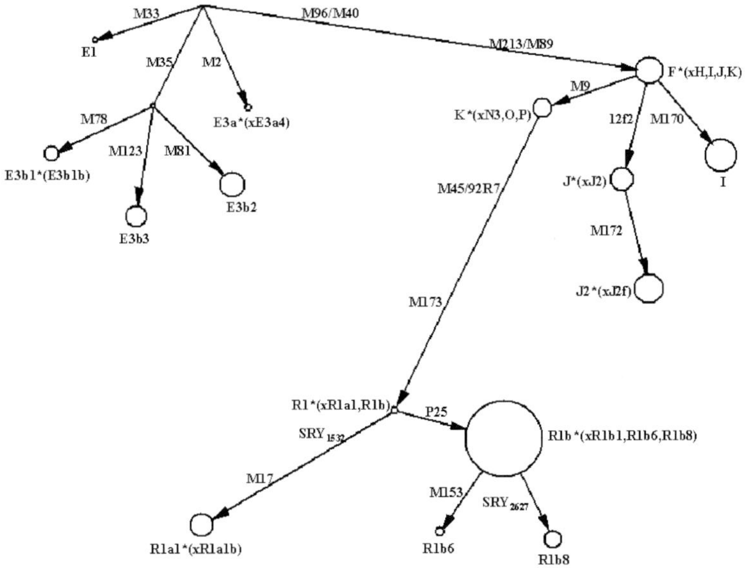

Fig. 1. Median-joining network based on 35 Y chromosome SNPs. The area of each circle is proportional to the frequency. The arrows indicate the likely direction of mutation events according to the YCC tree (2002).

following the protocol recommended by the International Forensic Y-User Group. Median-joining network was calculated using the program Network 3.111.

3. Results

We used the 35 Y-SNP package to type 348 unrelated Canary Islands males, and we observed 16 different haplogroups. Most of the haplogroups were one-step derivatives (Fig. 1). Haplogroup frequencies from 0.3% to 48% were identified. Two large haplogroups

Table 1
Observed SNP haplogroups and STR haplotypes among 269 Canary Islands people

Haplogroups	*N*	Frequency (%)	Number of different Y-STR haplotypes
E1	1	0.4	1
E3a*(xE3a4)	2	0.7	2
E3b*	1	0.4	1
E3b1*(E3b1b)	5	1.9	5
E3b2	19	7.1	11
E3b3	7	2.6	6
F*(xH,I,J,K)	15	5.6	12
I	30	11.2	27
J*(xJ2)	11	4.1	9
J2*(xJ2f)	15	5.6	14
K*(xN3,O,P)	10	3.7	9
R1*(xR1a1,R1b)	2	0.7	2
R1a1*(xR1a1b)	15	5.6	12
R1b*(xR1b1,R1b6,R1b8)	125	46.5	75
R1b6	3	1.1	3
R1b8	8	3.0	7

Table 2
Y-STR haplotypes that occurred three or more times in the most frequent haplogroups

Haplogroup	Allele at								Frequency
	DYS 19	DYS 389 I	DYS 389 II	DYS 390	DYS 391	DYS 392	DYS 393	DYS 385 I/II	
E3b2	13	14	30	24	9	11	13	13,14	5/19
E3b2	13	14	30	23	9	12	13	13,14	3/19
I	15	13	28	23	11	12	15	15,16	3/30
R1b*(xR1b1,R1b6,R1b8)	14	13	29	24	11	13	13	11,14	12/125
R1b*(xR1b1,R1b6,R1b8)	14	14	30	24	11	13	13	11,14	7/125
R1b*(xR1b1,R1b6,R1b8)	14	13	30	24	11	13	13	11,14	6/125
R1b*(xR1b1,R1b6,R1b8)	14	13	29	24	11	13	13	11,15	5/125
R1b*(xR1b1,R1b6,R1b8)	14	12	27	24	10	14	12	11,14	3/125
R1b*(xR1b1,R1b6,R1b8)	14	13	29	23	11	13	13	11,14	3/125
R1b*(xR1b1,R1b6,R1b8)	14	13	29	24	10	13	13	10,16	3/125
R1b*(xR1b1,R1b6,R1b8)	14	13	29	24	11	13	13	10,15	3/125
R1b*(xR1b1,R1b6,R1b8)	14	13	29	25	10	13	13	11,14	3/125
R1b*(xR1b1,R1b6,R1b8)	14	14	30	24	11	13	13	11,17	3/125

STR alleles are indicated by the number of repetitions.

assigned to the European lineage were found: R1b*(xR1b1,R1b6,R1b8) (47.6%) and I (9.7%). The major haplogroup E (~ 13%) and haplogroup J2*(xJ2f) (6.9%) was also detected. In addition to the SNP analysis, 269 of the samples were also typed for eight Y-STRs. A total of 190 different Y-STR haplotypes were observed; thus 79 males did not have an unique STR haplotype within this population (Tables 1 and 2). The 79 males without a unique haplotype belonged to 34 different haplotype groups. By combining SNP and STR results, the 79 males were divided into 40 haplotype groups.

4. Discussion

In the population from Canary Islands analysed here, almost half of the males belong to the haplogroup R1b and in most of the individuals where a unique haplotype could not be assigned to a sample, the individual belonged to this haplogroup. Additionally, we typed the minimal Y-STR haplotype defined in the European reference database (http://ystr.org). Only 70% of the 269 individuals had a unique haplotype. The combined use of Y-SNP and Y-STR markers increased the number of different haplotypes. However, it is clear that additional SNP markers are needed before the full potential of SNP markers can be exploited in forensic caseworks from Canary Islands.

Acknowledgements

We thank Ms. Annemette Holbo Birk for technical assistance. The work was supported by grants to Juan Sanchez from Ellen and Aage Andersen's Foundation, and from the "Consejeria de Educacion y Cultura (DGUI), Gobierno de Canarias" (PI2000/053), Spain. Ada Zurita is a fellow of the "Cabildo de Tenerife", Spain.

Reference

[1] J.J. Sanchez, C. Børsting, C. Hallenberg, A. Buchard, A. Hernandez, N. Morling, Multiplex PCR and mini-sequencing of SNPs—a model with 35 Y chromosome SNPs, Forensic Sci. Int. (2003) (in press).

International Congress Series 1261 (2004) 331–333

www.ics-elsevier.com

SNP genotyping with single base extension-tag microarrays

B. Sobrino, M. Lareu*, M. Brion, A. Carracedo

Institute of Legal Medicine, Unit of Forensic Genetics, Faculty of Medicine, University of Santiago de Compostela, San Francisco 15782, Santiago de Campostela, Spain

Abstract. During the last few years, there is an increasing interest in the use of Single Nucleotide Polymorphisms (SNPs) for forensic purposes as an alternative to STR analysis. At this moment, development of SNP genotyping technologies to analyse several markers in the same reaction with high accuracy, simplicity and reasonable cost is the key to progress in SNP typing for forensic genetics. A promising approach for this purpose is DNA microarrays. We have developed a microarray for typing a set of 29 Y-chromosome SNPs for European populations. Single Base Extension and Tags (SBE-Tag) has been the strategy selected. © 2004 Elsevier B.V. All rights reserved.

Keywords: Single nucleotide polymorphism (SNP); Y-chromosome; Microarrays; Single base extension (SBE)

1. Introduction

Single Nucleotide Polymorphisms (SNPs) represent the most abundant source of sequence variation in the human genome. This feature together with their low mutation rate and their simplicity make these markers suitable for forensic applications. Many methods are currently available for characterizing known SNPs [2]. The strategy selected for typing a set of 29 Y-chromosome SNPs is SBE-Tag [3]. With this method, SNPs are genotyped by minisequencing using primers with a 5′ tag sequence. Each SNP has its own specific tag. The multiplex SBE reaction is performed in solution and is analysed after hybridisation to a generic tag array. The use of tags allows us to use the same tag array to genotype different sets of SNPs for different purposes. The "array of arrays" concept [4] allows the simultaneous analysis on different samples in the same slide, saving money and time.

2. Material and methods

Oligonucleotides complementary to the tags of the SBE primers, with a stretch of 15 dT residues followed by a NH2 group at the 3′ end, were spotted onto CodeLink slides

* Corresponding author. Tel.: +34-981582327; fax: +34-981580336.
E-mail address: apimllar@usc.es (M. Lareu).

doi:10.1016/j.ics.2003.12.002

(Amersham Bioscience) with the Affymetrix 417 Arrayer. After spotting, the slides were prepared as described in the product protocol.

The 29 Y-SNPs were divided in 4 multiplexes. Each PCR reaction was performed in 25 μl using 1 × PCR buffer, 300 μM of dNTPs, 2 mM of MgCl2, 0.1–0.5 μM of primers, 2U of AmpliTaq Gold DNA polymerase (Applied Biosystem) and 10 ng of DNA. The PCR conditions were 95 °C for 10 min, 32 cycles of 94 °C for 30 s, 59 °C for 30 s, 70 °C for 30 s and a final extension at 65 °C for 15 min. The sequences of PCR and minisequencing primers are available from the authors upon request. The four PCR products were mixed and evaporated to a final volume of 20 μl to concentrate the sample. 4 μl of Exo-SapIT (Amersham Bioscience) were added to 10 μl of mixed PCR products and incubated at 37 °C for 15 min followed by 85 °C for 15 min.

2.5 μl of the treated PCR product was added to 10 μl of a SBE reaction mix containing 1X Thermosequenase buffer, 0.25 μmol of each TAG-SBE primer, 2U of Thermosequenase (APB) and one of the four JOE-labelled ddNTP and the other three ddNTPs unlabelled at a concentration of 0.5 μmol. The SBE reaction consisted of 30 cycles of primer extension (96 °C for 30 s, 50 °C for 30 s and 60 °C for 30 s).

The hybridization was performed as described on the slide protocol. The volume involved in the hybridization reaction was 7 μl of SBE products mixed with 8 μl of hybridization buffer. Arrays were scanned using the Affymetrix 418 Scanner, and analysed using ImaGene 4.1 (BioDiscovery).

3. Results and discussion

We selected 29 Y-chromosome SNPs, which appear to be the most important for European populations [1]. These SNPs were divided into 4 multiplex PCR reactions. The four PCR products were pooled in order to be used as template for the multiplex SBE reaction. The use of SBE-Tag strategy allows us to use a standard array of generic tags, which eliminates the need to design and manufacture custom arrays for specific sets of markers. The tags are immobilized covalently on microscope slides in an "array of arrays" format (Fig. 1) [4].

Fig. 2 shows the results of a sample. Four SBE reactions were performed per sample, one for each labelled ddNTP because only one fluorescent label for ddNTPs was used. We obtained results for 24 of 29 SNPs, although the signal of some SNPs needs to be

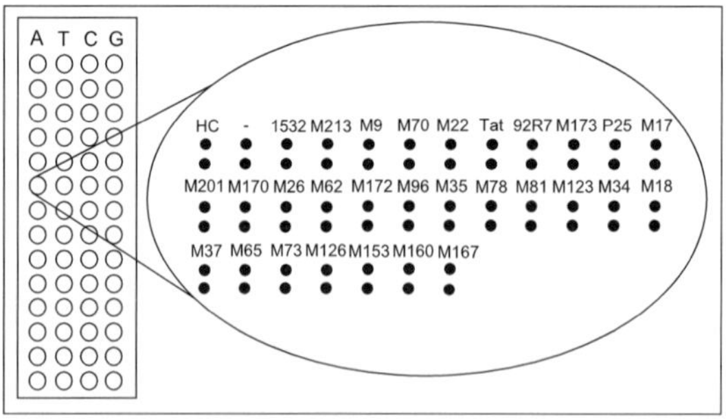

Fig. 1. Representation of an "array of arrays" format [4].

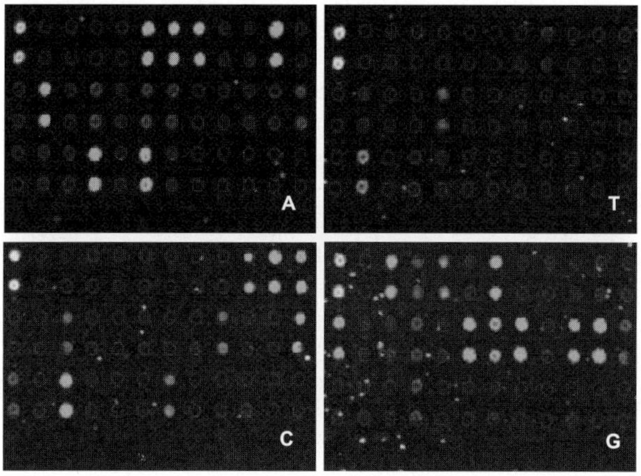

Fig. 2. Results of a sample.

increased. P25 shows signal in panels A and C because it is duplicated. However, the G signal of M22 is because of self-complementary of the primer.

In the light of the results, the SNP genotyping with SBE-Tag microarray is a promising strategy for different applications where a large number of SNPs are required such as forensic genetics. Nevertheless, much work remains to be done to validate SNP typing methods before they can be used in routine forensic analysis.

Acknowledgements

This work was supported by grants from Xunta de Galicia ((PGIDT01PXI20806 PR) and Ministerio de Educación y Ciencia (DGCYT.P4.BIO2000-0145-P4-02). B.S. has a fellowship from the Ramón Areces Foundation.

References

[1] The Y Chromosome Consortium. A nomenclature system for the tree of human Y-chromosomal binary haplogroups, Genome Research 12 (2002) 339–348.

[2] A.C. Syvanen, Accessing genetic variation: genotyping single nucleotide polymorphisms, Nature Reviews 2 (2001) 930–942.

[3] J.N. Hirschorn, et al., SBE-TAGS: an array-based method for efficient single nucleotide polymorphism genotyping, PNAS 97 (22) (2000) 12164–12169.

[4] T. Pastinen, et al., A system for specific, high-throughput genotyping by allele-specific primer extension on micorarrays, Genome Research 10 (2000) 1031–1042.

International Congress Series 1261 (2004) 334–336

www.ics-elsevier.com

SNP-genotyping on human Y-chromosome for forensic purposes: comparison of two different methods

R. Lessig[a,*], J. Edelmann[a], M. Zoledziewska[b], T. Dobosz[b], K. Fahr[c], M. Kostrzewa[c]

[a] Institute of Legal Medicine, University of Leipzig, Johannisallee 28, D-04103 Leipzig, Germany
[b] Institute of Legal Medicine, Medical University of Wroclaw, Poland
[c] Bruker Daltonik GmbH, Leipzig, Germany

Abstract. Y-chromosomal DNA polymorphisms and especially the Y-STRs are well established for forensic routine casework. Concern of our study was to use Y-SNPs for forensic purposes, which are mainly investigated in molecular anthropology for evolutionary studies. We compared two minisequencing methods with different detection principles.

Keywords: Y-chromosomal SNP; Minisequencing; SNaPshot; MALDI-TOF MS

1. Introduction

Whereas short tandem repeats on the human Y-chromosome (Y-STRs) are well established in forensic routine casework, Y-chromosomal single nucleotide polymorphisms (Y-SNPs) are mostly used in molecular anthropology for evolutionary research up to now. In recent studies, several Y-SNPs have been shown to be potentially useful for forensic purposes, as well. In the field of forensic routine, methods for genotyping Y-SNPs have to comply with strong quality requirements. In particular, high efficiency in the analysis of minimal DNA-amounts, extremely high reliability, automation and high-throughput capability as well as cost-efficient tests are important in forensic work. According to an international study by Kayser et al. (personal communication), eight Y-chromosomal SNPs were chosen and combined in a hierarchical system to two multiplex reactions: M9mut (M9, M74, M173, M46, M17) and M9anc (M170, M172, M35), respectively. The hierarchical genotyping strategy allows a correlation of samples to different European haplogroups. In a proof-of-principle study, the samples from four different European populations were analysed with both methods.

* Corresponding author. Tel.: +493419715118; fax: +493419715109.
E-mail address: lesr@medizin.uni-leipzig.de (R. Lessig).

0531-5131/
doi:10.1016/S0531-5131(03)01778-3

2. Materials and methods

Samples from routine casework were analysed. DNA extraction was performed using the QIAamp DNA Blood Kit (Qiagen, Hilden, Germany). To amplify the targeted sequences of DNA, the set of Y-SNPs chosen by M. Kayser (personal communication) was used. The sequences of the primers following M9: Kayser et al. (2000), M74: Kayser (pers. comm.), M46: Zerjal et al. (1997), M17, M172: Cordeaux (pers. comm.) and M173, M170, M35: unpublished. Allele identification was achieved by PCR amplification of 10–50 ng of genomic DNA.

2.1. SNaPshot minisequencing

The amplified products were purified from dNTPs and primers by shrimp alkaline phosphatase (SAP) and exonuclease I (EXO I) treatment to avoid participation in the subsequent primer-extension reaction. For the minisequencing reaction, the commercial kit SNaPshot Multiplex of ABI was used. After the extension and labelling reaction, the unincorporated ddNTPs were removed by enzymatic treatment using 0.2 U of SAP to avoid comigration of [F] ddNTPs with the fragment of interest. The sequences of the SNaPshot primers are of all markers are self-designed for a length of the product between 19 and 61 bp (Fig. 1).

2.2. Electrophoresis and detection

The products were analyzed on the ABI Prism™ 310/ABI Prism™ 3100 Avant Genetic Analyzers.

For MALDI-TOF MS-based Y SNP genotyping, the PCR-products containing the polymorphic site were treated with SAP and EXO I. In the following primer extension reaction, special primers with a biotin label at the 5′ end and a photocleavable building block at position 8 or 9 from the 3′ end were used. The extension primers hybridized directly adjacent to the SNP and were extended allelespecific by one nucleotide. Subsequently, the primer extension products were purified using the Bruker genostrep™ purification system. There by, the primer extension products were bound to streptavidin coated microtiter plates, salts and other undesirable components were removed by washing

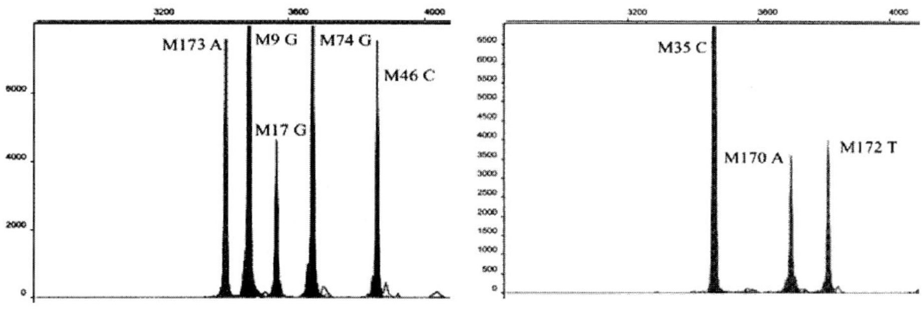

Fig. 1. Left: result of a pentaplex-reaction. Right: result of a triplex-reaction.

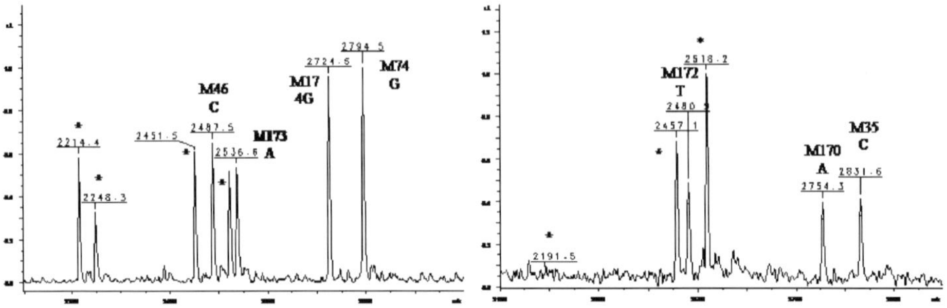

Fig. 2. Left: result of a quadruplex-reaction. Right: result of a triplex-reaction. The peaks marked with (*) show the remaining primers and the peaks labelled with the respective SNP and the genotype represent the primer extension products in all mass spectra.

and finally the purification plate was exposed to UV-light (366 nm, UV unit CL-366™, Bruker). Via UV-cleavage the 3′ part of the primer extension products containing the genotyping information was released to the elution buffer and could be transferred to the MALDI-TOF MS sample carrier. The shortened primer extension products were measured subsequently in a Bruker autoflex™ mass spectrometer in linear mode using 3-hydroxypicolinic acid (3-HPA) as matrix (Fig. 2).

3. Results

Fig. 1 shows results of the minisequencing with SNaPshot-reaction. An example of the pentaplex (left) shows the samples belong to the haplogroup Eu13/14 following the definition of Semino et al. (2000). In contrast, a result of the triplex for a sample of the haplogroup Eu4 is shown on the right.

Alternatively, Fig. 2 shows results of MALDI-TOF MS Y-SNP genotyping of the same samples. On the left the quadruplex-reaction (M74, M173, M46 and M17) detecting a sample representing the haplogroup Eu13/14 and on the right a result of the triplex-reaction (M35, M170, M172) of a sample representing the haplogroup Eu4.

4. Discussion

The results of our study show, that both fluorescent-based minisequencing using the ABI Prism SNaPshot multiplex kit and the MALDI-TOF MS-based genotyping in combination with the Bruker genoSNIP assay are well suited for genotyping Y-SNP markers. The European haplogroups could be accurately genotyped with the presented multiplex assays using both methods. The sample preparation procedure of both systems comprising PCR, SAP/*Exo*I-digest and single base extension reaction are very similar. To apply the SNaPshot minisequencing multiplex kit, the same equipment can be used as for genotyping STRs. The analysis costs for genotyping Y-SNPs are in the same range as for STR-analysis. In comparison to SNaPshot minisequencing, genotyping of Y-SNPs using the genoSNIP assay based on MALDI-TOF MS is less time consuming. Up to 384 samples can be prepared in parallel automatically using a dedicated pipetting robot (Bruker puredisk™) and measured with high accuracy and speed in the mass spectrometer.

International Congress Series 1261 (2004) 337–339

www.ics-elsevier.com

Validation of the Y-Plex 6™ kit

C. Gehrig*, A. Teyssier

Forensic Genetics, Institute of Legal Medicine, 9 Avenue de Champel, Geneva 1211, Switzerland

Abstract. With the aim of using Y-chromosomal polymorphic markers in Swiss crime cases and deficiency paternity cases, a validation study of the Y-Plex 6™ kit (Reliagene) was performed. The Y-Plex 6 kit is a commercial multiplex system for the simultaneous analysis of six tetranucleotide STR loci (DYS393, DYS19, DYS389II, DYS390, DYS391 and DYS385). In this study, we present the results of some forensic validation studies including the following aspects: sensitivity, influence of the increase of number of cycles (28–34 cycles), evaluation of stutter peaks, specificity study for different amounts of female DNA, analysis of female/male mixtures, analysis of male/male mixtures, analysis of father–son pairs, a forensic case application and quality control.

Keywords: Y-STR; Validation study; Forensic analysis

1. Introduction

Y-chromosomal STR polymorphisms are of increasing interest in the forensic field because of their possible application in stain analyses and in deficiency paternity cases. Since the majority of sexual offenses have a male perpetrator and a female victim, using Y-chromosome specific primers can improve the chances of being able to detect small amounts of perpetrator DNA in a high background of heterologous female DNA. We used the commercial kit Y-Plex 6™ developed by Reliagene. The PCR was carried out following the amplification conditions recommended by the manufacturer. Fragments were analyzed on an ABI310 instrument.

2. Sensitivity

Robust and reproducible amplification results for all six loci were obtained for a DNA template input of 150 pg (30 cycles) (Fig. 1). Increasing the number of cycles (32–34) made it possible to increase the sensitivity to amounts of < 150 pg.

* Corresponding author. Tel.: +41-22-379-55-80; fax: +41-22-372-96-53.
E-mail address: christian.gehrig@hcuge.ch (C. Gehrig).

0531-5131/ © 2003 Elsevier B.V. All rights reserved.
doi:10.1016/S0531-5131(03)01499-7

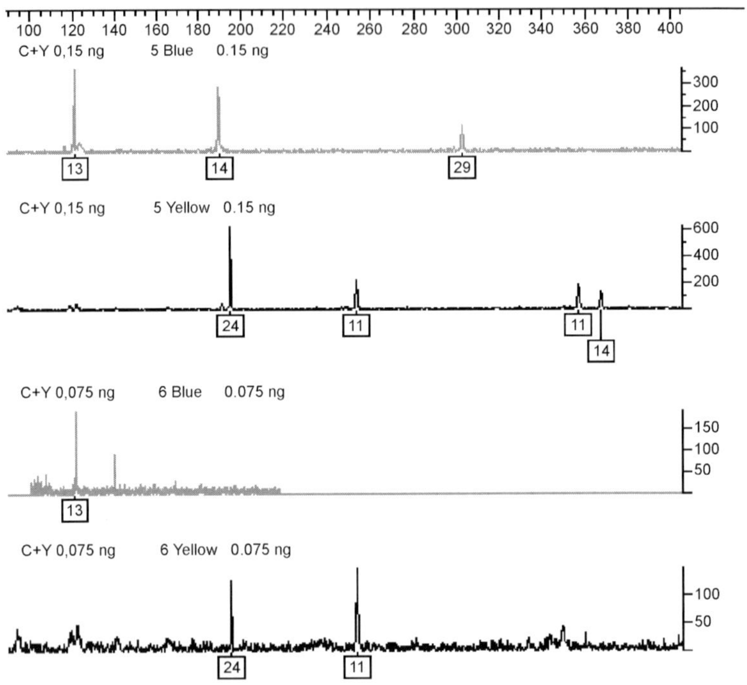

Fig. 1. 0.15 and 0.075 ng at 30 cycles.

3. Stutter peaks

Analysis of stutter peaks was calculated as the peak height of the stutter/peak height of the true allele of each locus (%). The stutter percentage is dependant on the allele length, the larger fragments having the highest stutter percentage. The locus DYS389II has the highest stutter percentage of all six loci, between 10% and 13%; this may complicate the interpretation of mixtures of male DNA.

4. Specificity: female DNA

Female DNA in concentrations ranging from 2 to 50 ng were amplified. When the input of female DNA was higher than 2 ng, two nonspecific peaks using the TAMRA dye (yellow) were observed. The first was at 255.8 bp. This peak was in the range of the DYS391 marker but not in an allelic window. A second constant nonspecific peak was observed at 450 bp, clearly outside the range of the DYS385 locus.

5. Specificity: mixture male/female DNA

The male/female mixtures were prepared in the proportions 1:0, 1:1, 1:5 and 1:20. A complete male profile was detected in male/female mixture samples down to the 1:20 ratio, which contained 1 ng of male DNA and 20 ng of female DNA.

6. Selectivity: mixture male/male DNA

The male/male mixtures were prepared in the proportions 1:0, 19:1, 9:1, 4:1, 2:1, 1:1, 1:2, 1:4, 1:9, 1:19 and 0:1. Male No. 2 showed not one but two alleles at the DYS389II locus (30 and 32), due probably to a duplication of the locus. The results indicated that the quantities of amplified products are generally proportional to the DNA present in the mixture. The complete DNA profile of male 2 was detected in mixtures up to 1:4 (male No. 2: male No. 1). An incomplete DNA profile of male 2 was detected in a mixture of 1:9 (male No. 2/male No. 1).

7. Father–son pairs

Twenty-five Swiss father–son pairs were typed; no inconsistencies were found. The father–son pairs had previously been investigated for 15 autosomal STRs, with paternity indices exceeding 100 000.

8. Swiss population data

Swiss population data have already been published [1,2].

9. Forensic case application

As an example of the application of Y-STRs, a case study is provided. Two blood stains found at a crime scene were typed using the SGM Plus kit. The two profiles were similar; it was suspected that the two men who left the blood stains at the crime scene were brothers. To investigate this theory, the DNA extracts of the crime scene material were typed with the Y-Plex 6™ kit. The two haplotypes were identical and when compared with the Y haplotype reference database (Berlin), a frequency of 0.00028 was calculated. Combining the autosomal data and the Y-STR data, it is extremely likely that the two men who left the blood stains at the crime scene are from the same paternal lineage (i.e. brothers).

10. Quality control

The Y-Plex 6™ kit was successfully used in the following proficiency testing: German proficiency test (GEDNAP 24 and 25), ISFG paternity testing 2003 and a Swiss quality control organized by the Swiss Society of Legal Medicine.

11. Conclusions

Our data indicate that the Y-Plex 6™ kit yielded sensitive (up to 150 pg of male DNA, 30 cycles), reproducible and reliable typing results for forensic casework and deficiency paternity testing.

References

[1] C. Gehrig, M. Hochmeister, B. Budowle, Swiss allele frequencies and haplotypes of 7 Y-Specific STRs, J. Forensic Sci. 45 (2) (2000) 436–439.

[2] L. Roewer, et al., Online reference database of European Y-chromosomal short tandem repeat (STR) haplotypes, Forensic Sci. Int. 118 (2–3) (2001 May 15) 106–113.

International Congress Series 1261 (2004) 340–343

www.ics-elsevier.com

Y-chromosomal STR haplotypes in an Arab population from Yemen

U.-D. Immel*, M. Kleiber, M. Klintschar

Institut für Rechtsmedizin, Martin-Luther University Halle-Wittenberg, Franzosenweg 1, 06112 Halle/Saale, Germany

Abstract. We analysed eight Y-chromosomal STRs (DYS385, DYS19, DYS 389I and II, DYS390, DYS391, DYS392, DYS393) in an Arabic population sample of 128 males from the Sana'a region (Yemen) and found 117 different haplotypes. One hundred five of these haplotypes were never observed in any population study so far.

Keywords: Population data; Microsatellite; Short tandem repeat; Y-chromosome

1. Introduction

Y-chromosomal STRs are increasingly used to study male-specific linkage evolution and for forensic applications [1]. For the last years, worldwide population data have been collected and protocols have been reported. However, forensic application of these linked markers requires knowledge of haplotype frequencies from different populations.

2. Material and methods

In the present study, a set of eight y-chromosomal STR loci (DYS19, DYS389-I, DYS389-II, DYS390, DYS391, DYS392, DYS393, DYS385) were analyzed in an Arabic population sample of 128 males from the Sana'a region. DNA was extracted from 128 unrelated male blood samples according to standard Qiagen procedures QiAmp Blood Kit. Amplifications were performed using fluorescent dye-labelled primers according to Elmoznino and Prinz [2]. The PCR products were analyzed by capillary electrophoresis using the ABI 310® Genetic Analyzer (Applied Biosystems) and genotyper software.

3. Results and discussion

Among the 128 Yemenian males studied 117 different Y-STR haplotypes were observed (Table 1). The most frequent haplotype occurred 4 times.

One feature of Y-STR haplotypes is the region-specific distribution qualifying these loci for estimating the ethnic origin of individuals. To identify haplotypes shared with other populations, searches in the Asian and European Y-STR databanks were performed for each Yemenian haplotype [3,4].

* Corresponding author. Tel.: +49-345-557-1833; fax: +49-345-557-1587.
E-mail address: uta.immel@medizin.uni-halle.de (U.-D. Immel).

0531-5131/
doi:10.1016/S0531-5131(03)01492-4

Table 1
Yemenian Y-STR haplotypes

Sample	DYS 19	DYS 389 I	DYS 389 II	DYS 390	DYS 391	DYS 392	DYS 393	DYS 385 a	DYS 385 b	Sample	DYS 19	DYS 389 I	DYS 389 II	DYS 390	DYS 391	DYS 392	DYS 393	DYS 385 a	DYS 385 b
Y 271	14	13	30	23	10	11	12	15	18	Y 97	13	12	28	23	10	11	13	13	18
Y 140	14	13	30	23	11	11	13	13	17	Y 196	13	12	31	24	11	11	12	13	18
Y 166	14	13	30	24	11	11	12	13	17	Y 369	13	13	29	22	11	11	12	13	13
Y 151	14	13	30	24	11	11	12	13	17	Y 411	13	13	29	23	9	11	13	15	17
Y 1	14	13	30	24	10	11	12	13	18	Y 404	13	13	30	23	9	11	12	13	17
Y 302	14	13	30	24	10	11	13	16	19	Y 63	13	13	30	24	10	11	11	13	17
Y 270	14	13	31	23	11	11	11	13	17	Y 266	13	13	30	24	10	11	13	15	15
Y 93	14	13	31	23	11	11	12	13	18	Y 283	13	13	30	24	10	11	13	17	18
Y 182	14	13	31	23	9	11	13	13	18	Y 301	13	13	30	25	10	11	13	15	16
Y 101	14	14	28	23	10	11	12	13	15	Y 389	13	13	30	25	11	11	13	15	16
Y 343	14	14	28	23	11	12	13	14	16	Y 398	13	13	30	25	10	11	13	16	16
Y 412	14	14	28	24	10	11	12	12	16	Y 405	13	13	31	23	9	11	13	16	16
Y 49	14	14	29	22	11	11	11	13	17	Y 402	13	13	31	23	9	11	13	16	16
Y 217	14	14	29	22	10	11	12	13	17	Y 211	13	13	31	24	10	11	13	15	18
Y 76	14	14	29	22	11	11	12	13	18	Y 84	13	13	31	24	15	11	13	13	15
Y 396	14	14	29	23	9	10	12	12	17	Y 408	13	13	31	24	10	11	14	16	16
Y 406	14	14	29	23	10	11	12	13	17	Y 409	13	13	32	24	10	11	14	16	16
Y 384	14	14	29	23	9	12	12	13	17	Y 407	13	13	32	24	10	11	14	16	17
Y 400	14	14	29	24	9	11	12	13	20	Y 277	13	13	32	25	10	11	13	16	16
Y 105	14	14	29	24	10	11	12	18	18	Y 300	13	13	33	24	10	11	13	15	16
Y 401	14	14	29	26	9	11	12	14	18	Y 79	13	14	30	24	11	11	11	13	17
Y 387	14	14	30	22	10	11	12	13	17	Y 275	13	14	31	25	11	11	12	13	18
Y 32	14	14	30	23	11	11	11	12	16	Y 258	13	14	31	25	9	11	12	15	18
Y 60	14	14	30	23	10	11	11	13	17	Y 290	13	14	31	25	10	11	13	13	17
Y 15	14	14	30	23	11	11	11	13	18	Y 280	13	14	31	25	9	11	13	15	16
Y 16	14	14	30	23	11	11	11	13	18	Y 225	13	14	31	25	10	11	13	15	16
Y 237	14	14	30	23	10	11	12	13	16	Y 250	13	14	31	25	9	11	13	15	17
Y 385	14	14	30	23	10	11	12	13	16	Y 247	13	14	32	25	10	11	13	16	17
Y 385	14	14	30	23	11	11	12	13	16	Y 226	14	12	28	22	11	12	13	14	14
Y 391	14	14	30	23	8	11	12	13	17	Y 101	14	12	28	23	11	11	12	13	16

Y 415	14	14	30	23	10	11	12	13	17	Y 95	14	12	28	23	11	11	12	13	16
Y 139	14	14	30	23	10	11	12	13	18	Y 285	14	12	28	23	10	11	13	14	15
Y 10	14	14	30	23	11	11	12	13	18	Y 165	14	12	29	22	11	11	12	13	18
Y 382	14	14	30	23	9	11	12	14	17	Y 138	14	12	29	23	10	11	12	13	17
Y 381	14	14	30	23	10	11	12	14	17	Y 120	14	12	30	23	10	11	12	13	18
Y 394	14	14	30	23	9	11	13	16	16	Y 230	14	13	28	23	11	11	12	12	16
Y 2	14	14	30	24	11	11	10	13	17	Y 121	14	13	29	22	10	11	12	13	18
Y 403	14	14	30	24	10	11	12	13	13	Y 76	14	13	29	22	11	11	12	13	18
Y 390	14	14	30	24	11	11	12	13	16	Y 273	14	13	29	22	11	11	12	17	17
Y 3	14	14	31	23	10	11	11	13	17	Y 310	14	13	29	23	11	11	12	13	18
Y 376	14	14	31	23	10	11	12	13	17	Y 215	14	13	29	23	11	11	13	13	17
Y 393	14	14	31	23	8	11	12	13	17	Y 135	14	13	29	23	10	11	13	13	18
Y 383	14	14	31	23	9	11	12	14	16	Y 246	14	13	29	23	10	11	13	15	16
Y 399	14	14	31	24	10	11	12	13	17	Y 303	14	13	29	23	10	11	13	15	17
Y 116	14	14	32	23	10	11	12	13	18	Y 85	14	13	29	23	10	11	13	15	18
Y 83	14	14	32	24	10	11	13	13	17	Y 188	14	13	29	23	10	11	13	16	19
Y 235	15	11	28	25	10	11	12	15	18	Y 183	14	13	29	24	10	11	12	10	16
Y 200	15	12	28	25	11	11	11	13	18	Y 256	14	13	29	24	10	11	12	12	18
Y 186	15	12	28	25	10	11	12	14	17	Y 264	14	13	29	25	9	11	13	15	16
Y 222	15	12	28	25	10	11	12	15	18	Y 107	14	13	30	21	11	11	12	13	16
Y 204	15	12	28	25	10	11	12	16	18	Y 308	14	13	30	22	11	11	12	13	18
Y 243	15	12	29	21	10	11	15	13	14	Y 41	14	13	30	23	11	11	11	13	18
Y 288	15	12	29	24	9	11	12	13	18	Y 133	14	13	30	23	10	11	11	14	17
Y 260	15	13	29	22	10	11	12	12	17	Y 136	14	13	30	23	10	11	12	13	17
Y 241	15	14	30	21	10	11	14	14	15	Y 153	14	13	30	23	11	11	12	13	17
Y 152	15	13	30	23	10	11	12	14	17	Y 167	14	13	30	23	11	11	12	13	17
Y 91	15	13	30	24	9	11	12	13	17	Y 287	14	13	30	23	11	11	12	13	17
Y 106	15	14	30	24	10	11	12	16	17	Y 79	14	13	30	23	11	11	12	13	17
Y 124	15	14	30	24	10	11	12	17	17	Y 36	14	13	30	23	11	11	12	13	18
Y 242	15	14	31	21	10	11	14	14	16	Y 149	14	13	30	23	11	11	12	13	18
Y 395	15	15	30	24	8	10	13	15	16	Y 154	14	13	30	23	11	11	12	13	18
Y 91	15	15	30	24	9	11	12	13	16	Y 312	14	13	30	23	10	11	12	14	17
Y 386	15	15	31	23	9	10	12	13	16	Y 171	14	13	30	23	10	11	12	14	17
Y 395	15	15	31	24	10	12	13	16	16										
Y 397	17	17	31	23	12	11	13	11	12										

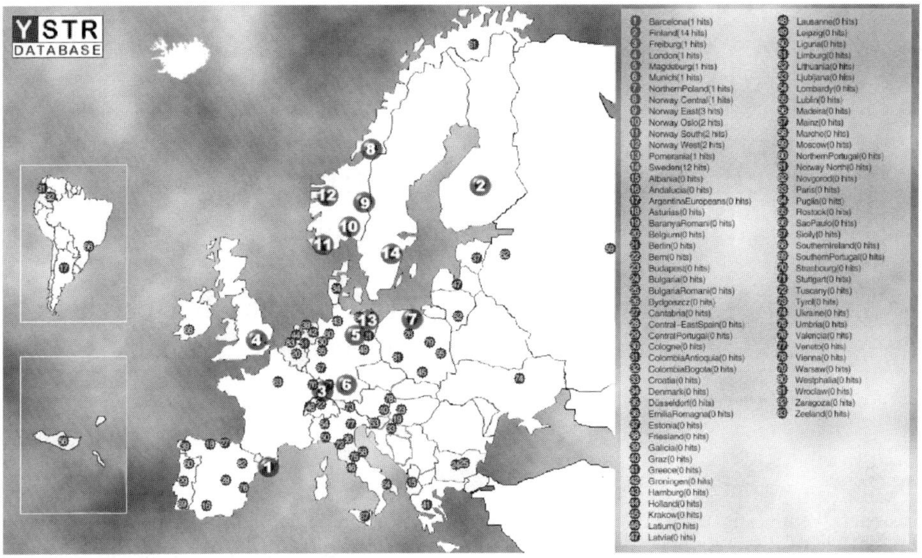

Fig. 1. Y285, 43 matches in the European database.

By doing so, eight matches were found in Asia. The haplotypes were found in 4 of 16 Asian population samples (Egypt, Syria, Turkey and Vietnam) with 2218 minimal haplotypes. Seven of the matching haplotypes were found in the Middle East, an area both geographically and culturally close to Yemen.

In Europe, we found 95 matches with 17 of the haplotypes from Yemen in 40 of 83 European population samples (12,802 individuals). Surprisingly, the geographical distribution of haplotype matches lacked the expected decline with growing geographical and cultural distance from Yemen. This finding is due to haplotype Y285, which was observed 43 times in Europe (Fig. 1), almost entirely in Scandinavia (in 36 of 1209 samples in the Y-STR database), whereas the remaining shared haplotypes show the expected south–north decline in frequency. The finding of a common Scandinavian haplotype in Yemen is surprising and might best be explained by a mere coincidence, i.e. two different lineages which have developed into matching haplotypes. This observation is a reminder not to overestimate the value of Y-STR haplotypes for estimating the ethnic origin of an individual.

Acknowledgements

The authors would like to thank A. Graul, A. Heide and S. Salostowitz for excellent technical assistance and G. Bothe for brilliant pictures.

References

[1] M.A. Jobling, A. Pandya, C. Tyler-Smith, The Y chromosome in forensic analysis and paternity testing, Int. J. Leg. Med. 110 (3) (1997) 118–124.
[2] M. Elmoznino, M. Prinz, 2003, http://ystr.charite.de/text/locus_pcr2_2.html.
[3] (http://www.ystr.org/europe/; http://www.ystr.org/asia/).
[4] R. Lessig, et al., Asian online Y-STR haplotype reference database, Legal Med. 5 (2003) 160–163.

International Congress Series 1261 (2004) 344–346

www.ics-elsevier.com

Y chromosome genetic structure in the Italian peninsula

C. Capelli*, B. Arredi, L. Baldassarri, I. Boschi, F. Brisighelli, A. Caglià, M. Dobosz, F. Scarnicci, V.L. Pascali

Forensic Genetics Laboratory, Istituto di Medicina Legale, Università Cattolica del S. Cuore, Largo F. Vito, 1-00168, Rome, Italy

Abstract. We investigated Y chromosome populations structure in the Italian peninsula by means of a number of microsatellites and SNPs markers. Genetic analysis revealed a certain degree of heterogeneity between samples at both haplotype (hpt) and haplogroup (hg) level. Implications in genetic history and forensic are discussed. © 2003 Published by Elsevier B.V.

Keywords: Y chromosome; SNP: single nucleotide polymorphism; STR: short tandem repeat; Population

1. Introduction

Y chromosome analysis has its own, well-established role in modern forensic DNA analysis. A vast consensus has been reached on the adoption of a 8-STRs haplotype (hpt), this being the base for the establishment of large national and continental databases. Y-STR databases have also been used to explore population genetic issues, either relevant to the forensic inference or of general concern. It is often stated that the distribution of Y hpts in large populations (such as national groups and big urban aggregates with homogenous ethnic composition) reflects the virtual absence of internal structure. We recently discussed the general validity of this assumption [1]. We in fact showed that significant differences actually exist between Central–North and Central–South Italian populations by the means of chromosome groups (haplogroups, hgs) defined by slowly evolving markers (Unique Event Polymorphisms, UEPs). This result is of central interest, in light of the fact that hpts and hgs are phylogenetically related to each other and haplotypes might mirror the same differential distribution shown by haplogroups. In order to investigate this specific issue in detail, we collected new samples from numerous local communities of Italy and carried out extensive Y-linked microsatellites and UEPs analysis.

* Corresponding author. Tel.: +39-6-35507031; fax: +39-6-35507033.
E-mail address: c.capelli.@rm.unicatt.it (C. Capelli).

0531-5131/ © 2003 Published by Elsevier B.V.
doi:10.1016/S0531-5131(03)01789-8

2. Sampling

Individuals were selected according to their father's father place of origin, to be within the area of interest. We included two samples from Central–North Italy (A and B), two samples from South Italy (D and E), and a Central–East location (C).

3. Y chromosome markers

The following SNPs were selected for the investigation: M35, M89, 12f2, M172, M170, M9, 92R7, M173, M17 [2–4]. Additionally, nine Y linked microsatellites were genotyped: DYS 388, 393, 392, 19, 390, 391, 389 I, 389 II and 385. The number of individuals genotyped for STRs/UEPs were: A 39/32; B77/58; C 57/58; D60/61; E 60/71.

4. Distribution of genetic variation

We investigated the issue of differential distribution of diversity across the samples areas by AMOVA and principal components (PC) analyses. The two approaches focused on microsatellite and SNP variation, respectively. The percentage of variation observed at haplotype level was largely within populations (96.71%), as usually observed in human populations. Interestingly, 3.29% was instead present between populations. This pattern was found to be significant ($p<0.01$) [5].

When focusing on SNPs, populations showed interesting differences in haplogroup frequencies. For comparison, we include populations from data available in literature [2,6]. In particular, two groups, namely, R1*xR1a1 and E3b were found to have inverse distribution along the peninsula. The former was the main type in the North, declining in frequency moving South, while the latter had its highest percentage in the South. HGs R1*xR1a1 and E3b, together with hg J2, were the three most common type along the peninsula (38%, 16% and 21%, respectively). Differently from the former two, J2 did not clearly show any pattern of differential distribution, with a range of frequency between 13% and 25%. In the PC plot, the northern samples (A and B) did tend to cluster with French and Basques, along axis 1, while C, D and E instead were together with other Mediterranean populations (Greeks and Calabrians). The main factors shaping the principal components plot were hg R1*xR1a1 and E3b (with loading factors of 0.443 and − 0.338) for axis 1, while R1*xR1a1 and I were on axis 2 (0.167 and − 0.35). Both A and B had the highest frequencies of R1*xR1a1 , around 50%, while C, D and E displayed the highest for E3b hg. The first two principal components summarised more than 62% of the total genetic variation (data not shown).

5. Differential distribution of haplotypes

The AMOVA results of significant amount of genetic variation across populations is raising the issue of nonrandom distribution of haplotypes across the different populations. Similarly, as haplotypes are evolutionary linked to the mutations defining haplogroups, the different frequencies of haplogroups in the analysed samples suggests that populations might have different frequencies for certain Y chromosome haplotypes. The haplotypes shared at least by two populations were eight. Only one type was shared across four populations, while none was present all across the five groups. Most of types were uniquely present in each population. This is possible to be related to the high level of resolution offered by the nine genotyped microsatellites. The highest haplotype frequency was 5% ,observed in the A sample, and showing frequencies ranging between 0% and 1% in the others.

6. Conclusions

We here report that significant differences emerge among local groups both at hpt and hg level, making the reality of Y lineages stratification in Italy highly complex. In particular, at least two hgs show significant different frequencies between North and South samples, namely, R1*xR1a1 and E3b. Those two are the main factors shaping populations distribution in PC plot. In the plot, it appears that there is a certain tendency for independent clustering of the North and South Italian samples. We envision that the whole issue that could reflect different historical demographic phenomena occurred in the Mediterranean basin and in the Italian Peninsula during past millennia. These results also raise concerns on the appropriateness of the use of all-purpose "Italian" databases for forensic casework inference. The AMOVA analysis seems to support this, as the distribution of genetic variation was found to be significant across different groups ($p<0.01$). Nonrandom distribution of Y haplotypes within national borders seems to be not unusual [4]. Our results, together with the observation in other countries, raise the issue of how appropriate would be the use of a single national database before exhaustively investigate the issue of population structure.

References

[1] A. Caglià, et al., in: B. Brinkmann, A. Carracedo (Eds.), Progress in Forensic Genetics 9, International Congress Series, vol. 1239, Elsevier, Amsterdam, 2003, pp. 307–310, January.
[2] O. Semino, et al., Science 290 (5494) (2000) 1155–1159.
[3] Y Chromosome Consortium, Genome Res. 12 (2) (2002) 339–348 (February).
[4] C. Capelli, et al., Curr. Biol. 13 (2003) 979–984.
[5] S. Schneider, et al., Genetics and Biometery Laboratory, University of Geneva, Geneva, 2000.
[6] E. Bosch, et al., Am. J. Hum. Genet. 68 (2001) 1019–1029.

ELSEVIER

International Congress Series 1261 (2004) 347–349

www.ics-elsevier.com

Y chromosome SNP haplogroups in Danes, Greenlanders and Somalis

J.J. Sanchez[a,*], C. Børsting[a], A. Hernandez[b], J. Mengel-Jørgensen[a], N. Morling[a]

[a] *Department of Forensic Genetics, Institute of Forensic Medicine, University of Copenhagen, 11 Frederik V's Vej 11, DK-2100 Copenhagen, Denmark*

[b] *Instituto Nacional de Toxicología, Departamento de Canarias, La Laguna, Tenerife, Spain*

Abstract. We have developed a PCR-based assay with co-amplification of 25 DNA fragments and detection of 35 Y chromosome SNPs with the SNaPshot technique. The Y SNP package can define 34 Y chromosome haplogroups and it can identify the majority of the Y chromosome haplogroups of interest in the populations relevant to forensic genetics in Denmark. We typed 194 Danes, 215 Greenlanders, and 201 Somalis, all males. A total of 21 different haplogroups were identified. In Danes, 11 haplogroups with frequencies from 0.5% to 38% were identified and three of the haplogroups, I, R1b*(xR1b1, R1b6, R1b8) and R1a1*(xR1a1b), were found in ~ 91% of the population. In Greenlanders, 10 haplogroups with frequencies from 0.5% to 50% were identified and the haplogroups P*(xQ3a, R1), R1b*(xR1b1, R1b6, R1b8) and I, were found in ~ 86% of the population. In Somalis, 14 haplogroups with frequencies from 0.5% to 79% were identified and the haplogroups E3b1*(xE3b1b) and K*(xN3, O, P) were found in ~ 88% of the population. The distribution of haplogroups was compared to the distribution found in 65 males from West Africa.

Keywords: Y chromosome; Single nucleotide polymorphism; Multiplex PCR; Minisequencing

1. Introduction

We have developed a multiplex PCR with 25 amplicons containing 35 known Y chromosome SNPs, and we have used the SNaPshot assay to detect all 35 SNPs in a single experiment [1]. We selected Y chromosome SNPs that were reported to be polymorphic in European and other populations relevant to forensic genetics in Denmark [2]. Here, we compare the haplogroup diversity in Somali, Danish and Greenlandic males using the 35 SNP package. These populations include Y haplogroups typically found in African and Eurasian populations.

* Corresponding author. Tel.: +45-35-32-6225; fax: +45-35-32-6120.
E-mail address: juan.sanchez@forensic.ku.dk (J.J. Sanchez).

doi:10.1016/S0531-5131(03)01635-2

2. Materials and methods

DNA samples from unrelated males (number of individuals are given in parenthesis) from Somalia (201), Greenland (215), Denmark (194) and a total of 65 Western Africans from Mali (38), Ghana (16), Mauritania (3), Guinea Conakry (2), Liberia (2), Côte d'Ivoire (1), Guinea–Bissau (1), Senegal (1), and Cameroon (1), were typed for 35 SNPs.

The PCR amplification, SNaPshot reaction and SNP typing was performed as previously described [1]. The relevant portion of the YCC tree is shown in Fig. 1.

3. Results

The genealogical relationship of the haplogroups and their relative frequency is shown in the Fig. 1. In Danes, 11 haplogroups with frequencies from 0.5% to 38% were identified

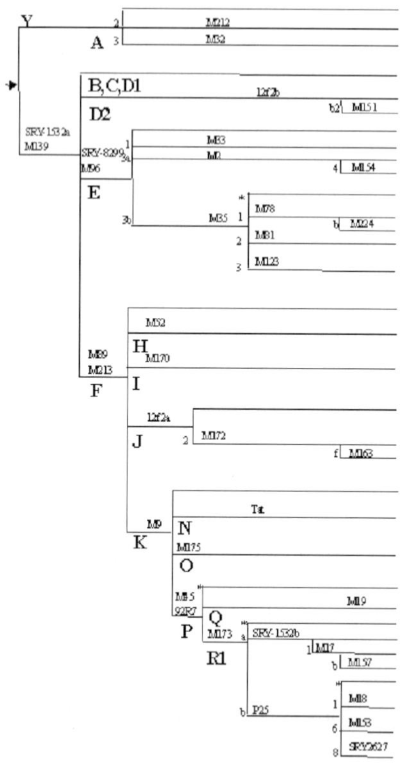

Haplogroup	Danes (N = 194)	Greenlanders (N = 215)	Somalis (N = 201)	Western Africans (N = 65)
Y*(xA2,A3,BR)				
A2				
A3	-	-	1 (0.5)	-
BR*(xD2,E,F)	-	1 (0.5)	2 (1.0)	-
D2*(xD2b2)				
D2b2				
E*(xE1,E3a,E3b)	-	-	1 (0.5)	1 (1.5)
E1	-	-	-	5 (7.7)
E3a*(xE3a4)	-	-	3 (1.5)	58 (89.2)
E3a4				
E3b*	1 (0.5)	-	3 (1.5)	1 (1.5)
E3b1*(xE3b1b)	2 (1.0)	1 (0.5)	156 (77.2)	-
E3b1b				
E3b2	-	-	3 (1.5)	-
E3b3	1 (0.5)	-	1 (0.5)	-
F*(xH,I,J,K)	1 (0.5)	-	1 (0.5)	-
H	-	-	1 (0.5)	-
I	75 (38.7)	36 (16.7)	-	-
J*(xJ2)	-	-	5 (2.5)	-
J2*(xJ2f2)	5 (2.6)	4 (1.9)	1 (0.5)	-
J2f2				
K*(xN3,O,P)	-	3 (1.4)	21 (10.4)	-
N3	1 (0.5)	-	-	-
O	-	1 (0.5)	-	-
P*(xQ3a,R1)	3 (1.5)	106 (49.1)	-	-
Q3a				
R1*(xR1a,R1b)	3 (1.5)	-	-	-
R1a*				
R1a1*(xR1a1b)	32 (16.5)	19 (8.8)	2 (1.0)	-
R1a1b				
R1b*(xR1b1,R1b6,R1b8)	70 (36.1)	43 (19.9)	-	-
R1b1				
R1b6▼				
R1b8▼	-	1 (0.5)	-	-

Fig. 1. Phylogenetic distribution of the 34 Y chromosome haplogroups that can be detected by the 35 biallelic markers. On the right is shown the distribution of Y chromosome haplogroups in Danes, Greenlanders, Somalis and people from West Africa. The relative frequency in percent is shown in parentheses. (ψ) The haplogroups R1b6 and R1b8 have been described as R1b3d and R1b3f in the new YCC tree 2003 [3].

and three of the haplogroups: I (38.7%), R1b*(xR1b1, R1b6, R1b8) (36.1%) and R1a1*(xR1a1b) (16.5%), were identified as the most abundant in this population. In Greenlanders, 10 haplogroups with frequencies from 0.5% to 50% were identified and the haplogroup P*(xQ3a, R1) (49.1%) was the most frequent followed by R1b*(xR1b1, R1b6, R1b8) (19.9%) and I (16.7%), which are characteristic of male Europeans.

In Somalis, 14 haplogroups with frequencies from 0.5% to 79% were identified and two of the haplogroups were found in 90% of the population: E3b1*(xE3b1b) (77.2%) and K*(xN3, O, P) (10.4%). In contrast, among the Western Africans, E3b1 was never observed. The most frequent haplogroup in West Africa was E3a (89%) (Fig. 1).

4. Discussion

Haplogroup P*(xQ3a, R1), found in almost 50% of males from Greenland, was also found in high frequencies among the North Americans and Siberian Inuits [4]. In contrast, the other three major haplogroups found in Greenland (haplogroup I, R1a1 and R1b) are found in high frequencies in the Danish population. This substantiates the notion that almost 50% of the male Greenlanders are of European (Nordic) descent [5] and that the other half may originate from Siberian and North American Inuits.

The Somali population have the highest frequency of the Y chromosome haplogroup E3b1* (79%) ever reported. Unfortunately, there are very few reports containing results from the subclades to E3b in the literature. However, the highest haplogroup frequencies reported for E3b is around 25% observed in Albanian, Greek, Lebanese and Ethiopian populations [2].

The haplogroup distributions found in the four different populations in this study are very different, demonstrating the efficiency of the 35 SNP package to separate various population groups.

Acknowledgements

We thank Ms. Annemette Holbo Birk for technical assistance. The work was supported by grants to Juan Sanchez from Ellen and Aage Andersen's Foundation and from the "Consejeria de Educacion y Cultura (DGUI), Gobierno de Canarias" (PI2000/053), Spain.

References

[1] J.J. Sanchez, et al., Multiplex PCR and minisequencing of SNPs—a model with 35 Y chromosome SNPs, Forensic Sci. Int. 137 (1) (2003) 74–84.

[2] P.A. Underhill, et al., Y chromosome sequence variation and the history of human populations, Nat. Genet. 26 (3) (2000) 358–361.

[3] M.A. Jobling, C. Tyler-Smith, The human Y chromosome: an evolutionary marker comes of age, Nat. Rev., Genet. 4 (8) (2003) 598–612.

[4] M.C. Bortolini, et al., Y-chromosome evidence for differing ancient demographic histories in the Americas, Am. J. Hum. Genet. 73 (3) (2003) 524–539.

[5] E. Bosch, et al., High level of male-biased Scandinavian admixture in Greenlandic Inuit shown by Y-chromosomal analysis, Hum. Genet. 112 (4) (2003) 353–363.

International Congress Series 1261 (2004) 350–352

www.ics-elsevier.com

Y chromosome STRs in the north of Portugal

M.L. Pontes[a], J.A. Peña[b], M.A. Alfonso Sanchez[b], D. Abrantes[a], G. Lima[a], M.J. Pereira[a], I. Fernández-Fernández[c], A. Castro[c], M.F. Pinheiro[a,d,*], M. Martínez de Páncorbo[e]

[a] *Delegação do Porto do INML, Jardim Carrilho Videira, 4050-167 Oporto, Portugal*
[b] *Dep. Biología Animal y Genética, Unid Antropología Física, Facultad de Ciencias, Univ. del País Vasco, Spain*
[c] *DataGene, Sondika, Spain*
[d] *ICBAS, Universidade do Porto, Oporto, Portugal*
[e] *Dep. Zoologia y Dinamica Celular Animal, Facultad de Farmacia, Univ. del País Vasco, Spain*

Abstract. The interest in Y chromosome polymorphisms has continuously increased, not only in evolutionary/genealogical studies, but also in forensic genetics. The objective of this study is to analyse the *loci* DYS19, DYS389I, DYS389II, DYS390, DYS391, DYS392, DYS393 and DYS385I/II in a population sample from the North of Portugal. One hundred one unique haplotypes were found and the haplotypic diversity was 0.998 ± 0.001 which reinforces the forensic utility of these markers. Phylogenetic analysis shows that our population can be included in the European Y chromosome lineages and distinct from the Asian ones. © 2003 Published by Elsevier B.V.

Keywords: Y-STR; Minimal haplotype; Population data

1. Introduction

The NRY part of the Y human chromosome is paternally inherited and haploid [1] and the interest in Y chromosome polymorphisms has continuously increased. From the forensic point of view, these markers, being passed down without any recombination, can be used in cases of unknown parentage [2]. Moreover, the Y chromosome specific markers are of election in cases of sexual assaults, since they permit the detection of male DNA in mixtures of male/female cells, even with a high background of female DNA, particularly if more than one male is involved [3]. From the evolutionary point of view, these markers are useful for tracing migration movements of populations, inferring the history of modern humans [4]. Having this in mind, we have studied the *loci* DYS19, DYS389I, DYS389II, DYS390, DYS391, DYS392, DYS393 and DYS385I/II in a population sample from the North of Portugal, involved in paternity testing.

* Corresponding author. Delegação do Porto do INML, Jardim Carrilho Videira, 4050-167 Oporto, Portugal. Tel.: +351-222073850; fax: +351-223325931.
E-mail address: correio@dpinml.mj.pt (M.F. Pinheiro).

0531-5131/ © 2003 Published by Elsevier B.V.
doi:10.1016/S0531-5131(03)01839-9

2. Material and methods

DNA was isolated from 122 unrelated healthy individuals, using Chelex or phenol-chloroform extraction methods. Amplification was performed in three PCR reactions: a pentaplex (DYS19, DYS389I, DYS389II, DYS390, DYS393), a triplex (DYS391, DYS392, DYS393) and a monoplex (DYS385I/II) [5,6]. The PCR products were typed by capillary electrophoresis (ABI 310 Genetic Analyser, Applied Biosystems). Haplotypes were determined by simple counting and several statistic parameters were calculated using Arlequin software ver. 2000: gene diversity and variance by AMOVA. Genetic distances were also calculated and the correspondent filogenetic tree obtained as well as multi dimensional scalling (MDS).

3. Results and discussion

The analysis of these Y-STR markers showed 111 unique haplotypes. The two most frequent haplotypes were repeated three times and seven others only two times. The highest gene diversity corresponds to DYS385I/II (0.847), followed by DYS389II (0.677), being the DYS389I the locus that presents the lowest value (0.535). The mean gene diversity was 0.626 and the value of the haplotypic diversity was 0.998 ± 0.001, probably due to the scarce repetition of haplotypes. So, the probability that two randomly chosen individuals from our population share the same haplotype is 0.002.

Comparisons of our population with others from Iberia, Europe and Asia were performed. We did not compare our haplotypic data with African populations. We share many haplotypes with Iberia: seven with Asturias (North Spain), six with Barcelona (Mediterranean part) and five with Andalusia (South Spain). The number of shared haplotypes decreases progressively with other European populations: four with Germany,

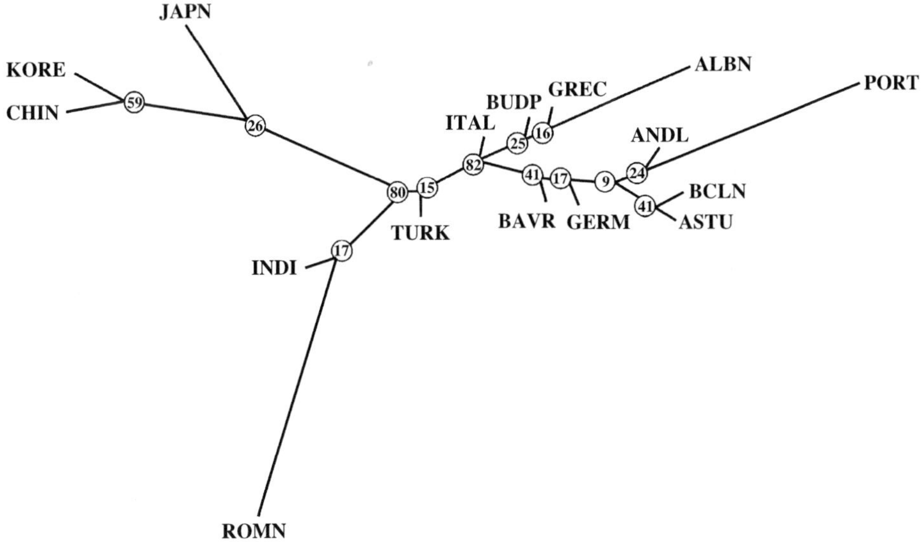

Fig. 1. Neighbour-joining tree based on Slatkin's distances.

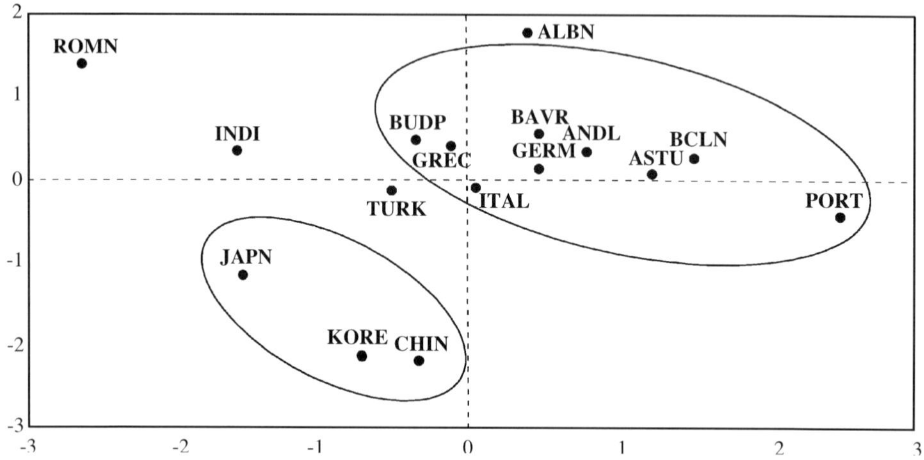

Fig. 2. Multi-dimensional scaling: total variance of 96.4% and the stress coefficient was 0.088.

three with Hungary, two with Italy and one with Turkey, Albania and Romanies. The haplotype 14-13-29-24-11-13-13-11/14 is the most frequent in our population and in all the other European ones compared in this study, with the exception of Italy. None of the haplotypes is shared with India, China, Korea or Japan. The AMOVA analysis shows that the biggest percentage of variance occurs within populations. The Slatkin's genetic distancies [7] between our population and the others were calculated and used to debug a dendrogram (Fig. 1) and a MDS diagram (Fig. 2). The phylogenetic analysis shows that our Y chromosomes can be included in the European lineages and are distinct from the Asian ones. In conclusion, we can reinforce the forensic utility of these markers, namely in sexual assaults. Additionally, the phylogenetic data allows to include the Y chromosomes from the North of Portugal into the European lineages and to distinguish them from the Asian ones.

References

[1] P. Grignani, et al., Int. J. Leg. Med. 114 (2000) 125–129.
[2] L. Roewer, et al., Forensic Sci. Int. 114 (2000) 31–43.
[3] J.M. Butler, et al., Forensic Sci. Int. 129 (2002) 10–24.
[4] M.A. Jobling, C. Tyler-Smith, Trends Genet. 11 (1995) 449–456.
[5] A. Carracedo, et al., Forensic Sci. Int. 119 (2001) 28–41.
[6] P. Schneider, et al., Forensic Sci. Int. 97 (1998) 61–70.
[7] M. Slatkin, Genetics 139 (1995) 457–462.

International Congress Series 1261 (2004) 353–356

www.ics-elsevier.com

Y chromosome in forensic casework and paternity testing

Farida Alshamali[a,*], Abdul Qader Alkhayat[a], Bruce Budowle[b], Nigel Watson[c]

[a] Crime Laboratory, G. Department Forensic Sciences, Dubai Police GHQ, Al-Itihad Street, P.O. Box 1493, Dubai, United Arab Emirates
[b] Laboratory Division, FBI, 2501 Investigation Pkwy, Quantico, VA 22135, USA
[c] Forensic Science Unit, Strathclyde University, Glasgow, UK

Abstract. The aim of the study is to demonstrate the power obtained by combining autosomal and Y chromosome STRs in certain case scenarios. Although autosomal STRs are in use and highly informative, Y STRs are extremely useful and provide additional information that could not be provided by autosomal STRs alone.

Keywords: Y STRs; Forensic casework; Paternity testing

1. Introduction

The determination of the gender of the source of forensic biological materials can be of investigative and evidentiary value [5]. Recently, Y STR loci have gained an increased attention from both forensic and paternity testing groups [3]. Y STRs loci typing is particularly useful for typing the male DNA component in male/female mixture evidence samples [4]. Typing closely linked loci that do not undergo recombination is of particular interest in deficiency paternity testing and in determining paternal lineages [2,6]. This study reports four example cases where Y STRs combined with autosomal STRs helped to reach a conclusion of potential source with greater confidence.

2. Material and methods

DNA was extracted using the standard organic procedure. Autosomal STRs were typed using either the AmpFLSTR® Profiler Plus™ and AmpFLSTR® Cofiler™ Kits, or the AmpFLSTR® Identifiler™ Kit (Applied Biosystems). Profiling of Y STRs was conducted

* Corresponding author. Tel.: +971-02013520; fax: +971-42014497.
E-mail address: shamali@emirates.net.ae (F. Alshamali).

doi:10.1016/j.ics.2003.12.101

using Y-Plex™ 6 STR kit and Y-Plex™ 5 STR kit (Reliagene, USA) according to the manufacturers' protocols.

2.1. Case 1: burned human remains

A fire and explosion took place in a firework games warehouse. Nine bodies were recovered of which relatives could identify four of them. Of the five remaining severely charred bodies, two examples are presented. In the first example, a corpse and five body fragments were recovered from under the fire debris 40 days after the incident. Autosomal STRs profiling showed a match among the recovered fragments and corpse. A man who reported his brother missing could not be excluded as a relative. Since only the brother was available for testing, Y STRs were typed and found to match the profile of the remains. The second example consisted of a partially burned body. A man whose full brother used to work in the same place visually identified one of the corpses to resemble his brother. Comparison at 15 autosomal STRs showed no shared alleles at seven loci. While the evidentiary value for sibship was not strong, the man could not be excluded as a possible

a

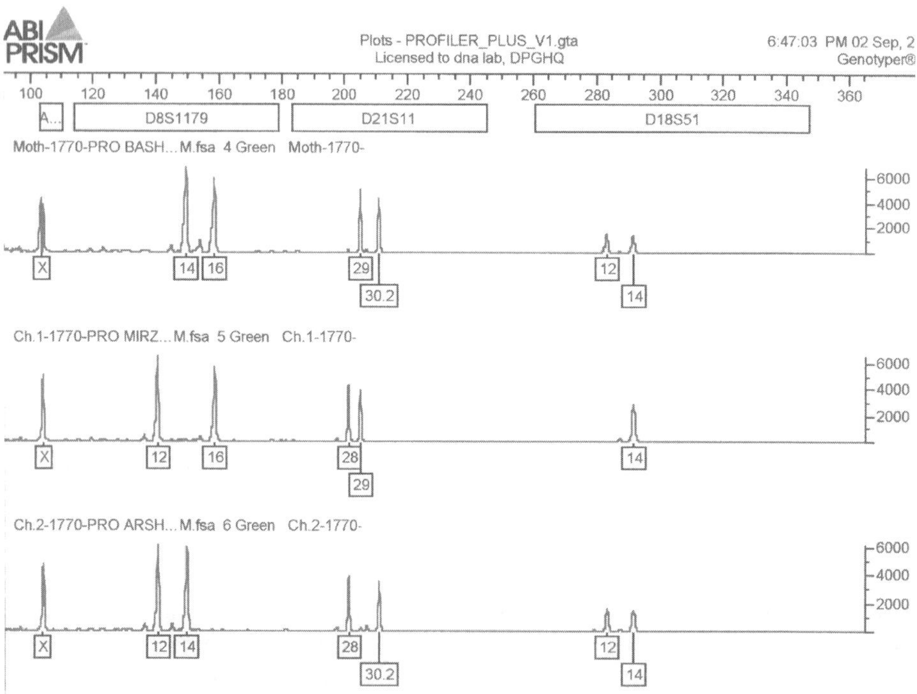

Fig. 1. (a) Autosomal STR profiles of the mother and two sons. (b) The YSTR profiles of the sons showing the same haplotype.

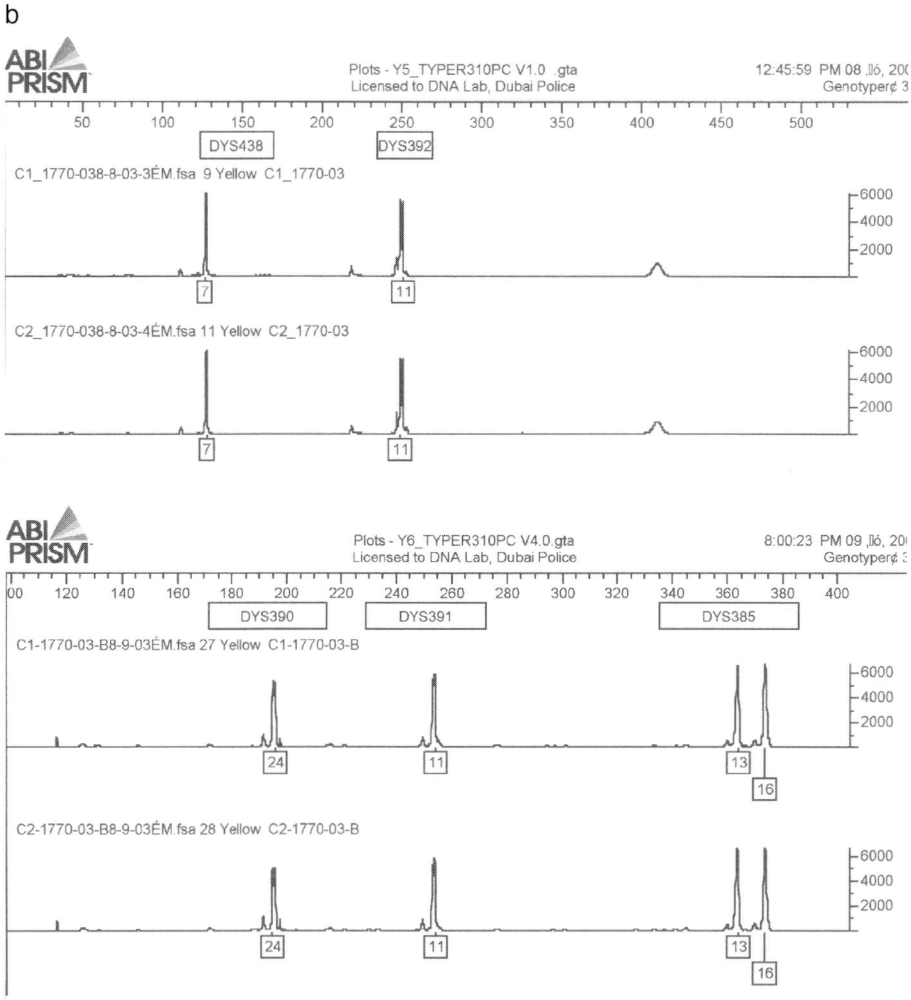

Fig. 1 (*continued*).

brother. The Y STR profile comparison clearly was different and provided a simple and a straightforward exclusion.

2.2. Case 2: sexual assault

A 14-year-old girl who had been missing from her home was found with an evidence of sexual abuse. The results obtained by autosomal STR analysis showed a mixture of more than one individual in the male fraction. The Y STR results were consistent with two males comprising the sample. One suspect was identified and could not be excluded as a contributor of the profile by both autosomal and Y STR typing. The second contributor has yet to be identified.

2.3. Case 3: forensic paternity

A woman accused a man of being the father of her child. The man denied the allegation. The trio was profiled using 15 autosomal STR markers. There were two differences found: a possible one step mutation at the CSF1PO locus on the mother's side and a null allele, i.e., a possible primer binding site mutation, at the D5S818 locus on the father side. The Y STR profiles were identical in the child and alleged father. Thus, the data could not exclude the alleged father as the biological father.

2.4. Case 4: gender confirmation

A putative mother and her two sons were referred to the lab to assess maternity. The father was not available for testing. The amelogenin results showed only an X in all three individuals. Testing with Y STR markers demonstrated that the putative sons did carry a Y chromosome and shared an identical Y haplotype at all 11 markers used (Fig. 1). The amelogenin anomaly is likely the result of a mutation or deletion in the region of the Y chromosome where the amelogenin primers reside [4].

3. Conclusion

Y STRs can supplement the highly robust autosomal STRs used in both forensic and paternity testing and in some instances provide information where autosomal markers fail to do so. Y STR typing could be used to assist in establishing kinship, to help resolve complicated paternity cases, to provide a simple straightforward means of exclusion in motherless paternities and in one of the most challenging applications in the field of forensics, i.e. mass disasters [1]. Although Y STRs are not as discriminating as autosomal STRs, they offer certain advantages in the analyses of different types of mixture samples. Autosomal STR profiles obtained in such cases at times provide inconclusive results. In conclusion, autosomal and Y STRs combined provide a powerful tool for certain forensic and paternity cases. Reliable Y STR typing has augmented the forensic arsenal for resolving complicated cases.

References

[1] D. Corach, et al., Mass disasters: rapid molecular screening of human remains by means of short tandem repeats typing, Electrophoresis 16 (1995) 1617–1623.

[2] P. de Knijff, et al., Chromosome Y microsatellites: population genetic and evolutionary aspects, Int. J. Leg. Med. 110 (1997) 134–149.

[3] M.A. Jobling, et al., The Y chromosome in forensic and paternity testing, Int. J. Leg. Med. 110 (1997) 118–124.

[4] M. Prinz, et al., Multiplexing of Y chromosome specific STRs and performance for mixed samples, Forensic Sci. Int. 85 (3) (1997) 209–218.

[5] P.E. Roffey, et al., A rare mutation in the amelogenin gene and its potential ramifications, J. Forensic Sci. 45 (5) (2000) 1016–1019.

[6] L. Roewer, The Y Chromosome: forensic application and evolutionary aspects, in: B. Olaisen, B. Brinkman, P.J. Lincoln (Eds.), Progress in Forensic Genetics vol. 7, Elsevier, 1998, pp. 407–412.

International Congress Series 1261 (2004) 357–359

www.ics-elsevier.com

No obvious geographical Y-chromosome gradient in the Swedish population

G. Holmlund[a,*], H. Nilsson[a], L. Engdahl[a], A. Götherström[b], B. Lindblom[a]

[a] The National Board of Forensic Medicine, Department of Forensic Genetics, University Hospital, SE-581 85 Linköping, Sweden

[b] Department of Evolutionary Biology, Uppsala University, SE-725 36 Uppsala, Sweden

Abstract. We have analysed 305 Y-chromosomes from seven regions in Sweden to find out if there is population stratification. The Y-STR-minimal haplotype markers including DYS385 a and b were analysed and haplogroups were defined by the SNPs TAT, 92R7, M9, M17 and SRY1532. The STRs were analysed on an ABI377 and the SNPs by Pyrosequencing. Y-haplogroups 1, 2, 3, 16 and 26 were found in approximately equal frequencies in the sub-populations. Also, the gene diversity within the STR-haplotypes, analysed by the Markov chain algorithm, showed no differences. Thus, the whole database can be used for frequency calculations. © 2003 Elsevier B.V. All rights reserved.

Keywords: Y-STR; Y-SNP; Haplotypes; Haplogroups; Population

1. Introduction

The Y-STR databases, including regional data, give invaluable means for the calculation of match probabilities. However, there is an apparent risk for an overestimation of the significance of a match, if there are no data on the genetic stratification of the population.

2. Materials and methods

2.1. Sub-populations and blood samples

Seven regions, shown in Fig. 1, were selected according to the demographic history of the Swedish people [1,2].

Three-hundred-five blood samples were collected, of which 109 were men from paternity cases, with known place of birth and typical Swedish names. The rest (196) were from blood donors having given their written consent and questioned about their origin.

2.2. Y-chromosome markers

The STR-markers DYS19, DYS389I, DYS389II, DYS390, DYS391, DYS392, DYS393 and DYS385 were analysed as described earlier [3]. The DYS385 was separated into DYS385a and DYS385b according to Kittler et al. [4]. All fragment lengths were analysed on an ABI377.

* Corresponding author. Tel.: +46-13-22-30-36; fax: +46-13-13-60-05.
E-mail address: gunilla.holmlund@rmv.se (G. Holmlund).

doi:10.1016/S0531-5131(03)01550-4

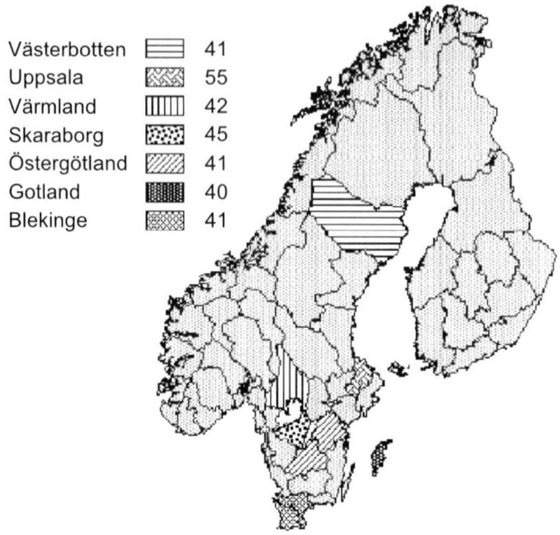

Fig. 1. Map of Sweden showing the number and the geographical origin of the Y-chromosomes.

The SNPs TAT, 92R7, M9, M17 and SRY1532 (=SRY10831) were amplified according to Thomas et al. [5]. For the Pyrosequencing [6] one primer was biotinylated and the amplicons purified by streptavidine bead binding filters. The Pyrosequencing strategy is shown in Table 1. In 96 samples, SNP-detection was also done with Denaturing High-Performance Liquid Chromatography (DHPLC) [7].

2.3. Statistical analyses

Arlequin [8] was used for population comparisons based on haplogroup data. The analysis is based on a Markov chain algorithm to estimate the gene diversity for the STRs within the haplogroups for each population.

3. Results

Twenty-eight Y-STR-haplotypes were found more than once. The most frequent haplotype, 14,12,28,23,10,11,13,14a,14b (16/305, 0.0524), was evenly distributed in six of the seven sub-populations, but missing in Östergötland. The other relatively frequent haplotypes (4-7/305) were also evenly distributed. For the more rare haplotypes (2-3/305), however, the distribution differs in that they are found within the same region, which shows relatedness between the men. Separating DYS385 into a and b elevated the power of discrimination from 75% to 79%.

Table 1
Polymorphisms and *primer-sites* used for Pyrosequencing of Y-SNPs

Marker	Sequence
TAT	CTGAGACTCACATCTGAACACTTAAGT T/C CAACAAAATTAAATTATAAAGT
92R7	TGCATGAACACAAAAGACGTAGAAG T/C TTGTCTTTGCTGGTCATATTTAACAATGC
M9	AAAGAAACGGCCTAAGATGGTTGAAT G/C CTCTTTATTTTTCTTTAATTTAGACATGTTCAA
M17	ACCAACGACCAACAATGCCCG G/- AAAAAAATTCACTTAAAACCCCAAACAATTC
SRY1532	GAAGACTGAAAAAGTGTGTCA G/A ATTGTAAAAGTTCCAAGTGG

Table 2
Y-STR gene diversity within each haplogroup in the sub-populations

Haplogroup	Västerbotten	Uppsala	Värmland	Skaraborg	Östergötland	Gotland	Blekinge
2	0.9532	0.9717	0.9625	0.9667	0.9641	0.9267	0.9640
3	(1)	0.8650	0.8101	0.7619	0.8415	0.8099	0.8650
1	0.8822	0.8959	0.8653	0.9222	0.8946	0.8431	0.8657
16	0.8657	(1)	(1)			0.7636	
26	0.7627	0.7636	0.6829	(2)			(2)

The standard error varied between 0.008 and 0.0161.
(1) Not calculated, only two haplotypes; (2) not calculated, only one haplotype.

The haplogroups were assigned according to Rosser et al. [9] and Weale et al. [10]. The relative haplogroup frequencies in the whole population were for hg3 0.118, hg2 0.600, hg1 0.190, hg16 0.049 and hg26 0.043. There were no significant differences between the geographical regions although hg16 is missing in Östergötland, Skaraborg and Blekinge and hg26 in Värmland, Gotland and Östergötland. Interestingly, hg3 is about half as frequent as in other European populations. SRY1532 is closely associated with DYS385a-11 and DYS385b-14 as shown by Kittler et al. [4]. Only minor gene diversity differences between the sub-populations were found, as shown in Table 2.

4. Conclusion

There were no statistical differences between the sub-populations, regarding both haplotype and haplogroup distributions. The Swedish population is accordingly not stratified and the complete database can be used for Y-chromosome STR-haplotype-frequency calculations.

There can, however, be some risk for an overestimation of match probabilities for the more rare haplotypes since they can locally be more frequent than in the whole population.

Acknowledgements

This work was supported by partial funding from the Board for Research and Development, The National Board of Forensic Medicine, Sweden.

References

[1] S. Erixon, Atlas över svensk folkkultur. Uppsala, 1957.
[2] S. Erixon, Svensk byggnadskultur. Lund, 1982.
[3] G. Holmlund, et al., Y-chromosome STR haplotypes in a Swedish population, in: B. Brinkmann, A. Carracedo (Eds.), Progress in Forensic Genetics, vol. 9, Elsevier, Amsterdam, 2003, pp. 343–348.
[4] R. Kittler, et al., Apparent intrachromosomal exchange of the Y chromosome explained by population history, Eur. J. Hum. Genet. 11 (4) (2003) 304–314.
[5] M.G. Thomas, N. Bradman, H.M. Flinn, High throughput analysis of 10 microsatellite and 11 diallelic polymorphisms on the human Y-chromosome, Hum. Genet. 105 (1999) 577–581.
[6] M. Ronaghi, et al., Real-time DNA sequencing using detection of pyrophosphate release, Anal. Biochem. 242 (1996) 84–89.
[7] P.A. Underhill, et al., Detection of numerous Y chromosome biallelic polymorphisms by denaturing high-performance liquid chromatography, Genome Res. 7 (1997) 996–1005.
[8] Arlequin, http://www.antrhro.unige.ch/arlequin.
[9] H.Z. Rosser, et al., Y-chromosomal diversity in Europe is clinal and influenced primarily by geography, rather than by language, Am. J. Hum. Genet. 67 (2000) 1526–1543.
[10] M.E. Weale, et al., Armenian Y chromosome haplotypes reveal strong regional structure within a single ethno-national group, Hum. Genet. 109 (2001) 659–674.

International Congress Series 1261 (2004) 360–362

www.ics-elsevier.com

Evaluation of the forensic usefulness of the separate analysis of DYS385a and DYS385b in an Austrian population sample

Harald Niederstätter[a], Burkhard Berger[a], Herbert Oberacher[a], Anita Brandstätter[a], Christian Huber[b], Walther Parson[a,*]

[a] *Forensic Molecular Biology, Institute of Legal Medicine, University of Innsbruck, Müllerstrasse 44, A-6020, Innsbruck, Austria*

[b] *Instrumental Analysis and Bioanalysis, Saarland University, Building 9.2, D-66123, Saarbrücken, Germany*

Abstract. The duplicated Y-STR DYS385 is one of the most informative markers on the Y-chromosome. It consists of two copies—DYS385a and DYS385b—that are located close to the inner borders of palindrome P4. The application of standard PCR protocols for DYS385 results in the simultaneous amplification of both copies. Hence, an explicit assignment of the alleles to their loci is not possible which causes a loss of information. Recently, a PCR strategy was published that allows the separate analysis of DYS385a and b, which we followed with modifications in our study on 133 unrelated Caucasian men from Tirol (Austria). Additionally all markers of the minimal haplotype (including DYS385) were amplified using standard PCR protocols. The non-allele-discriminating amplification strategy for DYS385 allowed the discrimination of 27 different genotypes (GD = 0.8616). By the separate analysis of the two DYS385 copies, this number increased to 34 (GD = 0.9185). However, the cumulative haplotype diversity of the complete minimal haplotype was 0.9951, regardless of the amplification strategy for DYS385. This indicates that in the context of the minimal haplotype, the separate analysis of DYS385a and b has no or only a marginally positive effect on the differentiation of paternal lineages.

Keywords: Y-chromosome; DYS385; Y-STR; Population study

1. Introduction

The analysis of polymorphic short tandem repeat (STR) markers that are located in the male specific region of the Y-chromosome has proven to be of great forensic relevance in special cases where the highly informative autosomal STRs are not applicable. However, the discrimination power of Y-STRs is lower than that of their autosomal counterparts since Y-chromosomal markers discriminate between different paternal lineages but not between individuals that belong to the same patriline. Furthermore, the analysis of the

Abbreviations: bp, base pair(s); GD, gene diversity; STR, short tandem repeat.

* Corresponding author. Tel.: +43-512-5073303; fax: +43-512-5072764.
E-mail address: Walther.Parson@uibk.ac.at (W. Parson).

0531-5131/
doi:10.1016/S0531-5131(03)01609-1

system with the highest gene diversity (GD) in the minimal haplotype—DYS385—does not utilise the full information content of this duplicated marker when conventional PCR strategies are used because both copies are amplified simultaneously, which makes the assignment of the alleles to the loci DYS385a and DYS385b impossible.

Recently, Kittler et al. [1] published a PCR strategy for the separate analysis of both copies of DYS385. The two DYS385 loci ‘a’ and ‘b’ lie on the long arm of the Y-chromosome in palindrome P4 close (~ 450 bp) to the proximal and distal inner borders that separate the duplicated arms form the interspersed unique spacer sequence [2]. This enables the design of allele-specific primers that hybridize to the spacer sequence. Using these primers in combination with a nondiscriminating primer that lies in the duplicated fragment allows the separate amplification of both DYS385 loci.

The major aim of this study was to specify to which extent the separate analysis of both DYS385 copies improves Y-STR haplotyping.

2. Materials and methods

2.1. DNA samples

Blood samples were obtained from 133 unrelated Caucasian men from Tirol (Austria). DNA was extracted using the QIAmp DNA Blood miniKit (Qiagen, Hilden, Germany) and quantitated by UV absorbance measurement.

2.2. Primers and PCR conditions

The PCR conditions and sequences of the primers that were used for the amplification of the Y-STRs comprising the minimal haplotype (DYS19, DYS385, DYS392, DYS393, DYS389 I and II, DYS390 and DYS391) were taken from Parson et al. [3].

The two allele-discriminating primers dys385a and dys385b were designed with the Primer Express 1.5 software (AB, Applied Biosystems, Warrington, UK) using the sequences of the clones RP11-143C1 (GenBank accession number AC007379) and RP11-569J3 (GenBank accession number AC022486), respectively.

For the separate amplification of the two DYS385 copies, either the primer dys385a or dys385b was used at a concentration of 300 nM in combination with the primer DYS385.2B (300 nM; 5′ -CCAATTACATAGTCCTCCTTTC-3′ , [4]). Thermal cycling comprised an initial denaturation step of 95 °C for 10 min followed by 30 cycles of 95 °C for 15 s, 54 °C for 1 min and 72 °C for 2 min.

The obtained PCR products had a length of approximately 700–780 bp. One-microliter aliquots of the first-round PCR product were subjected without further manipulations to semi-nested second-round PCR amplifications using the primers DYS385.A (5′ -FAM-AGCATGGGTGACAGAGCTA-3′ , [5]) and DYS385.2B at a concentration of 200 nM each. Thermal cycling was performed after an initial denaturation at 95 °C for 10 min for 7 cycles comprising 95 °C for 15 s, 58 °C for 1 min and 72 °C for 1 min and a final extension step of 72 °C for 60 min. The fluorescent labeled amplification products were separated by capillary gel electrophoresis on an ABI Prism 3100 DNA Analyzer (AB) under standard conditions and data analysis was performed with the software packages GeneScan Analysis Version 3.1 and Genotyper Version 2.5 (both AB).

3. Results

With the conventional PCR protocol, 27 different DYS385 genotypes were found in our population sample (GD = 0.8616). The genotype with the highest frequency was 11–14 (34.59%). The separate analysis of DYS385a and DYS385b increased the number of different genotypes to 34 (GD = 0.9185). The most common allele combination was DYS385a–DYS385b 14–11 (frequency = 23.31%), followed by DYS385a–DYS385b 11–14 (frequency = 11.28%). All samples that yielded only a single band when the conventional amplification strategy was used produced two bands of identical lengths when DYS385a and DYS385b were analysed separately. The discrimination capacity of the complete minimal haplotype was not affected, regardless of the strategy for the amplification of DYS385. With both PCR protocols, we could distinguish between 109 haplotypes corresponding to a cumulative haplotype diversity of 0.9951.

4. Conclusions

Our results show that the separate analysis of the two DYS385 loci improves the power of discrimination of this single marker when compared to the results obtained with the conventional nondiscriminating amplification strategy. However, in the forensically more relevant context of the minimal haplotype, the separate analysis of DYS385 had no positive effect on the differentiation of paternal lineages in our study. The gain of information due to the separate analysis of DYS385a and b becomes redundant by the analysis of the other markers included in the minimal haplotype.

Further, in the first round of amplification of the allele-discriminating PCR protocol for DYS385a and DYS385b, amplicons with lengths ranging from ~ 700 up to ~ 780 bp are obtained. Therefore, this method is not applicable for the typing of samples that contain only highly degraded DNA.

Acknowledgements

We thank Alexandra Lindinger (ILM, Innsbruck, Austria) for excellent technical assistance.

References

[1] R. Kittler, A. Erler, S. Brauer, M. Stoneking, M. Kayser, Apparent intrachromosomal exchange on the human Y chromosome explained by population history, Eur. J. Hum. Genet. 11 (4) (2003) 304–314.

[2] H. Skaletsky, T. Kuroda-Kawaguchi, P.J. Minx, H.S. Cordum, L. Hillier, L.G. Brown, et al, The male-specific region of the human Y chromosome is a mosaic of discrete sequence classes, Nature 423 (6942) (2003) 825–837.

[3] W. Parson, H. Niederstätter, S. Köchl, M. Steinlechner, B. Berger, When autosomal short tandem repeats fail: optimized primer and reaction design for Y-chromosome short tandem repeat analysis in forensic casework, Croat. Med. J. 42 (3) (2001) 285–287.

[4] P.M. Schneider, S. Meuser, W. Waiyawuth, Y. Seo, C. Rittner, Tandem repeat structure of the duplicated Y-chromosomal STR locus DYS385 and frequency studies in the German and three Asian populations, Forensic Sci. Int. 97 (1) (1998) 61–70.

[5] M. Kayser, A. Caglia, D. Corach, N. Fretwell, C. Gehrig, G. Graziosi, et al, Evaluation of Y-chromosomal STRs: a multicenter study, Int. J. Leg. Med. 110 (3) (1997) 125–129.

ELSEVIER

International Congress Series 1261 (2004) 363–365

www.ics-elsevier.com

Multiplex PCR development of Y-chromosomal biallelic polymorphisms for forensic applications

F. Alessandrini, M. Pesaresi, V. Onofri, L. Buscemi, A. Arseni, A. Tagliabracci*

Policlinico Torrette, Istituto di Medicina Legale, Università Politecnica delle Marche, via Conca, I-60020 Ancona, Italy

Abstract. The aim of this study is to set-up multiplex PCR of NRY single nucleotide polymorphisms (SNPs) suitable for forensic purposes. A first multiplex has been developed with SNP loci defining the European haplogroups (M35, M89, M172, M170, M9, M173, M45). PCR was performed with primers designed to produce amplicons in a range between 96 and 136 bp starting from 1 ng of DNA template. PCR product was minisequenced with tailed primers of different length and run in an automated five-colour capillary electrophoresis sequencer. © 2003 Published by Elsevier B.V.

Keywords: Y-SNPs; Multiplex PCR; Minisequencing; Geographical affiliation

1. Introduction

Such binary polymorphisms, also known as single nucleotide polymorphisms (SNPs), are of special interest for forensic purposes, because the amplification of short fragments including the single-base mutation which characterizes their polymorphism potentially allows a positive result. Underhill et al. [1] recently detected more than 200 biallelic variations screening a sample of 21 populations, with many of the markers showing regional specificity. The combination of these binary polymorphisms yielded a phylogenetic tree based on the principle of maximum parsimony, defining 18 haplogroups, indicated by capital letters from A to R (Fig. 1) [2].

The aim of this study was therefore to set up a multiplex PCR of Y-SNPs suitable for forensic purposes, employing materials, methods and technologies normally available in forensic laboratories.

2. Materials and methods

DNA was extracted from whole blood of 68 Europeans and 29 non-European subjects using the QIAamp (Qiagen, Chatsworth, CA) procedure [3]. The M35, M89, M172,

* Corresponding author. Tel.: +39-71-596-4727; fax: +39-71-596-4723.
E-mail address: medleg@mta01.univpm.it (A. Tagliabracci).

doi:10.1016/S0531-5131(03)01531-0

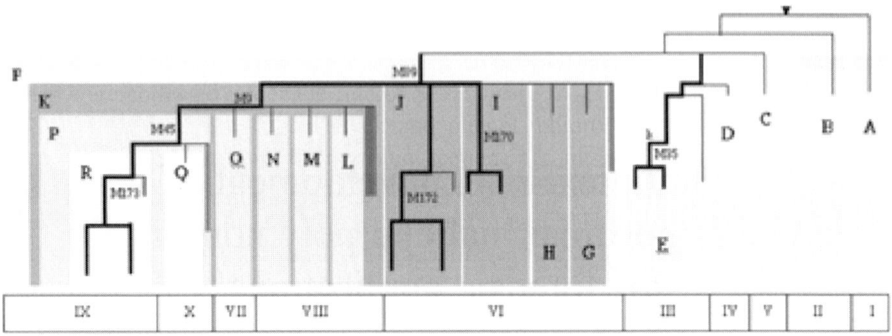

Fig. 1. Phylogeographic tree (YCC 2002, modified), showing loci investigated in this study: M35, M89, M172, M170, M9, M173 and M45.

M170, M9, M173 and M45 loci [1], characterizing European haplogroups, were chosen for this multiplex. One nanogram of DNA was submitted to amplification and 4 μl of the purified product was submitted to a dideoxy single-base extension of unlabelled oligonucleotide primers using the SnaPshot multiplex kit (AB) in the conditions recommended by the manufacturer. Moreover, multiplex was tested on low molecular weight DNA after fragmenting in a sonicator device (Labsonic, from B. Braun). Sonicated DNA was amplified with the AmpFlSTR Identifiler PCR Amplification kit (AB) and was analyzed on an ABI 310 (AB).

3. Results

For SNP genotyping, we used minisequencing, a single-base extension of an unlabeled oligonucleotide primer. Hot-start PCR was chosen for our multiplex, in place of Touchdown PCR, because it worked better and all the loci in the multiplex, starting from only 1 ng of DNA in our experimental conditions, could be amplified.

The first multiplex was designed to contain mutations capable of placing the Y chromosome of the subject under investigation within the known European haplogroups. Haplogroups F*(xK), R1 and E, that, although most highly represented in Europe, are not exclusive to Europeans. Of the 68 Europeans tested, 64 were correctly assigned to one of the three European haplogroups when typed with the multiplex we made.

Experiments to explore the suitability of the Y-SNP multiplex with low molecular weight DNA were performed by amplifying DNA fragments sized less than approximately 150 bp, produced by sonication. Positive amplifications were obtained from 1 ng of DNA for all seven SNPs included in our multiplex, whereas only pherograms with high noise background and questionable peaks below the rfu threshold of 50 were obtained (Fig. 2).

4. Discussion

Although the small number of people examined here does not allow conclusive results to be shown, the present work demonstrates the definite possibility of affiliating one subject to the geographical area of provenance by studying the biallelic markers of the Y-chromosome located in the lowest branches of phylogenetic tree.

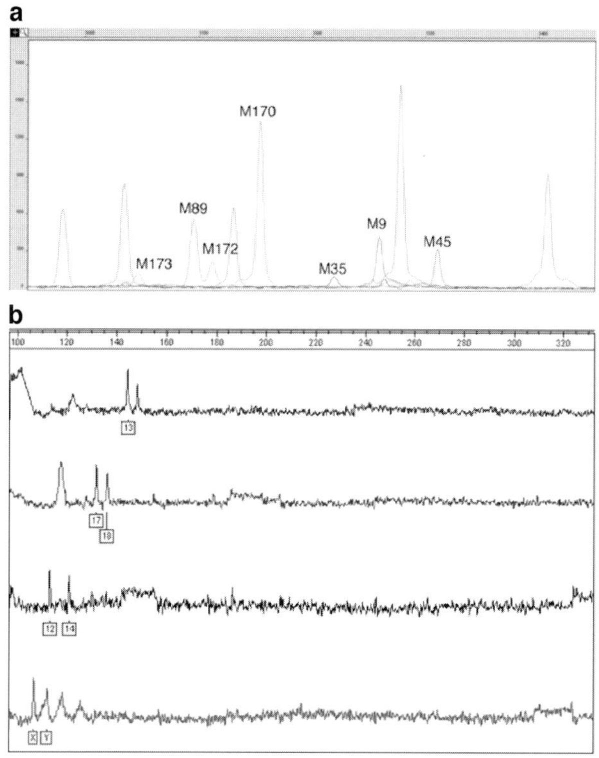

Fig. 2. Y-SNP-multiplex and microsatellites amplification from low molecular weight DNA fragmented by sonication. (a) Pherogram of Y-SNP multiplex obtained by amplification of 1 ng DNA sonicated for 200 min. All seven extension products are present in the pherogram. Typing results: K*(xP). (b) Microsatellites typing of 1 ng of fragmented DNA by sonication for 200 min from the same sample.

In conclusion, the main achievement of this work is the development of an effective, robust multiplex PCR of seven Y-chromosome SNPs starting from 1 ng of DNA template, exploring polymorphisms on fragments between 96 and 136 nucleotides in size, yielding positive results also with degraded DNA. SNPs, included in the multiplex, are hierarchically organized, capable of assigning the geographical area of the subject and guiding the choice of further polymorphisms to be analyzed for evolutionary or forensic purposes. This hierarchical strategy is an important feature of forensic work when only small amounts of DNA are available.

References

[1] P.A. Underhill, et al., The Phylogeography of Y chromosome binary haplotypes and the origins of modern human populations, Ann. Hum. Genet. 65 (2001) 43–62.

[2] The Y Chromosome Consortium. A nomenclature system for the tree of human Y-chromosomal binary haplogroups, Genome Res. 12 (2002) 339–348.

[3] C.A. Scherczinger, et al., DNA extraction from liquid blood using QIAamp, J. Forensic Sci. 42 (1997) 893–896.

ELSEVIER

International Congress Series 1261 (2004) 366–368

www.ics-elsevier.com

Analysis of the HVI and HVII regions of mitochondrial DNA in 100 individuals from North of Portugal

G. Lima[a], J.A. Peña[b], M.A. Alfonso Sanchez[b], M.L. Pontes[a], D. Abrantes[a], M.J. Pereira[a], I. Fernández-Fernández[c], A. Castro[c], M.F. Pinheiro[a,d,*], M. Martínez de Pancorbo[e]

[a] *Delegação do Porto do Instituto Nacional de Medicina Legal, Jardim Carrilho Videira s/n, 4050-167 Oporto, Portugal*

[b] *Dep. Biologia Animal y Genética, Unid. Antropologia Física, Facultad de Ciencias, Univ. del País Vasco, Bilbao, Spain*

[c] *DataGene, Sondika, Spain*

[d] *ICBAS, Univ. do Porto, Oporto, Portugal*

[e] *Dep. de Zoologia y Dinamica celular animal, Facultad de Farmacia, Univ. del País Vasco, Spain*

Abstract. The analysis of mitochondrial DNA (mtDNA) control region is of great importance in forensic casework and evolution studies. The aim of this study was to create a population database for the HVI and HVII regions of mtDNA in the population of North of Portugal. The HVI and HVII segments were studied in 100 unrelated and healthy individuals by direct sequencing. Nucleotide substitutions were found using Anderson's reference sequence. Length and position heteroplasmy were observed. The genetic structure of the population was analysed. The match probability and discrimination power values were calculated. The phylogenetic analysis for HVI segment was made following classification into haplogroups and genetic distances were calculated. These analyses place the North of Portugal population among the European Caucasoid populations. © 2003 Published by Elsevier B.V.

Keywords: Mitochondrial DNA; HVI–HVII; North of Portugal

1. Introduction

The control region of the human mitochondrial DNA (mtDNA) is highly polymorphic due to a rapid rate of evolution. The mtDNA does not undergo recombination and is present in high copy number per cell. For this reason, its analysis is an important tool for genetic identification and may provide results where the analysis of nuclear DNA fails.

* Corresponding author. Delegação do Porto do Instituto Nacional de Medicina Legal, Jardim Carrilho Videira s/n, 4050-167 Oporto, Portugal. Tel.: +351-222073850; fax: +351-223325931.

E-mail address: correio@dpinml.mj.pt (M.F. Pinheiro).

0531-5131/
doi:10.1016/j.ics.2003.12.006

Table 1
Diversity and genetic parameters in the population of North of Portugal

	HVI	HVII	HVI+HVII
No. of haplotypes	64	55	83
Polymorphic positions	59	45	104
Transitions	56	40	96
Transversions	5	1	6
Insertions	0	4	4
Deletions	1	0	1
Nucleotide diversity	0.012038 ± 0.006654	0.010187 ± 0.005767	0.011116 ± 0.005772
Gene diversity	0.9596 ± 0.0140	0.9739 ± 0.006	0.9882 ± 0.0054
Mean number of pairwise differences	4.32188 ± 2.156573	3.626465 ± 1.853745	7.948283 ± 3.725813

The haploid maternal inheritance of the mtDNA is also useful for the identification of maternally related individuals. The analysis of mtDNA is usually done by direct sequencing of PCR products. It is of great importance in forensic genetics because it has been applied successfully to different types of biological samples. The simultaneous occurrence of more than one type of mtDNA in a single individual is called heteroplasmy, being the length heteroplasmy the most frequent type observed. For purposes of genetic identification, its occurrence must be carefully evaluated. The great amount of variability accumulated in the control region represents a record of the human evolution history. In this sense, the analysis of mtDNA polymorphisms is particularly useful in human evolutionary studies and phylogenetic analysis between populations. The aim of this study was to create a population database for the HVI and HVII regions of mtDNA in the North of Portugal.

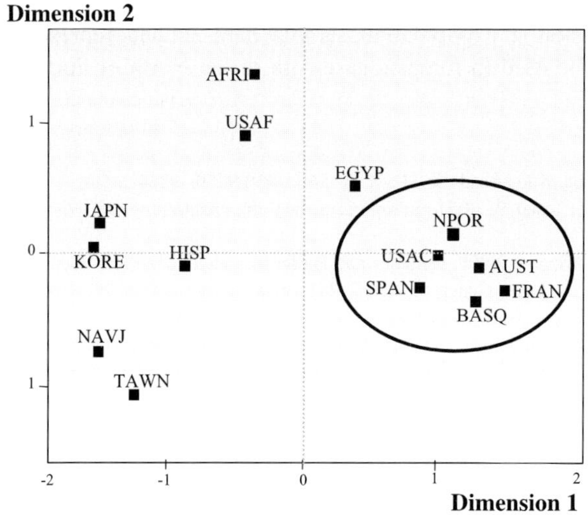

Fig. 1. Nonmetrical multidimensional scaling (MDS) applied on mismatch–intermatch pairwise distances. Total variance for the eigenvectorial reduction = 99.4%, stress = 0.0368.

2. Material and methods

Blood samples were collected from 100 unrelated and healthy individuals from the population of North of Portugal. DNA was extracted using the phenol–chloroform method. The HVI and HVII segments were amplified by PCR using the primers L15 996–H16 401 and L29–H408 [1], respectively, each modified. The two segments were sequenced by capillary electrophoresis (ABI PRISM 310 Genetic Analyser, Applied Biosystems) on both strands using the primers M13 and the "dRhodamine Terminator Cycle Sequencing Ready Reaction kit" (Applied Biosystems). Nucleotide substitutions were found by comparison with Anderson's reference sequence [2]. The genetic structure of the population was analysed [3]. The match probability (PM) and discrimination power (PD) values were calculated. The phylogenetic analysis for HVI segment was made following classification into haplogroups [4] and genetics distances were calculated using the mismatch–intermatch means of pairwise differences [5,6]. The analysis of both segments taken together was made using only their sequences. A nonmetrical multidimensional scaling (MDS) diagram was debugged [7,8].

3. Results and discussion

The sequences of mtDNA HVI and HVII segments were studied from positions 16033 to 16391 and 57 to 408, respectively. Population parameters are shown in Table 1.

Taken together both segments, PD is 0.9882 and PM is 0.0118. Length heteroplasmy was observed in 16 individuals. Position heteroplasmy was observed in 2 individuals (16038R and 16295Y). The MDS diagram for mtDNA haplogroups in 13 populations (USA Africans, Africans, Egypt, USA Caucasians, Spain, Basques, Austria, France, USA Hispanics, Japan, Korea, Taiwan and Navajo) [9] and North of Portugal is shown in Fig. 1. The phylogenetic analysis between the population of North of Portugal and other 13 populations demonstrates that this population is included in the European population cluster. In conclusion, the population sample here studied represents a mitochondrial database that can be used in forensic casework in the North of Portugal.

References

[1] Vigilant, et al., Proc. Natl. Acad. Sci. U. S. A. 86 (1989) 9350–9354.

[2] Thompson, et al., Clustal W (1.5) multiple sequence alignments program, Nucleic Acids Res. 22 (1994) 4673–4680.

[3] Schneider, et al., Arlequin 2.000, Genetics and Biometry Laboratory, Univ. Genebra, Switzerland, 2000.

[4] Richards, et al., Ann. Hum. Genet. 62 (1998) 241–260.

[5] C.R. Rao, Theor. Popul. Biol. 21 (1982) 24–43.

[6] M. Nei, Molecular Evolutionary Genetics, Columbia Univ. Press, New York, USA, 1987.

[7] W. Torgerson, Multidimensional scaling: I. Theory and method, Psychometrika 17 (1952) 401–419.

[8] J. Lalouel, Distance analysis and multidimensional scaling, in: J. Mielke, M. Crawford (Eds.), Current Developments in Anthropological Genetics, Theory and Methods, vol. 1, Plenum, New York, 1980, pp. 209–250.

[9] Budowle, et al., Forensic Sci. Int. 103 (1999) 23–25.

ELSEVIER

International Congress Series 1261 (2004) 369–371

www.ics-elsevier.com

Analysis of the single nucleotide polymorphisms of mitochondrial DNA by liquid bead array technology

Masayuki Nata*, Masaki Hashiyada

Division of Forensic Medicine, Department of Public Health and Forensic Medicine, Tohoku University Graduate School of Medicine, Seiryo-machi 2-1, Aoba, Sendai 980-8575, Japan

Abstract. Thirty single nucleotide polymorphisms (SNPs) in mitochondrial DNA were investigated in 105 unrelated Japanese by liquid bead array technology which is a detection method using microsphere and a flow cytometer. Nineteen SNPs were observed, and 50 different mt DNA types were observed, and 35 types were seen only once, and 15 types in multiple individuals. Genetic diversity was estimated as 0.943. This array system is simple and rapid, as well as suitable for high-throughput applications in a forensic investigative screening. © 2003 Elsevier B.V. All rights reserved.

Keywords: Single nucleotide polymorphism (SNP); Mitochondrial DNA; Liquid bead array; Screening

1. Introduction

DNA typing of mitochondria has been used as a useful technique in forensic caseworks. Signet™ Mitochondrial DNA Screening System (Marligen Biosciences, Ijamsville, USA) is a new array system based on liquid bead array technology. Thirty single nucleotide polymorphisms (SNPs) in human mitochondrial DNA can be analyzed rapidly by this system.

2. Materials and methods

DNA samples of 105 unrelated Japanese volunteers were extracted from buccal swabs using Chelex 100 method.

The assay consists of five steps as follows: (1) Amplify the mitochondrial DNA hypervariable regions. (2) Remove the PCR primers by digesting with Exonuclease I. (3) Label the PCR products with a fluorescently tagged oligonucleotide by primer extension. (4) Hybridize the labeled DNA with allele-specific oligonucleotide in a multiplex beads array. (5) Read the hybridized microspheres in a Luminex 100 Sysytem. Collected data was analyzed by a MasterPlex GT software (MiraiBaio, Alameda, USA). In this study, IB,

* Corresponding author. Tel.: +81-22-717-8110; fax: +81-22-717-8112.
E-mail address: nata@gonryo.med.tohoku.ac.jp (M. Nata).

doi:10.1016/S0531-5131(03)01829-6

Table 1
mt DNA tupes observed in 105 Japanese

IB	IC1	IC2	ID	IIA1	IIA2	IIB	IIC	IID	*N*
CRS	CRS	CRS	CRS	73G	CRS	CRS	CRS	263G	1
CRS	CRS	CRS	CRS	73G	CRS	CRS	195C	263G	1
CRS	CRS	CRS	16362C	73G	CRS	CRS	CRS	263G	2
CRS	CRS	CRS	16362C	73G	CRS	152C	CRS	263G	1
CRS	CRS	16311C	16362C	73G	CRS	CRS	CRS	263G	1
CRS	16304C	16311C	CRS	73G	CRS	CRS	CRS	263G	1
CRS	16304C	16311C	CRS	73G	CRS	CRS	195C	263G	1
CRS	16304C	16311C	CRS	73G	CRS	152C	CRS	263G	10
CRS	16304C	CRS	CRS	73G	CRS	CRS	CRS	263G	2
16217C	CRS	CRS	CRS	73G	CRS	CRS	CRS	263G	2
16217C	CRS	CRS	CRS	73G	CRS	CRS	195C	263G	1
16217C	CRS	CRS	CRS	73G	CRS	CRS	200G	263G	2
16217C	CRS	CRS	CRS	73G	CRS	146C	CRS	263G	1
16217C	CRS	CRS	CRS	73G	CRS	150T	CRS	263G	1
16217C	CRS	CRS	CRS	73G	CRS	150T	195C	263G	1
16217C	CRS	CRS	CRS	73G	CRS	150T/152C	CRS	263G	2
16217C	CRS	16311C	CRS	73G	CRS	CRS	CRS	263G	1
16217C	CRS	16311C	CRS	73G	CRS	150T	195C	263G	1
16217C	16298C	CRS	16362C	73G	CRS	152C	CRS	263G	1
16223T	CRS	CRS	CRS	73G	CRS	CRS	CRS	263G	4
16223T	CRS	CRS	CRS	73G	CRS	CRS	195C	263G	1
16223T	CRS	CRS	CRS	73G	CRS	146C	CRS	263G	1
16223T	CRS	CRS	CRS	73G	CRS	146C	199C	263G	1
16223T	CRS	CRS	CRS	73G	CRS	150T	CRS	263G	5
16223T	CRS	CRS	16362C	73G	CRS	CRS	CRS	263G	18
16223T	CRS	CRS	16362C	73G	93G	CRS	CRS	263G	1
16223T	CRS	CRS	16362C	CRS	CRS	CRS	CRS	263G	1
16223T	CRS	CRS	16362C	73G	CRS	CRS	CRS	CRS	1
16223T	CRS	CRS	16362C	73G	CRS	150T	CRS	263G	6
16223T	CRS	CRS	16362C	CRS	CRS	150T	CRS	263G	1
16223T	CRS	CRS	16362C	73G	CRS	152C	CRS	263G	7
16223T	CRS	CRS	16362C	73G	CRS	152C	CRS	CRS	1
16223T	CRS	CRS	16362C	73G	CRS	CRS	195C	263G	2
16223T	CRS	CRS	16362C	CRS	CRS	CRS	195C	263G	1
16223T	CRS	CRS	16362C	73G	CRS	CRS	199C	263G	1
16223T	CRS	CRS	16362C	73G	CRS	146C	CRS	263G	1
16223T	CRS	16311C	CRS	73G	CRS	146C/152C	CRS	263G	1
16223T	CRS	16311C	16362C	73G	CRS	150T	CRS	263G	1
16223T	CRS	16319A	CRS	73G	CRS	CRS	CRS	263G	4
16223T	CRS	16319A	CRS	73G	CRS	146C	195C	263G	2
16223T	CRS	16319A	CRS	CRS	CRS	146C	195C	263G	1
16223T	CRS	16319A	CRS	73G	CRS	152C	CRS	263G	1
16223T	CRS	16319A	16362C	73G	CRS	CRS	CRS	263G	2
16223T	CRS	16319A	16362C	73G	CRS	152C	200G	263G	1
16223T	16298C	CRS	CRS	73G	CRS	146C	195C	263G	1
16223T	16298C	16311C	CRS	73G	CRS	150T	199C	263G	1
16223T	16298C	16319A	CRS	73G	CRS	152C	CRS	263G	1
16223T	16304C	CRS	CRS	73G	CRS	150T	CRS	263G	1
16223T/16224C[a]	CRS	CRS	16362C	73G	CRS	146C	195C	263G	1
16224C	16294T	16309G	CRS	73G	CRS	152C	200G	263G	1

[a] No difference of relative intensity was observed between 16223T and 16224C.

IC1, IC2, and ID in HV1 regions, and IIA1, IIA2, IIB, IIC, and IID in HV2 regions were analyzed. IA in HV1 region was not analyzed.

3. Results and discussion

Nineteen SNPs were observed, and the frequencies of observed variations were approximately similar to previous report [1,2]. Fifty different mtDNA types were observed of which 35 types were seen only once. Fifteen types were seen in multiple individuals (Table 1). Genetic diversity [3] was estimated as 0.952. Seo et al. [2] and Imaizumi et al. [4] reported that the genetic diversity of Japanese mt DNA was estimated as 0.999 and 0.996, respectively. As compared to them, this study is not high polymorphic, because this system is designed to rapidly screening, not to detailed analyses. In forensic case work, this system excludes irrelevant mtDNA samples, and then, further sequencing analysis would be carried out about unexcluded samples. This array system is simple and rapid, as well as suitable for high-throughput applications in a forensic investigative screening.

Acknowledgements

Special thanks to Ms. Junko Tanoue, Mr. Seiichiro Tto (Hitachi Software Engineering) and Mr. Steven B. Lee (MiraiBaio).

References

[1] M. Nata, et al., Sequence polymorphism of the D-loop of mitochondrial DNA in Japanese and Chinese population, Acta Crim. Japan 65 (1999) 244–254.

[2] Y. Seo, et al., Sequence polymorphism of mitochondrrial DNA control region in Japanese, Forensic Sci. Int. 97 (1998) 155–164.

[3] F. Tajima, Statistical method for testing the neutral mutation hypothesis by DNA polymorphism, Genetics 123 (1989) 585–595.

[4] K. Imaizumi, et al., A new database of mitochondrial DNA hypervariable region 1 and II sequence from 162 Japanese individuals, Int. J. Leg. Med. 116 (2002) 68–73.

ELSEVIER

International Congress Series 1261 (2004) 372–373

www.ics-elsevier.com

Cabo Verde islands: different maternal and paternal heritage testifies the nature of its first settlers

R. Gonçalves, A.T. Fernandes, A. Brehm*

Centro de Estudos da Macaronésia, Biology, University of Madeira, Campus of Penteada, PT 9000-390 Funchal, Portugal

Abstract. The Cabo Verde Archipelago was colonized by the Portuguese in the 15th century. The first male settlers were mostly European males who never exceeded 1% of the total population mainly constituted by slaves brought from the West African coast. No European women were among the settlers who went to Cabo Verde without their families and formed liaisons with slaves creating a new class of individuals, the "mullato". Here, we compare the maternal and paternal heritage of present-day Cabo Verdeans, by looking to their mtDNA and Y-biallelic markers profile. There is a strong asymmetry concerning both markers. The sub-Saharan component account for 93% of the total mitochondrial lineages of Cabo Verdeans, but less than 21% of the Y-chromosomes. The high percentage of Y-chromosome markers with an European affiliation attests for the importance that few lineages existing at the beginning of the settlement became widespread in the population in just 500 years. © 2003 Published by Elsevier B.V.

Keywords: Cabo Verde; mtDNA; Y-SNPs

1. Introduction

The Cabo Verde islands were settled in 1460, by a few European males (mainly Portuguese) and sub-Saharan slaves brought from the West African coast. No women were among the European settlers so a crioulo population appeared as a consequence of liaisons with slave women, eventually becoming the majority of the population [1]. Recently, two studies analysed the genetic composition of the Cabo Verde population by looking at mtDNA and Y-chromosome biallelic markers. While almost all mitochondrial lineages (93%) were of sub-Saharan origin, the majority of Y-chromosomes were found to trace back to European and North African lineages (84%).

2. Materials and methods

The same individuals were typed for mtDNA and Y-biallelic markers. In the case of mtDNA, 292 samples were sequenced for their mitochondrial HVS-I and HVS-II regions. When necessary, RFLPs of diagnostic nucleotide positions were also performed in order to

* Corresponding author. Tel.: +351-291705380; fax: +351-291705399.
E-mail address: brehm@uma.pt (A. Brehm).

0531-5131/ © 2003 Published by Elsevier B.V.
doi:10.1016/S0531-5131(03)01770-9

Table 1
mtDNA haplogroup profiles (in %) in Cabo Verde

L1a	**L1b**	**L1c**	**L2a**	**L2b**	**L2c**	**L3b**	**L3d**	**L3e**	**L3***	U6	Eu[a]
1	**8**	**8**	**20**	**3**	**17**	**9**	**7**	**17**	**4**	3	3

In bold are the sub-Saharan typical haplogroups.
[a] Eurasian.

Table 2
Y-chromosome haplogroup profiles (in %) in Cabo Verde

A	E(xE3a,E3b)	**E3a**	E3b	R1b	F(xR1b)
2	8	**16**	21	17	36

In bold are the sub-Saharan typical haplogroups.

unambiguously determine their haplogroup assignment. Primers, sample's origin and PCR conditions are described in detail elsewhere [2]. Two hundred one individuals were typed for 36 Y-SNPs (single nucleotide polymorphisms) following the procedure described in Ref. [3].

3. Results and discussion

MtDNA and Y-haplogroup frequencies observed in Cabo Verdeans are summarized in Tables 1 and 2. This population is a perfect choice for studies of admixture and behaviour (spread) of nuclear and non-nuclear genes due to the particularity of the putative parental populations being known and also genetically distinct: West Africans (sub-Saharans) and Portuguese (Europeans). Several studies have been done recently with the aim of getting a clear picture of the genetics of Cabo Verdeans (STRs [4] and HLA [5]). MtDNA haplogroups present in the population testify the almost null contribution of women of European ascendancy to the making of Cabo Verde genetic profile but it is striking that in 500 years, non-sub-Saharan Y-haplogroups became by far the most widespread lineages present in the population contrary to a common belief that the few European settlers had a low impact in the population's genetic profile.

References

[1] V.M. Godinho, Os Descobrimentos e a Economia Mundial, Arcádia, hisbon vol. 1.2 (1965) 467–478.

[2] A. Brehm, L. Pereira, H.-J. Bandelt, M. Prata, A. Amorim, Mitochondrial portrait of the Cabo Verde Archipelago: the Senegambian outpost of Atlantic Slave Trade, Ann. Hum. Genet. 66 (2002) 49–60.

[3] R. Gonçalves, A. Rosa, A. Freitas, A. Fernandes, T. Kivisild, R. Villems, A. Brehm, Y-chromosome lineages in Cabo Verde Islands witness the diverse geographic origin of its first male settlers, Hum. Genet. 113 (2003) 467–478.

[4] A. Fernandes, R. Velosa, J. Jesus, A. Carracedo, A. Brehm, Genetic differentiation of the Cabo Verde Archipelago population analysed by STR polymorphisms, Ann. Hum. Genet. 67 (2003) 340–347.

[5] H. Spínola, A. Brehm, F. Williams, J. Jesus, D. Middleton, Distribution of HLA alleles in Portugal and Cabo Verde. Relationships with the slave trade route, Ann. Hum. Genet. 66 (2002) 285–296.

ELSEVIER

International Congress Series 1261 (2004) 374–376

www.ics-elsevier.com

Identification by mtDNA of exchanged human body remains

C. Cruz[a], T. Ribeiro[a], C. Vieira-Silva[a], I. Lucas[a], H. Geada[b], R. Espinheira[a,*]

[a] *Forensic Genetics, National Institute of Legal Medicine Institute, Rua Manuel Bento de Sousa, No. 3, 1159-219 Lisbon, Portugal*

[b] *Department of Legal Medicine, Faculty of Medicine, Lisbon, Portugal*

Abstract. This report presents an homicide case which occurred in an African country, involving five Portuguese citizens whose identification was suspected to have been exchanged. HVI and HVII control regions of mtDNA analysis was performed from bones from each of the five corpses in order to achieve identification by comparison with four alleged mothers. Two bodies shared the same sequence, which suggest a kinship relation. Results have confirmed the suspicion of body remains exchange.

Keywords: mtDNA; HVI/HVII; Human identification; Human remains; Degraded DNA

1. Introduction

Five Portuguese citizens were killed in Africa. Three of them were identified and subsequently removed to Portugal, where they were buried. Two children were reported as missing. One year later, two skeletons were found in a grave, 500 m from the crime scene. Genetic typing of DNA extracted from skeletal remains was performed in order to establish their identities. One of the mothers of the two missing minors was excluded from the maternity of the skeletal remains. The hypothesis was raised of an identity exchange of the three corpses previously removed to Portugal. These were then exhumed and subjected to genetic analysis to achieve biological identification.

In this report, we present the results of mtDNA sequence analysis of human body remains of five individuals and their presumptive mothers.

2. Material and methods

Bones and teeth from the five deceased individuals were powdered in a 6800 freezer mill (Fisher Bioblock) and DNA was extracted by an organic method. DNA extraction from bloodstains of the presumptive mothers was performed by Chelex method.

* Corresponding author. Tel.: +351-218811800; fax: +351-218809958.
E-mail address: bio.lisboa.inml@mail.pt (R. Espinheira).

0531-5131/
doi:10.1016/S0531-5131(03)01771-0

Table 1
HVI and HVII mtDNA sequences of the five individuals and four alleged mothers compared to the Anderson reference sequence

	Nucleotide position																		
	HVI																		
Sample origin	16069	16126	16129	16148	16168	16172	16187	16188	16189	16193	16223	16224	16230	16264	16270	16278	16293	16311	16320
Anderson	C	T	G	C	C	T	C	C	T	C	C	T	A	C	C	C	A	T	C
Body 1	.	.	A	T	T	C	T	G	C	.	T	.	G	.	.	T	G	C	T
Body 2	.	.	.	.	.	.	.	.	.	.	.	C	.	.	.	.	.	C	.
Body 3	.	C	.	.	.	.	T	.	C	.	T	.	.	T	T	T	G	C	.
Body 4	T	C	.	.	.	.	.	.	.	T	.	.	.	.	.	T	.	.	.
Body 5	.	.	.	.	.	.	.	.	.	.	.	C	.	.	.	.	.	C	.
Mother 1	.	.	A	T	T	C	T	G	C	.	T	.	G	.	.	T	G	C	T
Mother 2	.	C	.	.	.	.	T	.	C	.	T	.	.	T	T	T	G	C	.
Mother 3	.	.	.	.	.	.	.	.	.	.	.	C	.	.	.	.	.	C	.
Mother 4	T	C	.	.	.	.	.	.	.	T	.	.	.	.	.	T	.	.	.

	HVII																	
	73	93	95	114	150	152	182	185	189	195	198	236	247	263	295	309.1	315.1	316
Anderson	A	A	A	C	C	T	C	G	A	T	C	T	G	A	C	--	--	G
Body 1	.	G	C	.	.	.	.	G	G	.	.	C	A	G	.	C	C	.
Body 2	G	.	.	T	.	.	.	.	.	.	.	.	.	G	.	C	C	A
Body 3	G	.	.	.	.	C	T	T	.	C	T	.	A	G	.	.	C	.
Body 4	G	.	.	.	T	.	.	.	.	.	.	.	.	G	T	.	C	.
Body 5	G	.	.	T	.	.	.	.	.	.	.	.	.	G	.	C	C	A
Mother 1	.	G	C	.	.	.	.	G	G	.	.	C	A	G	.	C	C	.
Mother 2	G	.	.	.	.	C	T	T	.	C	T	.	A	G	.	.	C	.
Mother 3	G	.	.	T	.	.	.	.	.	.	.	.	.	G	.	C	C	A
Mother 4	G	.	.	.	T	.	.	.	.	.	.	.	.	G	T	.	C	.

A letter in each position indicates a nucleotide substitution relative to the reference sequence and the absence means that the sequence is according to the reference sequence. Double dash indicates the positions where there is no nucleotide on Anderson sequence.

For HVI region amplification, primers L15997 (A1), L16159 (A2), H16395 (B1) and H16236 (B2) were used [1]. Primers L048 (C1), L172 (C2), H408 (D1) and H 285 (D2) were applied for HVII region amplification [1]. PCR was carried out using the following thermal cycling conditions: 95 °C 11 min, 36 cycles (95 °C 10 s, 60 °C 30 s, 72 °C 30 s), 72 °C 10 min.

PCR products were sequenced with BigDye® Terminator v3.1 Cycle Sequencing Kit (Applied Biosystems) and purified with DYNAPURE™ Dye Terminator Removal ver.2 (Dynal®). Sequencing was carried out on an ABI PRISM™ 377 DNA Sequencer.

3. Results

We have obtained mtDNA sequences in all but one sample (a bone) after some changes of the protocol.

Almost all the samples were successfully amplified with the pairs of primers A1/B1 and C1/D1. Results were not obtained for HVII and for HVI regions from teeth of bodies 2 and 4, respectively. On these cases, shorter overlapping fragments were amplified with the pairs of primers C1/D2, C2/D1 (for body 2), A1/B2, A2/B1 (for body 4) and the reconstruction of HVII and HVI sequences were performed.

MtDNA sequence of each body matched always one of the alleged mothers sequence (Table 1). Nucleotide substitutions were the same in bodies 2, 5 and in presumptive mother 3, suggesting a kinship relation.

Results revealed that the three bodies buried in Portugal had been incorrectly identified.

4. Discussion

It was difficult to obtain results namely from teeth and bones retrieved in Africa. The state of bone samples was poor, probably due to humidity, temperature or other African environmental conditions and soil characteristics that accelerate the degradation process.

In some cases, increasing the amount of DNA helped to overcome the low amount of the DNA, but in some others lead to negative results, which can be explained by an increase of Taq polymerase inhibitors in the mix reaction. Several dilutions DNA extract were tested in order to decrease the hypothetical contaminants. Regarding the high fragmentation of DNA associated with this kind of samples [2], the application of different primers to the HVI and HVII regions allowed the amplification of two shorter overlapping fragments for each region and the reconstruction of HVI and HVII sequences.

MtDNA analysis was a useful tool to solve this case. Although it cannot be used to definitely identify the corpses, it provided evidence of maternal relationships and, consequently in this case, the previously exchange of human body remains.

References

[1] M.R. Wilson, J.A. DiZinno, D. Polanskey, et al., Validation of mitochondrial DNA sequencing for forensic casework analysis, Int. J. Legal Med. 108 (1995) 68–74.

[2] H.N. Poinar, The top 10 list: criteria of authenticity for DNA from ancient and forensic samples, Prog. Forensics Genet. 9 (2003) 575–579.

International Congress Series 1261 (2004) 377–379

www.ics-elsevier.com

Insights from pattern of mtDNA variation into the genetic history of São Tomé e Príncipe

Maria Jesus Trovoada[a,b], Luísa Pereira[a], Leonor Gusmão[a], Augusto Abade[b], António Amorim[a,c], Maria João Prata[a,c,*]

[a] *IPATIMUP, Institute of Pathology and Immunology of University of Porto, Rua Dr. Roberto Frias, s/n. 4200-465, Oporto, Portugal*

[b] *Department of Anthropology, University of Coimbra, Coimbra, Portugal*

[c] *Faculty of Sciences, University of Porto, Oporto, Portugal*

Abstract. Sequence data from the hypervariable segments I (HVS-I) and II (HVS-II) was obtained for 30 Angolares, 35 Forros and 38 Tongas, three self-reported ethnic groups from São Tomé e Príncipe, an African archipelago (Gulf of Guinea) whose settlement begun in the late 15th century. The repertory of mtDNA lineages denoted a fully African maternal pool primarily arisen from a Central/Southwestern substratum. The absence of any lineages of putative European descent means that the European impact at the mitochondrial pool was virtually nil. Angolares showed a clear reduction of mtDNA diversity and a slight genetic differentiation relatively to Tongas or Forros, whereas the two last groups did not present any signs of genetic boundaries between each other. The data now obtained reinforce the depiction of genetic substructuring in São Tomé e Príncipe previously derived from Y-chromosome STRs.

Keywords: MtDNA; Haplogroups; São Tomé e Príncipe; Population groups

1. Introduction

São Tomé e Príncipe is a small archipelago located on the Equator (Gulf of Guinea) that was uninhabited when first visited by Portuguese navigators in the early 1470s. Shortly afterward, the settlement was initiated with European colonist, mainly Portuguese, and an overwhelming number of slaves brought from the African Western mainland.

Among present day São Tomé e Príncipe inhabitants, the existence of three distinct population groups, Angolares, Forros and Tongas, is a common perception. Forros are referred to be "the sons of the land", the more ancient African inhabitants of the archipelago [1]. Tongas are the descendents from African contract labourers who, from the middle of the 19th century on with the development of the coffee and cocoa economy, massively entered the archipelago. The origin of Angolares is less clear notwithstanding the fact that the identification as a distinct community has the stronger

* Corresponding author. IPATIMUP, Institute of Pathology and Immunology of University of Porto, Rua Dr. Roberto Frias, s/n. 4200-465, Oporto, Portugal. Tel.: +351-225570700; fax: +351-225570799.

E-mail address: mprata@ipatimup.pt (M.J. Prata).

doi:10.1016/S0531-5131(03)01633-9

support from the geographical confinement to the southeastern tip of São Tomé, from cultural and livelihood traditions or from the own language.

Here we present sequence data from mtDNA detected by surveying HVS-I and HVS-II in individuals from the three São Tomean groups.

2. Material and methods

Blood samples were collected from 30 self-reported Angolares, 35 Forros and 38 Tongas. DNA was extracted from whole blood by standard phenol chloroform or Chelex methodologies. Primers, PCR and sequencing strategy as described in Ref. [2]. PCR products purified with Microspin™ S-300 HR columns (Pharmacia). Sequence reactions carried out with the kit Big-Dye™ Terminator Cycle Sequencing Ready Reaction (AB Applied Biosystems) and then a protocol based on $MgCl_2$/ethanol precipitation for purification of samples. Automatic sequencer: ABI Prism 3100 Genetic Analyzer. Sequence analysis: DNA Sequencing Analysis 3.7 software (AB Applied Biosystems).

3. Results and discussion

Among the 103 São Tomeans analysed, 71 different sequences were found (Fig. 1) belonging to 32 distinct haplogroups all specific from sub-Sahara, which testifies a full matrilineal African background. Previously we have detected some Y-STR haplotypes of likely European ancestry [3]. The combined results indicate that the European component of present São Tomé e Príncipe population was essentially mediated by males, signalling therefore the biased mating pattern that has prevailed in the archipelago.

Within the overall sample, four haplogroups, L1b, L1c, L2a1 and L3e1*, attained considerable high frequencies representing 56% of the sequences. The four haplogroups are common in West/Central Africa. Forros and Tongas, basically share the same mtDNA profile characterised by the presence of many different haplogroups. In contrast, the Angolares show a reduced number of different haplogroups and a particularly high frequency of L3e1* and L1c lineages.

Diversity levels in Forros, Tongas and in the overall São Tomean sample (Table 1) are very similar to those registered in mainland populations from the cluster of Central/Western ones at which São Tomé e Príncipe geographically belongs. Distinctly, Angolares show lower diversity, particularly concerning mean heretozygosity and proportion of different haplotypes, resembling what happens in Western African islands such as Cabo Verde NW or Bioko.

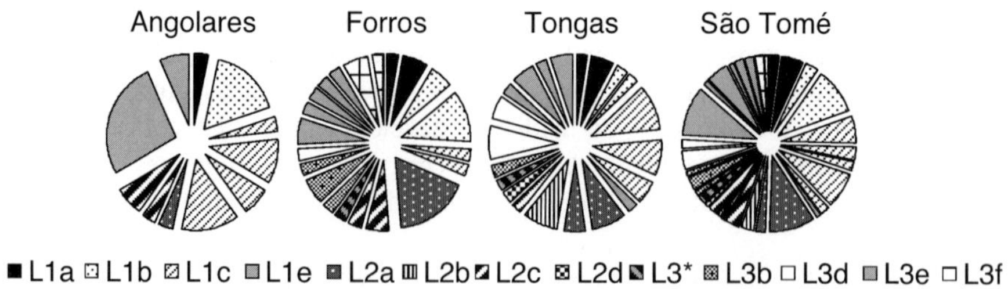

Fig 1. mtDNA haplogroup profiles in Angolares, Forros, Tongas and in overall São Tomé.

Table 1
Diversity and neutrality measures for HVS-I in African populations

Population/group	N^a	K (K/N)^b	H (S.E.)^c	M^d	Fu's Fs
Morocco [4]	32	29 (90.6)	0.988 ± 0.014	5.84	− 25.01*
Niger [5]	34	30 (88.3)	0.991 ± 0.010	6.19	− 24.70*
Nigeria [5]	60	38 (63.3)	0.972 ± 0.010	6.82	− 23.15*
Senegal [6]	110	46 (41.8)	0.963 ± 0.008	6.23	− 24.53*
C.Verde NW [7]	108	28 (25.9)	0.908 ± 0.013	5.84	− 5.58
C.Verde SE [7]	184	101 (54.9)	0.984 ± 0.003	6.29	− 24.85*
Mbuti [8]	13	5 (38.5)	0.756 ± 0.097	7.13	3.76
Biaka [8]	17	8 (47.1)	0.890 ± 0.043	7.81	1.67
Bioko [9]	45	16 (35.6)	0.910 ± 0.020	7.09	− 0.55
Angolares	30	16 (53.5)	0.913 ± 0.037	8.74	− 1.34
Forros	35	29 (82.9)	0.988 ± 0.010	7.52	− 18.66*
Tongas	38	28 (73.7)	0.984 ± 0.009	8.55	− 12.61*
São Tomé	103	61 (59.2)	0.985 ± 0.004	8.36	− 24.68*
Kenya [4]	36	32 (88.9)	0.991 ± 0.010	9.66	− 20.75*
Mozambique [2]	109	49 (45.0)	0.960 ± 0.008	7.78	− 23.62*

[a] N = sample size. [b] K = number of different sequences and percentage of sample size (N). [c] H = sequence diversity ± standard error. [d] M = average number of pairwise differences.
* $P<0.05$.

Analysis of population pairwise FSTs revealed statistically significant differences between Angolares and Forros (FST = 0.037, P = 0.04) or Angolares and Tongas (FST = 0.030, P = 0.04); while Tongas and Forros did not showed statistical differences (FST = 0.01, P = 0.14). The small level of genetic distinctiveness of Angolares can be attributable to genetic drift since, until recently, they lived in relative isolation in the southeastern tip of São Tomé e Príncipe, which is also reflected in their cultural and livelihood traditions or even in their own language.

For a small archipelago with a so recent population history, this is really a quite remarkable finding. In São Tomé e Príncipe, a complex net of social and historical forces must have interacted in order that a self-reported community like Angolares, with a presumable distinct origin from other São Tomé e Príncipe inhabitants, has retained and still preserves signs of genetic distinctiveness, despite the sharing of a so restricted territory with other people.

Acknowledgements

Financial support was granted by *Fundação para a Ciência e a Tecnologia, Programa Operacional Ciência, Tecnologia e Inovação (POCTI).*

References

[1] I.C. Henriques, São Tomé e Príncipe. A invenção de uma sociedade, Vega e Autor, 2000.
[2] L. Pereira, et al., Ann. Hum. Genet. 65 (2001) 439–458.
[3] M.J. Trovoada, et al., Ann. Hum. Genet. 65 (2001) 271–283.
[4] J.C. Rando, et al., Ann. Hum. Genet. 62 (1998) 531–550.
[5] E. Watson, et al., Am. J. Hum. Genet. 61 (1997) 691–704.
[6] L. Graven, et al., Mol. Biol. Evol. 12 (1995) 334–345.
[7] A. Brehm, et al., Ann. Hum. Genet. 66 (2002) 49–60.
[8] L. Vigilant, et al., Science 253 (1991) 1503–1507.
[9] E. Mateu, et al., Ann. Hum. Genet. 61 (1997) 507–518.

International Congress Series 1261 (2004) 380–382

www.ics-elsevier.com

Investigation of mtDNA heteroplasmy discordance between mother and child

K. Takayanagi*, H. Asamura, K. Tsukada, M. Ota, H. Fukushima

Department of Legal Medicine, Shinshu University School of Medicine, Asahi 3-1-1, Matsumoto, Nagano 390-8621, Japan

Abstract. Maternal mitochondrial DNA (mtDNA) heteroplasmy discordances were investigated by means of mtDNA hypervariable region 1 sequencing using hair shaft and blood samples obtained from eight mother–offspring pairs. Despite mtDNA's inheritance through the maternal line, heteroplasmic discrepancies appear to exist. Results also suggest that heteroplasmic mutations may be more common in hair than in blood. © 2003 Elsevier B.V. All rights reserved.

Keywords: mtDNA; Heteroplasmy; Mother–offspring pair; Hair shaft; Blood

1. Introduction

Mitochondrial DNA (mtDNA) sequencing has been validated for personal identifications in forensics analysis [1]. In recent years, improved DNA extraction methods and increased sequencing sensitivity have made possible the detection of heteroplasmic point mutations. While the results of one previous study suggest that heteroplasmy in the mtDNA control region is inherited and remains stable throughout life, other studies appear to indicate discrepancies among different samples obtained from a single individual or from maternally related individuals [2]. This study sought to analyze the mtDNA sequences of maternal lineages and to compare hair shaft and blood samples from individuals belonging to the same maternal lineage.

2. Material and methods

2.1. Samples

Hair shaft and blood samples were taken from eight mother–offspring pairs. Before DNA extraction from hair shaft samples, we provided the contamination by the serial washing procedure of water and ethanol. Moreover, all experiments were performed according to ISFG guidelines concerning mtDNA treatment to minimize DNA contamination.

* Corresponding author. Tel.: +81-26-337-3218; fax: +81-26-337-3084.
E-mail address: kayoko@sch.md.shinshu-u.ac.jp (K. Takayanagi).

doi:10.1016/S0531-5131(03)01784-9

2.2. DNA extraction

DNA was extracted from hair and blood by the silica beads method, and mtDNA control region 1 (position 15997–16401) was amplified by PCR using the following primers: 5′-FAM-CACCATTAGCACCCAAAGCT-3′ (15997) and 5′-CTTTGGAGTTGCAGTTGATG-3′ (16401).

2.3. Sequencing

BigDye Terminator Ver.3 was used as recommended by the manufacturer, and sequencing was performed in a 310 Genetic Analyzer. Analysis was performed with Sequence Analysis Ver.3.4.1.

3. Results

Heteroplasmic transitions were found among four of eight mother–offspring pairs, as shown in Table 1. For mother–offspring pairs who did not demonstrate heteroplasmy, mutation positions were found to correspond perfectly. In heteroplasmic point mutations, a heteroplasmic T/C transition at position 16189 was detected in three mother–offspring pairs, while a heteroplasmic G/A transition at position 16129 was detected in pair 2. In pair 4, a heteroplasmic T/C transition at position 16189 was observed only in the hair sample from the child. Although a heteroplasmic transition at 16189 was observed in both the mother's hair and blood samples, the proportions of the two nucleotides differed between hair and blood samples. In pairs 1, 3, and 4, length heteroplasmy was detected in all samples from both the mother and child in a C-stretch region, but a non-heteroplasmic

Table 1
Heteroplasmic positions found in the HV1 of mtDNA obtained from the four mother–offspring pairs

Base position		HV1			
Reference sequence		16129	16189	16189.1	16189.2
			T	–	–
Pair 1	mother's hair shaft		C>T	C/ –	
	mother's blood		C<T	C/ –	
	child's hair shaft		C>T	C/ –	
	child's blood		C>>(T)	C/ –	
Pair 2	mother's hair shaft	G/A			
	mother's blood	A			
	child's hair shaft	A			
	child's blood	A			
Pair 3	mother's hair shaft		C>T	C/ –	C/ –
	mother's blood		C>>(T)	C/ –	C/ –
	child's hair shaft		C>>(T)	C/ –	C/ –
	child's blood		C<T	C/ –	C/ –
Pair 4	mother's hair shaft		C	C	C/ –
	mother's blood		C	C/ –	–
	child's hair shaft		C>T	C/ –	–
	child's blood		C	C/ –	–

mutation consisting of a single cytosine insertion after position 16189 was detected only in a mother's hair sample of pair 4.

4. Discussion

MtDNA sequencing has been used as a tool for identifying individuals from minute quantities of DNA obtained from matter such as hair and bone [1]. However, the possibility of heteroplasmy has generally not been considered when considering whether two samples originate from the same maternal line. Our results indicated that discrepancies in heteroplasmy appear to occur despite maternal inheritance of mtDNA.

An earlier study reported no differences in intraindividual heteroplasmic point mutations in mtDNA sequences between hair and blood. The increasing sophistication and discriminating power of analysis has led to several recent reports that indicate extreme variability in the levels of heteroplasmy among hair roots from the same individual [3]. As with our study, heteroplasmic inconsistencies were found in the hair shaft and blood samples from the same individuals, suggesting that heteroplasmic mutations may occur more frequently in hair shafts than in blood.

These results suggest the need for careful consideration of heteroplasmy in mtDNA analyses and the need for multiple references and carefully scrutiny for the presence of heteroplasmy.

References

[1] A. Salas, M.V. Lareu, A. Carracedo, Heteroplasmy in mtDNA and the weight of evidence in forensic mtDNA analysis: a case report, Int. J. Legal Med. 114 (2001) 186–190.

[2] S. Lutz, H.J. Weisser, J. Heizmann, S. Pollak, Mitochondrial heteroplasmy among maternally related individuals, Int. J. Legal Med. 113 (2000) 155–161.

[3] T. Grzybowski, B.A. Malyarchuk, J. Czarny, D. Miscicka-Sliwka, R. Kotzbach, High levels of mitochondrial DNA heteroplasmy in single hair roots: reanalysis and revision, Electrophoresis 24 (2003) 1159–1165.

International Congress Series 1261 (2004) 383–385

www.ics-elsevier.com

Maternal and paternal contributions in Jewish populations

A. Picornell*, P. Giménez, G. Jiménez, J.A. Castro, M.M. Ramon

Laboratori de Genètica, Departament de Biologia, Universitat de les Illes Balears, Cra. Valldemossa, km. 7.5, 07122, Palma de Mallorca, Balears, Spain

Abstract. A total of 107 Jewish individuals (Ashkenazi, Sephardic, North African and Oriental) have been analyzed for the Y-chromosome minimal STR-haplotype and for the HVRI mtDNA. The results have been compared with autosomal microsatellite data obtained previously from the same population samples. Significative sex-specific differences could be observed in these Jewish populations.

Keywords: MtDNA (HVRI); Y-chromosome STRs; Jewish populations

1. Introduction

Modern Jews constitute one ethnic group split into several groups, the most numerous of which are the Ashkenazim, who have resided in north-eastern Europe for centuries; the Sephardim who, after their expulsion from Spain in 1492, lived in other Mediterranean countries, especially Turkey; the North African, where evidence exists of Jewish communities as early as the first centuries AD that were augmented as a consequence of the Spanish expulsion; and the Oriental Jews who have lived in Middle East countries throughout their history [1]. Geneticists have studied Jewish populations since the turn of the 20th century in an attempt to unravel what must be a complex system of interrelationships among Jewish communities and their non-Jewish neighbours. Several studies of "classical" and DNA markers have provided evidence both for the common genetic origin of Jewish communities and for admixture between Jewish communities and their host peoples. Studies based on low-resolution mtDNA RFLP or HVRI sequences have been published [2,3] but no mtDNA databases have been reported to date for Jewish populations, which are essential in order to estimate random match probabilities in forensic casework. Respect to Y-chromosome, there is also a lack of database containing the minimal Y-chromosome haplotype.

* Corresponding author. Tel.: +34-971-172050; fax: +34-971-173184.
E-mail address: apiconell@uib.es (A. Picornell).

doi:10.1016/S0531-5131(03)01631-5

The purpose of the present study were: (i) to develop a HVRI sequence mtDNA database from Jewish individuals, (ii) to study the Y-chromosome "minimal haplotype" in these populations and, (iii) to compare the differences in mtDNA found in Jews and non-Jews with those found using Y-chromosome and autosomal microsatellite data obtained from the same population samples.

2. Material and methods

We analyzed 107 Jewish individuals. Following the classical criteria, they were categorized in four groups: Ashkenazi, Sephardic, North African and Oriental. All these samples belong to the collection of The National Laboratory for the Genetics of Israeli Populations at Tel-Aviv University.

A 406-nt sequence in region I of the mtDNA D-loop (sites 15994–16400) was analysed. Amplification was performed on a 2400 GeneAmp Thermal Cycler (Perkin Elmer). A QIAquick PCR purification kit (Quiagen, Germany) and the Big Dye Terminator Ready Reaction kit (Perkin Elmer) was used. Sequencing reaction products were analysed using an ABI PRISM 310 (PE/ABD) automated DNA sequencer. Each template was sequenced in both directions.

The five Y-chromosome STRs DYS19, DYS389I and II, DYS390 and DYS391 were co-amplificated. PCR amplification of DYS393 was achieved in singleplex and coamplification of the loci DYS385 and DYS392 was performed in a duplex reaction. A GeneAmp PCR System 2400 and an ABI 310 automatic sequencer (PE Applied Biosystems) was used.

3. Results and discussion

In mtDNA a total of 74 different haplotypes in 107 individuals were observed, with a lower incidence of unique haplotypes (54.2%) than in other populations (Table 1). When compared to the CRS sequence, 75 transitions, seven transversions and one insertion were found. Three individuals with one position of sequence heteroplasmy at nucleotides 16 093, 16 134 and 16 169, respectively, were detected. The mean pairwise differences in the Jewish populations were in the range of 5.5–6.2, with the exception of Sephardic Jews that had a lower value of 4.8. The gene diversity showed values that ranged between 0.95 and 0.98, and the random match probability was between 5% and 10%.

The eight Y-specific loci showed 71 different haplotypes in 71 unrelated males, therefore all haplotypes were unique.The discrimination capacity was 100% and the haplotype diversity was 1.00.

The data on mtDNA and Y-chromosome were compared between them and with those on autosomical markers previously studied in these populations. With respect to mtDNA, Jewish populations showed a considerable differentiation between them. These results agree with Thomas et al. [3], who indicated that each of the different Jewish communities formed independently around distinct groups of maternal founders and that subsequent gene flow from the host populations was limited on the female side. Autosomal microsatellite data showed no significant differences between all four Jewish populations studied or between them and other circum-Mediterranean populations [4]. Y-chromosome data showed that all the Jewish populations grouped together, and presented a clear

Table 1
Frequencies (%) of the haplotypes observed in the Jewish populations found in at least two individuals

HVRI sequence (sites 15994–16400)	Ashkenazi (20)	Oriental (23)	N. African (33)	Sephardic (31)
CRS	10.0	0	9.1	9.7
224 (C), 234 (T), 311 (C)	15.0	0	0	0
224 (C), 311 (C)	15.0	0	0	0
223 (T), 224 (C), 234 (T), 311 (C)	10.0	0	0	0
129 (A), 223 (T), 264 (T), 270 (T), 311 (C), 319 (A), 362 (C), 391 (A)	10.0	0	0	0
126 (C), 292 (T), 294 (T), 296 (T)	0	17.4	0	0
69 (T), 145 (A), 261 (T), 290 (T)	0	8.7	0	0
284 (G), 362 (C)	0	17.4	0	0
134(T), 189 (A), 223 (T), 278 (T), 311 (C)	0	0	15.2	0
126 (C), 362 (C)	0	0	9.1	0
129 (A), 223 (T), 311 (C), 391 (A)	0	0	6.1	0
298 (C)	0	0	3.0	3.2
356 (C)	0	0	3.0	3.2
86 (C)	0	0	0	6.5
218 (T), 328 (A), 362 (C)	0	0	0	9.7
311 (C), 362 (C)	0	0	0	6.5

Modal haplotypes in each group are underlined. Number of individuals is in brackets.

differentiation with respect to the non-Jewish populations. Therefore, sex-specific differences can been observed in Jewish populations and this fact must be taken into account for a suitable choice of databases in order to weight correctly the value of the evidence of a mtDNA and/or Y profile match.

References

[1] H. Ben-Sasson, A History of the Jewish People, Harvard Univ. Press, Cambridge, 1976.

[2] U. Ritte, E. Neufeld, E.M. Prager, M. Gross, I. Hakim, A. Khatib, B. Bonné-Tamir, Mitochondrial DNA affinities of several Jewish communities, Hum. Biol. 65 (3) (1993) 359–385.

[3] M.G. Thomas, M.E. Weale, A.L. Jones, M. Richards, A. Smith, N. Redhead, A. Torroni, R. Scozzari, F. Gratrix, A. Tarekegn, J.F. Wilson, C. Capelli, N. Bradman, D.B. Goldstein, Founding mothers of Jewish communities: geographically separated Jewish groups were independently founded by very few female ancestors, Am. J. Hum. Genet. 70 (2000) 1411–1420.

[4] A. Picornell, C. Tomàs, G. Jiménez, J.A. Castro, M.M. Ramon, Jewish population genetic data in 20 polymorphic loci, Forensic Sci. Int. 125 (2002) 52–58.

International Congress Series 1261 (2004) 386–388

www.ics-elsevier.com

Microgeographic substructure of Northern Portuguese mitochondrial DNA lineages: the female perspective of this region history

S. Beleza[a,b,*], A. Salas[b], A. Amorim[a,c], L. Gusmão[a], A. Carracedo[b]

[a] *IPATIMUP, Instituto de Patologia e Imunologia da Universidade do Porto, R. Dr. Roberto Frias s/n, 4200 Oporto, Portugal*

[b] *Unidad de Genética Forense, Instituto de Medicina Legal, Universidad de Santiago de Compostela, R. San Francisco s/n, E-15705 Santiago de Compostela, Galicia, Spain*

[c] *Faculdade de Ciências da Universidade do Porto, Praça Gomes Teixeira, 4050 Oporto, Portugal*

Abstract. Mitochondrial DNA (mtDNA) lineages of 354 male samples from the five districts of Northern Portugal were defined. The aim was to obtain the female demographic history of this region and to compare it with the one obtained from Y chromosome haplotypes. The mtDNA landscape of North Portugal is in agreement with the one obtained from Y chromosome analysis, suggesting an East–West gradient in haplotype diversity. However, contrary to what happens with the Y chromosome, the easternmost district was the most diverse. Several explanations for this contrasting pattern are advanced.

Keywords: mtDNA; North Portugal; Microgeography; Substructure

1. Introduction

In a previous study of Y-chromosome STR markers in the five districts from Northern Portugal and two from Southern Galicia, we could detect signs of a slight microdiferentiation of the Easternmost district of North Portugal (Bragança), contrasting with the generally homogeneous genetic background of the region. In the present work, we analysed the mitochondrial DNA (mtDNA) variability in the same Northern Portuguese districts. The aim was to obtain the female genetic perspective of the North Portugal demographic history and to compare it with the one obtained with the Y chromosome haplotypes.

* Corresponding author. Population Genetics, IPATIMUP, Instituto de Patologia e Imunologia da Universidade do Porto, R. Dr. Roberto Frias s/n, 4200 Oporto, Portugal. Tel.: +351-225570700; fax: +351-225570799.

E-mail address: sbeleza@ipatimup.pt (S. Beleza).

doi:10.1016/S0531-5131(03)01502-4

2. Materials and methods

A total of 354 unrelated individuals from the five districts of Northern Portugal were analysed, distributed as follows: 117 from Porto, 69 from Braga, 68 from Viana do Castelo, 49 from Vila Real, and 51 from Bragança. HVS-I was amplified as described by Pereira et al. [1].

RFLP analysis of selected coding region positions was performed, whenever the assigned HVS-I sequence information alone to their corresponding haplogroups was insufficient. The typing was done with the use of standard protocols [2–5].

A stretch of 350 bp belonging to HVS-I segment (running from position 16050 to 16400; nomenclature according to Anderson et al. [6]) was analysed. Phylogenetic classification of the sequences was done according to Macaulay et al. [3], Richards et al. [4], Richards et al. [7], Quintana-Murci et al. [8], and Helgason et al. [9].

Haplotypes and haplogroups frequencies were determined by direct counting. Diversity indices, AMOVA, and pairwise F_{ST} values and associated p-values were calculated in Arlequin 2.0 [10].

Principal component (PC) analyses were performed using POPSTR (H. Harpending, personal communication) on the haplogroup composition (relative frequencies) of Northern Portuguese populations.

3. Results

Principal Component analysis (PC) was performed on the basis of the relative frequencies of mtDNA haplogroups (Fig. 1).

The first two PCs accounted for ≈ 70% of the variance, from which 43.7% corresponds to the first one and displays an East–West gradient, separating the interior (Bragança and Vila Real) from the coastal districts (Porto, Braga and Viana do Castelo);

When AMOVA was computed without any hierarchical grouping, the amount of variation among populations was not significant (0.17%, $p = 0.1896$). Performing

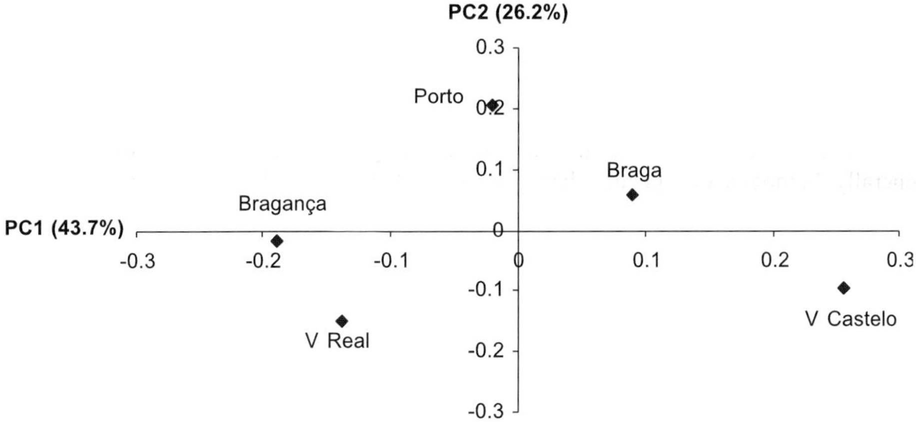

Fig. 1. Two-dimensional plot of the principal components of mtDNA haplogroup frequencies for Northern Portuguese samples.

AMOVA considering two groups, one composed by the easternmost districts and the other by the westernmost coastal districts, the percentage of variation among groups was slightly higher (0.18%, $p=0.1017$).

Nevertheless, pairwise F_{ST} values were significantly different when comparing Bragança and Viana do Castelo. Therefore, based on the pattern observed in the PC analysis as well as the pairwise FST values obtained (data not shown), AMOVA was repeated comparing Bragança with a single group composed by the other four districts. In this case, there was a two-fold increase in the proportion of genetic variation among groups (although statistically not significant). Other AMOVA designs considering one district (different from Bragança) against the others yielded lower among groups values (the next being 0.22% for Viana do Castelo).

Several diversity indices were calculated with HVS-I sequences for the five populations (data not shown). Bragança exhibited higher diversity values than the other districts regarding all diversity indices estimated. In contrast, Viana do Castelo, the most NW district is the one showing the most reduced diversity.

4. Discussion

The mtDNA landscape of North Portugal seems relatively homogenous, although suggesting an East–West gradient in haplotype diversity. This picture is in agreement with that obtained from Y chromosome analysis. However, in this case, contrary to what happens with the Y chromosome, the easternmost district is the most diverse.

Several (and not mutually exclusive) explanations for this contrasting pattern can be advanced: (a) different male/female effective population sizes; (b) differential migration patterns (coastal longer range migrations for males, shorter range continental movements for females); (c) different mating patterns and cultural practices between males and females. Since all the districts are closely related culturally and geographically, the first and the second options arise as the most plausible explanations.

Acknowledgements

This work was supported by POCTI, Programa Operacional Ciência, Tecnologia e Inovação. Sandra Beleza has a PhD grant (SFRH/BD/860/2000) from FCT.

References

[1] L. Pereira, et al., Ann. Hum. Genet. 64 (2000) 491–506.
[2] A. Torroni, et al., Genetics 144 (1996) 1835–1850.
[3] V. Macaulay, et al., Am. J. Hum. Genet. 64 (1999) 232–249.
[4] M. Richards, et al., Am. J. Hum. Genet. 67 (2000) 1251–1276.
[5] A. Torroni, et al., Am. J. Hum. Genet. 69 (2001) 844–852.
[6] S. Anderson, et al., Nature 290 (1981) 457–465.
[7] M. Richards, et al., Ann. Hum. Genet. 62 (1998) 241–260.
[8] L. Quintana-Murci, et al., Nat. Genet. 23 (1999) 437–441.
[9] A. Helgason, et al., Am. J. Hum. Genet. 68 (2001) 723–737.
[10] S. Schneider, et al., Genetics and Biometry Lab, Dept. of Anthropology, University of Geneva, 2000.

ELSEVIER

International Congress Series 1261 (2004) 389–391

ICS

www.ics-elsevier.com

Mitochondrial analysis of a British Afro-Caribbean population

D. Ballard[a,*], E. Musgrave-Brown[a], A. Salas[b], C. Thacker[a], D. Syndercombe-Court[a]

[a] *Department of Haematology, Barts and The London, Queen Mary's School of Medicine and Dentistry, Turner Street, London, E1 2AD, UK*

[b] *Institute of Legal Medicine-Faculty of Medicine, University of Santiago de Compostela, Galicia, Spain*

Abstract. Mitochondrial DNA (mtDNA) analysis has been used both to identify individuals and to infer patterns of human evolution. We have analysed a representative population of Afro-Caribbean individuals who are residents within the UK. Sequencing has been carried out on both the hypervariable regions I (HVI) and II (HVII). In addition, a set of informative mitochondrial single nucleotide polymorphisms (SNPs) have been investigated. Comparison of these results with published data for different African populations has enabled the samples to be classified into haplogroups. Analysis of the haplogroup distribution has suggested an ancestral geographical origin for these British Afro-Caribbean samples mainly from Western Africa with some influence from Southeast Africa.

Keywords: Mitochondrial DNA; British Afro-Caribbean population

1. Introduction

Mitochondrial DNA (mtDNA) analysis is becoming more widely used in forensic science, especially in cases of sample degredation and complex relationship issues. It is also proving to be a useful tool in the study of recent human evolution.

There are two areas of the mtDNA genome that are normally sequenced in forensic analysis, hypervariable regions I (HVI) and II (HVII). To interpret the results, the haplotypes obtained need to be compared against a representative database.

Migration into Britain has led to a multicultural society, with 2.2% of the population classing themselves as Black by the 2001 census [1]. A database of British Afro-Caribbeans was therefore established to allow assessment of haplotype frequency in cases involving families or individual from this racial group. By including some informative mitochondrial single nucleotide polymorphisms (SNPs), it is possible to further define these samples into

* Corresponding author. Tel.: +44-2073-777076; fax: +44-2073-777629.
E-mail address: d.j.ballard@qmul.ac.uk (D. Ballard).

0531-5131/
doi:10.1016/j.ics.2003.12.017

mitochondrial haplogroups. This enables a general picture to be built up regarding the composition of a British Afro-Caribbean population in relation to their African origins.

2. Method

DNA samples were obtained from 128 unrelated individuals resident in the United Kingdom who describe their ethnic origin as Black. Samples had previously been used for paternity testing and were randomly selected. Consent was obtained in all cases.

Following Chelex extraction, HVI and HVII were each amplified directly via PCR. The PCR products were incubated with ExoSAP-IT (Amersham Biosciences) to remove unincorporated primers and dNTPs and sequenced using the DYEnamic ET Terminator Cycle Sequencing kit (Amersham Biosciences). The same primers were used as in the initial PCR. In cases where length heteroplasmy was observed in the cytosine stretch from 16184 to 16193, alternative primers that bind to the region just downstream were used to provide additional sequencing data.

The sequence reaction products were precipitated with ethanol and sodium acetate/EDTA prior to separation via capillary electrophoresis on an ABI PRISM 3100 Genetic Analyser (Applied Biosystems). Sequence Analysis and Sequence Navigator software (Applied Biosystems) were used to compare the results obtained with the Anderson reference sequence [2], and any deviations from this were noted. The haplotypes produced could then be recorded to provide haplotype frequency information.

A mtDNA skeleton of African haplogroups derived by phylogenetic analysis (detailed by Salas et al. [3]) was used as a guide to classify samples based on the sequence information of HVI and HVII. In cases where the sequence information alone was insufficient for haplogroup classification, mtSNPs in the coding region were additionally typed.

Seven SNPs were selected for the ability to differentiate badly characterized African haplotypes. These were (with reference to the Anderson sequence):

3693—To distinguish haplogroup L2d
8701—To distinguish haplogroup L*
8618—To distinguish haplogroup L3d
10086—To distinguish haplogroup L3b
10400—To distinguish haplogroup M*
10819—To distinguish haplogroup L3e
12705—To distinguish haplogroup N*

Primers were designed and five products were amplified from two PCR reactions. The seven SNPs were typed using SNaPshot (Applied Biosystems) in one multiplex reaction. The SNaPshot products were separated by size on an ABI PRISM™ 3100 Genetic Analyser and GeneScan 3.1 software (Applied Biosystems) was used for assessing allelic designation.

3. Results

Of the 128 samples analysed, 93 different HVI haplotypes and 80 different HVII haplotypes were observed. When HVI and HVII were analysed together, this figure increased to 120 (a haplotype diversity value of 0.9990).

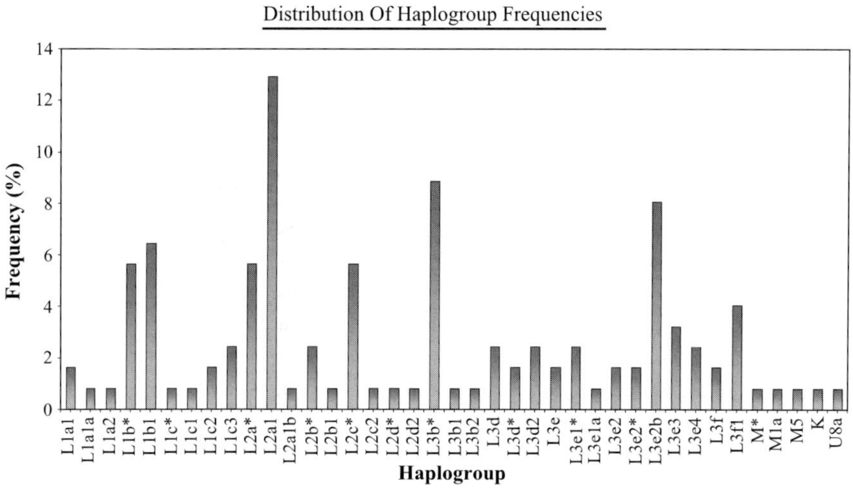

Fig. 1. Haplogroup frequency for British Afro-Caribbean samples.

The haplogroup classifications are represented graphically in Fig. 1. The most common haplogroups were L1b* (5.5%), L1b1 (6.5%), L2a* (5.5%), L2a1 (13%), L2c* (5.5%), L3b* (9%) and L3e2b (8%).

4. Discussion

As expected, the database of British Afro-Caribbeans shows a relatively high diversity. In most cases, the classification of the samples seem to generally point to an origin from West Africa (with some influence from Southeast Africa), whether through direct migration to Britain or via the Caribbean. While there are still large areas of Africa uncharacterized, this proposed distribution occurs despite the cultural and commercial links that Britain has with the Southern and Eastern African countries in the British Commonwealth and so may partly reflect the influence of the Atlantic slave trade.

References

[1] 2001 Census, UK Office of National Statistics.

[2] S. Anderson, A.T. Bankier, B.G. Barrell, M.H. de Bruijn, A.R. Coulson, J. Drouin, I.C. Eperon, D.P. Nierlich, B.A. Roe, F. Sanger, P.H. Schreier, A.J. Smith, R. Staden, I.G. Young, Sequence and organisation of the human mitochondrial genome, Nature 290 (1981) 457–465.

[3] A. Salas, M. Richards, T. De la Fe, M.V. Lareu, B. Sobrino, P. Sanchez-Diz, V. Macaulay, A. Carracedo, The making of the african mtDNA landscape, American Journal of Human Genetics 71 (2002) 1082–1111.

International Congress Series 1261 (2004) 392–394

www.ics-elsevier.com

Mitochondrial DNA analysis of ancient Yakut skeletons

F.X. Ricaut[a,b,*], C. Keyser-Tracqui[a], P. Blandin[a], E. Crubézy[b], B. Ludes[a,b]

[a] *Laboratoire d'Anthropologie Moléculaire, Institut de Médecine Légale, 11 rue Humann, 67085 Strasbourg, France*

[b] *Anthropobiologie, Université Paul Sabatier, CNRS, UMR 8555, Toulouse, France*

Abstract. The excavation of 10 frozen graves in central Yakutia (dated to be 300–600 years old) revealed 11 human bodies belonging to the ancient Yakut population. To investigate the origin and evolution of the Yakut population, DNA was extracted from these skeletons and analysed by sequencing of the hypervariable region 1 (HV1) of the mitochondrial DNA (mtDNA). Comparison of haplotypes obtained with those of 8774 Eurasian individuals suggested a relative continuity of the ancient mitochondrial Yakut lineages during the three last centuries, as well as their putative central Asian origin. © 2003 Elsevier B.V. All rights reserved.

Keywords: Yakuts; Ancient DNA; Mitochondrial DNA

1. Introduction

The Sakha (also known as Yakuts) are an enigmatic ethnic group living in northeastern Siberia in the Sakha republic, an autonomous republic within the Russian Federation. Their origin, in spite of numerous archaeological and recent genetic studies [1,2], is still fully debated.

The difficulties encountered by molecular biologists could arise from many historic and demographic events since the formation of the Sakha population, such as the Russian colonisation starting in the 17th century, as well as the high degree of isolation and genetic drift of the Siberian populations. These events could have obscured the ancestral Yakut gene pool. Consequently, a direct access to the gene

* Corresponding author. Laboratoire d'Anthropologie Moléculaire, Institut de Médecine Légale, 11 rue Humann, 67085 Strasbourg, France. Tel.: +33-390-243347; fax: +33-390-243362.

E-mail address: fx.ricaut@infonie.fr (F.X. Ricaut).

0531-5131/ © 2003 Elsevier B.V. All rights reserved.
doi:10.1016/S0531-5131(03)01630-3

Table 1
Modern Eurasian populations sharing ancient Yakut haplotypes

Population	*n*	References	Ancient Yakut samples					
			IM2, AD1, AD3s, AD3n	SS3	Yak 3	AD2	SS2	SS1, Yak2, IM1
Yakut	139	[1,5]	12%	1.4%	3.6%	0.7%	2.9%	–
Buryat	166	[1,6]	–	–	1.8%	0.6%	0.6%	–
Mongol	103	[7]	–	–	0.8%	–	–	–
Tuvan	36	[6]	–	–	13.6%	–	–	–
Kazakh	55	[8]	–	–	1.1%	–	–	–
Chinese	378	[9]	0.3%	–	–	–	–	–
Turks	218	[10]	–	–	–	–	1.4%	–
NW Europeans	456	[10]	–	–	–	–	1.3%	–
NE Europeans	510	[10,11]	–	–	–	–	2%	–

pool of ancient Sakha individuals could lead to a better understanding of the genetic history of this Siberian population.

2. Material and methods

During the summer 2002, a French-Yakut scientific expedition excavated 10 Yakut frozen graves dating back from the 15th to 18th century and located in central Yakutia. The human bodies were well-preserved, the frozen graves being in direct contact with permafrost.

DNA was extracted from bone fragments by the silica-based method according to Fily et al. [3]. Hypervariable region 1 (HV1) of the mtDNA control region was amplified using the L15989/H16239 and L16190/H16410 primers, and were sequenced by means of the ABI Prism BigDye® Terminator cycle sequencing Ready Reaction Kit (PE Applied Biosystems), as described previously by Ricaut et al. [2]. The sequence reaction products were analysed on an ABI Prism 3100 automatic sequencer (PE Applied Biosystems).

The nucleotide sequences obtained from the 11 ancient Yakut samples were compared with the mtDNA sequences of 8774 Eurasians individuals, using the Blast 2.0 program (www.ncbi.nlm.nih.gov). The reference sequences used for comparative analysis are listed in the Table 1 previously published by Ricaut et al. [2].

3. Results

A 366-base pair fragment of the mtDNA HV1 region was obtained for each of the 11 samples, and compared to the Cambridge Reference Sequence [4]. The current frequency distribution of ancient Yakut haplotypes in the reference populations presenting these haplotypes is indicated in Table 1.

4. Discussion

The distribution of the ancient Yakut haplotypes in Eurasian populations is principally limited to Yakut and central Asian modern populations. This suggests (i) a relative continuity of the mitochondrial Yakut lineage since the 15th–18th centuries and (ii) a putative central Asian origin of these ancient mitochondrial Yakut lineages, which is in accordance with the origin of Yakut population postulated by archaeological and recent genetic studies [1,2]. Moreover, the presence in a Yakut subject (SS2) buried in the 15th century of a haplotype affiliated to East European Caucasoid indicates that the Caucasoid part of the Yakut population was present two centuries before the Russian colonisation (starting in the 17th century).

Nevertheless, the absence of ancient Yakut haplotypes shared by Siberian populations is surprising because a part of these populations, and notably the Evenks, have contributed to the mitochondrial modern Yakut gene pool as reported by Pakendorf et al. [1]. A possible explanation could be that the smallness of our sample did not allow to detect the Siberian genetic contribution, but we cannot exclude a contribution of Siberian population to the mitochondrial Yakut gene pool subsequent to the 15th–18th centuries.

In conclusion, the molecular data obtained from the archaeological samples studied bring new elements to the understanding of origin and evolution of the mitochondrial Yakut gene pool. However, our results are inevitably constrained by the sample size, and the new archaeological samples could provide more comprehensive insights of the Yakut population history.

Acknowledgements

This work has been supported by the program of the French/Sakha cooperation from the Action Cooperation Integred from the French Minister of the research “le complexe spatial Altaï-Baïkal. Plaque tournante des flux géniques en Haute Asie de la période protohistorique à l'époque moderne”.

References

[1] B. Pakendorf, et al., Mitochondrial DNA evidence for admixed origins of Central Siberian populations, Am. J. Phys. Anthropol. 120 (2003) 211–224.

[2] F.X. Ricaut, et al., Genetic analysis of human remains found in two medieval Yakut graves (At-Dabaan site, 18th century), Int. J. Leg. Med. (in press).

[3] M.L. Fily, et al., Paleogenetic analysis of the skeletons from the sepulchral cave of Elzarreko Karbia (Bronze, Age Basque Country), C. R. Acad. Sci. Paris 321 (1998) 79–85.

[4] S. Anderson, et al., Sequence and organization of the human mitochondrial genome, Nature 290 (1981) 457–465.

[5] M.V. Derenko, G.F. Shields, Mitochondrial DNA sequence diversity in three north Asian aboriginal populations groups, Mol. Biol. (Mosk.) 31 (5) (1997) 665–669.

[6] M.V. Derenko, et al., Mitochondrial DNA variation in two South Siberian Aboriginal populations: implications for the genetic history of north Asia, Hum. Biol. 72 (6) (2000) 945–973.

[7] C.J. Kolman, et al., Mitochondrial DNA analysis of Mongolian populations and implications for the origin of new world founders, Genetics 142 (1996) 1321–1334.

[8] D. Comas, et al., Trading genes along the silk road: mtDNA sequences and the origin of Central populations, Am. J. Hum. Genet. 63 (1998) 1824–1838.

[9] Y.G. Yao, et al., Phylogeographic differenciation of mitochondrial DNA in Han Chinese, Am. J. Hum. Genet. 70 (2002) 635–651.

[10] M. Richards, et al., Tracing European founder lineages in the near eastern mtDNA pool, Am. J. Hum. Genet. 67 (2000) 1251–1276.

[11] V. Orekhov, et al., Mitochondrial DNA sequence diversity in Russians, FEBS Lett. 445 (1999) 197–201.

ELSEVIER

International Congress Series 1261 (2004) 395–397

www.ics-elsevier.com

Mitochondrial DNA control region polymorphism in Han, Yao, Li, Uygure and Tibetan groups in China

H. Tang[a,b], W.S. Ma[a], Y.Ch. Liu[a,*], J.W Yan[a,c], Y. Liu[b], Y.P. Hou[b]

[a] *Department of Biologic Evidence Division, Forensic Medical Examination and Identification Center, Beijing Public Security Bureau, 1# Longgang Street, 100085 Beijing, China*

[b] *Institute of Forensic Medicine, Sichuan University, Chengdu, China*

[c] *Xi An Jiao Tong University, Xian, China*

Abstract. In order to investigate the polymorphisms of mtDNA in different groups in China, we have sequenced mtDNA control region from 446 unrelated person. The polymorphic sites in Han, Li, Uygure, Tibetan and Yao groups were 269, 316, 159, 117, 141, respectively, and the pairwise difference, hyplotypes, etc. were calculated. The result showed that there were other hypervariable regions besides HVI and HVII. However, the HV III were located at different region in each group.

Keywords: mtDNA; Control region; Han group; Yao group; Li group; Uygure group; Tibetan group; China

1. Objective

The sequencing of mtDNA hypervariable region I and II has become a powerful tool to investigate biological evidence that cannot be analyzed by the use of nuclear DNA. However, the power of discrimination of mtDNA testing is limited. Studying additional diversity outside of mtDNA hypervariable regions will enhance the power and efficiency of mtDNA profiling. China is a multinational country, the living region and marriage habit of every ethnic group may influence the genetics diversity of mitochondrial DNA. In the context, the whole control region of mtDNA were studied in Han, Yao, Li, Uygure and Tibetan groups in China, in order to research the polymorphisms in different groups.

2. Materials and methods

2.1. Sample collection

100 unrelated Han samples were collected from Beijing. 105 unrelated Yao samples were collected from Du'an, Guangxi province. 100 unrelated Li samples were collected

* Corresponding author. Tel.: +86-10-62909016; fax: +86-10-62902582.
E-mail address: fyzhx6688@163.com (Y.Ch. Liu).

doi:10.1016/S0531-5131(03)01504-8

from Hainan province. 99 unrelated Uygure samples were collected from Kashi Xinjiang province. 42 unrelated Tibetan samples were collected from Nagqu Tibet province. The samples were collected under the rule of.

DNA was extracted by the Chelex and phenol–chloroform method. The following primers were used for amplification and sequencing: mt-1(15756-16087) H 5′-gaa tcg gag gac aac cag taa g-3′, L 5′-tag cgg ttg ttg tag ggt-3′; mt-0(16030-16481) H 5′-cat ggg gaa gca gat ttg-3′; L 5′-tta gct acc ccc aag tgt-3′; mt-2(16419-00270) H 5′-caa tat ccc gca caa gag tg-3′, L 5′-tgg aaa gtg gct gtg cag aca t-3′; mt-3(00132-00444) H 5′-ctt tga ttc ctg cct cat cc-3′, L 5′-tta gtt ggg ggg tga ctg tt-3′; mt-4(00374-00672) H 5′-cac cag cct aac cag att tc-3′, L 5′-tag aaa ggc tag gac caa acc t-3′. PCR was carried out under the following thermal cycle conditions: denature at 95 °C for 200 s; 94 °C for 30 s, 55 °C for 30 s, 72 °C for 90 s, for total 35 cycles; following 72 °C for 7 min.

PCR products were analyzed using BigDyeTerminator Cycle Sequencing Ready Reaction Kit and ABI 377.

3. Statistic analysis

The genetic diversity (GD) was calculated using the formula $GD = n(1 - \Sigma x^2)/(n-1)$, discrimination power (Dp) was calculated according to the equation $Dp = 1 - \Sigma x^2$, where n was the number of sample, x was the haplotype frequency.

4. Result

We determined the nucleotide sequence of a 1400-bp fragment of the mt-DNA (positions 15786-16569, followed by 1–660 bp). The polymorphic sites in Han, Li, Uygure, Tibetan and Yao groups were 269, 316, 159, 117, 141, respectively. In each group, sequence

Table 1
The polymorphisms of mtDNA control region in Han, Tibetan, Li, Uygure and Yao groups in China

Region	Han (n = 100)		Li (n = 100)		Uygure (n = 99)		Tibetan (n = 42)		Yao (n = 105)	
	N	Hyplo types	N	Hyplo types	N	Hyplo types	N	Hyplo types	N	Hyplo types
15786-16023	23	21	20	19	12	14	3	4	9	7
16024-16365	109	96	93	77	65	64	47	42	68	65
16366-00072	14	18	67	50	17	18	10	8	10	14
00073-00340	68	86	58	70	34	52	29	26	35	56
00341-00437	21	18	32	29	4	5	8	8	4	5
00438-00574	25	33	38	35	25	21	16	15	13	13
00575-00650	9	14	8	4	2	3	4	4	2	3

Region	Han (n = 100)		Li (n = 100)		Uygure (n = 99)		Tibetan (n = 42)		Yao (n = 105)	
	Dp	GD	Dp	GD	Dp	GD	Dp	GD	Dp	GD
15786-16023	0.4628	0.4675	0.4332	0.4376	0.4122	0.4164	0.1360	0.1393	0.2901	0.2927
16024-16365	0.9892	0.9991	0.9838	0.9937	0.9723	0.9823	0.9761	0.9999	0.9738	0.9832
16366-00072	0.6794	0.6863	0.9108	0.9200	0.6472	0.6538	0.5872	0.6015	0.6362	0.6423
00073-00340	0.9850	0.9949	0.9792	0.9891	0.9497	0.9594	0.9312	0.9539	0.9669	0.9762
00341-00437	0.4726	0.4774	0.6200	0.6263	0.1345	0.1358	0.3740	0.3831	0.0923	0.0932
00438-00574	0.8838	0.8923	0.8832	0.8921	0.8218	0.8302	0.7481	0.7663	0.7510	0.7582
00575-00650	0.5174	0.5226	0.0778	0.0786	0.0398	0.0402	0.1360	0.1393	0.1092	0.1103

N: the number of nucleotide substitution.

Table 2
The variation rate (%) of mtDNA control region in Han, Tibetan, Li, Uygur and Yao groups

Position variation		Uygur ($n=99$)	Yao ($n=105$)	Han (Beijing) ($n=100$)	Li ($n=100$)	Tibetan ($n=42$)
16086	T→C	/	1.90	/	/	4.76
16093	T→C	1.01	12.38	7	2	16.67
16111	C→T	/	0.95	3	/	7.14
16129	G→A	4.04	26.67	16	14	9.52
16183	A→C	23.23	26.67	/	29	2.38
16184	C→T	1.01	5.71	5	2	2.38
16189	T→C	29.29	37.14	26	35	7.14
16223	C→T	41.41	45.71	25	43	80.95
16234	T→C	2.02	0.95	6	3	30.95
16263	C→A	1.01	2.86	/	/	/
16290	C→T	2.02	1.90	7	1	9.52
16293	A→C	/	/	2	/	7.14
16298	T→C	14.14	12.38	11	4	4.76
16304	T→C	1.05	18.09	11	28	7.14
16311	T→C	6.06	9.52	17	20	11.90
16316	A→G	1.01	/	3	/	11.90
16319	G→A	2.02	1.90	14	4	9.52
16327	C→T	16.16	6.67	5	/	4.76
16362	T→C	19.19	24.76	47	17	21.43
16390	G→A	8.08	2.86	3	8	/
16519	T→C	67.67	53.33	57	50	45.24
00073	A→G	83.83	100	100	100	97.62
00152	T→C	17.17	10.48	32	14	35.71
00190	C→T	/	/	53	/	/
00235	A→G	2.02	5.71	6	2	14.29
00249	A→d	18.18	23.81	/	12	14.29
00263	A→G	93.93	97.14	97	98	100
00309.1	C	63.63	60.95	47	54	47.62
00315.1	C	94.94	97.14	90	93	100
00489	T→C	39.39	46.66	58	43	73.81

diversity was caused mainly by nucleotide substitution. The pairwise difference, hyplotypes and the GD, Dp value for every part of control region were presented in Table 1. Table 2 shows the variation rate of some hypervariation sites in different nationals.

5. Conclusion

The result showed that there were other hypervariable regions besides HVI and HVII. However, the HV III were located at different region in each group. In Han, Uygure, Tibetan groups, the HV III were located at 00483-00574. However, in Li and Yao groups, the HV III were between HV I and HV II. Also, the variation and power of discrimination of mtDNA were enhanced by detection of the whole region than HVI or HVII. We suggested that there should be more databases established which consisted of more samples and regions of mtDNA. When mtDNA sequencing was used in forensic field, we should analyze more regions besides HV I and HV II in order to improve the discrimination power. According to the nationality of the sample, different regions should be detected.

International Congress Series 1261 (2004) 398–400

ELSEVIER

www.ics-elsevier.com

Molecular identification of arthropods by cytochrome *b* analysis

M.M. de Pancorbo[a,b,*], A. Castro[b,c], I. Fernández-Fernández[b,c], N. Cuevas[c], M. Castillo[d], M. Saloña[a]

[a] *Dpto. de Z. Dinámica Celular A., Facultad de Farmacia, Universidad del País Vasco, Vitoria-Gasteiz, Spain*
[b] *Instituto Vasco de Criminología, Universidad del País Vasco, San Sebastián-Donostia, Spain*
[c] *DataGene Ltda. (Grupo Adirondack), Parque Tecnológico, Derio (Bizkaia) Spain*
[d] *Albalate St. 13, 2250 Binaced–Huesca, Spain*

Abstract. This work has been developed to improve the analysis of cadaveric entomofauna. Taking into account that the cytochrome *b* is widely use to identify vertebrates, we have used it for the identification of some necrophagous species involved in the postmortem process. © 2004 Published by Elsevier B.V.

Keywords: Cytochrome *b*; *Lucilia sericata*; *Piophila casei*; *Dermestes frischii*

1. Introduction

Entomological knowledge can reveal the manner or location of death, although is most often used to estimate the time of death, or postmortem interval (PMI). Insects collected as evidence during a postmortem investigation should be preserved as eggs, larva or adult. Preimaginal stages can be difficult or impossible to identify to specific level, and an incorrect or uncertain identification can seriously harm or impede an investigation. This is because adult arrival times, egg phase duration and larval growth rates can vary between species. Proper species identification is usually an essential first step in the use of entomological evidence in a legal investigation [1]. An alternative source for species identification information is mitochondrial DNA. We selected the mtDNA region that codes for cytochrome *b*. This gene contains species-specific information and has been used in phylogenetic as well as in forensic investigations in a number of studies [2].

The main objective of this work is to improve the analysis of cadaveric entomofauna. Taking into account the difficulty to identify eggs, larva and maggots, we have used the

* Corresponding author. Dpto. de Zoología y Dinámica Celular, Facultad de Farmacia, Universidad del País Vasco, Paseo de la Universidad 7, 01006 Vitoria-Gasteiz, Spain. Tel.: +34-945-013045; fax: +34-945-013756.
E-mail address: gcpmagom@lg.ehu.es (M.M. de Pancorbo).

0531-5131/ © 2004 Published by Elsevier B.V.
doi:10.1016/j.ics.2003.12.084

Table 1
Clustal W(1.5) multiple sequence alignment

L. sericata GACTAAG-AATAAAATAATTACTCCT-ACTAATCAAGTTGTGTGTAAATAAGTATGAAC
P. casei GACTAAG-A**T**TAAAAT**C**ATTACTCCT**C**ACTAATCAAGTT**T**G**G**TGTAAATAA**A**TATGAAC
D. frischii GACTAAG**GC**AATAAAATAATTACTCCT**C**ACTAATCAAGTTG-GTGTAAATAAGTATGAAC
L. sericata CGTAATATATTCCTCG-TCCTACATGTAAGT-AAATACAAATAAAGAAAAATGATGC**T**-C
P. casei CGTAATATATTCCTCG**A**TCCTACATGTAAGT**G**AAATACAAATAAAGAAAATGATGCG-C
D. frischii CGTAATATATTCCTCG-TCCTACATGTAAGT-AAATACAAATAAAGAAAAATGATGCG**T**C
L. sericata C**C**TTAGCATGTATAGTTCGTAATAATCAACCAT**C**ATTTACGTCTCGGCAAAT**C**ATGATTT
P. casei CATTAGCATGTATAGTTCGTAATAATCAACCATAATTTACGTCTCGGCAAAT-ATGATTT
D. frischii CATTAGCATGTATAGTTCGTAATAATCAACCATAATTTACGTCTCGGCAAAT-ATGATTT
L. sericata ACTCT**A**TTAAAAGCTA-GTCTAATATC**C**TGCTGTGTAATGT**C**TAGCTAAAAATAA
P. casei ACTCTGTTAAAAGCTA**A**GTCTAATATC-TGCTGTGTAATGTATAGCTAAAAATAA
D. frischii ACTCTATTAAAAGCTA-GTCTAATATC-TGCTGTGTAATGTATAGCTAAAAATAA

cytochrome b to identify some important necrophagous species involved in the postmortem process.

2. Methodology

Lucilia sericata, a pioneer, *Piophila casei* arriving during fat saponification of corpses and *Dermestes frischii*, responsible of feeding on advanced decayed and mummified corpses, have been studied. They were properly identified and preserved in 96% EtOH for further studies. Three specimens of each species were selected for genetic analysis. In order to avoid human contamination, we have extracted DNA from muscle of one leg of each specimen. Cell lysis was performed using proteinase K and SDS and the DNA was purified by the phenol–chloroform method. Cytb was amplified under the conditions described by Parson et al. [2]. All the samples were sequenced using the dRhodamine Terminator kit (Applied Biosystems) method in an automatic ABI Prism 310 DNA sequencer. The sequences of insects of the same species were aligned using the Clustal V

Table 2
Cytb sequences producing significant alignments using the online BLAST search engine

	Score bits	*E*-value
L. sericata		
gi | 13384216 | gb | AF352790.1| *Chrysomya putoria* mitochondrion, cytb	341	3e − 91
gi | 1166529 | gb | U37541.1 | DMU37541 *Drosophila melanogaster*	283	6e − 74
gi | 7799401 | emb | AJ400907.1 | DME400907 *Drosophila melanogaster*	283	6e − 74
P. casei		
gi | 13384216 | gb | AF352790.1| *Chrysomya putoria* mitochondrion, cytb	230	1e − 57
gi | 12923 | emb | X03240.1 | MIDYRRN *Drosophila yakuba* complete mt	190	9e − 46
gi | 5101664 | emb | AJ242872.1 | CCA242872 *Ceratitis capitata* comp mt	174	5e − 41
D. frischii		
gi | 13384216 | gb | AF352790.1| *Chrysomya putoria* mitochondrion, cytb	418	e − 114
gi | 12923 | emb | X03240.1 | MIDYRRN *Drosophila yakuba* complete mt	337	7e − 90
gi | 1166529 | gb | U37541.1 | DMU37541 *Drosophila melanogaster* com mt	329	2e − 87

program. The obtained sequences were used to identify the species of the samples by aligning to the cytb gene sequence entries using the online BLAST search engine of NCBI.

3. Results and discussion

Sequence data from a 358-bp region cytb were obtained for all specimens. The results of alignment by Clustal V showed that the sequences of insects, which are closest relatives, are almost indistinguishable. On the contrary, insects that belong to different species showed a high degree of divergence (Table 1). The cytb sequences of species here studied are not included in the database of GenBank. Thus, no significant coincidences were observed. However, the closest BLAST alignments were found between our species and *Chrisomia* and *Drosophila* genera (Table 2).

For insects, it is very common to sequence some or all of cytochrome oxidase subunits I and II (COI and COII). For vertebrates species, it is most common the cytochrome b gene analysis. Other gene commonly used to identify species is 16S RNA.

Our work has demonstrated that there are several differences in the base sequences of the cytb gene between arthropod species. Thus, the cytb gene can be added to the genes above mentioned to improve our ability to identify the insect species.

Acknowledgements

This work has been supported by the grant UE 14/01 of the Basque Country University.

References

[1] M. Benecke, B. Seifert, Forensic entomology exemplified by a homicide. A combined stain and postmortem time analysis, Arch. Kriminol. 204 (1999) 52–60.

[2] W. Parson, K. Pegorarto, H. Niederstatter, M. Foger, M. Steinlechner, Species identification by means of the cytochrome *b* gene, Int. J. Leg. Med. 114 (2000) 23–28.

ELSEVIER

International Congress Series 1261 (2004) 401–403

www.ics-elsevier.com

Mitochondrial DNA polymorphism in 103 unrelated Caucasian Danes

E.M. Rasmussen*, E. Sørensen, B. Eriksen, H.J. Larsen, N. Morling

Department of Forensic Genetics, Institute of Forensic Medicine, University of Copenhagen, 11 Frederik V's Vej DK-2100, Copenhagen, Denmark

Abstract. We describe a high-quality database containing data from the hypervariable regions HV1 and HV2 on the mitochondrial control region of 103 unrelated Caucasian Danes. Each sample was amplified in duplicates and sequenced twice in both the forward and reverse direction with primer and terminator chemistry, respectively. The data were analysed with the quality assessment program Phred. A total of 94 unique sequences were observed. Most of the observed mutations were T to C or C to T transitions compared to the Cambridge Reference Sequence (CRS). © 2003 Elsevier B.V. All rights reserved.

Keywords: DNA sequencing; Typing; MtDNA; Forensic genetics; Database

1. Introduction

Sequencing of the hypervariable regions HV1 and HV2 of mitochondrial DNA is commonly used in forensic casework. The statistical interpretation of the results depends on the population frequency of a particular haplotype in the population of interest. Thus, it is important to establish a database representing the different haplotypes present in the given population. Although sequencing of the mitochondrial control region has been performed routinely for years, recent reports indicate that some databases used also in the forensic genetics setting may include errors [1]. Recognising the problems reported concerning the validity of population data, we have established a high-quality database consisting of 103 Danes of Caucasian origin.

2. Materials and methods

Blood samples from 103 unrelated Caucasian Danes were each divided in two subsamples. DNA was extracted from each of the subsamples using either Chelex 100 or phenol/chloroform. HV1 and HV2 were amplified separately in two steps for each of the subsamples. In the first amplification, the primers L-15997/H-16401 and L-48/H-408 were used. In the second amplification, the primers L-15997(-21)-M13/H-16401-M13Rev and L-48(-21)-M13/H-408-M13Rev were used [2]. The first sample was sequenced twice

* Corresponding author. Tel.: +45-35326222; fax: +45-35326209.
E-mail address: michael.rasmussen@forensic.ku.dk (E.M. Rasmussen).

doi:10.1016/S0531-5131(03)01512-7

(forward and reverse) with the BigDye Primer chemistry, and the second sample was sequenced twice (forward and reverse) with the BigDyeTerminator Cycle Sequencing chemistry. Electrophoresis of the extension products was performed on either ABI 377 or ABI 310 (Applied Biosystems). If length heteroplasmy was detected, the sample was further sequenced as decribed by Rasmussen et al. [2]. Sequences were compared to the Cambridge Reference Sequence (CRS) [3] using the Sequencher (GeneCodes) software, and a quality score was obtained with the Phred (CodonCode) software. Base calls with Phred values above 20 were considered as being of sufficient quality. The final assignment at each base position was done when concordant results were obtained from both forward *and* reverse sequencing with one of the subsamples and forward *or* reverse with the other subsample, i.e., with at least three different combinations of the two chemistries and the two sequencing directions. This threefold consensus strategy combined with the use of Phred quality scores for each base call ensured a high quality of the base positions included in the database.

3. Results and discussion

The sequence data showed 94 different haplotypes in the 103 samples examined. One haplotype was present three times, and eight haplotypes were present twice. Each of the remaining haplotypes was observed only once. When comparing each of the sequences in the database to CRS [3], 73 mutations were observed in HV1 and 37 mutations were observed in HV2. The mutations were represented with a high number of transitions, but also transversions, deletions or insertions were present. Nineteen samples showed length heteroplasmy with poly C in positions 16,184–16,193 in HV1, in positions 303–315 in HV2 or in both. Table 1 presents an overview of the different types of mutations found.

Table 1
Sequence polymorphism in the hypervariable regions HV1 and HV2 of mtDNA of 103 unrelated Danish Caucasian individuals

	HV1	HV2
Transitions		
T–C	111	85
C–T	112	31
A–G	19	184
G–A	19	17
Transversions		
C–A	4	1
G–C	2	–
A–C	5	–
T–G	1	–
G–T	–	1
Insertions		
+2A	–	1
+1T	–	3
+1C	–	154
+2C	1	6
Deletions	–	
−1A	2	–

References

[1] H.-J. Bandelt, et al., The fingerprint of phantom mutations in mitochondrial DNA data, Am. J. Hum. Genet. 71 (2002) 1150–1160.

[2] E.M. Rasmussen, et al., Sequencing strategy of mitochondrial HV1 And HV2 DNA with length heteroplasmy, Forensic Sci. Int. 129 (2002) 209–213.

[3] S. Anderson, et al., Sequence and organization of the human mitochondrial genome, Nature 290 (1981) 457–465.

International Congress Series 1261 (2004) 404–406

ELSEVIER

www.ics-elsevier.com

Mitochondrial variation in the Bahia–Brazil population

M.V. Santos[a,*], C. Mendes[b], M. Carvalho[b], M.C. Vide[b], F. Corte-Real[c], D.N. Vieira[c]

[a] *Faculty of Medicine, University of Coimbra, CNPq, Coimbra, Brazil*
[b] *Service of Forensic Genetics, Delegation of Coimbra, National Institute of Legal Medicine, Coimbra, Portugal*
[c] *National Institute of Legal Medicine and Faculty of Medicine, University of Coimbra, Coimbra, Portugal*

Abstract. The variability of the mtDNA in 100 individuals from Bahia–Brazil was studied for the purpose of forensic investigation and population genetics. The mtDNA was extracted and amplified to obtain sequences of HVS-I and HVS-II. Amplified products were purified and sequenced, and the sequences were analysed. The differences between DNA sequences in comparison with the Cambridge Sequence Reference (CRS) are shown.

Keywords: Bahia–Brazil population; mtDNA; Population genetic data

1. Introduction

The analysis of the HVS-I, HVS-II and HVS-III regions of the mitochondrial D-Loop has been studied because of its copy number per cell and polymorphism, which are important for forensic investigation and population genetics. The mtDNA information is passed from mother to child allowing the maternal line to be traced. The mutation rates are higher than those observed in the nuclear DNA. The mtDNA inheritance pattern shows limitation in the discrimination power, although the distinct female lineage can be determined by different haplogroups. The Bahian population has become very diversified due to the inclusion of a wide range of ethnic backgrounds. In this study, a database of the Bahian population was established with HVS-I and HVS-II regions. The frequency of the nucleotide sequence variations and match probability were estimated.

* Corresponding author. Delagação de Coimbra, Instituto Nacional de Medicina Legal, Largo da Sé Nova, 3000-213 Coimbra, Portugal. Tel.: +351-239-814381; fax: +351-239-820549 or Tel./fax: +55-73-616-1809 (Post March, 2003).

E-mail address: diederiche@clix.pt (M.V. Santos).

doi:10.1016/S0531-5131(03)01785-0

2. Material and methods

The mtDNA was extracted [1] from blood samples of 100 unrelated (in three generations) healthy donors from Bahia–Brazil and amplified to obtain sequences of HVS-I and HVS-II according to Ref. [2] using a 9600 thermal cycler. Amplified products were purified and sequenced with BigDye™ v.3.0 Terminator Cycle Sequencing Ready Reaction Kit and primers described by Ref. [2] on the 9600 thermal cycler. The sequences were analysed on the ABI Prism 377 automatic sequencer or by capillary electrophoresis on the ABI PRISM 3100 Avant Genetic Analyzer employing ABI software [3]. The mtDNA results are provided in a DNA sequence analysis format and the intra- and inter-sequence differences are determined in comparison with the Cambridge Reference Sequence (CRS) [4]. The sequence variation from the Cambridge Reference Sequence was established by calculating nucleotide diversity and gene diversity [5]. The nomenclature and interpretation of the mtDNA profiles were according to Refs. [6,7].

3. Results and discussion

Sequence polymorphisms from the CRS sited between 16024 and 16390 in HVS-I and from 73 to 374 in HVS-II show a total of 82 different sequences for HVS-I and 74 for HVS-II. Considering both regions, 94 different sequences were observed and from these 86 sequences were found once, 4 were found twice and 2 were found 3 times. Table 1 summarizes the mutation events found in the Bahian population.

As regards HVS-I, 92 polymorphism sites were identified, of which the most frequent were 16223 (C/T = 85%), 16278 (C/T = 44%), 16311 (T/C = 39%), 16189 (T/C = 34%), 16294 (C/T = 22%), 16187 (C/T = 21%), 16362 (T/C = 19%), 16129 (G/A = 17%), 16270 (C/T = 16%), 16126 (T/C = 15%), 16390 (G/A = 14%), 16264 (C/T = 14%) and 16327 (C/T = 13%). One C insertion was found at 16188.1 (insC = 2%), 16192.1 (insC = 2%) and 16285.1 (insC = 1%), and one T deletion at 16325 (delT = 2%). The positions with more than one difference were 16114 (A = 6% and T = 1%), 16258 (T = 1% and G = 1%), 16259 (A = 1% and T = 2%), 16265 (T = 1% and C = 2%), 16325 (delT = 2% and C = 7%) and 16343 (T = 3% and G = 1%).

Instead, for HVS-II, 52 polymorphism sites were identified, of which the most frequent were 263 (G = 99%), 73 (G = 96%), 152 (C = 52%), 195 (C = 43%), 150 (T = 30%), 182 (T = 26%), 146 (C = 22%), 247 (A = 21%), 198 (T = 19%) and 357 (G = 11%). Lastly, one C insertion was found at 309.1 (insC = 40%) and 315.1 (insC = 90%), one A insertion was found at 316.1 (insA = 9%), and two C insertions at 309.1 and 309.2 (insC = 9%). The positions with more than one difference were 185 (A = 6% and T = 12%) and 189 (C = 8%

Table 1
Sequence polymorphisms and gene diversity in the Bahian population ($n = 100$)

	Pyrimidine transitions	Purine transitions	Transversions	Insertions	Deletions	Nucleotide diversity	Sequence diversity
HVS-I	450	85	29	5	2	0.01103	0.9940
HVS-II	220	304	45	157	15	0.01341	0.9917
HVS-I + HVS-II	669	390	73	163	17	0.01222	0.9979

and G = 23%). In addition, a singular pattern was observed in HVS-II in which five samples shared three A deletions at positions 249, 290 and 291.

A total of 144 polymorphism sites (nucleotide positions) were identified for HVS-I and HVS-II regions.

In comparison with other populations [9–16], the Bahian population shows higher values for number of different sequences (82 in HVS-I and 74 in HVS-II), number of variable nucleotide positions (92 in HVS-I and 52 in HVS-II) and sequence diversity (99.40% in HVS-I and 99.01% in HVS-II).

Length polymorphism or length heteroplasmy [8] occurred in nine different individuals in HVS-I and HVS-II.

HVS-II qualifies as a suitable tool for population genetics because of its polymorphism content, but this region shows a lower variability between individuals in comparison to HVS-I.

In accordance to Ref. [17], we found a higher mutation rate in HVS-II compared with HVS-I and this can be useful for practical applications in forensic genetics.

However, the differences permit us to understand the evolutionary process, but, in some differences, it was not possible to determine which mutation event occurred. In this work, these differences were considered as nucleotide substitutions.

Acknowledgements

Special thanks go to the donors of the samples. We would like to thank CNPq/Brazil for financial support and *Universidade Estadual de Santa Cruz* and *Departamento de Polícia Técnica*-SSP/BA.

References

[1] P.S. Walsh, D.A. Metzger, R. Higuchi, BioTechniques 10 (1991) 506–513.
[2] M.R. Wilson, et al., Int. J. Leg. Med. 108 (1995) 68–74.
[3] Applied Biosystems, ABI Prism 3100 Genetic Analyzer. User's Manual, Applera, CA, USA, 2001.
[4] S. Anderson, et al., Nature 290 (1981) 457–465.
[5] M. Nei, F. Tajima, Genetics 198 (1997) 145–163.
[6] A. Carracedo, et al., Forensic Sci. Int. 110 (2000) 79–85.
[7] G. Tully, et al., Forensic Sci. Int. 124 (2001) 83–91.
[8] K.E. Bendall, B.C. Sykes, Am. J. Hum. Genet. 57 (1995) 248–256.
[9] M.V. Santos, et al., VII Jornadas de Genética Forense. Junho, Barcelona, Spain (Publication in CD).
[10] M. Carvalho, et al., Int. Congr. Ser. 1239 (2003) 535–539.
[11] H.B.S.M. Côrte-Real, et al., Ann. Hum. Genet. 60 (1996) 331–350.
[12] A. Salas, et al., Eur. J. Hum. Genet. 6 (1998) 365–375.
[13] L. Pereira, M.J. Prata, A. Amorim, Ann. Hum. Genet. 64 (2000) 491–506.
[14] M. Carvalho, et al., VII Jornadas de Genética Forense. Junho, Barcelona, Spain (Publication in CD).
[15] E. Mateu, et al., Ann. Hum. Genet. 61 (2001) 507–518.
[16] L. Pereira, et al., Ann. Hum. Genet. 65 (2001) 439–458.
[17] A. Salas, et al., Prog. in Forensic Genet. 8 (2000) 329–331.

International Congress Series 1261 (2004) 407–409

ELSEVIER

www.ics-elsevier.com

Population variation of human mitochondrial DNA (HV1 and HV2) in Spanish unrelated individuals (Northeast Spain)

M. Crespillo*, M. Paredes, J.A. Luque, G. Luque, J.L. Valverde

Sección de Biología. Instituto Nacional de Toxicología. Ministerio de Justicia, Merced 1, E-08002, Barcelona, Spain

Abstract. A population database from 200 unrelated Caucasian individuals living in Spain was generated. Sequence polymorphisms of the mitochondrial DNA (mtDNA) control region, hypervariable regions I and II (HVRI and HVRII) were determined by polymerase chain reaction (PCR) and direct sequencing. A total of 175 different sequences were found as defined by 154 variable positions. The most common sequence occurred 10 times, this sequence is also the most frequent in other European populations such as Austrian, German and British. The mean pairwise difference for the two regions taken together was 8.25. The study revealed that transitions made up the majority of the deviations (88%), whereas we observed a significantly lower frequency of transversions (8%). A statistical estimate of the results for this Caucasian population showed a genetic diversity of 0.9965. The probability of two random individuals showing identical mtDNA haplotypes is 0.84%. In order to use the mtDNA analysis in forensic casework, we consider that it is of crucial importance to know the frequency of the different sequences of mtDNA, and this database study could be a useful tool to evaluate statistically the results. © 2003 Published by Elsevier B.V.

Keywords: Mitochondrial DNA; Database; Northeast Spain

1. Introduction

During the last 8 years in our laboratory we have used mitochondrial DNA (mtDNA) analysis to solve routine forensic casework where conventional DNA typing is unavailable. Mainly to type naturally shed hairs or hairs without roots and to confirm the identification of highly decomposed remains and skeletal remains. The present study shows a mtDNA database for the regions hypervariable regions I and II (HVRI and

* Corresponding author. Tel.: +34-93-3174061; fax: +34-93-3182530.
E-mail address: macrespillo@terra.es (M. Crespillo).

doi:10.1016/S0531-5131(03)01718-7

Table 1
Statistical data

	HV1	HV2	HV1 + HV2
Number of different haplotypes	131	100	175
Number of variable sites	99	55	154
Number of unique haplotypes	107	77	162
Frequency	0.0229	0.0459	0.0034
Average number of differences	4.555	3.697	8.252
Genetic diversity	0.97709	0.95497	0.99658
Randon match probability (%)	2.78	4.84	0.84

HVRII), from unrelated Caucasian individuals living in Spain. This database is being used to evaluate the results of mtDNA analysis in our laboratory.

2. Materials and methods

DNA was obtained from casework reference samples (blood, saliva, hair) of 200 unrelated Caucasians who live in the Northeast of Spain. DNA was extracted by standard

Table 2
Distribution of mutation distribution

Mutation type	Number of position	Total number of mutations
Transitions		
Py–Py		
C–T	47	257
T–C	39	314
Pu–Pu		
A–G	33	378
G–A	13	63
Total	132	1012
Transversions		
A–C	3	23
C–G	3	3
G–C	2	3
T–G	2	2
G–T	3	6
A–T	2	2
Total	15	39
Insertions		
+ C	3	297
+ 2C	1	18
+ 3C	1	1
Total	5	316
Deletions		
− A	3	6
− T	1	1
Total	4	7

Table 3
Most frequent haplotypes observed in Spanish population (northeast Spain)

Haplotypes HV1 + HV2	*n*
263G 315.1C	10
263G 309.1C 315.1C	5
16189C 263G 315.1C	3
16069T 16126C 73G 185A 228A 263G 295T 315.1C	2
16311C 263G 315.1C	2
16093C 16224C 16311C 73G 195C 263G 315.1C	2
16069T 16126C 16278T 73G 185A 188G 228A 263G 295T 309.1C 315.1C	2
16145A 16222T 263G 315.1C	2
16069T 16126C 16193T 73G 150T 152C 263G 295T 315.1C	2
263G 309.1C 309.2C 315.1C	2
16192T 16270T 16319A 73G 150T 263G 315.1C	2
200G 263G 315.1C	2
16224C 16311C 73G 263G 315.1C	2

phenol–chloroform method [1]. The mtDNA regions subjected to analysis were 16024–16365 (HVRI) and 73–340 (HVRII). Amplification reaction was performed as described previously [2] employing a GeneAmp System 2400 thermal cycler (Perkin-Elmer, Norwalk, CT).

The amplified products were purified and separated from unreacted primers and dNTPs by filtration in a Centricon-100 (Amicon Beverly, MA) following the manufacturer's recommendations. Sequencing fragments were generated using Taq DyeDeoxy™ Terminator Cycle Sequencing Ready Reaction kit (Foster City, CA, USA) and primers identical to those employed for amplification, according to the protocol provided by PE/ABD with the kit. Afterwards, DNA products were purified by ethanol precipitation and the fragments were analysed using an automated DNA sequencer ABI PRISM 310 (PE/ABD). Each template was sequenced from both directions and the consensus sequence was aligned and compared with the reference sequence [3] using the software SeqEd™ V. 1.0.3 (PE/ABD).

3. Results and discussion

Table 1 shows the statistical data (different haplotypes, variable sites, unique haplotypes frequency, genetic diversity and random match probability) obtained for each region and two region taken together. Table 2 shows the distribution of nucleotide substitution that we have obtained. Table 3 shows the haplotypes observed at least in two individuals in our population.

References

[1] J. Sambrook, E.F. Fristch, T. Maniatis, Molecular Cloning: A Laboratory Manual, 2nd ed., Cold Spring Harbor Laboratory Press, Cold Spring Harbor, NY, 1989.

[2] M.R. Wilson, J.A. DiZinno, D. Polanskey, J. Replogle, B. Budowle, Validation of mitochondrial DNA sequencing for forensic casework analysis, Int. J. Leg. Med. 108 (1995) 68–74.

[3] S. Anderson, A.T. Bankier, B.G. Barrel, M.H.L. de Bruijin, A.R. Coulson, I.C. Drouin, I.C. Eperon, D.P. Nierlick, B.A. Roe, F. Sanger, P.H. Schreider, A.J.H. Smith, R. Staden, I.G. Young, Sequence and organization of the mitochondrial genome, Nature 290 (1981) 457–465.

International Congress Series 1261 (2004) 410–412

www.ics-elsevier.com

Sequence analysis of mitochondrial DNA HVIII region in a Japanese population

A. Nagai*, I. Nakamura, Y. Bunai

Department of Legal Medicine, Gifu University School of Medicine, 40 Tsukasa-machi, Gifu 500-8705, Japan

Abstract. Sequence polymorphism of the hypervariable region HVIII of mitochondrial DNA (mtDNA) was analyzed in a sample of 150 unrelated Japanese individuals living in Gifu Prefecture (central region of Japan). A total of 21 different haplotypes resulting from 20 variable sites was observed. The most frequently observed nucleotide substitution was at position 489 (T to C transition).

Keywords: mtDNA; HVIII; Japanese population data

1. Introduction

The sequence analysis of the hypervariable region of mitochondrial DNA (mtDNA) is a very useful tool for forensic investigations. Recently, Lutz et al. [1] reported the existence of the third hypervariable region called HVIII (positions 438–574). The main aim of this study was to evaluate the variability of the HVIII region in the Japanese population.

2. Materials and methods

Blood samples were obtained from 150 unrelated Japanese individuals living in Gifu Prefecture (central region of Japan). DNA was extracted using the phenol–chloroform method. PCR amplification conditions were based on the method of Bini et al. [2]. The PCR products were directly sequenced using the Thermo Sequenase core sequencing kit (Amersham). The PCR primers labeled with Texas Red were used as the sequence primers. Sequence analysis was performed on an SQ5500-S DNA Sequencer (Hitachi Electronics Engineering). The resulting sequence data were compared with the reference sequence described by Anderson et al. [3].

* Corresponding author. Tel.: +81-58-267-2250; fax: +81-58-267-2957.
E-mail address: anagai@cc.gifu-u.ac.jp (A. Nagai).

0531-5131/
doi:10.1016/S0531-5131(03)01786-2

3. Results and discussion

The sequence polymorphisms of the mtDNA HVIII region observed in this study are summarized in Table 1. A total of 21 different haplotypes resulting from 20 variable sites was found in a sample of 150 unrelated Japanese individuals living in Gifu Prefecture. The most common haplotype was found in 38.0% ($n=57$) of the individuals. Transitions were more prevalent than transversions (Table 2). Screening CA repeat at positions 514–523 (−CA, +CA, +2CA), we found 53 sequences with $(CA)_{5-1}$, 92 with $(CA)_5$, 3 with $(CA)_{5+1}$ and 2 with $(CA)_{5+2}$ repeats (Tables 1 and 2). At C stretch at positions 568–573 (+C, +2C, +3C), we found 1 sequence with 5, 145 sequences with 6, 1 sequence with 7, 1 sequence with 8 and 2 sequences with 9 C residues (Tables 1 and 2). The most frequently observed nucleotide substitution was at position 489 (T to C transition), and secondly at positions 522 (C deletion) and 523 (A deletion). The genetic diversity and the genetic identity for this population sample were calculated to be 0.782 and 0.223, respectively, based on the calculation method described by Tajima [4].

Table 1
Sequence polymorphisms in the mtDNA HVIII region of 150 unrelated Japanese

456	469	482	483	489	493	499	501	522	523	523a	523b	523c	523d	542	573	573a	573b	573c	593	*n*
C	C	T	C	T	A	G	C	C	A	–	–	–	–	C	C	–	–	–	T	
•	•	•	•	C	•	•	•	•	•	•	•	•	•	•	•	•	•	•	•	57
•	•	•	•	•	•	•	•	del	del	•	•	•	•	•	•	•	•	•	•	26
•	•	•	•	C	•	•	•	del	del	•	•	•	•	•	•	•	•	•	•	24
•	•	•	•	•	•	•	•	•	•	•	•	•	•	•	•	•	•	•	•	22
•	•	•	•	C	•	•	•	•	•	C	A	•	•	•	•	•	•	•	•	3
•	•	•	•	C	G	•	•	•	•	•	•	•	•	•	•	•	•	•	•	3
•	•	•	T	•	•	•	•	•	•	•	•	•	•	•	•	•	•	•	•	1
•	•	C	•	C	•	•	•	•	•	•	•	•	•	•	•	•	•	•	•	1
•	•	•	•	C	•	•	•	•	•	•	•	•	•	•	•	C	C	•	•	1
•	•	•	•	•	•	•	•	•	•	C	A	C	A	•	•	•	•	•	•	1
•	•	•	•	C	•	•	•	del	del	•	•	•	•	•	•	C	C	C	•	1
•	•	•	•	•	•	A	•	•	•	•	•	•	•	•	•	•	•	•	•	1
•	•	•	•	C	•	•	T	•	•	•	•	•	•	•	•	•	•	•	•	1
•	G	•	•	C	•	•	•	•	•	•	•	•	•	•	•	•	•	•	•	1
•	•	•	•	C	•	•	•	•	•	C	A	C	A	•	•	•	•	•	•	1
•	•	•	•	C	•	•	•	•	•	•	•	•	•	•	•	C	C	C	•	1
•	•	•	•	C	•	•	•	•	•	•	•	•	•	•	del	•	•	•	•	1
•	•	•	•	C	•	•	•	•	•	•	•	•	•	•	•	•	•	•	C	1
T	•	•	•	C	•	•	•	•	•	•	•	•	•	•	•	•	•	•	•	1
•	•	•	•	•	•	•	•	del	del	•	•	•	•	T	•	•	•	•	•	1
•	•	•	•	•	•	•	•	del	del	•	•	•	•	•	•	C	•	•	•	1
Total																				150

The nucleotide in the reference sequence [3] is shown below the order for polymorphic sites. Letters following a number (a–d) indicate additions of nucleotides not found in the reference sequence.
(•) Identical nucleotide with the reference, (–) nucleotide absence in the reference, del: deletion from the reference, *n*: observed number.

Table 2
Nucleotide substitutions, insertions and deletions in the mtDNA HVII region of 150 unrelated Japanese

Mutation type	HVIII	
	Number of positions	Total number of mutations
Transition		
C → T	4	4
T → C	3	99
A → G	1	3
G → A	1	1
Total	9	107
Transversion		
C → G	1	1
Total	1	1
Insertion		
+CA	1	3
+2CA	1	2
+C	1	1
+2C	1	1
+3C	1	2
Total	5	9
Deletion		
− C	1	1
− CA	1	53
Total	2	54

This database of mtDNA HVIII region for Japanese population would be useful for forensic examinations and human genetic studies.

References

[1] S. Lutz, H.-J. Weisser, J. Heizmann, S. Pollak, Location and frequency of polymorphic positions in the mtDNA control region of individuals from Germany. Int. J. Leg. Med., 111 (1998) 67–77, Erratum, Int. J. Leg. Med., 112 (1999) 145–150.

[2] C. Bini, S. Ceccardi, C. Colalongo, G. Ferri, M. Falconi, S. Pelotti, G. Pappalardo, Population data of mitochondrial DNA region HNIII in 150 individuals from Bologna (Italy), in: B. Brinkmann, A. Carracedo (Eds.), Progress in Forensic Genetics, vol. 9, Elsevier, Amsterdam, 2003, pp. 525–528.

[3] S. Anderson, A.T. Bankier, B.G. Barrell, M.H.L. De Bruijn, A.R. Coulson, J. Drouin, I.C. Eperon, D.P. Nierlich, B.A. Roe, F. Sanger, P.H. Schreier, A.J.H. Smith, R. Staden, I.G. Young, Sequence and organization of the human mitochondrial genome, Nature 290 (1981) 457–465.

[4] F. Tajima, Statistical method for testing the neutral mutation hypothesis by DNA polymorphism, Genetics 123 (1989) 585–595.

International Congress Series 1261 (2004) 413–415

www.ics-elsevier.com

Sequence Polymorphisms of Mitochondrial Control Region DNA in Argentine population

S.E. Filippini, A. Castro, M.G. Fraga, F. Gagliardi, C. Echenique, A.M. Di Lonardo*

Banco Nacional de Datos Genéticos, Hospital Dr. C.G. Durand, J.B. Ambrosetti 743 Planta Baja, 1405 Buenos Aires, Argentina

Abstract. As mitochondrial analysis offers great potentials for individualization in forensics, it is sometimes the more convenient and more successful method to be considered, in particular, with low DNA samples. That is the reason why today, many efforts are made to build up mitochondrial databases for forensic purposes. In our study, we analyzed the Sequence Polymorphisms of Mitochondrial DNA Control Regions, HV1 and HV2, in Argentine individuals, most of them from the city of Buenos Aires, with the aim of creating our own database.

Keywords: Mitochondrial DNA; Forensics; Population; Polymorphisms

1. Introduction

Sequencing of Mitochondrial DNA D-Loop Region [1,2] has been incorporated since 1993 in our laboratory to study maternal lineage. Since then, it has become a tool of choice for forensic casework. Automated DNA Sequencing of PCR products have made mitochondrial DNA analysis easier and faster. The aim of this study is to analyze Sequence Polymorphisms of Mitochondrial Control Region DNA [3] in our population, and for that purpose, we studied the D-Loop Hypervariable Regions 1 and 2 (HV1 and HV2). Statistical interpretation of the results let us create a database with sequences of our own population.

2. Materials and methods

We studied 565 unrelated Argentine individuals, most from the city of Buenos Aires. DNA was extracted by Miller's method (salting out) and by chloroform/phenol/isoamyl alcohol extraction method.

Mitochondrial DNA D-Loop Region of approximately 1.300 bp was amplified from blood samples using the following primers: L-15926 and H-00580. For forensic samples, we amplified three fragments of HV1 Segment (253, 156 and 192 bp) and three fragments of HV2 Segment (233, 227 and 172 bp) using the following primers: L-15997/H-16255; L-

* Corresponding author. Tel.: +5411-4-982-1716; fax: +5411-4-982-0625.

E-mail address: bndg@infovia.com.ar (A.M. Di Lonardo).

0531-5131/
doi:10.1016/S0531-5131(03)01646-7

16099/H-16255; L-16209/H-16401; L-00030/H-00262; L-00140/H-00366; and L-00241/H-00412, respectively. PCR was performed in a GeneAmp PCR System 9700® (Perkin Elmer). PCR product was purified using Microspin S-300 HR Columns (Amersham/Pharmacia). Sequencing reaction was performed with "Big Dye Terminator Cycle Sequencing Kit" (PE BioSystems). Templates were purified using Centrisep-Spin Columns and analyzed in an ABI Prism 310 Genetic Analyzer (PE Applied BioSystems).

3. Results and discussion

We analyzed the Sequence Polymorphisms of Mitochondrial Control Region DNA in 565 unrelated individuals. We studied HV1 Region in all the samples and HV2 Region in 261 of them. For HV1 Region, we analyzed 390 bp (16023–16412), and for HV2 Region, 342 bp (060–401). In HV1 Region, we observed 325 different haplotypes (57.5%) and 262 individuals showed a unique haplotype (46.4%).The Cambridge Reference Sequence (CRS) was the most frequent haplotype observed, present in 35 unrelated individuals (11%). We calculated Genetic Identity (P = 0.013) and Genetic Diversity (h = 0.9887). We also found 143 polymorphic sites with 159 mutational events, being 135 of them transitions (84.9%) and 24 transversions (15.1%), and, in 13 polymorphic sites, we could observe both types of mutational events (8.17%). In our population, HV1 Region did not present either insertions or deletions. Transition C→T at position 16223 was the most frequent substitution, found in 283 individuals (50%).This mutational event is present in Amerindian, Asian and African haplotypes [4]. The haplotype 16223-T, 16298-C, 16325-C, 16327-T was frequent in our population (8.9%), as well as that described in Amerindians [5]. In 129 individuals, we found a transition C→T at position 16189 showing the polycitosine tract (from 16184 position to 16193 position). We found heteroplasmies in five samples at positions 16187C/T, 16210 A/G, 16261 C/T, 16265 C/T and 16179 T/C. All the mutational events found in HV1 Region are described in Table 1. The analysis of HV2 Region in 261 unrelated individuals displayed 146 different haplotypes, a value of P = 0.017 (Genetic

Table 1
Mutational events in HV1 Region

	16037	16038	16048	16051	16069	16071	16082	16083	16084	16086	16092	16093	16111	16114	16124	16125	16126	16129	16136	16137	16140	16142	16145	16147	16148	16150	16153	16156	16157	16160	16162	16163	16167	16168	16169	16171	16172	16173	16174	16176	16178	16179	16181	16182	16183	16184	16185
ANDERSON:	A	A	G	A	C	C	C	C	G	T	T	T	C	C	T	G	T	G	T	A	T	C	G	C	C	C	G	G	T	A	A	A	C	C	C	A	T	C	C	C	T	C	A	A	A	C	C
T					17	1	1	1					58				1					7		1	4	1							1	5	4			4	6	1		4				2	3
G	2	1		30																1										1	2	6				1				1			1				
C										3	21	26			3	1	59	1	7		4								3								18		1		7			14	47		
A			1						1					3				19					9				11	2												83							

	16186	16187	16188	16189	16190	16192	16193	16194	16197	16209	16210	16213	16214	16215	16217	16218	16219	16221	16222	16223	16224	16225	16230	16234	16235	16239	16240	16241	16242	16243	16245	16247	16248	16249	16254	16255	16256	16257	16260	16261	16263	16264	16265	16266	16269	16270	16271	16274
ANDERSON:	C	C	C	T	C	C	C	A	C	A	A	G	C	A	T	C	A	C	C	C	T	C	A	C	A	C	A	A	C	T	C	A	C	T	A	G	C	C	C	C	T	C	A	C	A	C	T	G
T	7	20	5		1	19	5	1	1				2	1		5		1	2	283		1		5		2			32		3						17	1	1	2		6	1	3		15		
G			8								1			115			6						1	1	7	2	1	6				1			4								1		1			
C				129						20					46						18									1				7						1	4		1				2	
A		3										3														4							1			1												3

	16278	16286	16287	16288	16290	16291	16292	16293	16294	16295	16296	16297	16298	16300	16301	16302	16304	16309	16310	16311	16312	16316	16319	16320	16323	16324	16325	16327	16342	16343	16344	16352	16354	16355	16356	16357	16359	16360	16362	16363	16366	16368	16381	16384	16390	16391	16399	16404
ANDERSON:	C	C	C	T	C	C	C	A	C	C	C	T	T	A	C	A	T	A	G	T	A	A	G	C	T	T	T	C	T	A	C	T	C	C	T	T	T	C	T	C	C	T	T	G	G	G	A	C
T	33	2	4		55	9	12		42	3	18				5					1				7				106			4		1	8				8		1	2							1
G		1		1				7						3				1			3	3								5																	4	
C				4								2	116			2	18			111					2	4	185		2			3			1	6	1		158			2	1					
A																			2				72	1										1										3	18	10		

Sample: 565 unrelated individuals. Mutational events: 159. Transitions: 135. Transversions: 24.

Table 2
Mutational events in HV2 Region

	0	0	0	0	0	0	1	1	1	1	1	1	1	1	1	1	1	1	1	1
	6	6	7	7	8	9	0	0	0	0	0	0	1	1	1	3	4	4	4	5
	4	6	2	3	9	3	3	6	7	8	9	9	0	1	9	9	0	3	6	0
ANDERSON:	C	G	T	A	T	A	G	del	del	del	G	del	del	del	T	T	C	G	T	C
T	13																			21
G				190		17		1	1			1					1			
C			7		2								1		1	1			53	
A		1					2			1	1			1				2		

	1	1	1	1	1	1	1	1	1	1	1	1	1	1	2	2	2	2	2	2
	5	5	5	6	8	8	8	8	8	9	9	9	9	9	0	0	0	0	1	1
	1	2	3	3	2	3	5	8	9	4	5	6	8	9	0	1	4	7	2	4
ANDERSON:	C	T	A	G	C	A	G	A	A	C	T	T	C	T	A	A	T	G	T	A
T	3				1					12			3							
G		1	23	1		2		2	6						6	2				2
C	1	50							1		34	1		2			8		1	
A							9											5		

	2	2	2	2	2	2	2	2	2	2	2	2	2	2	2	2	2	2	2	2
	1	1	2	2	2	2	2	3	3	3	3	4	4	4	5	5	5	6	6	7
	5	7	2	5	6	7	8	4	5	7	9	4	9	9	3	7	8	2	3	2
ANDERSON:	A	T	C	G	T	A	G	A	A	A	T	A	A	del	C	A	C	C	A	A
T			1				1										3	1		
G	2					2		1	22	1		1			1	1			258	1
C		3			1						4		1							
A				3			4							51						

	2	2	2	2	2	2	2	3	3	3	3	3	3	3	3	3	3	3	3	3
	8	9	9	9	9	9	9	0	0	0	1	1	1	1	1	2	2	3	4	7
	2	0	1	1	5	6	7	1	9	9	4	5	5	5	9	5	7	8	0	2
				1				1	1	2			1	2	2					
ANDERSON:	T	del	del	I	C	C	A	I	I	I	del	del	I	I	I	C	C	C	C	T
T					6	1										1	1	3	1	
G							1													
C	1							1	169	41	1	1	261	1	1					2
A		55	55	1	1															

Sample: 261 unrelated individuals. Mutational events: 85. Transitions: 58. Transversions: 8. Insertions: 7. Deletions: 11.

Identity) and a value of $h=0.9866$ (Genetic Diversity). We observed 69 polymorphic sites and 85 mutational events corresponding to 58 transitions (68.2%) and 9 transversions (10.6%). In contrast to HV1 Region, HV2 Region presented insertions and deletions.

The insertion of an additional cytosine at the cytosine tract 311–315 was found in all individuals, while 64.75% presented the insertion of an additional cytosine at the 303–309 cytosine tract. We observed 51 individuals sharing three deletion positions (249, 290 and 291), which are described in Mapuches [6]. This HV2 haplotype is associated with the following HV1 haplotype: 16223-T, 16298-C, 16325-C, 16327-T. In one case, we observed a 6-bp deletion (from nucleotide 106 to nucleotide 111), also found in Chibcha population (http.www.mitomap.org). All the mutational events found in HV2 Region are described in Table 2.

Considering the complete haplotype (HV1 and HV2) from 261 unrelated individuals, 224 different haplotypes were distinguished with $P=0.0058$ (Genetic Identity) and $h=0.9979$ (Genetic Diversity). A number of 107 polymorphic sites were detected in HV1 Region, and 69 in HV2 Region. We also analyzed the mutational events present in HV2 Region in association with the most frequent HV1 haplotypes in our population. For example, our most frequent HV1 haplotype, CRS (common in Europeans) [7], was associated with HV2 haplotypes which did not present the point mutation 073-G. Complete sequence analysis (HV1–HV2) showed a high level of diversity (99.8%), which let us conclude that sequencing of Mitochondrial DNA D-Loop Region is an essential marker to be considered in human identification.

References

[1] S. Anderson, et al., Nature 290 (1981) 457–465.
[2] R.L. Cann, et al., Nature (London) 325 (1987) 31–36.
[3] R. Hopgood, et al., BioTechniques 13 (1992) 82–92.
[4] E. Watson, et al., American Journal Genetics 61 (1997) 691–704.
[5] A. Torroni, et al., Human Genetics 53 (1993) 563–590.
[6] C. Ginther, et al., DNA fingerprinting, in: S.D.J. (Ed.), State of the Science, 1993.
[7] A. Salas, et al., European Journal of Human Genetics 6 (1998) 365–375.

International Congress Series 1261 (2004) 416–418

ELSEVIER

www.ics-elsevier.com

Subdividing mtDNA haplogroup H based on coding-region polymorphisms—a study in Iberia

L. Pereira[a,*], M. Richards[b], A. Alonso[c], C. Albarrán[c], O. Garcia[d], V. Macaulay[e], A. Amorim[a,f]

[a] *IPATIMUP (Instituto de Patologia e Imunologia Molecular da Universidade do Porto), Porto, Portugal*
[b] *Department of Chemical and Biological Sciences, University of Huddersfield, Huddersfield, UK*
[c] *Instituto de Toxicología, Sección de Biologia, Madrid, Spain*
[d] *Area de Laboratorio Ertzaintza, Gobierno Vasco, Bilbao, Spain*
[e] *Department of Statistics, University of Oxford, UK*
[f] *Faculdade de Ciências da Universidade do Porto, Portugal*

Abstract. Information on complete human mitochondrial DNA has revealed polymorphisms located in the coding region, which are useful for a more secure mtDNA haplogroup subdivision. We sequenced 1580 bp in the coding region informative for subclassification of haplogroup H, the most poorly resolved European haplogroup when studying only control-region variation. This revealed nine coding polymorphisms (at positions 3010, 3915, 3992, 4024, 4336, 4745, 4769, 4793 and 6776, besides the diagnostic position 7028) that allowed subclassification of around 80% of the 306 Iberian H samples in eight subhaplogroups. Frequencies for these haplogroups vary widely, with half of the samples sharing the substitution at position 3010 (but some structure is already apparent within this subhaplogroup). The HVRI diversity suggested the following age estimates for some subhaplogroups: 3010: 13,400 ± 3000 years; 6776: 8600 ± 2800 years; 4336: 4700 ± 2700 years; 3915: 17,300 ± 9100 years. Those ages indicate that these H subhaplogroups may be informative for different time scales of European demographic history.

Keywords: MtDNA; Coding region; Haplogroup H; Iberia

1. Introduction

The most common strategy used in the past to study the variation in population samples of mtDNA, the sequencing of one or both of the hypervariable regions located in the control region, has been insufficiently informative to reveal clear phylogeographic patterns in about a half of the European mtDNA pool. This is because the phylogeny of the most common European haplogroup, H, is poorly resolved. Recent data from mtDNA complete sequencing [1,2] have revealed informative polymorphisms at some coding-region positions, namely in the ND1, ND2 and CO1 genes and some tRNAs. We sequenced

* Corresponding author.
E-mail address: lpereira@ipatimup.pt (L. Pereira).

0531-5131/
doi:10.1016/S0531-5131(03)01651-0

four segments encompassing these diagnostic positions in three samples from the Iberian Peninsula, in the subset already classified as haplogroup H.

2. Material and methods

Iberian samples (194 from Portugal, 37 from Madrid in Central Spain and 75 from the Basque Country in Northeastern Spain) previously classified (by HVRI screening and checking of the diagnostic position 7028) as belonging to haplogroup H were sequenced for the following coding regions: nps 3001 – 3360, 3661 – 4050, 4281 – 4820 and 6761 – 7050. Primers used were, respectively: L2978 5′-GTC CAT ATC AAC AAT AGG GT-3′ and H3361 5′-CGT TCG GTA AGC ATT AGG AA-3′; L3640 5′-TCT AGC CAC CTC TAG CCT AG-3′ and H4051 5′-TAG AGT TCA GGG GAG AGT GC-3′; L4264 5′-CAT TCC CCC TCA AAC CTA AG-3′ and H4821 5′-AGA GGG GTG CCT TGG GTA AC-3′; L6740 5′-TGG TCT GAG CTA TGA TAT CA-3′ and H7051 5′-GAT GGC AAA TAC AGC TCC TA-3′. The temperature profiles for the PCR were: 95 °C for 10 s, 64 °C for 30 s and 72 °C for 30 s for 35 cycles for the third pair of primers, and the same except 58 °C as annealing temperature for the others. Automated sequencing was carried out in an ABI 3100 using the Kit Big-Dye Terminator Cycle Sequencing Ready Reaction (AB Applied Biosystems).

The HVRI diversity observed between 16,090–16,365 bp was used for age estimation, by assuming a mutation rate of one transition per 20,180 years and applying the rho statistics as described in [3]; calculations were carried out using the Network version 3.0 software.

3. Results

The haplogroup H frequencies in the Iberian samples analysed here are: 41% in Portugal; 49% in Madrid; and 50% in the Basque Country.

The sequencing of the 1580 bp in the coding region in the 306 H Iberian samples showed that nine polymorphisms were present in at least two of those populations, allowing the discrimination of eight H sub-haplogroups, the frequencies of which are displayed in Table 1.

There is still a wide range of subhaplogroup frequencies, with half of the individuals sharing the substitution at np 3010. But this subhaplogroup shows some diversity in the coding regions studied here, and potential further subdivisions within it can be defined. In Iberia, there is a lineage 3010 4733, the frequency of which was 0.015 in Portugal, 0.135 in Madrid and 0.107 in the Basque Country; and a subset of this with an additional substitution, 3010 4733 3849, with relative frequencies of 0.005, 0.027 and 0.067, respectively.

The second most frequent subhaplogroup in Portugal and the Basque country, defined by the substitution at position 6776, shows, curiously, a very low frequency in Madrid.

Table 1
Iberian frequencies of the H sub-haplogroups based on coding region polymorphisms (all transitions)

	Characteristic variants								
	3010	4769	6776	3992 4024	4336	3915	4745	4793	other/no
Portugal	0.459	0.041	0.191	0.021	0.031	0.031	0.010	0.026	0.190
Madrid	0.541	0.054	0.027	0.027	0.081	0.027	–	0.054	0.189
Basque Country	0.507	0.120	0.160	0.027	0.053	–	0.013	–	0.080

The Basque country presents a high frequency for the subhaplogroup defined by the 4769 polymorphism, and half of the samples presented an additional coding polymorphism at position 4592, that was not observed in the other two populations.

A proportion of 10 – 20% of the H samples were not further classifiable on the basis of variation in these coding-region segments.

This study showed that HVRI sites that have been previously used to define subclades (e.g., position 16,304) seem to have mutated more than once in haplogroup H. Nevertheless, the HVRI position 16,304 was present in all but one of the 13 individuals that presented the coding substitution 4336, while 16362 was present in all of the seven individuals bearing the 3915 substitution.

Using the HVRI diversity within the most frequent of these subhaplogroups, we estimated the following times for their most recent common ancestors: 3010: 13,400 ± 3,000 years; 6,776: 8600 ± 2800 years; 4336: 4700 ± 2700 years; 3915: 17,300 ± 9100 years.

4. Conclusions

This initial screening, by sequencing a considerable region (1580 bp long) around the coding positions potentially informative for haplogroup H subclassification, indicated a total of nine coding positions that enable the classification of 80% of the Iberian H samples in eight subhaplogroups. A more practical screening strategy (RFLP or mini-sequencing) can be designed for population genetic/forensic surveys of these polymorphisms, whenever HVRI diversity is poorly informative. In fact, the HVRI CRS haplotype appeared in different coding-defined haplotypes, probably due to the high recurrence in the control region. It is a priority to learn more about them in a wider geographical area, since the different ages seem to indicate that these H subhaplogroups may be informative for different time scales of European prehistory.

Acknowledgements

This work was partially supported by a research grant to LP (SFRH/BPD/7121/2001) from Fundação para a Ciência e a Tecnologia and IPATIMUP by Programa Operacional Ciência, Tecnologia e Inovação (POCTI), Quadro Comunitário de Apoio III. This study is included in the Project POCTI/ANT/45139/2002 financed by Fundação para a Ciência e a Tecnologia (Eixo 2, Medida 2.3 do POCTI, QCA III). VM has a Wellcome Trust Research Career Development Fellowship.

References

[1] M. Ingman, H. Kaessmann, S. Paabo, U. Gyllensten, Mitochondrial genome variation and the origin of modern humans, Nature 408 (2000) 708–713.

[2] C. Herrnstadt, J.L. Elson, E. Fahy, G. Preston, D.M. Turnbull, C. Anderson, S.S. Ghosh, J.M. Olefsky, M.F. Beal, R.E. Davis, N. Howell, Reduced-median-network analysis of complete mitochondrial DNA coding-region sequences for the major African, Asian, and European haplogroups, Am. J. Hum. Genet. 70 (2002) 1152–1171.

[3] J. Saillard, P. Forster, N. Lynnerup, H.-J. Bandelt, S. Norby, mtDNA variation among Greenland Eskimos: the edge of the Beringian expansion, Am. J. Hum. Genet. 67 (2000) 718–726.

International Congress Series 1261 (2004) 419–421

www.ics-elsevier.com

Typing mtDNA SNPs of forensic and population interest with snapshot

Beatriz Quintáns, Vanesa Álvarez-Iglesias, Antonio Salas, Maviki Lareu*, Ángel Carracedo

Institute of Legal Medicine, University of Santiago de Compostela, San Francisco s/n. 15782 Santiago de Compostela, Spain

Abstract. In last years, interest in Single Nucleotide Polymorphism (SNP) has increased due to their numerous applications: in medical genetics, in human and evolutionary genetics but also in forensic field. Polymorphisms placed in the mitochondrial genome are particularly important in a forensic context in part due to the fact that it is in high copy number per cell. Consequently, mtDNA is especially useful to the study of degraded samples with little or no nuclear DNA as being old skeletal remains and hair shafts. On the other hand, mtDNA SNPs have demonstrate its usefulness for human population studies. The development of new methodologies for high-throughput SNPs analysis is one of the most promising areas in genetics. Here, we describe a rapid and robust assay to simultaneously genotype 17 SNPs of mitochondrial DNA by minisequencing reaction using SNaPshot (Applied Biosystems). The methodology here described shows high accuracy and sensitivity, and avoid the use of alternative time-consuming classical strategies (i.e. RFLP typing) and the requirement of high quantities of DNA template.

Keywords: SNaPshot; SNPs; mtDNA; Hypervariable region; Human identification

1. Introduction

The development of new methodologies for high-throughput SNPs analysis is one of the most challenging areas in genetic research because their numerous applications. Most of these high-throughput technologies as DNA microarrays or MALDI-TOF are extremely expensive and therefore cannot be used by a great majority of standard labs. Furthermore, many of them are still in phase of development. Classical methods are time-consuming, costly and require high amounts of DNA. Here, we describe a rapid and robust assay to simultaneously genotyping 17 mitochondrial DNA coding region SNPs by minisequencing reaction using SNaPshot (Applied Biosystems), a methodology based on the dideoxy

Abbreviations: HVS-I, the first hypervariable region; HVS-II, the second hypervariable region; rCRS, revised Cambridge Reference Sequence.

* Corresponding author. Tel.: +34-981582327; fax: +34-981580336.

E-mail address: apimllar@usc.es (M. Lareu).

0531-5131/

doi:10.1016/S0531-5131(03)01825-9

(ddNTP) single base extension of an unlabeled oligonucleotide at the 3′ -end of the base immediately adjacent to the SNP. Each ddNTP is labeled with different fluorescent dyes. We have incorporated a set of SNPs in a multiplex that allow allocate common mitochondrial European types into the mtDNA phylogeny, including haplogroup H, the most frequent lineage in Europe (40–50%) and the worst phylogeneticaly characterized in the first and second hypervariable segments as well.

2. Materials and methods

A total of 266 individuals from Galicia (nothwest Iberia) were analyzed. First hypervariable segment (HVS-I) was sequenced from position 16024 to 16400 following conditions described by Salas et al. [1]. A preliminary classification of the sequences into haplogroups was done following phylogenetic criteria according to Richards et al. [2].

Two reactions of PCR were performed: Multiplex 1 includes SNPs defining common European haplogroups (4216, 4529, 4580, 7028, 10,398, 10,400, 10,873, 12,308, 12,705 and 14,766). Multiplex 2 includes SNPs defining subhaplogroups inside haplogroup H (3010, 3915, 3992, 4336, 4769, 4793 and 6776). After post-PCR purification with ExoSapIT (Amersham Biosciences), minisequencing reaction of 17 SNPs was carried out simultaneously. After post extension treatment with Sap (Amersham Biosciences), products were electrophoresed on an ABI PRISM 3100® Genetic Analyzer.

In some cases, two SNPs are placed very closely to each other within the mtDNA molecule and this allows its co-amplification in the same amplicon. The size of the PCR products ranged from 80 to 224 bp, which facilitate the analysis of degraded samples or with low quantities of DNA. The extended SNaPshot primers for different SNPs differ between them by size and color and they can be detected by capillary electrophoresis. The length of the extension primers were modified by the addition of non-homologous tails at the 5′ -end.

3. Results and discussion

Fig. 1 shows the electropherogram for the 17-coding region mtDNA SNPs minisequenced in a single reaction.

The advantages of the used of this set of SNPs in a forensic and anthropological context clearly manifest when looking at the most common European lineage (H) that represents 45% of the Galician samples. We can subtype this haplogroup in 6 different sublineages [3] (frequencies in Fig. 2). H7 (4793G) did not found. With the sub-classification of rCRS

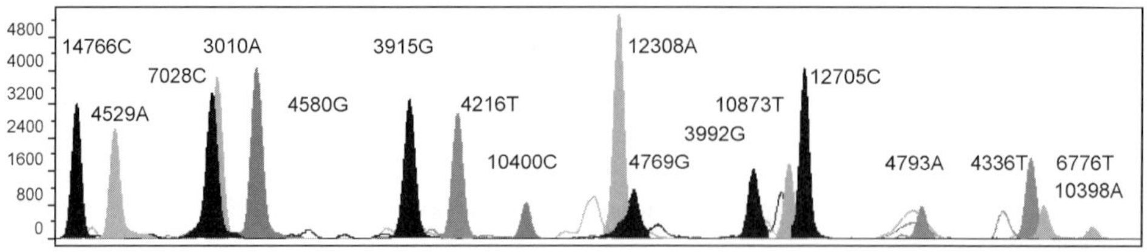

Fig. 1. Electropherogram for the minisequenced 17-coding region mtDNA SNPs.

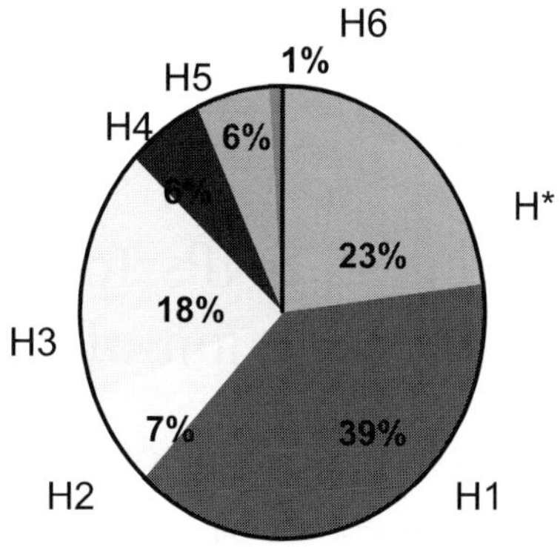

Fig. 2. Frequencies of sublineages of haplogroup H in Galician sample.

in HVS-I, the haplotype diversity increase from 0 to 0.737 in this set of samples. Other HVS-I haplotypes also gain in discrimanation power when using this coding region SNPs. In those cases where HVS-I is phylogenetically informative [2], we found a complete correlation with the coding region mtDNA SNP status.

The method for typing of 17 mitochondrial DNA coding region SNPs of forensic and population interest with SNaPshot shows to be rapid, robust and accurate and avoids both the use of alternative time-consuming classical strategies (i.e. RFLP typing) and the requirement of high quantities of DNA template. The electrophoresis performed on an ABI PRISM 3100® Genetic Analyzer providing and automatic, standardized and sensitive mode of detection and process of the results.

Acknowledgements

We thank Meli Rodríguez and Raquel Calvo for her technical assistance. This work was supported by grants from the Ministerio de Educación y Ciencia (DGCYT-P4. BIO2000-0145-P4-02), Ministerio de Sanidad (FIS 01/0024) and the Xunta de Galicia (PGIDT-01-PXI-20806-PR and PGIDIT02PXIC20804PN). AS has a research contract with the University of Santiago de Compostela.

References

[1] A. Salas, et al., mtDNA analysis of the Galician population: a genetic edge of European variation, Eur. J. Hum Genet. 6 (4) (1998) 75–365.

[2] M. Richards, et al., Tracing European founder lineages in the Near Eastern mtDNA pool, AJHG 67 (5) (2000) 1251–1276.

[3] C. Herrnstadt, et al., Reduced-median-network analysis of complete mitochondrial DNA coding-region sequences for the major African, Asian, and European haplogroups, AJHG 70 (5) (2002) 1152–1171.

ELSEVIER

International Congress Series 1261 (2004) 422–424

www.ics-elsevier.com

MtDNA coding region SNPs for rapid screening and haplogroup identification of forensic samples

Anita Brandstätter[a], Thomas J. Parsons[b], Walther Parson[a,*]

[a] *Forensic Molecular Biology, Institute of Legal Medicine, University of Innsbruck, Müllerstrasse 44, 6020, Innsbruck, Austria*

[b] *Armed Forces DNA Identification Laboratory, Armed Forces Institute of Pathology, Building 101, 1413 Research Boulevard, Rockville, MD 20850, USA*

Abstract. Analysis of single nucleotide polymorphisms (SNPs) is a promising application in forensic human identification. We selected 16 SNPs from the coding region of the human mitochondrial DNA in order to ascribe samples to 1 of the 9 major West European Caucasian mitochondrial haplogroups. The selected SNPs are targeted in two multiplex-systems, via the application of the SNaPshot™ kit, a multiplex method based on the dideoxy single-base extension of unlabeled oligonucleotide primers. By screening these SNPs prior to sequencing analysis of the hypervariable regions in the control region, we would be able to rapidly differentiate between stains or hairs in high volume case work or to eliminate multiple suspects from an inquiry.

Keywords: West European Caucasian mtDNA haplogroups; Mitochondrial SNPs; Multiplex SNP typing; Primer extension method; Forensic profiling

1. Introduction

Every European can trace his or her evolutionary history back to nine ancestral matriarchal groups, referred to as mitochondrial haplogroups, from which all Europeans appear to be descended. The assignment to these haplogroups relies on the identification of a series of phylogenetic informative single nucleotide polymorphisms (SNPs). The set of selected markers in this study had to meet certain conditions: to discriminate between major European mtDNA lineages, to have a substantial power of exclusion with a minimal set of SNPs that may be targeted in two multiplex reactions and to be sensitive for degraded DNA or for low amounts of intact DNA.

Snapshot™ (AB) is a mini-sequencing method that relies upon the single-base extension of a primer immediately adjacent to the SNP using fluorescently labelled ddNTPs. The fluorescently labeled extension products can then be separated and visualized by electrophoresis and fluorescence detection.

* Corresponding author. Tel.: +43-512-507-3303; fax: +43-512-507-2764.
E-mail address: Walther.Parson@uibk.ac.at (W. Parson).

0531-5131/ © 2003 Elsevier B.V. All rights reserved.
doi:10.1016/S0531-5131(03)01627-3

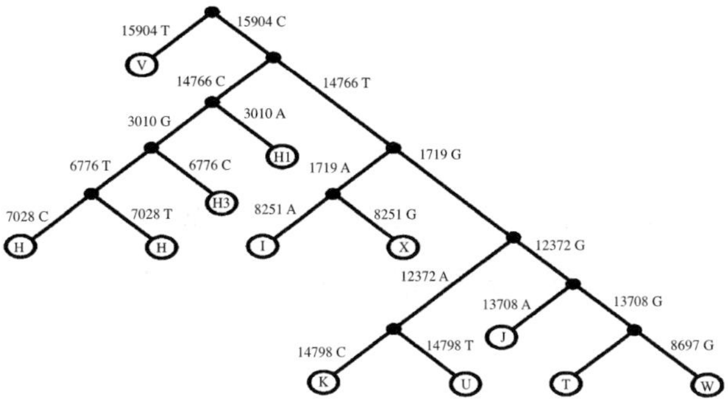

Fig. 1. Bifurcating decision tree for haplogroup assignment.

2. Materials and methods

For amplification, 19 μl of the PCR master mix (1.0 unit of Advantage 2 (Clontech), 1.0 unit of reaction buffer (Clontech), 200 μM each dNTP (AB); amplification primers and their concentrations are specified in Ref. [1]) was mixed with 1 μl DNA extract (containing 0.5–25 pg of genomic DNA). The amplification reaction was conducted in two eightplex PCR-reactions. Multiplex I comprised the SNP target sites G709A, G1719A, G3010A, C7028T, A11251G, G12372A, T14798C and C15904T. Multiplex II comprised the SNP target sites A1811G, T6365C, T6776C, G8251A, G8697A, G9055A, G13708A and C14766T. After an initial denaturation at 95 °C for 2 min, the reactions were put through 28–32 cycles of denaturation at 95 °C for 30 s, annealing at 66 °C for 30 s and extension at 72 °C for 30 s. PCR primers and unincorporated dNTPs were removed by adding ExoSAP-IT (USB). The reactions comprised 2.5 μl of the SNaPshot™ Multiplex Ready Reaction Mix, 2.0 μl of PCR product, 1.0 μl of pooled extension primers (0.2 μM final concentration for each primer) and water up to 10 μl. Thermal cycling and post-extension treatment were conducted following the manufacturers protocol. Unincorporated ddNTPs were removed

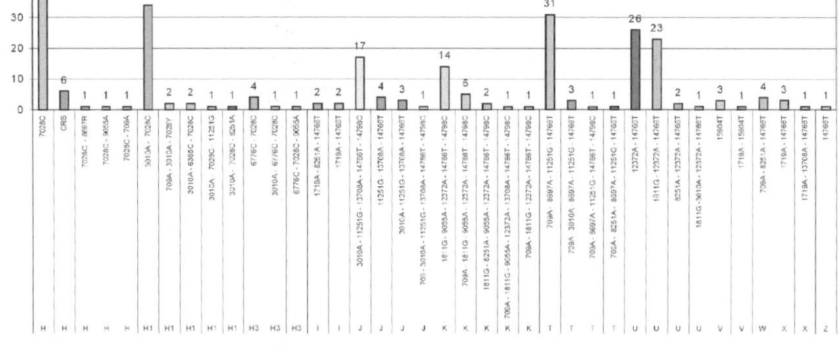

Fig. 2. Distribution mtDNA haplotypes in 277 unrelated Austrian Caucasians.

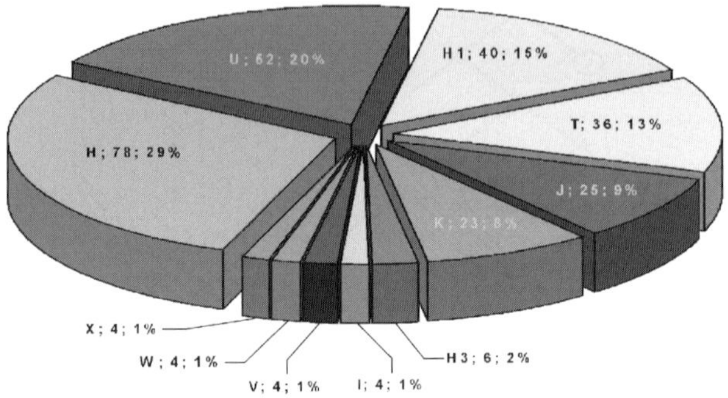

Fig. 3. Distribution of West European Caucasian haplogroups in 277 unrelated Austrian Caucasians.

with SAP (USB). The assignment to West European Caucasian haplogroups and was performed by following the branches of a bifurcating tree (Fig. 1).

3. Results

All 277 samples were successfully typed with the two multiplexes. The haplotypes found in this study are summarized in Fig. 2. All nine major West European Caucasian haplogroups (and two sub-haplogroups) were observed in our sample (Fig. 3). The most common haplotype found was a profile matching the rCRS, thus assigned to haplogroup H (24.5%). Overall, 37 different lineages were found in 277 individuals and 16 of them appeared only once in the dataset. The probability of a random match between two unrelated individuals was calculated as 11.4%.

The screening procedure presented here proved to be practical for unambiguously ascribing haplogroup origin to unknown DNA samples, and the method itself was shown to be very sensitive and suitable to type samples containing at least 1 pg genomic DNA. The entire procedure may be completed in 1 day and integrates easily with existing laboratory equipment. In addition, the assay is well suited for use on high degraded samples, as the amplicon lengths do not exceed 100 bp. Apart from the ability to eliminate non-probative DNA samples from further investigations, the assignment of a sample to a certain haplogroup gives the investigator the possibility to target specific control region fragments, which show a higher variability for certain haplogroups. This novel, multiplex PCR amplification and typing system for 16 mtDNA coding region SNPs promises to be a convenient and informative new DNA profiling system in the forensic field.

Acknowledgements

We thank H. Niederstätter (ILM Innsbruck) for helpful comments; M.D. Coble, R.S. Hamm (both AFDIL, USA) and P.M. Vallone (NIST, USA) for technical advices. This research was supported by a research grant (no. 14031/89-02) from the University of Innsbruck, Austria.

Reference

[1] A. Brandstätter, et al., Rapid screening of mtDNA coding region SNPs for the identification of West European Caucasian haplogroups, Int. J. Leg. Med. (2003) (Online First: DOI:10.1007/s00414-003-0395-2).

International Congress Series 1261 (2004) 425–427
www.ics-elsevier.com

MtDNA: a successful identification case in burned remains

N. Cerri*, A. Verzeletti, F. De Ferrari

Institute of Legal Medicine, University of Brescia, Piazzale Spedali Civili 1, 25123 Brescia, Italy

Abstract. Some human carbonized remains were found in a wood near a lake. Investigations and a macroscopic analysis of the remains led suspicions to a killed and burned 20-year-old man. To identify with certitude the remains, nuclear DNA from the remains and from the alleged mother were analysed. Only at vWA locus an exclusion was found. Because of the delicacy of the case (a murder) and since only the alleged mother's DNA was available, a mt-DNA analysis was performed. It was found a good correlation in both HV1 and HV2 regions between the DNA from the remains and the mother's.

Keywords: STR; mtDNA; Identification

1. Introduction

Some human carbonized remains were found in a wood near a lake in Northern Italy (Fig. 1). The remains examination led to the recognitions of some bones and pieces of organs such as the liver and a kidney. According to bones morphology and investigations, the remains were ascribable to a killed and burned 20-year-old man.

To establish with certitude the identity of the found body, a genetic analysis was carried out between the remains' and alleged mother's DNA (the only relative available) regarding both nuclear DNA and the mitochondrial one.

2. Materials and methods

DNA was obtained from the carbonized remains (liver and kidney) and from an oral swab for the alleged mother. DNA was extracted using Chelex®-100 method according to Walsh colleagues.

For nuclear DNA, amplification was carried out applying AmpFlSTR® Profiler Plus™ and SGM Plus™ PCR Amplification Kits (Applied Biosystems) in a Perkin Elmer 2400 thermal cycler, according to manufacturer's recommendations. Products were

* Corresponding author. Tel.: +39-030-3995480; fax: +39-030-3995839.
E-mail address: deferrar@med.unibs.it (N. Cerri).

0531-5131/
doi:10.1016/S0531-5131(03)01528-0

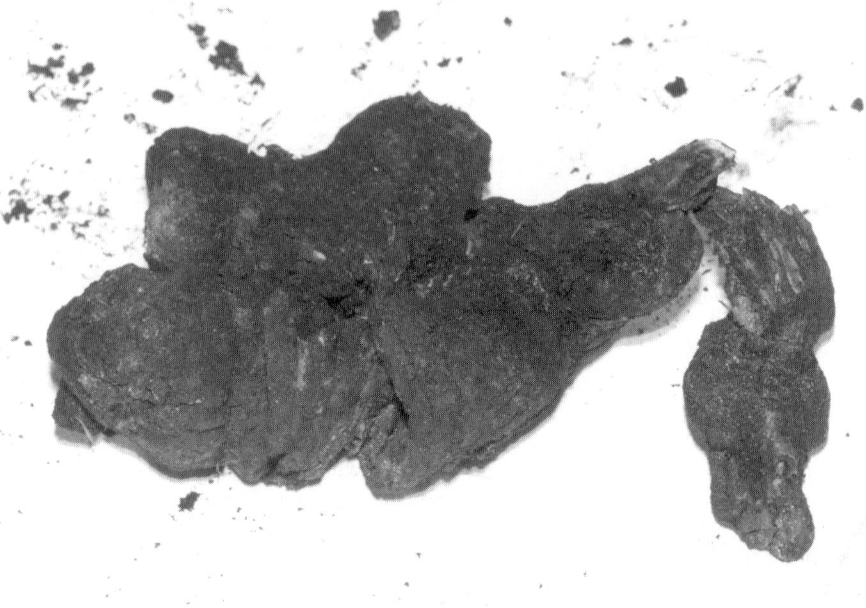

Fig. 1. The remains.

loaded on the ABI Prism 310 Genetic Analyser and analysed with GeneScan analysis software V.3.2.1.

For mt-DNA, HV1 and HV2 regions were analysed. HV1 PCR products were generated by using Primer L15971: 5′-TTAACTCCACCATTAGCACC-3′ and Primer H16414: 5′-CACGGAGGATGGTGGTCAAG-3′. HV2 PCR products were generated by using Primer L15: 5′-CACCCTATTAACCACTCACG-3′ and Primer H389: 5′-CTGGTTAGGCTGGTGTTAGG-3′ according to Buscemi et al. [1] PCR amplification was performed in a total volume of 50 μl: 5 μl 10 × PCR-Buffer (Applied Biosystem), 3 μl 25 mM $MgCl_2$ (Applied Biosystems), 4 μl 10 mM dNTPs (Applied Biosystems), 0.4 μl 50 μM of both Fw and Rv Primers, 0.5 μl Taq-Gold (Applied Biosystems). The amount of DNA was 1 ng for each reaction. Amplification was performed on a P-E 2400 Thermal Cycler. The conditions were as follows: 94 °C for 30 s, then 94 °C for 1 m, 56 °C for 10 s, 72 °C for 30 s for 38 cycles. The PCR product was purified with a Microcon 100 device (Amicon) and then it was evaluated from a quantitative point of view on a 2% agarose gel.

BigDye Terminator cycle sequencing of PCR products was performed according to manufacturer's protocol. Both strands were sequenced using the Primers F15971 and R16414 for HV1 region; F29 5′-CTCACGGGAGCTCTCCATGC-3′ and R381 5′-GCTGGTGTTAGGGTTCTTTG-3′ were used for HV2 region. PCR sequencing was performed in a total volume of 20 μl: 4 μl BigDye Terminator RR Mix (Applied Biosystems), 1 μl of F or R Primers and 3–5 μl PCR product. PCR conditions were the following: 96 °C for 15 s, 50 °C for 5 s, 60 °C for 2 min for 25 cycles. Analysis was carried

Table 1
STR analysis

Loci	Remains	Alleged mother
D3S1358	18–18	17–18
VWA	16–16	14–14
FGA	21–23	23–23
D8S1179	13–14	13–14
D21S11	30–32.2	30–32.2
D18S51	16–18	14–16
D5S818	9–13	9–11
D13S317	11–12	8–11
D7S820	8–10	8–10
D16S539	13–13	9–13
D2S1338	17–25	17–17
D19S433	13–15.2	13–13
TH01	8–8	8–9.3
Sex	M	F

out by capillary electrophoresis on an ABI Prism 310 (Applied Biosystems); data were analysed by Sequencing Analysis Software 3.4.1 (Applied Biosystems).

3. Results and discussion

STRs analysis gave a successful attribution, but an exclusion at vWA locus was found in the nuclear DNA of the remains (Table 1). The paternity testing supplied a good value (0.9999182), but because of the delicacy of the case (a murder) and since only the alleged mother's DNA was available, a mt-DNA analysis was performed.

Human mt-DNA is a small molecule with circular structure, containing 16,569 bp, entirely sequenced [2], it is well known that it is very resistant to extreme environmental conditions, and as a consequence, it can be used in forensic applications [3,4].

The two samples were analysed for both HV1 and HV2 regions and their sequence was compared with the Anderson's one. A perfect compatibility was found in both HV1 and HV2 regions between the DNA from the remains and the mother's.

This work evidence the importance of mt-DNA in cases where a maternal transmission is involved and STR analysis is limited by an "incompatibility". Otherwise, it is clear that another approach could have been done: the vWA sequencing to demonstrate the mutation at this locus.

References

[1] L. Buscemi, C. Turchi, G. Benedetto, C. Sassaroli, M. Paoli, A. Tagliabracci, Polymorphism of mitochondrial DNA: creation of a database of genotype frequencies in a population sample from Central Italy, in: A. Carracedo, B. Brinkmann (Eds.), Progress in Forensic Genetics, vol. 8, Elsevier, Amsterdam, 2000, pp. 341–343.

[2] S. Anderson, et al., Sequence and organization of the human mitochondrial genome, Nature 290 (1981) 457–465.

[3] M.R. Wilson, et al., Validation of mitochondrial DNA sequencing for forensic casework analysis, Int. J. Leg. Med. 108 (1995) 68–74.

[4] R. Piercy, K.M. Sullivan, N. Benson, P. Gill, The application of mitochondrial DNA typing to the study of white Caucasian genetic identification, Int. J. Leg. Med. 106 (1993) 85–90.

International Congress Series 1261 (2004) 428–430

www.ics-elsevier.com

Mitochondrial DNA profiling of modern Malay and Orang Asli populations in peninsular Malaysia

Z. Zainuddin[a], W. Goodwin[b,*]

[a] *Department of Forensic Medicine and Science, University of Glasgow, Glasgow, UK*
[b] *Department of Forensic and Investigative Science, University of Central Lancashire, Preston, PR1 2HE, UK*

Abstract. A study was undertaken to assess the utility of mtDNA as a forensic tool in the Malay Peninsular. Two populations, modern Malay and Orang Asli, were sampled and their mitochondrial DNA (mtDNA) analysed. Comparing the different haplogroups that were found, there are clear differences between the two populations. As a forensic tool, the use of mtDNA in the Orang Asli is limited as many individuals share the same haplotype, reducing the power of discrimination. In the Malay population, the power of discrimination is sufficiently high to make it a valuable tool.

Keywords: mtDNA; Hypervariable region I; Malay; Orang Asli

1. Introduction

Mitochondrial DNA has proven to be a useful tool for human identification as well as understanding modern human evolution and migrations. Malaysian populations are underrepresented in the published data, and therefore, before using mtDNA as a forensic tool in Malaysia, it is important to study the population. This is particularly so when there are distinct populations within the main population, such as the Orang Asli. In addition to providing useful information for forensic studies, this information will also provide information on the relationships of the Malay population with neighboring populations.

2. Materials and methods

In total, 102 samples were collected from 11 states of Peninsular Malaysia and 58 samples from two populations of Orang Asli (Kensiu and Jahai) were collected. DNA was extracted using Puregene® DNA Extraction kit. The HVI region was amplified using L15926 and H16431 primers and sequenced. Polymorphisms were reported by

* Corresponding author. Tel.: +44-1772-894254; fax: +44-1772-894981.
E-mail address: whgoodwin@uclan.ac.uk (W. Goodwin).

0531-5131/
doi:10.1016/S0531-5131(03)01725-4

Table 1

Population	Samples	Haplotypes[a]	Power of exclusion[b]
Malay	102	73 (6)	0.0203
Orang Asli	58	12 (18)	0.1961

[a] Total number of haplotypes observed (most frequently occurring haplotype in brackets).
[b] The probability that two samples chosen at random would have the same haplotype.

aligning the sequence obtained to the Anderson Reference Sequence [1]. RFLP analysis of the coding region was performed to examine the following mutations: + 10394/ + 10397 *DdeI/AluI* [2,3], + 13262 *AluI* [4], − 5176 *AluI* [4,5], − 12406 *HincII* [6], + 12308 *HinfI* [7], − 1715 *DdeI* [7,8] and − 7025 *AluI* [5,8]. The haplogroups were determined using a combination of the HVI sequence and RFLP analysis (haplogroup nomenclature was in accordance with the above references and M. Richards, personal communication).

3. Results

Analysis of the hypervariable region I was used to place the samples into haplogroups. A summary of the mtDNA diversity is shown in Table 1.

Additional information from RFLP sites located outside of the hypervariable regions was used, in some cases, to place the samples into more highly resolved haplogroups. The different haplogroups along with their defining polymorphisms and the frequencies of these haplogroups in the tested populations are shown in Table 2.

From the data, it is clear that there are large differences between the modern Malay and the Orang Asli populations, both in the power of discrimination and in the haplogroups composition.

Table 2
The distribution of haplogroups within the modern Malay and Orang Asli populations

Haplogroup	Defining polymorphisms	Population frequencies	
		Malay	Orang Asli
M[a]	+ 10394/ + 10397 *DdeI/AluI*	39.12	5.17
M21a	+ 10394/ + 10397 *DdeI/AluI*	5.88	34.48
M21b	+ 10394/ + 10397 *DdeI/AluI*	–	1.72
M-D	+ 10394/ + 10397 *DdeI/AluI*, − 5176 *AluI*	1.96	–
M-C	+ 10394/ + 10397 *DdeI/AluI*, + 13262 *AluI*	0.98	–
B4	9-bp deletion	7.84	–
B5	9-bp deletion	10.78	6.90
E	+ 10394/ + 10397 *DdeI/AluI*, − 7598 *HhaI*	1.96	–
F1a	− 10394/ − 10397 *DdeI/AluI*, − 12406 *HincII*	16.67	–
N9a	− 10394/ − 10397 *DdeI/AluI*	2.94	3.45
R	− 10394/ − 10397 *DdeI/AluI*	7.84	–
R21	+ 10394/ − 10397 *DdeI/AluI*, − 1715 *DdeI*	1.96	48.28
Y	+ 10394/ − 10397 *DdeI/AluI*	1.96	–

[a] Includes all variations of the M super haplogroup that are not specified.

4. Discussion

As in other populations, mtDNA can be a powerful tool for human identification when used in the Malay population. However, the differences between the Malay and Orang Asli populations highlight the need for care in interpreting any results in a forensic context. Further studies examining the nuclear autosomal and Y-chromosome loci will provide an improved understanding of the genetic composition in different populations in Peninsular Malaysia.

References

[1] S. Anderson, A.T. Bankier, B.G. Barrell, M.H. de Bruijn, A.R. Coulson, J. Drouin, I.C. Eperon, D.P. Nierlich, B.A. Roe, F. Sanger, P.H. Schreier, A.J.H. Smith, R. Staden, I.G. Young, Sequence and organisation of the human mitochondrial genome, Nature 290 (1999) 457–465.

[2] A. Torroni, T.G. Schurr, M.F. Cabell, M.D. Brown, J.V. Neel, M. Larsen, D.G. Smith, C.M. Vullo, D.C. Wallace, Asian affinities and continental radiation of the four founding Native American mtDNAs, Am. J. Hum. Genet. 53 (1993) 563–590.

[3] T. Kivisild, H.-V. Tolk, J. Parik, Y. Wang, S.S. Papiha, H.-J. Bandelt, R. Villems, The emerging limbs and twigs of the East Asian mtDNA tree, Mol. Biol. Evol. 19 (10) (2002) 1737–1751.

[4] A. Torroni, T.G. Schurr, C.-C. Yang, E.J.E. Szathmary, R.C. Williams, M.S. Schanfield, G.A. Troup, W.C. Knowler, D.N. Lawrence, K.M. Weiss, D.C. Wallace, Native American mitochondrial DNA analysis indicates that the Amerind and Nadene populations were founded by two independent migrations, Genetics 130 (1992) 153–162.

[5] A. Torroni, D.C. Wallace, Mitochondrial DNA variation in human populations and implications for detection of mitochondrial DNA mutations of pathological significance, J. Bioenerg. Biomembranes 26 (1994) 261–271.

[6] T. Kivisild, K. Kaldma, M. Metspalu, J. Parik, S. Papiha, R.Villems, The place of the Indian mitochondrial DNA variants in the global network of maternal lineages and the peopling of the old world, in: S. Papiha, R. Deka, R. Chakraborty (Eds.), Genomic Diversity: Applications in Human Population Genetics, Kluwer Academic/Plenum Publisher, New York, 1999, pp. 135–152.

[7] A. Torroni, K. Huoponen, P. Francalacci, M. Petrozzi, L. Morelli, R. Scozzari, D. Obinu, M.L. Sarontaus, D.C. Wallace, Classification of European mtDNAs from an analysis of three European populations, Genetics 144 (1996) 1835–1850.

[8] V. Macaulay, M. Richards, E. Hickey, E. Vega, F. Cruciani, V. Guida, R. Scozzari, B. Bonne-Tamir, B. Sykes, A. Torroni, The emerging tree of West Eurasian mtDNAs: a synthesis of control-region sequences and RFLPs, Am. J. Hum. Genet. 64 (1999) 232–449.

International Congress Series 1261 (2004) 431–433

www.ics-elsevier.com

Collaborative exercise on mitochondrial DNA by laboratories in the GEFI group☆

L. Buscemi[a], S. Presciuttini[b], A. Tagliabracci[a,*]

[a] *Institute of Legal Medicine, University of Ancona, Via Conca Torrette, I-60020 Ancona, Italy*
[b] *Center of Statistical Genetics c/o C. Retrovirus, University of Pisa, S.S. Abetone e Brennero 2I, 56127, Italy*

Abstract. This work presents preliminary results concerning a collaborative exercise on mitochondrial DNA by laboratories of the GeFI group. © 2003 Published by Elsevier B.V.

Keywords: Mitochondrial DNA; Population study; Heteroplasmy; Collaborative exercise

1. Introduction

Since 1991, the Italian Group of Forensic Genetists (GeFI) has carried out several collaborative exercises aiming at study of DNA polymorphisms, in order to standardize analytical procedures and to set up Italian databases for use in forensic cases of personal identification and controversal paternity. The present work illustrates results obtained during such an exercise on analysis of hypervariable regions HVR1 and HVR2 of mitochondrial DNA. The exercise consisted of typing three blood stains, of which one was used as a positive control, and samples from at least 50 subjects, locally resident and not related to each other, for each participating laboratory. A satellite project was also linked to the exercise, involving analysis of at least 20 mother–child pairs.

2. Materials and methods

Eleven laboratories, all belonging to centres for forensic genetics in Northern and Central Italy, participated in the project. The sample population was composed of 593 subjects, distributed as follows: Northern Italy: 50 Bologna (BO), 50 Brescia (BR), 51 Florence (FI), 56 Genova (GE), 50 Modena (MO), 50 Padova (PD), 50 Pavia (PV), 50 Turin (TO); Central Italy: 83 Ancona (AN), 53 Rome (RM), 50 Terni (TR). Seven laboratories participated in the satellite project, analysing 173 mother–child pairs: 23

☆ Contributors: Turchi, C. (Ancona); Pelotti, S. (Bologna); Cerri, N. (Brescia); Ricci, U. (Florence); Verdiani, S. (Genova); Alù, M. (Modena); Caenazzo, L. (Padova); Previderè, C. (Pavia); Boschi, I. (Rome); Carnevali, E. (Terni); Robino, C. (Turin).

* Corresponding author. Tel.: +39-71-5964722; fax: +39-71-5964723.
E-mail address: tagliabr@mta01.univpm.it (A. Tagliabracci).

0531-5131/ © 2003 Published by Elsevier B.V.
doi:10.1016/S0531-5131(03)01522-X

Table 1
Materials and methods used by 11 participating laboratories

DNA extraction	Phenol–chloroform (AN-BO-GE-PV-RM-TO)	Chelex (AN-BO-BR-MO-RM)	Other (FI-MO-PD-TR)
DNA quantification	Quanti-blot (AN-BO-BR-MO-TO)	Agarose minigel (AN-GE-RM-TR)	Spectrophotometer (AN-FI-PD-PV-TR)
PCR conditions	Holland '94 [1] with minor modifications		
Sequencing			
Dye terminators	ABI 310(AN-BO-BR-PD-PV-RM-TR-TO)	ABI 377 (MO-GE)	
Dye primers	LICOR 4200 (FI)	ABI 377 (MO-GE)	ALFexpress (RM)

Ancona, 50 Bologna, 20 Modena, 20 Padova, 20 Pavia, 20 Rome and 20 Turin. Table 1 shows materials and methods used by the participating laboratories.

3. Results

Of the 11 laboratories taking part in this exercise, 2 did not correctly type the control stains. Observed mutations (Table 2) included substitutions, with transitions prevailing over transversions in both polymorphic regions, a well-known phenomenon in mitochondrial DNA. Heteroplasmic positions were observed and related to: the HVR1 and HVR2 of one sample of the study population study, i.e., 16366 C (T-70%; C-30%) and 199 T (T-70%; C-30%); the HVR2 of three mother–child pairs: 199 T (Mother T-70%/C-30%; Child T-50%/C-50%); 251 g (Mother A-70%/g-30%; Child A-40%/g-60%); 204 T (Mother T; Child T-60%/C-40%). Heteroplasmy was observed at a frequency—both in study population and mother–child pairs—which was lower than that found in similar

Table 2
Observed mutations in an Italian sample population of 593 individuals

Mutations	HVR1		HVR2	
	Number of positions	Total number of mutations	Number of positions	Total number of mutations
Transitions				
C–T	65	568	23	156
T–C	34	617	25	382
A–g	34	102	23	957
g–A	14	96	13	106
Total	147	1383	84	1601
Tranversions				
C–A	11	15	4	4
A–C	8	36	3	5
C–g	6	12	–	–
g–C	2	4	–	–
T–g	1	1	1	2
g–T	1	1	1	1
A–T	7	9	1	1
T–A	–	–	3	3
Total	36	78	13	6
Insertions				
+1C	1	2	4	826
+2C			1	56
+1T			2	3
+1A			1	1
Total	1	2	8	886
Deletions				
−1A			1	1
Total			1	1

Table 3
HVR1/HVR2 haplotype frequency spectrum of 593 individuals from 11 Italian regions

Number of individuals per haplotype	North								Center		
	BO	BS	FI	GE	MO	PD	PV	TO	AN	RM	TR
7									1		
4											1
3	1		1					1		1	
2	3		2		1		3		2	2	3
1	41	50	44	56	48	50	44	47	72	46	40
% Unique haplotypes	82.0	100	86.3	100	96.0	100	88.0	94.0	86.7	86.8	80.0
Number of different haplotypes (*H*)	45	50	47	56	49	50	47	48	75	49	44
%	90.0	100	92.2	100	98.0	100	94.0	96.0	90.4	92.5	88.0
Number of individuals (*N*)	50	50	51	56	50	50	50	50	83	53	50
H/*N*	0.90	1	0.92	1	0.98	1	0.94	0.96	0.90	0.92	0.88

previous studies [2]. Table 3 shows a summary of the diversity found in each sample in terms of the number of haplotypes that have been observed in one individual, in two individuals,. . ., in *k* individuals (the frequency spectrum of the haplotypes).

A simple parameter related to haplotype diversity is the rate (*H*/*N*) of the total number of different haplotypes, *H*, to the total number of individuals in a sample. One sample only showed a value of this parameter lower than 90%, whereas all sequences were unique in three subsamples (*H*/*N*= 100%). All the six instances of haplotypes observed in three or more subjects (top three data rows in Table 3) included the two most frequent haplotypes observed in the global sample, namely "CRS,263G,309insC,315insC" and "CRS,263G,315insC". These two haplotypes were observed in 25 and 13 individuals of the global sample, respectively, and together represented 6.4% of it. The ratio *H*/*N* in the total sample was 460/593, or 84.7%, and the percentage of unique haplotypes was 74.6%, testifying a situation very far from sample saturation (when practically all haplotypes existing in a population are present in a sample).

4. Discussion

Most of the errors in published mtDNA sequences have been noted [3], with grave consequences for the purposes at which forensic investigations aim. For these reasons, the results of this exercise emphasize the need to continue collaboration and quality control exercises, for: (a) retesting of original pherograms by each laboratory; (b) establishing a task force for centralized collection and checking of pherograms; (e) verification of whether haplotypes are in line with European haplogroups.

References

[1] M.M. Holland et al., Identification of human remains using mitochondrial DNA sequencing: potential mother–child mutational events, in: W. Bar, Fiori, U. Rossi (Eds.), Advances in Forensic Haemogenetics, vol. 5, Springer, Berlin, 1994, pp. 399–406.
[2] T.J. Parsons et al., A high observed substitution rate in the human mitochondrial DNA control region, Nat. Genet. 15 (4) (1997) 363–368.
[3] C. Dennis, Error reports threaten to unravel databases of mitochondrial DNA, Nature 421 (2003) 773–774.

International Congress Series 1261 (2004) 434–436

www.ics-elsevier.com

Forensic identification of two murderers by DNA multi-reverse parental analysis

M. Pizzamiglio, A. Mameli, C. Bellino, D. My, L. Garofano*

Raggruppamento Carabinieri Investigazioni Scientifiche, Reparto di Parma, Parco Ducale 3, 43100, Parma, Italy

Abstract. In this paper, we present a murder case committed by three men in a small town in northern Italy in which two of the murderers were identified by means of a multi-reverse parental analysis approach. Four different complete male profiles for 17 STRs were obtained from the bloodstains and other evidence collected at the crime scene, one of which belonged to the victim. Two of the three unknown profiles revealed similar characteristics for many alleles/loci tested, which could be explained by a possible parental linkage. The investigators focused their attention on some families in gypsy communities with records of robberies. All donors were excluded except for two individuals whose profiles were very similar to the two unknown DNA profiles obtained from the crime scene. We then decided to type the close relatives of these two individuals. Among the relatives typed, four of them appeared to belong to the parents of the two unknown men involved in the murder. As a consequence, one murderer was arrested after a few weeks, the other more than 2 years. © 2003 Published by Elsevier B.V.

Keywords: Reverse parental analysis; DNA typing; STRs

1. Materials and methods

DNA was extracted and purified from bloodstains, cigarette butts and saliva samples of about 100 reference samples, using Qiagen automated extraction [1] and subsequently quantified by slot-blot hybridization [2] with the chemiluminescent signals recorded by GeneGnome CCD imaging systems [3]. For the amplification and typing, we used the *AmpFlSTR Identifiler PCR Amplification Kit* [4] and the *Powerplex 16.2 PCR Amplification Kit* [5]. Electrophoresis was carried out on an ABI Prism 310 Genetic Analyzer. Data were analysed by Gene Scan v.3.1 analytical software.

* Corresponding author. Tel.: +39-521-230023; fax: +39-521-206396.
E-mail address: risparma@provincia.parma.it (L. Garofano).

0531-5131/ © 2003 Published by Elsevier B.V.
doi:10.1016/S0531-5131(03)01890-9

2. Reverse paternity and parental analysis

All the STRs profiles obtained from evidence collected and from reference samples were studied and compared to each other, to look for the presence of a consistent number of same genotypes and/or identical alleles, in order to identify any possible killer's relative. All the allele/genotype counts were hand-made. Reverse paternity analysis was conducted using the Program "Pater version 2.0" [6].

3. Results and discussion

Two of the bloodstains collected at the crime scene were found to belong to two unknown individuals and, with respect to the numbers of same genotypes (two) and identical alleles (nine) of their profiles, a possible parental linkage was suggested. All the remaining evidence came from the victim, excluding one cigarette butt, which showed a third unknown profile, suspected to belong to the third perpetrator. According to the elements found during the preliminary investigation as well as from the genetic results we achieved, the investigators concentrated their attention on some individuals of a gypsy community. Many reference saliva samples were then collected and delivered to our lab, to be submitted for DNA typing. Among the profiles we obtained, two of them, which belonged to two cousins of the same family group, showed a very interesting similarity with those of the two bloodstains found at the crime scene.

As shown in Table 1, this unusual similarity consisted in 8 matching loci plus 8 identical alleles between the first individual (first cousin) and one of the two bloodstains and 5 matching loci plus 12 identical alleles, between the second individual (second cousin) and the second bloodstain, pointing out clear and strong evidence of parental linkage which indicated that the two unknown profiles, could come from the same family group. According to these results and looking at the family trees we asked to study in the meantime, we suggested to the investigators to collect more appropriate samples of reference saliva, especially from the two related families of the two cousins previously mentioned. The genetic results obtained were then subjected to statistical calculations [7] (as shown in Table 2), which strongly supported the hypothesis that among the family samples typed, there were the four parents (father and mother) of the two unknown individuals who left the bloodstains at the crime scene.

As a consequence of these results, we then typed all saliva samples of the available sons of the two families considered, but no complete matches were achieved indicating that the

Table 1
Common genotype/allele between the two unknown profile and the I°/II° cousins

	I° unknown profile	II° unknown profile
Common genotype		
I° cousin	2	8
II° cousin	5	2
Common allele		
I° cousin	10	8
II° cousin	12	8

Table 2
Likelihood ratio (LR) and probability of paternity (*P*, %) values

Samples considered for statistical analyses			No. of STRs-typed	*P* (%)	LR (odds)
I° father	I° mother	I° unknown blood profile	17	99.99999999999916%	$1.19951*10^{14}$
II° father	II° mother	II° unknown blood profile	17	99.99999999999980%	$5.99221*10^{14}$

only two missing sons should be the two killers. The statistical calculations for these family groups were made according to the reverse parental approach. The 2 suspects at large were then found and arrested and asked to give a sample of their saliva, which was submitted to DNA analysis, providing a full match for all 17 STRs typed. These results definitively proved that they were the two criminals who had left the bloodstains at the crime scene after a violent fight with the victim. All this confirmed the validity of our initial hypothesis and showed it was fundamental to apply the multi reverse parental analysis approach to identify the culprits of a murder, stressing once more the huge power of DNA in the forensic field.

References

[1] Qiagen, QIAamp 96 DNA Blood BioRobot Kit Handbook.
[2] P.S. Walsh, et al., A rapid chemiluminescent method for quantitation of human DNA, Nucleic Acid Research 20 (19) (1992) 5061–5065.
[3] B. Budowle, et al., Using a CCD camera imaging system as a recording device to quantify human DNA by slot blot hybridization, BioTechniques 30 (2001) 680–685.
[4] Applied Biosystems, AmpFlSTR Identifiler PCR Amplification Kit.
[5] Promega, Powerplex 16.2 PCR Amplification Kit.
[6] Program "Pater version 2.0" by Petter F. Mostad and Thore Egeland, Norwegian Computing Center.
[7] The Evaluation of Forensic DNA Evidence, National Research Council, pp. 127–132.

ELSEVIER

International Congress Series 1261 (2004) 437–439

www.ics-elsevier.com

Forensic identification of a murderer by LCN DNA collected from the inside of the victim's car

M. Pizzamiglio, A. Mameli, D. My, L. Garofano*

Raggruppamento Carabinieri Investigazioni Scientifiche, Reparto di Parma, Parco Ducale, 3, Parma 43100, Italy

Abstract. In this paper, we report a real case of a murder, committed in northern Italy whose culprit was identified through unusual evidences. The scene of crime did not show any traces. There were no signs of sexual assault on the body. The cause of death was determined to be manual strangulation. The investigators focused their attention inside the victim's car because they found some stains, to be presumably referred to blood. Subsequently, the victim's car was transferred to our lab for the analysis. In order to collect some sweat/skin residuals of the murderer, the surface of the steering wheel, as well as the gear lever and the handbrake, were sampled using FTA-Paper. A few days later, the investigators sent to our lab the oral swab of a suspect. A complete female profile of 15 STRs was obtained from blood stains on the upholstery and in the ashtray. The same complete male profile of 15 STRs was obtained from the sweat/skin residuals collected from the surface of the steering wheel and the gear lever. This profile was recognized as identical to that of the saliva obtained from the suspect who, afterwards, confessed the crime. These results are very important as they highlight that it is possible to type even low copy number (LCN) DNA if a proper and immediate collection of biological evidence is performed. © 2003 Published by Elsevier B.V.

Keywords: DNA typing; STRs; LCN DNA

1. Introduction

In the afternoon of 21 September 2002, the naked body of a young woman was found in the countryside near Bagnocavallo, a small village in northern Italy. There were no signs of sexual assault on the body. The cause of death was determined to be manual strangulation. Her clothes were found nearby and her car was found later, abandoned not far from the body. The investigators focused their attention inside the victim's car because they found some stains, presumably blood, located on the upholstery and in the ashtray. Also, some witnesses said that, during the same morning, they had seen the victim together with a man in the victim's car, as they left the car park of a supermarket. Subsequently, the victim's car was transferred to our lab in order to analyse the alleged

* Corresponding author. Tel.: +39-521-230023; fax: +39-521-206396.
E-mail address: risparma@provincia.parma.it (L. Garofano).

0531-5131/ © 2003 Published by Elsevier B.V.
doi:10.1016/S0531-5131(03)01855-7

blood stains and to collect some sweat/skin residues of the murderer, probably left on the surface of the steering wheel, as well as in the gear lever and in the handbrake. At the same time, it was presumed that a credit card and all of her money had been stolen. Investigators asked the company which had issued the credit card to track it down. On the same day, a man tried to use the victim's credit card at a cash dispenser and was thus filmed by the closed circuit cameras of the banks. Because of the very low quality of the camera recordings, it was only possible to recognise height and sex. It was also possible, however, to see the model and colour of the car driven by the man, including some of the licence plate numbers. All these elements allowed the investigators to focus their attention on a middle-aged man who lived in the same town as the victim. He was followed and filmed, and it was proved that he used a car of the same type and colour as that used by the alleged killer, with corresponding car plate numbers. Thanks to these results this man thus became the main suspect for the murder and a sample of his saliva was collected for comparison with biological traces still present in the victim's car.

2. Materials and methods

2.1. Inspection of the victim's car

A first general examination of the victim's car, was carried out by a squad of crime scene officers: they found some stains, presumably blood, located on the upholstery and in the ashtray. A more accurate inspection then followed in a specialized area of our labs, aimed at identifying latent biological traces. It was conducted by means of a Crimescope CS-16 [1] tunable forensic light source used in a specific darkroom at a wavelength ranging from 415 to 490 nm, but no interesting results were obtained.

2.2. Blood identification

In order to confirm the presence of blood, a small portion of the above traces underwent the *Combur test strip* [2], which gave positive results.

2.3. Trace collection, DNA extraction and typing

The blood stains were collected by *Sterile Dacron Polyester Tipped Applicators* [3]. The potential sweat/skin traces of the murderer were collected by *FTA classic cards* [4], which were scraped twice on the steering wheel, as well as on the gear lever and handbrake, in order to increase the quantity of cells sampled. All samples, including the saliva collected from the suspect, were submitted to phenol–chloroform extraction [5] and then purified using the QIAamp DNA mini kit [6]. DNA quantitation was carried out by slot-blot hybridization [7] with the chemiluminescent signals recorded by GeneGnome CCD imaging systems [8]: the amount of DNA extracted was <100 pg for the traces collected from the steering wheel and the gear lever, while the blood stains and the oral swab showed a quantity ranging between 20 and 30 ng. For the amplification and typing, we used the *AmpFlSTR Identifiler PCR Amplification Kit* [9]. Electrophoresis was carried out on ABI Prism 310 Genetic Analyzer. Data were analysed by Gene Scan v.3.1 analytical software.

3. Results and discussion

The profiles we obtained from the biological material collected from the steering wheel, as well as on the gear lever, even if the DNA extracted was very low, equal to less than 100 pg were both fully interpreted for the 16 loci markers we studied, and showed to be consistent with the suspect's profile. Based on these results, the suspect was then arrested and confessed to the murder. In this case, it is important to stress, once more, how crucial it was to have the immediate availability of the victim's car in order to carry out an accurate and extensive inspection of the internal surfaces from which it seemed much more probable to collect biological residues left by the perpetrator. Not less important was a particular strategy for LCN DNA extraction [10], amplification and typing, which made it possible to obtain full and a easy to interpret profiles, even starting from a few cells, which were fundamental to highlight the suspect's responsibility and solve the crime.

References

[1] Crimescope CS-16 "Application manual". Section 6.2.
[2] Roche "Combur^3 Test E".
[3] Puritan "Sterile Dacron Polyester Tipped Applicators".
[4] Whatman BioScience "FTA Classic Card".
[5] P. Gill, A.J. Jeffreys, D.J. Werrett, Forensic application of DNA fingerprints, Nature 318 (1985) 577–579.
[6] Qiagen "QIAamp DNA mini kit".
[7] P.S. Walsh, et al, A rapid chemiluminescent method for quantitation of human DNA, Nucleic Acids Research 20 (19) (1992) 5061–5065.
[8] B. Budowle, et al, Using a CCD Camera Imaging System as a recording device to quantify human DNA by slot blot hybridization, BioTechniques 30 (2001) 680–685.
[9] Applied Biosystems "AmpFlSTR Identifiler PCR Amplification Kit".
[10] P. Gill, Application of low copy number DNA profiling, Croatian Medical Journal 42 (3) (2001) 229–232.

International Congress Series 1261 (2004) 440–442

ELSEVIER

www.ics-elsevier.com

Forensic identification of a murderer by typing volunteers of a small village of Northern Italy

M. Pizzamiglio, A. Mameli, D. Denari, L. Garofano*

Raggruppamento Carabinieri Investigazioni Scientifiche, Reparto di Parma, Parco Ducale, 3, Parma 43100, Italy

Abstract. In this paper, we report the real case of a murder, committed in a small village (about 1000 people) in Northern Italy, whose culprit was identified through the paternity test. The corpse of an elderly female (75 years old) was found in her house. The cause of death was determined to be a violent blow. There were also signs of sexual assault to the body. The investigators sent much evidence to our lab: it also included some stains, presumably consistent with semen, collected from the victim's pubic hair. Microscopic analysis of the semen residues permitted the identification of spermatozoa with tails attached; the subsequent DNA typing allowed us to obtain a complete male profile for 17 STRs. The investigators focused their attention on some men with criminal records of sexual crimes who were suspected of the murder, but they were all excluded by DNA profiling. However, the profiles we obtained from those people showed a characteristic similarity for many alleles/loci, due to possible inbreeding. Hence, we suggested to both the prosecutor and the investigators that the people ranging 18–65 years of age living in the village be invited to give a sample of their saliva. We received a total of 400 saliva samples, which underwent genetic analysis. All donors but one were excluded. Sample 47 in fact suggested a possible parentage linkage (father–child) with the murderer, showing at least one identical allele for any STR locus analysed, with the profile obtained from semen. Due to these results, the investigators took more information and established that the donor numbered as sample 47 had a 19-year-old son, who had not been typed because he was serving in the military. Immediately, the investigators collected and sent an oral swab of the suspect to our lab. Before the analytical results, he confessed to the crime: his DNA profiling was recognized as identical to that of the semen collected from victim. This is the first example in Italy of parental test used to identify a murderer. Moreover, this is the first report on DNA typing, of the entire population of a small Italian village used for crime investigation. © 2003 Published by Elsevier B.V.

Keywords: Reverse paternity analysis; DNA typing; STRs; Probability of paternity

* Corresponding author. Tel.: +39-521-230023; fax: +39-521-206396.
E-mail address: risparma@provincia.parma.it (L. Garofano).

0531-5131/ © 2003 Published by Elsevier B.V.
doi:10.1016/S0531-5131(03)01854-5

1. Materials and methods

Stains which were likely due to semen were analyzed by the Sema™ Kit [1] for the detection of the seminal vescicle specific antigen and then submitted to microscopic observation. DNA was isolated from cigarette butts, seminal stains and reference saliva samples from 400 donors, using Qiagen automated extraction [2] and then quantified by slot-blot hybridization [3] with the chemi-luminescent signals recorded by GeneGnome CCD imaging systems [4]. For the amplification and typing we used the AmpFlSTR Identifiler PCR Amplification Kit [5] and the Powerplex 16.2 PCR Amplification Kit [6]. Electrophoresis was carried out on ABI Prism 310 Genetic Analyzer. Data were analysed by Gene Scan v.3.1 analytical software.

2. Reverse paternity and parental analysis

All the STRs profiles obtained were accurately studied and compared to the one from the sperm to look for the presence of a consistent number of same genotype and/or identical alleles, in order to find out any possible relative of the killer. All the allele/genotype counts were hand made. Reverse paternity analysis was conducted using the Program "Pater version 2.0" [7].

3. Results

A mixed profile was obtained from the sperm evidence, in which the main contributor was an unknown male, and the minor being the victim. In order to obtain the male profile which could be interpreted as best as possible, multiple PCR mixtures were conducted at different dilution of the extracts obtained from the semen traces. All DNA profiles obtained from the cigarette butts did not match the one from the sperm. No other matches were achieved from the first group of felons suspected of the crime, but it was clear and interesting that there was some similarity with the sperm STRs profile. Based on these considerations, after a meeting to which both the prosecutor and the investigators were invited, it was decided that to try to identify the perpetrator, it might be useful to obtain saliva voluntary samples from all males living in the town and compare the genetic data, with the unknown profile obtained from the sperm. All profiles were accurately studied to detect a sufficient number of alleles/loci matches. After almost 300 reference saliva samples tested, two individuals corresponding to two brothers showed a characteristic genetic similarity with the sperm profile, consistent with two loci and nine alleles in common. At this point, looking at the donor list, we decided to analyze a middle-aged man with the same surname of the two brothers, corresponding to their uncle. The profile we obtained from the latter, compared to the killer's sperm, showed at least the same allele for each of the 17 markers tested, with a likelihood ratio [8] 225,213 odds equal to a probability of paternity of 99.9995559%, hence leading to the hypothesis that he could be the killer's father. The day after we presented our results, his son, when visited by the investigators, immediately confessed to the murder and gave a saliva sample that, once analyzed, showed to be fully compatible with the one extracted from the sperm left on the victim's body.

4. Discussion

A cruel murder without any apparent reason was solved only by a large amount of DNA analyses of male individuals living in the town where the murder took place. After dedicated steps for typing the mixed stains which were consistent with both male and female material left on the victim's body and long and complex work of typing hundreds of reference samples coupled with an exhausting allele count, some hypothetical parental linkages could be achieved. The results obtained from DNA analyses, while exculpating the first group of individuals suspected to be the guilty parties, led to the identification of the alleged father of the killer, given the number of common genotypes/alleles of the DNA profiles obtained. According to this hypothesis, the only son of this man supposed to be the killer's father, was then captured and confessed to the murder, giving a saliva sample which confirmed a complete match with the profile achieved from the semen traces. Once more, this case highlights the importance of very close cooperation between investigators and forensic scientists whose skill, together with an appropriate and affordable analytical strategy, are able to make a fundamental contribution to the truth.

References

[1] Humagen Fertility Diagnostic, SEMA Kit Application Manual.
[2] Qiagen QIAamp 96 DNA Blood BioRobot Kit Handbook.
[3] P.S. Walsh, et al., A rapid chemiluminescent method for quantitation of human DNA, Nucleic Acid Research 20 (19) (1992) 5061–5065.
[4] B. Budowle, et al., Using a CCD Camera Imaging System as a recording device to quantify human DNA by slot blot hybridization, BioTechniques 30 (2001) 680–685.
[5] Applied Biosystems, AmpFlSTR Identifiler PCR Amplification Kit.
[6] Promega, Powerplex 16.2 PCR Amplification Kit.
[7] Program Pater version 2.0 by Petter F. Mostad and Thore Egeland, Norwegian Computing Center.
[8] The Evaluation of Forensic DNA Evidence. National Research Council, pp. 127–132.

ELSEVIER

International Congress Series 1261 (2004) 443–445

www.ics-elsevier.com

Identifying the culprit from LCN DNA obtained from saliva and sweat traces linked to two different robberies and use of a database

M. Pizzamiglio, A. Mameli, G. Maugeri, L. Garofano*

Raggruppamento Carabinieri Investigazioni Scientifiche, Reparto di Parma, Italia, Parco Ducale, 3, 43100, Parma, Italy

Abstract. This work refers to the identification of a criminal who committed, during a period of 6 months, two robberies in two different towns in Northern Italy. In the first robbery, we analyzed traces on a pillowcase used to carry the stolen goods. As the pillowcase showed no visible traces, we made a specific search for latent traces by means of a Crimescope CS-16 tunable forensic light source used in a special darkroom at a wavelength ranging from 415 to 490 nm: it revealed some interesting luminescent areas possibly due to biological traces (saliva). Subsequently, the latent stains were analysed with the alpha-amylase test, which gave positive results. The evidence available for the second robbery consisted in a pair of glasses left by the criminal in a bank. The glasses showed no visible traces, however, the surface in contact with the nose and ears were sampled using FTA-Paper to collect any residual sweat. The use of the database for the management of DNA profiles allowed us to link the two crimes that had occurred in two different places and at different times. In fact, the same complete male profile for 15 STRs was obtained both from the traces of saliva identified on the pillowcase used to carry the stolen goods (first robbery) and from the glasses frame surface which had been in contact with the nose (second robbery). Moreover, these results enabled the extraction of low copy number (LCN) DNA from uncommon evidence left at the crime scene, increasing the possibilities to identify the culprits.

Keywords: Latent traces; DNA database; DNA profiles; STRs; LCN DNA

1. Introduction

Two real cases once again highlight the importance of STR analysis from extremely low levels of human DNA. Low copy number (LCN) DNA profiling [1,2] is a technique sensitive enough to analyze just a few cells, so that the range of forensic evidence is increased. Moreover, the increasing number of profiles that it is possible to obtain from trace evidence collected at the crime scene stresses even more the great necessity for a DNA

* Corresponding author. Tel.: +39-521-230023; fax: +39-521-206396.
E-mail address: risparma@provincia.parma.it (L. Garofano).

0531-5131/
doi:10.1016/S0531-5131(03)01853-3

database: through the automatic comparison of millions of genetic data it is fast and easy to link scene to scene and identify criminals, starting just from minute biological traces.

In this case, the evidence collected at crime scenes included:

- First robbery: one pillowcase used by the robber to carry the stolen goods and then left in an abandoned house.
- Second robbery: a pair of glasses worn by the robber and left inside the bank.

The DNA profiles we obtained were registered into our local DNA database [3].

2. Materials and methods

2.1. Latent traces detection

In order to identify latent biological traces, the pillowcase and the glasses underwent a Crimescope CS-16 inspection, a tunable forensic light source used in a specific darkroom at a wavelength ranging from 415 to 490 nm [4]: both evidence revealed some interesting luminescent areas possibly due to biological traces (saliva/sweat).

2.2. Saliva identification

In order to confirm the presence of saliva left on the pillowcase, the latent traces previously revealed were submitted to the *ACP Amylase Kinetic Test* [5], which gave positive results.

2.3. DNA extraction and typing

The saliva traces found on the pillowcase were cut and submitted to phenol–chloroform extraction [6]. The potential sweat residues in the glasses' surface in contact with the nose and the ears were first collected by FTA classic cards [7] and then submitted to the same phenol–chloroform extraction procedure. The products obtained were then purified using the QIAamp DNA mini kit [8] and quantified by slot-blot hybridization [9] with the chemi-luminescent signals recorded by GeneGnome CCD imaging systems [10]. For the amplification and typing, we used the *AmpFlSTR Identifiler PCR Amplification Kit* [11] following the manufacturer's recommendations. Electrophoresis was carried out on ABI Prism 310 Genetic Analyzer. Data were analysed by Gene Scan v.3.1 analytical software.

3. Results and discussion

The recent introduction of LCN DNA profiling using STRs has resulted in an expansion of the range of evidence types that may be analysed, concurrently improving the success rates of DNA profiling techniques on evidence collected at the crime scene that were known to be problematic or largely unsuccessful in the recent past. The results we obtained show that it is now possible to type successfully unusual evidence such as saliva traces as well as sweat residues even if, in both cases, the DNA amount extracted from the evidence was very low (<100 pg).

Furthermore, to achieve positive results it is still essential to provide continuing education in training crime scene officers for proper collection, careful preservation and packaging of the items. The same attention is needed in the lab where it is necessary to manage each case using appropriate analytical strategies in order to detect traces that are still present or need to be developed. We have also found that the use of convenient procedures for DNA extraction is still very crucial as well as its purification and quantitation. Above all, a dedicated step for the amplification of DNA extracted from evidence, in order to obtain a complete profile and to avoid any stochastic effects which may occur when amplifying samples with very low DNA quantities, is essential. In this regard, the use of *AmpFlSTR Identifiler PCR Amplification Kit* was the system of choice due to its high sensitivity and robustness.

Finally, the availability of a DNA database seems to be crucial for rapid solutions of many crimes, especially when they are committed in different areas: as soon as we entered the genetic results of the second robbery into our local DNA database, we were able to link the same profile to the two robberies, committed by the same criminal during a period of 6 months, in two different towns in Northern Italy. This produces a positive impact on citizens, as well as a consistently saves money because no other expensive investigations need to be performed.

References

[1] P. Gill, et al., An investigation of the rigor of interpretation rules for STRs derived from less than 100 pg of DNA, Forensic Science International 112 (2000) 17–40.
[2] P. Gill, Application of low copy number DNA profiling, Croatian Medical Journal 42 (3) (2001) 229–232.
[3] L. Garofano, M. Pizzamiglio, et al., Italian population data on thirteen short tandem repeat loci: HUMTH01, D21S11, D18S51, HUMVWAFA31, HUMFIBRA, D8S1179, HUMTP0X, HUMCSF1P0, D16S539, D7S820, D13S317, D5S818, and D3S1358, Forensic Science International 97 (1998) 53–60.
[4] Crimescope CS-16, Application manual.
[5] Sclavo Diagnostics International BNP-Amylase application manual.
[6] P. Gill, A.J. Jeffreys, D.J. Werrett, Forensic application of DNA fingerprints, Nature 318 (1985) 577–579.
[7] Whatman BioScience, FTA Classic Card.
[8] Qiagen, QIAamp DNA mini kit.
[9] P.S. Walsh, et al., A rapid chemiluminescent method for quantitation of Human DNA, Nucleic Acids Research 20 (19) (1992) 5061–5065.
[10] B. Budowle, et al., Using a CCD camera imaging system as a recording device to quantify human DNA by slot blot hybridization, BioTechniques 30 (2001) 680–685.
[11] Applied Biosystems, AmpFlSTR Identifiler PCR Amplification Kit.

International Congress Series 1261 (2004) 446–448

www.ics-elsevier.com

A triplet pregnancy case with a complete hydatidiform mole and two fetuses diagnosed by polymorphic STR markers

Toshimichi Yamamoto [a,*], Masaki Suzuki [b], Atsuo Itakura [c], Shigehiko Mizutani [b], Yoshinao Katsumata [a]

[a] *Department of Legal Medicine and Bioethics, Nagoya University Graduate School of Medicine, 65 Tsurumai-cho, Showa, Nagoya 466-8550, Japan*

[b] *Department of Obstetrics and Gynecology, Nagoya University Graduate School of Medicine, 65 Tsurumai-cho, Showa, Nagoya 466-8550, Japan*

[c] *Maternity and Perinatal Care Center, Nagoya University Hospital, 65 Tsurumai-cho, Showa, Nagoya 466-8551, Japan*

Abstract. We encountered a triplet pregnancy case with a mole and two normal fetuses, analyzed their karyotypes, and genotyped 15 STR markers and amelogenin after their termination in early pregnancy. The results of genotypes indicated that the triplets were trizygotic. The molar tissue lacked any of the maternal alleles at seven loci and, at one (D2S1338) of the seven loci, transmissions of the heterozygous paternal alleles to the mole were observed. These findings indicated that the mole resulted from dispermic androgenesis. The diagnosis with STR markers should prove very useful to better understand the zygosity of gestation and the genetic origin of hydatidiform moles. © 2004 Elsevier B.V. All rights reserved.

Keywords: STR polymorphism; Diagnosis

1. Introduction

It is well known that the presence or absence of fetal tissue has been used to classify hydatidiform moles into complete (CHM) and partial moles [1]. Both moles are essentially different as to cytogenicity and the risk of trophoblastic neoplasma. The incidence of molar pregnancy is known to be associated with increased maternal age. Recent reports have indicated that CHM occurs in approximately 1 in 1200 pregnancies in the United States, 1 in 500 in Japan and 1 in 100 in Indonesia [2,3]. However, the incidence of CHM in twin pregnancies is not as frequent, about 1 in 22,000–100,000 pregnancies and that in triplet is even rarer. We report here a triplet pregnancy involving a CHM mole and two

* Corresponding author. Tel.: +81-52-744-2119; fax: +81-52-744-2121.
E-mail address: yamachan@med.nagoya-u.ac.jp (T. Yamamoto).

doi:10.1016/j.ics.2003.12.078

normal fetuses with a diagnosis in early pregnancy with an analysis of the polymorphic marker-based genotyping.

2. Materials and methods

2.1. Case

A 34-year-old Japanese woman was treated for infertility for 3 years. She became pregnant after artificial insemination from her husband. An ultrasonographic examination at 7 weeks revealed the two living fetuses in separate gestational sacs but also a small gestational sac without a fetus. At 9 weeks, the patient felt a pain with slight genital bleeding. Further ultrasonographic examination revealed two living fetuses and uniformly thickened cystic areas without doppler signal. After hospitalization owing to her extremely high serum β-HCG level, termination of the pregnancy was decided. Both fetuses (fetuses 1 and 2) and the bulk of the mole were removed by aspiration (Fig. 1). Pathological examination of the molar tissue confirmed the presence of a CHM.

2.2. Karyotyping and genotyping

A piece of skin tissue from each fetus and the molar villi were cultured and karyotyped with the standard methods. DNA was extracted from the placenta of each fetus, the molar tissue and from blood of the parents. The DNA (2 ng) was amplified using a AmpFlSTR

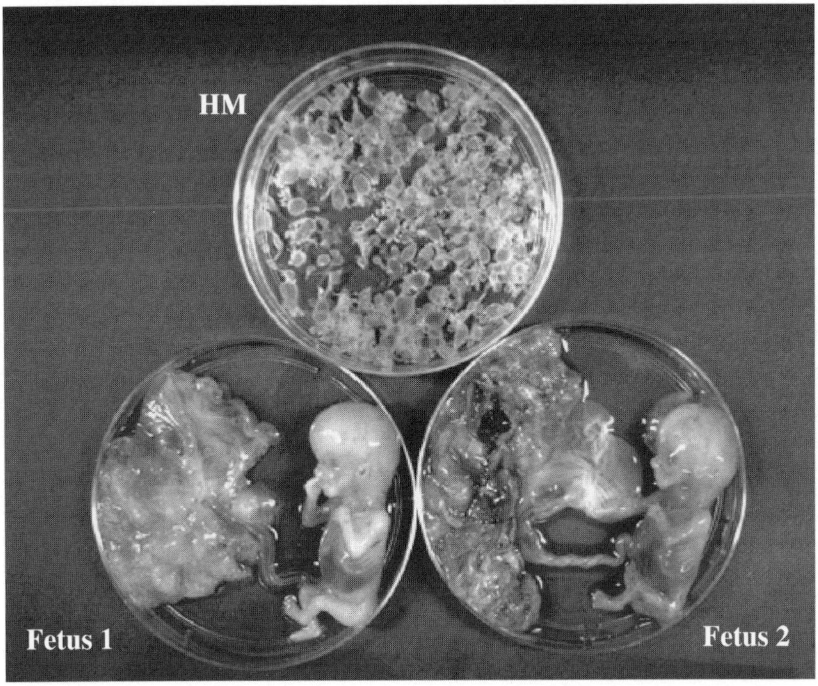

Fig. 1. Photograph of the hydatidiform mole (HM) and two normal fetuses (fetus 1 and fetus 2).

Table 1
Genotypes of the two fetuses, the mole tissues and the parents at 15 STR loci and amelogenin

Locus (karyotype)	Father (46,XY)	Mother (46,XX)	Fetus 1 (46,XX)	Fetus 2 (46,XX)	Mole (46,XY)
D8S1179	13,15	10,13	13,15	10,15	13,13
D21S11	30,32.2	29,30	29,30	30,32.2	32.2,32.2[a]
D7S820	8,12	11,12	8,12	8,12	8,12
CSF1PO	11,12	12,12	12,12	11,12	12,12
D3S1358	15,18	16,17	16,18	15,17	18,18[a]
TH01	6,8	6,7	7,8	6,7	6,6
D13S317	8,8	10,11	8,10	8,11	8,8[a]
D16S539	9,12	11,12	9,12	9,12	9,12
D2S1338	17,18	24,24	17,24	17,24	17,18[a,b]
D19S433	13,14	13,14	13,13	13,13	13,14
vWA	15,17	19,19	17,19	17,19	17,17[a]
TPOX	8,11	11,11	8,11	11,11	8,11
D18S51	13,14	13,17	13,13	13,14	14,14[a]
Amelogenin	X,Y	X,X	X,X	X,X	X,Y
D5S818	12,12	10,12	12,12	10,12	12,12
FGA	22,23	21,22	21,22	21,22	23,23[a]

[a] Evidence of androgenesis.
[b] Evidence of dispermic origin.

Identifiler™ PCR amplification kit with 15 STR markers and a gender determination marker (amelogenin) according to the user's manual, and analyzed with a Genetic Analyzer 310 and genotyped with Genotyper.

3. Results and discussion

To determine the zygosity of gestation and the genetic origin of the mole, karyotyping and genotyping of the fetal and molar tissues were performed (Table 1). Karyotypes of fetus 1, fetus 2 and the molar tissue were 46,XX, 46,XX and 46,XY, respectively, the same as the genotyping results of amelogenin. Thirteen loci were helpful in differentiating genotypes among the triplets (Table 1). Genotypes of the two fetuses were distinct at nine loci and those between the male fetus 1 and the XY mole were different at nine loci. The results confirmed that the triplets were trizygotic. The molar tissue lacked any of the maternal alleles at seven loci. Furthermore, transmissions of the heterozygous paternal alleles to the mole were observed at one of the seven loci (D2S1338), and homozygous paternal alleles at six loci. These findings indicated that the mole resulted from dispermic androgenesis. A diagnosis with STR markers should prove very useful to know the zygosity of gestation and the genetic origin of hydatidiform moles.

References

[1] A.E. Szulman, U. Surti, The syndromes of hydatidiform mole: I. Cytogenetic and morphologic correlations, American Journal of Obstetrics and Gynecology 131 (1978) 665–671.

[2] Y. Shiina, K. Ichinoe, The age incidence of hydatidiform mole and secondary occurrence rate of invasive mole and choriocarcinoma, Acta Obstetrica et Gynaecologica Japonica 31 (1979) 82–86.

[3] B.H. Guen, W. Cannon, Molar pregnancy in British Columbia: estimated incidence and postevacuation regression patterns of the β-subunit of human chorionic gonadotropin, American Journal of Obstetrics and Gynecology 139 (1981) 316–319.

ELSEVIER

International Congress Series 1261 (2004) 449–451

www.ics-elsevier.com

Allele sharing in related and unrelated individuals: implications in kinship analysis

M.J. Farfán*, V. Prieto, P. Sanz

Servicio de Biología, Instituto Nacional de Toxicología, Apdo. 863, E-41080 Sevilla, Spain

Abstract. The 13 STRs included in CODIS are of extensive use in kinship analysis and forensic DNA testing. Investigation of relationships different from paternity/maternity are in increasing demand in forensic casework. In this study, we evaluate how the determination of allele sharing between two individuals can assist in the discrimination between a first-degree relationship and non-relationship. We have determined the number of shared alleles (0, 1 or 2) among a sample of 400 unrelated individuals, as well as in 205 parent–child pairs and 114 full-sibs pairs for the 13 mentioned STRs. The obtained results on probability of sharing a number of alleles given a relationship and likelihood ratios of a first-degree relationship vs. non-relationship are shown. An exponential correlation between the total number of shared alleles and full-sib index was observed. © 2003 Elsevier B.V. All rights reserved.

Keywords: Allele sharing; CODIS; Kinship analysis; First-degree relationship; Unrelated

1. Introduction

Kinship analyses different from paternity/maternity testing are in increasing demand. These analyses have the drawback that there is no possibility of exclusion, e.g., sibling analysis. In those cases, a more complex statistical analysis is required and sometimes the results are of a low evidentiary weight. In this paper, we make a preliminary evaluation of the practical usefulness of determination of the total number of shared alleles when typing for CODIS, in assisting in discrimination between first-degree related and unrelated individuals.

2. Material and methods

DNA extraction: phenol/chlorophorm method or GFX™ columns (Amersham-Pharmacia-Biotech). *DNA quantitation*: Quantiblot® (Applied Biosystems). *PCR conditions*: according to manufacturer's instructions for kits Profiler Plus™, COfiler™ and Identifiler™ (Applied Biosystems) or PowerPlex®16 (Promega). *DNA capillary electrophoresis*: ABI PRISM™ 310 (Applied Biosystems). *Analysis of DNA fragments*: Genescan® and Genotyper® (Applied Biosystems). *Data analysis*: Microsoft® Excel 2000 (pairing analysis) [1]; PATCAN v. 1.1 (full-sib index calculations) [2].

* Corresponding author. Tel.: +34-954371233; fax: +34-954370262.
E-mail address: farfan@us.es (M.J. Farfán).

doi:10.1016/S0531-5131(03)01842-9

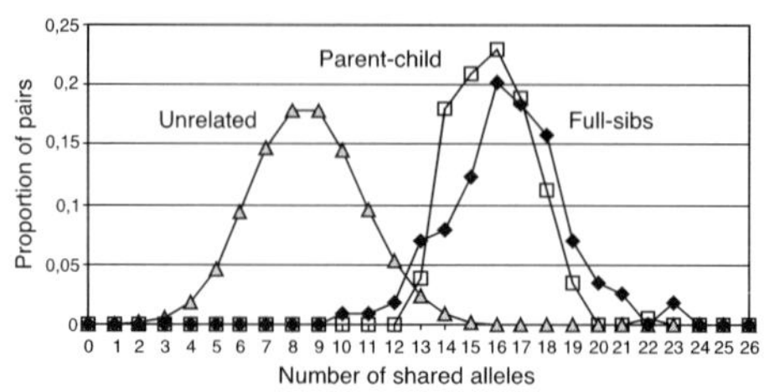

Fig. 1. Distribution of the total number of shared alleles for the 13 STRs in all the possible pairs (79 800) among a sample of 400 unrelated individuals, as well as in 205 parent–child pairs and 114 full-sibs pairs.

3. Results

Additionally, full-sib index for 114 true full-sibs pairs and 114 pairs of unrelated persons obtained by shuffling the same individuals (false full-sib pairs) were estimated. Full-sib index is actually the LR of both individuals in the pair being full-sibs vs. unrelated, having into account genotype combinations and allele frequencies. An exponential correlation (correlation coefficient: 0.969) between the total number of shared alleles and full-sib index was observed (data not shown).

4. Discussion

The results are shown in Figs. 1 and 2 and Tables 1 and 2.

In this study, first-degree and unrelated individuals typed for CODIS are easily discriminated by the allele sharing test with some restrictions: for sibling analysis there is an ambiguous range between 10 and 13 shared alleles (see Fig. 1 and Table 1). Regardless of the total number of shared alleles, sharing at least 1 allele in more than 10 loci supports the hypothesis of a full-sib relationship vs. unrelated ($LR \geq 7.4$) (Fig. 2A, Table 2). The same applies to sharing both alleles in more than three loci ($LR \geq 21.2$) (Fig. 2B, Table 2). On the

Table 1
Results on likelihood ratios (LRs) of a first-degree relationship vs. non-relationship, given the total number of shared alleles in the 13 CODIS STRs (see Fig. 1)

Shared alleles	Likelihood ratios	
	PC/U	FS/U
0	–	–
1–9	0	0
10	0	0.1
11	0	0.1
12	0	0.3
13	1.6	2.9
14	19.1	8.4
15	83.7	49.0
16	397.7	350.0
17	2168.8	2100.0
18	2984.4	4200.0
19–26	–	–

LRs were calculated as the ratios between the two probabilities involved: PC/U, parent–child vs. unrelated; FS/U, full-sibs vs. unrelated.

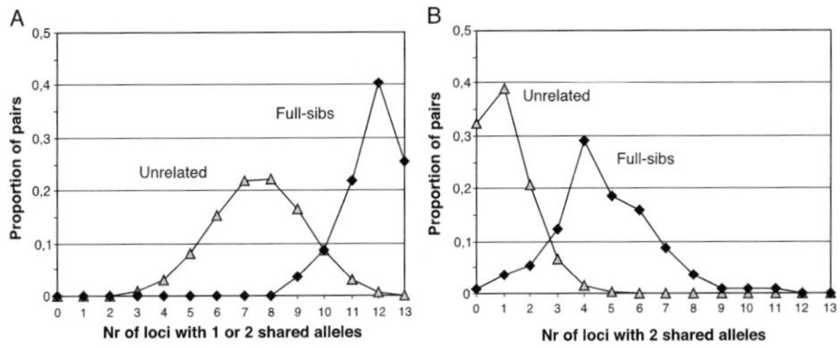

Fig. 2. Proportion of pairs vs. the number of loci in which both members share at least one allele (A) or both alleles (B).

other hand, 65% of the full-sibs pairs shared at least 1 allele in 13 or 12 loci (Fig. 2A), as in a parent–child relation, assuming a single mutation in the later case. This could be a serious problem in some identification cases (e.g., common graves, mass disasters). An exponential correlation between the total number of shared alleles and full-sib index was observed.

Acknowledgements

We thank S. Presciuttini for kindly providing the Excel worksheets for pairing analysis and J.A. Riancho and M.T. Zarrabeitia for kindly providing the PATCAN software.

References

[1] S. Presciuttini, et al., Allele sharing in first-degree and unrelated pairs of individuals in the Ge.F.I. AmpFlSTR® Profiler Plus™ database, Forensic Sci. Int. 131 (2003) 85–89.

[2] J.A. Riancho, M.T. Zarrabeitia, A Windows-based software for common paternity and sibling analyses, Forensic Sci. Int. 135 (2003) 232–234.

Table 2
Likelihood ratios of a first-degree relationship vs. non-relationship, given the total number of loci in which both members share at least one allele or both alleles (results in Fig. 2A and B)

Number of loci	Likelihood ratios			
	1 or 2 shared alleles		2 shared alleles	
	PC/U	FS/U	PC/U	FS/U
0	–	–	0.1	0.03
1	0	0	0.5	0.1
2	0	0	1.0	0.3
3	0	0	3.5	1.9
4	0	0	13.9	21.2
5	0	0	53.9	88.6
6	0	0	151.4	700.0
7	0	0	–	–
8	0	0	–	–
9	0	0.2	–	–
10	0	1.0	–	–
11	0	7.4	–	–
12	0	65.8	–	–
13	2280.0	580.0	–	–

LRs were calculated as in Table 1.

International Congress Series 1261 (2004) 452–453

www.ics-elsevier.com

Twin zygosity studies with the formula from DNA-View's Kinship Module after molecular analyses by polymorphic markers

U. Ricci[a,*], E. Lapi[a], S. Guarducci[a], E. Andreucci[a], C. Bacci[a], B. Toschi[a], C. Brenner[b], M.L. Giovannucci Uzielli[a]

[a] *Genetics and Molecular Medicine Unit, University of Florence, Via Luca Giordano, 13, Azienda Ospedaliera 《A. Meyer》, Florence I-50132, Italy*

[b] *Consultant in Forensic Mathematics, California, USA*

Abstract. Human Monozygotic (MZ) Twins estimated to occur once in 250 live births, result from an abnormal behavior by embryonic cell(s) to develop as separate embryos. The MZ twins are considered genetically identical and the reduced phenotypic, genetic or chromosomal concordance represents a very important challenge for geneticists. Determination of zygosity by molecular studies usefully provides a superior replacement for the conventional studies of placenta and chorionic membranes. We utilized a protocol based on the CODIS polymorphic markers battery, by using an infrared LI-COR 4200 instrument (LICOR, Nebraska, USA), and we associated the statistical analysis method with formulae derived by the DNA-View's Kinship Module to better evaluate the genetic identity in a group of MZ twins.

Keywords: Monozigosity twins; Monozigosity discordance; Zygosity analysis; Polymorphic markers

1. Introduction

Human Monozygotic (MZ) twins originate from the cleavage of a single fertilised zygote into two separate zygotes, during the early embryogenesis. Human MZ twins estimated to occur once in 250 live births. Their genome is considered identical. Discordance for well-defined syndrome, or isolated birth defects, or chromosomal abnormalities in MZ twins as well as for complex multifactorial traits and diseases, was described in several instances, in the literature. Environmental factors, but also the origin, development, genetic and epigenetic factors possibly involved in the reduced concordance, must be considered in future studies on MZ twins. A skewed or non-random X-inactivation was also assumed as possible event for discordance in intrapair MZ female twins.

The reduced concordance between MZ twins remains in fact poorly understood, and we need now to compare the genome sequence of MZ twins carefully, in the light of modern

* Corresponding author. Tel.: +39-555662941; fax: +39-555662931.

E-mail address: ricciugo@tin.it (U. Ricci).

doi:10.1016/S0531-5131(03)01523-1

molecular insight of the human genome, to reveal any possible variation and difference between a set of human MZ twins.

2. Materials and methods

We report the preliminary results of a study we are performing in a series of MZ twins referred to the Genetics and Molecular Medicine Unit for different reasons.

In all cases, we performed the zygosity test by using the CODIS polymorphic markers (TPOX, D3S1358, FGA, CSF1PO, D7S820, D8S1179, THO1, D13S317, D16S359, D18S51, D21S11) typed as previously described [1].

In three cases, the MZ twins were concordant for the same genetic disorder: Rett syndrome with the same MECP2 mutation, the same, nonspecific form of mental retardation, a form of autism.

In one case, the intrapair MZ twins showed discordance for a congenital cardiac defect (pulmonary valvular atresia). In another MZ set, the clinical spectrum of an Oculo Auricolo Vertebral syndrome (OAV) was expressed in different way, while in a third MZ twin set, a mosaicism 46,XX/45,X was finally confirmed in both fetuses, but with different percentages of cells with chromosomal defect.

Moreover, we applied the methods to study other four pair of twins, in which the parents are interested just for curiosity.

The scenarios we wish to compare for the twin zygosity study are: (a) **MZ**: C and V are genetically one person; (b) **DZ**: C and V are genetically ordinary full siblings.

The likelihood ratio favoring MZ over DZ is the ratio $P(E|\mathbf{H}_1)/P(E|\mathbf{H}_0)$, where **E** is the event; **E**: Genotypes as stated are observed in the twins C and V.

This likelihood ratio can be evaluated one locus at a time and is the product of the per-locus likelihood ratios. There are only two kinds of locus of concern. Either C and V are identically homozygous QQ or identically heterozygous PQ; the likelihood ratio formulas are respectively $4/(1+q)^2$ and $4/(1+p+q+2pq)$ [2].

3. Results

The molecular analysis of zygosity, performed on the basis of a different number of DNA polymorphic markers of CODIS, confirmed that in all set of twins included in the study, the subjects were MZ twins. The application of the formula from the Kinship Module of the DNA-View program gave us the following results: the likelihood ratio (LR) for MZ for the twins with different mosaicism for 46,XX/45,X was 36,800 (11 markers analysed).

The twins discordant for the cardiac congenital defects were MZ by a LR of 1950, with the use of only nine DNA polymorphic markers. The LR obtained in the MZ control set gave values between 177,000 and 418,000, with the analysis of 13 DNA polymorphic markers. These preliminary data are useful to well evaluate the results of LR with the number of the DNA polymorphic markers included in the molecular zygosity study. The study we performed has never been extended to the parents of the twins, to avoid a paternity/maternity test which was not requested.

References

[1] U. Ricci, et al., Infrared fluorescent automated detection of thirteen short tandem repeat polymorphisms and one gender-determining system of the CODIS core system, Electrophoresis 21 (2000) 3564–3570.

[2] C. Brenner, Symbolic kinship program, Genetics 145 (1997) 535–542.

International Congress Series 1261 (2004) 454–456

www.ics-elsevier.com

Banco Nacional de Datos Genéticos and human identification of forensic cases

S.F. Valente, S.E. Filippini, O.A. Santapá, M.G. Fraga, F. Gagliardi, C. Echenique, A.M. Di Lonardo*

Banco Nacional de Datos Genéticos, Hospital Dr. C.G. Durand, J.B. Ambrosetti 743, 1405 Buenos Aires, Argentina

Abstract. Molecular techniques based on DNA technology such as STRs typing (nuclear and Y chromosomes) and Mitochondrial DNA Sequencing are used today for human remains identification depending its success, mainly, on the type and the state of the sample. In this study, we describe the work of Banco Nacional de Datos Genéticos (Buenos Aires, Argentina) on bones, teeth and other forensic samples and evaluate the rate of success for each marker analyzed.

Keywords: Human identification; STRs; Y chromosome; Mitochondrial DNA; Forensics

1. Introduction

Human identification from forensic samples often presents difficulties due to the poor quality and quantity of DNA obtained, caused by contamination and degradation. That is the reason why new molecular technologies of DNA multiplex PCR amplification of nuclear STRs [1–5] and automated DNA Sequencing of Mitochondrial D-Loop Region [6–8] have become strong tools to be used in forensic science.

2. Materials and methods

We analyzed forensic samples from 45 cases: 121 samples including bones and teeth and 10 samples including swabs, stains of biological fluids and paraffin embedded tissue (Fig. 1). Bones and teeth were pulverized in a Freezer Mill 6 800, digested with proteinase K and SDS buffer, extracted by chloroform/phenol/isoamyl alcohol method, and then purified with Centricon 100 columns. DNA from paraffin embedded tissue was extracted with QIAmp DNA Mini kit (QIAGEN). In all cases, we used controls of extraction to avoid contamination.

Mitochondrial DNA D-Loop Region was amplified for HV1 and HV2 Regions. The symmetric PCR reaction was performed in a thermal cycler GeneAmp PCR System

* Corresponding author. Tel.: +54-11-4-982-1716; fax: +54-11-4-982-0625.
E-mail address: bndg@infovia.com.ar (A.M. Di Lonardo).

doi:10.1016/S0531-5131(03)01617-0

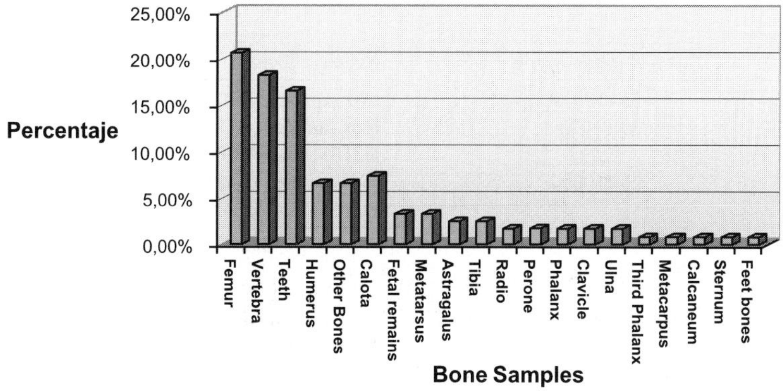

Fig. 1. Bone samples ($n = 121$).

9700® (Perkin Elmer). PCR product was run in agarose gel, dyed with ethidium bromide, visualized with UV light and photographed. It was purified using Microspin S-300 HR Columns (Amersham/Pharmacia). Sequencing reaction was performed with "Big Dye Terminator Cycle Sequencing Kit" (PE Applied Biosystems). For forensic samples, the primers used were: L-15997/H-16255; L-16099/H-16255; L-16209/H-16401 for D-Loop Region HV1 Segment and L-00030/H-00262; L-00140/H-00366, L-00241/ H-00412 for D-Loop Region HV2 Segment. Templates were purified using Centrisep-Spin Columns (Princeton Separations) and subsequently analyzed in an ABI PRISM 310 Genetic Analyzer (PE Applied Biosystems) following manufacturer's specifications.

Autosomal STRs were amplified using Amp FlSTR® Profiler Plus™ and Amp FlSTR® Cofiler™ Kits (PE Applied Biosystems) [3–5] in duplicate, with negative and positive controls. The following loci were analyzed: D3S1358, vWA, FGA, D8S1179, D21S11, D18S51, D5S318, D13S317, D7S820, D16S539, TPOX, THO1, CSF1PO and Amelogenin.

For the Y chromosome STRs analysis, we used Y-Plex™ 6 Reliagene Kit which amplified the following loci: DYS393, DYS19, DYS389 II, DYS390, DYS391, and DYS385. PCR products for all these markers were analyzed in an ABI PRISM 310

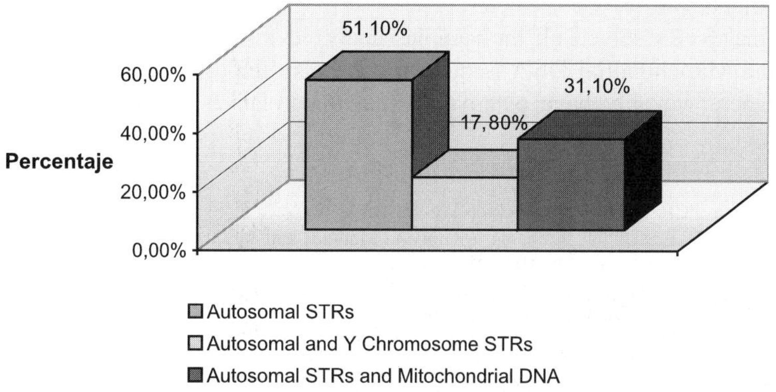

Fig. 2. Genetic markers analyzed.

Table 1

Samples	Positive results	Negative locus
Femur (25)	25 (100%)	two samples (TH01; CSF1PO; D21S11 and D18S51)
Vertebra (22)	20 (91%)	four samples (D18S51; D7S820; CSF1PO; D8S1179; D21S11 and TPOX)
Teeth (20)	20 (100%)	four samples (D18S51; D7S820; CSF1PO; D8S1179; D21S11; FGA; D16S539 and TH01)

Genetic Analyzer (PE Applied Biosystems) using Genescan® Analysis 3.1 software and Genotyper® Analysis 2.5.2 software following manufacturer's specifications.

3. Results and discussion

In all the forensic samples studied for autosomal STRs, Y chromosome STRs and Mitochondrial DNA D-Loop Region (Fig. 2), we analyzed the rate of success for each marker.

Among the 121 forensic samples including bones and teeth we analyzed for autosomal STRs: 25 (20.6%) femur samples, obtaining successful results in all of them except for two that were incompletely typed for loci CSF1PO, D21S11 and D18S51; 22 (18.2%) vertebra samples with successful results for 20 (91%) and with incomplete typing for 4 of them (20%) for loci D18S51, D7S820, D21S11, D8S1179 and CSF1PO; 20 (16.5%) teeth samples with successful results in all of them but 5 (25%) with incomplete typing for loci: D21S11, D18S51, CSF1PO, FGA, D7S820, D16S539 and D8S1179 (Table 1).

From data obtained, we conclude that incomplete typing are represented by loci of higher molecular weight (higher than 200 bp), which demonstrates the poor quality of the sample analyzed due to its state of degradation. The paternity and/or maternity probabilities calculated were always over 99.99% when all the loci were amplified. In the 33 (27.3%) samples where it was necessary Mitochondrial DNA D-Loop Region Sequencing, we obtained successful results in 27 (82%) of them for HV1 Region. In 9 of them, we obtained sequences of about 150–200 bp (20–25 years old samples) and in 18 of them we sequenced fragments longer than 200 bp. Only 8 of them could be analyzed for HV2 Region (samples with 5 years old or less).

The age of the samples and its conservation and are factors closely related which affect DNA viability.

Autosomal STRs solved all the samples analyzed in our study, but Y chromosome analysis and Mitochondrial DNA Sequencing are also important and necessary markers in cases where we only have paternal or maternal relatives, respectively.

References

[1] H.A.M. Erlich, PCR Technology, Stockton Press, USA, 1989.
[2] M.A. Innis, et al. (Eds.), PCR Protocols: A Guide to Methods and Application, Academic Press, UK, 1990.
[3] A. Edwards, et al., Genomics 12 (1992) 241.
[4] H. Hammond, et al., Am. J. Hum. Genet. 55 (1994) 175–189.
[5] A. Urquhart, et al., BioTechniques 18 (1995) 116–121.
[6] S. Anderson, A.T. Bankier, B.G. Barrell, M.H.L. de Bruijn, A.R. Coulson, J. Drouin, I.C. Eperon, D.P. Nierlich, B.A. Roe, F. Sanger, A.J. Smith, R. Staden, I.G. Young, Nature 290 (1981) 457–465.
[7] R.L. Cann, M. Stoneking, A.C. Wilson, Nature (Lond.) 325 (1987) 31–36.
[8] R. Hopgood, K.M. Sullivan, P. Gill, BioTechniques 13 (1992) 82–92.

International Congress Series 1261 (2004) 457–459

ELSEVIER

www.ics-elsevier.com

Bayesian analysis of mixed stains when there are two related contributors

A. Peñafiel*, J.M. Ruiz de la Cuesta

Laboratorio de Biopatología Médico Legal, Departamento de Toxicología y Legislación Sanitaria, Universidad Complutense de Madrid, Ciudad Universitaria, 28040 Madrid, Spain

Abstract. The analysis of DNA extracted from biological evidence is today one of the most important tools in forensic science. Particularly usual in casework is to find mixed biological stains. Their mathematical study has already been done, including the case of subestructured populations. Here we present a set of formulae valid for the case where we know there are only two contributors and these are genetically related. Furthermore, we extract some interesting links between mixed biological stains belonging to two or more related people and those coming from unrelated people. The analysis rests on probability theory and mathematical genetics well described in scientific literature. © 2003 Elsevier B.V. All rights reserved.

Keywords: Likelihood ratio; Mixed stains; Relatedness; Bayesian evaluation; Forensic casework

1. Introduction

It is usual to find in forensic casework biological stains coming from two or more people [1–4]. If we are facing offences against sexual freedom, as is the case of a violation, in which two non-typed and perhaps genetically related offenders have participated, it is necessary to evaluate the genetic evidence taking this possibility carefully into account. The objective of this work is to obtain a set of expressions allowing us to assign probabilities to the allelic configuration for some given markers studied under the hypothesis that the contributors have a given relatedness between them.

2. Methodology and results

2.1. Theoretical aspects

According to Evett and Weir [1], the joint genotypic probability of the several pairs of genotypes for the different kinds of relatedness is:

$$P(aa,aa) = a^4 + 4\theta_{XY}a^3(1-a) + 2\Delta_{X+Y}a^3(1-a)^2$$
$$P(aa,bb) = (1-4\theta_{XY}+2\Delta_{X+Y})a^2b^2$$
$$P(aa,ab) = 2(1-4\theta_{XY}+2\Delta_{X+Y})a^3b + 4(\theta_{XY}-\Delta_{X+Y})a^2b$$

* Corresponding author. Tel.: +34-91-7738532; fax: +34-91-3051593.
E-mail address: armandomatematicas@hotmail.com (A. Peñafiel).

doi:10.1016/S0531-5131(03)01510-3

Table 1
Values of parameters θ_{XY} and Δ_{X+Y}

Relatedness	θ_{XY}	Δ_{X+Y}
Parent–offspring	1/4	0
Full sibs	1/4	1/8
Uncle–nephew	1/8	0
Half sibs	1/8	0
Grandparent–grandchild	1/8	0
First cousins	1/16	0

$$P(aa,bc) = 2(1-4\theta_{XY}+2\Delta_{X+Y})a^2bc$$
$$P(ab,ab) = 4[(1-4\theta_{XY}+2\Delta_{X+Y})a^2b^2+(\theta_{XY}-\Delta_{X+Y})ab(a+b)+\Delta_{X+Y}ab]$$
$$P(ab,ac) = 4[(1-4\theta_{XY}+2\Delta_{X+Y})a^2bc+(\theta_{XY}-\Delta_{X+Y})abc]$$
$$P(ab,cd) = 4(1-4\theta_{XY}+2\Delta_{X+Y})abcd$$

where the parameters θ_{XY} and Δ_{X+Y} take different values according to the presumed relatedness (Table 1).

With this as a starting point we will study mixed stains in those cases where a relatedness is presumed. Since we have applied the method for only two contributors, there will appear four alleles at most. Let M_α denote the stain which has the alleles $\alpha = a,b,c,d$. If G_{S_1} and G_{S_2} are the contributors' genotypes and H_p represents the hypothesis of relatedness between contributors, we will have:

$$P(M_\alpha|H_p) = \sum_{G_{S_1},G_{S_2}} P(G_{S_1},G_{S_2}/\alpha,H_p)$$

where the sum is done over all the genotypes compatible with the alleles which are found in the stain. Here we present the calculated expressions along with those corresponding to the non-relatedness case (Table 2).

2.2. Example

Let us suppose we are facing a crime-scene piece of evidence having one, two or three alleles. This makes us formulate the hypothesis of two contributors related as parent and offspring. In order to calculate the L.R. (likelihood ratio) properly [5,6], we should use the rows 2 and 3 of the previous table:

$$\text{L.R.}_{\cdot a} = \frac{1}{a} \Rightarrow \text{if we take } a = 0.25 \Rightarrow \text{L.R.} = 4$$

Table 2
Calculated expressions for $P(M_\alpha | H_p)$

	$P(M_a)$	$P(M_{ab})$	$P(M_{abc})$	$P(M_{abcd})$
Genetically unrelated	a^4	$2ab[2(a+b)^2-ab]$	$12abc(a+b+c)$	$24abcd$
Parent–offspring	a^3	$3ab(a+b)$	$6abc$	–
Full sibs	$(1/4)a^2(1+a)^2$	$(1/2)ab[2(a+b)^2 + 3(a+b)-ab+1]$	$3abc(a+b+c+1)$	$6abcd$
Uncle–nephew, half sibs, grandparent–grandchild	$(1/2)a^3(1+a)$	$(1/2)ab[4(a+b)^2 - 2ab+3(a+b)]$	$3abc[2(a+b+c)+1]$	$12abcd$
First cousins	$(1/4)a^3(1+3a)$	$(3/4)ab[4(a+b)^2 - 2ab+a+b]$	$(3/2)abc[6(a+b+c)+1]$	$18abcd$

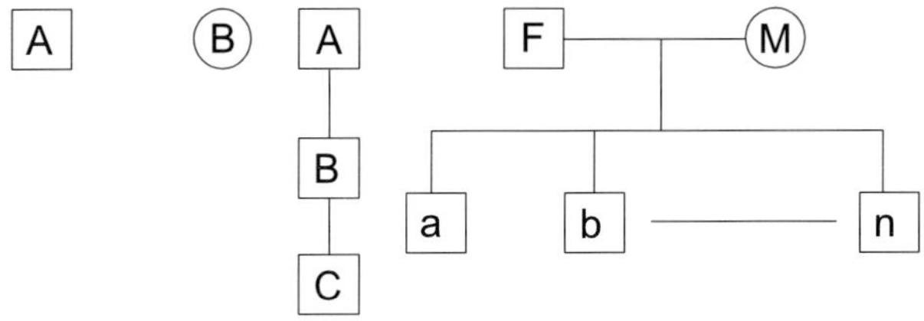

Fig. 1. Examples of equivalent genetic configurations.

$$\text{L.R.}_{a,b} = \frac{3(a+b)}{2[2(a+b)^2 - ab]} \Rightarrow \text{if we take } a = 0.3, b = 0.4 \Rightarrow \text{L.R.} = 1.22$$

$$\text{L.R.}_{a,b,c} = \frac{1}{2(a+b+c)} \Rightarrow \text{if we take } a = 0.10, b = 0.15, c = 0.20 \Rightarrow \text{L.R.} = 5.42$$

With these values, the total likelihood ratio is, assuming independence, 26.45.

3. Discussion

The deduced expressions are useful to analyse forensic casework in which it is presumed that contributors are related. We still have to determine the minimum threshold for the L.R. suitable to accept the hypothesis H_p, a problem which is still open in the bayesian evaluation of results from forensic genetic analyses. There is, however, one relatively important restriction when the circumstances of the case are unknown. The following configurations would give identical results, preventing their distinction: two non-related people; parents and offspring; grandparent, parent and offspring... Generally speaking, all those cases having the same number of independent alleles—i.e. non inherited by a contributor from another—cannot be discriminated (Fig. 1).

Acknowledgements

The authors want to express all their gratitude to Dr. Fernando Bandrés and Dr. Félix Gómez-Gallego (Laboratorio de Biopatología Médico-Legal, Departamento de Toxicología y Legislación Sanitaria, Facultad de Medicina, UCM) for their support during this work, as well as to Dr. Lourdes Prieto (Laboratorio de ADN, Servicio Central de Analítica, Comisaría General de Policía Científica, Madrid) and Elíes Hernandis Oltra for their invaluable technical support.

References

[1] I.W. Evett, B.S. Weir, Interpreting DNA Evidence: Statistical Genetics for Forensic Science, Sinauer, Saunderland, MA, 1998.

[2] B.S. Weir, C.M. Triggs, L. Starling, L.I. Stowell, K.A.J. Walsh, J.S. Buckleton, Interpreting DNA mixtures, J. Forensic Sci. 42 (1997) 113–122.

[3] B.S. Weir, Genetic Data Analysis II, Sinauer, Sunderland, MA, 1996.

[4] B.S. Weir, Forensics, in: D.J. Balding, M. Bishop, C. Cannings (Eds.), Handbook of Statistical Genetics, Wiley, England, 2001, pp. 721–740.

[5] C.G.G. Aitken, Statistics and the Evaluation of Evidence for Forensic Scientists, Wiley, New York, 1995.

[6] B. Robertson, G.A. Vignaux, Interpreting Evidence: Evaluating Forensic Science in the Courtroom, Wiley, Chichester, 1995.

ELSEVIER

International Congress Series 1261 (2004) 460–462

www.ics-elsevier.com

Case study: paternity testing—when 21 loci are not enough

W. Goodwin[a,*], D. Ballard[b], K. Simpson[c], C. Thacker[b], D. Syndercombe Court[b], J. Gow[c]

[a] *Department of Forensic and Investigative Science, University of Central Lancashire, Maudland Building, Preston PR1 2HE, UK*

[b] *Department of Haematology, Barts and the London, Queen Mary's School of Medicine and Dentistry, Turner Street, London E1 2AD, UK*

[c] *Glasgow University Department of Neurology, Southern General Hospital, Glasgow G51 4TF, UK*

Abstract. A seemingly routine paternity case which involved the testing of a mother, child and man led to inconclusive results as an exclusion involving only a single repeat was found at one of the 14 loci tested. This led to the testing of further loci. Only the single exclusion was found after profiling a total of 21 loci, with the addition of a further single locus providing a second exclusion. Even with both mutation events incorporated into the calculation a paternity index (PI) of 4957 was calculated, still a significant figure. However, when a second likelihood ratio was calculated assessing the likelihood of the results if the biological father of the child was the tested man or the tested man's brother, then the results were not significant, only 0.15. This analysis led to the profiling of the tested man's brother who matched at all 19 loci that were profiled and was concluded to be the biological father.

Keywords: Paternity testing; STR; Mutation

1. Introduction

Laboratories that are involved in undertaking paternity testing often work with limited information about individual cases; this at times can potentially lead to incorrect conclusions. The situation has been alleviated to some degree in recent years with the introduction of kits that allow the easy typing of multiple loci, the more advanced multiplex kits such as the Identifiler™ (ABI) and the Powerplex® 16 (Promega) simultaneously profiling 15 and 16 STR loci. However, in some cases, it is desirable to increase the number of loci that are profiled in order to resolve complex scenarios. Here, we present a case where 22 loci were typed before a case could be resolved.

* Corresponding author. Tel.: +44-1772-894254; fax: +44-1772-894981.
E-mail address: whgoodwin@uclan.ac.uk (W. Goodwin).

0531-5131/
doi:10.1016/S0531-5131(03)01724-2

2. Material and methods

2.1. STR profiling

DNA was extracted from buccal swabs using QiAMP® DNA extraction Kit (Qiagen). The samples were profiled using the Powerplex® 1.1 and 2.1, Powerplex® 16 Powerplex® FFFL kits (Promega) and the ABI Identifiler™. The additional locus, SE33, was tested using custom made primers. Products were analysed using the Hitachi FMBIO® and the ABI Prism™ 310 Genetic Analyzer. Because of the highly variable nature of SE33 the PCR products from all the individuals involved in the case were sequenced using the ABI BigDye™ Terminator sequencing kit.

2.2. Statistical analysis

PIs were calculated according to standard formulas. The mutation frequencies were incorporated into the PIs as a likelihood ratio, using the formulae suggested by Charles Brenner [1]. A mutation frequency of 0.0025 was used for a single step D21 locus and 0.0015 for a multiple step SE33 locus [2].

Table 1
The DNA profiles of the mother, child and first tested man

	Loci	Mother		Child		Tested Man 1		PI	PI*
1	D3S1358	16	16	16	16	14	16	2.222	1.384
2	vWA	14	17	16	17	14	16	2.531	1.459
3	D16S539	11	12	11	12	11	11	1.68	0.772
4	D2S1338	19	25	17	19	17	21	2.816	1.483
5	D8S1179	10	13	10	13	12	13	0.719	0.589
6[a]	D21S11	30	30	28	30	29	29	0.0038	0.015
7	D18S51	12	16	12	12	12	18	3.508	1.563
8	D19S433	15.2	15.2	14	15.2	14	14	3.053	1.658
9	THO1	9	9.3	8	9	6	8	5.405	1.688
10	FGA	23	23	20	23	20	24	3.077	1.509
11	D7S820	11	11	8	11	8	8	5.714	1.742
12	D13S317	10	12	10	11	11	13	1.6	1.299
13	D5S818	11	12	12	13	12	13	3.03	1.505
14	CSF1PO	10	12	12	12	12	12	3.361	1.543
15	TPOX	11	11	8	11	8	8	2.326	1.399
16	PENTA D	9	9	9	14	13	14	9.26	1.761
17	PENTA E	15	16	12	16	7	12	2.146	1.365
18	LPL	10	10	10	12	12	12	3.716	1.582
19	F13B	8	10	8	9	9	10	2.146	1.365
20	FES	11	11	11	12	11	12	2.023	1.319
21	F13A01	6	6	6	6	6	7	1.532	1.211
22[a]	SE33	23.2	28.2	23.2	27.2	15	24.2	0.0036	0.018
Total PIs								4957	0.15

Two paternity indices are shown; the PI is the standard paternity index and is the likelihood ratio of the probability of the results if the tested man is the father compared to the probability of the results if an unrelated man is the father. The second PI* is the likelihood of the probability of the tested man being the father compared to the likelihood of the tested man's brother being the father.

[a] Tested loci that led to exclusions.

3. Results

The profiles of the mother, child and first tested man are shown in Table 1. All loci were successfully typed. Three of the loci, D2S1338, D19S433, PENTA D, initially profiled for the mother, child and first tested man were not repeated for the second tested man (results not shown). The alleles of the SE33 loci were sequenced to verify the interpretation from the allelic ladder, which can be difficult due to the complex nature of the loci; in all cases, the results of the sequencing confirmed the original findings.

With both mutation events incorporated into the calculation, a paternity index (PI) of 4957 was calculated; this is still relatively high due to the large number of matching loci. Without additional information and testing, it would be very difficult to make any firm conclusions about the results.

In this case, a dialog with the individuals involved in the test revealed that the tested man's brother could possibly be the biological father. Testing this hypothesis was possible and when the probability of the tested man being the father was compared to the probability that the tested mans brother was the father a much lower likelihood ratio was calculated, the results are presented in Table 1. A sample from the tested man's brother was obtained and profiled using 19 of the loci. No exclusions were found at any of the 19 loci, making it much more likely that he was the biological father, a PI of 140 million was calculated.

4. Discussion

This case illustrates one of the problems that face paternity testing laboratories when dealing with civil rather than criminal cases, namely that the information provided is often incomplete.

The case illustrates the value for a paternity testing laboratory to carry as many loci as possible in order to help to resolve complex cases. It also illustrates the benefit in trying to ascertain all the information that is relevant to the case before making any conclusions; however, because of the sensitive nature of many cases, such information will not always be forthcoming.

References

[1] Brenner C. Mutations in paternity, 1998. http://dna-view.com.

[2] English Speaking Working Group Paternity Testing Workshop, 2003-personal communication.

International Congress Series 1261 (2004) 463–464

www.ics-elsevier.com

Databases: the real importance in paternity testing

A.T. Fernandes*, R. Gonçalves, A. Brehm

Department of Biology, Madeira University, Campus da Panteada, Funchal 9000-390, Portugal

Abstract. Five databases with 15 short tandem repeats (STRs) from populations belonging to Madeira Islands, Açores, Cabo Verde and Guiné-Bissau were separately employed to calculate paternity indexes in thirty case studies from Madeira. The five populations show significant differences among them. For all cases, the results of paternity probability showed no differences when each of the five databases was employed. Due to the high number of loci surveyed and the resolution achieved, the results suggest that there is no need to use databases from specific populations when the goal is to determine the probability of paternity. The results are even more striking if we take into account that two of the databases are of African populations and were employed against cases from a European genetic background. © 2003 Published by Elsevier B.V.

Keywords: Paternity test; Database; Short tandem repeat (STR)

1. Introduction

Databases are important for population studies but are not all-important for paternity analysis. Five databases with 15 short tandem repeats (STRs) of different populations were used, with some populations showing significant differences among them, like the two Cabo Verde populations and the one in Guiné [1,2], and those with the Madeira and Açores [3,4]. There are significant differences between Madeira and Açores and also between the two groups of Cabo Verde islands.

We used 30 paternity cases, from which 20 have data on father, mother and child, in which paternity was confirmed. Two of the cases show a single exclusion (we considered a mutation and used the 10^{-4} value to the mutation rate). In two cases, in the absence of the father, data from paternal grandparents was used. In six cases, we had only the father/son pair, and in three of these paternity was confirmed and in three others excluded.

2. Material and methods

We used the Powerplex 16 from Promega to type all the 15 STRs for the databases. The results were done by ABI Prism 310. The paternity probability was calculated according to statistics group of GEP-ISFG.

* Corresponding author. Tel.: +351-96-7040332; fax: +351-291-705399.
E-mail address: atgf@uma.pt (A.T. Fernandes).

0531-5131/ © 2003 Published by Elsevier B.V.
doi:10.1016/S0531-5131(03)01766-7

3. Results

In all cases, the differences between the results with the five databases are not statistically significant. In the positive cases, we had a result higher than 99.99% equivalent to "Paternity practically proved" and in cases of exclusion values almost zero. In one case, we had a single exclusion and used more STRs to increase the paternity probability. It will be necessary to do the same when we used the other databases.

References

[1] A.T. Fernandes, R. Velosa, J. Jesus, A. Carracedo, A. Brehm, Genetic differentiation of the Cabo Verde Archipelago population analysed by STR polymorphisms, Annals of Human Genetics (in press).

[2] R. Gonçalves, J. Jesus, A.T. Fernandes, A. Brehm, Genetic profile of a multi-ethnic population from Guine-Bissau (west African Coast) using the new Powerplex16 system kit, Forensic Science International 129 (2002) 78–80.

[3] A.T. Fernandes, A. Brehm, C. Alves, L. Gusmão, A. Amorim, Genetic profile of the Madeira Archipelago population using the new Powerplex16 System Kit, Forensic Science International 125 (2002) 281–283.

[4] R. Velosa, A.T. Fernandes, A. Brehm, Genetic profile of the Açores Archipelago population using the new Powerplex16 System Kit, Forensic Science International 129 (2002) 68–70.

International Congress Series 1261 (2004) 465–467

www.ics-elsevier.com

DNA analysis in a case of serial murderers

A. Barbaro[a,*], P. Cormaci[a], A. Barbaro[b], S. Louahlia[c]

[a] *Department of Forensic Genetics, SIMEF, Reggio Calabria, Italy*
[b] *SIMEF Director-SIMET, 89128 Reggio Calabria, Italy*
[c] *National Legal Medicine Institute, Casablanca, Italy*

Received 31 August 2003; received in revised form 8 September 2003; accepted 15 September 2003

Abstract. At the beginning of 2003, in Casablanca (Morocco), three persons (two men and one woman) were found dead in different places and in different slots: they were horribly mutilated. The man suspected for the murders was found hanged. We performed DNA analysis for the identification of each victim by comparison with the alleged relatives to test the paternity of the woman's son, to verify the siblings relation, and to discover to whom some hairs belonged that were found on the scene of the 3rd homicide. © 2003 Elsevier B.V. All rights reserved.

Keywords: Human remains; Identifiler kit; Y-STRs

1. Introduction

At the beginning of 2003, in Casablanca (Morocco), three persons were found dead in different places and in different slots: a man (T11) from whom only the legs were found, a woman (G1) and a young man (S1) whose body was horribly mutilated. All bodies were found stored inside identical big cardboard boxes: inside one of them, four hairs were found. After some weeks of investigations, the man suspected (C1) for the murders was found hanged by the police: it was supposed that he killed himself. Some samples were sent to our laboratory and we performed DNA analysis useful to: (1) identify the victims by comparison with their relatives; (2) verify if T11 and the suspect C1 were cousins; (3) verify who was the father of the G1 son (H1) since the victim was supposed to be the girlfriend of the suspect; (4) verify the presence of semen on the vaginal swab taken from the victim G1; (5) compare hairs found in the crime scene with the ones of the young victim S1 and of the criminal C1.

2. Materials and methods

2.1 . DNA extraction

DNA analysis has been performed from the root of four hairs, found inside the cardboard box containing S1 body, and from tissues (skin or muscle) belonging to the

* Corresponding author. Department of Forensic Genetics, SIMEF-Via Nicolo'da Reggio 4, 89128, Reggio Calabria, Italy. Tel.: +39-965891184-5; fax: +39-965891125.

E-mail addresses: simef@tiscali.it (A. Barbaro and A. Barbaro), saidlouahlia@voila.fr (S. Louahlia).

URL: http://www.simef.com.

0531-5131/
doi:10.1016/S0531-5131(03)01540-1

victims using "DNA IQ-Tissue and Hair Extraction kit" (Promega). Hair roots were incubated at 56° in an Incubation Buffer/Proteinase K solution containing DTT for 1 h, while about 1 mg of minced cadaveric tissues was incubated overnight in the same buffer. Then all samples were treated by different solutions (lysis, washing and eluition) and a special paramagnetic resin according to the manufacturer's protocol [1]. DNA was extracted from oral swabs belonging to the alleged parents of the victims by "Instant Gene Matrix"(Biorad) treatment. Samples were incubated at 56 °C for 30 min and then boiled for 8 min [2]. All extracts were then quantified by the ALU Quant-Human DNA Quantitation System (Promega) that uses a specific human DNA probe and a luciferase reaction to produce light proportional to the amount of human DNA in the samples analysed [3].

2.2. DNA amplification

DNA amplification was carried out in a laboratory different from the one dedicated to the extraction, so that amplified products never entered the extraction laboratory. STRs amplification was carried out by Gene Amp 9700 and 2400 thermal cyclers (Applied Biosystems), using the *AmpFLSTR Identifiler kit* (Applied Biosystem) that coamplifies the repeat regions of 15 STRs repeat loci plus Amelogenin. According to the kit protocol, positive and negative controls were enclosed during the amplification step [4]. To verify if the suspect and one of the male victims were cousins, we analysed six STRs localized on the chromosome Y: DYS388, DYS390, DYS391, DYS392, DYS393 and DYS319. Amplification has been performed using the GeneAmp PCR System 2400 (Applied Biosystems) according to Kayser et al. [5].

2.3. Electrophoretic analysis

Amplified products were analysed by capillary electrophoresis onto two ABI PRISM 310 Genetic Analyzer (Applied Biosystems) employing ABI softwares (DATA Collection, GeneScan Analysis, Genotyper Fragment Analysis).

For fragment length determination of the PCR products obtained by Amp*FlSTR Identifiler* kit, the orange-fluorescent internal lane DNA standard LIZ 500 was used for calibration, while for Y-STRs detection, we used the red-fluorescent internal size standard ROX 350.

3. Results and discussion

In homicide investigations, if there is a tissue sample from an unidentified deceased individual and investigators have an idea of who may be the sample's source, if the decedent's parents or children are available, it will be possible to compare the related survivors' DNA profiles with that of the deceased to conclusively determine whom the remains came from. There are two possible testing outcomes. An exclusion is a simple statement that the alleged father is excluded from the group of men who could be the father.

In the case of an inclusion, a statistical analysis is performed based on how common or rare are the obligate genes. These are the genes that the alleged father could have contributed to the child and that must have come from the child's biological father.

The inclusionary results are expressed as Probability of Paternity while the Exclusion power shows the probability, given the mother and child results, that a non-father would be excluded from paternity by the set of analysed markers. In this casework, we performed the calculation using the Moroccan frequencies reported by Huckenbeck et al. [6].

1. DNA analysis of biological material belonging to the victim G1 and of her alleged relatives showed a compatibility among DNA profiles. The probability of paternity of the alleged father versus the victim G1 was *0.99999999 (99.999999%)*. The exclusion power of the examined systems was 0.99999999 (99.999999%). Vaginal swab analysis did not show any trace of seminal fluid (negative results for Florence, acid phosphatase and PSA tests) but only the presence of epithelial cells which showed the same DNA profile than the victim.
2. DNA analysis of biological material belonging to the victim S1 and of his alleged relatives showed a compatibility among DNA profiles.
The probability of paternity of the alleged father versus the victim S1 was *0.99971220 (99.971220%)*.
The exclusion power of the examined systems was 0.99982780 (99.982780%).
3. The comparison between DNA profile of H1 and the ones of S1 and of C1 showed that: (a) there was a compatibility, for the analysed loci, between DNA profile of H1 and the one of G1; (b) there were six incompatibilities, for the analysed loci, between DNA profile of H1 and the one of C1; (c) there was a compatibility, for the analysed loci, between DNA profile of H1 and the one of S1; (d) theprobability of S1 paternity of S1 (the alleged father) versus H1 was *0.99957940 (99.957940%)*. The exclusion power of the examined systems was 0.99986390 (99.986390%).
4. DNA analysis of biological material belonging to the victim T11 and of his alleged relatives showed a compatibility among DNA profiles.
The probability of paternity of the alleged father versus the victim T11 was **0.99971740 (99.971740%)**. The exclusion power of the examined systems was 0.99983220 (99.983220%).
5. The analysis of Y-STRs markers (that are inherited along the male offspring) showed that C1 and T11 had, for the analysed loci, an haplotype condivision, so presumably they belong to the same male line. This was compatible with the occurrence that they could be son of two brothers, that, in their turn, has inherited the same Y-STRs from the same father (the grandfather of the cousins).
6. DNA analysis of hairs showed that they were belonging to a man different from S1 and from C1.
DNA profile frequency was estimated on data from the population to which the individuals typed were belonged, since a different population study would probably lead to a different frequency estimate.
In particular, using the Moroccan frequencies reported by Huckenbeck et al. [6], the calculated value of profile frequency was 1:1,000,000,000.

References

[1] DNA IQ-Tissue and Hair Extraction kit Protocol.
[2] Instant gene Matrix Manual.
[3] ALU Quant-Human DNA Quantitation System Protocol.
[4] AmpFlSTR Identifiler kit User's Manual.
[5] S. Kayser, et al., Evaluation of Y-chromosomal STRs: a multicenter study, Int. J. Leg. Med. 110 (1997) 125–133.
[6] W. Huckenbeck, K. Kuntze, H.-G. Scheil, The Distribution of the Human DNA-PCR Polymorphisms, Supplement Volume IV (1998/1999/2000/2001).

International Congress Series 1261 (2004) 468–470

www.ics-elsevier.com

DNA analysis of sex chromosomal aberration: curious mutation found in Turner syndrome

K. Honda[a,c,*], T. Nakamura[a], E. Tanaka[a], K. Yamazaki[b,c], Z. Tun[a], S. Misawa[c]

[a] *Department of Legal Medicine, Tsukuba University School of Medicine, 1-1-1 Tennnodai, Tsukuba, Ibakari, 305-8575 Japan*

[b] *Tsukuba Medical Examiner's Office, 1-3-1 Amakubo, Tsukuba, 305-0005 Japan*

[c] *Tokyo Medical Examiner's Office, 4-21-18 Ootsuka, Bunkyo, Tokyo-to, 112-0012 Japan*

Abstract. The clear evidence that curious fashion of mitochondrial DNA (mtDNA) inheritance was reported in sex chromosomal aberration. Human mtDNA is located outside the nucleus of the cell producing energy for the cell. In the recent years, mtDNA is being used in forensic DNA identification because each cell has many copies of mitochondria, and is easy to be amplified by PCR. Human mtDNA has polymorphic sites in hypervariable regions (HVR) I, II and III. However, human mtDNA evokes some problems, such as heteroplasmic point mutations and questionable maternal inheritance. To investigate this phenomenon, we had a chance to perform a mtDNA testing on 1-month-old infant, diagnosed as Turner Syndrome which was confirmed to be 45XO karyotype by X-STR testing. As a result, two remarkable evidences were obtained. The first, an intermarriage, is seemed to be related in the genesis of the sex chromosomal aberration. The second, the exact maternal inheritance of mtDNA was not maintained in Turner syndrome, as well as in Klinefelter syndrome reported by us previously. In these cases, although paternal influence of mtDNA inheritance was deniable, mutations of mother's mtDNA were excluded or repaired to the usual type in child's mtDNA.

Keywords: Turner syndrome; MtDNA; Maternal inheritance; Mutation; X-STR

1. Introduction

In 1938, Turner presented a syndrome composed of a variety of congenital anomalies such as small stature, delayed sexual maturity, congenital lymphedema, wing-like neck, etc. Afterwards this syndrome was found to be missing one of the sex chromosomes and its karyotype being 45XO. It has been ever said that Turner Syndrome occurs in 1/2500 newborn females and its incidence is increasing recently.[1] In addition, sudden death is sometime occurred in these infants and are needed to submit for forensic analysis in case there is suspicion about the death.

* Corresponding author. Tel.: +81-29-853-3043; fax: +81-29-853-3264.
E-mail address: k-honda@md.tsukuba.ac.jp (K. Honda).

0531-5131/
doi:10.1016/S0531-5131(03)01716-3

2. Materials and method

Blood samples from an infant with Turner Syndrome and her parents were collected for DNA analysis. First, we performed X–Y Amelogenin DNA testing (106/112 bp) and five kinds of X STR tests (HPRTB, HumARA, STRX1, DXS6789, and DXS6807).

HVR (hypervariable regions) I and II of human mtDNA were analyzed by direct sequencing using ABI PRISM 377 DNA sequencer (Perkin Elmer) after cycle sequencing of Big Dye Primer method.

3. Results

X chromosomal STR analysis showed that this infant had only one X chromosome, supporting the diagnosis of pure Turner syndrome, excluding mosaic type. By repetitive testing, the possibility of mosaic was almost negative.

In the testing of inheritance pattern of X chromosome from the parents, the origin of inherited X was not easily determined because the parents interestingly have many identical alleles. So, it was suspected that the father and the mother were related in a way, that is,

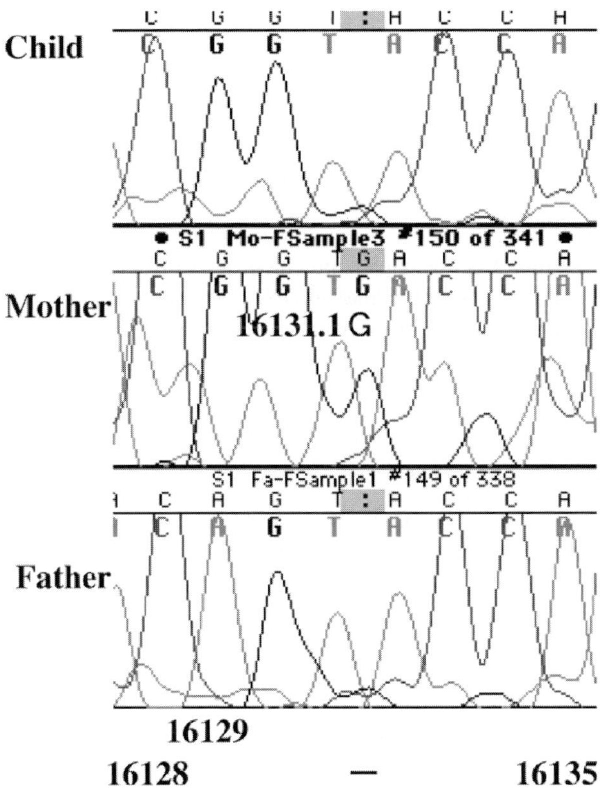

Fig. 1. The G insertion of nps16131 (mutation) in mother is disappeared in child. In addition, as for nps16129, the mother and child agrees in G, but father is A. It means that mitochondrial DNA sequence is different with child and father definitely, child and mothter slightly.

accidental intermarriage was not deniable. Fortunately, one (DXS 6789) out of five X-STRs tested showed that X chromosome of the infant was inherited from mother, in other words, a paternal sex chromosome was rejected.

Analysis of mtDNA HVR I and HVR II revealed that mtDNA of the infant was derived from mother. Curiously, mother's mtDNA has strange insertions, which were not found normal population yet. It was noted in G/C sequences of 16095-6, 16132-3 and 16150-1, disappeared in the child (Fig. 1).

Therefore, undeniable small difference of mtDNA between mother and the infant was recognized, that was, mutations of mother's mtDNA were excluded or repaired to usual type in child's mtDNA.

In conclusion, our data implied that mtDNA of maternal origin could generate some variations after fertilization.

4. Discussion

Turner's syndrome is an abnormality of a sex chromosome, and it is thought that the problem has no relevance with mtDNA. However, in our case, mutations were seen in mtDNA of mother, and it suggests that one cannot say that mt DNA has nothing to do with the genesis of sex chromosomal aberration [2,3].

It was thought that mtDNA and nuclear DNA have completely different origin, but our data suggest that both are related closely, and they might be relevant to each other. In more details, mtDNA might partially affect the fertilization and cell division. In our previous study, the similar phenomenon was found with Klinefelter's syndrome[4–6], supporting this hypothesis.

In mammals including humans, it has been believed that a child inherited mtDNA directly from the mother and constantly remained in its original state. However, it cannot be denied that there is a possibility that mtDNA can be varied by growth after having inherited the original DNA from the mother.

References

[1] A. Uematsu, T. Yorifuji, J. Muroi, et al, Parental origin of normal X chromosomes in Turner syndrome patients with various karyotypes: implications for the mechanism leading to generation of a 45, X karyotype, Am. J. Med. Genet. 111 (2002) 134–139.

[2] A.A. Morris, R. Lightowlers, Can paternal mtDNA be inherited? Lancet 355 (2001) 1290–1291.

[3] L. Frederick, A. Renee, Male sperm mortality dictated by mother's mtDNA, Am. J. Hum. Genet. 67 (2000) 543–548.

[4] K. Honda, Z. Tun, R. Matoba, DNA testing of Klinefelter's syndrome in a criminal case using XY chromosomal STR multiplex-PCR, J. Forensic Sci. 46 (5) (2001) 1235–1238.

[5] K. Honda, Z. Tun, D. Young, T. Terao, Examination of Y-STR mutations in sex chromosomal abnormality in forensic cases, Forensic Sci. Int. 118 (2001) 136–140.

[6] H. Oikawa, Z. Tun, D. Young, H. Ozawa, K. Yamazaki, E. Tanaka, K. Honda, The specific mitochondrial DNA polymorphism found in the Klinefelter's syndrome, Biochem. Biophys. Res. Commun. 297 (2002) 341–345.

International Congress Series 1261 (2004) 471–472

www.ics-elsevier.com

DNA extraction assays from formalin fixed tissues: paternity testing from a 3-week-old embryo

L. Delpech*, G. Garcin, C. Giacometti, O. Marie, S. Frackowiak, P.-E. Coiffait

Laboratoire de Police Scientifique, 97 Boulevard Camille Flammarion, 13248 Marseille Cedex 04, France

Keywords: Formalin; Extraction; Embryo; Multiplex STR PCR; Paternity testing

DNA forensic samples are generally critical in terms of quantity and quality. In a recent criminal case, we had to fingerprint a very early embryo (less than 4 weeks old) included in the chorion issued from the dead pregnant victim, to test paternity of two alleged fathers. Multiple difficulties appeared: (1) the selective dissection of the embryo (1 mm length) among the chorionic material; (2) the 6 months formalin treatment of the autopsic tissue; (3) the necessity to have most informative DNA profile (many loci) with minimum biological material. In this way, use of multiplex amplification kits was greatly recommended instead of several singleplex PCR.

Prior to the investigations on the critical sample, some assays were realised using autopsic test tissues as liver and cardiac muscle, formalin fixed for a long term, and on the chorionic tissue around embryo. Two extraction protocols were tested: Qiagen Tissues Protocol and an organic phenol-chloroform like technique after treatment of the samples in a GTE buffer to neutralise formalin excess. DNA was then quantified (Quantiblot) and typed using SGM+ and/or Identifiler multiplex PCR kits revealed on Capillary Electrophoresis with ABI 310 genetic analyser (Applied Biosystems).

Although significative DNA amounts have been detected from liver and cardiac tissue, no profile was obtained in STR fluorescence detection. However a complete profile was obtained from the chorion, providing mother fingerprint. So a tricky dissection of the chorion was attempted in order to remove the 1 mm long embryo. Several "suspected samples" were extracted, quantified and STR typed: some of them exhibited a partial profile mixture (10/15 STR markers) with a clear Y peak, the others showed a partial profile compatible with the mother DNA fingerprint.

* Corresponding author. Tel.: +33-4-91-62-85-38; fax: +33-4-91-62-97-70.
E-mail address: laure.delpech@interieur.gouv.fr (L. Delpech).

doi:10.1016/S0531-5131(03)01549-8

In conclusion, suitable DNA amplified fragments (<250 pb) were obtained in multiplex PCR from formalin fixed samples. In further assays, we try to type specifically Y STR on the samples issued from the "embryo-chorion" fragments. We also look forward to perform, on the questioned sample, singleplex PCR of the largest discriminant markers between the two alleged fathers.

International Congress Series 1261 (2004) 473–475

www.ics-elsevier.com

DNA typing from steel cable

L. Saravo [a,*], S. Spitaleri [a], D. Piscitello [a], S. Travali [b]

[a] *Laboratory of Molecular Biology, Raggruppamento Carabinieri Investigazioni Scientifiche (RaCIS) Reparto di Messina, Italy*

[b] *Department of Biomedical Sciences, University of Catania, Italy*

Abstract. The aim of this study is to analyze the possibility of DNA typing, on the specimen recovered at the crime scene. The optimization of extraction was carried out via an experimental system to reproduce the contact with the victim. The results obtained will be described in detail.

Keywords: Low copy number; Identifiler; PCR; Drop out

1. Introduction

We report a homicide attempt case which occurred in February 2003 in Sicily. The victim was assaulted with a steel cable put around the neck, but was able to run away, and the contact was only for a few moments. Police found a 3-m-long cable, which was 0.6 cm in diameter, at the suspect's house and immediately submitted it to our laboratory for the DNA typing. Results were immediately transmitted to the Public Prosecutor and the assailant was soon arrested.

Before the final analysis on the above specimen, we performed various types of experiments, according to LCN recommendation, to optimize the extraction phase and PCR DNA typing on different reference samples [1]. We set several experimental conditions to evaluate the minimum time of contact with the skin necessary to transfer sufficient quantities of biological material onto a steel cable similar to that described in the case report. DNA extraction and PCR conditions were optimized for low copy DNA typing on a different cable used as reference samples. Experimental time points were different. Sufficient DNA to perform the STR analysis was obtained from samples to complete DNA typing. The untreated cable, used as negative control, did not give any amplified product. Our result demonstrates that a brief contact of some objects with the human skin is sufficient to determine the transfer of some biological material and support the possibility to type DNA in a low copy number on specimens recovered at the crime scene.

* Corresponding author. Tel.: +39-905725388; fax: +39-905725690.
E-mail address: kunitz@libero.it (L. Saravo).

0531-5131/ © 2003 Elsevier B.V. All rights reserved.
doi:10.1016/S0531-5131(03)01715-1

2. Materials and methods

We utilized various kinds of steel cables, in order to better the reproduction of the original conditions of our case and to evaluate eventual differences in DNA quality and yield.

The specimen cables were at first cut into 10 bits and each bit was washed for 3 h in an ultrasonic bath in 1 ml of lysis buffer (10 mM Tris–HCl pH 8, 10 mM EDTA pH 8, 100 mM NaCl, 2% SDS, 40 mM DTT) in a single tube, with 15 ul di PK (20 mg/ml). The mix was vortexed at 1000 rpm to separate the lubricating grease. The surnatant was purified Microcon 100 Amicon following the manufacturer's recommendation. DNA extraction from the specimen and reference samples was carried out essentially by chelex procedure [2].

The amplification of the DNA extracted was performed by use of an *AmpFLSTR Identifiler kit* (Applied Biosystem), in 12.5 ul final volume. PCR followed in a Perkin Elmer Gene Amp PCR System cycler 2400 and 9700 [3]. According to the kit protocol, positive and negative controls were enclosed during the amplification step.

The product of reaction after 28 cycles was then analyzed and non-repurified with Microcon 100 Amicon and the analysis of amplified was performed following standard parameters on ABIPRISM 3100 DNA Sequencer Allele. Sizes were determined using Gene Scan v.2.1 software. Automatic allele designation was achieved by use of Genotype v.3.7 software (Applied Biosystems).

3. Results and discussion

The procedure we have described above, chosen after optimization on various kinds of steel cable, permitted the correct identification of the DNA extracted. Blood tests were negative and the DNA, perhaps, resulted from contact with the skin.

To obtain a suitable sample, we chose not to swab the cable surface, but to cut the steel cable into small pieces to treat with ultrasound in order to increase the extraction effectiveness and to decrease interference with potential contaminants (oil, dirt, etc.) the mix was vortexed at 1000 rpm to separate the lubricating grease.

The procedure utilized, which gave the maximum sensitivity, was as follows:

- Extraction using a strong buffer and sample sonication;
- Inhibitors removal through filtration;
- Single tube amplification with chelex;
- Reaction volume reduction;
- Post-amplification filtration;
- Electrophoresis on ABI 3100.

The experiment conducted with various steel cables in different experimental conditions permitted us to demonstrate that the 30-s contact between the cable and the human epidermis was sufficient to permit the extraction of amplifiable DNA (Fig. 1). Some artifacts were observed, such as; allelic drop out, but the influence on the interpretation was minimum.

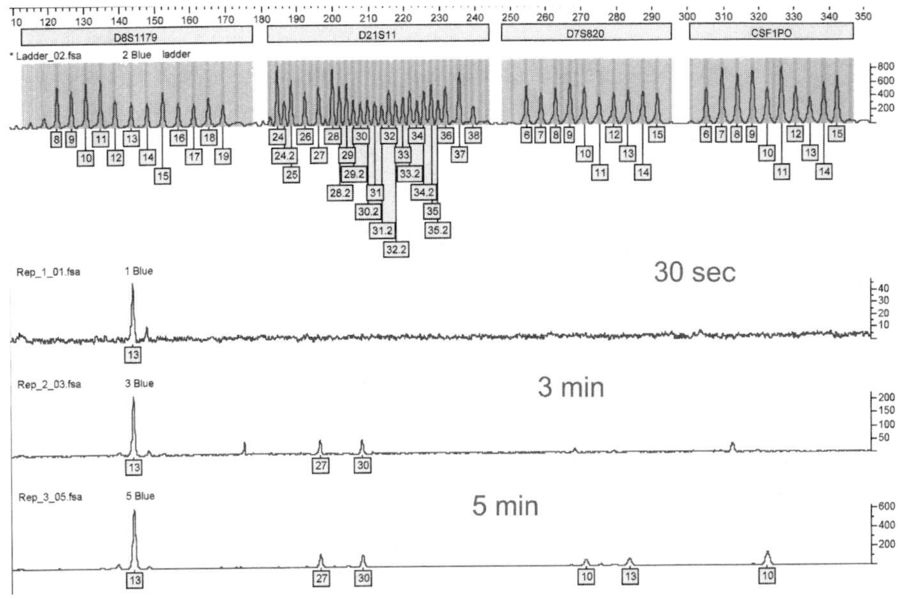

Fig. 1. DNA genotyping from different time of contact.

Conditions that can affect the amount of biological material transferred to the cable need to be experimentally evaluated; at this moment we are studying the influence of contact time on DNA recovery [4–6].

Acknowledgements

This research was supported by grant of Dr. R.A. Recupido and Dr. F. Sottosanti, Judge and Public Prosecutor of the Court of Catania.

References

[1] P. Gill, J. Whitaker, C. Flaxman, N. Brown, J. Bukleton, An investigation of the rigor of interpretation rules for STRs derived from less than 100 pg of DNA, Forensic Sci. Int. 112 (2000) 17–40.

[2] P.S. Walsh, D.A. Metzger, R. Higuchi, Chelex 100 as a medium for simple extraction of DNA for PCR-based typing from forensic material, BioTechniques 10 (1991) 506.

[3] Amp*Fl*STR Identifiler PCR Amplification Kit. User's Manual, PE Biosystems, 2001.

[4] A.D. Kloosterman, P. Kersbergen, Efficacy and limits of genotyping low copy number DNA samples by multiplex PCR of STR loci, Progress in Forensic Genetics, vol. 9, Elsevier, Amsterdam, 2003, pp. 795–798.

[5] P. Gill, Application of low copy number DNA profiling, Croatian Medical Journal 42 (3) (2001) 229–232.

[6] J. Butler, Forensic DNA Typing, Academic Press, San Diego, CA, 2001.

International Congress Series 1261 (2004) 476–478

www.ics-elsevier.com

Effect on paternity index of substituting the biological father by his brother—preliminary report

J. Berent*, R. Jacewicz, S. Szram

Department of Forensic Medicine, Medical University of Lodz, ul. Sedziowska 18a, 91-304 Lodz, Poland

Abstract. *Background*: In cases of analysis of trios with the biological father, inconsistencies never appear (barring the possibility of a mutation occurring). The paternity index (PI) calculated for such trios always has a value greater than zero. If in such a trio the biological father is substituted by his brother, it can cause a change in PI if the brother's genotype is different from the genotype of the biological father. The purpose of this study was to determine what the effect on PI for a trio would be if the biological father in the trio was replaced by his brother. In the study, a computer simulation was used of all theoretically possible trios with the biological father and his brother. For all the simulated trios, PIs were calculated and compared. The calculations were based on SGM Plus systems. It was determined that PI calculated for the trio with the biological father's brother can only have one of four possible relations to PI for the trio with the biological father. Most often, there was no change in the PI—this occurred in over half the cases (53.7%, SD = 0.9%). Significantly less frequent was the situation in which the result of the substitution was an inconsistency (32.3%, SD = 3.8%). The remaining two possibilities—twice greater or lesser PI resulting from substituting the father in the trio—were very rare and appeared with medium frequency of only a few percent (4.7%, SD = 1.0% and 5.3%, SD = 2.0%, respectively). Substituting, for the biological father in a trio, his brother, in so far as no inconsistency appears as a result, does not cause any change in PI in the majority of cases. Thus, distinguishing the biological father from his brother can occur practically only by means of excluding the brother.

Keywords: Paternity index; Avuncular index; Relatives; SGM Plus; Population data

1. Introduction

The rare cases where even DNA testing does not resolve the question of paternity are almost always those in which the true and alleged fathers are related [1]. Older publications remark only that in this situation the analysis is more difficult, since the results may provide little information [2]. In 1988, Morris et al. [3] defined the Avuncular Index (AI), which brought certain possibilities of a more analytical approach to the problem. The aim of this study was to determine how the substitution, for the true father in a trio, of a brother affects paternity index (PI) for the trio.

2. Materials and methods

In the study, a computer simulation was run on all theoretically possible trios with a true father and his brother. The analysis was based on 10 DNA systems from SGM Plus

* Corresponding author. Tel.: +48-42-6544536; fax: +48-42-6544293.
E-mail address: J.Berent@eranet.pl (J. Berent).

0531-5131/
doi:10.1016/S0531-5131(03)01452-3

Table 1
Population genetics of SGM Plus multiplex—population sample of 100 unrelated persons (200 alleles) from central Poland

Allele	D3S1358	VWA	D16S539	D2S1338	D8S1179	D21S11	D18S51	D19S433	TH01	FGA
6									0.260	
7									0.145	
8			0.005		0.015				0.120	
9			0.100		0.010				0.215	
9.3									0.250	
10			0.035		0.070		0.010		0.010	
11			0.290		0.065		0.010	0.005		
12			0.325		0.200		0.060	0.065		
13	0.005		0.220		0.290		0.100	0.210		
13.2								0.020		
14	0.140	0.150	0.025		0.215		0.175	0.340		
14.2								0.035		
15	0.220	0.070		0.010	0.095		0.190	0.145		
15.2								0.060		
16	0.220	0.165		0.075	0.030		0.135	0.075		
16.2								0.035		
17	0.265	0.300		0.235	0.010		0.150			
17.2								0.005		
18	0.145	0.225		0.065			0.080			
18.2								0.005		
19	0.005	0.080		0.075			0.050			0.095
20		0.010		0.115			0.020			0.120
21				0.055		0.005	0.015			0.190
22				0.025						0.205
22.2										0.030
23				0.105						0.135
23.2										0.005
24				0.120			0.005			0.135
25				0.105		0.005				0.055
26				0.015						0.020
27						0.060				0.010
28						0.200				
29						0.185				
30						0.220				
30.2						0.035				
31						0.050				
31.2						0.085				
32.2						0.105				
33.2						0.040				
34.2						0.010				

multiplex. Allele frequencies came from the authors' own population from central Poland of 100 non-related persons (200 alleles) and are shown in Table 1.

In the systems studied for all theoretically possible combinations of genotypes, the PI for the true father and his brother, and the frequency of each combination of genotype in the population were calculated. Then, on that basis was calculated the frequency of change in PI values in the population F_{PI} between trios with the true father and the true father's brother, i.e., how often the quotient: PI of true father's brother over PI of true father had the values: 0, 0.5, 1 or 2, since only these values are possible, and where: 0 means exclusion of the brother; 0.5 means that the brother's PI is two times lower than the father's PI; 1 means that the brother's PI is equal to the father's PI; and 2 means that the brother's PI is two times greater than the father's PI. The F_{PI} values thus obtained and corresponding minimal, maximal and average values, along with the standard deviation, were arranged in Table 2.

3. Results

Table 2
Results of F_{PI} calculations for the 10 microsatellite systems from SGM Plus multiplex (for symbols see Materials and methods)

System	$F_{PI}(0)$	$F_{PI}(0.5)$	$F_{PI}(1)$	$F_{PI}(2)$
D3S1358	0.293007	0.109571	0.542637	0.054785
VWA	0.302522	0.104207	0.541167	0.052104
D16S539	0.260491	0.124407	0.552899	0.062203
D2S1338	0.376388	0.065232	0.525764	0.032616
D8S1179	0.315245	0.097600	0.538354	0.048801
D21S11	0.350989	0.078971	0.530554	0.039486
D18S51	0.368379	0.069603	0.527217	0.034801
D19S433	0.314204	0.097511	0.539529	0.048756
TH01	0.289647	0.111212	0.543535	0.055606
FGA	0.356737	0.075863	0.529468	0.037932
Average	0.322761	0.093418	0.537112	0.046709
S.D.	0.038452	0.019908	0.008647	0.009954
Minimum	0.260491	0.065232	0.525764	0.032616
Maximum	0.376388	0.124407	0.552899	0.062203

4. Discussion

The study has shown that in the case of replacing the true father with his brother, most often, there was no change in the PI. For the SGM Plus systems, this occurred in over half the cases (0.537112, SD = 0.008647). Significantly less frequent was the situation in which the result of the substitution was an inconsistency (0.322761, SD = 0.038452). The remaining two possibilities—twice greater or lower PI values—were very rare and appeared with medium frequency of only a few percent (0.046709, SD = 0.009954 and 0.053418, SD = 0.019908, respectively). Furthermore, it is worth emphasizing that—as was noted by Presciuttini et al. [4]—the results of an analysis are easily carried over to other systems or STR system sets, and therefore also permit generalizations which go beyond the loci sets chosen for this study.

5. Conclusion

Substituting, for the true father in a trio, his brother, in so far as no inconsistency appears as a result, does not cause any change in PI values in the majority of cases. Thus, distinguishing the biological father from his brother can occur practically only by means of excluding the brother.

Acknowledgements

This project was supported by the Medical University of Lodz grant no. 502-11-785(35).

References

[1] M. Czarny, et al., Is DNA analysis always useful: problems in paternity testing in case of closely related alleged fathers, Arch. Med. Sad. Kryminol. 45 (1995) 287–295.

[2] J.W. Morris, Probability of paternity: Logic I, in: H. Silver (Ed.), Probability of Inclusion in Paternity Testing, American Association of Blood Banks, Arlington, 1982, pp. 45–59.

[3] J.W. Morris, et al., The avuncular index and the incest index, in: W.R. Mayr (Ed.), Advances in Forensic Haemogenetics, vol. 2, Berlin, 1988, pp. 607–611.

[4] S. Presciuttini, et al., Allele sharing in first-degree and unrelated pairs of individuals in the Ge.F.I. AmpFlSTR® Profiler Plus™ database, Forensic Sci. Int. 131 (2003) 85–89.

ELSEVIER

International Congress Series 1261 (2004) 479–481

www.ics-elsevier.com

Evaluation of stain cases of the Swiss DNA Database

A. Kratzer, C. Brun, C. Haas*, P. Voegeli, W. Bär

Institute of Legal Medicine, University of Zurich, Winterthurerstrasse 190, 8057 Zurich, Switzerland

Abstract. Since the Swiss federal DNA profile information system (EDNA) has been launched in July 2000 the number of stain cases increased considerably: 337 cases in 1999 compared to 1386 cases in 2001. Before the Swiss DNA database was in use, stain cases were examined only if a suspect was present. Now also stain cases with unknown perpetrators are being examined. In this study 500 stain cases comprising 1270 single stains from 2001 were evaluated. From 1270 stains 1104 were analyzed by PCR (18% were mixed profiles), 837 displayed a DNA profile and finally 395 were entered into the database. A total of 224 of 395 profiles (57%) that were entered into the database resulted in a hit. The changes in types of stains and crime categories as a result of the implementation of the database are documented and discussed. © 2003 Elsevier B.V. All rights reserved.

Keywords: Forensic genetics; STR typing; DNA database; Switzerland

1. Introduction

The Swiss DNA database is operational since July 2000. DNA profiles of persons who are suspected of having committed a crime according to the Swiss crime catalogue and DNA profiles of stains from unknown perpetrators are entered into the database [1].

The goal of this study was to evaluate to what extent the implementation of the DNA database has changed our case material (type of stain and crime category) and to find out the success rate of the database. Therefore 500 stain cases comprising 1270 single stains from 2001 were evaluated and the results were compared with 205 stain cases investigated before the Swiss DNA database had been launched [2].

2. Material and methods

DNA from the 500 stain cases was extracted according to standard procedures and amplified using the commercially available Multiplex PCR kit Amp*Fl*STR SGM Plus.

3. Results

3.1. Types of stains and crime category

A total of 505 of the 1270 examined stain samples were from touched objects, e.g. from hafts of tools and weapons, gloves and clothes (so-called contact stains). The second

* Corresponding author. Tel.: +41-1-635-56-56; fax: +41-1-635-68-58.
E-mail address: haco@irm.unizh.ch (C. Haas).

doi:10.1016/S0531-5131(03)01536-X

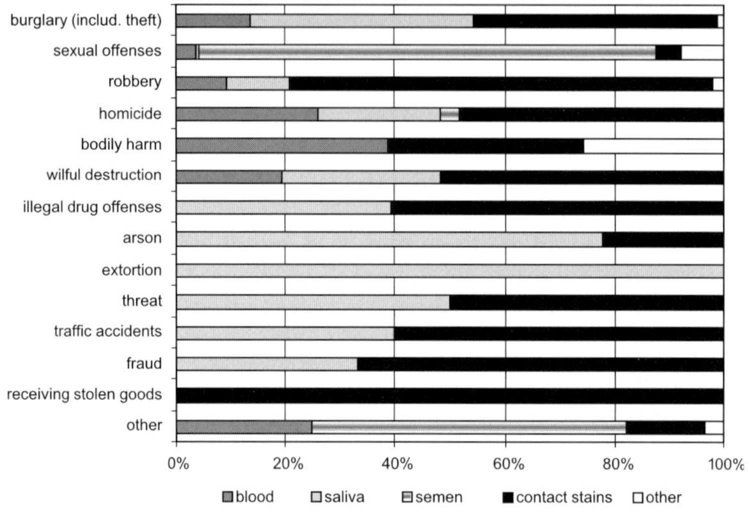

Fig. 1. Distribution of types of stains among crime categories.

category was saliva stains (380 samples), followed by semen (199 samples) and blood stains (149 samples). The remaining 37 samples originated from tissues, hairs, fingernails, faeces and urine. Fig. 1 illustrates how the different types of stains were distributed among the crime categories. Only contact stains and saliva stains could be found in nearly all crime categories.

3.2. Results of STR typing

From the 1270 stain samples 166 were not subjected to a DNA analysis mainly because preliminary tests to detect the presence of blood, saliva or semen were negative or the client only required the results of the preliminary tests. 1104 stains were subjected to a DNA

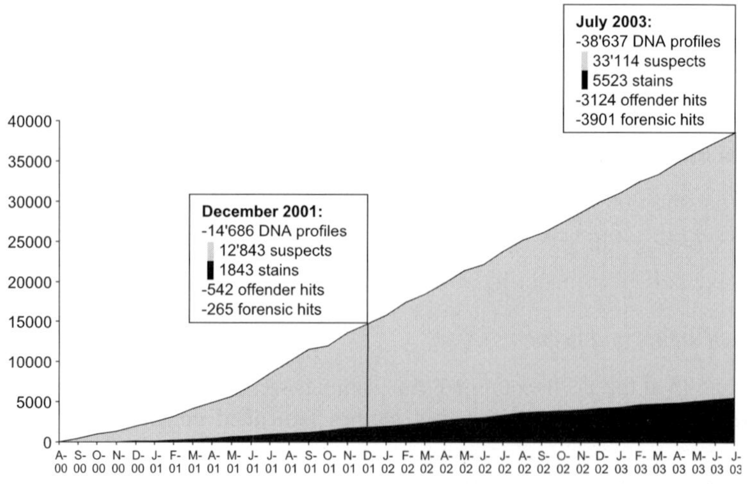

Fig. 2. Number of DNA profiles in the Swiss DNA database since August 2000.

analysis, whereof 837 were successful. The analysis of 267 samples provided no result. Most of the 837 successfully typed samples showed male profiles (562 samples), 73 showed female profiles and about one quarter of the samples (202) resulted in mixed profiles.

A total of 395 of the 837 DNA profiles were entered into the Swiss DNA database. For the inclusion of a DNA profile into the database a minimum of six typed STR loci and for mixed profiles a minimum of eight loci limited to four alleles per locus is required. 442 DNA profiles were not sent to the database for the following reasons: several typed samples resulted in identical DNA profiles, the PCR analysis results were inconclusive or not interpretable or the obtained DNA profiles did not fulfil the admission requirements.

3.3. Hits and success rate

395 DNA profiles were sent to the Swiss DNA database for data recording and comparison. 57% of the profiles that were entered into the database resulted in hits. 36% of the DNA profiles complied with the DNA profile of a person and resulted in the identification of the perpetrator. Several crime scenes could be linked by stain-to-stain hits (21% of the DNA profiles). Considering the 1104 stains subjected to a DNA analysis not counting the 372 identical profiles within the cases, about every third stain sample resulted in a hit.

4. Discussion

The implementation of the Swiss DNA database led to a considerable increase of examined stain cases (337 cases in 1999 compared to 1386 cases in 2001). Now also stains from crime scenes with unknown perpetrators are being examined. In comparison to an evaluation study investigating stain cases from 1991 to 1994 a new type of stains now dominates the case material: the contact stains. They even represent the main part (39%) of the routinely analyzed stains, followed by saliva (30%), semen (16%) and blood stains (12%). In former times blood stains (64%) made up the majority of the analyzed stain samples corresponding to the then major crime category "homicide". Nowadays the major crime category is "burglary and theft" with the contact stains as the largest group of analyzed stain samples.

5. Actual statistical data and outlook

The actual statistical data from the Swiss DNA database are shown in Fig. 2. Every month approximately 1400 profiles (1100 from suspects and 300 from stains) are entered into the database. At the end of July 2003 the total number of profiles from suspects in the database was 33,114 and the number of stain profiles amounted to 5523. Since the start of the database in July 2000, 3124 hits between profiles from persons and stains allowed the identification of the unknown perpetrators. In addition 3901 forensic hits were reported.

References

[1] M. Strehler, A. Kratzer, W. Bär, Swiss federal DNA profile information system, Progress in Forensic Genetics, vol. 9, Elsevier Science B.V., Amsterdam, 2003, pp. 777–781.

[2] D. Boller, Die Analyse von Kriminalspuren mit der PCR-Technik (1991-1994). Dissertation Med. Fakultät der Universität Zürich, 1998.

International Congress Series 1261 (2004) 482–484
www.ics-elsevier.com

Evaluation of STR typings (TH01, TPOX and CSF1PO loci) using urine obtained from bladder cancer patients

Y. Itoh[a,*], K. Satoh[a,b], N. Iizuka[a,b], R. Kobayashi[a,c], K. Nagao[d], M. Fujime[d]

[a] *Department of Forensic Medicine, Juntendo University School of Medicine, 2-1-1 Hongo, Bunkyo, Tokyo 113-8421, Japan*
[b] *Medico-Legal Section, Criminal Investigation Laboratory, Metropolitan Police Department, Tokyo, Japan*
[c] *Department of Microbiology, Tokyo Medical University, Tokyo, Japan*
[d] *Department of Urology, Juntendo University School of Medicine, Tokyo, Japan*

Abstract. We examined urine and blood DNA obtained from bladder cancer patients with commercially available STR kits such as those for TH01, TPOX and CSF1PO loci. These loci were amplified by PCR, and polymorphic alleles were visualized as bands on gels. The results were compared with each paired DNA. Microsatellite alternation was observed in 5 out of 52 (9.6%) urine DNAs from the patients with bladder cancer. These loss of heterozygosity (LOH) and microsatellite instability (MSI) were observed such as the combination of an intense and a faint band. Complete LOH causing incorrect typing results was not observed. We were able to avoid incorrect typing results when using urine DNA under careful observation.

Keywords: Microsatellite; Urine DNA; Loss of heterozygosity; Instability; Bladder cancer

1. Introduction

In forensic casework, microsatellite analysis of urine provides important information for DNA profiling [1–4]. Several investigators using polymorphic microsatellite markers have reported microsatellite alternations such as loss of heterozygosity (LOH) and microsatellite instability (MSI) in urine sediments from patients with bladder cancer and urologic diseases [5–7]. Microsatellite alteration is characterized by expansion or deletion of a repeat unit which has been related to malignancy and inflammatory condition. It should be considered to affect the microsatellite typing results.

* Corresponding author. Tel.: +81-3-5802-1050; fax: +81-3-5802-1050.
E-mail address: yitoh@med.juntendo.ac.jp (Y. Itoh).

doi:10.1016/S0531-5131(03)01525-5

This study was performed to evaluate commercially available kits for microsatellite typing of urine DNA.

2. Materials and methods

All samples from Japanese patients with urologic disease were obtained with informed consent and were collected at the Depart. of Urology, Juntendo Univ. School of Medicine.

Blood DNA was isolated from whole blood using the QIAamp DNA Mini Kit (QIAGEN, Germany). Urine DNA was isolated from urine as follows. Two to five milliliters of urine was centrifuged for 5 min at 5000 rpm and the pelleted cells were used for extraction by the phenol–chloroform method.

PCR amplification was completed with reagents and protocols provided by Promega GenePrint STR kits (Promega, Tokyo) TH01, TPOX and CSF1PO for loci located on chromosomes 11, 2 and 5, respectively. The amplified products were separated by polyacrylamide gel electrophoresis and visualized using Promega's DNA silver staining system (Promega, Tokyo).

3. Results and discussion

Microsatellite alternations such as LOH and MSI were observed in 5 out of 52 (9.6%) urine DNAs from the patients. In two out of five urine DNAs, the alternation was simultaneously observed at the TH01 and TPOX loci (Table 1). The remaining three urine DNAs showed two instances at the TH01 locus and one instance at the CSF1PO locus. As shown in Fig. 1, microsatellite alternation was observed, such as the combination of an intense and a faint band. Complete LOH causing incorrect typing results was not observed.

The frequency of microsatellite alternation in our study was lower than that found by other investigators [5–7]. This might have been due to differences in choice of microsatellite loci, or number of microsatellite markers studied. Our results may be attributed to a panel of three microsatellite markers. Furthermore, as the DNA derived from urine is contained in leukocytes and exfoliated cells including renal tubular, transitional urothelial, squamous and cancer cells, the mixture ratio of cancer or inflammatory cells in the urine may also have an influence. This may be attributable to the preparation of DNA samples.

Table 1
Microsatellite alternation in urine DNA

Sample no.	Microsatellite markers		
	TH01	TPOX	CSF1PO
19	MSI	MSI	–
44	LOH	–	–
52	–	–	LOH
56	LOH	LOH	–
59	MSI	–	–

–: no genetic alternation detected between blood and urine DNA; LOH: loss of heterozygosity, MSI: microsatellite instability.

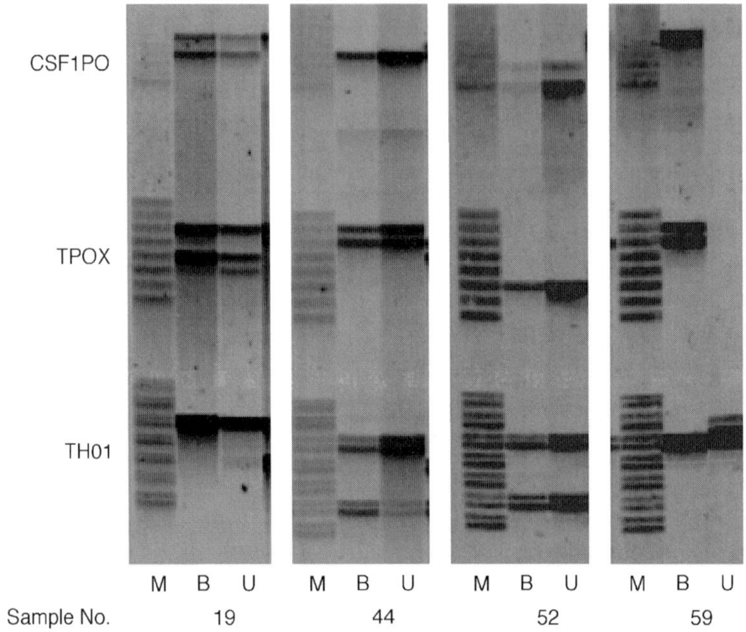

Fig. 1. Electrophoretic patterns of microsatellite analysis of paired blood DNA (B) and urine DNA (U). Sample No. 19; MSI of urine DNA in TH01 and TPOX loci, No. 44; LOH of urine DNA in TH01 locus, No. 52; LOH of urine DNA in CSF1PO locus; No. 59; MSI of urine DNA in TH01 locus.

Microsatellite analysis of urine represents a novel and potentially powerful clinical tool for the detection of recurrent bladder cancer. For this purpose, choice of microsatellite loci, number of microsatellite markers studied and preparation of urine DNA were considered to be important factors to detect a high frequency of microsatellite alternation.

Microsatellite alternation in urine DNA is presumed to affect the DNA typing results. In this study, however, we were able to avoid incorrect typing results under careful observation.

References

[1] B. Brinkmann, et al., Forensic identification of urine samples, Int. J. Leg. Med. 105 (1992) 59–61.

[2] M. Prinz, et al., DNA typing of urine samples following several years of straggle, Int. J. Leg. Med. 106 (1993) 75–79.

[3] D.R. Linfert, et al., The effect of Pathologic substances and adulterants on the DNA typing of urine, J. Forensic Sci. 43 (1998) 1041–1045.

[4] A. Milde, et al., Improved DNA typing of human urine by adding EDTA, Int. J. Leg. Med. 112 (1999) 209–210.

[5] L. Mao, et al., Molecular detection of primary bladder cancer by microsatellite analysis, Science 271 (1996) 659–662.

[6] G. Steiner, et al., Detection of bladder cancer recurrence by microsatellite analysis of urine, Nat. Med. 3 (1997) 621–624.

[7] M. Christensen, et al., Microsatellite alterations In urinary sediments from patients with cystitis and bladder cancer, Int. J. Cancer 85 (2000) 614–617.

International Congress Series 1261 (2004) 485–487

www.ics-elsevier.com

Forensic DNA analysis of a foetal histological section and chromosome sample from chorionic villi (CV) in Down syndrome

H. Pamjav[a,*], B. Egyed[b], S. Füredi[b], J. Woller[b], Zs. Pádár[b], E. Susa[a], B. Baraczka[a]

[a] *Institute of Forensic Medicine, Ministry of Justice, DNA Laboratory, 1363 Budapest, Pf. 31, Hungary*
[b] *Institute of Forensic Sciences, Hungarian National Police HQ, Budapest, Hungary*

Abstract. According to the opinion of a plaintiff (Mrs. B) and a co-plaintiff (Mrs. A), two samples had been exchanged during cytogenetic investigation of foetal chorionic villi (CV), because the child of Mrs. A was born with Down syndrome in spite of the negative CV result (46, XY). The CV investigation of Mrs. B had given a positive result (47, XY, +21), so the pregnancy was terminated, but histological sections of her abortus showed no pathological changes. DNA profiles were successfully obtained from the participants and both of the slides. Two complicating factors were observed during the investigation. Between mother (Mrs. A) and the Down syndrome child, a one-step germ line mutation was found together with a three-allele D3S1358 pattern in the same child's profile. The genetic investigation and its statistical interpretation strongly support the hypothesis that the putative exchange of samples did not occur.

Keywords: Three-banded pattern; Paternity testing; Down syndrome; STR; Germline mutation

1. Case report

A civil liability claim was initiated against one of the Budapest hospitals in 1992. According to the opinion of the plaintiff (Mrs. B) and the co-plaintiff (Mrs. A), two samples had been exchanged during cytogenetic investigation of foetal chorionic villi (CV), because the child of Mrs. A was born with Down syndrome in spite of the negative CV result (46, XY). The CV investigation of Mrs. B had given a positive result (47, XY, +21) and so the pregnancy was terminated, but histological sections of her abortus showed no pathological changes.

* Corresponding author. Tel.: +36-1-457-0183; fax: +36-1-201-6166.
E-mail address: phorolma@hotmail.com (H. Pamjav).

0531-5131/
doi:10.1016/j.ics.2003.11.011

2. Materials and methods

Forensic DNA analysis was carried out on the Giemsa-stained CV slide (chromosome sample) from Mrs. A, the histological slide stained with hematoxylin–eosin from the abortus of Mrs. B and on blood samples from Mrs. A, her husband Mr. A, their child with Down syndrome and Mrs. B.

The histological slide and the chromosome sample were placed in xylene and acetone, respectively, until the cover glasses could be easily removed. The slides were then placed in ethanol solutions of decreasing concentration, and finally in distilled water. The tissue and mitotic chromosomes were removed with cotton swabs. DNA was isolated by phenol–chloroform extraction and Microcon YM-100 (Millipore, USA) purification. DNA was extracted from blood samples using the QIAmp DNA Blood Mini Kit (Qiagen, Germany). STR loci were amplified with the ProfilerPlus AmpF1STR kit (Applied Biosystems). All samples were analysed on an ABI Prism 310 Genetic Analyzer (Applied Biosystems).

3. Results and discussion

Profiles were successfully obtained from the participants and off the slides originated from Mrs. A and Mrs. B (Table 1). The child of Mrs. A had three different alleles at the locus D21S11, consistent with Down syndrome. The profiles indicated that Mr. and Mrs. A were the biological parents of the child (PP>99.99%), although there were two complicating factors. First, one allele of the child (D8S1179) did not match either parent but could have arisen as a one-step mutation within the mother. Second, a three-allele pattern was found at the locus D3S1358 from the child's blood, hair and buccal samples, indicating that a second mutation had also occurred (Table 1). The DNA profile from the CV slide matched that of the child's, except that only two alleles at D3S1358 were present, suggesting that the third allele (allele 19) had arisen as a one-step somatic mutation in embryoblast cells during embryonic life (Table 1). The histological slide from the abortus also showed three alleles at D21S11, consistent with the original cytogenetic diagnosis of Down syndrome. The DNA profiles justified that the histological slide had been prepared from the abortus of Mrs. B. The genetic investigation and its statistical interpretation [1,2] therefore strongly support the hypothesis that the putative exchange of samples did not occur.

Table 1
Genotypes

Locus	Father "A"	Mother "A"	Child	CV Sample	Mother "B"	Abortus Sample
D3S1358	17-18	15-16	16-18-19	16-18	14-15	14-17
VWA	16-17	17-19	16-19	16-19	15-19	15-18
FGA	21-23	19-21	21-21	21-21	-	-
D8S1179	13-14	13-16	13-17	13-17	13-14	13-14
D21S11	30-32.2	30.2-31.2	30.2-31.2-32.2	30.2-31.2-32.2	28-29	28-29-30
D5S818	10-10	11-12	10-12	10-12	12-13	13-13
D13S317	9-12	12-12	12-12	12-12	-	-

Acknowledgements

Authors express their gratitude to Dr. Chris Tyler Smith and Dr. Charles Brenner for providing essential help with consultation on the subject.

References

[1] B. Egyed, S. Füredi, M. Angyal, L. Boutrand, A. Vandenberghe, J. Woller, Z. Pádár, Analysis of eight STR loci in two Hungarian populations, Int. J. Leg. Med. 113 (2000) 272–275.

[2] C. Brenner, Paternity calculation with 3-banded pattern, Available at: http://www.dna-view.com/3band.htm, 1999.

International Congress Series 1261 (2004) 488–490

www.ics-elsevier.com

Genetic inconsistencies in paternity cases

A.M. Di Lonardo*, M.B. Rodríguez Cardozo, M.V. Cólica, M.A. Abovich, C. Echenique

Banco Nacional de Datos Genéticos, Hospital Dr. C.G. Durand, J.B. Ambrosetti 743, 1405 Buenos Aires, Argentina

Abstract. Knowledge about mutation rates and mutational process of short tandem repeats (STRs), microsatellite loci used in paternity testing and forensic analysis, is crucial for the correct interpretation of resulting genetic profiles. Therefore, this study was carried out in 629 paternity cases, from 2000 to 2003, in which more than 2000 individuals were studied and genetic inconsistencies discovered during biological relationship testing.

Keywords: Paternity Testing; STRs; Microsatellites; Mutations

1. Introduction

Short tandem repeats (STRs) polymorphisms have become a powerful tool for human identification, and actually are the genetics markers more useful. However, as the STR markers are more mutable than the classical serological or molecular markers, parentage-testing laboratories are observing sporadic exclusion caused by mutations during maternal or paternal meiosis events.

Genetic inconsistencies discovered during biological relationship testing can add complexity to the analysis and resolution of a case [4–6].

2. Materials and methods

This study was carried out in 629 paternity cases, from 2000 to 2003 in which more than 2000 individuals were studied.

Genomic DNA was isolated from blood samples with salting out Miller's method [15]. The samples were amplified at the loci FGA, VWA, D3S1358, D5S818, D7S820, D8S1179, D13S317, D18S51 and D21S11 using the AmpFlSTR® Profiler Plus Kit (PE Biosystems, Foster City, CA) and at the loci CF1PO, TPOX, TH01, D3S1358, D7S820, and D16S539 using the AmpFlSTR® Cofiler TM kit (PE Biosystems). The same loci and the D2S1338 and D19S433 were amplified with the AmpFlSTR® Identifiler™ Kit (PE Biosystems) Samples were analyzed using the ABI PRISM® 310 Genetic Analyzer (PE Biosystems), according to the manufacturer's recommendations using as separation medium Performance

* Corresponding author. Tel.: +54-11-4982-1716; fax: +54-11-4-982-0625.
E-mail address: bndg@infovia.com.ar (A.M. Di Lonardo).

doi:10.1016/S0531-5131(03)01611-X

Table 1
The mutation rates at the individual STR loci

Locus	No. of meiosis		No. of mutation		Mutation rate		Type of mutation
	Male	Female	Male	Female	Male	Female	
vWA	562	309	1	–	0.18%	–	Addition
CSF1P0	562	309	1	–	0.18%	–	Deletion
D7S820	562	309	1	–	0.18%	–	Addition
D21S11	562	309	2	–	0.35%	–	Addition (2)
D8S1179	562	309	1	–	0.18%	–	Addition
FGA	562	309	1	–	0.18%	–	Deletion
D13S317	562	309	1	–	0.18%	–	Null allele
D2S1338	562	309	1	–	0.18%	–	Deletion
D3S1358	562	309	1	–	0.18%	–	Null allele

Optimized Polymer (POP) 4TM (PE Biosystems). The data was acquired by 1.0.2 software ABI PRISM® 310 Collection and analyzed by GeneScan® Analysis software 3.1 and Genotyper® 2.5 according to the manufacturer's recommendations [1–3,13,14].

3. Results

From more than 600 studies, only 1.6% showed inconsistent results for one of the locus investigated. These inconsistencies were present at vWA, CSF1P0, D7S820, D8S1179, FGA, D13S317, D2S1338 and D3S1358 loci. The mutations observed were the following ones:

1. Most of them were either gains or losses of complete repeats.
2. The number of additions was significantly major than the number of deletions.
3. We assume the presence of null alleles at D3S1358 and D13S317 in two paternity cases where the alleged father had a homozygous genotype.

The mutation rates at the individual STR loci are given in Table 1.

In these cases, we made the mathematical and statistical calculations of Paternity Probability with and without the presence of the mutation. In all of the cases, the percentage of Paternity Probability [10–12], including the inconsistency, was greater than 99,99% [7–9].

4. Conclusion

For this number of investigated markers, our exclusion criteria is based on the presence of more than three inconsistencies in the paternity investigation.

References

[1] K. Lazaruk, et al., (PE AB) genotyping of forensic short tandem repeat (STR) systems based on sizing precision in a capillary electrophoresis instrument, Electrophoresis 19 (1998) 86–93.

[2] O. Henegariu, et al., Multiplex PCR: critical parameters end step-by-step protocol, Biotechniques 23 (3) (1997) 504–511.

[3] J. Wallin, et al., TWAGDAM validation of AmpFlSTR® blue PCR amplification kit for forensic casework analysis, J. Forensic Sci. 43 (4) (1998) 1–17.
[4] B. Brinkman, et al., Mutation rate in human microsatellites: influence of structure and length of tandem repeats, Am. J. Hum Genet. 62 (1998) 1408–1415.
[5] Henke-Henke, Mutation in human microsatélites, Am. J. Hum Genet. 64 (1999) 1473.
[6] Annual report summary for 1999-AABB parentage Testing Standard Program Unit.
[7] A. Carracedo, Problemas Bioestadísticos en Genética Forense, Universidad Santiago de Compostela, España, 1996.
[8] Ch. Brenner, Symbolic kinship program, Genetics 145 (1997) 535–542.
[9] Ch. Brenner, et al., Calculation of paternity probabilities from multilocus DNA profile, Electrophoresis 15 (1994) 170–174.
[10] Ch. Brenner, www.dnaview.com.
[11] Ch. Brenner, Calculation of paternity index, Inclusion Probabilities in Paternity Testing. Amer. Assoc. of Blood Banks-Arlington, pp. 632–638.
[12] Ch. Brenner, Kinship analysis by DNA when there are many possibilities, in: G. Sensabough, et al., (Eds), Progress in Forensic Genetics 8.
[13] AmpFlSTR®Cofiler™-Profiler™, PCR Amplification Kit User's Manual, Applied Biosystems, Foster City, CA, 2001.
[14] AmpFlSTR®Identifiler™, PCR Amplification Kit User's Manual, Applied Biosystems, Foster City, CA, 2001.
[15] S.A. Miller, et al., Nucleic Acids Res. 16 (1988) 1215.

International Congress Series 1261 (2004) 491–493

www.ics-elsevier.com

Human identification using DNA purified from residues in used toothbrushes

M.R. Jobim[a], F. Gamio[a], G. Ewald[a], M. Jobim[a], L.F. Jobim[a,b,*]

[a] *Laboratório DNA Reference Ltda, Pôrto Alegre, Brazil*

[b] *Serviço de Imunologia, Hospital de Clínicas de Porto Alegre, Universidade Federal do Rio Grande do Sul, Pôrto Alegre, Brazil*

Abstract. This article describes human identification using DNA purified from residues in used toothbrushes. © 2003 Published by Elsevier B.V.

Keywords: DNA; Toothbrush

1. Introduction

There are cases of paternity and maternity investigation where there is no available biological material to reconstruct the genetic profile of the alleged father and/or mother. In these cases, exhumation is usually the necessary step in order to determine sibling correlation. Obtaining material from exhumed bodies is not always possible besides being complex technically, bureaucratically and psychologically. In order to find more amenable alternatives, we tested toothbrushes used by subjects as source of DNA.

Our first case was a woman who had been deceased 6 months earlier and whose putative son brought in some of her hairs for analysis. He also brought the woman's last toothbrush (Fig. 1).

2. Materials and methods

By using the Salting Out technique and NaOH treatment method, we extracted the DNA from the toothbrush and hair roots, respectively (Fig. 2). The genetic profile was obtained with AmpFLSTR Identifiler PCR Amplification KIT (Applied Biosystems ABI, Foster City, CA).

* Corresponding author. Serviço de Imunologia, Hospital de Clínicas de Porto Alegre, Universidade Federal do Rio Grande do Sul, Rua Ramiro Barcelos, 2350, Pôrto Alegre, RS 90035-903, Brazil. Tel.: +55-51-32221350; fax: +55-51-33465009.

E-mail address: jobim.ez@terra.com.br (L.F. Jobim).

doi:10.1016/j.ics.2003.11.013

MATERNITY TESTING

STR	Mother	Alleged Son
D8S1179	13/14	14/15
D21S11	29/30	28/29
D7S820	8/11	12
CSF1PO	11/12	10/12
D3S1358	15/17	15
TH01	7/9	9/9.3
D13S317	11/12	10/11
D16S539	9/11	12/14
D2S1338	17/22	19/24
D19S433	13/15	14/16.2
vWA31	16/17	18/19
TPOX	7/10	8
D18S51	16/19	14/16
FGA	20/25	22/25
D5S818	11/12	10/11
Amelogenina	XX	XY

Fig. 1. STRs in alleged mother and child.

To test the reproducibility of toothbrush as a source of genetic material for use in human identification, we sampled toothbrushes used by 33 different individuals while normally collecting their peripheral blood sample. The labelled STR's were fractionated with an ABI Prism 310 Genetic Analyzer (ABI) and the profile analysed with Genotyper (ABI) after image obtention with GeneScan (ABI) (Fig. 3).

3. Conclusions

We could observe that in six loci analysed, the alleged mother did not match to those of the putative son. However, the "hair" and "toothbrush" genetic profiles matched indicating that both belonged to the same woman.

Fig. 2. Toothbrushes.

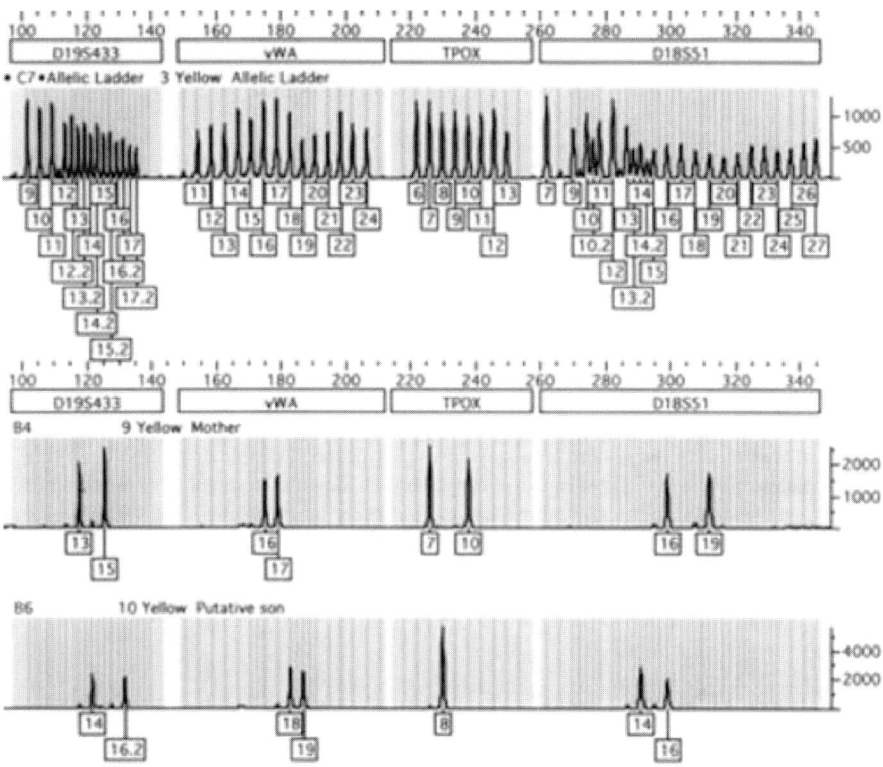

Fig. 3. STRs in ABI.

We were able to obtain 23 STR profiles out of the 33 toothbrushes samples or success rate of about 70% (Fig. 4). Moreover, all 23 STR profiles matched the profiles obtained with the respective blood samples.

In conclusion, used toothbrush is a viable alternative source for obtaining DNA samples. In most cases, there are enough preserved biological material in used toothbrushes to give DNA in quantities and quality good enough for all kinds of DNA work related to human identification.

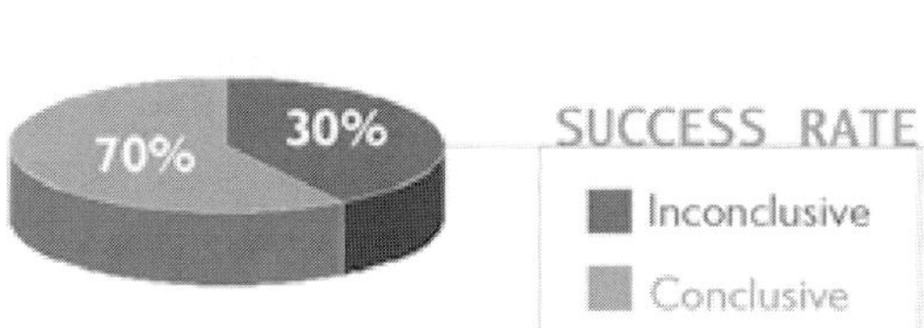

Fig. 4. Success rate.

International Congress Series 1261 (2004) 494–496
www.ics-elsevier.com

Identification of a carbonized body by DNA profiling

N. Staiti[a], S. Spitaleri[a], C. Vecchio[b], L. Saravo[a,*]

[a] *Laboratory of Molecular Biology, Raggruppamento Carabinieri Investigazioni Scientifiche (RaCIS), Reparto di Messina, S.S. 114 Km 6400, Tremestieri, 98128 Messina, Sicilia, Italy*
[b] *Technical Laboratory, Raggruppamento Carabinieri Investigazioni Scientifiche (RaCIS), Rome, Italy*

Abstract. In the South of Italy, there are many cases of kidnapped people that, after a longtime, are found completely burned in order to cancel every trace. The aim of the present work is to identify the body of a man found inside a car, without head, completely burned down. The DNA typing was performed on a bone taken from the backbone, as the internal organs were not useful for traditional analysis due to their high DNA degradation. For comparison, we obtained DNA specimen from saliva of hypothetical related and personal effect samples of the victim.

Keywords: Human identification; Burnt tissue; Identifiler; DNA profiling

1. Introduction

In south of Sicily (Italy), a man was found in a car, completely burnt down and without head. It was very difficult for the medical examiner to identify the body as no marks were found for recognition.

The police had a list of few missed people, with particular interest focused on a man that was supposed dead 4 months before.

Due to the bad condition of the body, it was quite hard to choose the samples to be analyzed. We finally decided to use a lombar vertebra, heavily contaminated by burnt material from the car, for the DNA extraction [1].

2. Materials and methods

DNA extraction from the unidentified body was carried out on a vertebra; the bone was washed for 3 h in ultrasonic bath and the burnt material was totally removed. Later the bone was cut and a small part of tissue taken from the inner part of the bone was used for the nuclear DNA analysis. This analysis was performed with I.Q. procedure "Tissue and Hair extraction Kit Protocol (Promega)" [2]; the protocol includes simple steps for DNA extraction by an Incubation buffer, DNA capture by using a special resin, DNA washing

* Corresponding author. Tel.: +39-905725388; fax: +39-905725690.
E-mail address: kunitz@libero.it (L. Saravo).

0531-5131/
doi:10.1016/S0531-5131(03)01542-5

by a washing Buffer and then DNA eluition by an Eluition Buffer. The samples (less to 0.5 mg of tissue) were then put into a 1.5-ml tube with the Incubation buffer, at 56 °C for 3 h, with 50 μl twice of PK (20 mg/ml) and 100 μl of 1 M DTT. For the following steps, we used the IQ protocol.

DNA from saliva samples belonging to the parents and the brothers and from toothbrush recovered into the house of the man of the missing man were extracted with chelex treatment (Biorad) [3].

The amplification of DNA extracted was performed by use of "AmpFLSTR Identifiler" kit (Applied Biosystem), in 23 μl final reaction in a Perkin Elmer Gene Amp PCR System cycler 2400 and 9700. The product of reaction after 28 cycles was then analyzed and further repurification with Microcon 100 Amicon as performed to follow [4].

According to the kit protocol, positive and negative controls were enclosed during the amplification step. Automatic allele designation was achieved by the use of Genotyper v.3.7 software. (Applied Biosystems).

3. Results and discussion

The results of the DNA fingerprinting are reported below (Table 1). It was possible to uniquely identify the burnt body. The analysis was found to be faster than other methods used for similar applications.

The sample, a lombar vertebra, taken by the medical examiner was found to be a good source for DNA extraction. Moreover, the cells into the bone and their DNA content were well protected by both the burnt material dropped from the car and some other tissues (fats) from the body.

The personal identification was performed by comparing the DNA profile with those from the victim's tooth brush and from paternity tests.

Table 1
The results of the DNA fingerprinting

Locus	Father	X	Mother
Amelogenina	X–Y	X–Y	X–X
D8S1179	13–14	13–13	11–13
D21S11	25.2–32.2	29–32.2	29–31.2
D18S51	14–21	14–17	15–17
D3S1358	16–18	15–18	15–16
VWA	16–17	17–19	18–19
FGA	25–25	22–25	22–22
D5S818	11–11	11–12	12–12
D13S317	11–12	11–11	11–11
D7S820	8–10	10–10	9–10
THO1	8–9.3	6–9.3	6–9
TPOX	8–8	8–11	11–11
CSF1PO	11–11	11–11	10–11
D16S539	10–10	9–10	9–10
D2S1338	18–20	18–19	19–20
D19S433	14–14	13–14	13–16

The paternity test on the DNA samples from missing man's family showed that the genetic profile from the carbonized body was compatible with the DNA profiles from the parents. The probability of paternity calculated by using Sicily allele frequencies was 0.9999998 (99.9998%) [5].

Acknowledgements

This research was supported by Dr. Matteo Donghi for the statistics application in the paternity calculations.

References

[1] M. Holland, Extraction of DNA from Dried Skeletal Remains, Workshop June 9, 1998, Innsbruck.
[2] DNA IQ™ Tissue and Hair Extraction Kit. User's Manual, Technical Bulletin, vol. 307, Promega, 2002.
[3] P.S. Walsh, D.A. Metzger, R. Higuchi, Chelex 100 as a medium for simple extraction of DNA for PCR-based Typing from forensic material, BioTechniques 10 (1991) 506.
[4] Amp*Fl*STR Identifiler PCR amplification kit, User's manual, PE Biosystems, 2001.
[5] J. Butler, Forensic DNA Typing, Academic Press, San Diego, CA, 2001.

International Congress Series 1261 (2004) 497–498

www.ics-elsevier.com

Localization of DNA on a dishcloth used as a strangulation tool allowed perpetrator identification within a family

Isabella Spinetti[a], Chiara Toni[a], Silvano Presciuttini[b,*], Ranieri Domenici[a]

[a] Unit of Legal Medicine, School of Medicine, University of Pisa, Pisa, Italy
[b] Inherited Disease Research Branch, NHGRI, NIH, Baltimore, MD, USA

Abstract. A case report of a domestic murder is presented. The victim was strangled with a kitchen cloth; the suspect, victim's ex-husband, who still frequented the house, admitted of having used that cloth, though to dry his hands only. The pattern of DNA amplified from the cloth, belonging to both victim and suspect, allowed suspect's version to be rejected. © 2003 Published by Elsevier B.V.

Keywords: Strangulation; DNA pattern; STR

1. Introduction

In cases of strangulation by ligature, it is often possible to extract DNA of both the victim and the assailant from the tool used in the homicide [1,2]. In the case presented here, the dead body of a woman 37 years old was found on the floor of her bedroom whit a dishcloth knotted around her neck. Postmortem examination ascribed death to asphyxia. The last individual to see her alive was her ex-husband. He admitted to have had an altercation with her, from which he had suffered some scratches (he showed finger nail scratches on his face), but denied any involvement in the homicide. He also claimed to have used a kitchen cloth to wipe his hands, so that it was not unlikely that his DNA could be found on the body of evidence.

2. Materials and methods

DNA was extracted from blood and nails of the victim, from a cigarette butt smoked by the suspect, and from samples of the cloth. In particular, small fragments were obtained from the cloth edges clutched by the murderer, whereas other fragments were randomly taken from the center and from the two other edges. DNA was extracted using the QIAamp DNA mini kit (Qiagen, Hilden, Germany). We use Profiler plus AND Cofiler plus kit for the

* Corresponding author. Postal address: Via Roma no. 55, Scuola Medica, U.O. Medicina Legale, 56126 Pisa, Italy. Tel.: +39-50-560527; fax: +39-50-560677.

E-mail address: ranieri@biomed.unipi.it (R. Domenici).

0531-5131/ © 2003 Published by Elsevier B.V.
doi:10.1016/S0531-5131(03)01642-X

Table 1
The victim's DNA profile (2nd column), suspect's DNA profile (4th column) and the mixture of DNA obtained from the cloth edges

DNA markers	Victim	Dishcloth	Ex-husband
D3S1358	15–17	14–15–17	14–14
vWA	15–17	14–15–16–17	14–16
FGA	20–25	20–23–25–26	23–26
D8S1179	12–15	11–12–13–15	11–13
D21S11	30–31	29–30–31	29–31
D18S51	12–17	12–13–14–17	13–14
D5S818	12–12	12–13	12–13
D13S317	11–11	11–13	11–13
D7S820	11–12	8–11–12	8–12
D16S539	9–12	9–11–12	9–11
TH01	8–8	7–8–9.3	7–9.3
TPOX	8–11	8–11	8–8
CSF1PO	11–12	10–11–12	10–10
AMEL (sex)	XX	XY	XY

amplification of 13 STR loci; electrophoresis was carried out in the ABI 310 automated sequencer (Applied Biosystem) following standard protocols. The DNA profiles were compared with those of the victim and the suspect. The biostatistical analysis of the mixed profile was in accordance with Ref. [3], assuming that the victim was one of the contributors.

3. Results

Both a profile identical to that of the suspect (5th right finger) and other profiles compatible with a mixture of victim's and suspect's genotypes (1st right finger and 2nd, 3rd, 4th left fingers) were obtained from the nails of the victim. A mixture compatible with a combination of DNA of both victim and suspect ($LR = 1.9 \times 10^{11}$) was also obtained from the edges of the cloth held by the murderer; on the contrary, only victim's DNA was obtained from all other cloth fragments (Table 1).

4. Discussion

Whereas the DNA evidence from the nails of the victim was compatible with the statement of the suspect, the localization of DNA on the cloth rejected his version. In fact, it was extremely improbable that the ex-husband could have used only the diagonally opposite ends of the cloth to dry his hands, precisely the same ends used by the murderer in the strangulation. In addition, no alleles of anyone other than the victim and the suspect appeared in the mixed profiles (the suspect afterwards confessed to the crime).

This case is an example of the importance of studying the distribution of DNA on crime weapons.

References

[1] M. Bohnert, M. Faller-Marquardt, S. Lutz, R. Amberg, H.J. Weisser, S. Pollak, Transfer of biological traces in cases of hanging and ligature strangulation, Forensic Sci. Int. 116 (2–3) (2001 Feb. 15) 107–115.

[2] R. Szibor, M. Michael, I. Plate, D. Krause, Efficiency of forensic mtDNA analysis. Case examples demonstrating the identification of traces, Forensic Sci. Int. 113 (1–3) (2000 Sept. 11) 71–78.

[3] I.W. Evett, B.S. Weir, Interpreting DNA Evidence, Sinauer, Sunderland, MA, 1998.

ELSEVIER

International Congress Series 1261 (2004) 499–501

www.ics-elsevier.com

Loss of heterozygosity and microsatellite instability of forensically used STR markers in human cervical carcinoma

J. Edelmann[a,*], R. Lessig[a], S. Hering[b], L.-C. Horn[c]

[a] *Institut für Rechtsmedizin, Universität Leipzig, Leipzig, Germany*
[b] *Institut für Rechtsmedizin, Technische Universität Dresden, Dresden, Germany*
[c] *Institut für Pathologie, Universität Leipzig, Leipzig, Germany*

Abstract. Analysing tumor materials and normal tissues from 27 patients with carcinoma of the uterine cervix for loss of heterozygosity (LOH) and microsatellite instability (MSI) on 11 chromosome X loci (DXS6800, DXS6807, DXS8377, DXS101, DXS7424, GATA172D05, DXS10011, DXS7130, DXS6803, HPRTB, and ARA), we found the highest frequency of LOH for DXS10011 (20%) and ARA (17%). MSI was seen up to 11% for DXS10011. Mostly, X-chromosomal LOH and MSI were observed at Xq28 and Xq12. Testing 14 autosomal loci (D3S1358, vWA, D16S539, D2S1338, D8S1179, D21S11, D18S51, D19S433, TH01, FGA, SE33, D3S1768, D3S2456, and D17S1537), 4–40% of the informative cases represented LOH. The highest frequency was seen for markers in 3p (21–40%), suggesting putative tumor suppressor gene at this region. © 2003 Elsevier B.V. All rights reserved.

Keywords: Cervical carcinoma; Loss of heterozygosity; X-chromosome

1. Introduction

The mutation rates of polymorphic microsatellites are well known, which makes the risk of mistakes for forensic application calculable. The stability of STR alleles, however, is not realised, for example, in well-known trinucleotide expansions and many carcinomas.

The prevalence of human papillomavirus (HPV) infection in cervical carcinoma (CX) is high, but only 2% of infected women develop high dysplasia or invasive carcinoma. Thus there must exist additional factors needed for tumor development resulting in genomic instability. Common forms of genomic instability are loss of heterozygosity (LOH) and microsatellite instability (MSI). Among chromosomes involving LOH or MSI, the X-

* Corresponding author. Tel.: +49-341-9715111; fax: +49-341-9715109.
E-mail address: edej@medizin.uni-leipzig.de (J. Edelmann).

doi:10.1016/S0531-5131(03)01717-5

chromosome may be affected in ovarian carcinomas [1], but limited information exists for CX [2,3].

2. Materials and methods

DNA was extracted from fresh, snap-frozen materials ($n = 17$), tissue blocks containing formalin-fixed and paraffin-embedded tumor materials ($n = 10$), and normal tissues from patients ($n = 27$) with carcinoma of the uterine cervix, surgically staged as pT1b1 to pT2b. We used the QIAamp tissue kit and the nonorganic Chelex 100 extraction protocol recently published [4]. LOH was assessed by polymerase chain reaction (PCR) analysis of the matched pairs of normal and tumor DNA with polymorphic microsatellite markers. Resulting PCR products were detected by capillary electrophoresis (ABI 310). Loss of one allele of a polymorphic marker or a very strong decrease in signal intensity of one allele in tumor DNA was considered as evidence for LOH. MSI was identified when novel alleles of microsatellite markers appeared in tumor DNA compared to the matching germ line DNA [5].

3. Results and discussion

Genetic alterations could be detected in 19 of 27 patients (70%) in at least one of the investigated STR loci; nine patients represented LOH as well as MSI, nine patients represented either LOH or MSI, and one patient represented only MSI. For chromosome X loci, we found LOH up to 20% of informative cases (Table 1). The highest frequency of LOH could be detected for DXS10011, ARA, and DXS8377. X-chromosomal MSI was seen mainly for DXS10011 and DXS8377. Thus the most observed X-chromosomal alterations were detected in the region at Xq28 and Xq12. Testing of 14 autosomal loci of different chromosomal location up to 40% of informative cases represented LOH (Table 2). The highest frequency was seen for markers in 3p (D3S1768: 40%; D3S1358: 24%; D3S2456: 21%), 4q28 (FGA: 24%), 11p (TH01: 23%), and 19q (D19S433: 20%). Genetic alterations for D19S433 (19q12–

Table 1
Chromosome X marker testing (27 patients)

Marker	Number of cases (LOH positive/informative)	LOH (%)	MSI (%)
DXS6800	1/20	5.0	3.7
DXS6807	2/14	14.3	0
DXS8377	4/26	15.4	7.4
DXS101	3/24	12.5	0
DXS7424	1/26	3.8	0
GATA172D05	1/22	4.5	3.7
DXS10011	5/25	20.0	11.1
DXS7130	2/21	9.5	0
HPRTB	1/19	5.3	3.7
DXS6803	1/21	4.8	0
ARA	4/23	17.4	0

Table 2
Autosomal STR marker testing (27 patients)

Marker	Number of cases (LOH positive/informative)	LOH (%)	MSI (%)
SE33	0/25	0	7.4
D3S1358	5/21	23.8	3.7
D3S1768	8/20	40.0	0
D3S2456	4/19	21.0	0
D17S1537	2/21	9.5	0
VWA	1/24	4.2	3.7
D16S539	1/20	5.0	0
D2S1338	3/24	12.5	0
D8S1179	1/24	4.2	0
D21S11	0/23	0	3.7
D18S51	2/25	8.0	0
D19S433	4/20	20.0	3.7
TH01	6/26	23.1	0
FGA	6/25	24.0	0

13.1), coupled with LOH for the FGA locus (4q28) and DXS10011 (Xq28), were found in four patients (15%).

4. Conclusion

LOH in CX on several genetic loci is a common phenomenon, even in CIN lesions, suggesting the existence of tumor suppressor genes in these regions. Further studies are necessary to identify chromosomal regions, which are associated with tumor progression and metastatic diseases, or in alteration of the susceptibility of the host for HPV infection. Furthermore, great care should be taken in the evaluation of typing results obtained from clinical tissue specimens, in particular when no reference samples are available, because genetic instability is a very common event observed in different tumors and the STRs used for individual identification could sometimes be affected.

References

[1] C. Choi, M.H. Kim, S.W. Juhng, Loss of heterozygosity at chromosome Xp22.2–p22.13 and Xq26.1–q27.1 in human breast carcinomas, J. Korean Med. Sci. 13 (1998) 311–316.

[2] R. Chuaqui, M. Silva, M. Emmert-Buck, Allelic deletion mapping on chromosome 6q and X chromosome inactivation clonality patterns in cervical intraepithelial neoplasia and invasive carcinoma, Gynecol. Oncol. 80 (2001) 364–371.

[3] L. Cheng, J. Gu, T.M. Ulbright, et al, Precise microdissection of bladder carcinomas reveals divergent tumor subclones in the same tumor, Cancer 94 (2002) 104–110.

[4] B. Legrand, P. de Mazancourt, M. Durigon, et al, DNA genotyping of unbuffered formalin fixed paraffin embedded tissue, Forensic Sci. Int. 125 (2002) 205–211.

[5] R.C. Boland, S.N. Thibodeau, S.R. Hamilton, et al, A National Cancer Institute workshop on microsatellite instability for cancer detection and familial predisposition: development of international criteria for the determination of microsatellite instability in colorectal cancer, Cancer Res. 58 (1998) 5248–5257.

International Congress Series 1261 (2004) 502–504

www.ics-elsevier.com

Maternity testing in a chimerical child

M.B. Rodríguez Cardozo, M.V. Cólica, M.A. Abovich, A. Szöcs, A.M. Di Lonardo*

Immunologia, Banco Nacional de Datos Genéticos, Hospital Dr. C. G. Durand, Juan B. Ambrosetti, 743 Planta Baja 1405 Buenos Aires, Argentina

Received 5 September 2003; received in revised form 12 September 2003; accepted 17 September 2003

Abstract. Human congenital chimerism is due to the coexistence of two genetically different cell lines either in the whole body or limited to the blood. We present a case of maternity in which the alleged child has ambiguous genitalia, and chimerism was suspected. The maternity was dubious and the father was not available for the study. STR typing of the child revealed the presence of X an Y chromosomes at Amelogenin locus and a double maternal and paternal alleles contribution in certain autosomical loci. We could not exclude maternal relationship between the alleged mother and the child. Molecular analysis performed with highly discriminating STR systems allowed us to clarify the origin of a chimerical individual.

Keywords: Maternity testing; STRs; Chimerism; Typing

1. Introduction

Human congenital chimerism is due to the coexistence of two genetically different cell lines either in the whole body or limited to the blood. These cells are from different genetic patterns originated from two or more zygotes. Within permanent chimerical individuals "blood chimeras" or "twin chimeras", which result from in-uterus junctions of twins and "whole body chimeras" where the coexistence of the different cell lines is not restricted to hematological cells but spread over various tissues, can be distinguished [1–3].

Whole body chimerism (tetragametic or dispermic chimerism) is characterized by double paternal contribution of markers. In very rare cases, double maternal contribution has also been detected [2].

We present a case of maternity in which the alleged child had ambiguous genitalia, and chimerism was suspected. The maternity was dubious and the father was not available for the study.

* Corresponding author. Tel.: +5411-4982-1716; fax: +5411-4982-0625.
E-mail address: bndg@infovia.com.ar (A.M. Di Lonardo).

doi:10.1016/S0531-5131(03)01624-8

Table 1
STR typing for mother and child

Locus	Child	Alleged mother
D8S1179	14/13/12/11	11/12
D21S11	31/30/29	31/30
D7S820	12/11/9	11/9
CSF1P0	10/10	10/10
D3S1358	18/15	18/15
TH01	6/6	6/6
D13S317	12/11/9	9/9
D16S539	11/10/9	11/9
D2S1338	19/19	21/19
D19S433	15/12	15/12
vWA	17/16/15	16/15
TPOX	12/11	12/8
D18S51	16/13/12	18/13
D5S818	13/11/10	11/10
FGA	25/23/21/19	23/21
Amelogenin	X/Y	X/X

2. Materials and methods

Genomic DNA was isolated from blood samples with salting out Miller's method. The samples were amplified with the AmpFlSTR™ Identifiler Kit (PE Biosystems, Foster City, CA). Samples were analyzed using the ABI PRISM™ 310 Genetic Analyzer (PE Biosystems), according to the manufacturer's recommendations using as separation medium Performance Optimized Polymer (POP) 4™ (PE Biosystems). The data was acquired by 1.0.2 software ABI PRISM™ 310 Collection and analyzed by GeneScan® Analysis software 3.1 and Genotyper® 2.5 according to the manufacturer's recommendations [4,5].

3. Results

STR typing for mother and child are given in the Table 1.

4. Discussion

STR typing revealed the presence of two maternal and two paternal alleles at two loci in blood of the proposita. In another locus (D13S317), two paternal alleles were present, while the other 11 systems investigated revealed double maternal contribution.

Amelogenin showed the presence of a Y chromosome in misbalance with the X chromosome.

5. Conclusion

We could not exclude maternal relationship between the alleged mother and the child. We confirmed the double maternal contribution, and the possibility that the chimerism of our proposita was the result of the double parental alleles contribution [6,7].

Molecular analysis performed with highly discriminating STR systems allowed us to clarify the origin of a chimerical individual.

References

[1] Yu. Neng, et al., N. Engl. J. Med. 346 (20) (2002) 1546–1552.
[2] J.C. Giltay, et al., Am. J. Hum. Genet. 62 (1998) 937–940.
[3] A.J. Green, et al., J. Med. Genet. 31 (10) (1994 Oct.) 816–817.
[4] K. Lazaruk, et al., Electrophoresis 19 (1998) 86–93.
[5] O. Henegariu, et al., BioTechniques 23 (3) (1997) 504–511.
[6] A. Milde, et al., Int. J. Leg. Med. 112 (5) (1999) 333–335.
[7] L.M. Repas-Humpe, et al., Ann. Hematol. 78 (9) (1999 Sept.) 431–434.

ELSEVIER

International Congress Series 1261 (2004) 505–507

www.ics-elsevier.com

Microsatellite instability detection in hereditary colorectal cancer: is it possible in a public hospital?

S. Filippini[a], G. Jankilevich[b], M. Barugel[c], O. Santapá[a], S. Valente[a], E. Roca[c], A.M. Di Lonardo[a,*]

[a] *Banco Nacional de Datos Genéticos, Unidad Inmunología Hospital Carlos G. Durand, J.B. Ambrosetti 743 (1405), Buenos Aires, Argentina*

[b] *Servicio de Oncología del Hospital Carlos G. Durand, J.B. Ambrosetti 743 (1405), Buenos Aires, Argentina*

[c] *Servicio de Oncología del Hospital Bonorino Udaondo, Buenos Aires, Argentina*

Abstract. Microsatellite analysis is emerging as an important tool in the study of cancer. The addition of novel microsatellite alleles is referred as microsatellite instability (MSI) indicating possible mutations in cellular DNA repair mechanism. The detection of these genetic changes demonstrates the presence of a clonal population of cells that share altered genetic information, which is characteristic of cancer cells. In this study, we analyzed the five MSI markers: D2S123, D5S346, D17S250, BAT 25, BAT 26 recommended at the 1997 National Cancer Institute in a patient with suspicious familiar history of Non-Polyposic Hereditary Colorectal Cancer (NHPCC), Lynch syndrome, and high instability MSI-H was confirmed.

Keywords: Colorectal cancer; DNA; PCR; Microsatellite instability; NHPCC

1. Introduction

Colorectal cancer is one of the principal causes of cancer-related death in Caucasian society. Non-Polyposic Hereditary Colorectal Cancer (NPHCC) [1–3], one of the hereditary syndromes related with this disease, is an autosomal dominant disorder accounting for about 3–5% of all colorectal cancer cases caused by mutation of one of the DNA mismatch repair genes. Clinical features include familiar history of colorectal, endometrial, ovarian and transitional tumors. The genetic hallmark is microsatellite instability (MSI), a replication error in genomic repeated sequences of one or two nucleotides present all along chromosomes and DNA sequences enlarges or gets shorter, but cells have mechanisms to repair this damage. HNPCC is cause by germiline mutation of the DNA mismatch repair genes (hMLH1, hMLH2, hPMS1, hPMS2, hMSH6).

* Corresponding author. Tel.: +54-11-4982-1716; fax: +54-11-4982-0625.
E-mail address: bndg@infovia.com.ar (A.M. Di Lonardo).

doi:10.1016/S0531-5131(03)01702-3

Microsatellite instability (MSI) is found in the colorectal cancer DNA of most individuals with germiline mismatch repair genes mutations [4,5].

The aim of our study was to detect MSI in a patient with history that suggests Lynch syndrome (NPHCC) [1–3].

2. Materials and methods

A patient with suspicious familiar history of Lynch syndrome signed an informed consent form. DNA sample was extracted by salting out method [7,8], tumoral DNA from paraffin-embedded tissue with QIAmp DNA kit (QIAGEN). DNA samples were amplified in a Perkin Elmer Gene Amp PCR System 9700® (PE Applied Biosystems) for the following loci D2S123, D5S346. D17S250, BAT-25, BAT-26, BAT-40, TP53, D18S58, D18S69, D13S175, and D10S197 markers recommended at the 1997 National Cancer Institute (NCI)-sponsored conference on MSI [4]. The PCR products were detected and

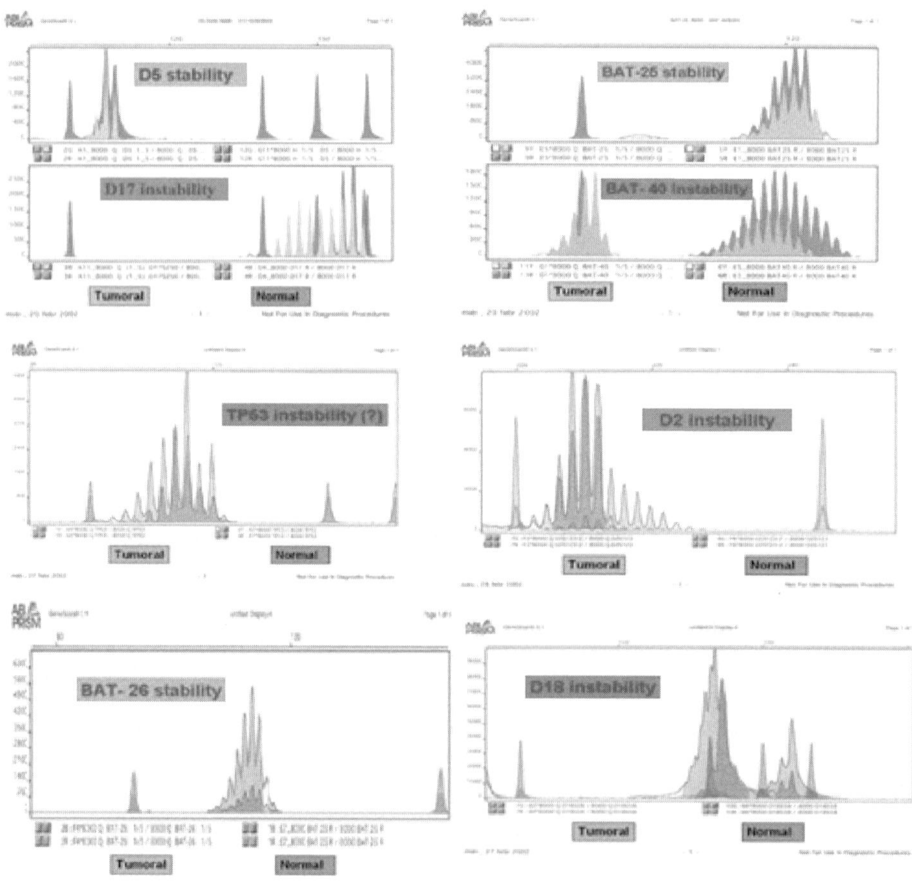

Fig. 1. Microsatellite markers studied.

analyzed using Capillary electrophoresis in an ABI PRISM™ 310 Genetic Analyzer and GeneScan® Analysis software 3.1 (PE Applied Biosystems) [7,8].

3. Results

In 1997, the National Cancer Institute Workshop on Hereditary Nonpolyposis Colorectal Cancer Syndrome proposed specific markers for MSI testing [4,6]. The microsatellite markers used for the diagnosis of MSI recommended by NCI were: D2S123, D5S346, D17S250, BAT-25, BAT-26 and defined MSI-high (MSI-H) when the tumor DNA sample present shifting of at least two of the five loci.

MSI-low (MSI-L) is identified by only one marker showing instability and more loci have to be analyzed. MSI testing using these markers should be performed on the tumor tissue of individuals who meet the Bethesda criteria [4], modified putatively affected with HNPCC. A result of MSI-high in tumor DNA usually leads to consideration testing by sequencing for mutation in DNA repair genes. In our case, the tumor sample of the patient showed MSI at two loci: D2S123, and D17S050, which means high instability (MSI-H), but also other microsatellite markers were studied and loci BAT 40 and TP 53, were also instable (Fig. 1).

4. Conclusions

The detection of MSI was successful and possible in our hospital; we could detect MSI-H in the patient studied. The method based on capillary electrophoresis and fluorescent markers detect 10% of tumoral cells in the sample, which means that the high sensitivity of this technology compares to the standard polyacrylamide gel electrophoresis and radioactive detection. Consensus panel and expert opinion suggests evaluation for MSI as the first step in the genetic work-up of pedigrees suspected to be affected by HNPCC.

References

[1] H.T. Lynch, T.C. Smyrk, P. Watson, et al., Genetics, natural history, tumor spectrum, and pathology of hereditary nonpolyposis colorectal cancer, an updated review, Gastroenterology 104 (1993) 1535–1549.

[2] H.T. Lynch, T.C. Smyrk, Hereditary nonpolyposis colorectal cancer (Lynch syndrome). An updated review, Cancer 78 (1996) 1149–1167.

[3] H.T. Lynch, T.C. Smyrk, An update of Lynch syndrome, Current Opinion in Oncology 10 (1998) 349–356.

[4] M.A. Rodriguez Bigas, C.R Boland, S.R. Hamilton, D.E. Henson, J.R. Jass, P.M. Khan, H. Lynch, M. Perucho, T. Smyrk, L. Sobin, S. Srivastava, A national cancer institute workshop on hereditary nonpoliposis colorectal cancer institute workshop on hereditary nonpoliposis colorectal cancer syndrome: meeting highlights and Bethesda guidelines, Journal of the National Cancer Institute 89 (1997) 1758–1762.

[5] L.A. Aattonen, R. Salovaara, P. Kristo, F. Cauzian, A. Hemminki, P. Peltomaki, R.B. Chadivick, M. Kaariainen, M. Eskelinen, M. Jarvinen, J.P. Mecklin, A. de la Chapelle, Incidence of hereditary nonpoliposis colorectal cancer and the feasibility of molecular screening for the disease, New England Journal of Medicine 338 (1998) 1481–1487.

[6] Efficient detection of hereditary nonpolyposis colorectal cancer gene carriers by screening for tumor microsatellite instability before germiline genetic testing, Gastroenterology 120 (2001) 21–30.

[7] K.B. Mullis, et al., Methods Enzymol. 155 (1987) 335–350.

[8] S.A. Miller, et al., Nucleic Acid Research 16 (1988) 1215.

International Congress Series 1261 (2004) 508–510

www.ics-elsevier.com

Mosaicism as a possible reason for poor amplification of amelogenin-Y in three human male individuals

E.M. Dauber[a,*], S. Wenda[a], B. Glock[b], G. Dorner[a], W.R. Mayr[a]

[a] *Division of Blood Group Serology, Department of Blood Group Serology and Transfusion Medicine, University of Vienna, Medical School, Vienna 1090, Austria*

[b] *Laboratory for Molecular Biology, Blood Donation Centre for Vienna, Lower Austria and Burgenland, Austrian Red Cross, Vienna, Austria*

Abstract. Unusual peak height ratios of the two amplified fragments in the X–Y homologous amelogenin gene in two multiplex STR kits (16 loci) required further investigations in three male Caucasoid individuals. Mosaicism is discussed as a possible reason for these findings.

Keywords: Amelogenin; Mosaicism; Peak height ratio; Peak imbalance

1. Introduction

A complete loss of the Y-specific PCR product of the X and Y homologous amelogenin gene [1] has already been detected in 0.018% of the males in the Austrian national DNA database. This loss was suggested to be due to a deletion on the Y-encoded gene [2]. Further failures of the amelogenin sex test have been found in Indians, which were found to be due to large deletions on the p-arm of the Y-chromosome [3].

This study reports three cases of unusual peak height ratios of the two amplified fragments of the amelogenin gene in three male Caucasoid individuals and suggests possible reasons for this phenomenon. The first case reported is a monozygotic twin suffering from a malign lymphoma (B-CLL). STR loci were investigated in our laboratory to find out whether the patient (*421) and his healthy brother (*420) were monozygotic or dizygotic twins, which is, in addition to HLA typing, relevant for bone marrow transplantation. Further two healthy, unrelated male Caucasoid individuals (*1514, *1703) showed the same phenomenon. All persons investigated were of normal male appearance.

* Corresponding author. Klinische Abteilung für Blutgruppenserologie, Waehringer Guertel 18-20, A-1090 Wien, Austria. Tel.: +43-1-40400-5320; fax: +43-1-40400-5321.

E-mail address: eva.maria.dauber@univie.ac.at (E.M. Dauber).

doi:10.1016/S0531-5131(03)01658-3

2. Materials and methods

DNA was extracted from blood samples using the salting out or the Chelex method. Multiplex PCR was carried out with the AmpFlSTR Identifiler PCR Amplification Kit (Applied Biosystems) and the Geneprint Powerplex 16 System (Promega), which applies published primer sequences [4]. A singleplex amelogenin PCR with the original primers [1], a DYS19 PCR [5] and the amplification of a male-specific SRY marker situated in the Y-chromosomal sex determining region [6] were added. The singleplex PCR products were detected by horizontal native polyacrylamide gel electrophoresis and silver staining. More Y-chromosomal STR loci including another amelogenin sex test were investigated with the genRES DYSplex-1 (Amelogenin, DYS390, DYS385 (I/II), DYS389 (I+II), DYS391) and the genRES DYSplex-2 (DYS393, DYS19, DYS389 (I/II), DYS392) kit (Serac, Germany).

Modified amelogenin-Y specific primers (GenBank acc. no. M55419) were designed using the Primer Express software (Applied Biosystems): the modified forward primer (5′ TTG CAT TAG CAG TCC CCT GG 3′) partially overlapped (6 bp) the 5′ end of the original forward primer, while the modified reverse primer (5′ GAG CAA CAC AGG CTT GAG GC 3′) binded downstream of the original reverse primer binding site. The PCR products were sequenced with the same primers (Big Dye Terminator Cycle Sequencing Ready Reaction Kit, Applied Biosystems).

In a next stage of analysis, a PCR applying an alternative amelogenin primer pair binding to the X- and Y-homologue was carried out [2]. Fragment analysis of multiplex PCR kits, the singleplex amelogenin sex test applying alternative primers and sequencing were performed on an ABI Prism 310 Genetic Analyzer.

3. Results and discussion

The AmpFlSTR Identifiler PCR Amplikation Kit and the Geneprint Powerplex 16 System revealed reproducible peak imbalances of the X- and Y-fragment at the amelogenin locus in three males. The ratios of the peak height values are given in Table 1. If possible, these findings were confirmed by PCR analysis from another DNA sample (*1514, *1703). A singleplex PCR of the amelogenin gene gave the same results. At the DYS-19 locus, an allele was detectable in all cases.

Amplification of the male-specific SRY gene and two multiplex Y-STR Kits (genRES DYSplex-1 and genRES DYSplex-2, Serac) including amelogenin revealed normal results

Table 1
Ratios of the peak height values (quotient of relative fluorescence units Y-fragment/X-fragment) of samples *421, *1514, *1703, showing abnormal results of amelogenin-Y, and *420, the monozygotic twin of *421, showing normal results

Sample	% rfu AmY/X Idfiler	% rfu AmY/X Powerplex16	% rfu AmY/X DYSplex-1	% rfu AmY/X alternative
*420	0.98	1.12	0.90	1.02
*421	0.08	0.16	0.09	0.07
*1514	0.19	0.30	0.14	0.16
*1703	0.54	0.61	0.54	0.58

(3 different Y-STR haplotypes), except for the imbalanced amelogenin peaks (Table 1). In the case of *421, both twins were identical in all STR loci with exception of the abnormal amelogenin results. Sequencing with the modified Y-specific primers revealed no differences to the GenBank sequence (acc. no. M55419). Therefore, a base substitution between the non-overlapping part of the modified forward primer and the modified reverse primer could be excluded as a single reason for the observed phenomenon. To rule out a sequence variation in the overlapping part of the primer sites, too, another amelogenin PCR was carried out, which applies an alternative primer pair, binding to the X- and Y-homologue. It revealed a poor amplification of the Y-specific peak, too, which resulted in the same peak imbalances as they were observed initially. Therefore, the insufficient amplification of the Y-fragment could not be explained by a mutation in a primer annealing site.

A possible explanation for these findings might be mosaicism: the coexistence of at least two cell lines, a normal cell line and a somatically mutated cell line. A deletion including the Y-chromosomal amelogenin gene, as it was already suggested in cases of a complete loss of the Y-fragment, might be the difference between the two cell lines. In this case, the mutated cell line might not have been amplified at all, while the normal cell line was amplified to a lower extent compared with the X-fragment. As males possess one X and one Y chromosome, the weaker intensity of the Y-specific signals compared with the signals of the X-fragment corresponds to the proportion of the normal to the mutated cell line. The malign disease of one of the monozygotic twins (*421), who could possess a somatic mutation, speaks also in favour of this theory. Furthermore, gonosomal mosaicism leading to different ratios of X- and Y-chromosomes cannot be ruled out as a reason for the observed phenomenon.

References

[1] A. Mannucci, K.M. Sullivan, P.L. Ivanov, P. Gill, Forensic application of a rapid and quantitative DNA sex test by amplification of the X–Y homologous gene amelogenin, Int. J. Leg. Med. 106 (4) (1994) 190–193.

[2] M. Steinlechner, B. Berger, H. Niederstätter, W. Parson, Rare failures in the amelogenin sex test, Int. J. Leg. Med. 116 (2002) 117–120.

[3] K. Thangarajay, G. Reddy, L. Singh, Is the amelogenin gene reliable for gender identification in forensic casework and prenatal diagnosis? Int. J. Leg. Med. 116 (2002) 121–123.

[4] K.M. Sullivan, A. Manucci, C. Kimpton, P. Gill, A rapid and quantitative DNA sex test: fluorescence-based PCR analysis of X–Y homologous gene amelogenin, BioTechniques 15 (1993) 636–641.

[5] L. Roewer, J.T. Epplen, Rapid and sensitive typing of forensic stains by PCR amplification of polymorphic simple repeat sequences in casework, Forensic Sci. Int. 53 (1992) 163–171.

[6] Y.M.D. Lo, M.S.C. Tein, T.K. Lau, C.J. Haines, T.N. Leung, P.M.K. Poon, J.S. Wainscot, P.J. Johnson, A.M.Z. Chang, N.M. Hjelm, Quantitative analysis of fetal DNA in maternal plasma and serum: implications for noninvasive prenatal diagnosis, Am. J. Hum. Genet. 62 (1998) 768–775.

International Congress Series 1261 (2004) 511–513

www.ics-elsevier.com

Non-exclusion paternity case with a triple genetic incompatibility☆

R. Jacewicz[a,*], J. Berent[a], A. Prosniak[a], T. Dobosz[b], E. Kowalczyk[b], S. Szram[a]

[a] *Department of Forensic Medicine, Medical University of Lodz, Sedziowska 18a, Lodz 91-304, Poland*
[b] *Department of Forensic Medicine, Medical University of Wroclaw, Poland*

Abstract. This work presents a paternity determination case in which the total analysis of 30 DNA markers detected three genetic inconsistencies between the putative father and the child, two in STR markers, D8S1179 and D18S51, and one in RFLP marker, D7S21. The paternity index, including the mutation rates of the systems mentioned above, amounted to 2.374×10^{10}, which corresponds with the paternity probability higher than 99.99999999%. The case proves that great care should be taken when the non-fatherhood status is ascertained on the basis of the "three exclusion rule". It suggests also that the best solution is to calculate the appropriate statistical estimations in every case.

Keywords: Paternity investigation; Poland; Triple mutation; D8S1179; D18S51; D7S21

1. Introduction

A mutation event of DNA markers caused by losses or gains repetitive units is quite a common phenomenon in forensic practice. It must be taken into careful consideration in genetic paternity determination. With the increase in the number of genetic loci investigated, the presence of a single genetic inconsistency between a child and his biological father has become relatively frequent and cases with double paternal genetic inconsistencies have been reported more and more often [1,2]. The aim of this paper was to show a non-exclusion paternity case with three paternal genetic incompatibilities found in our material.

2. Materials and methods

The case was encountered during routine paternity tests. Samples of blood were taken from the alleged father, his child and the child's mother. The DNA was isolated with the use of the salt extraction procedure as described by Lahiri [3]. Minisatellite analysis was

☆ This project was supported by the Medical University of Lodz grant no. 502-11-702.

* Corresponding author. Tel.: +48-42-6544536; fax: +48-42-6544293.
E-mail address: r.jacewicz@post.pl (R. Jacewicz).

doi:10.1016/S0531-5131(03)01649-2

performed by restriction with *Hin*fI and hybridization with MS43A, G3, YNH24, TBQ7, MS1, MS205, MS31 (Cellmark Diagnostics) and measurement of restriction fragments by software BIO1D (Vilber Lourmat). The amplification of STR markers was performed using the Identifiler system (Applied Biosystem) and Power Plex 16 system (Promega) with a detection on 310 ABI Prism and ABI Prism 377 sequencers. The additional six loci included in AmpliTypePM + DQA1 Typing Kit (Applied Biosystem) were co-amplified and typed utilizing reverse dot-blot.

Paternity index (PI) was calculated including the mutation rates according to Brenner [4].

3. Results

The results observed in a paternity case with three inconsistencies between the father and the child with the paternity index (PI) value are given in Table 1. The combined

Table 1
A non-exclusion paternity case with three paternal genetic inconsistencies in D8S1179, D18S51 and D7S21 loci

L.p.	Locus	Father	Child	Mother	PI
1	D8S1179	13–13	14–15	10–15	0.004[a]
2	D16S539	9–13	9–11	11–12	8.929
3	D21S11	29–30	28–30	28–30.2	2.315
4	vWA	18–19	16–18	15–16	1.984
5	TH01	7–8	6–7	6–8	4.032
6	D18S51	15–15	15–16	14–15	0.001[a]
7	D13S317	11–12	12–12	9–12	1.953
8	D7S820	9–10	10–10	10–10	1.666
9	CSF1PO	10–11	11–13	12–13	2.193
10	D19S433	12–13	13–13	13–16	2.451
11	D2S1338	20–20	20–24	16–24	6.579
12	Penta D	10–11	11–14	10–14	3.215
13	D3S1358	16–17	14–17	14–14	3.205
14	FGA	19–25	19–23	20–23	7.353
15	Penta E	9–13	13–14	12–14	2.933
16	D5S818	12–13	13–14	11–14	4.032
17	TPOX	11–11	8–11	8–8	3.968
18	LDLR	BB	BB	AB	0.806
19	GYPA	AB	AB	AA	1.000
20	HBGG	AA	AA	AB	0.960
21	D7S8	AB	AB	AB	1.000
22	GC	AA	AC	CC	2.083
23	DQA1	2–4.1	1.1–2	1.1–4.2/4.3	5.618
24	D12S11	10.4–3.5 kb	10.4–7.4 kb	10.2–7.4 kb	50.000
25	D7S22	10.5–4.6 kb	10.5–2.9 kb	9.3–2.9 kb	25.000
26	D2S44	4.5–1.9 kb	4.5–2.7 kb	3.3–2.7 kb	12.500
27	D10S28	4.7–2.0 kb	4.7–3.0 kb	3.0–1.4 kb	14.286
28	D1S7	9.7–2.3 kb	9.7–6.8 kb	8.3–6.8 kb	15.625
29	D16S309	3.4 kb	3.4–2.6 kb	2.9–2.6 kb	10.526
30	D7S21	8.4 kb	8.9–7.6 kb	7.6–5.9 kb	0.264[a]
Total					2.374×10^{10}

PI—paternity index value.

[a] Value of PI with consideration of appropriate average paternal mutation rates.

paternity index in the case after inclusion of the mutation index for D8S1179, D8S51 and D7S21 was 2.374×10^{10}, which corresponded with final probability of paternity value higher than 99.99999999%. From this statistical calculation, we concluded the presence of a triple mutation event in the investigated case.

4. Discussion

Though the triple mutation theoretically seems to be an extremely rare incident, it does not appear impossible in our practice. Minisatellites such as D7S21 are considerably mutable regions in the human DNA with an average paternal mutation rate of 1.9×10^{-2} and the lack of maternal mutation event [5]. For STR markers, an average paternity mutation rate of 3.4×10^{-3} is 10 times higher than the maternal one [1]. Taking into consideration mentioned values of mutation rates, combined frequency of observed triple mutation event appears in 1 out of 4.5 million cases on average, as previously reported Thomson and Pilotti [6].

5. Conclusion

We proved that "three exclusion rule" is not safe enough. We suggest to rule out any arbitrary decision point and to calculate the appropriate statistical estimations in every case.

References

[1] H. Geada, L. Viriato, STR mutations in paternity investigations: a study of 1-year consecutive cases, Prog. Forensic Genet. 9 (2003) 657–660.

[2] C. Brandt-Casadevall, M. Gene, Presence of two mutations between father/child in two cases paternity testing, Prog. Forensic Genet. 9 (2003) 647.

[3] D.K. Lahiri, J.I. Nurnberger Jr., A rapid non enzymatic method for RFLP studies, Nucleic Acids Res. 19 (1991) 5444.

[4] C. Brenner, available at: http://dna-viev.com/mudisc.htm.

[5] R. Jacewicz, DNA polymorphism of the three VNTR systems: D7S21, D12S11, D5S110 in the population of central Poland and usefulness in paternity testing, PhD thesis. The Ludwik Rydygier's Medical University in Bydgoszcz, Bydgoszcz 2001.

[6] J.A Thomson, V. Pilotti, Validation of short tandem repeat analysis for the investigation of cases of disputed paternity, Forensic Sci. Int. 100 (1999) 1–16.

ELSEVIER

International Congress Series 1261 (2004) 514–516

www.ics-elsevier.com

On the power of excluding relatives of the true father from paternity

Yue-Qing Hu[a,*], Wing K. Fung[b], C.T. Yang[b]

[a] *Department of Mathematics, Southeast University, Si Pai Lou 2#, Nanjing 210096, China*
[b] *Department of Statistics and Actuarial Science, The University of Hong Kong, Pokfulam Road, Hong Kong, China*

Abstract. The power of excluding a random man from paternity in a structured population for genetic tests for each of the with-mother and no-mother cases is considered. The situation in which a paternal relative of the child is to be excluded from paternity in such a population is also addressed. A simple relationship is found to hold between the power of excluding a random man from paternity and that of excluding a paternal relative of the child. Population allele frequency data for 12 STR loci in the Hong Kong Chinese are used to show numerically the effect of population structure on the exclusion probabilities. © 2003 Elsevier B.V. All rights reserved.

Keywords: Coancestry coefficient; Paternity testing; Population structure; Power of exclusion

---

1. Introduction

The necessity of taking account of genetic differences between subpopulations for forensic DNA investigation was addressed by various researchers [1–4]. For persons originating from the same subpopulation, Balding and Nichols [2] derived a formula for assigning probabilities to a set of alleles, incorporating the coancestry coefficient θ into the calculation, where the parameter θ is essentially the same as Wright's F_{ST} [5].

A genetic marker can be characterized by its ability to exclude a random man or a relative of the child from paternity in a standard trio (with-mother) or no-mother case. Formulae for the power of excluding (PE) a random man from paternity were provided by Ohno et al. [6]. However in many situations, particularly immigration cases, the false father is more likely to be a relative, e.g. brother, of the true father than an unrelated man. In view of this, Fung et al. [7] considered the probability of excluding a relative of the true father from paternity and provided formulae for estimating such probability under different circumstances. All the above work, however, is premised on the Hardy–Weinberg law which essentially assumes a structureless population. In subdivided populations, the expressions of the power of excluding a random man from paternity in the with-mother

* Corresponding author. Tel.: +86-25-3792315; fax: +86-25-7712719.
E-mail address: huyq@seu.edu.cn (Y.-Q. Hu).

doi:10.1016/S0531-5131(03)01449-3

and no-mother cases were derived in this study. A linear relationship between the power of excluding a random man and that of excluding a paternal relative of the child was exhibited. The Hong Kong Chinese population database of 12 STR loci was used to show numerically the effect of population structure on the probabilities of exclusion.

2. Results

Recently, Ayres [8] and Hu et al. [9] independently derived equivalent expressions of $Q_1(\theta)$ and $Q_2(\theta)$, though look differently, the power of excluding an unrelated man from paternity in a structured population for the with-mother and no-mother cases, respectively. The details of derivation of $Q_1(\theta)$ and $Q_2(\theta)$ can be referred to in Hu et al. [9], and the formulae can be found in Ayres [8] and Hu et al. [9].

It is not uncommon in immigration cases that the false father is more likely to be a paternal relative, e.g. a brother of the true father (TF) than an unrelated man. Thus in the following, we like to evaluate the probability of excluding a paternal relative from paternity, $Q_3(\theta)$ for the with-mother case and $Q_4(\theta)$ for the no-mother case, in a structured population. Here, we use symbol R to stand for a paternal relative of the true father of the child (C). The mother (M) is assumed to be independent on both TF and R.

Let $(k_0, 2k_1, k_2)$ be the kinship coefficients of individuals TF and R, Fung et al. [7] has derived P [none of the alleles of C and R is identical by descent (ibd)]= k_0+k_1. Since R is excluded from the parentage of C, R and C cannot share ibd alleles. Given R and C share no ibd alleles, R can be treated as a random man, i.e. R is unrelated to both M and C, in the process of calculating joint genotype probabilities. Thus, it leads immediately to $Q_3(\theta)=(k_0+k_1)Q_1(\theta)$, and $Q_4(\theta)=(k_0+k_1)Q_2(\theta)$.

The powers of exclusion $Q_1(\theta)$, $Q_2(\theta)$, $Q_3(\theta)$, and $Q_4(\theta)$ for each locus yields immediately the overall powers for several loci. The powers of exclusion allowing for one or two mismatches can also be yielded at once [7].

3. Example and discussion

For the allele frequency data at 12 STR loci for the Hong Kong Chinese [10] and $\theta=0$ and 0.03, the overall powers of exclusion for 0, 1, and 2 mismatches are presented in Table 1. $Q_3(\theta)$ and $Q_4(\theta)$ in Table 1 give the powers of excluding an uncle of the child from paternity. From Table 1, it is observed that the power of exclusion decreases as θ increases.

Table 1
Powers of exclusion for 0, 1 and 2 mismatches, $Q_1(\theta)$, $Q_2(\theta)$, $Q_3(\theta)$, and $Q_4(\theta)$ for Hong Kong Chinese with coancestry coefficient θ

PE	θ	Overall	At most 1 mismatch	At most 2 mismatches
$Q_1(\theta)$	0	0.99998	0.99957	0.99622
	0.03	0.99994	0.99953	0.99590
$Q_2(\theta)$	0	0.99849	0.98636	0.93537
	0.03	0.99682	0.97484	0.89644
$Q_3(\theta)$	0	0.98357	0.90213	0.71846
	0.03	0.97814	0.89991	0.71396
$Q_4(\theta)$	0	0.93659	0.74707	0.46705
	0.03	0.91746	0.69622	0.40435

This is expected as a bigger θ virtually means a higher level of relatedness among members of the population, so it is more difficult to exclude a false father from paternity.

$Q_1(\theta)$ in Table 1 shows that the panel of the 12 STR systems has a high ability to exclude an unrelated man from paternity of the child. In the motherless case, as expected, the power of exclusion $Q_2(\theta)$ in each entry becomes smaller compared to $Q_1(\theta)$.

It is noted that some of the overall powers of exclusion $Q_3(\theta)$ and $Q_4(\theta)$ are rather small, particularly in the case that makes allowances for two mismatches. When θ changes from 0 to 0.03, the overall power of exclusion $Q_4(\theta)$ drops, for 0, 1, and 2 mismatches, by respectively, 2.0%, 6.8%, and 13%. From the results of $Q_3(\theta)$ and $Q_4(\theta)$, it is obvious that the panel of the 12 STR systems may not be very informative for distinguishing close relatives from paternity in a structured population. For doubtful cases, it seems that more loci need to be used.

Acknowledgements

The authors are grateful to Mr. D.M. Wong, Dr. D.G. Clarke, and Mr. S.C. Leung for their helpful comments, administrative support and proofreading the draft. This work was supported in part by the SEU Science Foundation (9207011146) and Hong Kong RGC Competitive Earmarked Research Grant.

References

[1] N.E. Morton, Genetic structure of forensic populations, Proc. Natl. Acad. Sci. U. S. A. 89 (1992) 2556–2560.

[2] D.J. Balding, R.A. Nichols, DNA profile match probability calculation: how to allow for population stratification, relatedness, database selection and single bands, Forensic Sci. Int. 64 (1994) 125–140.

[3] K.L. Ayres, Relatedness testing in subdivided populations, Forensic Sci. Int. 114 (2000) 107–115.

[4] W.K. Fung, Y.Q. Hu, Interpreting forensic DNA mixtures: allowing for uncertainty in population substructure and dependence, J. R. Stat. Soc., Ser. A 163 (2000) 241–254.

[5] S. Wright, The genetical structure of population, Ann. Eugen. 15 (1951) 323–354.

[6] Y. Ohno, I.M. Sebetan, S. Akaishi, A simple method for calculating the probability of excluding paternity with any number of codominant alleles, Forensic Sci. Int. 19 (1982) 93–98.

[7] W.K. Fung, Y.K. Chung, D.M. Wong, Power of exclusion revisited: probability of excluding relatives of the true father from paternity, Int. J. Leg. Med. 116 (2002) 64–67.

[8] K.L. Ayres, Paternal exclusion in the presence of substructure, Forensic Sci. Int. 129 (2002) 142–144.

[9] Y.Q. Hu, D.M. Wong, W.K. Fung, Power of exclusion in structured populations, Technical Report, Department of Statistics and Actuarial Science, The University of Hong Kong, July, 2002.

[10] D.M. Wong, M.Y. Law, W.K. Fung, K.L. Chan, C. Li, T.S. Lun, K.M. Lai, K.Y. Cheung, C.T. Chiu, Population data for 12 STR loci in Hong Kong Chinese, Int. J. Leg. Med. 114 (2001) 281–284.

ELSEVIER

International Congress Series 1261 (2004) 517–519

www.ics-elsevier.com

Parental investigation in a child with abnormal karyotype

M.B. Rodríguez Cardozo, M.V. Cólica, M.A. Abovich, A. Szöcs, A.M. Di Lonardo*

Banco Nacional de Datos Genéticos. Hospital Dr. C.G. Durand, J.B. Ambrosetti 743 (1405), Buenos Aires, Argentina

Abstract. We present a parental investigation where the father and the mother are dubious, and the alleged child had a previous karyotype with a partial deletion at 13 chromosome (46XX del13). STR typing at D13S317 locus revealed homozygosity alleles in the three individuals involved in this study. The homozygosity of the alleged child at this locus was assumed as the result of a null allele, due to the partial deletion at 13 chromosome. This results showed a paternal inheritance of the chromosomal anomaly. In cases like this, the parental investigation with highly discriminating STR markers could be an additional contribution to the genetic diagnosis as well as an accurate genetic advice to the couple.

Keywords: Paternity testing; Chromosomal anomaly; STRs

1. Introduction

There are several situations in which the assessment of paternity may vary depending on whether a one-banded pattern or only one pick on the electropherogram is assumed as an homozygous allele. Another possibility is to consider that it could represent a gene with two different alleles, one of which is invisible, overlapped or has run off.

"Silent allele", of course, includes the possibility of an invisible band and the occurrence of "primer drop out" during the microsatellite amplification by PCR.

In this study, we present a parental investigation where the father and the mother are dubious and the alleged child has a partial deletion of chromosome 13 (46XX del13) in a previous karyotype.

* Corresponding author. Tel.: +54-11-4982-1716; fax: +54-11-4982-0625.
E-mail address: bndg@infovia.com.ar (A.M. Di Lonardo).

doi:10.1016/S0531-5131(03)01637-6

2. Materials and methods

Genomic DNA was isolated from blood samples with salting out Miller's method. The samples were amplified at the loci FGA, VWA, D3S1358, D5S818, D7S820, D8S1179, D13S317, D18S51 and D21S11 using the AmpFlSTR™ Profiler Plus Kit (PE Biosystems, Foster City, CA) and at the loci CF1PO, TPOX, TH01, D3S1358, D7S820 and D16S539 using the AmpFlSTR Cofiler™ kit (PE Biosystems). The same loci and the D2S1338 and D19S433 were amplified with the AmpFlSTR™ Identifiler Kit (PE Biosystems). Samples were analyzed using the ABI PRISM™ 310 Genetic Analyzer (PE Biosystems), according to the manufacturer's recommendations using as separation medium Performance Optimized Polymer (POP) 4™ (PE Biosystems). The data was acquired by 1.0.2 software ABI PRISM™ 310 Collection and analyzed by GeneScan® Analysis software 3.1 and Genotyper® 2.5 according to the manufacturer's recommendations [1–4].

3. Results

STR-typing at D13S317 locus (Fig. 1) revealed the following results (Table 1).

4. Discussion

The homozygosity of the alleged child at D13S317 locus was assumed as the result of a null allele due to a partial deletion at 13 chromosome. Thus, we considered that allele 8 at D13S317 locus was from maternal origin and that the partial deletion at 13 chromosome (13q 22–31) was by paternal inheritance.

This study revealed a non-exclusion of the maternal–paternal relationship for the other investigated markers.

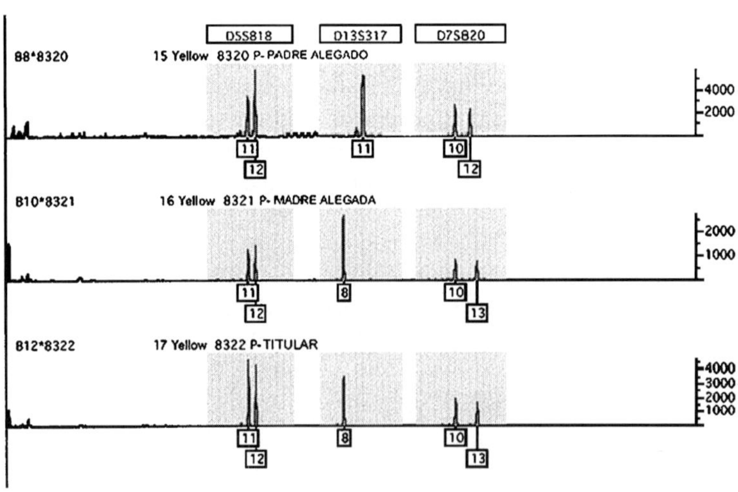

Fig. 1. STR-typing at D13S317 locus.

Table 1
STR-typing at D13S317 locus

Locus		Alleles		
		Mother	Child	Alleged father
1	D8S1179	15–12	13–12	16–13
2	D21S11	31–30	31.2–30	31.2–29
3	D7S820	13–10	13–10	12–10
4	CSF1PO	12–10	12–10	12–10
5	D3S1358	15–15	17–15	17–17
6	TH01	7–6	8–6	8–6
7	D13S317	8–8	8–8	11–11
8	D16S539	12–12	12–12	12–11
9	vWA	18–18	19–18	19–18
10	TPOX	12–11	11–10	11–10
11	D18S51	16–12	14–12	17–14
12	D5S818	12–11	12–11	12–11
13	FGA	25–21	25–24	24–24

In agreement with statistics–mathematics analysis of the obtained results (using Ch. Brenner formulas) [5], the parental probability was 999.999% (without D13S317 marker) and considering a null allele was 99.995%.

5. Conclusion

In cases like the previously described, the parental investigation with highly discriminating STR markers could be an additional contribution to genetic diagnosis as well as an accurate genetic advice to the couple.

References

[1] K. Lazaruk, et al., (PE AB): genotyping of forensic short tandem repeat (STR) systems based on sizing precision in a capillary electrophoresis instrument, Electrophoresis 19 (1998) 86–93.

[2] O. Henegariu, et al., Multiplex PCR: critical parameters end step-by-step protocol, Biotecniques 23 (3) (1997) 504–511.

[3] J. Wallin, et al., TWAGDAM validation of AmpFlSTR blue PCR amplification kit for forensic casework analysis, J. Forensic Sci. 43 (4) (1998) 1–17.

[4] AmpFlSTR®Cofiler™-Profiler™ PCR Amplification Kit User's Manual 2000, Applied Biosystems.

[5] Brenner, Ch: www.dnaview.com.

International Congress Series 1261 (2004) 520–522

www.ics-elsevier.com

Paternity cases when the alleged father is missing

M.V. Cólica, M.B. Rodríguez Cardozo, M.A. Abovich, A. Szöcs, A.M. Di Lonardo*

Department of Immunology, Banco Nacional de Datos Genéticos-Hospital Durand, Juan B. Ambrosetti 743 Planta Baja, 1405 Buenos Aires, Argentina

Abstract. New technologies of DNA analysis by STRs, LTRs and MHC genes, and the advance in statistical and mathematical calculations of complex paternity cases allowed paternity cases resolution when the alleged father is missing (AFM). Cases of civil state suppression during the dictatorial government (1976–1983) are investigated in our laboratory. In them, family groups are often incomplete in one or two generations. This study presents 31 cases of paternity testing with AFM carried out during 2001–2002 years. In these cases, only first grade relative of AFM and/or siblings or half siblings of the titular were available. In only 19 of them, alleged child's mother was available for the study. In all the 31 cases presented here, we could assign biological relationship between the alleged child and the alleged father's family members whose genetic information allowed us to reconstruct total or partially alleged father genotype.

Keywords: Paternity testing; STRs; Statistics; Forensics

1. Introduction

New technologies of DNA analysis by STRs, LTRs and MHC genes, and the advance in statistical and mathematical calculations of complex paternity cases allowed paternity cases resolution when the alleged father is missing (AFM).

Cases of civil state suppression during the dictatorial government (1976–1983) are investigated in our laboratory. In them, family groups are often incomplete in one or two generations.

This study presents 31 cases of paternity testing with AFM carried out during 2001–2002 years. In these cases, only first grade relative of AFM and/or siblings or half siblings of the titular were available. In only 19 of them, alleged child's mother was available for the study.

* Corresponding author. Tel.: +54-11-4982-1716; fax: +54-11-4982-0625.
E-mail address: bndg@infovia.com.ar (A.M. Di Lonardo).

0531-5131/
doi:10.1016/S0531-5131(03)01622-4

2. Materials and methods

Genomic DNA was isolated from blood samples with salting out Miller's method [21]. The samples were amplified at the loci FGA, VWA, D3S1358, D5S818, D7S820, D8S1179, D13S317, D18S51 and D21S11 using the AmpFlSTR™ Profiler Plus Kit (PE Biosystems, Foster City, CA) and at the loci CF1PO, TPOX, TH01, D3S1358, D7S820 and D16S539 using the AmpFlSTR Cofiler™ kit (PE Biosystems, Foster City, CA). The same loci and the D2S1338 and D19S433 were amplified with the AmpFlSTR™ Identifiler Kit (PE Biosystems, Foster City, CA) Samples were analyzed using the ABI PRISM™ 310 Genetic Analyzer (PE Biosystems, Foster City, CA), according to the manufacturer's recommendations using as separation medium Performance Optimized Polymer (POP) 4™ (PE Biosystems, Foster City, CA). The data was acquired by ABI PRISM™ 310 Collection 1.0.2 software and analyzed by GeneScan® Analysis 3.1 software and Genotyper® 2.5 according to the manufacturer's recommendations [1–3,13,14].

For the study minisatellite loci (SLPs) NICE™ Chemiluminiscent Probes (Llifecodes) was employed for the loci D7S22, D7S21, D12S11, D16S309, D4S163 and D2S44 [15–17].

Histocompatibility Major Complex's analysis was carried out with PCR-SSP (Peel Frez™) for A, B and DR loci [18–20].

3. Results

In eight cases, alleged father genotype reconstruction was performed from the grandparents. In many of these cases, other relatives (legal sons, brothers and sisters of AFM) were available. Reconstructions were performed from one grandparent and from one to three alleged uncles in seven cases. Another nine cases had only alleged uncles available for the study.

A number of three studies were carried out with only one grandparent, and one study was performed with an alleged half sibling. Furthermore, three full sibling cases were studied.

When the alleged father genotype reconstruction was possible, the Paternity Probability value was higher than 99.99% [5,7–12].

Kinship Analysis [4] (uncle–niece, grandparent–child, half siblings) was carried out when the alleged father genotype reconstruction was incomplete or impossible.

In these cases we obtained an index value higher than 1.000; and for the siblings cases we obtained a Sibling Probability value higher than 99.999999% [6].

4. Conclusion

In all the 31 cases presented here, we could assign biological relationship between the alleged child and the alleged father's family members whose genetic information allowed us to reconstruct total or partially alleged father genotype.

These cases were highly interesting for the advance of statistical and mathematical analysis of biological information.

References

[1] K. Lazaruk, et al., (PE AB): genotyping of forensic short tandem repeat (STR) systems based on sizing precision in a capillary electrophoresis instrument, Electrophoresis 19 (1998) 86–93.

[2] O. Henegariu, et al., Multiplex PCR: critical parameters end step-by-step protocol, BioTechniques 23 (3) (1997) 504–511.
[3] J. Wallin, et al., TWAGDAM validation of AmpFISTR blue PCR amplification kit for forensic casework analysis, Journal of Forensic Science 43 (4) (1998) 1–17.
[4] R.E. Wenk, et al., Determination of sibship in any two persons, Transfusion 36 (1996) 259–262.
[5] A. Carracedo, Problemas bioestadísticos en genética forense, Univeridad Santiago de Compostela, España, 1996.
[6] J.A. Luque, et al, Indice de Hermanidad II. Estudio y valoración mediante STRs, 4° Jornada de Genética Forense, La Gomera, 1999.
[7] Ch. Brenner, Symbolic kinship program, Genetics 145 (1997) 535–542.
[8] Ch. Brenner, et al., Calculation of paternity probabilities from multilocus DNA profile, Electrophoresis 15 (1994) 170–174.
[9] Ch. Brenner, A note on paternity computation case lacking a mother, Transfusion 33 (1993) 51–54.
[10] Ch. Brenner, www.dnaview.com.
[11] Ch. Brenner, Calculation of paternity index. In: Inclusion Probabilities in Paternity Testing. Amer. Assoc. of Blood Banks, Arlington, 1983, pp. 632–638.
[12] Ch. Brenner, Kinship analisys by DNA when there are many possibilities. G. Sensabough, et al. (Eds.), Progress in Forensic Genetics, vol. 8, 1999.
[13] Ch. AmpFISTR®Cofiler™-Profiler™, PCRAmplification Kit User's Manual, Applied Biosystems, Foster City, 2000.
[14] Ch. AmpFISTR®Identifiler™, PCRAmplification Kit User's Manual, Applied Biosystems, Foster City, 2001.
[15] E.M. Souther, et al., Journal of Molecular Biology 98 (1975) 503–527.
[16] A.J. Jeffreys, et al., Nature 314 (1985) 67–73.
[17] A.J. Jeffreys, et al., Genomics 7 (1990) 449–452.
[18] Albert, et al., Histocompatibily Testing, Springler-Verlag, 1972.
[19] P. Terasaki, Histocompatibily Testing, UCLA Tissue Typing Lab., 1980.
[20] P. HLA, 1991 Proceedings of XI International Histocompatibity Workshop and Conference vols. I–II, Oxford Science Publications, 1992.
[21] S.A. Miller, et al., Nucleic Acids Research 16 (1988) 1215.

International Congress Series 1261 (2004) 523–525

ELSEVIER

www.ics-elsevier.com

Paternity determination of the deceased defendant in STR against RFLP analysis☆

R. Jacewicz[a,*], J. Berent[a], A. Prosniak[a], T. Dobosz[b], E. Kowalczyk[b], S. Szram[a]

[a] *Department of Forensic Medicine, Medical University of Lodz, Sedziowska 18a, Lodz 91-304, Poland*
[b] *Department of Forensic Medicine, Medical University of Wroclaw, Poland*

Abstract. This work shows a paternity examination a deceased defendant carried out on the basis of his two sisters DNA profile determination. STR and RFLP analyses were used and their efficiency was compared. The statistical evaluation proved the defendant's paternity with the probability of more than 99,999% (PI>100,000). The restriction analysis appeared considerably more informative than the amplification one, which means seven RFLP markers correspond with the same paternity indices to the 15 STR markers. © 2003 Elsevier B.V. All rights reserved.

Keywords: Deficiency case; Paternity determination; Statistical approach; RFLP/STR analysis

1. Introduction

Paternity determination cases, where the DNA profile of the defendant is not available, belong to the cases of the highest level of difficulty. Considerably larger sets of genetic markers have to be examined than in standard casework and the statistical evaluation of the DNA evidence is more difficult [1].

The aim of this work was to check the differences between RFLP and STR methods in the value of the paternity index in the deficiency case in which, instead of the defendant, his two sisters were investigated.

2. Materials and methods

The paternity determination in the deficiency case was carried at the Department of Forensic Medicine, Medical University of Lodz, Poland. Samples of blood were taken from two sisters of the deceased alleged father as well as from the child and the child's mother. DNA was isolated with the use of the salt extraction procedure as described by Lahiri [2]. Amplification of 15 STRs was performed using the Identifiler system (Applied

☆ This project was supported by the Medical University of Lodz grant no. 502-11-702.

* Corresponding author. Tel.: +48-42-6544536; fax: +48-42-6544293.
E-mail address: r.jacewicz@post.pl (R. Jacewicz).

doi:10.1016/S0531-5131(03)01650-9

Biosystem) with detection on ABI Prism 377 sequencer. For minisatellite (RFLP) analyses, DNA was restricted with *Hin*dI and hybridized single locus probes (SLP): MS31 (D7S21), MS43A (D12S11), MS1 (D1S7), TBQ7 (D10S28), YNH24 (D2S44), G3 (D7S22), D5S43 (MS8) (Cellmark Diagnostics) and analysed with software BIO1D (Vilber Lourmat). Restriction fragments were grouped in fixed bins taking into account the measurement error of ± 2.3% [3].

Statistical evaluation was made using the paternity index value (PI) and the probability of paternity [W-Wahrscheinlichkeit] devised by Essen-Möller on the basis of Bayes's theory [4].

3. Results

The genotypes observed in the reported deficiency paternity case with appropriative value of PI for RFLP and STR analyses are given in Table 1.

Table 1
The genotypes and paternity index (PI) in a deficiency case in STR and RFLP analyses

N_{STR}	Locus	S_I	S_{II}	Ch	M	PI value
1	D8S1179	10/12	12/14	12/16	13/16	1.36
2	D21S11	30/32.2	30/32.2	30.2/32.2	30.2/30.2	2.15
3	D7S820	10/12	10/10	8/12	8/10	1.56
4	CSF1PO	10/11	11/11	11/12	10/12	2.19
5	D3S1358	15/18	15/18	16/16	16/17	0.50
6	TH01	9.3/9.3	9.3/9.3	7/9.3	9.3/9.3	0.50
7	D13S317	11/13	11/13	12/13	12/12	3.12
8	D16S539	11/11	11/13	12/13	12/13	0.74
9	D2S1338	24/25	24/25	20/25	20/24	2.02
10	D19S433	13/16	13/13	16/16	15/16	6.25
11	vWA	18/18	17/20	16/18	16/18	1.49
12	TPOX	8/8	8/8	8/10	8/10	0.69
13	D18S51	17/18	17/18	15/18	15/17	3.29
14	D5S818	10/11	10/11	11/13	10/11	0.50
15	FGA	21/23	23/23	21/23	21/23	2.73
Total						335.42
N_{RFLP}	Locus	S_I	S_{II}	Ch	M	PI value
1	D7S21	10.2/8.5	8.5/4.7	8.8/7.3	8.8/–	0.25
2	D12S11	7.4/7.2	7.4/7.2	7.2/7.1	10.6/7.1	6.58
3	D1S7	5.3/2.8	5.3/4.3	7.3/7.1	10.7/7.1	0.25
4	D10S28	1.6/–	4.3/1.6	1.6/1.4	2.0/1.4	4.00
5	D2S44	5.2/3.9	3.9/3.0	5.2/2.6	4.8/2.6	4.17
6	D7S22	7.2/1.6	7.7/1.6	7.8/1.6	7.8/1.6	6.83
7	D5S43	6.6/–	5.5/4.8	6.6/4.7	4.7/2.4	7.69
Total						360.37

$N_{STR/RFLP}$—following number of STR/RFLP loci applied; S_I—first sister of deceased defendant; S_{II}—second sister of deceased defendant; Ch—child; M—mother of child; PI—paternity index value
Sizes of restriction fragments for RFLP loci were given in kb.

4. Discussion

Paternity determination, when the alleged father's genotypes are unavailable, is performed on the basis of his family investigations. The most convenient situation is when the genetic profile of the defendant's both parents can be established. It is much more difficult to investigate a fatherhood status when, instead of the defendant, his siblings or/and his other children are available [5].

In the reported case, we applied seven markers RFLP and a set of 15 STRs to judge the fatherhood status of the deceased man. The statistical evaluation proved the defendant's paternity with the probability of more than 99,999% (PI>100,000). In the child we found very informative (allele frequencies 0.01–0.065) five RFLP alleles shared with the first or/ and second sister of the alleged father. After analyzing the seven markers, the paternity value was 99.72%, (PI = 360.37). The corresponding value of paternity indices (W = 99.70%, PI = 335.42) was received for 15 STRs markers. The considerable superiority of PI/W values in RFLP analysis with respect to STR analysis in a parentage testing was reported earlier. Thomson et al. [6] indicate that 16 STR systems are required to provide equivalent paternity indices to the six SLP (RFLP) systems.

5. Conclusion

The authors regard the RFLP analysis as helpful in deficiency cases because it allows to obtain higher value of probability of paternity than the STR analysis, and thus it should remain to be applied when the genetic profile of the defendant is unavailable.

References

[1] J.W. Lee, H.-S. Lee, Paternity determination when the alleged father's genotypes are unavailable, Forensic Sci. Int. 123 (2001) 202–210.

[2] D.K. Lahiri Jr., J.I. Nurnberger, A rapid non enzymatic method for RFLP studies, Nucleic Acids Res. 19 (1991) 5444.

[3] R. Jacewicz, DNA polymorphism of the three VNTR systems: D7S21, D12S11, D5S110 in the population of central Poland and usefulness in paternity testing, Ph.D. thesis. The Ludwik Rydygier's Medical University in Bydgoszcz, Bydgoszcz, 2001.

[4] E. Essen-Möller, Die Beweiskraft der Ähnlichkeit im Vaterschaftsnachweis: theoretische Grundlagen, Mitt. Anthropol. Ges. Wien 68 (1938) 2–53.

[5] R. Slomski, K. Dziechciowska, Paternity disputes based on analysis of DNA after the death of alleged father or mother, Arch. Med. Sad. Kryminol. 47 (1997) 307–314.

[6] J.A. Thomson, K.L. Ayres, V. Pilotti, M.N. Barrett, J.I.H. Walker, P.G. Debenham, Analysis of disputed single-parent/child and sibling relationships using 16 STR loci, Int. J. Leg. Med. 115 (2001) 128–134.

International Congress Series 1261 (2004) 526–528

www.ics-elsevier.com

Phenotype versus genotype reporting for DNA polymorphisms

C. Harrison*, R. Allen, A. Eisenberg, H. Polesky, R. Roby, C. Te Young, R. Walker, D. Zeagler

Parentage Testing Committee, College of American Pathologists, Northfield, IL, USA

Abstract. In the College of American Pathologists' (CAP) 2001 PI-A survey, consensus was not achieved for the child's phenotype at the HUMTH01 locus. Two alleles (6 and 9.3) were reported by 37 laboratories, and only one allele (9.3) by 30 laboratories. Analysis of the results showed that this discrepancy was related to the kits used. This was attributed to a primer binding site mutation. The mother's phenotype was 8,9.3 and the tested man's 9,9.3. Participants who detected the "6" allele in the child reported a PI of 0, while participants who did not detect it reported a median PI of 1.43. Two participants reported the inferred genotype of 9.3,9.3. This is clearly an incorrect response. This case illustrates that for DNA polymorphisms the phenotypes detected may depend on the testing method used. Thus reporting phenotypes only is sound and scientifically accurate.

Keywords: Phenotype; Genotype; Homozygous; Proficiency survey; Parentage testing

1. Introduction

Historically the Parentage Testing Community has consistently reported the phenotype of tested individuals and not their inferred genotype. When testing relied mostly on blood groups and HLA typing, it was very well recognized that a variety of genotypes could be attributed to a single phenotype. Since the publication of the 1st edition of the Standards for Parentage Testing Laboratories in 1990, the AABB has required that the reports display the "phenotypes established for each individual in each genetic system examined".

With DNA polymorphisms testing methodology, it was argued that the testing directly established a genotype. It became relatively common, specifically in the forensic

* Corresponding author. Department of Pathology, UTHSCSA 7703 Floyd Curl Dr., San Antonio, TX 78284-7750, USA. Tel.: +1-210-567-4090; fax: +1-210-567-2367.

E-mail address: harrisonc@uthscsa.edu (C. Harrison).

0531-5131/
doi:10.1016/j.ics.2003.12.066

community, to report a homozygous genotype (i.e. two identical alleles) when only one allele was detected.

Since the inception of the parentage testing proficiency survey (PI) in 1993, the CAP Parentage Testing Committee has encouraged the reporting of phenotypes by giving direct instructions on reporting format and downgrading a result reported as a genotype to "acceptable" instead of "good".

2. Methods

The participant summary reports of all three yearly mailings of the CAP Parentage Testing Survey program for years 1998–2002 were reviewed. Apparently homozygous phenotypes at all STR loci tested by PCR technology were examined for reporting format. The total number of single allele phenotypes was tabulated for each mailing as an absolute number and a percent reported as a genotype (i.e. two identical alleles).

Results on the four individuals tested were also examined to determine whether homozygosity determination influenced the interpretation and/or PI calculation.

3. Results

In the 2001 PI-A survey at the HUMTH01 locus the interpretation of a single allele in the child did influence the PI calculation. A tabulation of the results reported by the participants is listed in Table 1.

Participants using the STR kits from Promega Corporation detected the "6" allele in the child and reported a PI of 0. Participants using the STR kits from Applied Biosystems did not detect the "6" allele and reported a median PI of 1.43. Two participants reported a homozygous genotype of 9.3, which is clearly inaccurate.

Table 1
Results at the HUMTH01 locus 2001 PI-A survey

Specimen	Phenotype	Participants		Performance grade
		No.	%	
Mother	8,9.3	65	92.8	Good
	8,9.3/10	2	2.9	Acceptable
	8,10	2	2.9	Unacceptable
	8	1	1.4	Unacceptable
Child	6,9.3	35	50.0	
	6,9.3/10	2	2.9	
	9.3	28	40.0	
	9.3,9.3	2	2.9	Non-Consensus
	6,10	2	2.9	
	6	1	1.3	
Tested man	9,9.3	63	91.4	Good
	9,9.3/10	2	2.9	Acceptable
	9,10	2	2.9	Unacceptable
	9	1	1.4	Unacceptable
	9.3	1	1.4	Unacceptable

Table 2
Phenotype versus genotype reporting of single allele phenotypes

Year	Single allele phenotypes observed	Total no. of reported as genotypes	% Reported as genotypes
1998	1611	116	7.2
1999	1693	71	4.2
2000	2428	210	8.6
2001	2462	168	6.8
2002	2927	165	5.6

The data collected from 15 mailings are depicted in Table 2.

4. Discussion

In the PI 2001A mailing at the HUMTH01 locus the child's allele had a primer site mutation, causing a lack of amplification with one of two manufacturer's kits. The sample did not achieve consensus as 39 laboratories reported two alleles, while 31 reported a single allele. It is clear from the results that the child was heterozygous for 6 and 9.3. The mother's phenotype was 8,9.3 and tested man's was 9,9.3, thus this locus' results should lead to an inconsistency interpretation. For the laboratories that did not detect the "6" allele, it was reasonable to report the child's phenotype as 9.3 and to calculate a non-0 paternity index. However it was inaccurate to report the child's genotype as 9.3,9.3. Lack of detection of alleles due to primer site mutation can result in apparent homozygosity at a locus. This phenomenon is now well recognized and is not restricted to a single manufacturer's reagents [1,2].

There seemed to be a decreasing trend in the frequency of reporting single allele phenotypes as inferred genotypes before 2000. This frequency increased in 2000. The possibility that this was due to an influx of new laboratories into the survey program in 2000 was entertained. A review of the number of laboratories reporting STR results for the most frequently reported locus, VWA31, did not support this theory. After 2000, the frequency is again decreasing.

References

[1] R.W. Allen, J. Pritchard, J. Harman, et al., Phenotypic differences at the HUMvWA locus amplified with different STR kits, (Letter to the Editor), J. Forensic Sci. 45 (2000) 1166–1167.

[2] B. Budowle, C. Sprecher, Concordance study on population database samples using the PowerPlex™ 16 kit and AmpFlSTR® Profiler Plus™ and AmpFlSTR® COfiler™ kit, J. Forensic Sci. 46 (2001) 637–641.

International Congress Series 1261 (2004) 529–531

www.ics-elsevier.com

Sequencing of FES, vWA and SE33 STRs in mother–child incompatibilities

M.J. Anjos[a,*], M. Carvalho[a], F. Balsa[a], L. Andrade[a], V. Lopes[a], A. Serra[a], J. Gamero[b], F. Corte-Real[c], D.N. Vieira[c], M. Vide[a]

[a] *Service of Forensic Genetics, Delegation of Coimbra, National Institute of Legal Medicine, Largo da Sé Nova, Coimbra, 3000-213, Portugal*

[b] *Department of Legal Medicine, Faculty of Medicine, University of Cádiz, Spain*

[c] *National Institute of Legal Medicine, Largo da Sé Nova, Coimbra, 3000-213, Portugal*

Abstract. Our casuistic in paternity testing showed several isolated incompatibilities present in different STRs like FES, SE33, vWA, among others, include homozygote and heterozygote situations, and appear both in father–child and mother–child pairs. As we assume, in paternity testing, that the mother is the real one, most of incompatibility situations are assigned to a mutation in putative father. In fact, only sequencing allows the real explanation for the event.

Keywords: STR; Mutation; Sequencing

1. Introduction

In this work, we present some cases of mother–child incompatibilities, one of them (3) that seems to be in a first analysis due to a mutation in the father–child pair.

2. Material and methods

DNA from four families was extracted using Chelex 100 [1]. PCR singleplex reaction of each STR was prepared with primers and amplification conditions according to the authors (FES [2], SE33 [3] and vWA [2]) and carried out in a thermocycler GeneAmp® PCR System 9600 (Perkin Elmer). Allele designation was made using sequenced allelic ladders.

PCR product was purified with MicroSpin Sephadex G-50. Manual electrophoresis was done to separate the alleles in cases 2 to 4. Re-amplification of each one was carried out using the same primers followed by other purification.

* Corresponding author. Tel.: +351-239-854-230; fax: +351-239-820-549.
E-mail address: geneforense@dcinml.mj.pt (M.J. Anjos).

doi:10.1016/j.ics.2003.11.014

Cycle sequencing of the re-amplified product was made using the ABI Prism Big Dye V3.0 Terminator Cycle Sequencing Ready Reaction Kit with AmpliTaq DNA Polymerase, FS (Applied Biosystems). After sequencing, samples were purified by $MgCl_2$/ethanol precipitation. Detection was carried out using an ABI PRISM® 377 DNA Sequencer.

3. Results

Case 1 (FES) P. father: 10, 12 mother: 12 child: 10, 13.
Case 2 (SE33) P. father: 18, 29.2 mother: 17, 31.2 child: 29.2, 32.2.
Case 3 (vWA) P. father: 18, mother: 14, 18 child: 17, 18.
Case 4 (vWA) P. father: 15, 17 mother: 14, 18 child 1: 15, 18 child 2: 17.

4. Discussion and conclusions

Case 1—Mother's allele 12 revealed a consensus structure [4,5] in 12 repeats with an overlapping of bases after that—seems that there are two different sequences: one of allele 12 (with flanking region) and the other of allele 13. The child's sequence revealed an overlapping of two sequences that could correspond to alleles 10 and 13 (Fig. 1).

Case 2—Mother–child alleles (31.2 and 32.2) revealed a type II structure [6]. In Fig. 2, we can observe an "N" in the last repeat before the 3′ -flanking region: the G to A transition (a possible deamination) caused an increment of one repeat unit.

Case 3—Analysis of mothers allele 14 revealed the structure described for this allele [4,5]. In child's sequence (Fig. 3), we can see an identical structure to mother's allele 14 (flanking region included) instead of the expected structure for allele 17.

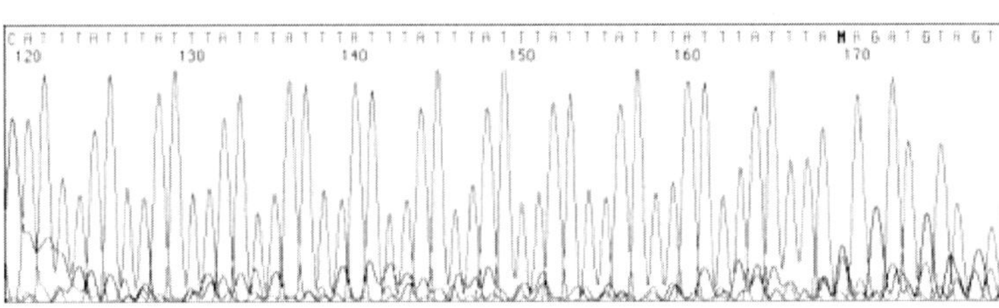

Fig. 1. FES: electropherogram of mother's allele 12.

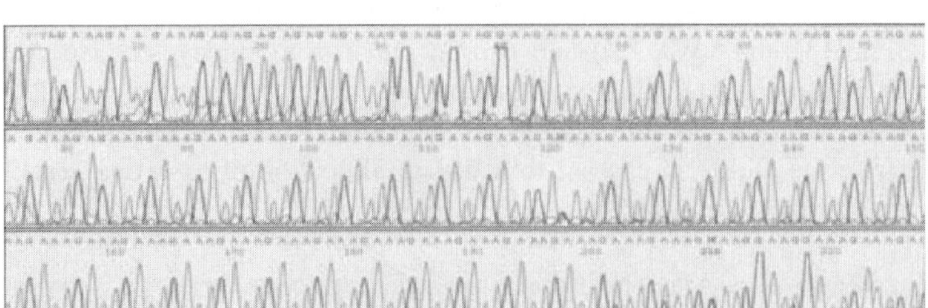

Fig. 2. SE33: electropherogram of child's allele 32.2.

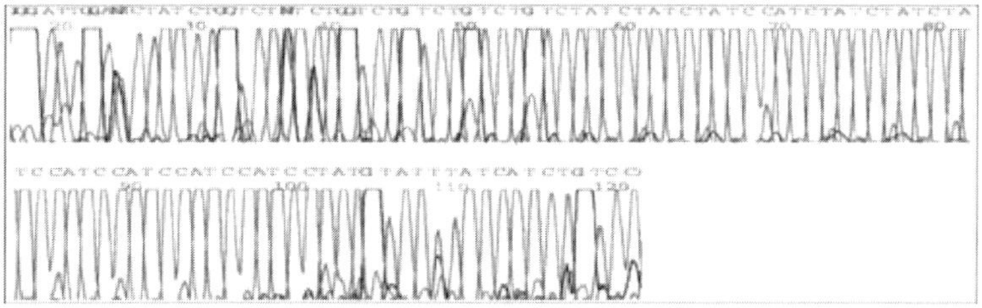

Fig. 3. vWA: electropherogram of child's allele 17.

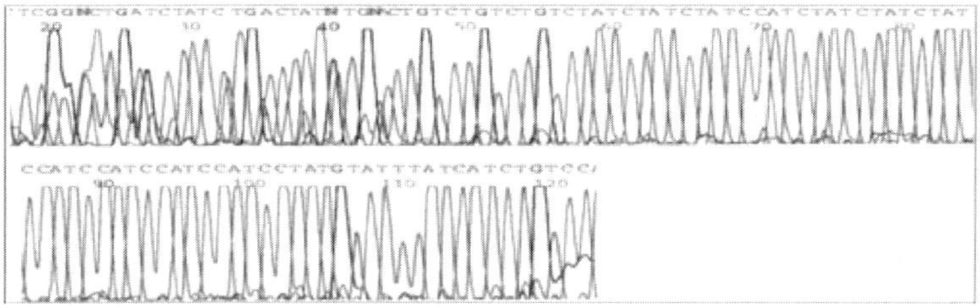

Fig. 4. vWA: electropherogram of child's 2 allele 17.

Case 4—Mothers allele 14 showed the structure already described. The child's 2 allele 17 (Fig. 4) revealed an overlapping of sequences where we can distinguish one structure identical to allele 14. It could be a false homozygote with alleles 14 and 17.

Several phenomena for human diversification are described like meiotic recombination and errors during replication [7]. Possible mechanisms like the unequal crossover between alleles or sister chromatids and point mutations could be a possible explanation for incompatibilities (detected in cases 4 and 2, respectively).

When a mutation is present in the primer binding region for any particular allele there are several possible results for PCR: no effect on amplification; weak amplification of the mutant sequence, resulting in peak signal imbalance in a heterozygote; non-amplification of the mutant allele, resulting a homozygous genotype in a true heterozygote [8]. Probably, cases that showed homozygote PCR products (cases 1 and 4) could have such a kind of mutation. However, we cannot explain what happened in case 3: sequencing of child's allele 17 (150.92 bp) revealed an identical structure to mother's allele 14 (138.76 bp).

In conclusion, we think that sequencing alleles in incompatibility cases should always be done for confirmation, especially in the father–child ones.

References

[1] P.S. Walsh, et al., BioTechniques 10 (4) (1991) 506–513.
[2] C. Kimpton, et al., Forensic Sci. Int. 71 (1995) 137–152.
[3] P. Wiegand, et al., Int. J. Leg. Med. 105 (1993) 315–320.
[4] A. Urquhart, et al., Int. J. Leg. Med. 107 (1994) 13–20.
[5] A. Möller, et al., Int. J. Leg. Med. 106 (1994) 319–323.
[6] A. Möller, et al., Int. J. Leg. Med. 106 (1994) 262–267.
[7] A.J. Jeffreys, et al., EMBO J. 17 (14) (1998) 4147–4157.
[8] S. Walsh, J. Forensic Sci. 43 (5) (1998) 1103–1104.

ELSEVIER

International Congress Series 1261 (2004) 532–534

www.ics-elsevier.com

Consensus profiles and databasing of casework samples amplified with 34 PCR cycles: an empirical approach

V. Castella*, N. Dimo-Simonin, C. Brandt-Casadevall, P. Mangin

Institut universitaire de médecine légale, Rue du Bugnon 21, CH-1005 Lausanne, Switzerland

Abstract. Forensic laboratories commonly have to analyze samples that contain minute amounts of DNA (Low Copy Number DNA). LCN samples can be amplified with increased numbers of PCR cycles, but stochastic variations of their profiles are generally observed. Here, we compare some characteristics of the AmplSTR SGM Plus profiles from casework samples amplified with 28 and 34 cycles in order to evaluate the interpretation guidelines used in our laboratory to genotype LCN samples. A first striking result was that 60% of the 563 casework samples considered yielded DNA concentrations <200 pg/μl DNA and were considered as LCN. Conclusive profiles were recovered for 142 of them (42%). At the end, 142 profiles amplified with 28 cycles and 119 profiles amplified with 34 cycles were sent to the Swiss data base. Respectively, 43.66% and 43.70% of them made a hit. This suggests that reliable LCN profiles can be obtained when using an adapted strategy.

Keywords: STR; LCN; Consensus profile; Multi-tube; Data base

1. Introduction

Forensic laboratories commonly have to analyze samples that contain minute amounts of DNA (Low Copy Number DNA). Furthermore, part of this DNA may be degraded and/or some PCR inhibitors may be present in the extract. Consequently, although it is theoretically feasible to amplify the genetic content of a single cell (~ 6 pg DNA), it may be problematic to obtain reliable AmplSTR SGM Plus (Applied Biosystems) profiles when concentrations of template DNA are <200 pg/μl. Increasing the number of PCR cycles enables to enhance the sensitivity of the PCR. Nevertheless, the benefit of increased sensitivity has to be balanced against a stochastic variation of the profiles (heterozygous imbalance, allelic dropout and false alleles) [1]. Here, we compare some characteristics of SGM Plus profiles from casework samples amplified with 28 or 34

* Corresponding author. Tel.: +41-21-314-70-58; fax: +41-21-314-70-90.
E-mail address: Vincent.Castella@hospvd.ch (V. Castella).

0531-5131/
doi:10.1016/S0531-5131(03)01640-6

Table 1
Information concerning the 563 casework samples considered

Categories of samples	Number of samples	Extraction protocol	[DNA] ≥ 200 pg/μl	CODIS Profiles[a]
Blood stains	100	Chelex	86%	94%
Semen stains	8	Chelex	88%	88%
Saliva stains	238	Chelex	65%	84%
Epidermal stains on clothes	56	Phenol/chloroform	54%	55%
Epidermal stains on swabs	155	Chelex	6%	19%
Hairs	6	Phenol/chloroform	17%	17%
Overall	563		40%	64%

[a] ≥ 6 and 8 loci scored for profiles of respectively one and two persons.

cycles in order to evaluate the interpretation guidelines used in our laboratory to genotype LCN samples.

2. Materials and methods

A total of 563 casework samples analyzed during the first semester of 2002 were considered. Their DNA was extracted using chelex or phenol/chloroform protocols (Table 1). One microliter of each extract was used to estimate the DNA concentration of the samples with the Quantiblot method (Applied Biosystems). Samples with DNA concentrations ≥ 200 and < 200 pg/μl were amplified with the SGM Plus kit in 25 μl reaction volume with 28 or 34 PCR cycles, respectively. One microliter of the amplicons was analyzed with an ABI Prism 310 Gene Sequencer using standard protocols.

Profiles obtained with 28 cycles were confirmed with a second amplification, generally performed with the same PCR conditions. When DNA concentrations were < 200 pg/μl, the first 34 cycles amplification was always performed using 1 μl extracted DNA. The PCR was then replicated, sometimes with different amount of template DNA, in order to apply a multi-tube approach [2,3]. The interpretation guidelines adopted in our laboratory were the following. Each locus was evaluated independently and the heterozygous loci were checked first. The two alleles present at one heterozygous locus were considered only when they appeared together at least three times (minimum three positive amplifications per locus) or when they appeared together twice and the two alleles were further detected at least once each (minimum four positive amplifications per locus). The allele present at one homozygous locus was considered only when no other allele was detected more than once over all the amplifications available.

3. Results

Overall, DNA concentrations ≥ 200 pg/μl were obtained for 226 out of the 563 casework samples considered (40%, Table 1). The vast majority (97%) of the stains with DNA concentrations ≥ 200 pg/μl enabled the obtainment of profiles suitable for the Swiss data base. Contrastingly, 42% of the stains with < 200 pg/μl DNA enabled to recover such profiles. Negative profiles were generally not reproducible over amplifications or contained more than four alleles at some loci.

For each category of stains, the percentages of profiles suitable for the Swiss data base (overall 64%) were always ≥ to the proportions of stains with substantial amounts of DNA (overall 40%; Table 1). Interestingly, several samples with DNA concentrations ≥ 200 pg/μl could not be amplified with 28 cycles. Once these extracts were diluted and amplified with 34 cycles, full SGM Plus profiles were obtained.

A total of 142 profiles amplified with 28 cycles and 119 profiles amplified with 34 cycles were sent to the Swiss data base. At the end of July 2002, respectively 43.66% and 43.70% of these profiles have made a hit in this data base.

4. Discussion

Samples that contain < 200 pg/μl DNA may be difficult to genotype with the SGM plus kit using 28 PCR cycles. In fact, with such conditions, conclusive profiles would have been expected for about 40% of the 563 stains considered here (i.e. those with DNA concentrations ≥ 200 pg/μl). Thanks to the enhanced sensitivity of the 34 cycles, this percentage was increased to 64%. No difference between the data base hits' rates of the casework samples amplified with 28 or 34 cycles was observed. This suggests that reliable LCN profiles were obtained with our interpretation guidelines.

In some cases, the use of smaller volumes of template DNA with enhanced number of PCR cycles improved the PCR reaction. In fact, the amount of PCR inhibitors present in the reaction mix is also diminished when less extract is used for the amplification. The PCR with 34 cycles may thus represent a strategy to analyze inhibited samples, even when they contain substantial amounts of DNA.

Acknowledgements

The authors gratefully acknowledge, Catherine Jan Cabrita, Syndie Delessert, Marie-Laure Morerod, Annelise Grini and Carmelo Simili for their assistance and contributions to this work.

References

[1] J.P. Whitaker, E.A. Cotton, P. Gill, A comparison of the characteristics of profiles produced with the AMPFlSTR SGM Plus multiplex system for both standard and low copy number (LCN) STR DNA analysis, Forensic Sci. Int. 123 (2001) 215–223.

[2] P. Taberlet, et al, Reliable genotyping of samples with very low DNA quantities using PCR, Nucleic Acids Res. 24 (16) (1996) 3189–3194.

[3] P. Gill, et al, An investigation of the rigor of interpretation rules for STRs derived from less than 100 pg of DNA, Forensic Sci. Int. 112 (2000) 17–40.

ELSEVIER

International Congress Series 1261 (2004) 535–537

www.ics-elsevier.com

STR and HLA analysis in paternity testing

Zorana Grubic*, Katarina Stingl, Natalija Martinez, Biserka Palfi, Vesna Brkljacic-Kerhin, Andrija Kastelan

National Referral Organ Transplantation and Tissue Typing Center, University Clinical Hospital Zagreb, Kispaticeva 12, HR 10000, Zagreb, Croatia

Abstract. During the 3-year period, 111 cases of paternity disputes were processed in our laboratory. The analysis was performed on nine STR (TH01, VWA31, FES/FPS, F13A01, SE33, D1S1656, D12S391, D18S535, and D22S683) loci and one VNTR (D1S80) locus. Out of 111 cases, 22 were exclusions. In all cases, exclusion was confirmed on at least five loci. STR loci that were informative in majority of cases were SE33 and D12S391. The least informative loci were FES/FPS and F13A01. In 21 cases exclusions were also confirmed by HLA class I, while only in 17 cases HLA class II alleles excluded the alleged father.

Keywords: Paternity testing; HLA; STR

1. Introduction

HLA system is the most polymorfic genetic system in human genome so far known and for that reason it was used in paternity testing for a long time. However, due to the predominance of certain HLA alleles and linkage disequilibrium, in some cases HLA was not informative enough. During the past decade STR loci became a valuable tool in paternity testing because of their high polymorphism and heterozygosity [1]. The mutation rate of STR loci is higher than that of HLA or some other genetic markers. Combination of these two systems offers higher informativeness and also diminishes the possibility of false exclusion due to mutations.

The aim of this study was to investigate and compare the usefulness of these two systems in cases of paternity dispute.

2. Material and methods

One hundred and eleven triplets (mother, child, and alleged father) were processed in our laboratory during the 3-year period. Nine STR loci (TH01, VWA31, FES/FPS,

* Corresponding author. Tel.: +385-1-23-88-689; fax: +385-1-23-12-684.
E-mail address: zgrubic@kbc-zagreb.hr (Z. Grubic).

0531-5131/
doi:10.1016/S0531-5131(03)01654-6

Table 1
The list of informativeness for nine STR loci and one VNTR locus

Locus	Percentage of informativeness
TH01	62.4
VWA31	62.2
FES/FPS	55.6
F13A01	57.9
SE33	85.7
D1S80	66.3
D1S1656	74.3
D12S391	82.9
D18S535	68.5
D22S683	76.2

F13A01, SE33, D1S1656, D12S391, D18S535, D22S683) and one VNTR locus (D1S80) were tested using four different PCR amplification protocols [1–4]. The analysis of the PCR products was performed by electrophoresis on a 6% polyacrilamide gel in an automated laser fluorescence sequencer (ALFexpress, Pharmacia Biotech). Assignment of alleles was done with Allele Locator program. HLA class I (HLA-A, -B) and class II (HLA-DR) antigens were detected by standard Microlymphocytotoxicity test in Terasaki plates using local and commercial sera.

3. Results

As one can see from Table 1, STR loci that were informative in majority cases were SE33 (85.7%) and D12S391 (82.9%). The least informative loci were FES/FPS (55.6%) and F13A01 (57.9%).

Out of 111 cases, 22 (19.8%) were exclusions. In all cases, exclusion was confirmed on at least five STR loci (five triplets). Ten exclusions were confirmed on six loci, four exclusions at seven loci while three exclusions were documented on eight loci (Fig. 1). We did not find any triplet with exclusion on all 10 loci.

The distribution of exclusions for each STR locus is presented in Fig. 2. The highest number of exclusions was observed at SE33 (18 cases) as opposed to TH01 (7 cases). On the other hand, analysis of HLA polymorphism showed exclusions in 21 out of 22 exclusions.

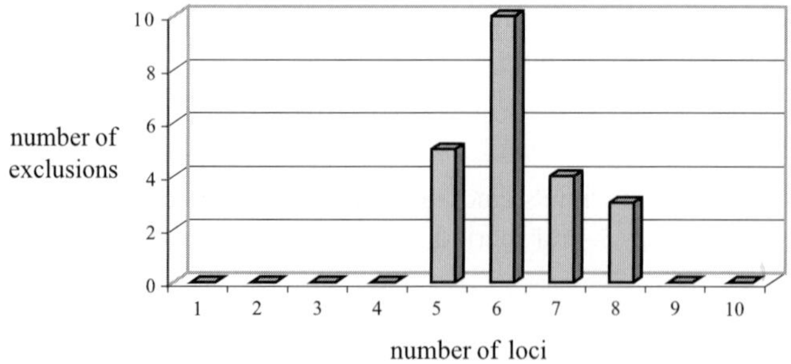

Fig. 1. Distribution of cases according to the number of exclusions.

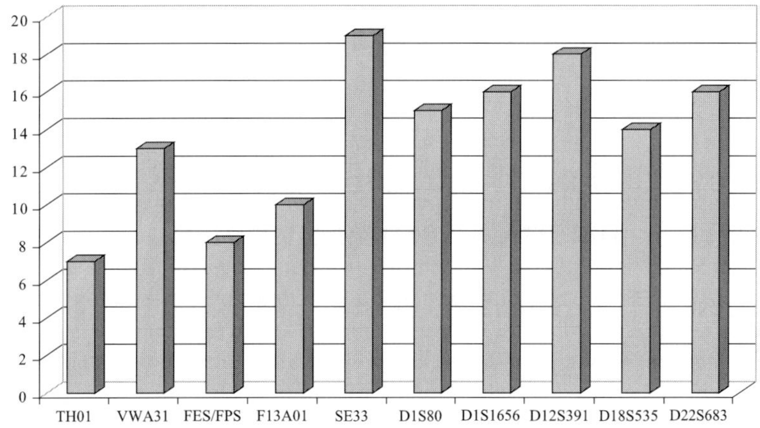

Fig. 2. The distribution of STR loci according to the number of exclusions.

In conclusion, analysis of STR loci combined with HLA polymorphism offers more reliable results for resolving paternity disputes.

References

[1] A. Urquhart, C.P. Kimpton, T.J. Downes, P. Gill, Variation of short tandem repeat sequences—a survey of twelve microsatellite loci for use as forensic identification markers, Int. J. Leg. Med. 107 (1994) 13–20.

[2] M.V. Lareu, S. Barral, A. Salas, M. Rodriguez, C. Pestoni, A. Carracedo, Further exploration of new STRs of interest for forensic genetic analysis, in: G.F. Sensabaugh, P.J. Lincoln, B. Olaisen (Eds.), Progress in Forensic Genetics 8 Elsevier, Amsterdam, 2000, pp. 198–200.

[3] K. Kasai, Y. Nakamura, R. White, Amplification of highly polymorphic VNTR locus (pMCT 118) by the polymerase chain reaction (PCR) and its application to forensic science, J. Forensic Sci. 35 (1990) 1196–1200.

[4] P. Wiegand, B. Budowle, S. Rand, B. Brinkman, Forensic validation of the STR systems SE33 and TC11, Int. J. Leg. Med. 105 (1993) 315–320.

International Congress Series 1261 (2004) 538–540

ELSEVIER

www.ics-elsevier.com

The evaluation of the IDENTIFILER system in paternity testing in Poland

R. Jacewicz*, J. Berent, A. Prosniak, M. Kadlubek, S. Szram

Department of Forensic Medicine, Medical University of Lodz, Sedziowska 18a, 91-304 Lodz, Poland

Abstract. The analysis of the IDENTIFILER system usefulness in paternity determination in the population of central Poland was carried out. An empirical and a theoretical approach have been taken into consideration, aimed at evaluating the exclusion efficiency of 15 STR markers as well as establishing the value of the paternity index. The combined values of PE and PI exceed 0.999999 and 8.4×10^9, respectively.

Keywords: Multiplex STR; Paternity testing; Poland

1. Introduction

The IDENTIFILER system is one of the two currently available multiplexes containing a panel of 15 STR loci in paternity determination [1]. This paper assesses the validity of STR loci included in the IDENTIFILER system for the use in paternity testing in Poland. An empirical and a theoretical approach were taken into consideration in order to validate 15 loci and the whole system for the resolution of paternity cases.

2. Materials and methods

Samples used in the validation for paternity testing were obtained from routinely performed cases at the Department of Forensic Medicine, Medical University of Lodz, Poland. In each case, the blood samples were taken from the mother, one child and one alleged father. DNA extraction was carried out using a salt method described by Lahiri and Nurnberger [2]. Analysed data contained 51 inclusion cases and 117 exclusion cases constructed by linking several mother/child pairs with random, unrelated men.

Amplification of 15 STRs was performed using the IDENTIFILER system with a detection on ABI Prism 377 sequencer (Applied Biosystem). Statistical evaluation was made using the following statistical parameters: power of exclusion (PE) [3] and paternity index value (PI) [4].

* Corresponding author. Tel.: +48-42-6544536; fax: +48-42-6544293.
E-mail address: r.jacewicz@post.pl (R. Jacewicz).

doi:10.1016/S0531-5131(03)01648-0

3. Results and discussion

3.1. Exclusion paternity cases

The power of exclusion (PE) is the parameter evaluating the loci/system efficiency of exclusion in parentage testing. Fig. 1 presents the observed and expected value of the power of exclusion for each marker in a sample population of Poland. A high value of exclusion efficiency was noticed for D2S1338 locus (75.17% expected PE and 77.78% observed one) and than for D18S51, FGA and D21S11 loci. Locus TPOX in theory (PE = 36.09%) and in practice (PE = 20,51%) was the poorest in exclusion efficiency. The average observed PE for locus—57.60% is very similar to the expected one—59.21%.

If a panel of 15 systems is applied in combination, the value of PE (theoretical and practical) reaches 99.9999%, meaning that, on average, only 1 out of million of non-fathers would remain unexcluded. The most frequently we observed nine exclusions (in 23.08% of all exclusion cases). We did not find any exclusion trio cases with only one, two or even three exclusions, which seems to be enough protection before the mutation event. For example, the investigation of 14 STRs gives one excluding result in 0.01% and exclusion in two loci in 0.14% [5].

3.2. Inclusion paternity cases

An evaluation of paternity testing (PI) index in 51 inclusion cases is contained in Fig. 2.

The highest observed and expected PI values were noticed for FGA system (7.3 vs. 8.4) and then for D18S51,D21S11 and D2S1338. Clearly, the lowest observed and expected PI value was obtained for TPOX locus (2.8 vs. 2.1).

The combined value of the expected average paternity index—8.4×10^9 is very near to the one observed in the analysis of 51 inclusions cases—9.2×10^9. The minimum PI combined value received in the analysis of 51 inclusion paternity trio cases was 3.4×10^5 . The maximum value of PI received in analysed cases was

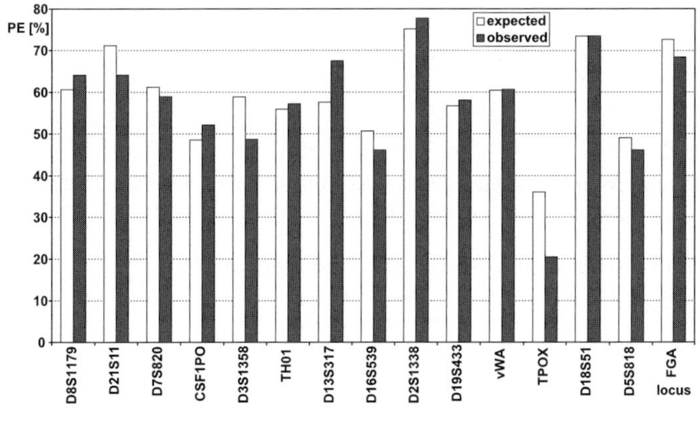

Fig. 1. Power of exclusion (PE) for STR IDENTIFILER loci examined in 117 exclusion cases. □—expected value; ■—observed value.

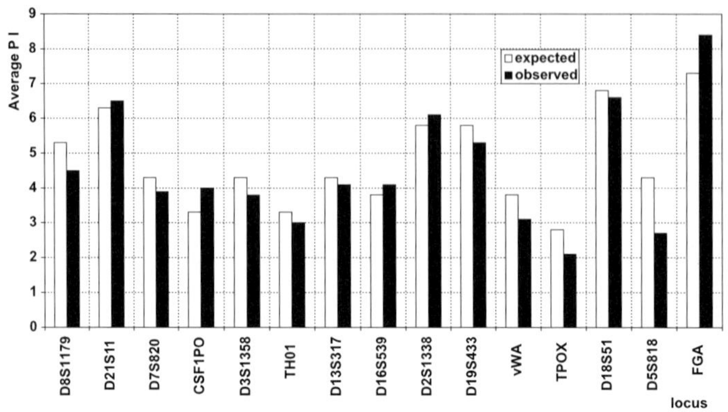

Fig. 2. Average paternity index (PI) for STR IDENTIFILER loci examined in 51 inclusion cases. □—expected value; ■—observed value.

4.4×10^{11}. In majority of the investigated trio cases (60.39%) after the examination of 15 STRs markers, the value of PI varies between million and milliard. When 12 STRs markers are investigated, analogous values vary between 10 thousands and 10 millions [6].

4. Conclusion

The analysis performed on Polish population proved that the panel of 15 STR loci included in IDENTIFILER system was sufficient to satisfactorily resolve all investigated trio paternity cases. The received number of excluding loci, not less than 4, is suitable, in our opinion, to protect from the mutation event when a judgment of non-paternity is formed. The obtained in inclusion cases value of the paternity index, greater than 100,000, according to our laboratory standards is sufficient to ascertain fatherhood status.

Acknowledgements

This project was supported by the Medical University of Lodz grant no. 502-11-702.

References

[1] Paternity testing workshop of the English Speaking Working Group of the IFSG, 2003 (draft report).
[2] D.K. Lahiri Jr., J.I. Nurnberger, A rapid non-enzymatic method for RFLP studies, Nucleic Acids Res. 19 (1991) 5444.
[3] B.S. Weir, Genetic data analysis II, Sinauer, Associates, Sutherland, MA, 1996, pp. 209–211.
[4] C. Brenner, J.W. Morris, Paternity index calculation in single locus hypervariable DNA probes: validation and other studies, Proceedings from the International Symposium on Human identification 1989. Promega, Madison, 1990, pp. 21–53.
[5] F. Calafell, The probability distribution of the number of loci indicating exclusion in a core set of STR markers, Int. J. Leg. Med. 114 (2000) 61–65.
[6] J.A Thomson, V. Pilotti, Validation of short tandem repeat analysis for the investigation of cases of disputed paternity, Forensic Sci. Int. 100 (1999) 1–16.

International Congress Series 1261 (2004) 541–543

ELSEVIER

www.ics-elsevier.com

The number of STR markers necessary to resolve relationships in deficiency paternity cases

Silvano Presciuttini[a,*], Chiara Toni[b], Fabio Marroni[a], Isabella Spinetti[b], Joan E. Bailey-Wilson[a], Ranieri Domenici[b]

[a] *Inherited Disease Research Branch, NHGRI, NIH, Baltimore MD, USA*
[b] *Unit of Legal Medicine, School of Medicine, University of Pisa, Pisa, Italy*

Abstract. The inference about the biological relationship between pairs of individuals using genetic markers plays a central role in many areas of human genetics. We investigated the number of markers (M) that are necessary to assign a given proportion of pairs (50%, 60%, 70%, 80%, 90%, 95%, and 99%) to their correct relationship at three predefined probability levels (99%, 99.9%, and 99.99%) against several alternative hypotheses. The following relationships were considered: (1) full sibs (FS), (2) second degree (2D, including half-sibs, grandparent–grandchild and avuncular pairs), (3) first cousins (FC), (4) unrelated individuals (UR). © 2003 Published by Elsevier B.V.

Keywords: STR; Familial relationships; DNA markers; Deficiency paternity

1. Introduction

Deficiency paternity cases are not unusual in the forensic practice. Typically, these situations arise when the alleged parent of a claimant is not available (in most cases this person is deceased), and one of his or her undisputed relatives acts as a defendant, i.e. s(he) denies claimant's contentions. Most of these cases reduce, at least at first examination, to determine the likelihood ratio of two alternative hypotheses about the relationship between a single pair of individuals. We have encountered instances in which the contrasting propositions about the two contenders were as follows: half-sibs vs. unrelated; avuncular pair vs. unrelated; full sibs vs. half-sibs; first cousins vs. unrelated; full sibs vs. unrelated. Here, we addressed the question of the number of autosomal DNA markers needed to resolve common relationships at specified probability levels by computer simulations.

* Corresponding author. Permanent address: Center of Statistical Genetics, c/o Centro Retrovirus, S.S. Abetone e Brennero 2, 56127 Pisa, Italy. Tel.: +39-50-2213797; fax: +39-50-2213524.
E-mail address: sprex@biomed.unipi.it (S. Presciuttini).

0531-5131/
doi:10.1016/S0531-5131(03)01664-9

2. Materials and methods

2.1. Computer simulations

The genotypes of 10 000 pairs of relatives were obtained by Monte Carlo simulations of pedigrees for the four considered relationships, FS, 2D, FC, and UR. Simulations were carried out separately for 25 commonly used markers, which were repeated a second time to reach a total number of 50 markers, thus representing a possible future expansion of validated markers. The markers were sorted by decreasing heterozygosity separately for the first set (including the 13 CODIS markers) and the second set (other 12 markers commonly used in the forensic practice). Genotype probabilities were obtained as provided [1,2], except for the FC relationship that required a elaborating new formulas.

2.2. LR calculation

The probability of the correct relationship for all pairs of genotypes at each locus was divided by the probability of each of the other relationships, thus obtaining the likelihood ratio (LR) that a pair was correctly attributed to its true relationship rather than to any of the others. For instance, in the case of FS vs. UR, we simulated 40 000 individuals (10 000 true FS pairs and 10 000 UR pairs) and calculated the LR(FS/UR) for all pairs and for all loci. LRs were multiplied across increasing number of loci. We settled several probability levels (99%, 99.9%, and 99.99%) and several limits for the proportion of pairs that were correctly discriminated (50%, 60%, 70%, 80%, 90%, 95%, and 99%); then, we determined the number of markers that allowed reaching these limits for each pair of contrasting hypotheses.

Table 1

	Probability	Percentage of pairs						
		50%	60%	70%	80%	90%	95%	99%
FS/2D	99%	13	16	18	24	33	41	>50
	99.9%	20	24	32	39	47	>50	>50
	99.99%	28	34	41	49	>50	>50	>50
FS/FC	99%	4	5	7	9	12	14	18
	99.9%	7	9	12	14	16	18	26
	99.99%	9	13	15	16	19	23	29
FS/UR	99%	4	5	6	8	11	14	17
	99.9%	7	8	10	14	15	18	24
	99.99%	9	10	14	16	19	20	28
2D/FC	99%	33	44	>50	>50	>50	>50	>50
	99.9%	>50	>50	>50	>50	>50	>50	>50
	99.99%	>50	>50	>50	>50	>50	>50	>50
2D/UR	99%	16	18	22	28	39	44	>50
	99.9%	28	31	39	45	>50	>50	>50
	99.99%	31	37	41	>50	>50	>50	>50
FC/UR	99%	>50	>50	>50	>50	>50	>50	>50
	99.9%	>50	>50	>50	>50	>50	>50	>50
	99.99%	>50	>50	>50	>50	>50	>50	>50

3. Results

Table 1 shows the number of markers necessary to assign a given percentage of pairs (second row) to each of six possible relationships (first column) at the specified level of probability (second column).

4. Discussion

Full sibs (FS) are discriminated from nonrelatives (UR) and first cousins (FC) with a reasonable number of markers; for instance, 90% of FS pairs are discriminated from UR pairs with probability of 99.99% using 18 markers (which are easily found in commercial kits); the same number of markers allows discriminating more than 50% of FS from FC at the same probability level. Discrimination between full and half sibs (FS/HS) is more problematic, in accordance with published data [3,4]; 18 markers can solve more than 50% of cases but only with a probability of 99%. First cousins (FC) are poorly discriminated from second degree (2D) and nonrelatives (UR), even in the hypothesis of the availability of 50 validated markers. Future extensions of this work will include the use of X- or Y-chromosome markers, which can allow solving particular cases of disputed relationships (for instance, two males that share the same Y-haplotype have a very low probability of being non relatives [5,6], whereas X-chromosome markers provide paternity indexes higher than similar autosomal markers in the case of female pairs).

References

[1] S. Presciuttini, C. Toni, E. Tempestini, S. Verdiani, L. Casarino, I. Spinetti, F. De Stefano, R. Domenici, J.E. Bailey-Wilson, Inferring relationships between pairs of individuals from locus heterozygosities, BMC Genet. 3 (1) (2002 Nov. 20) 23.

[2] I.W. Evett, B.S. Weir, Interpreting DNA Evidence, Sinauer, Sunderland, MA, 1998.

[3] M.G. Ehm, M. Wagner, A test statistic to detect errors in sib-pair relationships, Am. J. Hum. Genet. 62 (1998) 181–188.

[4] M. Boehnke, N.J. Cox, Accurate inference of relationships in sib-pair linkage studies, Am. J. Hum. Genet. 61 (1997) 423–429.

[5] L. Gusmao, M. Brion, A. Gonzalez-Neira, M. Lareu, A. Carracedo, Y chromosome specific polymorphisms in forensic analysis, Leg. Med. (Tokyo) 1 (2) (1999 Apr.) 55–60.

[6] R. Szibor, M. Krawczak, S. Hering, J. Edelmann, E. Kuhlisch, D. Krause, Use of X-linked markers for forensic purposes, Int. J. Legal Med. 117 (2) (2003 Apr.) 67–74.

International Congress Series 1261 (2004) 544–546

www.ics-elsevier.com

DNA research in sexual offences: experience in Ecuador

Fabricio González-Andrade[a,*], Dora Sánchez-Q[a], Begoña Martínez-Jarreta[b]

[a] *Molecular Genetics Department, Metropolitan Hospital, Av. Mariana de Jesus y Occidental, Meditropoli Medical Center, Quito 2119, Ecuador*

[b] *Department of Legal Medicine, University of Zaragoza, Spain*

Abstract. To assess the technical and judicial consequences resulting from the practical application of *DNA testing* in forensic research in the numerous sex crimes in Ecuador. Twenty-six sex offence cases were studied using the DNA technique and were analysed in the Genetics Department of the Ecuadorian Red Cross. For the tissue mixtures, we performed differential extraction using one separation solution for the female fraction and another for the male fraction, in accordance with our protocols. An ABI 310 sequencer was used for typing. The fragment size was determined and the allelic designation of the different loci made by comparing them with the PowerPlex 16 kit allelic ladders; the software package Grape 1.1 was used for analysis of the mixtures and for DNA fingerprinting, Statistical Evaluation. Only 15% of all cases reach the stage of Public Investigation, and the sentence is incriminating in only 12.5% of these cases.

Keywords: Ecuador; STR; Criminality; Sex offences; PCR; Justice

1. Introduction

The DNA analysis technique has not been in use for many years in Ecuador and filiation and paternity studies have been carried out more than any other kind so far [1,2]. However, in the sphere of criminality the application of this technique is still at the early stages, despite an increase since the establishment of the new Criminal Procedural Code [3]. Furthermore, there is a high rate of reports, which, together with the absence of a legal, social and family response, contribute to establishing impunity and covering-up as the norm [4]. In the year 2002, the National System of Legal Medicine and Forensic Science was created in Ecuador [5,6].

2. Material and methods

Samples: Twenty-six cases of sexual offences were studied by means of the DNA technique and analysed in the Molecular Genetics Department between July 2002 and

* Corresponding author. Tel./fax: +593-2-2248902.
E-mail address: fabriciogonzales@usa.net (F. González-Andrade).

0531-5131/ © 2003 Published by Elsevier B.V.
doi:10.1016/j.ics.2003.11.031

Table 1
Legal situation of sexual offences tried by the public prosecution nationally between July 2001 and December 2002

Type of offence	Prior investigation	Rejection	Public Prosecutor's examination	Conversion	Acquittal	Accusation
Indecent assault	732	46 (6.2%)	166 (22.7%)	0	38 (5.2%)	106 (14.5%)
Rape	2239	161 (7.2%)	416 (18.6%)	3	165 (7.4%)	430 (19.2%)
Rape of a minor	205	11 (5.4%)	51 (24.9%)	0	12 (5.9%)	33 (16%)
Procurement and corruption of minors	133	3 (2.3%)	16 (12%)	0	3 (2.3%)	5 (3.8%)
Abduction	1574	38 (2.4%)	90 (5.7%)	0	32 (2%)	38 (2.4%)
Total	4883	259 (5.3%)	739 (15.1%)	3 (0.06%)	250 (5.1%)	612 (12.5%)

August 2003 [7]. *DNA extraction*: Phenol–Cloroform–Isoamilic Alcohol, and proteinase K was used for the remains. For the unquestioned samples, we used the Wizard Genomic DNA Purification Kit System© method. The DNA was quantified by means of UV absorbance. For the tissue mixtures, we made a differential extraction using a separation solution for the female fraction Tris/EDTA/NaCl 400 μl, sarkosyl 25 μl, proteinase k (20 mg/ml), and for the male fraction Tris/EDTA/NaCl 150 μl, sarkosyl at 20%, proteinase k (20 mg/ml) and DTT 0.39 M, in accordance with our protocols. *PCR*: Amplification was carried out in a Genius© thermocycler. We used an ABI 310 sequencer. The fragment size and the allelic designation of the different loci were established by comparison with the allelic ladders of the PowerPlex 16 kit (Promega) and they were subsequently interpreted with the Gene Scan Analysis Software® programme. We followed the recommendations of the *DNA Commission of the International Society of Forensic Genetics* for STR analysis. *Analysis of data*: The Grape 1.1 software, for DNA fingerprinting, Statistical Evaluation was used for analysis of the mixtures.

3. Results and discussion

DNA analyses have mainly been useful for the exclusion of suspects and to clarify the role of each person involved in a sexual offence. An interesting fact is that a high percentage of the victims are under the age of 18, and the fact that there is a considerable number of boys among these. In all inclusion cases, the Likelihood Ratio was over one million. The criteria we used in the interpretation of the mixture profiles were: firstly, to

Table 2
DNA studies carried out by type of offence and legal proceedings

Legal procedure		Type of offence	
Prior investigation	5 (0.19)	Sexual offence	20 (0.76)
Public prosecutor's examination	14 (0.54)	Sexual offence plus theft	1 (0.04)
Criminal magistrate	1 (0.04)	Sexual offence plus homicide	4 (0.16)
Juvenile magistrate	2 (0.08)	Sexual offence plus abduction	1 (0.04)
Officers of court	4 (0.15)	Total	26
Total	26		

Table 3
Origin of samples for DNA analysis in the 26 cases analysed and individuals analysed

Origin of the samples	Number of samples	Individuals contrasted	Number
Vaginal swabs on slides	9 (0.31)	Victim plus suspect	13 (0.50)
Victim's underwear	7 (0.24)	Victim and two or more suspects	5 (0.19)
Articles of victim and/or aggressor's clothing	9 (0.31)	Two victims and two or more suspects	3 (0.12)
Foetal remains or placenta (following abortion)	1 (0.034)	Suspect plus exhibit	4 (0.15)
Sanitary pad	1 (0.034)	Exhibit with exhibit	1 (0.04)
Condoms	1 (0.034)	Total 26	
Unquestioned blood from family members	1 (0.034)		
Total	29		

identify the presence of a mixture profile; secondly, to identify the possible number of contributions to the mixture; thirdly, to estimate the relative proportion of the individuals that comprise the mixture and the combinations of possible genotypes; fourthly, to compare with genetic profiles obtained in the reference samples and, fifthly, to assess the results obtained and make statistical calculations where relevant (Tables 1–3).

References

[1] F. González-Andrade, D. Sánchez, B. Martínez-Jarreta, et al., Evaluation of 1495 cases of disputed paternity in Ecuador resolved with STR-PCR polymorphisms, Proc. IAFS, (2002) 261–265.
[2] F. González-Andrade, D. Sánchez, B. Martínez-Jarreta, Population genetic of 12 STR loci in a sample of Mestizos from Ecuador (South America), J. Forensic Sci. 48 (2).
[3] E. Legales, Código de Procedimiento Penal. RO 360, del 13 de enero del 2000.
[4] G. León, Del Encubrimiento a la Impunidad, diagnóstico sobre violencia de género, CEIME, 1a ed. (1995) 69.
[5] Estado Ecuatoriano. Reglamento del Sistema Nacional de Medicina Legal y Ciencias Forenses. Quito-Ecuador, RO. 157, del 6 de junio del 2002.
[6] P. Reilly, Legal and public policy issues in DNA forensics, Nat. Rev., Genet. (2001) 313–321.
[7] B. Martínez-Jarreta, El consentimiento informado, Revista Ciencia Forense, Institución Fernando El Católico, 2002.

International Congress Series 1261 (2004) 547–549

www.ics-elsevier.com

Robust STR multiplexes for challenging casework samples

James W. Schumm*, Robyn S. Wingrove, Elizabeth K. Douglas

The Bode Technology Group, Research and Development, 7364 Steel Mill Rd., Springfield, VA 22150, USA

Abstract. The presence of amplification inhibitors and degraded DNA in many World Trade Center (WTC) victim bone fragment samples motivated us to create STR multiplex sets displaying more robust amplification with challenging casework samples. We developed multiplex sets that co-amplify smaller versions of the larger amplicons present in commercial sets. They generate well-balanced profiles with at least five-fold the typical signal using 0.25 ng of human DNA template and generated three times the genetic information derived from commercial kits using the more challenging WTC samples. Sensitivity of the systems approaches detection of individual DNA fragment templates, requiring implementation of appropriate interpretation guidelines for this low copy number, high throughput environment.

Keywords: Short tandem repeat; PCR; World Trade Center; Low copy number

1. Introduction

Many World Trade Center (WTC) disaster bone samples had been exposed to extensive moisture in combination with substantial heating for periods of up to 2 months. Limited or degraded DNA and amplification inhibitors in some samples lead to limited profile determination using commercial multiplex systems. Here, we describe the design, development and application of new multiplex sets that generated substantially more robust genotype determination with degraded DNA, low copy number samples and samples containing amplification inhibitors.

2. Results and discussion

We processed 12 392 bone samples during the first phase of analysis of World Trade Center remains. Using the QIAamp 96 DNA Blood Kit DNA extraction method [1] in combination with Profiler Plus and COfiler multiplex systems, we generated full 13-locus profiles with 27% of samples. Another 17% produced 7–12 loci, while 22% revealed 1–7

* Corresponding author. Tel.: +1-703-644-1200x303; fax: +1-703-644-2319.
E-mail address: james.schumm@bodetech.com (J.W. Schumm).

doi:10.1016/S0531-5131(03)01776-X

loci and 34% of samples provided negative results. We initiated two projects to improve genotyping success rates. We previously reported development of a modified bone sample DNA extraction procedure [1], and here describe the design, development, testing, manufacture and validation of new multiplex sets providing more robust genotype determination with challenged samples.

We reasoned that re-design of the larger loci of Profiler Plus and COfiler into smaller amplicons in two multiplex sets, BodePlex 1 and BodePlex 2 (Fig. 1) and modifying protocol and primer mix parameters to optimize performance at reduced DNA templates would alleviate limitations due to DNA degradation or inhibition. In development, we demanded robust amplification with 0.25 ng template or less, complete polymerase-directed non-templated addition and no inappropriate primer-generated products.

We used some previously described primer sequences [2], but found about half the sequences required re-design to meet the demands of high product yield in a low template environment. Evaluation of primer set combinations necessitated additional primer design. In all, more than 100 different primer sequences from six different oligonucleotide vendors were evaluated in dozens of combinations to generate operationally useful multiplex sets. The extremely successful performance of the first two systems encouraged us to complete the set of the 13 core STR loci of the CODIS system by developing a third multiplex (data not shown). We employed previously identified primers [3] for the smaller loci of the PowerPlex 16 system and modified only the vWA locus primers of this set.

Fig. 1 displays the locus combinations and typical profiles generated with 0.25 ng template for the BodePlex 1 and BodePlex 2 systems, respectively. Note that the average peak height displayed in each case is similar to a typical amplification of 1–2 ng template using standard commercial multiplex systems. This increased product yield is due not only to modified primer selection, but also to protocol modifications such as increased enzyme concentration, prolonged elongation times and 32 cycles of amplification.

Primer-generated artifacts were not detected. However, low-RFU dye artifacts could not be completely eliminated despite vendor selection based primarily on this trait. On the

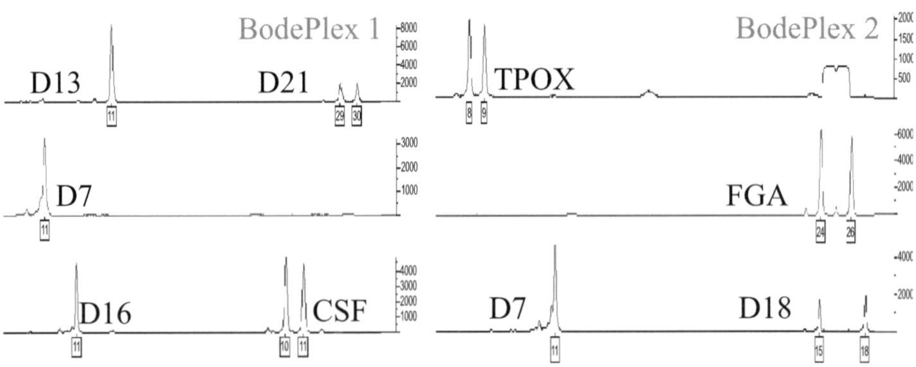

Fig. 1. BodePlex 1 and BodePlex 2 contain smaller versions of the large amplicon loci of Ampl*F*/STR Profiler Plus and COfiler. The amplified product of 0.25 ng DNA template is shown for each multiplex, respectively. Fluorescein-labeled (top), HEX-labeled (middle) and NED-labeled (bottom) loci are indicated.

positive side, these artifacts have low RFU values and can be readily discounted in profile determination since they are reproducibly present even in negative controls.

Validation of all three BodePlex systems was conducted according to United States DNA Advisory Board guidelines, including demonstration of accuracy, precision, reproducibility and concordance with other systems. Species-specificity and performance with non-probative samples and mixed DNA samples was characterized. Sensitivity experiments indicate alleles are generated with as little as one to three copies of DNA (data not shown). With such low copy number (LCN) situations, stochastic processes often generate allele imbalance or allele dropout. Therefore, our interpretation guidelines include a required minimum 400 RFU for homozygote calls and 100 RFU for individual allele calls. When one allele between 100 and 400 RFU is observed at a locus, it is called but the presence or absence of a second allele is considered unknown.

LCN projects with other systems have revealed "allele drop-in" in negative controls and samples [4]. This phenomenon is distinguished from general contamination in that only one or possibly two foreign fragments are observed rather than a full or substantially full profile. The alleles observed are random in nature and are not derived from the analyst performing the work. With BodePlex systems, we observe allele drop-in in 1–2% of negative samples. However, to insure proper assignment, allele designations are made only if the same allele is observed in two separate amplification reactions of the sample. This requirement for redundancy limits the number of identified alleles, but insures the highest quality of the accepted data in LCN situations.

In summary, these multiplex sets support high throughput, low copy number casework with extremely challenged samples.

References

[1] M.M. Holland, C.A. Cave, C.A. Holland, T.W. Bille, Croat. Med. J. 44 (3) (2003) 264–272.

[2] J. Butler, Y. Shen, B.R. McCord, J. Forensic Sci. 48 (5) (2003 Sep.) 1054–1064.

[3] A. Masibay, T.J. Mozer, C. Sprecher, J. Forensic Sci. 45 (6) (2000 Nov.) 1360–1362.

[4] P. Gill, J. Whitaker, C. Flaxman, N. Brown, J. Buckleton, J. Forensic Sci. Int. 112 (2000) 17–40.

ELSEVIER

International Congress Series 1261 (2004) 550–552

www.ics-elsevier.com

Collecting and processing buccal cell samples

James W. Schumm*, Eun Young Song, Martha Burger, Jangbir Sangha

The Bode Technology Group, Research and Development, 7364 Steel Mill Road, Springfield, VA 22150, USA

Abstract. Recently, we developed a new device and method of buccal sample collection. This device supports efficient sample collection, accessioning, and preparation for DNA amplification. The collection process is very simple and an individual can be trained in its effective use in just a few moments. New extraction methods were developed for use with the collector to provide rapid preparation of samples for amplification. © 2003 Elsevier B.V. All rights reserved.

Keywords: Buccal; Sample; Forensic; Product; Short tandem repeat; Validation

1. Introduction

There is a vital need for a reliable, noninvasive, and efficient method of DNA sample collection that feeds directly into automated downstream processes. Blood collection and deposition onto membranes currently provides an reliable automation-compatible collection method, but this approach is invasive and expensive, requiring trained personnel. Buccal cell collection with cotton or Dacron swabs retains sufficient sample while providing a less expensive and less invasive alternative. However, current buccal cell collection methods either require a secondary transfer of collected cells to a flat membrane with concordant risk of material loss or are not readily adapted either to automated tracking or automated extraction. We describe a new device to overcome these shortcomings employing direct collection of buccal samples for automation-compatible analysis and long-term storage.

2. Materials and methods

The Buccal DNA Collector, Bode**X**tract DNA Extraction Reagent, and Bode**E**lute DNA Extraction Reagent were obtained from The Bode Technology Group (TBTG) (Springfield, VA) and used as recommended. Amplification was performed using Profiler Plus, COfiler (Applied Biosystems, Foster City, CA), or PowerPlex 16 System

* Corresponding author. Tel.: +1-703-644-1200x303; fax: +1-703-644-2319.
E-mail address: james.schumm@bodetech.com (J.W. Schumm).

doi:10.1016/S0531-5131(03)01485-7

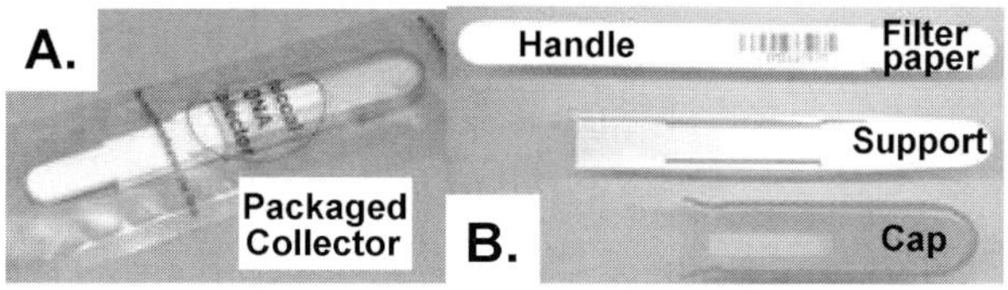

Fig. 1. Assembled and packaged Bode DNA Buccal Collector (A) and separated components (B).

(Promega) as described. Amplification products were separated and detected using the 3100 Genetic Analyzer and analyzed with GeneScan and Genotyper (Applied Biosystems).

3. Results and discussion

We designed, developed, manufactured, characterized, and validated a new device and accompanying protocols for rapid and simple buccal cell collection (Fig. 1). The collector is assembled, packaged, and sterilized for transport prior to use (Fig. 1A). It consists of three component parts: (1) a plastic handle holding a piece of filter paper, (2) a plastic support piece, and (3) a cap (Fig. 1B). The support snaps onto the handle to provide a firm support behind the filter paper during sample collection. It can be readily removed for sample analysis and storage.

To use the collector, one places a thumb on the back of it, puts the filter paper firmly against the inside of the cheek, and swipes with pressure against the cheek while pulling the device out of the mouth. This is repeated several times. Then the cap is placed over the filter paper to keep it clean during drying or transport (Fig. 2).

We have learned the following useful information after performing experiments to characterize and validate the collection process: (a) All positions on the collector collect enough sample material to provide reliable profiles. However, DNA yields are approximately twice as much near the tip of the paper versus near the handle. (b) Samples collected and stored in paper envelopes at room temperature for 12 months provided full profiles in 100% of cases (52 of 52) with allele peak heights similar to those in the original test profiles. (c) The number of cells collected is several-fold fewer than with blood collection. (d) Different individuals vary significantly in cell deposition generally yielding between 15- and 300-ng DNA from a 6-mm punch extracted with Bode**E**lute. (e) Two- to threefold variation in DNA yield was observed from the same person collected on 4 consecutive days. (f) Using either two or eight swipes of the cheek

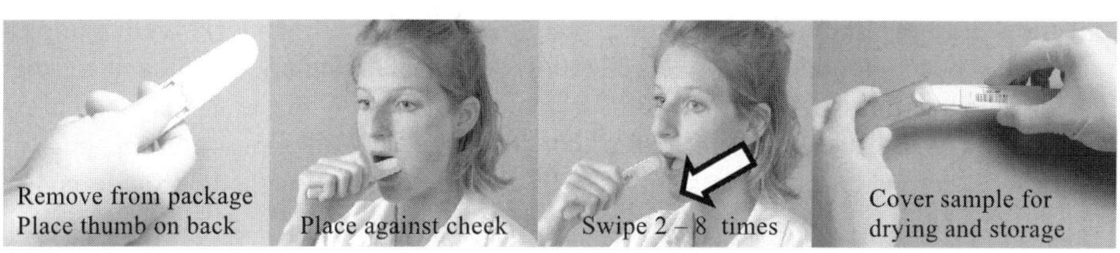

Fig. 2. Summarized instructions for use of Bode DNA Buccal Collector.

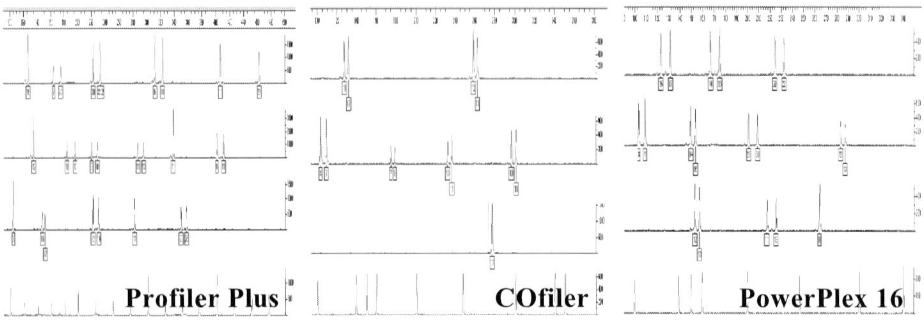

Fig. 3. Commercial kits were used to amplify punches from the Bode Buccal DNA Collector prepared using Bode**X**tract DNA Extraction Reagent.

generated full profiles. However, the DNA yield from two swipes was, on average, one-half to two-thirds of the yield of eight swipes; (g) Five consecutive collections of eight swipes each from the same cheek all yielded full profiles. However, the second and subsequent collections averaged yield of about one-third to two-thirds of the initial collection.

To simplify the extraction of DNA from the Buccal DNA Collector, two extraction reagents have been prepared. The Bode**X**tract DNA Extraction Reagent is used in preparation of small punches from the Buccal DNA Collector that are to be used directly in an amplification reaction. Protocols for preparation of one 3-mm punch or alternatively two 1.2-mm punches have been developed. The Bode**E**lute DNA Extraction Reagent is a one-step process that removes DNA from a 6-mm punch from the Collector. The DNA contained within the approximately 40-μl elution volume is immediately available for amplification without additional processing. Both extraction methods require minimal hands-on processing time, are compatible with tube or microplate format, and neither requires instrumentation beyond a plate heater.

Following collection and DNA extraction, samples prepared with Bode**X**tract were amplified with Profiler Plus and COfiler (Applied Biosystems) and with PowerPlex 16, PowerPlex 1.1, and PowerPlex 2.1 (Promega). All systems provided complete profiles. Examples of three of these multiplex systems amplified from punches prepared with Bode**X**tract are displayed in Fig. 3.

4. Conclusions

We have designed, developed, manufactured, and characterized a Buccal DNA Collection device for collection, processing, and storage of buccal cell samples. Training in collection and use of the collection device is extremely simple and reliable. Two DNA extraction reagents have been formulated for use with the Collector to allow amplification of processed punches either directly or following elution into an amplification-compatible reagent solution. These materials and methods provide convenient approaches to both large and small reference sample and databanking analysis requirements.

ELSEVIER

International Congress Series 1261 (2004) 553–555

www.ics-elsevier.com

Novel method of DNA extraction from bones assisted DNA identification of World Trade Center victims

T. Bille, R. Wingrove, M. Holland, C. Holland, C. Cave, J. Schumm*
The Staff of The Bode Technology Group

The Bode Technology Group, Research and Development, 7364 Steel Mill Drive, Springfield, VA 22150, USA

Abstract. DNA identification of many mass fatality victims of the 11 September 2001 attack on the World Trade Centers (WTC) in New York City required development of new analytical methods. Development of novel STR multiplex sets with improved performance using challenged DNA samples is described in an accompanying paper. Here we describe modifications and improvements to procedures used to extract DNA from bone fragments found at the site. © 2003 Elsevier B.V. All rights reserved.

Keywords: World Trade Center; Bone; Short tandem repeat; PCR

1. Introduction

The WTC DNA Identification Project required an effective high-throughput method of DNA extraction from bones. Many of the WTC samples had been abused not only by the enormous force of the towers collapse, but also by the long-lasting fires and substantial exposure to water that lasted for many weeks afterward. The solution came in two phases. Phase I included implementation of more traditional DNA extraction methods re-designed to accommodate the high-throughput requirements. Phase II focused on protocol changes to improve DNA yield and lower retention of inhibiting substances.

2. Results and discussion

Phase I included adaptation to a rapid DNA extraction method for 12849 WTC bone fragments. Once tissue was removed from the surface of each bone fragment with a scalpel and the bone was cleaned with bleach, we employed a drill to remove a portion of the outer surface of the bone. This outer material was discarded as potential surface contamination. A clean drill bit was used to pulverize an inner portion of bone.

* Corresponding author. Tel: +1-703-644-1200x303; fax: +1-703-644-2319.
E-mail address: james.schumm@bodetech.com (J. Schumm).

0531-5131/ © 2003 Elsevier B.V. All rights reserved.
doi:10.1016/S0531-5131(03)01831-4

Table 1

Results of initial STR analysis (AmpFlSTR Profiler Plus and COfiler)	WTC victim remains (100% = 12,849)	AA Flight 587 victim remains (100% = 442)
Full STR Profile (13 loci)	27.2%	73.1%
High Partial STR Profile (7–12 loci)	17.4%	11.8%
Low Partial STR Profile (1–6 loci)	21.1%	7.2%
No STR Profiles (0 loci)	34.3%	7.0%

Approximately 25–50 mg of this inner powder was extracted in a 96-well format using a modification of the QIAamp® 96 DNA Blood Kit (QIAGEN, Valencia, CA). This extraction includes a lysis step in the presence of SDS and Proteinase K followed by the bind-wash-elute QIAGEN technology [1].

STR results using this method were incomplete due to a combination of poor yield and possible inhibition of amplification. The same method was employed on remains of victims of American Airlines flight 587 that occurred in New York during this period. The much higher success rate with these materials reassured us that the method itself was very effective, but that the sample quality was much more challenging with the WTC samples (Table 1).

Phase II incorporated modifications to the Phase I extraction procedure to provide higher sample yield and quality. Treatment of the bone powder with EDTA assisted decalcification of the bone. Then overnight cell lysis without proteases was followed by a 3-h Protease K digestion step. The digested material was then captured onto a QIAamp membrane, washed, and eluted. Additional details of the method may be found in Holland et al. [1]. These modifications allowed use of up to 150 mg bone powder for extraction and provided an extracted product that was more amenable to PCR amplification.

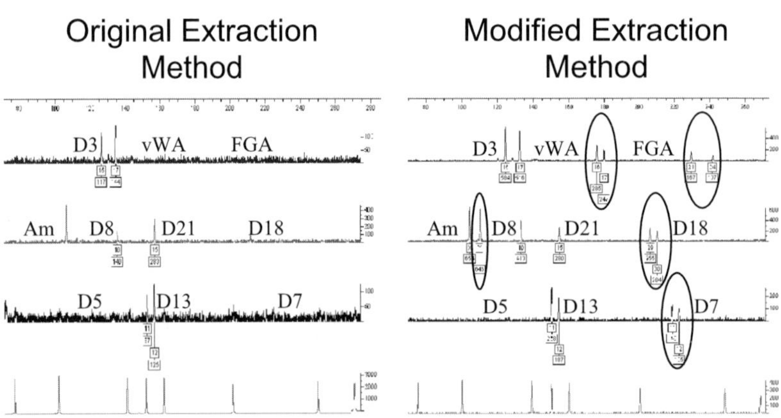

Fig. 1. Separate portions of one bone fragment sample were extracted using the original modified QIAamp® 96 DNA Blood Kit protocol or the modified extraction method. Products of each extraction were amplified with AmpFlSTR Profiler Plus. New alleles observed following amplification of DNA extracted with the new method are marked with ovals.

A total of 5335 samples that originally generated either Low Partial STR Profiles (1–6 loci in 13 attempted) or No STR Profiles were re-extracted with the improved method and re-amplified with the Profiler Plus and COfiler multiplex systems, respectively. Of these, 2.9% (i.e., 154) provided Full STR Profiles, 7.3% (i.e., 388) High Partial STR Profiles, 14.0% Low Partial STR Profiles, and 78.5% generated No STR Profiles. Thus, 542 new profiles were generated using the second extraction with the modified method. An example of an individual bone sample extracted with the two methods, respectively, and amplified with Profiler Plus is illustrated in Fig. 1.

In sum, high-throughput methods for extraction of DNA from bone fragments for STR analysis have been developed and then improved.

Reference

[1] M.M. Holland, C.A. Cave, C.A. Holland, T.W. Bille, Croatian Medical Journal 44 (3) (2003) 264–272.

International Congress Series 1261 (2004) 556–558

www.ics-elsevier.com

AB0 blood group genotyping of multiple single nucleotide polymorphisms using SNaPshot

G. Ferri*, C. Bini, S. Ceccardi, S. Pelotti

Department of Medicine and Public Health, Section of Legal Medicine, University of Bologna, via Irnerio 49, 40126 Bologna, Italy

Abstract. A novel reproducible strategy to type the AB0 blood group system by the minisequencing of five nucleotide positions using SNaPshot (Applied Biosystem, USA) is described. This new technique has been successfully applied on 30 blood donors and the results agree with the known serologically based predicted genotypes.

Keywords: AB0; Polymorphism; PCR; Single nucleotide polymorphism (SNP); Minisequencing

1. Introduction

AB0 gene on chromosome 9 consists of seven exons ranging in size from 28 to 688 bp and mutations critical for AB0 blood group phenotypes have predominantly been found in exons 6 and 7 [1]. We describe here a novel reproducible strategy based on a duplex PCR assay followed by multiplex PCR minisequencing protocol that simultaneously allows genotyping of the well-established single nucleotide polymorphisms (SNPs) at five nucleotide positions 261, 297, 467, 646 and 703 to reveal six common alleles (A1, A2, B, 01, 01V and 02). We tested this technique on 30 blood donors with known serologically based predicted genotypes in family studies.

2. Materials and methods

Blood samples were collected from 30 healthy individuals with known serologically AB0 genotypes in family studies. Genomic DNA was isolated from 200 μl of whole blood using QIAamp DNA Mini Kit (Qiagen,Germany). All primer sequences and final concentrations are listed in Table 1. PCR amplification of the 10 ng of DNA template was performed in a 25-μl reaction mixture with 1.5 mM $MgCl_2$, 200 μM dNTPs, 1 × Gold Buffer (Applied Biosystem, USA) and 1 U of Taq Gold Polymerase (Applied Biosystem) at 10 min at 95 °C for one cycle; 1 min at 94 °C, 1 min at 59 °C, 1 min at 72 °C for 34 cycles

* Corresponding author. Tel.: +39-51-243250; fax: +39-51-248896.
E-mail address: labemat@medleg.unibo.it (G. Ferri).

0531-5131/
doi:10.1016/j.ics.2003.11.012

Table 1
Primer sequences and concentrations used

Locus	Sequence	Final concentration (μM)
AB0 6F 20 mer	5′ -GCCTCTCTCCATGTGCAGTA-3′	0.3
AB0 6R 20 mer	5′ -AACCCAATGGTGGTGTTCTG-3′	0.3
AB0 7F 20 mer	5′ -TGGCTTTCCTGAAGCTGTTC-3′	0.3
AB0 7R 19 mer	5′ -GATGTAGGCCTGGGACTGG-3′	0.3
Extension primers		
261 27 mer F	5′ -$(T)_8$GGAAGGATGTCCTCGTGGT-3′	0.15
297 21 mer R	5′ -GTTGAGGATGTCGATGTTGAA-3′	0.4
467 38 mer F	5′ -$(T)_{16}$TACTATGTCTTCACCGACCAGC-3′	0.5
646 44 mer F	5′ -$(T)_{24}$GCGTGGACGTGGACATGGAG-3′	0.4
703 33 mer F	5′ -$(T)_{17}$CGGCACCCTGCACCCC-3′	0.075

and 7 min of final extension at 72 °C Minisequencing by SNaPshot Multiplex kit (Applied Biosystem) and post-extension treatment were performed as described by manufacturer. All samples were run on ABI PRISM 310 Genetic Analyzer (Applied Biosystem).

3. Results

The DNA template of 131/132 bp on exon 6 and 389 bp on exon 7 was successfully amplified in a duplex PCR reaction. Each extension primer was first tested by uniplex reaction then multiplex SNaPshot was utilized and the interpretation of the electrophoretic pattern from minisequencing (Fig. 1) with a table of reference (Table 2) allowed to assign

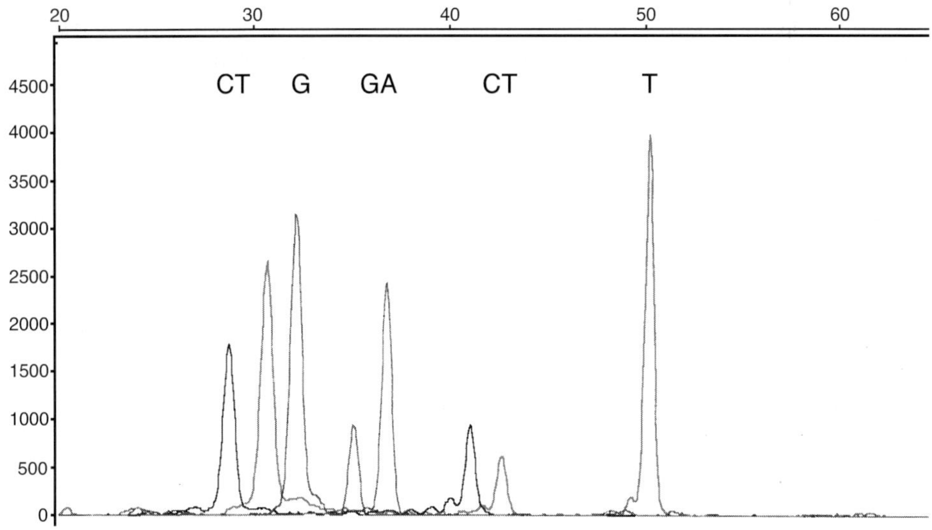

Fig. 1. AB0 blood group genotyping of multiple single nucleotide polymorphisms using SNaPshot: A2-B genotype (CT G GA CT T).

Table 2
AB0 genotype interpretation by minisequencing

Genotype	R 297 (22 bp)	F 261 (28 bp)	F 703 (34 bp)	F 467 (39 bp)	F 646 (45 bp)
A1 A1	T	G	G	C	T
A2 A2	T	G	G	T	T
B B	C	G	A	C	T
01 01	T	A	G	C	T
01V 01V	C	A	G	C	A
02 02	C	G	G	C	T
A1 A2	T	G	G	C T	T
A1 B	C T	G	G A	C	T
A1 01	T	G A	G	C	T
A1 01V	C T	G A	G	C	T A
A1 02	C T	G	G	C	T
A2 B	C T	G	G A	C T	T
A2 01	T	G A	G	C T	T
A2 01V	C T	G A	G	C T	T A
A2 02	C T	G	G	C T	T
B 01	C T	G A	G A	C	T
B 01V	C	G A	G A	C	T A
B 02	C	G	G A	C	T
01 01V	C T	A	G	C	T A
01 02	C T	G A	G	C	T
01V 02	C	G A	G	C	T A

the AB0 genotype without difficulties on 30 blood donors with known serologically based predicted genotypes in family studies.

4. Discussion

Via SNaPshot multiplex reaction we have developed a reproducible strategy to type the AB0 blood group system based on a duplex PCR assay followed by multiplex primers extension analysis. The well-established SNPs investigation at five nucleotide positions 261, 297, 467,646 and 703 permits the identification of A1, A2, B, 01, 01V and 02 alleles.

This method shows several advantages: first, one reaction mixture is required for DNA template amplification and one for minisequencing analysis that is a viable system for typing candidate SNPs at a moderate throughput level. Second, it is more practical, rapid than RFLP analysis, resulting unambiguous the interpretation of AB0 genotypes with a table of reference.

The molecular approach for typing AB0 blood group allows the direct determination of the AB0 genotype without family studies on the same DNA sample that can be also typeable for STRs and it may provide an additional information in identification case-works where AB0 blood group record is the only available data.

The present method may be very useful for personal identification as well as for paternity testing in forensic science.

Reference

[1] M.L. Olsson, M.A. Chester, Polymorphism and recombination events at the ABO locus: a major challenge for genomic AB0 blood grouping strategies, Transfus. Med. 11 (2001) 295–313.

International Congress Series 1261 (2004) 559–561

www.ics-elsevier.com

Capillary electrophoresis reveals DNA damage in aged forensic samples

P. Fattorini[a,*], F. Tomasella[a], E. Albertini[a], P. Grignani[b], C. Previderè[c]

[a] *Department of Sciences of Public Health, University of Trieste, Via molino a vento 123, 34137 Trieste, Italy*
[b] *IRCCS Policlinico S. Matteo, Department of Legal Medicine Pavia, Italy*
[c] *Department of Legal Medicine and Public Health, University of Pavia, Italy*

Abstract. Capillary electrophoresis was used to analyse aged forensic DNA samples. A good correlation between DNA damage and reliability of PCR typing results was found. © 2003 Elsevier B.V. All rights reserved.

Keywords: Capillary electrophoresis; DNA damage; PCR fidelity

1. Introduction

PCR fidelity is influenced by several factors with the integrity of the primary structure of the template playing a major role [1,2]. DNA damage, studied by reversed-phase HPLC/MS, showed that aged forensic samples exhibited reduced amounts of the four canonical DNA bases and the presence of several molecular products of DNA oxidation [3]. Capillary electrophoresis (CE) has shown to be a powerful tool to identify DNA bases and their analogous [4]. In the present work, we used this technical approach to analyse aged forensic samples. In addition, to investigate a correlation between DNA damage and the reliability of the PCR typing results, we analysed the DNA extracted from several different forensic specimens.

2. Materials and methods

In order to evaluate the robustness of CE, 200 nM of each DNA bases (C, G, A and T) and 5-BrU (employed as internal standard) were dissolved in 1% HCl and injected by pressure (10 s) in an uncoated fused silica capillary (length 57 cm, ϕ 50 μm). A P/ACE 5000 (Beckman) apparatus was employed and the detection of the effluents was performed at 254 nm. The raw data were analysed by the System Gold

* Corresponding author. Tel./fax: +39-040-946153.
E-mail address: fattorin@univ.trieste.it (P. Fattorini).

doi:10.1016/S0531-5131(03)01790-4

Table 1
Forensic samples analysed in this study

Sample	DNA source	Age	uDNA bases	PCR results
PV1A*	B	0.5	0.43	–
PV1B*	B	0.5	0.53	–
PV1C*	B	0.5	0.64	–
PV2A^	B	20	0.45	–
PV2B^	B	20	0.39	–
PV3A§	B	5	0.61	–
PV3B§	B	5	0.64	–
PV4	B	50	0.20	–
PV5	BS	0.5	0.31	–
TS1	BS	13	0.64	–
TS2	BS	12	0.43	–
TS146A	M	5	0.56	±
TS367D#	M	33	0.23	–
TS367F#	C	33	0.58	–
TS26	C	5	0.26	–
TS133A	C	5	0.84	+
TS2188	B	3	0.36	–
TS2189	B	2	0.87	+
CTRL	blood	–	>0.95	+

DNA source refers to the biological tissue from which DNA was extracted: B: bone, BS: bloodstain, M: muscle, C: cartilage. Age refers to the presumptive post-mortem time (given in years). uDNA bases refers to the relative amounts of undamaged DNA bases [3] found in the samples. PCR results refers to the reliability of the multiple PCR typing determinations: + reproducible results; – no genetic profiles; ± presence of PCR artefacts. Marks *, ^, § and # refer to samples collected from the same biological donor.

(Beckman). Replicate tests of this standard solution showed an error standard deviation <2%.

DNA extraction was performed following standard methods [3]. About 1 g (estimated by EtBr staining) [5] of the DNA samples listed in Table 1 was hydrolysed in 90% formic acid at 170 °C for 30 min. After lyophilisation, the samples were redissolved in 25 μl of 1% HCl containing 25 nM of 5-BrU and analysed as reported above. As controls, eight DNA samples extracted from fresh blood were employed.

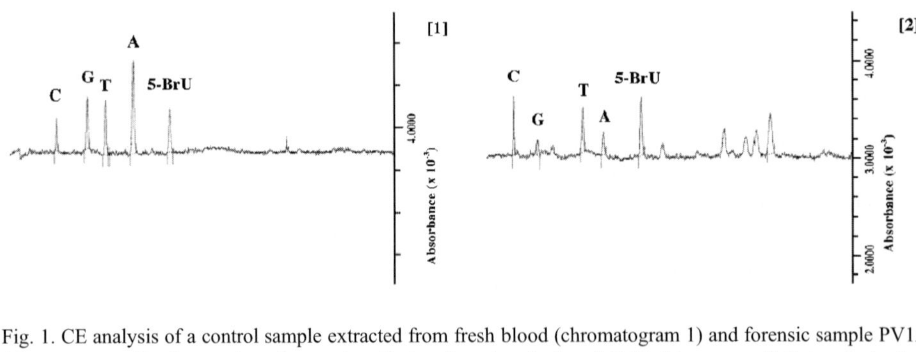

Fig. 1. CE analysis of a control sample extracted from fresh blood (chromatogram 1) and forensic sample PV1A (chromatogram 2). C: cytosine, G: guanine, T: thymine, A: adenine, 5-BrU: 5-bromouracil (internal standard control). Lower relative amounts of the four canonical bases and additional peaks are shown.

Comparable amounts (from 100 to 5 ng) of each forensic sample were amplified using the AmpF/STR *Identifiler* commercial kit (PE Applied Biosystem). Thirty cycles of PCR were performed. The PCR products were analysed by CE using an ABI Prism 310 Genetic analyser (PE Applied Biosystem).

3. Results

CE analysis of the forensic samples showed low relative amounts of undamaged DNA bases [3] compared to control samples (see Table 1). In addition, also the presence of several additional peaks was observed (see Fig. 1).

Replicate PCR amplifications provided reliable results only from samples TS133A and TS2189, while, in sample 146A, several PCR artefacts, such as allele "drop-out" and "drop-in", were found. No PCR products were obtained from the remaining samples tested in this study.

4. Discussion

In this work, we provide our experience on the employment of CE to analyse the integrity of the primary structure of the DNA extracted from aged forensic samples.

Our preliminary data confirm that CE is an accurate and sensitive method to detect chemical modification of the DNA recovered from aged forensic samples. The sensitivity of our method allows a powerful evaluation of the chemical integrity of less than 1 g of genetic material. Data from Table 1 strongly suggest that reliable STR typing can be achieved only from templates whose chemical composition is preserved. This is confirmed by other experimental data showing that both the processivity and the fidelity of *Taq* polymerase are influenced by the chemical integrity of the template [2,3,5,6].

In conclusion, our results show that CE is a powerful tool to investigate the molecular decay of forensic samples.

Acknowledgements

Part of this work was supported by MURST, 40% granted to P. Fattorini and C. Previderè (CIP 20011065132).

References

[1] K.A. Eckert, T.A. Kunkel, DNA polymerase fidelity and the polymerase chain reaction, PCR Methods Appl. 1 (1991) 17–24.

[2] S. Pääbo, et al., Ancient DNA and the polymerase chain reaction. The emerging field of molecular archaeology, J. Biol. Chem. 264 (1989) 9709–9712.

[3] P. Fattorini, et al., Fidelity of polymerase chain reaction-direct sequencing analysis of damaged forensic samples, Electrophoresis 20 (1999) 3349–3357.

[4] C.B. Norwood, et al., DNA adduct research with capillary electrophoresis, Anal. Biochem. 213 (1993) 194–199.

[5] C. Previderè, et al., Molecular characterisation of the nucleic acids recovered from aged forensic samples, Int. J. Leg. Med. 116 (2002) 334–339.

[6] M. Höss, et al., DNA damage and DNA sequence retrieval from ancient tissues, Nucleic Acids Res. 24 (1996) 1304–1307.

International Congress Series 1261 (2004) 562–564

www.ics-elsevier.com

DNA profiling by different extraction methods

A. Barbaro[a,*], N. Staiti[b], P. Cormaci[a], L. Saravo[b]

[a] *Department of Forensic Genetics, Studio Indagini Mediche E Forensi (SIMEF), 89128 Reggio Calabria, Italy*

[b] *Laboratory of Molecular Biology, Raggruppamento Carabinieri Investigazioni Scientifiche (RaCIS), 98128 Messina, Italy*

Abstract. The aim of this study is to compare the efficiency of different validated methods for DNA extraction using commercial kits. DNA extraction was performed on fresh liquid blood, old bloodstains, cigarettes butts, semen stains and hairs. Samples were quantified by the AluQuant Human DNA Quantitation System. Amplification was carried out by GeneAmp 2400 and 9700 Thermal Cyclers using the AmpFlSTR Identifiler kit. Amplified products were analyzed into both ABI PRISM 310 and 3100 Genetic Analyzers employing ABI softwares.

Keywords: Extraction methods; Forensic samples; STRs

1. Introduction

In recent years a number of different forensic kits for recovering small amounts of DNA from a variety of specimens (saliva, sperm stain, clotted blood) has been developed in order to improve the final quantity of DNA recovered, thus substantially reducing the cost per analysis.

The aim of this study was to evaluate the ability of each method to extract DNA from different samples; the quantity of human DNA extracted from each sample; any potential interference due to the substrate; the possibility to obtain reliable DNA typing results; and the quality of profiles obtained.

The present paper is intended to be the first step of an exhaustive research that will be soon extended to more systems, therefore here we will report our preliminary results and evaluations.

* Corresponding author. Department of Molecular Genetics–SIMEF Via Nicolo' da Reggio 4, 89128 Reggio Calabria, Italy. Tel.: +39-965891184-5; fax: +39-965891125.

E-mail addresses: simef@tiscali.it (A. Barbaro), kunitz@libero.it (P. Cormaci).

URL: www.simef.com.

doi:10.1016/S0531-5131(03)01647-9

2. Material and methods

We used 16 bloodstains (from 4 to 1 years old) upon cotton, denim, wood; 10 cigarette butts (6 months old); 10 anagen and 14 telogen single hair with roots; 10 semen stains on paper and tissue (3 months old).

For referencing, we spotted 30 μl of fresh blood on surfaces like cotton, denim, wood.

We took a piece of bloodstains and semen-stains in a known quantity with Harris UNI-CORETM cutter 2.0 mm.

DNA was extracted with DNA IQTM Systems (Promega), Invisorb Forensik Kit I (Invitek), Chelex (Biorad), QIAamp DNA Blood Mini kit (Quiagen, Hilden, Germany) and phenol–chloroform treatment according to the manufacture's protocol. [1–6] Quantification of human DNA was provided by the AluQuant Human DNA Quantitation System (Promega), following the manufacture's protocol [7].

Amplification was carried out in a different laboratory from the one dedicated to the extraction, so that amplified products never entered the extraction laboratory.

STRs amplification was carried out by GeneAmp 9700 and 2400 thermal cyclers, by the AmpFLSTR Identifiler kit (Applied Biosystem), according to the kit protocol, positive and negative controls were enclosed during the amplification step [8].

Amplified products were analyzed by capillary electrophoresis into both ABI PRISM 310 and 3100 Genetic Analyzers employing ABI softwares (DATA Collection, GeneScan Analysis, Genotyper Fragment Analysis).

3. Results and discussion

Our evaluations are summarized as follows: (a) the commercialized protocols should be adapted to improve the sensitivity when working either with difficult samples (old blood or old bloodstains on surfaces like wood or denim) or samples containing small DNA amount (telogen single hairs); (b) all the five procedure performed gave good and reproducible results in presence of fresh bloodstains. (c) the system based on colon like QIAamp kit constitutes an excellent method of purification, mainly for traces containing inhibitors; nevertheless, we observed a loss in DNA recovering (around 30%) that however is dependent from different factors (quantity of eluition buffer, no. of eluitions, eluition time and temperature). (d) for blood traces on denim and on nude wood (inhibitors presence) the QIAamp system gave the best results in comparison with the other methods, being able to purify completely the sample; however, the success of the analysis is also highly dependent on the modality of sampling (blood eluition or scraping). The kind of denim fiber and its color (clear or dark) are very relevant for the success of DNA extraction, since different tissues differently release DNA inhibitors. (e) systems like IQ allow a better surrender and an excellent reproducibility since the paramagnetic IQ resin used binds a known quantity of DNA and there is a low number of variable factors; the use of a single tube for DNA extraction reduces the loss of material. The process of lysis is excellent, thanks to an excellent buffer because of it the method is optimal for hard samples like single hair and semen stains too; we obtained a positive result for all 10 anagen single hair and for 9 of the 14 telogen hairs analyzed. Such a strong lysis solution may however interfere with the extraction of samples like cigarette butts since a prolonged exposition to it can destroy the filter that may link aspecifically the chelating resin. However, the strong IQ lysis solution (that contains DTT and PK), if efficiently opens sperm cells, nevertheless, may destroy the stain substrate (especially paper) and produce interferences that reduce the extraction output. (f) Chelex represents the optimal method when referred to low cost and rapidity of execution in a single tube; therefore its use is suggested with common samples as cigarette butts, semen stains, bloodstains. However, a single step does not remove DNA inhibitors that could interfere with DNA typing and so in their presence, a passage in centricon or microcon could be required to purify the sample. A successful DNA extraction of blood traces on jeans and nude wood has been observed using Chelex only when the blood sampling was performed by eluition of the stain from the surface. A similar situation was observed employing DNA IQ or Invisorb procedures. The main problem using chelex for old bloodstains is to make the stain soluble: since the reagent is not very strong, the procedure may require a prolonged incubation time to eluite the trace. IQ treatment permits to solubilize better the old stain since it uses a very strong extraction buffer. Semen stains gave similar good results using IQ or Chelex procedures. (g) Phenol–chloroform procedure employs many dangerous reagents, it is time-consuming since it requires many steps and a particular accuracy to avoid the loss of material, especially when they are analyzed samples containing LCN such as cigarette butts, hairs or semen stains. Organic extraction is restricted to a few complex cases only when samples are very degraded (old washed bloodstains, bones, putrefied tissues) since this procedure plus Centricon concentration, in comparison with other ones, permits to obtain a better DNA extract. (h) Invisorb procedure uses a soft buffer so we did not observe optimal results using it for extracting old bloodstains or bloodstains on wood or denim. However, it can be used with excellent results for cigarette butts and fresh blood.

4. Conclusion

A forensic laboratory often has to deal with samples that are less than ideal since the evidence may have been left exposed to hard environment for a long time or can be found on varied surfaces. In fact, a biological sample found on a crime scene as a liquid blood sample or more often as a bloodstain or semen stain or hair can be degraded or contains a number of substance besides DNA that can inhibit PCR amplification.

For example, materials like textile dyes or hemoglobin can remain with the DNA throughout the sample preparation process and compromise successful PCR.

Our paper shows that a right choice of the DNA extraction method and an accurate DNA quantification are very important steps in the analytical procedure to ensure optimal results.

References

[1] P.S. Walsh, D.A. Metzger, R. Higuchi, Chelex 100 as a medium for simple extraction of DNA for PCR-based Typing from forensic material, Biol. Tech. 10 (1991) 506.

[2] DNA IQ™ Tissue and Hair Extraction kit. User 's manual. Promega (2002).

[3] DNA IQ™ System-Small Sample Casework Protocol Extraction kit. User's manual. Promega (2002).

[4] QUIAamp DNA Mini Kit and QUIAamp DNA Blood Mini Kit Handbook, Quiagen (2001).

[5] Invisorb Forensic Kit I, Technical Bulletin, Invitek (2001).

[6] J. Sambrook, E.F. Fritsch, T. Maniatis, Molecular Cloning: A Laboratory Manual, CSH Press, New York.

[7] ALU Quant-Human DNA Quantitation System—User's manual. Promega (2002).

[8] Amp*Fl*STR Identifiler PCR amplification kit. User 's manual. PE Biosystems (2001).

ELSEVIER

International Congress Series 1261 (2004) 565–567

www.ics-elsevier.com

DNA profiling on fabrics: an in-situ method

Lay Hong Seah*, Mohd Izuan Othman, Primulapathi Jaya, N. Hithaya Jeevan

Forensic Division, Malaysian Department of Chemistry, Jalan Sultan, Petaling Jaya, Malaysia

Abstract. In the presence of sufficient DNA (from biological stains) on a binding substrate, multiplex PCR can be carried out in-situ without an extraction step. In this study, blood dried on six different fabrics, namely, cotton, rayon, nylon, wool, acrylic and polyester were tested. Multiplex PCR using the AmpF*l*STR Identifiler kit on a 2- to 3-mm square bloodstain successfully amplified the DNA from cotton, rayon, nylon and wool. A partial profile was obtained from the bloodstain on acrylic. No profile was obtained from the bloodstain on polyester. The binding properties of these various fabrics with DNA were investigated in this study.

Keywords: Fabrics; Cotton; Rayon; Nylon; Wool; Acrylic; Polyester; AmpF*l*STR identifiler; In-situ DNA profiling; STR

1. Introduction

Natural cellulose fibers, e.g. cotton or man-made cellulose fibers, e.g. rayon chemically consists of linked glucose units with free hydroxyl units which can provide sites for linkages. Polyamide fibers like nylon are a synthetic fiber with amide (–CONH–) linkages. Wool is a protein fiber made up of amino acids. Polyester is a synthetic fiber composed of units of an ester of a substituted aromatic carboxylic acid. Acrylic is a synthetic polymer composed of acrylonitrile units ($-CH_2-CHCN-$) [1]. The presence of biological fluids, e.g. blood, semen or saliva on fabrics (clothing or bedding items) present one of the most important evidentiary materials from a crime scene [2]. The ability to type DNA directly from various types of fabrics was investigated in this study.

2. Materials and method

A preserved blood sample (with normal blood counts) was loaded and dried on six types of fabrics, namely cotton, rayon, nylon, wool, acrylic and polyester. A 2-mm square bloodstain was taken from the cotton, rayon, nylon and wool fabrics, and a 3-mm square bloodstain was taken from acrylic and polyester fabrics due to the relatively bigger stain area. The stains were purified in-situ and subsequently amplifed directly (at days 1 and 14)

* Corresponding author. Tel.: +603-79853840; fax: +603-79581173.
E-mail address: lhseah@kimia.gov.my (L.H. Seah).

0531-5131/
doi:10.1016/S0531-5131(03)01832-6

using the AmpFlSTR Identifiler kit. The DNA typing was carried out on the ABI 3100 Genetic Analyzer and profiles were analyzed by GeneScan (version 3.7) and Genotyper 3.7 software [3].

3. Results and Discussion

At day 1, the DNA from cotton, nylon, rayon and wool fabrics were successfully amplified generating full DNA profiles (Fig. 1) with more intense profiles from cotton and

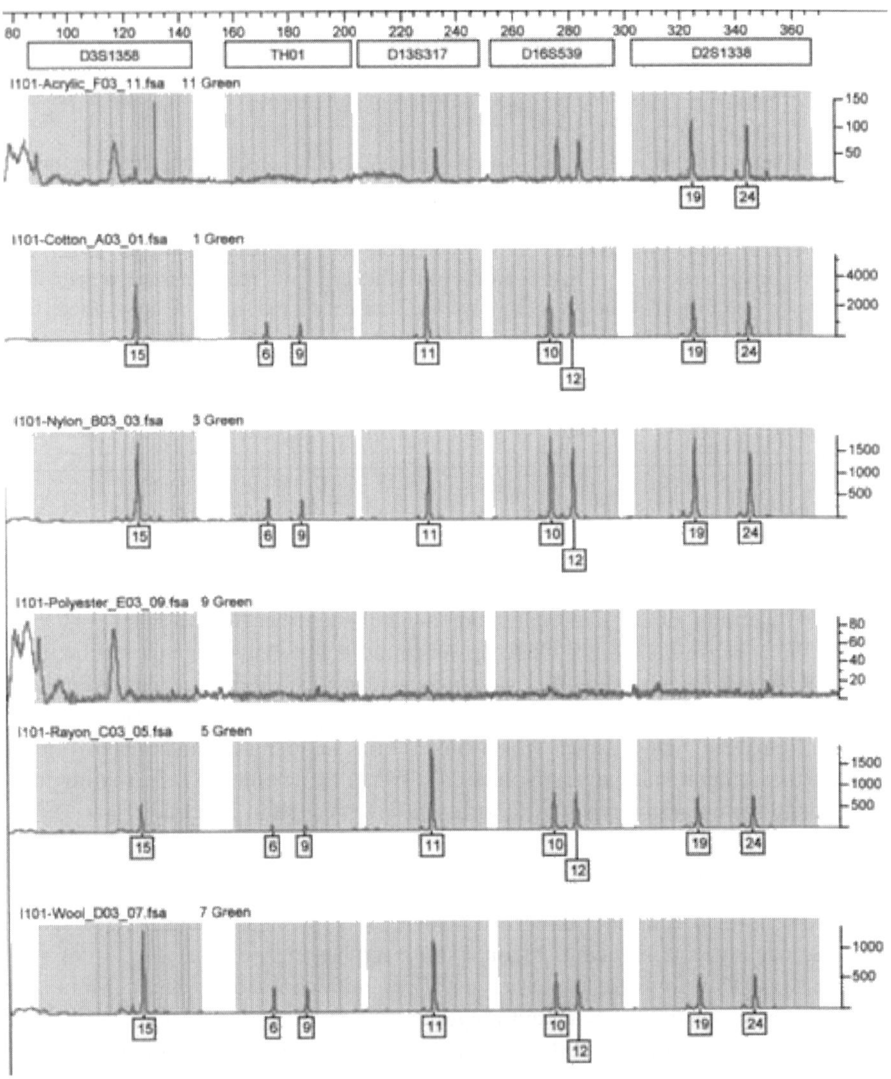

Fig. 1. Day 1—DNA profiles at the green loci D3S1358, TH01, D13S317, D16S539 and D2S1338 of AmpFlSTR Identifiler typing kit for (top to bottom) acrylic, cotton, nylon, polyester, rayon and wool.

nylon. A partial profile was obtained from acrylic and no DNA profile was derived from polyester. It is interesting to note that for DNA on acrylic amplification for the bigger alleles were generally more successful.

Amplification on the 14-day old bloodstains generated almost complete DNA profiles for cotton and nylon and a less complete profile for rayon but relatively less intense profiles compared to the fresh bloodstains (figure not shown). The DNA profile from acrylic showed no significant variation after 14 days.

The presence of functional groups on fibers permit molecular chains (intrinsic or extrinsic) to be held together by the operation of strong intermolecular forces–hydrogen bonding, dipole–dipole attractions and van der Waals forces [4,5]. The O–H groups of cotton and rayon and the N–H groups of nylons and wool are capable of strong hydrogen bonding with nucleic acid chains resulting in powerful intermolecular attractions, hence facilitating an in-situ amplification on the solid template with possible deterioration of the attractive forces with time. Polyesters and acrylics contain polar carbonyl (C=O) and cyano (C≡N) groups which permit relatively weaker dipole–dipole attraction with nucleic acid chains. The null amplification from polyesters could be due to inefficient intermolecular forces between polyesters and nucleic acids. The efficiency of the in-situ technique for the six different fabrics in decreasing order are cotton = nylon > rayon > wool > acrylic > polyester.

The ability to obtain a DNA profile by in-situ amplification from a small stained area (1–10 mm^2 area) without extraction of DNA from the fabric becomes important when biological stains are available on a small area where recovery of usable DNA for typing may be adversely reduced by an extraction process and when quick results are demanded. Biological stains on fabrics like cotton and nylon can be typed directly and stains on non-absorbent surfaces like glass and plastics can be swabbed up onto cotton cloth.

References

[1] D.S. Lyle, Modern Textiles, 2nd ed., Wiley, New York, 1982.

[2] H.C. Lee, et al., Forensic applications of DNA typing: collection and preservation of DNA evidence, Am. J. Forensic Med. Pathol. 19 (1998) 10–18.

[3] L.H. Seah, et al., STR Data for the AmpF/STR Identifiler loci in three ethnic groups (Malay, Chinese, Indian) of the Malaysian population, Forensic Sci. Int. In press.

[4] L. Mandelkern, Introduction to Macromolecules, Springer, New York, 1972.

[5] R.T. Morrison, R.N. Boyd, Organic Chemistry, 4th ed., Allyn and Bacon, Boston, 1983.

ELSEVIER

International Congress Series 1261 (2004) 568–570

www.ics-elsevier.com

DNA technology application procedures in forensic practice: social and ethical conditioning I

J.J. Gamero[a,*], J.L. Romero[a], J.L. Peralta[a], F. Corte-Real[b], M.C. Vide[b]

[a] *Legal Medicine Department, Faculty of Medicine, Cádiz University, Fragela s/n, Cádiz 11003, Spain*
[b] *National Institute of Legal Medicine, Largo da Sé Nova, 3000-213 Coimbra, Portugal*

Abstract. In the study carried out it is intended, in accordance with the preliminary draft of the International Declaration on Human Genetic Data, that information be gathered concerning the diverse questions regarding DNA analysis and its application in the identification of individuals (sample extraction, laboratory treatment, sample analysis and storage, information from the obtained results, etc.) that different social groups in our country may have. This would enable the establishment of a starting point for public debate and the development of public awareness proposals that may serve as an aid, not in the elaboration of a draft law for DNA database regulation in Spain which we consider to be outside our responsibility, but in the elaboration of later regulations which take into account all the details related with the process previously described.

Keywords: Public opinion; Forensic genetics; Ethics; Database

1. Introduction

The information obtained from DNA genetic analysis may furnish a large quantity of data which could result in discriminatory consequences in such areas as health, insurance, employment and the law as well as social and family life [1,2]. Among those rights that may be affected are those involving intimacy, liberty, equality and nondiscrimination [1]. The lack of protection afforded to personal health databases as well as the need to regulate the area of forensics (Draft Bill for the regularization of DNA databases in Spain, 1999) must be pointed out.

In the study carried out it is intended, in accordance with the preliminary draft of the International Declaration on Human Genetic Data [3], that information be gathered concerning the diverse questions regarding DNA analysis and its application in the identification of individuals (sample extraction, laboratory treatment, sample analysis and

* Corresponding author. Fax: +34-56-223-139.
E-mail address: joaquin.gamero@uca.es (J.J. Gamero).

0531-5131/
doi:10.1016/j.ics.2003.10.001

storage, information from the obtained results, etc.) that different social groups in our country may have [4].

2. Materials and methods

Once the general aims of the work had been specified and the tasks to be performed had been planned, the development of the task was begun in the following order: production of an opinion questionnaire and the selection of a homogenous group of interviewers; the selection of the sample in accordance with a criteria of randomness and representativity; the purging of non-random errors that do not concern the survey; the analysis of the data obtained, using statistical methods for their summarized description. As a means of collecting the data, the questionnaire form was chosen, since, as well as being convenient for the interviewees, it is an efficient means of coding, purging and an easy way to obtain a large amount of data. The sample choice was performed by using random criteria and by trying to find a cross-section nature in the different sexes and age groups. A stratified survey of the Spanish population was carried out and 1656 questionnaires were completed. Among those interviewed (809 women and 845 men) different age groups were represented (from 18 years of age upward).

The data collected was stored on a computer and statistically analysed with the help of the Statgraphics Plus 5.0 (Statistical Graphics November, 2000) programme. The statistical methods that were used were basically of a descriptive kind, firstly endeavouring to classify and tabulate the data obtained in absolute and relative frequency tables, with both simple and double input. The chi-square test was done to analyze the responses by sex and age.

3. Results

As for the opinion of the surveyed population regarding the need to regulate the obtention of biological samples (blood, saliva, sperm, etc.), when no consent is given 77% were in favour of such regulation. It must be pointed out that when the same question was analyzed in terms of different levels of education and groups of professions, highly significant differences were observed ($p<0.001$) due mainly to the fact that the percentage of interviewees who agreed with the need to regulate Spanish legislation regarding the obtention of biological samples without the consent of the individual increased as the level of education increased. This same increase was observed when taking into account the different analysed professions (Others: 74.4%; Health: 79.0%; Police: 83.5%; Law: 85.5%).

When the interviewees were asked about the necessity of a national database and DNA analysis for forensic purposes of *all the citizens*, without consent, 57.00% expressed disagreement with the need for such a database. The differences are significant when the different groups of professions are taken into account ($P\leq0.05$); the interviewees (only 26%) working in the field of law showed little support for a national DNA data bank for all the citizens and without their consent, followed by other professions (32.1%), professions involved in the health sector (38.2%) and professions involved in local and national security and law enforcement (41.4%).

When the interviewees were questioned about the type of samples or persons that should be included in the databases the highest percentage obtained was for the biological samples found in the place where an unsolved crime had been committed (75.85%); for persons condemned in court for having intentionally committed a crime (71.98%); for biological samples from unidentified corpses and from persons who voluntarily supply such samples (64.99%). When this same question was analysed in relation with the different age groups the answers were seen to be quite homogeneous. For the inclusion of biological samples found in the place of an unsolved crime P=0.02585, for biological samples from unidentified corpses P=0.7976, for victims of unsolved crimes P=0.1557, for persons condemned for criminal negligence P=0.0803, for volunteers P=0.3522 and for all citizens, including unconsenting persons P=0.3168. When the questions asked were related to the different groups of professions, homogeneity in the answers was observed in the cases of biological samples being taken from the scene of an unsolved crime (P=0.7000), biological samples from unidentified corpses (P=0.2022), victims of unsolved crimes (P=0.0574), citizens who voluntarily give samples (P=0.0660) as well as in the case of all citizens, including those who do not consent (P=0.0567). With regard to this latter group of figures, it must be pointed out that the highest percentages for the inclusion of all the different proposed groups in databases are to be found for those professions involved in local and state security, while those professions involved in the legal system expressed greater doubts, compared to the other studied professional groups, about such a proposal (except in three cases: biological samples found in the scene of an unsolved crime, samples taken from unidentified corpses and persons who voluntarily give samples).

References

[1] A. Aparisi, El proyecto Genoma Humano: algunas reflexiones sobre sus relaciones con el derecho. Tirant lo Blanch, Universitat de València, 139, 1997.

[2] M. Kite, Insurance firm admits using genetic screening, Bionews 8 (2001 February).

[3] UNESCO, Comité Internacional de Bioética Anteproyecto Revisado de Declaración Internacional sobre datos Genéticos Humanos, Paris 22 Enero, 2003.

[4] J.J. Gamero, et al., Study of Spanish awareness regarding DNA database in forensic genetic, International Congress Series 1239 (2003) 773–776.

ELSEVIER

International Congress Series 1261 (2004) 571–573

www.ics-elsevier.com

DNA technology application procedures in forensic practice: social and ethical conditioning II

J.J. Gamero[a], J.L. Romero[a], J.L. Peralta[a], F. Corte-Real[b], M.C. Vide[b], Joaquín J. Gamero Lucas[a,*]

[a] *Faculty of Medicine, Forensic and Legal Medicine Department, Cádiz University, Plaza Fragele s/n, Cádiz 11003, Spain*

[b] *National Institute of Legal Medicine, Largo da Sé Nova, 3000-213 Coimbra, Portugal*

Abstract. In the study carried out it is intended, in accordance with the preliminary draft of the International Declaration on Human Genetic Data, that information be gathered concerning the diverse questions regarding DNA analysis and its application in the identification of individuals (sample extraction, laboratory treatment, sample analysis and storage, information from the obtained results, etc.) that different social groups in our country may have. This would enable the establishment of a starting point for public debate and the development of public awareness proposals that may serve as an aid, not in the elaboration of a draft law for DNA database regulation in Spain which we consider to be outside our responsibility, but in the elaboration of later regulations which take into account all the details related with the process previously described.

Keywords: Public opinion; Forensic genetics; Ethics; Database

1. Introduction

There exists a general agreement concerning the fact that human genetics research may affect the community in general [1]. It is therefore necessary that society as a whole and not only its scientists should debate and decide what is to be accepted or rejected [2,3].

Finally, in the study carried out it is intended, in accordance with the preliminary draft of the International Declaration on Human Genetic Data [4], that information be gathered concerning the diverse questions regarding DNA analysis and its application in the identification of individuals (sample extraction, laboratory treatment, sample analysis and storage, information from the obtained results, etc.) that different social groups in our country may have [3].

* Corresponding author. Tel.: +34-956-01-51-87; fax: +34-56-223-139.
E-mail address: joaquin.gamero@uca.es (J.J. Gamero Lucas).

doi:10.1016/S0531-5131(03)01780-1

2. Materials and methods

Once the general aims of the work had been specified and the tasks to be performed had been planned, the development of the task was begun in the following order: production of an opinion questionnaire and the selection of a homogenous group of interviewers; the selection of the sample in accordance with a criteria of randomness and representativity; the purging of non-random errors that do not concern the survey; the analysis of the data obtained, using statistical methods for their summarized description. As a means of collecting the data, the questionnaire form was chosen, since, as well as being convenient for the interviewees, it is an efficient means of coding, purging and an easy way to obtain a large amount of data. Ten questions were analyzed in this study. These questions were of standard comprehension and interviewers were chosen if they had a suitable standard of education in order to form a homogenous group. The sample choice was performed by using random criteria and by trying to find a cross-section nature in the different sexes and age groups. A stratified survey of the Spanish population was carried out and 1656 questionnaires were completed. Among those interviewed (809 women and 845 men), different age groups were represented (from 18 years of age upwards).

The data collected was stored on a computer and statistically analysed with the help of the Statgraphics plus 5.0 (Statistical Graphics November, 2000) programme. The statistical methods that were used were basically of a descriptive kind, firstly endeavouring to classify and tabulate the data obtained in absolute and relative frequency tables, with both simple and double input. The statistical analysis of the data was completed with the calculation of the parameters of centralization, location, dispersion and asymmetry which allowed us to summarize the information contained in the surveys. The chi-square test was done to analyze the responses by sex and age.

3. Results and discussion

When the interviewees were asked about what institution or institutions should protect and maintain confidentiality of the data stored in a data base 60.15% considered that custody should remain in the hands of a Ministry of Justice Institution; 57.28% answered that the Institute of Legal Medicine should be responsible for this; 50.00%, a Ministry of Health Institution and 46.18%, the National Institute of Toxicology. On the other hand, homogeneity was observed for the different educational levels with regard to who should be the custodian of such data bases, except for the discrepancies found when the interviewees expressed their opinion about the capacity different institutions (involved in security) have for data base custody and confidentiality (Local Police, $P=0.0103$; National Police, $P=0.0067$; Police Forces of Autonomous Regions, $P=0.0345$; Civil Guard, $P=0.0001$).

When the interviewees were asked who or which institutions may have access to the forensic DNA data of an individual, 74.07% considered that the data may be handed over to judges and law courts, 54.40% to examining magistrates or those authorized by the latter and 53.66% to a public prosecutor. Again, the homogeneity observed between educational levels when the latter levels were related to the persons or institutions who may have access to data of individuals that is stored in a data base is noteworthy, with the exception of the discrepancies that emerged when the interviewees assessed the possibility of handing over said data to members of those professions involved in local and state security (Local Police, $P=0.0008$; National Police, $P=0.0244$; Police forces of Autonomous Regions, $P=0.0018$; Civil Guard, $P=0.0011$). When this question was related to the groups of analyzed professions the discrepancies shown by these different groups with regard to the different hypothesis included in the survey were noteworthy, with the exception of the circumstances in which Judges and Law Courts ($P=0.3814$) or Prosecuting Lawyers ($P=0.0557$) are permitted access to personal forensic data.

Another question put to the surveyed population referred to the type of research in which the personal data contained in these data bases may be used. Eighty-eight percent of the surveyed population considered that such data may be used in penal research.

Finally, the lack of attention that is generally paid in scientific forums to society's perception about the different biotechnology's applications should be pointed out. Sometimes, it seems that scientists do not know the influence that social perception, particularly in Europe, could have on technology and investigation policies that the government could develop and consequently, the support, or by contrary, the lack of it, given to the public investigation. According to what has been mentioned above, it is necessary, among other questions, the design of some mechanisms that obtain opinions of different social groups, before adopting legal decisions in relation to biotechnology, as to have a consensus, it is essential that the information become widely spread.

References

[1] C.M.C. Romeo, Introduction Journal of Law and Human Genetics 1 (1994) 16–20.

[2] M. Guillen, M.V. Lareu, C. Pestoni, A. Salas, A. Carracedo, Ethical-legal problems of DNA databases in criminal investigation, Journal of Medical Ethics 26 (2000) 266–271.

[3] J.J. Gamero, J.L. Romero, J.L. Peralta, M.A.C. Vide, Study of Spanish awareness regarding DNA database in forensic genetic, International Congress Series 1239 (2003) 773–776.

[4] UNESCO, Comité Internacional de Bioética, Anteproyecto Revisado de Declaración Internacional sobre datos Genéticos Humanos, Paris 22 Enero, 2003.

International Congress Series 1261 (2004) 574–576

www.ics-elsevier.com

Evaluation and comparison of deoxyribonucleic acid typing methods on human tissue fixed with different fixatives

E. Ginestra[a], L. Saravo[a,*], I. Ciuna[a], G. Sciacca[b], A. Finocchiaro[b], G. Lo Menzo[b]

[a] *Raggruppamento Carabinieri Investigazioni Scientifiche, S.S. 114 Km 6400, Tremestieri 98128, Reparto di Messina, Sicily, Italy*

[b] *Department of Legal Medicine, University of Catania, Italy*

Abstract. Commonly employed fixing fluids result in very satisfactory histomorphologic analysis; however, they don't allow deoxyribonucleic acid (DNA) typing methods to provide good results. This study investigated the effect of eight fixatives on DNA extracted from placenta samples. Fresh tissue (placenta) specimens were fixed by immersion in different fixing fluids for different periods (from 24 h to 60 days). Different DNA extraction methods were assayed. Gene Amp 2400 and 9700 Thermal Cyclers coupled to AmpFLSTR Identifier kit (Applied Biosystems), that allows the simultaneous amplification of 15 STRs loci, was used for quantification. Amplified products were analyzed by capillary electrophoresis on ABI PRISM 310 and 3100 Genetic Analyzers (Applied Biosystems).

Keywords: Tissue; Formalin; IQ; Fixative solution

1. Introduction

The possibility of typing DNA has been of great interest in personal identification, particularly for organs and tissues taken from autopsies and preserved for very long periods of time. In these cases, it is necessary to obtain very good fixing, preserving the molecular structure of tissues during the exam. The aim of the present work is to study and search for fixatives, which permit excellent utilization of tissues in forensic science.

2. Materials and methods

Fresh tissue (placenta) specimens were fixed by immersion in different fixing fluids for different periods (from 24 h to 60 days). DNA extractions were performed according to two different procedures: one incubation in PK with deproteinization in phenol–chloro-

* Corresponding author. Tel.: +39905725388; fax: +39905725690.
E-mail address: kunitz@libero.it (L. Saravo).

doi:10.1016/S0531-5131(03)01705-9

form, and the use of paramagnetic particles covered with silice (DNA IQ™ System, Promega) [1]. Prior to DNA extraction with phenol–chloroform, samples of placenta were washed several times with phosphate buffered saline (PBS) and homogenized in the same solution. Tissues fixed by Bouin fixative were washed several times with 50% ethanol to eliminate yellow colour of the picric acid. Cytoscreen™ was purchased by Ddk Italia. Specimens were then incubated overnight at 40 °C in a solution of lysis buffer (10 mM Tris–HCl, pH 8; 10 mM EDTA, pH 8; 100 mM NaCl, 2% SDS) containing Proteinasi K (100 mg/ml). The mixture was extracted twice with phenol–chloroform, in according to Ref. [2]. Prior to DNA typing, all samples were purified using DNA and Gel Band Purification Kit (Amersham Pharmacia Biotech) in accordance with the manufacturer's instructions. The evaluation of quality and approximate yield of DNA extracted was performed by 1% agarose gel electrophoresis and ethidium-bromide staining. Another extraction method used was DNA IQ™ System; this extraction was applied in accordance with the manufacturer's instructions [1]. STR amplification was carried out by Gene Amp 9700 and 2400 thermal cyclers (Applied Biosystems), with the "AmpFLSTR Identifier" kit (Applied Biosystems) [3]. Amplified products were analyzed by capillary electrophoresis on two ABI PRISM 310 and 3100 Genetic Analyzer (Applied Biosystems) employing ABI software (DATA Collection, GeneScan Analysis, Genotyper Fragment Analysis).

3. Results

Our results indicate that in specimens fixed with formaldehyde or with other fixative containing different concentrations of formaldehyde, there is a significant reduction in DNA extraction, both quantitatively and qualitatively, as compared to specimens treated with alcoholic fixatives; this reduction is less pronounced when using an IQ System for the extraction. Results from typing of DNA extracted with phenol–chloroform from samples fixed in 10% formaldehyde were less significant after 24 h due to the lack of amplification in a few polymorphisms or to the presence of particular phenomes such as "allelic drop-outs". These results can appear less significant if compared with DNA extraction by IQ System, which permitted good typing using samples treated with other fixatives containing formaldehyde.

Similar results were obtained with specimens fixed with 2,5 glutaraldehyde in SSPE at 4 °C and 4% paraformaldehyde in SSPE at 4 °C; in these samples, a small amount of degraded DNA could be detected in 24 h. In samples fixed with a Bouin liquid, a certain amount of highly degraded DNA can be detected after 24 h. This data might be caused by picric acid.

DNA typing detected on samples treated with alcohol fixatives, using extraction with phenol–choloroform and with IQ System, has provided good and reliable results, also after two mounts and four mounts for Citoscreen™.

4. Discussion

Our data on quantitative and qualitative yield, on typing DNA extracted with fixing fluids containing formaldehyde, are confirmed by international scientific literature [4–6]. DNA structure is damaged by formaldehyde, which produces an interaction with hydrogen links, tissue nuclease, and with fixed histonic proteins, causing damage to polymerase chain reaction (PCR). In our experience, and according to others, fixatives containing formaldehyde cause more damage on less marked DNA structures. The authenticity of the typing results must be based on the use of fixing fluid and on the DNA extraction method: IQ System seems quite convincing for samples treated with formaldehyde [7]. The series of result obtained suggest that fixatives with alcohol, and in particular with Citoscreen™, permit a better qualitative and quantitative conservation of DNA and an optimum typing with forensic genetic methods.

References

[1] DNA IQ™ system—small sample casework protocol extraction kit, User's manualTechnical Bulletin 296Promega.
[2] J. Sambrook, E.F. Fritsch, T. Maniatis, 2nd ed., Molecular Cloning: a Laboratory Manual, vol. 2, Cold Spring Harbor Laboratory Press, New York, 1989.
[3] AmpFLSTR Identifier PCR amplification kit. User's manual PE Biosystems, 2001.
[4] G. Sciacca, A. Finocchiaro, L. Liuzzo, L. Saravo, S. Spitaleri, G. Lo Menzo, DNA typing from human remains to different distance from deathFive Days Medical–legal Europe, Terrasini (Pa) Italy, 29 May to 2 June 2002.
[5] A.J.W. Gillespie, C.J. Best, et al. Evaluation of non-formalin tissue fixation for molecular profiling studie-sAmerican Journal of Pathology 160 (2) (2002) 449–457.
[6] B.M.P. Douglas, S.O. Rogers, DNA damage caused by common cytological fixativesMutation Research 401 (1998) 77–88.
[7] D.J.W. Gillespie, C.J. Best, V.E. Bichsel, K.A. Cole, S.F. Greenhut, S.M. Hewitt, M. Ahram, Y.B. Gathright, M.J. Merino, R.L. Strausberg, J.I. Epstein, S.R. Hamilton, G. Gannot, G.V. Baibakova, V.S. Calvert, M.J. Flaig, R.F. Chuaqui, J.C. Herring, J. Pfeifer, E.F. Petricoin, W.M. Linehan, P.H. Duray, G.S. Bova, M.R. Emmert-Buck, Evalutation of non-formalin tissue fixation for molecular profiling studiesAmerican Journal of Pathology 160 (2) (2002, February) 449–457.

International Congress Series 1261 (2004) 577–579

www.ics-elsevier.com

Extracting DNA from all forensic samples with KingFisher® technologies

T. Delefosse*, R. Hienne

Laboratoire CODGENE, Department of Human Genetic Identification, 11 Rue Humann, 67085 Strasbourg, Bas-Rhin, France

Abstract. Many of the forensic DNA extraction methods appeared to have limitations, such as inability to remove inhibitors of PCR reaction, or appeared to be time-consuming by needing too many steps and multiple tube transfers (which increase the risk of contaminations by exogenous DNA). We report here that by using technology based on paramagnetic silica particles which bind DNA in presence of chaotrophic salts, we are able to standardize and validate less kinds of DNA extraction methods for forensic samples. These new extraction methods allow us to reduce significantly number of steps, reagents, additional procedures, and time. Moreover, it allows us to avoid the classical and quite dangerous organic extraction method for most of forensic samples. Finally, these methods seem to give better quality of DNA in a shorter time.

Keywords: Forensic; Human DNA; STR

1. Introduction

In the field of forensic science, a wide range of biological samples are encountered. This leads to the use of as many different DNA extraction protocols. By now, several DNA extraction methods have been developed by the forensic community, but many of them appeared to have limitations such as inability to remove inhibitors of PCR reaction [1], or to be time-consuming by needing too many steps and multiple tube transfers which increase the risk of contaminations by exogenous DNA [1]. By using KingFisher® technologies, we were able to standardize and validate DNA extraction methods for almost all forensic samples. Thus, samples are treated with just one protocol [2] which allow us to (1) avoid the quite dangerous organic extraction method (e.g., phenol/chloroform method), (2) reduce significantly number of steps, reagents, or additional procedures (e.g., Centricon®), (3) reduce cost of experiments, and (4) save time.

* Corresponding author. Tel.: +33-3-90-24-31-67; fax: +33-3-88-24-00-85.
E-mail address: tdelefosse@codgene.com (T. Delefosse).

doi:10.1016/S0531-5131(03)01788-6

2. Methodology

Several forensic-like samples (home-made samples hairs, oral cotton swabs, gloves, cigarette butts, nails, etc.) were tested to improve the new extraction method using buffers from the Genomic DNA Purification Kit associated to the KingFisher® mL Automate [2]. Incubation steps were simplified to obtain only four kinds of incubation steps for all forensic samples (no incubation, 2 and 5 h or overnight [12 h] incubation time at 56 °C). Results show that quality and quantity of DNA were good enough to perform multiplex PCR with conventional kits (e.g., AmpFLSTR® SGM Plus® PCR Amplification Kit, Applied Biosystems). Thus, we were able to obtain only 6 different extraction protocols instead of the 10 which were routinely used in our lab. Encouraged by the results, we enlarged samples types to all kind of real forensic samples. Only fragments of clothes remain treated by classical techniques because of the size of those fragments incompatible with an extraction on the KingFisher® mL Automate [3].

Table 1
Summary of protocols used with and without KingFisher technologies

Samples		Steps					
		S	L	E 1	P/C 1	E 2	P/C 2
Blood		GFX Kit (Amersham)					
Nails, cotton swab			Buffer A	PCI	Centricon 30	Chelex 20%	μcon 100
Oral cotton swab/histobrush			Chelex 10%				
Cigarette butt			Chelex 20% Over Night				μcon 100
Blood stain			Buffer A	PCI	Centricon 30	Chelex 20%	μcon 100
Hair			Buffer D	PCI	(a) or (b)		
Human tissue[1] and clothes			Buffer A	PCI			
Sperm stain	UP	Buffer B		PCI		(c) or (d)	
	LP		Buffer C				
Blood, fresh human tissue[1] Nails, cotton swab, oral cotton swab/histobrush, cigarette butt, blood stain		KF ml					μcon 100*

1 = Muscle, fresh flesh; Buffer A = NaCl, Tris–HCl, EDTA, DTT, PK; Buffer B = PBS 1X, SDS, PK; Buffer C = PBS 1X, Sarcosyl, EDTA, DTT, PK; Buffer D = NaCl, Tris–HCl, EDTA, SDS, Urea, PK; KF ml = Protocol A (see user's manual); PCI = organic extraction method. *optional step. UP = upper phase, LP = lower phase. The different steps are defined as follows: W = washing, S = split L = lysis, E = extraction and P/C = purification/concentration. (a) = without KingFisher technologies (KF): Cleamix (TALENT); (b) with KF: KF ml; (c) = without KF: PC 1, E 2 and P/C 2 are Centricon 30, Chelex 20% and μcon 100, respectively; (d) with KF: PC 1, E 2 and P/C 2 are KF ml and an optional step with μcon 100.

3. Results

3.1. Standardization of extraction protocols

Table 1 shows how samples are treated with or without KingFisher® Technologies. It clearly appears that by using this new technologies, many protocols are simplified in number of steps, reagents or additional procedures. Moreover, for most of the forensic samples, it lets us avoid the use of quite dangerous organic extraction method.

3.2. Principle of automated magnetic particle processing

This method is based on paramagnetic silica particles which bind DNA in the presence of chaotrophic salts. Forensic samples are first incubated at 56 °C (2–12 h) in a lysis buffer with the addition (or not) of Protease K and/or DTT. Some samples—as fresh blood, muscle or oral histobrushes—do not need incubation step. DNA extracts are then purified on the KingFisher® mL Automate, according to the manufacturer's procedure [3].

3.3. Quantity and quality of extracted DNA

Total amount of extracted DNA is measured with AluQuant® Kit [4]. Results show that extractions with KingFisher® methods give DNA for all types of samples tried. Moreover, DNA amounts are less spread in wide ranges as classical extraction methods. Such kind of less spread ranges are also obtained for peak amplitudes (data not shown). Thus, whatever the type of samples analyzed, it appears that extractions with KingFisher® methods seem to give better DNA quality.

4. Discussion

Because forensic studies are taking a bigger place in courtyard investigations, it is crucial for laboratories to use modern technologies. Since its creation 15 years ago, CODGENE develops or adapts new techniques and technologies for the purpose of reducing time and cost of experiments with the same or better DNA quality. With the help of KingFisher® technologies [2], CODGENE was able to reduce extraction time by three! Thus, most samples give us results in less than 72 h. Actually, we are working to reduce the number of extraction methods to only three different protocols: one for hard human tissues (bones/teeth), a second one for sperm stains, and a third one for all other forensic samples. We also work to avoid all phenol/chloroform treatment and reduce steps in the way to have less tube transfers as possible.

References

[1] Willard, et al, Recovery of DNA for PCR amplification from blood and forensic samples using a chelating resin, in: P.J. Lincoln, J. Thomson (Eds.), Forensic DNA Profiling Protocols: Methods in Molecular Biology™, Humana Press, Totowa, NJ, 1998, pp. 1–18.

[2] Genomic DNA Purification Kit for KingFisher® and KingFisher® mL, ThermoLabsystems, 00810 Helsinki, Finland.

[3] Instructions for use of the Genomic DNA Purification Kit, ThermoLabsystems.

[4] AluQuant®, Human DNA Quantitation System on Centro LB 960 from Berthold.

International Congress Series 1261 (2004) 580–582

www.ics-elsevier.com

Forensic applications of the genomic matching technique: profiling the alpha block in the major histocompatibility complex

R. Laird[a,b], R.L. Dawkins[b], N. Jacobsen[b], S. Gaudieri[b,*]

[a] *Centre for Forensic Science, School of Anatomy and Human Biology, Faculty of Life and Physical Sciences, University of Western Australia, Crawley Avenue, Nedlands 6009, Australia*

[b] *Centre for Molecular Immunology and Instrumentation, Faculty of Medicine and Dentistry, University of Western Australia, Australia*

Abstract. The genomic matching technique (GMT) was developed to characterize polymorphic sequences within the human major histocompatibility complex (MHC), known as polymorphic frozen blocks (PFBs). PFBs are 200–300 kb sequences containing duplications, indels and SNPs. The power of the GMT to differentiate between individuals at the DNA level means that it can be applied as an exclusion tool in forensic science. Here, the GMT is applied to the alpha block in the MHC. © 2003 Elsevier B.V. All rights reserved.

Keywords: Alpha block; Polymorphic frozen block; Ancestral haplotypes; Genomic matching technique; Major histocompatibility complex

1. Introduction

Polymorphic frozen blocks (PFBs) were first observed in the major histocompatibility complex (MHC), and have since been described elsewhere in the genome [1,2]. The sequences within the PFBs are extremely polymorphic with increased numbers of SNPs, indels, and duplications when compared to flanking sequences [3,4]. Haplospecific geometric elements (HGEs) are polymorphic sequences within blocks that can be used as markers for the entire block sequence [4,5]. A profiling technique termed genomic matching technique (GMT) utilises primers that target HGEs, which differ in size, content and number, within the PFBs [4]. Thus, by utilising a single primer set, a complex haplospecific profile may be utilised in forensic science as a cost-effective exclusion tool.

Primer sets have previously been developed for the beta (containing HLA-B) and delta block (containing HLA-DR) of the MHC [6]. Here, the technique is extended to the alpha block (spanning HLA-A to HLA-F) of the MHC.

* Corresponding author. Present address: Centre for Forensic Science, School of Anatomy and Human Biology, Faculty of Life and Physical Sciences, University of Western Australia, Crawley Avenue, Nedlands 6009, Australia. Tel.: +61-8-9224-2920; fax: 61-8-9224-2899.

E-mail address: gaudieri@cyllene.uwa.edu.au (S. Gaudieri).

doi:10.1016/S0531-5131(03)01706-0

2. Methods

Sequence for the alpha block region from HLA-A to HLA-F (AF055066) was plotted against itself using the Dotter program [8]. Priming sites were selected within duplicated regions.

Selected primer sequences were searched against the alpha block regions for the ancestral haplotypes (AHs) 7.1 (PGF-HLA-A*0301; -B*0702; -DRB1*15011) and 8.1 (COX-HLA-A*0101; -B*0801; -DRB1*0301) (http://www.sanger.ac.uk/HPG/Chr6/MHC/index.shtml) using BLASTn (http://www.ncbi.nlm.nih.gov).

DNA samples were taken from cell panels [7] and an internal panel of Caucasian samples.

PCR was performed in a 20 μl volume containing 200 ng DNA, 1.5 mM $MgCl_2$, 1.3 U Taq Polymerase (Fisher Biotec) and 1.25 pmol primers (Falph1 5′CCATGCTGAGTCTTGTGATAC-3′ and Ralph2 5′ACAGGAAGCTTAAAAACCAGC-3′). The reactions involved 95 °C, 2 min; then 30 cycles of 95 °C, 30 s; 52 °C, 30 s; 72 °C, 1 min; and a final cycle at 72 °C, 1 min. PCR products were visualised as previously described [5,9].

3. Results

Multiple duplications within the alpha block were identified [3] and primers selected within duplicated regions that flanked HGEs.

Priming sites within the 8.1 and 7.1 AHs revealed unique HGEs (Table 1). Products differ in length and content.

Previous studies have shown that samples matched by GMT have concordant HLA typing, and discordant HLA-typed samples are GMT mismatched. Disparity arises between GMT mismatches and HLA matches, indicating that GMT detects greater

Table 1
AHs have unique priming sites and alpha block HGEs

Cell and AH	Product Sequence[a]	Product Size (bp)
COX / 8.1 AH	CCATGCTGAGTCTTGTGATACTTATTCCTTTGTATTTCTTCAAGATTTGTGCAATAAG(TA)$_5$ATACA(TA)$_5$TGTAT(GT)$_3$(AT)$_5$ATCCCCAAAACAAATATCAGTTTGTTTGCTGGTTTTTAAGCTTCCTGT	153
	CCATCCTGAGTCTTCTGATACTTATTCCTTTGTATTTCTTCAAGATTTGTGCAATAAG(TA)$_{20}$TCTCCCAAAACAAATATCAGTTTGTTTGCTGGTTTTTAAGCTTCCTGT	149
	CCATGCTGAGTCTTGTGATACCTTATTCCTTTGTATTTCTTTAAAGATTTGCACAATAAG(TA)$_6$TGTAC(AT)$_5$CTGAAAAAAAATTATTTGCTGGTTTTTAAGCTTCCTGT	129
PGF / 7.1 AH	ACAGGAAGCTTAAAAACCAGCAAAACAAACTGATATTTGTTTGGGG(AT)$_6$(AC)$_3$ATAC(AT)$_5$(GT)$_5$(AT)$_3$ACA(CATA)$_2$TACACA(TA)$_3$C(AT)$_3$(GT)$_2$(AT)$_3$(AC)$_2$(AT)$_3$AC(AT)$_3$GGATAC(AT)$_3$(GT)$_2$(ATATATACAC)$_2$(AT)$_3$GTAT(ATATATACAC)$_2$(AT)$_3$(GT)$_2$(AT)$_4$ACTTATTGCACAAATCTTTGAAGAAATACAAAGGAATAAGTATCACAAGACTCAGCATGG	296[b]
	CCATCCTGAGTCTTCTGATACATATTCCTTTGTATTCCTTCAAAGATTTGTGTCAATAA(AT)$_9$CTCCCCAAAACAAACCTCAGTTAGTTTGCTGGTTTTTAAGCTTCCTGT	124

[a]Primer sequences boxed.

[b]Primers acting in the opposite orientation to all other products.

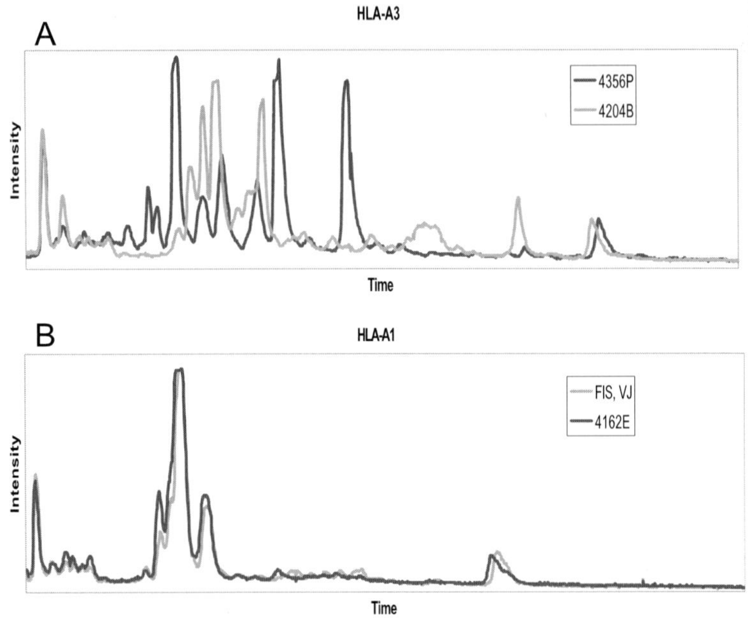

Fig. 1. Alpha block profiles are more discriminatory than HLA-A typing alone. (A) Samples typed as HLA-A3 but with different alpha block GMT profiles. (B) Samples with same HLA-A typing and alpha block profile. Horizontal axis is a relative time scale as products move through the gel and vertical axis is intensity of ethidium bromide fluorescence. First peak in profile corresponds to 59 bp internal standard.

polymorphism than HLA typing alone [9]. Seventy-two samples profiled at the alpha block produced results supporting these findings (Fig. 1).

4. Discussion

The application of the GMT has been shown to characterize polymorphism within the alpha block of the MHC, more so than HLA-A typing alone. Multiplexing for PFBs within the genome will produce economical, individual specific profiles, which can be utilised in forensic science as a powerful exclusion tool.

Acknowledgements

SG was supported by a Healy Fellowship from the Raine Medical Research Foundation. Publication 0306 from the CMII.

References

[1] R. Dawkins, et al., Immunological Reviews 167 (1999) 275–304.
[2] A. Kong, et al., Nature Genetics 31 (2002) 241–247.
[3] S. Gaudieri, et al., Genome Research 10 (2000) 1579–1586.
[4] S. Gaudieri, et al., Human Immunology 62 (2001) 279–285.
[5] N. Ketheesan, et al., Human Immunology 60 (1999) 171–176.
[6] G.K. Tay, et al., Bone Marrow Transplantation 15 (1995) 381–385.
[7] S.K. Cattley, et al., European Journal of Immunogenetics 27 (2000) 397–426.
[8] E. Sonnhammer, R. Durbin, Gene 167 (1996) 1–10.
[9] C. Witt, et al., Human Immunology 61 (2000) 85–91.

International Congress Series 1261 (2004) 583–585

www.ics-elsevier.com

Forensic toxicology: development of an SNP-assay for genotyping *CYP2D6* and *CYP2C19* variants

M. Verrecas, K. Knaepen, A. Gilissen, J.-J. Cassiman, R. Decorte*

Laboratory for Forensic Genetics and Molecular Archaeology, Department of Human Genetics, K.U. Leuven, Campus Gasthuisberg O&N, Herestraat 49, B-3000 Leuven, Belgium

Abstract. A procedure was developed for genotyping one *CYP2C19* and eight *CYP2D6* polymorphisms. After multiplex PCR of the exons containing the SNPs, a mini-sequencing reaction was performed with the SNapShot™ Multiplex Kit and the resultant primer-extension products were analyzed on an ABI PRISM® 3100 Genetic Analyzer. The developed procedure was validated in a population of 199 Caucasians.

Keywords: Pharmacogenetics; Single nucleotide polymorphism; Mini-sequencing; Cytochrome *P450*

1. Introduction

Forensic toxicology can contribute substantially to the interpretation and the determination of the causes and manners of death. Most fatal intoxications concern suicidal overdoses, but during recent years, chronic high dosage has attracted much attention. A high ratio between the parent drug and the metabolite could be interpreted not only as an overdose but could also be the result of a reduced metabolism of the parent drug by enzymes belonging to the cytochrome *P450* family. Several of these enzymes, such as *CYP2D6* and *CYP2C19,* are known to be polymorphic resulting in a different metabolic behaviour. The presence of the polymorphism is population dependent with about 5–10% of the Caucasian population belonging to the poor metabolisers [1]. Determination of the presence of a mutation in *CYP2D6* or *CYP2C19* may provide answers concerning the circumstances of death in cases with suspicion of overdose [2]. The present study describes the first results of the development of an Single Nucleotide Polymorphism (SNP)-assay for genotyping one *CYP2C19* and eight *CYP2D6* alleles. These assays are capable to identify at least 83% (*CYP2C19*) to 95% (*CYP2D6*) of the poor metabolizers in a Caucasian population.

2. Materials and methods

DNA was extracted by the chelex method from blood samples of 199 anonymous donors and quantified with the Quantiblot DNA Quantification Kit (Applied Biosystems).

* Corresponding author. Tel.: +32-16-346077; fax: +32-16-345997.
E-mail address: ronny.decorte@med.kuleuven.ac.be (R. Decorte).

doi:10.1016/S0531-5131(03)01775-8

Two multiplex PCR-reactions were developed for the amplification of the coding sequences of *CYP2C19* and *CYP2D6*. Exons 4 (198 bp) and 5 (168 bp) of the *CYP2C19* were amplified in one reaction while exons 1 (519 bp), 3 and 4 (460 bp), and 5 and 6 (609 bp) of *CYP2D6* were amplified in a second PCR. The sequences of the PCR-primers and the SNapShot™ primers are available upon request. The amplification was done in a 25-μl reaction containing 1.5 mM $MgCl_2$, 200 μM dNTPs, 2.5 U AmpliTaq Gold DNA-polymerase (Applied Biosystems), 1 × PCR-Gold-buffer, primers and 5 ng DNA. The PCR-conditions were as follows: denaturation of 10 min at 94 °C, 30 cycles of 1 min at 94 °C, 1 min at 55 °C and 1 min at 72 °C and final extension of 10 min at 72 °C in a GeneAmp® PCR System 9700.

The primers for genotyping *CYP2C19*2* and the *CYP2D6* alleles were selected with the READIT® Interrogation Probe Design software from Promega (http://www.promega.com/readit/probedesign/default.asp). The 10 detection primers (Table 1) for *CYP2D6* genotyping were combined into two SNapShot™ reactions. Free dNTPs and primers from the PCR-reaction were removed with Shrimp Alkaline Phosphatase (SAP) and Exonuclease I as described in the SNapShot™ manual. The SNapShot™ reactions and a final treatment with SAP were done according to the recommendations of the manufacturer. Sizing of the extension products was done in POP-6™ on an ABI PRISM® 3100 Genetic Analyzer with GeneScan™-120 LIZ™ as the internal size marker. The results were analyzed with GeneScan® v3.7.

3. Results and discussion

A multiplex PCR was developed for exons 4 and 5 of the *CYP2C19* gene, which contain, respectively, the *CYP2C19*2* and *CYPC19*3* alleles. The *CYP2C19*3* allele was not yet included in the SNapShot™ reaction due to its low occurrence in a Caucasian population (0.2%). Validation of the developed method in a population of 199 individuals showed in total 6 individuals (3%) homozygous for the mutation (PM). The allele frequency for *CYP2C19*2* was 13.8% which was in accordance to other studies in Caucasian populations [2].

Table 1
Detected mutations (header) for *CYP2D6* and their corresponding alleles (first column)

Allele	2549delA	1846G>A	100C>T	1661G>C	1707delT	2935A>C	124G>A	2850C>T	138-139insT	1979T>C
CYP2D6*3	■									
CYP2D6*4		■	■	■						
CYP2D6*6					■					
CYP2D6*7						■				
CYP2D6*10			■	■						
CYP2D6*12				■			■	■		
CYP2D6*15									■	
CYP2D6*20				■				■		■

Gray boxes indicate the presence of the mutated position.

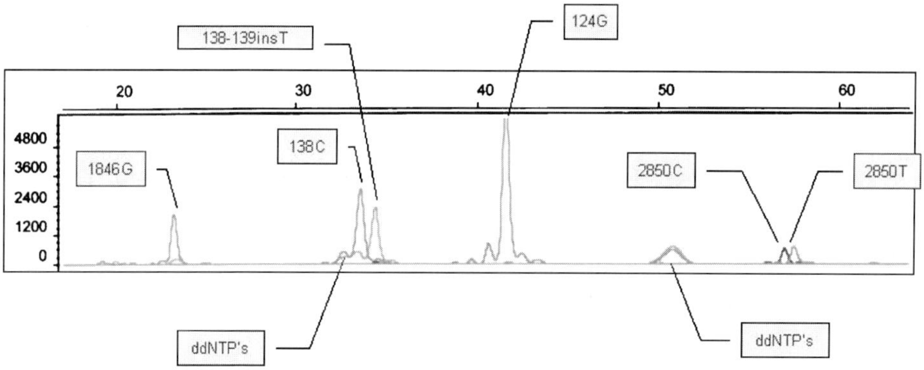

Fig. 1. SNaPshot™ result for genotyping *CYP2D6* (individual heterozygous for 2850C>T).

Exons 1, 3 and 4, and 5 and 6 of the *CYPDC6* gene were co-amplified in one PCR reaction. The primers for exon 1 co-amplified also several pseudogenes (*CYP2D7AP*, *CYP2D7BP* and *CYP2D8P*) of *CYP2D6*. Theoretically, it was possible to identify individuals homozygous for the *CYP2D6*5* allele (deletion of the complete gene; frequency of 2% in Caucasian populations). The 10 SNapShot™ primers were split into 2 SNapShot™ reactions after some initial experiments: one with 4 primers showing a high signal (Fig. 1) and one with 6 primers showing a lower signal. Validation of this assay in the population sample of 199 individuals showed a "clear" result for only 57 individuals. Several problems were encountered: (1) some SNapShot™ primers did not give any signal; (2) a background signal from free [F]-ddNTPs was seen that coincided with some of the SNapShot™ primers (Fig. 1); (3) the primer detecting mutation 138–139insT showed in most individuals a heterozygous result. The SNapShot™ primers showing a weak or no result hybridized to the "Exon 3–4" PCR-fragment indicating a not optimal amplification of this fragment. The background signal from the free [F]-ddNTPs could only be removed by replacing the SAP-treatment after the extension reaction with gel filtration through Sephadex G-50. The 138–139insT mutation is localized in exon 1 of the *CYP2D6* gene and is also present in several pseudogenes. As the multiplex PCR was set up to identify individuals with the gene deletion (*CYP2D6*5*), it was not possible to avoid initially this problem. Further experiments to overcome these problems are in progress and the results of the final *CYP2D6* assay will be reported elsewhere.

Acknowledgements

We would like to thank Dr. M.-P. Emonds (Bloodtransfusion Centre of Leuven, Belgium) who provided the population sample. J.-J. Cassiman is a holder of the "Arthur Bax and Anna Vanluffelen chair of Human Genetics".

References

[1] H. Druid, et al., Cytochrome *P450 2D6* (*CYP2D6*) genotyping on postmortem blood as a supplementary tool for interpretation of forensic results, For. Sci. Int. 99 (1999) 25–34.

[2] W.J. Tamminga, et al., The prevalence of *CYP2D6* and *CYP2C19* genotypes in a population of healthy Dutch volunteers, Eur. J. Clin. Pharmacol. 57 (2001) 717–722.

International Congress Series 1261 (2004) 586–588

www.ics-elsevier.com

Graphic SSCP analysis of ABO genotypes for forensic application

K. Honda[a,c,*], T. Nakamura[a], E. Tanaka[a], K. Yamazaki[b,c], Z. Tun[a], S. Misawa[b]

[a] *Department of Legal Medicine, Tsukuba University School of Medicine, 1-1-1 Tennnodai, Tsukuba, Ibaraki, 305-8575, Japan*

[b] *Tokyo Medical Examiner's Office, 4-21-18 Ootsuka, Bunkyo, Tokyo-to, 112-0012 Japan*

[c] *Tsukuba Medical Examiner's Office, 1-3-1 Amakubo, Tsukuba, 305-0005 Japan*

Abstract. Nowadays, many of the DNA sequences of ABO blood group system have been disclosed to perform DNA testing, and one-base mutations or variations among different ABO genotypes could be detected for genotyping. For this purpose, single-strand conformation polymorphism (SSCP), which detects only one-base difference between different genotypes, is applied to detect ABO genotypes and is one of the choices among ABO genotyping technology. For practical application in forensic DNA testing, we tried to apply SSCP method using high-resolution ALF express DNA sequencer (Pharmacia Biotech). High-resolution SSCP is extremely sensitive and reliable that almost all cases of trace evidence obtained from criminal investigation were able to be genotyped visually. The denatured single-stranded amplicons were electrophoresed in sequencing gel, analyzed by laser detector, and visualized the peak patterns of chromatogram. With this method, we are able to classify ABO genotypes into 15 groups and additional subtypes. In addition, analysis of ABO genotypes of 400 DNA samples extracted from individuals living in Japan, Mongolia, and Colombia revealed a remarkable regional difference in allele frequency of A101 versus A102, and O^A vs. O^G. © 2003 Elsevier B.V. All rights reserved.

Keywords: ABO genotype; SSCP; DNA polymorphism; Allele frequency

1. Introduction

The greatest advantage of using ABO blood group system in forensic identification is that ABO blood type to be screened is almost always known beforehand [1 2]. Therefore, we can narrow down the focus of crime investigation from the very beginning. The gene of transfer enzyme, which encodes ABO blood group was identified on the long arm of ninth chromosome (9q34) and composed of seven exons. Various genotypes based on a lot of

* Corresponding author. Department of Legal Medicine, Tsukuba University School of Medicine, 1-1-1 Tennnodai, Tsukuba, Ibaraki, 305-8575, Japan. Tel.: +81-29-853-3043; fax: +81-29-853-3264.

E-mail address: k-honda@md.tsukuba.ac.jp (K. Honda).

doi:10.1016/S0531-5131(03)01779-5

nucleotide substitutions have been reported in exon6 and exon7 so far. Until now, 5 major alleles and more than 70 subtypes including rare ones were discovered [3]. Although several methods of detecting single-base difference in ABO genotypes have been developed [4 5], Multiplex primer extension, their procedures are usually complicated, and we must perform the many steps to obtain the clear results. Therefore, we developed PCR-SSCP analysis using ALF express DNA sequencer (Pharmacia Biotech) for clear, easy, and quick analysis of trace/insufficient amount of DNA samples, which are either trace or insufficient in amount.

2. Materials and methods

The DNA samples of this study were collected from 686 Japanese, 155 Mongolian, and 117 Colombian in South America.

2.1. Polymerase chain reaction

In this method, three sets of fluorescent labeled primers were used in PCR
For exon6 (fragment I)

Primer1-F Cy5′ -TGCAGTAGGAAGGATGTCCTC-3′
Primer2-R Cy5′ -AATGTCCACAGTCACTCGCC-3′

For exon7 (fragments II and III)

Primer3-F Cy5′ -GTGGCTTTCCTGAAGCTGTT-3′
Primer4-R Cy5′ -AAGTCACTGATCATCTCCATG-3′
Primer5-F Cy5′ -TGGAGATCCTGACTCCGCTG-3′
Primer6-R Cy5′ -GTAGAAATCGCCCTCGTCCTT-3′

2.2. Single-strand conformational change polymorphism

After amplifying exon6 and exon7, SSCP was conducted by using a DNA sequencer (ALF Express, Amersham Pharmacia Biotech) equipped with a short gel ($173 \times 317 \times 0.5$ mm thick). The data were then analyzed after visualization of peak patterns of chromatogram. This method is rapid and economic. We can perform electrophoresis simultaneously within 4 h, 40 samples at the most can be analyzed at the same time, and we can use the old gel for more than three times.

3. Results and discussion

Ten kinds of fundamental genotypes (AA, AO^A, AO^G, BB, BO^A, BO^G, O^AO^A, O^AO^G, O^GO^G, and AB) by the combination of a base substitution of np261 (G/del) and np297 (A/G) were detected (Fig. 1). These genotype patterns result from the difference in the mobility shift of sense chain and anti-sense chain based on one base substitution or deletion.

In addition, examination of 400 DNA samples from Japan, Mongolia, and Columbia revealed a remarkable regional deviation in allele frequency of A101 versus A102, and O^A

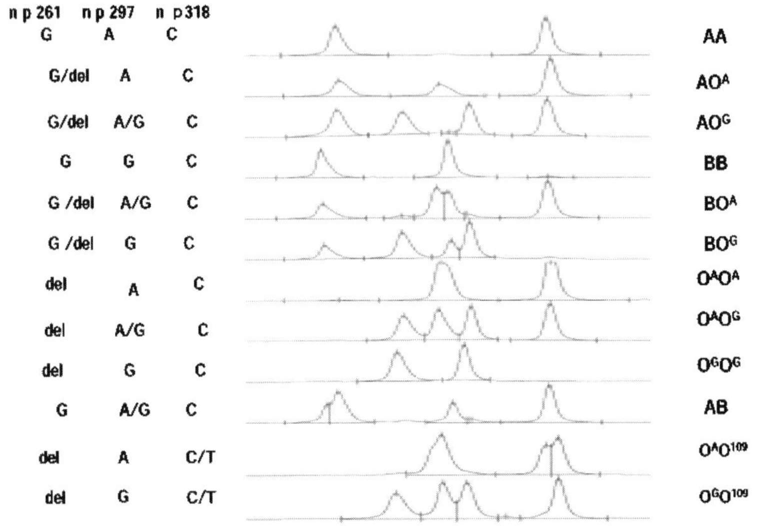

Fig. 1. SSCP pattern of fragment I and their corresponding nucleotide substitution and defined genomic types.

vs. O^G. In Japanese, although the frequency of O^A allele and O^G allele were almost the same in general (51% vs. 49%), the difference was seen between Kagoshima prefecture and Gifu prefecture (Kagoshima: $O^A/O^G = 47:53\%$, Gifu: $O^A/O^G = 57:43\%$). When compared to other population, O^G allele is more frequent than O^A allele in Mongolian ($O^A/O^G = 43:57\%$) and in Colombian ($O^A/O^G = 39:61\%$) by this study. After examination of exon6 and in exon7 including nps 703, we can classified ABO genotype in 15 groups and additional subtypes; that is, three types of AA (A101/A101, A101/A102, A102/A102), four types of AO (A101O^A, A101O^G, A102O^A, A102O^G), BB, two types of BO (BO^A, BO^G), three types of O (O^A O^A, O^G O^G, O^A O^G), two types of AB (A101B, A102B).

References

[1] K. Ogasawara, M. Bannai, N. Saitou, R. Yabe, K. Nakata, M. Takenaka, K. Fujisawa, M. Uchikawa, Y. Ishikawa, T. Juji, K. Tokunaga, Extensive polymorphism of ABO blood group gene: three major lineages of the alleles for the common ABO phenotypes, Hum. Genet. 97 (6) (1996) 777–783.

[2] F. Yamamoto, H. Clausen, T. White, J. Marken, S. Hakomori, Molecular genetic basis of the hist-blood group system, Nature 345 (6272) (1990) 229–233.

[3] S.P. Yip, Sequence variation at the human ABO locus, Ann. Hum. Genet. 66 (2002) 1–27.

[4] J.C.I. Lee, J.G. Chang, ABO genotyping by polymerase chain reaction, J. Forensic Sci. 37 (1992) 1275–1296.

[5] G. Watanabe, K. Umetsu, I. Yasuda, T. Suzuki, Amplified product length polymorphism (APLP): a novel strategy for genotyping the ABO blood group, Hum. Genet. 99 (1) (1997) 34–37.

International Congress Series 1261 (2004) 589–591

www.ics-elsevier.com

HumTHO1 and blood pressure. An obstacle for forensic applications?

M. Klintschar*, U. Immel, D. Stiller, M. Kleiber

Institut für Rechtsmedizin, Martin Luther-Universität Halle-Wittenberg, Franzosenweg 1, 06097 Halle an der Saale, Germany

Received 28 August 2003; received in revised form 28 August 2003; accepted 8 September 2003

Abstract. HumTH01 is reported to be associated with arterial hypertension (HT). As forensic polymorphisms must not reveal information about the personality of the tested individual in Germany, this finding is a potential obstacle for applying this locus to casework. We thus tested whether HumTH01 is associated with myocardial hypertrophy or with increased incidence of blood pressure (BP)-related diseases such as myocardial infarction. As we found no influence, it is argued that the use of TH01 for forensic purposes is legitimate.

Keywords: TH01; Forensic DNA typing; STR; Hypertension; Myocardial hypertrophy

1. Introduction

From the legal point of view, it is essential that DNA polymorphisms should not reveal information concerning the phenotype of the person analysed. A recent order of the German Federal Constitutional Court [1] stated that it is "decisive ... (to ensure that a DNA investigation is not in conflict with the civil rights of a citizen) ... that conclusions concerning the personality, like ... diseases ... are not permitted".

However, in clinical studies, a positive association between THO1 alleles 9.3 and 10 and essential hypertension (HT) [2] was reported. The goal of the present study was thus to further evaluate potential consequences from the reported association with hypertension.

2. Materials and methods

The case group comprised 172 unrelated cases of unexpected death from blood pressure (BP)-related diseases (myocardial infarction, left heart failure, stroke, aortic rupture) in Halle/Saale, Germany. Control group 1 comprised 124 cases of death from natural causes other than those qualifying for inclusion in the case group. Control group 2 comprised 348

* Corresponding author. Tel.: +49-345-557-1591; fax: +49-345-557-1587.
E-mail address: michael.klintschar@medizin.uni-halle.de (M. Klintschar).

0531-5131/
doi:10.1016/S0531-5131(03)01494-8

healthy babies, representing the average population. In 275 cases, the heart weight was measured. TH01 typing was performed as described [3].

3. Results and discussion

Essential HT is a risk factor for several potentially lethal events such as myocardial infarction, spontaneous intracerebral bleeding, etc. A genetic finding associated with substantially increased BP can thus be expected to result in an increased incidence of those events. Moreover, hypertrophy of the left myocardial wall should result, with increased heart weight as morphological equivalent.

Nevertheless, we found no differences in THO1 allelic frequencies between a case group with casualties from HT-related events and two control groups (Fig. 1). Moreover, we failed to demonstrate a correlation between THO1 genotypes and heart weights in 275 autopsy cases. (Table 1). These findings suggest that the association of THO1 with HT be weak and not capable of producing significant increases in HT-related deaths or organ malfunction.

But how could a non-coding polymorphism influence HT?

TH01 is located in intron 01 of the tyrosin hydroxylase gene, the rate limiting enzyme in the synthesis of catecholamines, which are pivotal in the regulation of blood pressure [4]. There are at least two indirect ways TH01 could influence blood pressure: Firstly, an allele could be in close linkage disequilibrium (LD) to a gene variant associated with HT. One fact fostering this possibility is the extremely low rate of spontaneous repeat array mutations of this marker leading to conservation of LD [5]. However, up to now, no such gene variant was identified.

The second possibility would be a functional activity of the THO1 sequence via gene regulation [6]. This possibility is supported by recent in vitro investigations, which proved that THO1 acts as a quantitative genomic effector modulating the activity of the tyrosin hydroxylase gene: The THO1 alleles inhibit transcription, and the inhibition is propor-

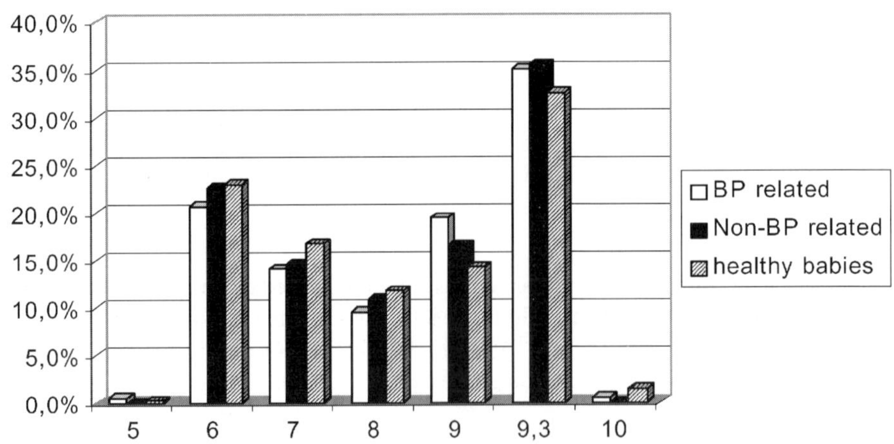

Fig. 1. Allelic frequencies for THO1 in the case group (BP-related causes of death) and two control groups (non-BP-related cause of death and healthy babies).

Table 1
Mean weight of the heart and THO1 alleles 9.3 and 10 in 275 autopsy cases

Genotype	Heart weight (g)	S.D.
Without alleles 9.3/10	430	130
Heterozygous for alleles 9.3/10	420	115
Homozygous for alleles 9.3/10	410	120

tional to the number of repeats [7]. It is assumed that the effect on transcription is specifically due to the repeat sequence by interaction with factors such as ZNF191 binding to the (TCAT)n repeat, and that other STRs with this repeat motif might have similar effects on other genes. Although it remains to be established whether such STRs influence transcription in vivo, the fact that the regulatory effect might depend on the sequence of the repeat motif is of special interest for forensic DNA profiling: (TCAT) is a rather uncommon motif for forensic STRs. Among the 8 German database systems, only TH01, and of the 13 CODIS loci, only THO1 and TPOX, show this repeat motif.

Nevertheless, the THO1 marker should thus not reveal any substantial "conclusions concerning the personality, ... (or) ...diseases" as demanded by the Federal Constitutional Court of Germany [1]. Based on the current knowledge, we are thus convinced that the use of this useful marker for forensic purposes is legitimate and should not be discontinued. It can nevertheless be expected that the ongoing research in the field of human genetics will reveal undesired associations for some of the polymorphisms used for forensic purposes, and we want to propose a discussion about possible consequences in forensic panels.

Acknowledgements

The authors would like to thank A. Graul, A. Heide and S. Salostowitz for their excellent technical assistance.

References

[1] Order of the Federal Constitutional Court of Germany (2 BvR 1741/99 9, Dec. 14th 2000), Neue Juristische Wochenschrift (12) 879: 882.
[2] P. Sharma, A. Hingorani, H. Jia, M. Ashby, R. Hopper, D. Clayton, M.J. Brown, Positive association of tyrosine hydroxylase microsatellite marker to essential hypertension, Hypertension 32 (1998) 676–682.
[3] M. Klintschar, M. Kubat, A study on the short tandem repeat systems HumTH01 and HumVWA in an Austrian population sample, Int. J. Leg. Med. 107 (1995) 329–330.
[4] K.H. Rahn, M. Barenbrock, M. Hausberg, The sympathetic nervous system in the pathogenesis of hypertension, J. Hypertens. 3 (1999) 11–14.
[5] B. Brinkmann, M. Klintschar, F. Neuhuber, J. Huhne, B. Rolf, Mutation rate in human microsatellites: influence of the structure and length of the tandem repeat, Am. J. Hum. Genet. 62 (1998) 1408–1415.
[6] Y. Kashi, D. King, M. Soller, Simple sequence repeats as a source of quantitative genetic variation, Trends Genet. 13 (1997) 74–78.
[7] V. Albanese, N.F. Biguet, H. Kiefer, E. Bayard, J. Mallet, R. Meloni, Quantitative effects on gene silencing by allelic variation at a tetranucleotide microsatellite, Hum. Mol. Genet. 10 (2001) 1785–1792.

International Congress Series 1261 (2004) 592–594

www.ics-elsevier.com

Cytochrome *b* for identification of animal species in processed food

M.M de Pancorbo[a,b,*], A. Castro[b,c], I. Fernández-Fernández[b,c], N. Cuevas[c]

[a] *Dpto. de Z. Dinámica Celular A., Facultad de Farmacia, Universidad del País Vasco, Paseo de la Universidad 7, 01006, Vitoria-Gasteiz, Spain*

[b] *Instituto Vasco de Criminología, Universidad del País Vasco, San Sebastián-Donostia, Spain*

[c] *DataGene Ltda. (Grupo Adirondack), Parque Tecnológico, Derio (Bizkaia) Spain*

Abstract. The objective of this work has been to develop a suitable methodology based on mitochondrial cytochrome *b* gene (cytb) to allow the identification of animals species used as raw material in the manufacture of processed food. In some cases, more detailed information on the kind of food sample found in the stomach of a victim may be of particular importance. A number of specimens of processed food with bovine, pork and chicken origin were analyzed. DNA was extracted by two methods: (1) Cell lysis using proteinase K and SDS, and phenol-chloroform DNA purification; (2) NucleoSpin Food (Macherey-Nagel™). PCR amplification of 358 pb of the cytb was done. The species of the samples were identified by aligning to the cytb gene sequence entries using BLAST of the National Center for Biotechnology Information. Both the DNA extraction procedures yielded enough DNA to be analyzed by PCR. Sequences obtained were searched against nucleotide sequence database (GenBank). With this procedure, it is possible to classify each sample correctly according to its biological species. © 2003 Published by Elsevier B.V.

Keywords: Cytochrome *b*; Processed food; Bovine; Pork; Chicken

1. Introduction

The cytochrome *b* gene (cyt b) from the mitochondrial genome contains species-specific information and has been used in phylogeny as well as in forensic investigations in previous studies. Thus, it has been confirmed the usefulness of cytb analysis in identifying the biological origin of casework specimens [1]. In some cases, more detailed information on the kind of food sample found in the stomach of a victim may be of particular importance. This information can be used to estimate the postmortem interval and may provide information about the place of decease itself.

* Corresponding author. Dpto. de Z. Dinámica Celular A., Facultad de Farmacia, Universidad del País Vasco, Paseo de la Universidad 7, 01006, Vitoria-Gasteiz, Spain. Tel.: +34-945-013045; fax: +34-945-013756.

E-mail address: gcpmagom@lg.ehu.es (M.M. de Pancorbo).

0531-5131/ © 2003 Published by Elsevier B.V.
doi:10.1016/S0531-5131(03)01657-1

In addition, identification of processed food is necessary as the customer has the right to be informed about products being bought and consumed [2]. Law requires that products should be labeled with official names, thus creating a foundation for discouraging fraud. Also, enforcement of protected species requires techniques to verify authenticity.

Improved techniques for the identification of food components are urgently required, and DNA-based technologies are providing answers to many of the questions being asked [3].

The objective of this work has been to develop a suitable methodology based on mitochondrial cytochrome *b* gene to allow the identification of animals species used as raw material in the manufacture of processed food.

2. Methodology

A number of specimens of processed food with bovine, pork, chicken and fish origin were analyzed. DNA was extracted by two methods: (1) Cell lysis was performed using proteinase K and SDS. The DNA was purified using the phenol-chloroform method. (2) NucleoSpin Food (Macherey-Nagel™) was used following the manufacturer's protocol. PCR amplification of 358 pb of the cytb was done under conditions described by Parson et al. (2000). All the samples were sequenced using the dRhodamine Terminator kit (Applied Biosystems) method, in an automatic ABI Prism 310 DNA sequencer. The obtained sequences were used to identify the species of the samples by aligning to the cytb gene sequence entries using the online BLAST search engine of the National Center for Biotechnology Information (NCBI).

3. Results and discussion

DNA was extracted from processed food using the methods above described. In both the cases, DNA extraction procedures yielded enough DNA to be analyzed by PCR. PCR products were sequenced. The sequencer identified most of the bases unambiguously (Fig. 1).

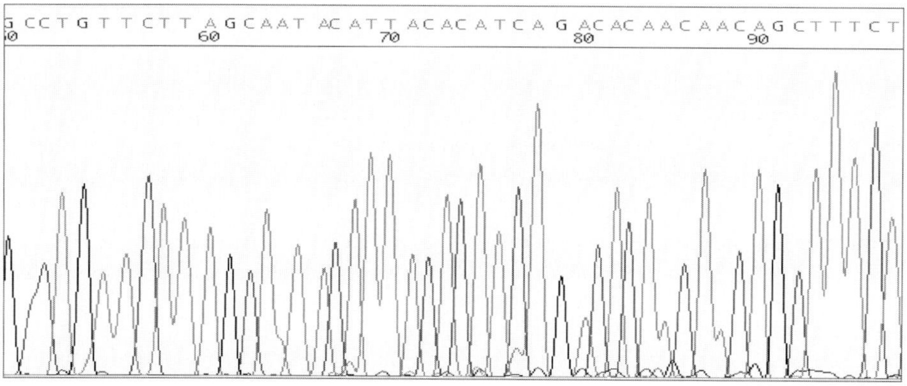

Fig. 1. Partial sequence of cytb obtained of DNA from sausage extracted by Proteinase K and SDS and purified with phenol-chloroform.

Table 1
Results from BLAST for identification of species from processed food

Processed food	Label of manufacturer	Species GenBank	Score (bits)	*E* value	Coincidence between label and DNA cytb analysis
Sausage	Pork	*Sus scrofa*	563	e − 158	+
Hard pork sausage	Pork	*Sus scrofa*	563	e − 158	+
Meatball	Bovine	*Box taurus*	525	e − 147	+
Stew chicken	Chicken	*Gallus gallus*	517	e − 144	+

Sequences obtained from processed food were searched against nucleotide sequence database (GenBank). The results of a sequence search contains a list of database entries, the score and e-value displayed high similarity between the laboratory results and the corresponding gender or species specified by the manufacturer (Table 1).

These results indicate that animal samples extracted from processed food can be successfully identified to specific level, even from degraded material using the cytb analysis. With this procedure, it is possible to classify each sample correctly according to its biological species.

Acknowledgements

This work has been supported by the grant UE 14/01 of the Basque Country University.

References

[1] W. Parson, et al., Int. J. Leg. Med. 114 (2000) 23–28.
[2] G.K. Weder, et al., Eur. Food Res. Technol. 213 (2001) 139–144.
[3] P. Bossier, J. Food Sci. 64 (1999) 189–193.

International Congress Series 1261 (2004) 595

www.ics-elsevier.com

Identification of rhino from 'medicinal' powders and sculptures

A. Linacre[a,*], H.-M. Hsieh[b], L.-H. Huang[b], L.-C. Tsai[b], Y.-C. Kuo[b], H.-H. Meng[b], J.C.-I. Lee[b]

[a] *Forensic Science Unit, University of Strathclyde, Glasgow, 204 George Street, G1 1XW, Scotland, UK*
[b] *Forensic Science, Central Police University, 56 Shu-Jen Road, Kwei-San, Taoyuan 33334, Taiwan, ROC*

Keywords: Rhino; DNA; Forensic wildlife studies

Material suspected of originating from species of Rhinoceros is frequently seized by forensic organisations investigating trade in endangered species. Rhino species, of which there are currently five, are on the verge of extinction in the wild. Trade in Rhino is contrary to CITES and should be investigated if suspected Rhino material is seized. This report details the use of DNA profile to unambiguously identify the presence of Rhino and SEM-EDX to determine that the seizure was from horn material. At present identification of the species is possible by DNA sequencing of the material, such as powdered rhinoceros horns. The unambiguous identification of Rhino products using a 402 bp fragment of cytochrome *b* gene was investigated. This DNA sequence may not only assist in the identification of the unknown sample, but can be used to determine the phylogenetic relationships of rhinoceros species. The results of this phylogenetic study showed that there were four major branches among rhinoceros species from a common origin with the greatest distance between the Indian and the Black Rhino. The amplification of the 402 bp fragment of the cytochrome *b* gene was found to be able to detect rhinoceros DNA even in the ratio of 1:19 with Holstein cow DNA. SEM-EDX was used successfully to determine that the sample was from hair or horn. The method used in this study can be applied in the identification of processed products of rhinoceros horns, such as sculptures, daggers, powders or even mixture powdered prescriptions.

* Corresponding author. Tel.: +44-1415-484377; fax: +44-1415-482532.
E-mail address: a.m.t.linacre@strath.ac.uk (A. Linacre).

doi:10.1016/S0531-5131(03)01662-5

International Congress Series 1261 (2004) 596–598

www.ics-elsevier.com

Features of expression of iNOS mRNA in postmortem brain

Valeri Kozhemyako[a,b,*], Galina Dirlam[a], Irina Smolina[b], Inessa Duyizen[c], Valeri Rasskazov[b]

[a] *Primorsky Forensic Medical Bureau, 3 Lazo Str., Vladivostok, Russia*
[b] *Pacific Institute of Bioorganic Chemistry, Far East Division of Russian Academy of Science, 159 Stoletya Str., Vladivostok 690022, Russia*
[c] *Marine Biology Institute, Far East Division of Russian Academy of Sciences, 17 Palchevskogo Str., Vladivostok, Russia*

Abstract. The purpose of this research was to use RNA as a subject of legal medicine. Tissue samples were obtained from postmortem human brains collected from cadavers, whose reasons of death were exactly determined. Total RNA was isolated by the standard method and used for reverse transcription-polymerase chain reaction analysis (RT-PCR). The subject of our special concern was NOS and its expression in various brain tissues during some pathological processes. In this study, we showed that postmortem brain tissue can yield good quality mRNA for the successful application of traditional molecular biology methods from postmortem brain tissue even with prolonged postmortem intervals (up to 7 days). The relationship between a level of inducible NOS expression and intensity of pathomorphologic development in organs and tissues of people who died from different reasons was detected.

Keywords: iNOS; RNA expression; RT-PCR

1. Introduction

Technological advances in molecular biology and genetics allowed scientists from different fields to use them for solving their own goals. DNA is successfully used as a subject of legal medicine as the individual stabile code of a person. Reversely, the regulation of mRNA gene expression represents an important and growing field in biological research. Messenger RNAs may elucidate features of processes, which took place before and on the moment of death. There are dozens of individual genes of interest which are all expressed in human tissues. As a subject of our investigation, we chose the NO^- synthesis system.

* Corresponding author. Laboratory of Marine Biochemistry, Pacific Institute of Bioorganic Chemistry, Far East Division of Russian Academy of Science, 159 Stoletya Str., Vladivostok 690022, Russia.Tel: +7-4232-209-739; fax: +7-4232-222-074.

E-mail address: kozhemyako@piboc.dvo.ru (V. Kozhemyako).

0531-5131/
doi:10.1016/j.ics.2003.11.009

The aim of the present study was to investigate the pattern of expression of inducible nitric oxide-synthase (iNOS) in various tissues of postmortem human brain.

2. Materials and methods

Tissue samples were obtained from postmortem human brains, lungs, hearts, livers and kidneys collected from cadavers, whose reasons of death were determined. Total RNA was isolated by guanidine isothiocyanate lysis and phenol:chloroform extraction by a method based on Chomczynski and Sacchi [1]. The RNA samples were used for reverse transcription-polymerase chain reaction analysis (RT-PCR). To normalize cDNA amounts used during the PCR amplification, a parallel amplification was performed using glyceraldehyde-3-phosphate dehydrogenases (G3PDH) specific primers (Clontech, USA). For amplification, $iNOS^-$ transcripts were used as specific primers.

3. Results

At first, we had to determine whether the high-molecular weight RNA could keep its stability or not in the main human organs, such as liver, lung, heart, kidney and brain after death (Fig. 1).

Our results showed that the high-molecular weight RNA appear to be rather stable in lung and heart, whereas the resistance of RNA within kidney and liver is slightly less. The brain tissues were the steadiest after the postmortem changes: we managed to isolate high-molecular weight RNA from the samples of brain tissues which were stored at 4 °C up to 7 days.

RNA, isolated from the postmortem brain, was found in good quantity and the samples taken from the brains 1, 2 or 3 days after death, were revealed to be not different from one another. Some degradation of RNA isolated from the brain has been found only after storing it 7 days following death. cDNA library, obtained by using reverse transcription of RNA, was isolated from the samples of the postmortem brains and displayed the content of a set of mRNAs, encoded by the "housekeeping genes". However, the amplification with primers for iNOS mRNA demonstrated a reply from only two brains and only some structures of brain, namely hippocampus and cerebellum in this case.

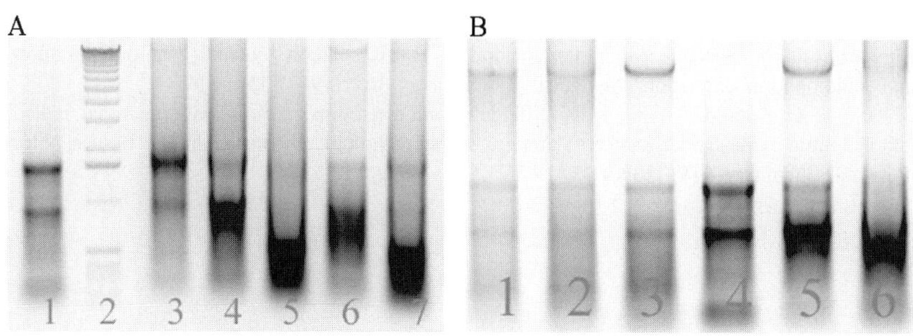

Fig. 1. Electrophoresis of RNA. (A) 1—Standard human RNA; 2—1 kb ladder; 3, 4, 5—liver (1, 2 and 3 days after death); 6, 7—kidney (1 and 2 days). (B) 1, 2—lung (1 and 3 days); 3—brain (5 days); 4—standard human RNA; 5, 6—heart muscle (1 and 3 days).

The reason for death of the first person was a drug overdose. But the second person died after a road accident without brain damage. Drugs and alcohol in the blood and urine of the last person were not detected.

4. Discussion

Our investigations for stability of RNA in the main organs corresponded to theoretical notions. It depended on nuclease activity in tissue. Nuclease content in a human brain was almost not detected. Therefore, DNA and RNA were the successfully isolated brain samples of various ages. In this study, we showed that postmortem brain tissue can yield good quality mRNA for the successful application of traditional molecular biology methods from postmortem brain tissue even with prolonged postmortem intervals (up to 7 days). Besides this, RNA from the other tissues potentially could be used but only at the first 1–3 days after death.

The amplitude of bands and the number of PCR cycles applied to get uniform bands for "housekeeping genes" were consistent with differences in the mRNA contents. A relationship was detected between level of iNOS expression and intensity of pathomorphologic development in tissues of people who died from different reasons. Besides that, RT-PCR analysis demonstrated a structure-specific picture. A matter of interest was that data obtained by different groups of scientists appeared very contradictory. Especially when they used commercial RNA which seemed to be a sum of RNAs, isolated from the same tissue of many bodies. For example, Park et al. [2], who used samples of commercial RNA, found the presence of iNOS mRNA within the different structures of the normal brain, taken after the death of a human.

No statistical evaluation of the data was performed due to the qualitative nature of this study, but we suppose that iNOS expression in some tissues could serve as a marker of toxic influence before the death of a human.

In conclusion, we showed that high-quality RNA, suitable for routine molecular analyses, could be obtained from postmortem brain tissue even with prolonged postmortem intervals. We would suggest further research of different human marker RNA for an ascertaining of the reason, in some cases, of a conjecturable time of death.

References

[1] P. Chomczynski, N. Sacchi, Single step method of RNA isolation by acid guanidinium thiocyanate–phenol–chlorophorm extraction, Analytical Biochemistry 162 (1987) 156–159.

[2] C.-S. Park, G. Krishna, M.-S. Ahn, et al., Differential and constitutive expression of neuronal, inducible, and endothelial nitric oxide synthase mRNAs and proteins in pathologically normal human tissues, Nitric Oxide, Biology and Chemistry 4 (5) (2000) 459–471.

International Congress Series 1261 (2004) 599–601

www.ics-elsevier.com

Molecular evaluation of victims of sudden death: a promising approach for excluding criminal responsibility

E. Polisecki[a], M. Marino[a], J. Ravioli[b], J. Cámera[b], A Sala[a], D. Corach[a,*]

[a] Servicio de Huellas Digitales Genéticas (SHDG) and Cátedra de Genética y Biología Molecular, Facultad de Farmacia y Bioquímica, Universidad de Buenos Aires, Buenos Aires, Argentina
[b] Cátedra de Medicina Legal, Facultad de Medicina, Universidad de Buenos Aires, Buenos Aires, Argentina

Abstract. Sudden death constitutes one of the most frequent causes of death in adults. In order to look for genetic markers that could play a role in the sudden death in adults (SDA), the common deletions of 4977 bp in the mitochondrial DNA and variations in the apoB gene were studied. The correlation of mtDNA common deletion with SDA victims might offer a rapid and simple tool to provide additional information in complex SDA investigations

Keywords: Mitochondrial DNA; Sudden death; 4977-bp deletion; ApoB gene

1. Introduction

One of the most frequent causes of death is the so-called sudden death in adults (SDA). The victims die by no apparent causes and without clinical information that might establish its cause. Data for some countries show approximately 88% SDA are of cardiac origin. An epidemiological study on coronary heart disease (CHD) has indicated that mother's age at death was more significant predictor of age at sudden CHD death than father's age [1]. This suggests that the maternally transmitted mitochondrial genotype may influence the susceptibility to adult-onset disease. In contrast to the nuclear DNA, mitochondrial DNA (mtDNA) have rendered 10–20 times more vulnerable to mutation and oxidative damage. MtDNA mutations have been proposed to contribute to the aging process. The occurrence in human tissues, with age-associated manner of a particular large mtDNA 4977-bp deletion (mtDNA4977-deletion) was first reported in 1990 [2]. This deletion accumulates preferentially in post-mitotic tissue such as muscle and brain [3]. Previous studies showed high levels of mtDNA4977-deletion in cardiac muscle from patients suffering from CHD. Recently, it was hypothesized that mtDNA damage is a common mechanism by which risk factors such as diabetes mellitus, hypertension, hypercholesterolemia and age contribute to atherogenesis [4]. ApoB is the main lipid transport protein in the blood. Several studies have shown that

* Corresponding author. Tel.: +54-114-9648281; fax: +54-114-9648282.
E-mail address: shdg@ffyb.uba.ar (D. Corach).

0531-5131/
doi:10.1016/S0531-5131(03)01652-2

genetic variation at the apoB gene locus is associated with altered circulating cholesterol, apoB levels and risk of CHD [5]. Until now, the association studies between apoB gene polymorphism and risk of CHD have reported contradictory results among populations.

In order to evaluate some mutations and polymorphisms potentially linked with SDA, the common mtDNA4977-deletion, the nuclear mutation Arg3500Gln/apoB and the polymorphism *Msp*I/apoB in codon 3611 were selected to analyze cardiac muscle samples from SDA and controls.

2. Materials and methods

2.1. Samples

Genomic DNA was isolated from a set of 13 cardiac muscle tissue from victims of SDA (18–70 years), and 9 muscle tissue sample from corpses not affected by SDA (22–71 years).

The extracted DNA was quantified by spectrophotometric analysis.

2.2. 4977-bp 'common' deletion

The dilution-PCR method was used to estimate the proportion of the total mtDNA harboring the mtDNA4977-deletion. DNA was prior digested with *Pst*I and *Eco*RI to avoid amplification of wild-type products. Serial dilutions of the digested were performed for the amplification of D-loop and mtDNA 4977-bp deletion. D-loop: primers 5′ caccattagcacccaaagct3′ (forward) and 5′ tgatttcacggaggatggtg3′ (reverse) amplify a 440-bp fragment and were used to quantify the total mtDNA. In order to detect mtDNA 4977-bp deletion, the 5′ ctcagagcccactgtaaagc3′ (forward) and 5′ cttgtcagggaggtagcgat3′ (reverse) primers amplify a 389-bp fragment. The PCR products were separated on 2% agarose gels and detected using a Foto/Analyst® and quantified using an Image Quant 5.1 software.

With all samples, the decline in optical density (OD) of the PCR products for each dilution series versus the amount of mtDNA fitted a semi-logarithmic plot according to a regression line, r^2>0.9. The percent of deleted mtDNA with respect to total mtDNA was determined by the ratio of the DNA dilutions that reduced the PCR product OD of the deleted mtDNA and total mtDNA curves to the same level. All PCR products were sequenced by the Big Dye terminator System.

2.3. Arg3500Gln/apoB and polymorphism MspI/apoB

This method is based on the selective creation of an artificial *Msp*I restriction site in the wild-type allele, but not in the mutant allele, to observe the Arg3500Gln. In the same fragment, there is a polymorphism *Msp*I/apoB (RFLP) in codon 3611showing the allele M− or M+. PCR was carried using the forward 5′ cttacttgaattccaagagcaccc3′ and reverse 5′ tggtaggatgatatttttgaggaa3′ primers.

The PCR product was digested with *Msp*I and were separated in a high resolution gel, GeneAmp™ Detection Gel and silver stain detection.

3. Results and discussion

MtDNA4977-deletion percent (%) (mean ± S.D.) was higher in victims of SDA (0.00488 ± 0.0011) than those not affected by SDA (0.00223 ± 0.0037) (P<0.05).

Moreover, when SDA victims were divided into two subgroups according to age distribution, no differences were found in mtDNA4977-deletion percent between victims <39 and >51 years. By sequence analysis, we confirmed in all samples affected that a single breakage point was detected between positions 8482 and 13460, which defines the deletion of the 4977-bp fragment.

Regarding ApoB gene, none of the samples tested showed the Arg3500Gln/apoB mutation. Detection of *Msp*I/apoB polymorphisms shows that 3 out of 13 SDA and 2 out of 9 not SDA presented the rare allele M – .

This preliminary investigation was mainly focused to search an association between SDA and oxidative damage, evidenced by an increase of mtDNA4977-deletion.

Our results indicate that samples from SDA have a significant percent increase of mtDNA4977-deletion in comparison to samples from victims not affected by SDA. Mitochondrial disease can be due to either a homoplasmic or a heteroplasmic mutation. In the case of a heteroplasmic mutation, the disease state develops only after a threshold level of mutation has been achieved. When the percent-mutated DNA far exceeds the threshold level, then an acute (and sometimes lethal) condition will be observed [3]. These results are probably related to the high incidence of CHD among SDA; in turn, cardiac ischemia is associated with high oxidative stress.

In this study, no differences were found in the percent of mtDNA4977-deletion between samples from young and old victims of SDA. The fact that samples from young victims showed high level of such deletion would indicate that this deletion may be associated with SDA, irrespective of age. On the other hand, it was considered necessary to study other genetic variations related to CHD. Herein we proposed some apoB gene variation such as Arg3500Gln and *Msp*I polymorphism. As expected, applying both mutation and polymorphisms of ApoB gene to a small sample tested did not correlate neither with SDA victims tissues nor with control samples. In order to correlate genetic variations with sudden death as an association study, a bigger sample would be required. The correlation of mtDNA common deletion with SDA victims might offer a rapid and simple tool to provide additional information in complex SDA investigations. Although the cause of sudden death may be probably due to multiple genetic effect, energy reduction led by anomalous (faster) mutated mtDNA replication may play a remarkable role in the SDA.

Acknowledgements

This work was supported, in part, by grants 0746-CONICET and UBACyT.B-038, to DC. DC and AS are members of CIC-CONICET.

References

[1] F. Brand, D. Kiely, W. Kannel, R. Myers, Family patterns of coronary heart disease mortality: the Framingham Longevity Study, J. Clin. Epidemiol. 45 (2) (1992) 169–174.

[2] G. Cortopassi, N. Arnheim, Detection of a specific mitochondrial DNA deletion in tissues of older humans, Nucleic Acids Res. 18 (23) (1990) 6927–6933.

[3] C. Berdanier, H. Everts, Mitochondrial DNA in aging and degenerative disease, Mutat. Res. 475 (2001) 169–184.

[4] S. Ballinger, et al., Mitochondrial integrity and function in atherogenesis, Circulation 106 (2002) 544–549.

[5] J. Rajput-Williams, et al., Variation of apolipoprotein-B genes is associated with obesity, high blood cholesterol levels, and increased risk of coronary heart disease, Lancet 24–31 (2) (8626–8627) (1988) 1442–1446.

International Congress Series 1261 (2004) 602–604

www.ics-elsevier.com

Multiplex PCR with confronting two-pair primers for Se genotyping

Y. Itoh[a,*], K. Takahashi[a,b], K. Satoh[a,b], K. Nagao[c], M. Fujime[c]

[a] *Department of Forensic Medicine, Juntendo University School of Medicine, 2-1-1 Hongo, Bunkyo Tokyo 113-8421, Japan*

[b] *Medico-Legal Section, Criminal Investigation Laboratory, Metoropolitan Police Department, Tokyo, Japan*

[c] *Department of Urology, Juntendo University School of Medicine, Tokyo, Japan*

Abstract. Multiplex PCR with confronting two-pair primers (PCR-CTPP) for Se genotyping classified into Se, se1 (G428A), se2 (A385T), and se5 (fusion gene) alleles has been developed. Genotyping was performed using the electrophoretic patterns of the PCR products. The incidences of the Se, se1, se2 and se5 alleles were 55.75% (223/400), 0% (0/400), 39.75% (159/400) and 4.5% (18/400) in Japanese subjects, respectively. We were not able to find the se1 non-functional alleles among our Japanese samples. Se genotyping may be a useful marker for ethnic discrimination of biological stains obtained from Japanese, Caucasian, African and Iranian individuals. This method is simple, rapid and accurate.

Keywords: Se genotyping; DNA typing; Population genetics; Blood group

1. Introduction

The ethnic specificity of Secretor genotypes has been given special attention in recent years. The se1, G428A [1], is a unique non-functional allele in Caucasians, Africans and Iranians. Both the se2, A385T [2] and se5, fusion gene [3] are also unique non-functional alleles in Asians. In this paper, we developed a multiplex PCR with confronting two-pair primers (PCR-CTPP) [4,5] for Se genotyping classified into Se, se1, se2, and se5 alleles. This assay provides a rapid, accurate and simple method for Se genotyping that can provide useful information on ethnic specificity.

2. Materials and methods

All samples from Japanese subjects were obtained with informed consent and were collected at the Department of Urology, Juntendo University School of Medicine.

Lewis phenotypes were determined for fresh blood samples by standard hemagglutination methods. Typing was carried out with monoclonal Le^a and Le^b antibodies (Seraclone: Biotest, Germany).

* Corresponding author. Tel.: +81-3-5802-1050; fax: +81-3-5802-1050.
E-mail address: yitoh@med.juntendo.ac.jp (Y. Itoh).

0531-5131/
doi:10.1016/S0531-5131(03)01535-8

DNA was isolated from blood using the QIAamp DNA Mini Kit (QIAGEN, Germany) or the standard phenol/chloroform extraction procedure. The extracted DNA was stored at 4 °C until the genotypes analysis.

Seven kinds of primers were designed, including T5-F: TCT CCC AGC TAA CGT GTC CCG (AC: U17894, the nucleotide sequences from position 24 to 44), T1-F: TGG GCA TAC TCA GCC CGT GT (AC: 82933, the nucleotide sequences from position 196 to 215), T2-R: CGG ACG TAC TCC CCC GGG AT (AC: U17894, the nucleotide sequences from position 500 to 481), NA1-F: GGA GGA GGA ATA CCG CCA CT (AC: U17894, the nucleotide sequences from position 462 to 481), T6-R: CAA TCC CTG TCC ACT CCG GCA (AC: U17894, the nucleotide sequences from position 1063 to 1043), T7-F: TGG GCA TAC TCA GCC CGT GT (AC: U17894, the nucleotide sequences from position 505 to 524), and T8-R: CGG ACG TAC TCC CCC GGG AT (AC: U17894, the nucleotide sequences from positions 544 to 524).

PCR-CTPP (confronting two-pair primers) was developed to perform secretor genotyping. DNA amplification was performed in 25 μl reaction volumes. PCR-CTPP for Se, se2 and se5 typing: 30 ng of template DNA was added to the reaction mixture containing PCR buffer (Invitorogen Life Technologies, Japan), 1.5 mM $MgCl_2$ (Invitorogen Life Technologies), 0.2 mM dNTPs (Promega Japan), 0.625 U platinum Taq DNA polymerase (Invitorogen life technologies). Primers (10 pmol) of T5-F and T1-F, 5 pmol primers of T2-R and NA1F, and 20 pmol primer of T6-R were used. PCR-CTPP for Se and se1 typing, 10 pmol primers of T5-F, T6-R, T7-F and T8-R was used as the primer pairs instead of the above pairs. After an initial denaturation step at 94 °C for 2 min, 35 cycles were performed consisting of 50 s at 94 °C, 1 min at 65 °C, and 1 min at 72 °C, followed by a 2-min extension at 72 °C in a TAKARA PCR Thermal Cycler MP (TP3000). Ten milliliters of each amplified PCR product was analysed by electrophoresis on 2% agarose gel stained with ethidium bromide.

3. Results and discussion

Genotyping was performed using the electrophoretic patterns of PCR products as follows, 1042 and 479 bp for Se/Se genotype, 1042, 602, and 479 bp for Se/se2 genotype,

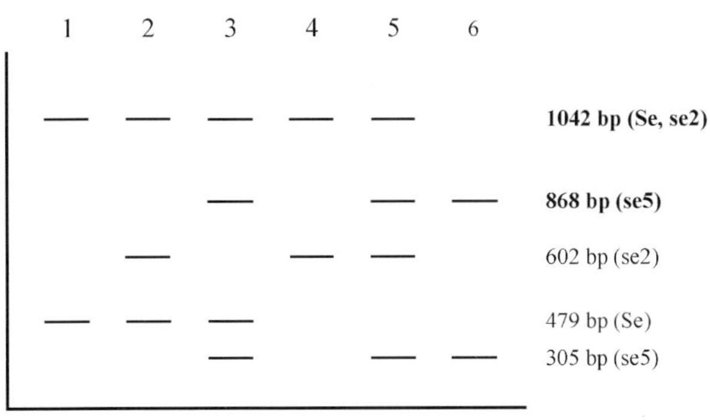

Fig. 1. Electrophoretic diagrams of PCR-CTPP products for Se, se2 and se5 genes. Genotypes of lanes; 1 = Se/Se, 2 = Se/se2, 3 = Se/se5, 4 = se2/se2, 5 = se2/se5, 6 = se5/se5.

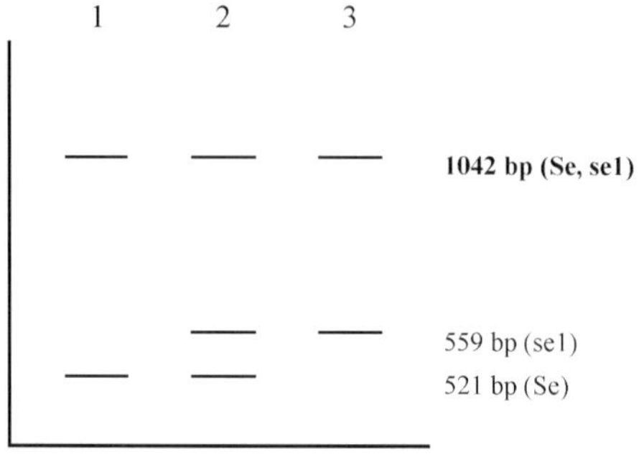

Fig. 2. Electrophoretic diagrams of PCR-CTPP products for Se and se1. Genotypes of lanes; 1 = Se/Se, 2 = Se/se1, 3 = se1/se1.

1042, 868, 479 and 305 bp for Se/se5 genotype, 1042 and 602 bp for se2/se2 genotype, 1042, 868, 602, and 305 bp for se2/se5A (Fig. 1). A 1042-bp positive control product is generated in the Se, se1 and se2 (Fig. 2). Similarly, a 868-bp positive control product was also generated in se5. The incidences of the Se, se1, se2 and se5 alleles were 55.75% (223/400), 0% (0/400), 39.75% (159/400) and 4.5% (18/400) in the Japanese subjects, respectively. Genotypes of Se/Se (54 cases), Se/se2 (104 cases), and Se/se5 (11 cases) belonged to phenotypes of Le(a − b+) or Le(a − b −). Those of se2/se2 (24 cases) and se2/se5 (7 cases) belonged to phenotypes of Le(a + b −) or Le(a − b −). No discrepancies were observed between the phenotypes and genotypes. We were not able to find the se1 non-functional alleles among our Japanese samples, consistent with the previous report [2]. Se genotyping may be a useful marker for ethnic discrimination of biological stains obtained from Japanese, Caucasian, African and Iranian individuals. This method is simple, rapid and accurate for forensic purposes.

References

[1] T. Kudo et al., Molecular genetic analysis of the human Lewis histo-blood group system: II. Secretor gene inactivation by a novel single missense mutation A385T in Japanese nonsecretor individuals, J. Biol. Chem. 271 (1996) 9830–9837.

[2] Y. Koda et al., Molecular basis for secretor type alpha (1,2)-fucosyltransferase gene deficiency in a Japanese population: a fusion gene generated by unequal crossover responsible for the enzyme deficiency, Am. J. Hum. Genet. 59 (1996) 343–350.

[3] R.J. Kelly et al., Sequence and expression of a candidate for the human Secretor blood group alpha (1,2) fucosyltransferase gene (FUT2). Homozygosity for an enzyme-inactivating nonsense mutation commonly correlates with the non-secretor phenotype, J. Biol. Chem. 270 (1995) 4640–4649.

[4] N. Hamajima et al., Polymerase chain reaction with confronting two-pair primers for polymorphism genotyping, Jpn. J. Cancer Res. 91 (2000) 865–868.

[5] K. Takahashi et al., Se genotyping by PCR with confronting two-pair primers (PCR-CTPP), DNA polymorphism 11 (2003) 139–142.

International Congress Series 1261 (2004) 605–607

ELSEVIER

www.ics-elsevier.com

PCR-based diagnosis of adenovirus and Epstein–Barr virus in paraffin-embedded heart tissue

R. Dettmeyer*, S.A. Padosch, A. Baasner, B. Madea

Institute of Forensic Medicine, University of Bonn, Stiftsplatz 12, 53111 Bonn, Germany

Abstract. Immunohistochemical and molecular-pathological techniques have improved the diagnosis, but the incidence of virus-induced lethal myocarditis still remains unclear. Therefore, it is of great interest to investigate postmortem myocardial samples in cases of sudden infant death syndrome (SIDS). Adenoviruses and Epstein–Barr viruses are known as possible agents of myocarditis. Viral DNAs were specifically isolated and amplified from formaldehyde-fixed material. At autopsy, myocardial samples were taken from 62 SIDS cases from different regions and investigated with PCR. Adenoviral DNA was detected in 2/62 and Epstein–Barr viruses in 3/62 cases. Our results emphasize the importance of modern molecular-pathological methods in cases of sudden unexpected death.

Keywords: Adenoviruses; Epstein–Barr virus; PCR; Paraffin-embedded tissue; Myocarditis

1. Introduction

Studies of myocarditis in adults demonstrated that numerous cases of acute myocarditis can not be diagnosed, according to the Dallas criteria [1], by traditional hematoxylin–eosin staining of endomyocardial biopsies. Previously, we reported on detection of enteroviruses (EV) including coxsackieviruses B3 (CVB3) and parvovirus B19 (PVB19) [2–5]. We analysed adenovirus (AV) DNA and Epstein–Barr virus (EBV) DNA from paraffin-embedded heart tissue with PCR. Therefore, we established a reliable method to isolate DNA from formaldehyde-fixed and paraffin-embedded material.

2. Materials and methods

Postmortem myocardial samples were obtained from 62 autopsy cases with suspected sudden infant death syndrome (SIDS). Eight myocardial samples were taken from each heart at standardized locations. Viral DNA was extracted from paraffin-embedded myocardial, liver and spleen samples with the Genial First-DNA-Kit (Genial, Troisdorf, Germany). The prerequisite for virus PCR was the amplification of cyclophilin (cyc) [6]. To avoid false-positive results due to contamination, negative controls were performed in

* Corresponding author. Tel.: +49-228-73-8331; fax: +49-228-73-8339.
E-mail address: rdettmey@uni-bonn.de (R. Dettmeyer).

doi:10.1016/S0531-5131(03)01505-X

Table 1
Details of PCR primers used to amplify viral genes; AV(3); EBV(29); cyc(9)

Primer	Nucleotide sequences (5′ to 3′)	Product size (bp)
AVF	GCC GCA GTG GTC TTA CAT GCA CAT	300 bp
AVR	CAG CAC GCC GCG GAT GTC AAA GT	(AVF/AVR; first round)
AV3	AGA CGT ACT TCA GCC TGA A	130 bp
AV4	CCT TGT ACG AGT ACG CAG TA	(AV3/AV4; second round)
EBV1	AAG GAG GGT GGT TTG GAA AG	309 bp
EBV2	AAC AGA CAA TGG ACT CCC TTA	(EBV1/EBV2; first round)
EBV3	ATC GTG GTC AAG GAG GTT CC	208 bp
EBV4	ACT CAA TGG TGT AAG ACG AC	(EBV3/EBV4; second round)
CycF	CGTC CAG CAT TTG CCA TGG A	180 bp
cycR	GAC AAG GTC CCA AAG ACA G	

Table 2
Details of PCR conditions used to amplify viral genes; AV [9]; EBV [12]; cyc [6]

Primer	Denaturation (°C)	Annealing (°C)	Extension (°C)	Number of cycles
AVF	94 (60 s)	58 (60 s)	72 (60 s)	30 (first round)
AVR				20 (second round)
AV3				
AV4				
EBV1	94 (60 s)	58 (60 s)	72 (60 s)	30 (first round)
EBV2				20 (second round)
EBV3				
EBV4				
CycF	94 (60 s)	56 (60 s)	72 (60 s)	55
CycR				

all experiments [7]. For each assay, positive controls were added. For details of PCR, see Tables 1 and 2. PCR products were sequenced on an ABI 310 sequencer. Sequence comparison was performed by BLAST search of NCBI Gen-Bank. PCR products were also analysed on polyacrylamide gels (Fig. 1).

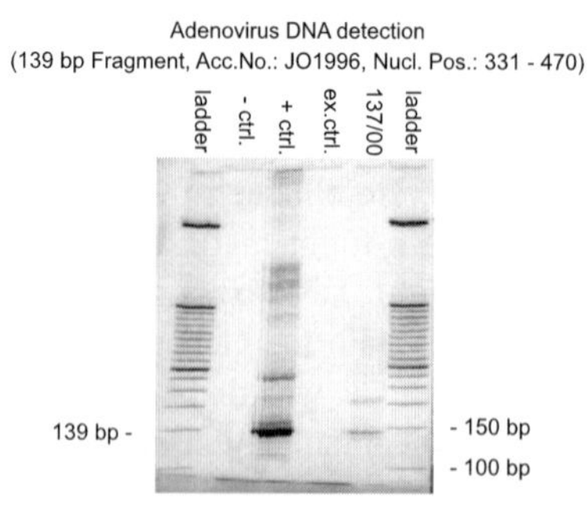

Fig. 1. Adenovirus DNA detection.

3. Results

Adenoviral DNA was detected in 2 out of 62 cases of suspected SIDS, whereas 3 out of these 62 cases were positive for EBV DNA. In all SIDS cases, the myocardial samples revealed no signs of myocarditis according to the Dallas criteria using conventional histologic stainings.

4. Discussion

Acute myocarditis can be diagnosed by PCR as a rapid method [8]. Given the fact that in endomyocardial biopsies, the detection of adenoviruses and EBV would be regarded as a pathological finding [9], this can be regarded as the cause of death in cases of SIDS. In our study, the myocardial tissues had been fixed in neutral buffered formaldehyde (pH 7.4) or Notox (Earth Safe Industries) for a maximum of 48 h. This was crucial for the extraction of intact nucleic acids. After longer fixation times, reproducible PCR for viruses was not possible. The ability to isolate intact viral DNA and RNA from paraffin-embedded tissue permits the analysis of several cardiotropic viruses. Although the pathomechanisms of virus-induced myocarditis are still a matter of great scientific interest, in clinical practice it is a widely recognized fact that EBV is without any doubt cardiopathogenic when detected in endomyocardial biopsy samples [10]. Recently, a cDNA clone that encodes the common coxsackie- and adenovirus receptor (CAR) was discovered [11]. Intriguingly, this receptor is downregulated after birth and is not detectable in adults. This observation offers a molecular basis for the explanation for the cardiopathogenity of the abovementioned viruses. Our results emphasize the importance of the PCR-based diagnosis in cases of SIDS.

References

[1] H.T. Aretz, Myocarditis—the Dallas criteria, Human Pathol. 18 (1987) 619–624.

[2] A. Baasner, R. Dettmeyer, M. Graebe, B. Madea, PCR-based diagnosis of enterovirus and parvovirus B19 in paraffin-embedded heart tissue, Int. Congr. Ser. 1239 (2003) 715–717.

[3] R. Dettmeyer, R. Kandolf, P. Schmidt, M. Schlamann, B. Madea, Lympho-monocytic enteroviral myocarditis: traditional, immunohistological and molecular pathological methods for diagnosis in a case of suspected sudden infant death syndrome (SIDS), For. Sci. Int. 119 (2001) 141–144.

[4] R. Dettmeyer, et al., Fatal parvovirus B19 myocarditis in an 8-year-old boy, J. For. Sci. 48 (2003) 183–186.

[5] R. Dettmeyer, et al., Coxsackie B3 myocarditis in 4 cases of suspected sudden infant death syndrome: diagnosis by immunohistochemical and molecular-pathologic investigations, Pathol. Res. Pract. 198 (2002) 689–696.

[6] J. Ben-Ezra, et al., Effect of fixation on the amplification of nucleic acids from paraffin-embedded material by the polymerase chain reaction, J. Histochem. Cytochem. 39 (1991) 351–354.

[7] S. Kwok, R. Higuchi, Avoiding false positives with PCR, Nature 339 (1989) 237–238.

[8] A.B. Martin, et al., Acute myocarditis: rapid diagnosis by PCR in children, Circulation 90 (1994) 330–339.

[9] G.M. Lozinski, et al., Adenovirus myocarditis: retrospective diagnosis by gene amplification from formalin-fixed, paraffin-embedded tissues, Human Pathol. 25 (1994) 831–834.

[10] M.M. Hebert, et al., Fatal Epstein–Barr virus myocarditis in a child with repetitive myocarditis, Pediatr. Pathol. Lab. Med. 15 (1995) 805–812.

[11] J.M. Bergelson, J.A. Cunningham, G. Droguett, et al., Isolation of a common receptor for coxsackie B viruses and adenoviruses 2 and 5, Science 275 (1997) 1320–1323.

[12] K.L. Chang, et al., EBNA-1 gene sequences in Brazilian and American patients with Hodgkin's disease, Blood 94 (1999) 244–250.

International Congress Series 1261 (2004) 608–610

www.ics-elsevier.com

Selective detection of parental alleles in imprinted gene, *H19*

Nori Nakayashiki*, Jun Kanetake, Masataka Takamiya, Yasuhiro Aoki

Department of Legal Medicine, Iwate Medical University School of Medicine, 19-1 Uchimura, Morioka 020-8505, Japan

Abstract. An autosomal polymorphism, designated H19FR which located upstream of imprinted *H19* gene, was investigated. Three allelic bands of H19FR system were detected by PCR amplification followed by constant denaturing gel electrophoresis (CDGE). In digested genomic DNA by methylation-sensitive endonuclease or *Mcr*BC, paternal or maternal allele of H19FR was selectively detectable, respectively. This parental typing was applicable to the DNA isolated from oral swab and hair with sheath in one individual with heterozygous genotype, but failed in the fingernail DNA. The DNA from bloodstain showed a tendency to obscure the parental discrimination.

Keywords: Polymorphism; *H19* gene; Parent-of-origin; Genomic imprinting; Methylation

1. Introduction

Genomic imprinting is defined as an epigenetic modification that leads to parent-of-origin-specific expression of a gene. It is assumed that main causative mechanism of genomic imprinting would be related to methylation of cytosine residue in CpG dinucleotide of the imprinted gene. A number of imprinted genes have been found and investigated so far. We describe here the H19FR polymorphism in paternally imprinted *H19* gene and the selective detection of parental allele in the H19FR system.

2. Materials and methods

Genomic DNA was extracted from peripheral blood, oral swab, hair with sheath, fingernail and bloodstain by routine phenol/chloroform method.

* Corresponding author. Tel.: +81-19-651-5110x3383; fax: +81-19-622-2826.
E-mail address: nnakaysk@iwate-med.ac.jp (N. Nakayashiki).

0531-5131/
doi:10.1016/S0531-5131(03)01500-0

2.1. H19FR polymorphism detected by constant denaturing gel electrophoresis (CDGE)

The PCR cocktail (25 μl) was composed of following reagents: 1 × PCR buffer (QIAGEN), 2.5 mM $MgCl_2$, 200 μM of each dNTP, 10 pM of each primer (H19F, 5′-ggctcttgca tagcacatgt-3′ and H19R-GC, 5′-cgcccgccgc gccccgcgcc cgtcccgccg cccccgccgc tccccatcat ccatggaact-3′), 0.5 U of Taq DNA polymerase (QIAGEN) and 10–20 ng of genomic DNA. After pre-heating the cocktail at 94 °C for 15 min, PCR by 32 cycles of 94 °C for 30 s, 61 °C for 30 s and 72 °C for 1 min, and post-extension at 72 °C for 4 min was carried out. In CDGE analysis [1,2], the PCR product was mixed with the same volume of 2 × loading dye (70% glycerol, 0.05% bromophenol blue and 0.05% xylene cyanol) and separated in a polyacrylamide gel (6% T and 2.6% C, 160 × 100 × 1 mm in size), including 45% denaturant (final concentration of 3.15 M urea and 18% formamide) and 1 × TAE buffer (40 mM Tris, 20 mM acetic acid, 1 mM EDTA, pH 8.0), in the 1 × TAE buffer at 60 °C, at 120 V for 3 h. After run, the band was visualized by silver staining.

2.2. Selective detection of parental allele by enzymatic pre-treatment of genomic DNA

One of two methylation-sensitive restriction enzymes (msRE), *Hpa*II (recognition site, $C^{m}CGG$) and *Hha*I ($G^{m}CGC$) was used to cleave a non-methylated allele, while *Mcr*BC [5′ ...$Pu^{m}C(N_{40-3000})Pu^{m}C$...3′] was used to digest a methylated allele [2,3]. 10–20 ng of genomic DNA was treated with 5 U of each enzyme at 37 °C for 2 h, and subjected to the PCR–CDGE analysis.

3. Results and discussion

From the SNP and genome databases, the region including three SNPs (nucleotide positions 7523, 7547 and 7591, accession no. AF125183) was amplified and designated H19FR, which located 2.5 kb upstream of paternally imprinted *H19* gene. The H19FR polymorphism was analyzed by CDGE technique, and three alleles were observed in the Japanese population (Fig. 1A) [2]. The frequencies of *H19FR**1, *H19FR**2 and *H19FR**3 were 0.5093, 0.3426 and 0.1481, respectively, accompanying the useful statistical values of heterozygosity (0.6013), polymorphic information content (0.5238) and probability for paternity exclusion (0.3161) [2].

Selective detection of parental allele was referred to the reports that upstream region of the human *H19* gene was widely and highly methylated in paternal allele [4–6]. The strategy of genomic DNA digested by either msRE or *Mcr*BC was subjected to H19FR analysis [3]. As a result, paternal allele or maternal allele was exclusively amplified from msRE- or *Mcr*BC-treated DNA samples, respectively [2] (Fig. 1B). No inconsistency was observed in 17 family studies (data not shown). Moreover, we investigated the H19FR typing and selective parental detection for forensic DNA samples isolated from oral swab, hair with sheath, fingernail and bloodstains (stored at 4 °C, room temperature and 37 °C for 1 day, 1 week, 1 month and 3 months). Though the correct genotype was detected from all of the samples, the parental typing was not succeeded in the fingernail DNA showing both alleles and in bloodstain DNA with faint appearance of another allele (data not shown). In the nail DNA, relatively slow growing would affect the methylated

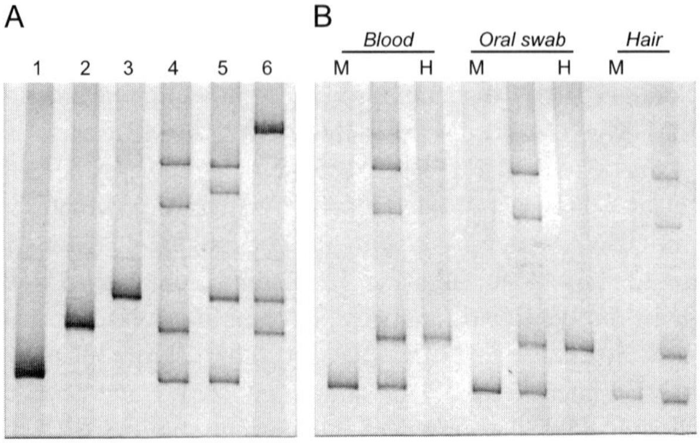

Fig. 1. Electrophoretic band pattern of H19FR genotypes detected by CDGE analysis. (A) Lanes 1–6 are six common genotypes 1–1, 2–2, 3–3, 2–1, 3–1 and 3–2, respectively. (B) Selective detection of parental allele from one individual with type 2–1. Genomic DNA was pre-digested by *Mcr*BC (M) or *Hpa*II (H) and subjected to the CDGE analysis. Single band amplified from *Mcr*BC-digested DNA and that from *Hpa*II-digested DNA were corresponding to the maternal and paternal alleles, respectively.

situation, or a possibility of different modification mode might be remained, because most of imprinted genes exhibit a manner of organ- or tissue-specific methylation status. On the other hand, the bloodstain DNA showed unstable results that the other parental band was becoming visible even in the bloodstain stored at 4 °C for 1 day, although the discrimination was still possible in bloodstain stored over 1 month. The reason was not clear, however, the methylated status in bloodstain DNA might be denaturated in early period after preparation.

As described above, the H19FR polymorphism will be a practical genetic marker with a possibility of selective detection of parental allele. By choosing suitable DNA sources, this typing method would supply effective information of parental origin not only to paternity test and pedigree investigation but also to the study on the genomic imprinting.

References

[1] S.G. Fischer, L.S. Lerman, DNA fragments differing by single base pair substitutions are separated in denaturing gradient gels: correspondence with melting theory, Proc. Natl. Acad. Sci. U. S. A. 80 (1983) 1579–1583.

[2] N. Nakayashiki, et al., A parent-of-origin detectable polymorphism in hypermethylated region upstream of the human *H19* gene (submitted for publication).

[3] K.A. Chotai, et al., A rapid, PCR based test for differential molecular diagnosis of Prader-Willi and Angelman syndromes, J. Med. Genet. 35 (1998) 472–475.

[4] Y. Jinno, et al., Mouse/human sequence divergence in a region with a paternal-specific methylation imprint at the human *H19* locus, Hum. Mol. Genet. 5 (1996) 1155–1161.

[5] M.A.E. Frevel, S.J. Sowerby, G.B. Petersen, A.E. Reeve, Methylation sequencing analysis refines the region of *H19* epimutation in Wilms Tumor, J. Biol. Chem. 274 (1999) 29331–29340.

[6] T.H. Vu, T. Li, D. Nguyen, B.T. Nguyen, X.-M. Yao, J.-F. Hu, A.R. Hoffman, Symmetric and asymmetric DNA methylation in the human IGF2-H19 imprinted region, Genomics 64 (2000) 132–143.

International Congress Series 1261 (2004) 611–612

www.ics-elsevier.com

STR typing of fixed human tissue: formalin vs. an alcohol-based method

Sarah Gino*, Simona Varacalli, Carlo Robino, Carlo Torre

Laboratorio di Scienze Criminalistiche Dipartimento di Anatomia, Farmacologia, Medicina Legale, Università degli Studi di Torino C.so Massimo D'Azeglio 52, 10126 Turin, Italy

Abstract. In this study, we evaluated the effect on DNA typing of storage of human tissue in formalin versus an alcohol-based method (Complucad®). Samples of tissue were collected at different time from fixation. DNA was isolated and, after quantitation, was amplified by quadruplex PCR including four STR loci (LPL, F13B, FESFPS and F13A01). For alcohol-fixed tissue, quantitation showed that DNA yield remained unchanged regardless of storage time and complete profiles were obtained. Instead, the DNA amount recovered from those fixed with formalin was lower and DNA looked very degraded. Actually, for these samples, we observed a lack of amplification of > 200 bp loci.

Keywords: Tissue fixation; STR; Forensic casework; Paternity testing

1. Introduction

DNA analysis of human tissues fixed for histopathological studies is not infrequently performed in forensic casework and paternity testing. However, it is well known that the most widely used fixative, formaldehyde, heavily interferes with PCR-based STR typing because of time-dependent degradation and cross-linking of DNA often leading to no results after fixation longer than 72 h [1], whereas it was observed that ethanol fixation is a most suitable method for preserving DNA integrity over time [2].

Considering the above, we evaluated the effect on DNA typing of storage ($\geq$ 72 h) of human tissue in formalin, in comparison with a commercially available fixative containing organic peroxides and alcohol (Complucad®) [3].

2. Materials and methods

Samples of brain, lung, heart, kidney and liver tissue were collected from five individuals at post-mortem examination. Before fixation, DNA was isolated from fresh brain tissue in order to obtain reference genetic profiles. Twenty-five milligrams of each

* Corresponding author. Tel.: +39-0-116707731; fax: +39-0-116707732.
E-mail address: sarah.gino@unito.it (S. Gino).

0531-5131/
doi:10.1016/S0531-5131(03)01660-1

fixed sample were collected after 3, 7, 30 and 90 days of storage at room temperature for tissues in Complucad® and after 3 and 7 days for those in formaldehyde. DNA was extracted using spin columns (Macherey-Nagel), quantified spectrophotometrically and with the Quantiblot Human Quantitation Kit (Applied Biosystem) and then amplified by quadruplex PCR including the STR loci LPL, F13B, FESFPS and F13A01 (Promega). Amplification products were separated by capillary electrophoresis on the ABI PRISM™ 310 Genetic Analyzer (Applied Biosystems). Electophoretic data were analysed using GeneScan™ software (Applied Biosystems).

3. Results and discussion

The results of quantitation showed that the DNA yield of Complucad® fixed tissues, though ranging from 5 to 35 μg according to the type of tissue, remained unchanged in each sample, regardless of storage time, up to 90 days. The total amount of DNA recovered from formalin-fixed samples was decidedly lower, varying between 6.25 and 25 ng after a fixation time of 7 days, with agarose gel electophoresis showing clear signs of DNA degradation.

As for STR typing, complete profiles corresponding to fresh brain standards were obtained from tissues fixed with Complucad for 90 days. Profiles from tissues fixed with formalin for 7 days, though consistent with those from controls, showed lack of amplification of >200 bp loci (FESFPS and F13A01).

This preliminary study showed that Complucad®, an alternative alcohol based fixation method, allowed to isolate high molecular weight DNA—even after a long time—useful for genetic analysis in forensic casework and paternity testing.

References

[1] R.L. Romero, A.C. Juston, J. Ballantyne, B.E. Henry, The applicability of formalin-fixed and formalin fixed paraffin embedded tissues in forensic DNA analysis, J. Forensic Sci. 42 (4) (1997) 708–714.

[2] C.E. Greer, S.L. Peterson, N.B. Kiviat, M.M. Manos, PCR amplifications from paraffin-embedded tissues: effects of fixative and fixation time, Am. J. Clin. Pathol. 95 (1991) 117–124.

[3] E. Muniz, A. Romero, L. Rodriguez-Mateo, R. Martinez-Rodriguez, R.R. Gragera, A novel non-toxic fixative solution of Complucad for histology and immunohistochemistry, J. Histotechnol. 23 (2000) 29–36.

International Congress Series 1261 (2004) 613–615

www.ics-elsevier.com

Strategies to improve the estimation of donor chimerism

D. Syndercombe Court[a,*], A. Butcher[b], G. Wright[b], C. Thacker[a], D. Ballard[a], M. Barnett[c], J. Cavenagh[c]

[a] *Haematology Department, Barts and The London, Queen Mary's School of Medicine and Dentistry, Turner Street, London E1 2AD, UK*

[b] *Haematology Department, The Royal London Hospital, UK*

[c] *Division of Haemato-Oncology, St. Bartholomew's Hospital, UK*

Abstract. *Background*: Reduced intensity conditioning regimens in peripheral blood stem cell transplantation (PBSCT) result in a period of mixed chimerism. Its regular monitoring is important to the patient's clinical assessment and measurement precision is essential to that process. 'Stutter' artefact peaks hinder chimerism estimation by mimicking minor proportions of DNA. We wished to assess the value of adding more loci to our current protocol and to look at the value of selecting only those markers unaffected by stutter artefact. *Methods*: Donor chimerism was monitored in 32 patients post PBSCT on five occasions using the Profiler Plus (Applied Biosystems) and Powerplex 16 (Promega) short tandem repeat (STR) kits. *Results*: Mean donor chimerism was not significantly altered by increasing the numbers of loci, but precision increased significantly ($p = 0.0002$). Removing loci affected by stutter from the Powerplex 16-associated measure increased error significantly ($p = 0.0024$), due to decreased sample size. *Conclusions*: Increasing available autosomal loci from 9 to 15 has increased precision of chimerism measurement and the time-consuming selection of loci compromised by stutter position alleles has proved unnecessary.

Keywords: Chimerism; Peripheral blood stem cell transplantation (PBSCT); Short tandem repeat (STR)

1. Introduction

Peripheral blood stem cell transplantation (PBSCT) is an effective method of treatment for haematological malignancies, but conditioning regimens result in a treatment-related mortality of 20–30%, deaths generally being related to infection or graft-versus-host disease (GVHD). Reduced intensity conditioning results in lower mortality and this produces a slower transformation from recipient to donor types, resulting in mixed chimerism continuing over several months. Serial chimerism studies are essential to monitor this process, to exclude non-alloimmune mechanisms of marrow suppression,

* Corresponding author. Tel.: +44-2073-777076; fax: +44-2073-777629.

E-mail address: y.d.syndercombe-court@qmul.ac.uk (D. Syndercombe Court).

0531-5131/
doi:10.1016/j.ics.2003.12.100

such as drug toxicity or viral infections, to predict graft failure [1] and schedule appropriate therapeutic interventions. We have been using the nine STR loci currently provided by Profiler Plus (Applied Biosystems) to monitor chimerism for more than 7 years [2].

For an accurate and precise assessment, sufficient numbers of polymorphic markers must be used to enable selection of enough informative splits between individuals, who are often closely related. 'Stutter' artefact peaks, four base pairs smaller than the true peak, can hinder chimerism estimation by mimicking minor proportions of DNA, making it difficult to get a true reflection of donor proportion where donor or recipient types are coincident with a stutter. We wished to assess the value of adding more loci and, in addition, the value of selecting only those markers unaffected by stutter artefact.

2. Materials and methods

2.1. Patient selection

Patients with a range of haematological malignancies treated by PBSCT were selected for study, including those with acute leukaemia, myeloma and lymphoma, under the care of St. Bartholomew's Hospital, London. Thirty-two patients who exhibited mixed chimerism from 1 month post PBSCT, and for whom five sequential assessments were available, were selected for the study.

2.2. Methods

DNA was extracted using Chelex 100 resin. Donors and recipients were profiled pre-transplant and recipients post-transplant, using both the Profiler Plus (PR) kit (Applied Biosystems) and the Geneprint Powerplex 16 (PO) kit (Promega) retrospectively. Analysis was undertaken using an ABI Prism 3100 Genetic Analyser (Applied Biosystems) and typed by reference to an allelic ladder run concurrently.

Percentage donor chimerism was calculated from the observed peak areas, making the assumption that the area contributed by one heterozygous allele, visible distinct in the mixed profile, was identical to that area contributing to a mixture of donor and recipient. In addition to calculation of donor chimerism using each of the STR kits, PR and PO respectively, values were also calculated for informative loci in the Powerplex 16 kit, but omitting loci where a donor allele coincided with the stutter peak region of the recipient allele, or vice versa (no stutter—PONST). In certain circumstances such removal seemed unnecessary: for example, leaving out a locus where the average donor chimerism was greater than 80% and where a particular donor allele was coincident with the stutter peak of the recipient. A further assessment was therefore made leaving out only those 'important' stutters (important stutter–POIST).

A repeated measures analysis of variance (ANOVA) was used to compare the 'between occasion' and 'between measure' means and standard errors (used as an assessment of precision) of the donor chimerism values at each of the five sequential time points.

3. Results

There was no significant difference in mean donor chimerism values obtained from each kit, whether or not selective loci were deleted ($p = 0.78$). Mean values did vary at the

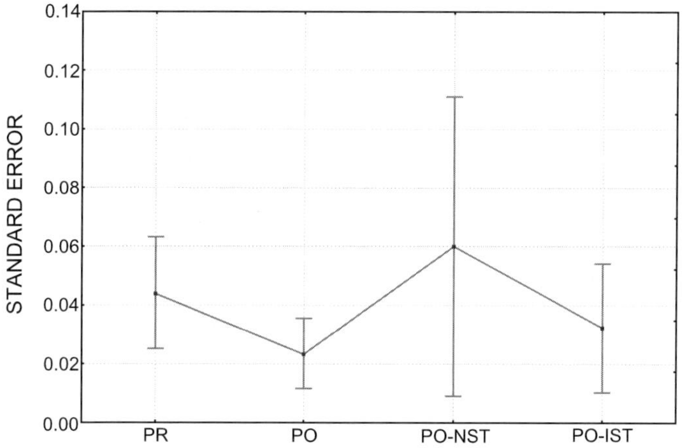

Fig. 1. Mean standard error of the mean donor chimerism, specific to method at all time points. Vertical bars denote 95% confidence interval.

different time points, which was to be expected as these reflected changes in clinical progress and the standard error was similar at different time points. There was, however, a significant difference in error between the different assessment measures ($p = 0.0002$), PO providing the smallest standard error (Fig. 1).

4. Conclusions

Increasing the number of available loci for our chimerism studies has allowed us to improve the precision of the measures that we provide for our clinicians, without any shift in mean values, enabling a trouble-free transition to the new methodology. Having a larger number of loci appears far more useful than methods to reduce the error produced by stutters, the selection of which is necessarily patient specific and therefore time-consuming.

References

[1] I.W. Blau, N. Basara, A. Serr, C. Seidl, E. Seifried, M. Bischoff, M. Roemer, A.A. Fauser, A second unrelated bone marrow transplant: successful quantitative monitoring of mixed chimerism using a highly discriminative PCR-STR system, Clinical and Laboratory Haematology 21 (1999) 133–138.

[2] J. Hasskamp, D. Syndercombe Court, C.P. Phillips, S.M. Kelsey, A.C. Newland, Short tandem repeat analysis to monitor chimerism after bone marrow transplantation, Progress in Forensic Genetics 7 (1998) 162–164.

ELSEVIER

International Congress Series 1261 (2004) 616–618

www.ics-elsevier.com

Surprising stability of DNA in stains at extreme humidity and temperature

S. Lund, J. Dissing*

Research Laboratory, Institute of Forensic Medicine, University of Copenhagen, Frederik V Vej 11, DK-2100 Copenhagen, Denmark

Abstract. The stability of DNA in air-dried blood and buccal stains at various conditions of relative humidity and temperature was tested by the ability to amplify 1600 and 273 bp DNA fragments by PCR and a 147 bp DNA fragment by real time PCR. Surprisingly it was observed that even the long DNA fragment was amplifiable after incubation for more than 1 month at 100% humidity and temperatures up to 65 °C. The 273 bp fragment was amplifiable after 3 months at 65 °C, 100% humidity. Fungal/microbial growth was observed on some stains after incubation at room temperature or 35 °C at 100% humidity, but never at lower humidity. However, in wet stains DNA degraded rapidly. Thus, even at extreme humid and hot conditions simple air-drying is adequate for the preservation for month of stains and reference samples to be analysed for STRs and SNPs.

Keywords: DNA; Stability; Stains; Humidity; Temperature

1. Introduction

Most forensic laboratories have experienced the inability to detect or amplify DNA from moist biological stains or reference samples on cotton buds, which had been stored and/or shipped at soaking wet conditions. It has been shown that the inactivation rate of a protein (acid phosphatase) in semen stains is exponentially related to the relative humidity, the rate being 1,000,000-fold higher at 100% humidity than at 40% [1]. The degradation of DNA often parallels the degradation of proteins, and many of the processes that degrade DNA depend on the presence of water [2,3]. Therefore, we expected that DNA in biological stains and reference samples would show a rapid decay at high relative humidity. To see if this was true, stains of whole blood or buccal cells were incubated at various conditions of relative humidity and temperature. The quality and quantity of the remaining DNA was assessed by PCR.

2. Methods and materials

Whole blood (5 μl) or buccal cells were spotted onto pieces (4 × 4 mm) of Whatman filter paper No. 3 and air-dried overnight. The stains were incubated in closed boxes at 0%,

* Corresponding author. Tel.: +45-35326125; fax: +45-35326150.
E-mail address: joergen.dissing@forensic.ku.dk (J. Dissing).

0531-5131/
doi:10.1016/S0531-5131(03)01641-8

50%, 80% and 100% relative humidity at room temperature, 35, 45, 55 and 65 °C. Constant humidity was maintained by the inclusion of H_2O, saturated solutions of $(NH_4)_2SO_4$ (80% humidity), $NaHSO_4$, H_2O (50% humidity) or silica gel. One series of bloodstains on microscopic slides was transferred to soaking wet (Milli-Q grade water) cotton buds and incubated at 100% humidity at room temperature. DNA was extracted from the stains using QIAamp® DNA Mini Kit (Qiagen, Germany). PCR of a 1600 bp segment was performed using primers targeting the human ACP1 locus from intron 4 to exon 5 and a 273 bp segment was amplified using primers targeting exon 4 at the human HFE-locus. Real time PCR was performed using ABI-Prism-7000 SDS (Applied Biosystems) and primers and probe targeting a 147 bp segment in exon 4 of the human HFE-gene.

3. Results

3.1. Dry bloodstains

Five sets of bloodstains on filter paper were prepared during the spring, summer and autumn month and incubated at various nonsterile conditions of temperature and relative humidity. Amplification of the 1600 bp fragment was possible from all dry stains after incubations for up to at least 1 month (Fig. 1A) even at the most extreme conditions (65 °C and 100% humidity). The 273 bp fragment was amplifiable after 3 months, even at 65 °C, 100% humidity. Fungal and/or microbial growth was observed on some of the bloodstains at 100% humidity after 1 month at room temperature or 35 °C. Real time PCR showed a decrease in the number of DNA templates in 5 μl extract from about 3000 copies to about 30 copies after incubation for 6 months at 35 °C, 100% humidity, and

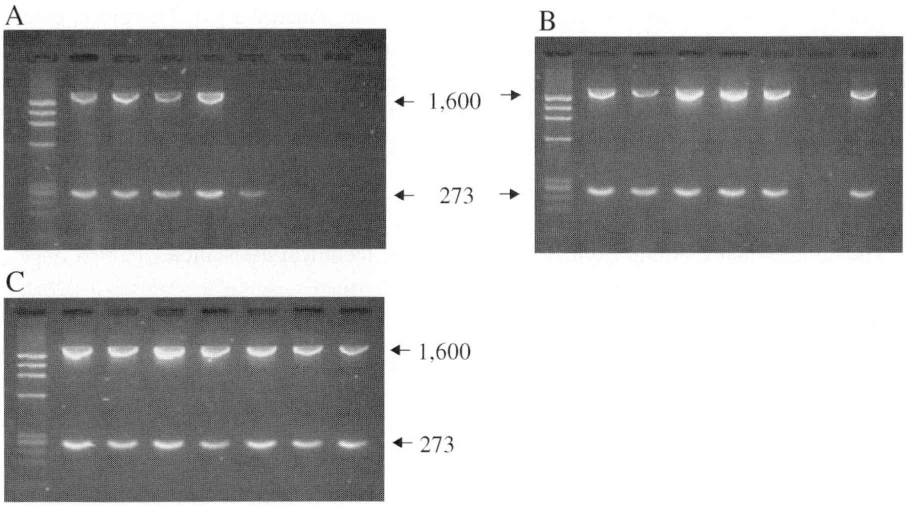

Fig. 1. Bloodstains incubated at 35 °C and controlled relative humidity. PCR of 1600 and 273 bp fragments (37 cycles). Lane assignments (left to right) 1: ΦX174 RF DNA HaeIII-digested; 2: 0 month; 3: 1 month; 4: 2 months; 5: 3 months, 6: 4 months. (A) 100% humidity. Lanes 7–8: 6 months; 7 months. (B) 80% humidity. Lane 7: void; Lane 8: 1 ng DNA template. (C) 50% humidity. Lanes 7–8: 6 months; 7 months.

approximately 10 copies after 7 months. As expected, the stability of the DNA increased at lower humidity and fungal and/or microbial growth was not observed at these conditions (Fig. 1B and C).

3.2. Dry buccal stains

Buccal stains were incubated at 35 °C and the long DNA fragment was amplifiable up to 3 months at 100% humidity; the short fragment was amplifiable after 6 months, 100% humidity.

3.3. Wet cotton buds with blood

Rapid degradation of DNA was observed in soaking wet cotton buds with blood. After 1 week at room temperature it was no longer possible to amplify the long fragment, and the short fragment was only amplifiable up to 4 weeks of incubation.

4. Discussion

The results showed a surprising stability of DNA in stains even at extreme environmental conditions (35–65 °C, 100% relative humidity), provided the stains had been dried prior to incubation. We had expected a rapid decay of DNA at high relative humidity but observed, on the contrary, that even long DNA fragments were amplifiable after month of incubation. The appearance of fungal/microbial growth on some of the stains at 100% humidity may explain the decrease in amplifiable DNA observed for these stains. However, the average environmental humidity is well below 100% even during wet seasons, e.g. the average value is 90% for the winter month in Denmark [4] and it does not exceed 82% at any time of the year in tropical Darwin, Australia [5]. Therefore, even in humid climates simple air-drying seems to be adequate for the preservation for month of DNA in stains and reference samples to be analysed for STRs and SNPs. This may be especially attractive to developing countries that want to implement modern DNA-profiling techniques but find the purchasing of expensive sampling kits prohibitive.

Acknowledgements

The authors thank Annie Søndervang for skilful technical assistance.

References

[1] G.F. Sensabaugh, The utilisation of polymorphic enzymes in forensic science. Isozymes, Curr. Top. Biol. Med. Res. 11 (1983) 137–154.
[2] H.N. Poinar, et al., Amino acid racemization and the preservation of ancient DNA, Science 272 (1996) 864–866.
[3] H.N. Poinar, B.A. Stankiewicz, Protein preservation and DNA retrieval from ancient tissues, Proc. Natl. Acad. Sci. 96 (1999) 8426–8431.
[4] J. Cappelen, B. Vraa Jørgensen, The Climate of Denmark 2002. Technical Report 03-02, Danish Meteorological Institute, Ministry of Transport, Copenhagen, 2003, pp. 1–88.
[5] Commonwealth Bureau of Meteorology at: http://www.bom.gov.au/cgi-bin/climate/cgi_bin_scripts/idl_RH_graphs/rh_script.cgi?14015.

International Congress Series 1261 (2004) 619–621

www.ics-elsevier.com

Three points detection of short fragments derived from the amelogenin gene for gender determination—new possibilities for the capillary electrophoresis system

M. Zoledziewska*, A. Jonkisz, A. Lebioda, B. Bartnik, E. Kowalczyk, G. Dmochowska, B. Swiatek, T. Dobosz

Medical University of Wroclaw, Institute of Forensic Medicine, Mikulicza-Radeckiego 4, 50-345 Wroclaw, Dolnoslaskie, Poland

Abstract. The sex-typing technique described allows detection of conventionally used fragments from first intron, shortened by Alonso to the 62/68 bp (for the X and Y, respectively) and fluorescently labelled. Additionally, two mutation points along the fragments, which differs for the X and Y copies, are detected with minisequencing. The challenge compromises also possibility of single injection analysis of fluorescently labelled fragments and mutation points with the use of the same matrix/filter set. In the present study, the new developed technique for gender-typing was tested on fresh and partially degraded forensic samples.

Keywords: Amelogenin; Sex-typing; Minisequencing

1. Introduction

According to Sasaki and Shimokawa [2], the homology of the X and Y copies of the amelogenin gene is 91%. The sex chromosomes arose 300 millions years ago and now, when comparing human amelogenin gene with its copy on Y chromosome, 19 regions of homology can be seen [1]. Regions carrying one deletion are useful for PCR sex determination methods. Fragments derived from the amelogenin gene (GeneBank acc. no. M55418 for the Amel X and M 55419 for the Amel Y) have been widely used for sex determination in forensic and archaeological samples. The primers which flank a 6-bp deletion in first intron of the X and Y homologous sequences (106 bp for X and 112 bp for Y copies) described by Sullivan et al. [3] are used as a part of commercially systems. The intronic sequences of amelogenin gene consist a panel of different polymorphisms

* Corresponding author. Tel.: +48-717841475; fax: +48-717840095.
E-mail address: magdaz@forensic.am.wroc.pl (M. Zoledziewska).

doi:10.1016/S0531-5131(03)01852-1

X:
CCCTGGGCTCTGTAAAGAATAGTGTGTTGA
TTCTTTATCCCAGAT**GTTTCTCAAGTGGTCCT**
Y:
CCCTGGGCTCTGTAAAGAATAGTGGGTGGATTC
TTCATCCCAAAT*AAAGTG***GTTTCTCAAGTGGTCCC**

Fig. 1. The sequences derived from X and Y chromosomes (60/66 bp, respectively). The sequences in bold represent the primers; the differences between X and Y are on bold and big letters; the 6-bp deletion is in cursive.

including ins/del and single nucleotide exchanges allowing various techniques of detection and differentiation of two sequences to be applied. However, the commercial multiplex systems are designed to flank fragments from 100 up to 400 bp and the space between 0 and 100 bp is available for detection.

2. Materials and methods

DNA was extracted from 4 frozen venous blood samples with a standard phenol–chloroform method, from 35 stain and 20 hair samples with chelex method and from 5 bone samples with slightly modified Ivanov et al. protocol.

2.1. DNA amplification

PCR was performed with Qiagen Multiplex PCR Reaction Kit on Biometra thermocycler. Fig. 1 presents the sequences of the primers redesigned by Alonso. The reversal primer was labelled with 6FAM. The reaction was carried out in 10 μl total volume containing 0.4 μM of each primer. The amplification consisted of 95 °C denaturation for 15 min and 95, 60 and 72 °C was repeated for 28 cycles. The amplification has ended after 30 min at72 °C.

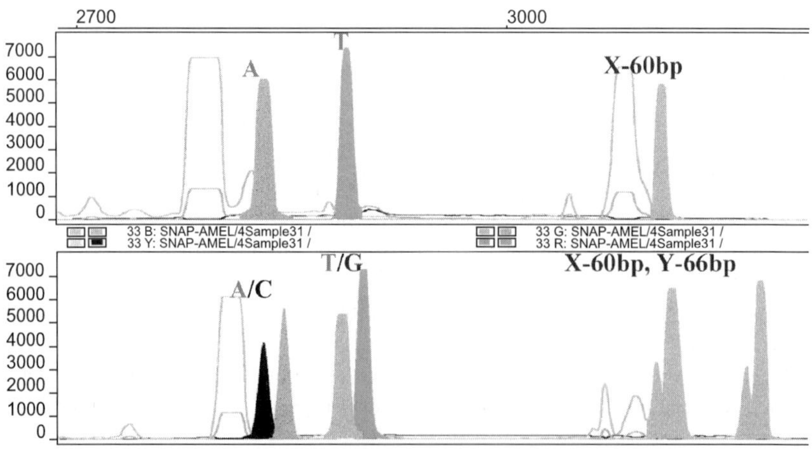

Fig. 2. The results of electrophoresis and detection of two partially degraded DNA samples; a profile of female and male (first and second rows, respectively).

2.2. Minisequencing

Products of the PCR reaction were cleaned from dNTPs and primers with SAP and EXO I (USB, USA). For 5 μl of product, 0.5 units of SAP and 2 units of EXO I were used. Reaction was performed on Biometra at 37 °C for 1 h and 75 °C for 15 min. After cleaning, the products were subjected to minisequencing reaction with an ABI Prism SNaPshot Multiplex Kit of AB Applied Biosystems. The single base extension reaction was conducted in 5 μl total volume containing 0.2 μM of each snap primer. For reaction, the forward (24 bp) and unlabeled reversal (17 bp) primers were used (Fig. 1). After enzymatic cleaning, the products were applied to detection.

2.3. Electrophoresis and detection

The products were analysed on ABI Prism 310 Sequencer with the use of the filter set E or E5 and designed for the SNaPshot chemistry matrix with GeneScan 3.1. The time of retention was 15 min with 4 s of injection.

3. Results

Fig. 2 presents an example of data obtained for two partially degraded samples. The efficiency of typing of DNA extracted from frozen blood and bone samples was 100% and was in agreement with the data obtained using standard commercial kits. Whereas, the efficiencies of DNA-typing from stain samples were 75% and 85% for hair samples.

4. Discussion

The choice of the method usually depends on investigation. Our study showed that it was technically possible to amplify and detect fragments and single base differences in the same reaction/injection. That information could be valuable for further studies. In some cases, the information provided on SNPs is very useful with those on STRs and could give more full information in identification cases.

References

[1] H. Haas-Rochholz, G. Weiler, Additional primer sets for an amelogenin gene PCR-based DNA sex test, Int. J. Leg. Med. 110 (1997) 312–315.

[2] S. Sasaki, H. Shimokawa, The amelogenin gene, Int. J. Dev. Biol. 39 (1995) 127–133.

[3] K. Sullivan, A. Mannucci, C. Kimpton, P. Gill, A rapid and quantitative DNA sex test: fluorescence-based PCR analysis of X–Y homologous gene amelogenin, BioTechniques 15 (1993) 636–641.

International Congress Series 1261 (2004) 622–624

ELSEVIER

www.ics-elsevier.com

Typing of teeth with two different amplification systems

N. Cerri[a,*], U. Ricci[b], A. Verzeletti[a], B. Falconi[a], F. De Ferrari[a]

[a] *Institute of Legal Medicine, University of Brescia, Piazazale Spedali Civili 1, 25123, Brescia, Italy*
[b] *Genetics and Molecular Medicine Unit, University of Florence, A.O. "A. Meyer", Florence, Italy*

Abstract. Two different automated procedures (capillary electrophoresis and infrared automated sequencer) for STR analysis on DNA obtained from highly degraded teeth were compared. Even with these two automatic protocols, negative or not much informative results were obtained. Our results confirm that in extreme conditions, it is necessary to perform more sensitive analysis (i.e. SNPs, mt-DNA) to obtain informative genetic profiles.

Keywords: Teeth; STRs; Infrared and capillary electrophoresis analysis

1. Introduction

Many studies showed that the particular dental resistance to environmental factors and to putrefactive phenomena allows to obtain suitable DNA from dental pulp and to achieve a genetic profile for identification [1–3].

In the past, dot-blot analysis (Dqalpha and Polymarker), VNTR or STR with manual procedures showed differences in all situations where a too small amount of substance was available, depending both on the subject's age and on the type of tooth. When dental pulp was not integer (decayed or infected tooth), in carbonised specimens or in the case of teeth exposed directly to high temperature or aggressive conditions, no results were obtained [4].

In this study, DNA extracts, previously obtained from different kinds of teeth and evaluated by dot-blot analysis, were reanalysed with two different automated procedures: capillary electrophoresis in an ABI-Prism 310 instrument (Applied Biosystems) and an Infrared automated DNA sequencer LI-COR 4200 (LI-COR, Nebraska, USA).

* Corresponding author. Tel.: +39-30-3995480; fax: +39-30-3995839.
E-mail address: deferrar@med.unibs.it (N. Cerri).

0531-5131/
doi:10.1016/S0531-5131(03)01714-X

2. Materials and methods

Human teeth, extracted for orthodontic or periodontology reasons, were obtained from oral surgeons' patients of various age. We exposed teeth to standard and aggressive conditions (freezer, various humidity conditions, dry environment, chemical substance, carbonisation).

DNA extraction was carried out using two different protocols: Chelex method and phenol/chloroform method after incubation with proteinase K (20 mg/ml).

DNA was amplified and analysed by two different automatic procedures: 1. AmpFlSTR® Profiler Plus™, SGM Plus™ and Green I from Applied Biosystems kit, according to manufacturer's procedures, analysed by capillary electrophoresis in an ABI-Prism 310

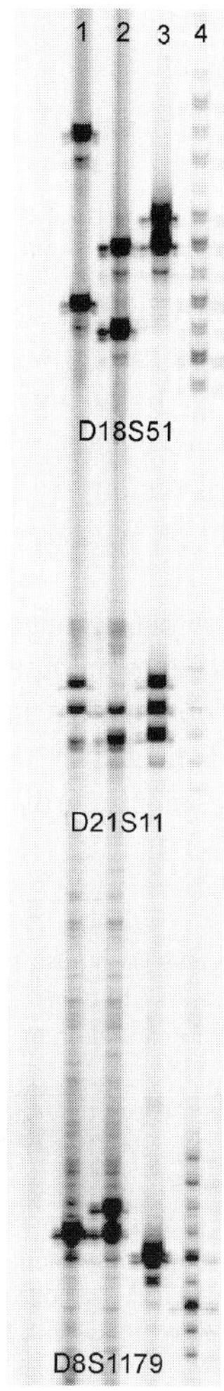

Fig. 1. Results obtained with MU3 system: 1—sample A; 2—sample B; 3—K562 cell line; 4—allelic ladder.

instrument (Applied Biosystems). 2. Amplification of four independent PCR multiplex systems and analysis with an Infrared automated DNA sequencer LI-COR 4200 (LI-COR).

Nonquantified extract (1 μl) was employed for the analysis, according to the previously described protocol [5,6]. For LI-COR analysis, we used the QIAGEN® Multiplex PCR kit to amplify the whole STRs of CODIS system. The amplifications were performed in a total volume of 12.5 μl, using 5.8 μl of Master Mix containing buffer, dNTPs, magnesium, HotStarTaq DNA polymerase and 5.8 μl of primer mix as previously described [5]. DNA (0.9 μl) was added before PCR. When samples gave negative results, 0.9 μl of a 1:10 dilution was used for PCR. The following amplification conditions were used: 95 °C for 15 min, then 94 °C for 30 s, 60 °C for 1 min and 30 s, 72 °C for 1 min and 30 s, for 32 cycles, with final extension at 72 °C for 10 min. Stop solution (6 μl) containing 95% formamide, 10 mM EDTA and 0.1% blue bromophenol were added at the end of the amplification cycles. Gel electrophoresis was performed in a LI-COR® model 4200 monolaser automated fluorescent DNA sequencer as previously described [5]. The result of the run appeared in an autoradiogram-like image as shown in Fig. 1.

3. Results and discussion

Our results do not seem to support significant differences between the two amplification systems. The minor variation in typing seems to occur because of a random fluctuation (e.g. pipetting). Good results with both methods were obtained in the samples that showed a positivity even by using a dot-blot analysis; no significative differences were found in all situations where a too small amount of substance was available nor in samples obtained from various age patients (presence or not of atrophic matter), from different type of teeth or with regard to the integrity of dental pulp (healthy or infected).

Even with these two automatic protocols, negative or no informative results were obtained when teeth were submitted to extreme conditions (e.g. incinerated tooth at 800 C°), while incomplete profiles were obtained in teeth exposed to 250 °C. Our results confirm that in extreme conditions, it is necessary to perform more sensitive analysis (i.e. SNPs, mt-DNA) to obtain informative genetic profiles.

References

[1] R. Mukoyama, et al., HLA Dqalpha genotyping on human teeth by the polymerase chain reaction amplification, in: B. Jacob, W. Bonte (Eds.), Advances in Forensic Sciences, Koster, Berlin, 1995, pp. 256–259.

[2] D.J. Sweet, C.H.W. Sweet, DNA analysis of dental pulp to link incinerated remains of homicide victim to crime scene, JSFCA 40 (1995) 310–314.

[3] P. Sanz, V. Prieto, M.V. Andres, PCR genotyping in dental pulp from old human skeletal remains and fire victims, in: A. Carracedo, B. Brinkmann, W. Bar (Eds.), Advances in Forensic Haemogenetics, vol. 6, Springer, Berlin, 1996, pp. 319–321.

[4] N. Cerri, et al., Genetic identification from dental pulp by using DNA amplification (PCR), in: W. Bar, A. Fiori, U. Rossi (Eds.), Advances in Forensic Haemogenetics vol. 5,Springer, Berlin, 1994, pp. 268–270.

[5] U. Ricci, et al., Infrared fluorescent automated detection of thirteen short tandem repeat polymorphisms and one gender determining system of the CODIS core system, Electrophoresis 21 (2000) 3564–3570.

[6] U. Ricci, et al., Identification of forensic samples by using an infrared-based automatic DNA sequencer, CMJ 44 (3) (2003) 299–305.

International Congress Series 1261 (2004) 625–627

www.ics-elsevier.com

Uniparentally inherited genetic markers as tools for ethnic and geographical origin detection of forensic samples

A. Sala[a], M. Marino[a], C. Arguelles[b], A. Fenocchio[b], D. Corach[a,*]

[a] *Servicio de Huellas Digitales Genéticas (SHDG), Facultad de Farmacia y Bioquímica, Universidad de Buenos Aires, Junin 956-7 Piso, Buenos Aires 1113, Argentina*

[b] *Laboratorio de Citogenética Humana, Facultad de Ciencias Quimicas, Exactas y Naturales, Universidad de Misiones, Argentina*

Abstract. Uniparentally inherited polymorphic genetic markers opened a new scope in the human forensic identification. These genetic markers may display geographic and/or ethnic specific characteristic features that may provide a clue about the origin of the donor of a given sample. Maternally inherited mitochondrial (mtDNA) polymorphisms and paternally transmitted Y-chromosome specific polymorphic sequences when investigated in combination may provide relevant information concerning the ethnic/geographical origin of a person. Some populations are particularly more suited for these investigations due to their differential attributes. South American aboriginal are a good example. In this contribution, we provide information about an isolated aboriginal community that depicts ethnic specific attributes. The combined use of matri and patri lineage markers allowed to estimate the admixture at the individual level.

Keywords: Ethnic group–DNA polymorphism; mtDNA; Y-chromosome polymorphisms

1. Introduction

Human identification by DNA typing is based on the analysis of highly polymorphic autosomal short tandem repeats (STRs). Although highly informative, these markers are unable to provide information concerning the ethnic or geographic origin of the donor of a sample. In those cases in which no suspects are available, such as rape cases, homicides or burglary, or when fragmentary human remains are the sole source of genetic material, as in suicide terrorist attacks cases, it would be desirable to detect at least the ethnicity or geographic origin of these evidentiary material. Uniparentally inherited genetic markers

* Corresponding author. Tel.: +54-11-49648281; fax: +54-11-49648282.
E-mail address: shdg@ffyb.uba.ar (D. Corach).

doi:10.1016/S0531-5131(03)01524-3

(e.g. Y-chromosome specific or maternally inherited mitochondrial (mtDNA) polymorphisms) may provide a clue for such identification. Since males perpetrate most violent crimes, gender-specific genetic markers may represent a valuable identification tool [1]. Mammalian Y-chromosomes are characterized by the absence of recombination in the major extension of the chromosome (except PAR 1 and 2 in the telomers, of both arms) and by the presence of a wide range of different types of polymorphic loci. These markers include alphoid satellite variants, minisatellites (MYS1) and microsatellites (Y-STR) all of them with high mutation rate, as well as others, with low mutation rate, included within the so-called Unique Event Polymorphisms (UEP). These biallelic markers are the Single Nucleotide Polymorphism (Y-SNP) and the Insertion/deletion events (Ins/del), like Y Alu Polymorphism (YAP), and may provide additional information when analyzed in combination with highly variable Y-STRs. In order to investigate this relevant forensic aspect, different geographically isolated aboriginal communities inhabiting North Eastern Argentina were investigated. Three communities of the Guarani M'Byá tribe from different localities were investigated by Y-STR nonaplex (DYS19, DYS385, DYS389 I and II, DYS390, DYS391, DYS392 and DYS393), the ins/del YAP, the SNP DYS199, as well as the mtDNA Region V 9bp ins/del. In order to confirm the Amerindian mtDNA haplogroup B, HVRI sequencing of those samples with 9-bp deletion was carried out. The overall information was compared with the results obtained with a set of Argentinean samples randomly chosen from different regions of the country.

2. Materials and methods

2.1. Samples

Three communities belonging to the Guarani M'Byá tribe inhabiting Misiones Province (North Eastern Argentina) were selected, (M'Bororé, $N=52$; Yriapu, $N=10$; and Ybaté, $N=6$). Blood samples were obtained by finger puncture from unrelated male donors. In addition, 50 samples randomly chosen from different regions of Argentina were also analyzed.

Blood samples collected onto FTA paper were processed according with manufacturer's protocol.

Y-STRs: DYS19, DYS389 I/II, DYS390, DYS391, DYS392, DYS393 and DYS385 were amplified using one fluorescent dye labeled primer. Amplicons were detected with an ABI310.

DYS199: Amplification using allele-specific primers was performed according to Underhill (1996) [2]. The amplification products were separated in 2% agarose gels and detected by Ethidium Bromide staining through UV light.

Ins/del YAP: amplification using specific primers followed by agarose gel electrophoresis was employed.

mtDNA analysis: Hipervariable Region I was amplified, purified and then sequenced by means of Big Dye Terminator system, employing an ABI 310 sequencer.

Nine-base pair deletion mt DNA Region V was amplified as previously described [3] using forward primer labeled with TET. The detection was made in an ABI 310 sequencer.

3. Results and discussion

Within the sample investigated ($N = 68$ individuals) for the Y-STR minimal haplotype, a reduced value of haplotype diversity was detected (78%). Accordingly, a minimal Y-STR haplotype defined as: DYS19/13, DYS389I/14, DYS389II/31, DYS390/24, DYS391/11, DYS392/14, DYS393/11 and DYS385/14.16, denoted a high frequency (35%). This haplotype is neither present in other Argentina aboriginal tribes such as Mapuche, Tehuelche and Wichi nor in the Reference Y-STR Database http://www.ystr.charite.de) in which population data of Metropolitan areas of Argentina are also included [4]. This particular Guaraní haplotype is combined with the UEPs variants DYS199/T and YAP (−). When a reduced combined haplogroup including DYS19, DYS392, DYS393 and DYS199 is considered, a still higher frequency is detected (43%). This Ethnic Specific Combined Haplogroup (ESCH) may represent the effect of a bottleneck resulting in a founder effect that might be interpreted under the light of the history of this region. In addition, it may be used as an informative approach for tracing and identifying patrilineages from male-produced evidences, in forensic casework.

In contrast, the Metropolitan sample of Argentina shows a different picture. The haplotype diversity is, in this group, 98%, and the most frequent haplotype is represented in 3 out of 50 individuals (6%). Fourteen percent of these samples are DYS199/T in contrast with 87% in the Guaraní sample.

In average, 17% of the samples investigated in both groups depicted the mitochondrial Region V 9-bp deletion. The sequence of the HVR I confirmed that these samples belonged to the Amerindian B haplogroup [5]. Since in this work only haplogroup B was taken into account, further analysis would be required to assess the frequencies of the other Amerindian haplogroups.

The results emerging from the uniparentally inherited genetic markers might suggest: (a) that the Guarani community may represent a newcomer ethnic component, (b) that the metropolitan areas population has a much higher aboriginal component than expected and (c) the ESCH identified may represent a suitable male-specific haplogroup to be used in forensic casework.

Acknowledgements

This work was supported, in part, by grants 0746-CONICET, and UBACyT.B-038, to DC. DC and AS are members of CIC-CONICET.

References

[1] D. Corach, et al., Routine Y-STR typing in forensic casework, For. Sci. Int. 118 (2–3) (2001 May) 131–135.

[2] P.A. Underhill, et al., A pre-Columbian Y chromosome-specific transition and its implications for human evolutionary history, Proc. Natl. Acad. Sci. U. S. A. 93 (1996) 196–200.

[3] L.A. Wrischnik, et al., Length mutations in human mitochondrial DNA: direct sequencing of enzymatically amplified DNA, Nucleic Acids Res. 15 (2) (1987 Jan 26) 529–542.

[4] M. Kayser, et al., An extensive analysis of Y-chromosomal microsatellite haplotypes in globally dispersed human populations, Am. J. Hum. Genet. 68 (4) (2001 Apr) 990–1018.

[5] A. Stone, M. Stoneking, mtDNA analysis of a prehistoric Oncata population: implications for the peopling of the New World, Am. J. Hum. Genet. 62 (1998) 1153–1170.

International Congress Series 1261 (2004) 628–630

ELSEVIER

www.ics-elsevier.com

EasyDNA: user-friendly paternity and kinship testing programs

Wing K. Fung*, C.T. Yang, Wei Guo

Department of Statistics and Actuarial Science, University of Hong Kong, Pokfulam Road, Hong Kong, China

Abstract. EasyDNA is a family of four computer programs developed for handling paternity and kinship determinations, and statistical calculations for (a) alleged fathers, (b) alleged fathers but without DNA typing, (c) incest cases, and (d) missing persons. These programs have been named EasyPA, EasyPAnt, EasyIN, and EasyMISS, respectively. The programs have wide applicability, and users can save results for checking and/or reporting purposes. The programs employ the distinctive pull-down manual, making them very user-friendly. In this paper, we are going to demonstrate the programs using a missing person example. © 2003 Elsevier B.V. All rights reserved.

Keywords: DNA profiling; Paternity; Kinship determination; Missing person

1. A case of missing person

EasyDNA consists of four different computer programs [1]. Here we demonstrate one of them, EasyMISS, using a missing person example. Consider a case that a person (X) goes missing and his family members report his disappearance to the local police force [2]. A dead body is found later, and the police likes to establish if the dead man is *X* using genetic testing. The DNA profiles of X's mother, two children, and three siblings are typed. The spouse (S) of X is not available, and instead her father and two siblings are typed. A total of 10 persons are typed. The hypotheses of interest are H_0: the dead man (alleged X) was X, and H_1: the dead man is not X. Although the problem looks complex, EasyMISS can handle it easily.

Scheme 1 gives the DNA profiles at locus D3S1358. For brevity, only one locus is considered though the program can handle any number of loci. The genotypes are inputted easily using the built-in pull-down manual. After clicking the box Calculate, the likelihood ratio is obtained immediately as 18.06. If we click the box Generate Output, the summary

* Corresponding author. Tel.: +852-2859-1988; fax: +852-2858-9041.
E-mail address: wingfung@hku.hk (W.K. Fung).

doi:10.1016/S0531-5131(03)01486-9

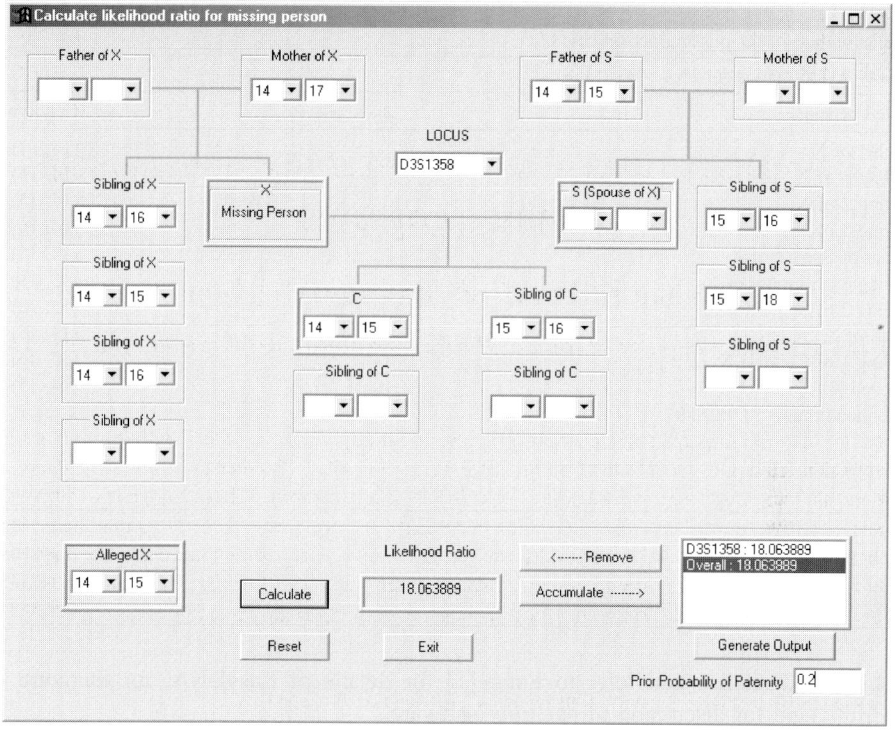

Scheme 1. A missing person case example.

results will be saved in a file and they are shown in Table 1. This is very useful for checking and reporting purposes.

2. Concluding remarks

The developed software EasyDNA employs the distinctive pull-down manual, which makes the programs easy to use. The relationships of the people involved can be easily visualized using the provided pedigree diagram. We can also save the output for clients, for easy checking, and/or for legal purposes. The programs can handle both civil and criminal paternity cases, and kinship determinations for disasters such as air-crashes. The developed programs have wide applicability, e.g. motherless paternity case, motherless case with relatives of the mother typed, different alternative hypotheses H_1 (e.g. the true father is a relative of the alleged father), paternity testing when the alleged father cannot be typed, alleged parents, various kinship determinations such as three or more alleged sibs, incest case, and inheritance dispute case.

Besides giving the common likelihood ratios, the programs can also provide the posterior probabilities of paternity if required (see Table 1 of the missing person example). They can also allow for one or two mismatches of DNA profiles due to mutation. The residual and overall paternity indices are provided.

Table 1
Results output for the missing person case

Genotype information for locus: D3S1358	
Tested person	Genotype
Mother of X	(14, 17)
Sibling 1 of X	(14, 16)
Sibling 2 of X	(14, 15)
Sibling 3 of X	(14, 16)
Father of Spouse of X	(14, 15)
Sibling 1 of Spouse of X	(15, 16)
Sibling 2 of Spouse of X	(15, 18)
Child of X	(14, 15)
Sibling 1 of Child of X	(15, 16)
Alleged X	(14, 15)
Likelihood ratio = 18.063889	
Paternity probability	
Prior	Posterior
0.100	0.667454
0.200	0.818708
0.500	0.947545
0.900	0.993887

Interested readers can refer to Fung [1] for details of EasyDNA, for literature on paternity, and for discussion of paternity software.

Acknowledgements

This work was supported in part by the Hong Kong RGC Competitive Earmarked Research Grant.

References

[1] W.K. Fung, User-friendly programs for easy calculations in paternity testing and kinship determinations, To appear in Forensic Science International (2003).

[2] D.M. Wong, M.Y. Law, W.K. Fung, K.L. Chan, C. Li, T.S. Lun, K.M. Lai, K.Y. Cheung, C.T. Chiu, Population data for 12 STR loci in Hong Kong Chinese, Int. J. Leg. Med. 114 (2001) 281–284.

International Congress Series 1261 (2004) 631–633

www.ics-elsevier.com

Validation of forensic DNA analysis from bloodstains treated by presumptive test reagents

A. Barbaro[c,*], P. Cormaci[a], A. Teatino[b], A. Barbaro[a]

[a] *Department of Forensic Genetics, SIMEF, 98128 Reggio Calabria, Italy*
[b] *Department of Chemistry and Toxicology, SIMEF, 98128, Reggio Calabria, Italy*
[c] *SIMEF, Director-SIMEF, 98128 Reggio Calabria, Italy*

Abstract. Dilute bloodstains that cannot be seen by the eye may be detected at the crime scene using different presumptive tests. In this study, we tested the effect of two presumptive blood enhancement reagents (luminol and fluorescein) on the subsequent chemical and genetic analysis of fresh or aged bloodstains treated or not treated by soap.

Keywords: Dilute bloodstains; Presumptive tests; Hemoglobin detection; STRs

1. Introduction

The enhancement reagents often provide valuable aid in crime scene analysis and laboratory examination: in fact, they are able to detect minute traces of blood even when attempts have been made to wash away the incriminating evidence. By the luminol test, the bloodstains can be made to glow with a blue light due to the chemiluminescent reaction of the luminol reagent with hemoglobin iron while fluorescin is converted by the catalytic action of hemoglobin into fluorescein, a bright-yellow fluorescent chemical. We evaluated the effect of the reagents above on the hemoglobin detection by spectrophotometry, chromatography and immunodiffusion; the ability to extract DNA using DNA IQ System (Promega), Chelex (Biorad) and phenol–chloroform treatment; any potential detrimental effect on STRs analysis using the Amp*FlSTR Profiler Plus* and *Identifiler* kits (Applied Biosystems); the possibility to obtain consistent and reliable DNA typing results.

2. Material and methods

We used an old blood sample to prepare some bloodstains (of about 3 × 3 cm) on the following surfaces: moquettes carpet, tissue, paper, wood, skin, glass, and tile. As a reference, we used a fresh blood sample belonging to the same donor above. All bloodstains were dried for about 1 week, and each one was used at natural and after

* Corresponding author. Department of Forensic Genetics, SIMEF Via Nicolo'da Reggio 4, 89128, SIMEF, 98128 Reggio Calabria, Italy. Tel.: +39-965891184-5; fax: +39-965891125.

E-mail address: simef@tiscali.it (A. Barbaro).

URL: http://www.simef.com.

0531-5131/
doi:10.1016/S0531-5131(03)01539-5

washing with water and soap. Each surface was divided in two different fields, and each one was sprayed with luminol or fluorescein. From each area were taken three different samples.

Fluorescein and luminol preparation was performed, respectively, following the procedures described by Cheeseman et al. [1] and Eckert and James [2]. Detection limit using homemade reagents was 1:1,000,000. For immunodiffusion, we prepared a 3% agar solution following the protocol described by Hochmeister et al. [3]. DNA was extracted by DNA IQ System, Chelex, and by organic/centricon treatment.

As a reference, we extracted DNA from fresh and old blood samples, without any treatment. All samples were quantified by the Alu Quant Human DNA Quantitation System, then amplified by *AmpFlSTRs Identifiler* and *Profiler Plus* kits and PCR products analyzed onto two ABI PRISM 310 Genetic Analyzer.

3. Results and discussion

3.1. Spectrophotometry

To observe any eventual modification of hemoglobin typical spectra produced by reagents, each dilution was analysed (in the range 200–800 nm) by an HP spectrophotometer at 412 nm (Soret peak), 589–667 and 553–525 nm (Fraunhofer peaks). We determined also soap, luminol and fluorescein spectra. In the presence of soap, typical hemoglobin peaks were variably detectable with the kind of cleaning we performed, while in the presence of luminol and fluorescein, typical hemoglobin peaks become NOT REVEALABLE also on NOT WASHED bloodstains.

3.2. Chromatography

As confirmatory test for the presence of human hemoglobin, we use an immunochromatographic rapid test OC-Hemocard (Alfa Wassermann). The eluate obtained by distilled water from an untreated bloodstain showed pH 7 and gave a positive result with Hemocard test. The eluate obtained by distilled water from a bloodstain sprayed with luminol showed pH 11 and gave negative results with Hemocard test. The eluate obtained by distilled water from a bloodstain sprayed with fluorescein showed pH 8.5 and gave a weakly positive result. In both cases, adjusting pH to 7 by Tris–HCl or NaOH treatment before adding the sample to Hemocard, we obtained a positive result. When about 200 Al of IQ or phenol–cloroform extraction buffers were added to the Hemocard, a negative result was found.

Lysis buffers above require SDS, Proteinase K or DTT that interfere with the test presumably damaging hemoglobin. We found similar circumstances using Chelex sovranatant.

Results from washed and unwashed bloodstains were comparable: the possibility to obtain a positive result is dependent from the cleaning modality or intensity.

3.3. Immunodiffusion

We evaluated the possibility to detect hemoglobin on washed/unwashed bloodstains after reagent treatment using a commercially available anti-human hemoglobin antiserum.

Luminol and fluorescein do not interfere with the possibility to detect hemoglobin.

3.4. DNA analysis

We evaluated the ability to extract DNA using DNA IQ System, Chelex and organic/centricon procedure from bloodstains treated by luminol or fluorescein, any potential detrimental effect on STRs analysis and the possibility to obtain consistent and reliable DNA typing results. (a) Washed and unwashed samples treated by presumptive reagents were successfully quantified by the Alu Quant Human DNA Quantitation System. (b) Differences were noted on the ability to obtain DNA suitable for STRs analysis from the surfaces used in this study depending on the nature of the substrate. (c) The organic/centricon extraction method gave higher yields of DNA than Chelex or DNA IQ. (d) Profiles from fresh or old bloodstains treated were comparable to the ones of the untreated fresh or old blood samples. (e) Results obtained after luminol or fluorescein spraying were comparable (no evidence of degradation correlated to the reagents applications). (f) Differences were noted between DNA profile of old blood samples (partial profile, allelic dropout, unbalanced peaks) and the ones of fresh samples (full profile). (g) Soap does not interfere with the ability to recover DNA: the quality of DNA profile is dependent from the washing modality or intensity.

4. Conclusion

Luminol or fluorescein enhancement of bloodstains interferes with the possibility to perform spectrophotometrical determination of hemoglobin, probably because the absorption peaks of reagents above cover the hemoglobin peaks and prevent from discovering them. Both reagents do not interfere with the confirmatory tests that use antihuman hemoglobin monoclonal antibody: it is very important to adjust pH to values around 7 so as to obtain a good test working.

Reagents do not interfere with the ability to obtain DNA suitable for PCR analysis: the substrate, the cleaning, the age of the sample and the choice of the DNA extraction method are the major factors that can affect the success of DNA analysis. Results obtained from washed and unwashed bloodstains were comparable: a positive result can be dependent from the washing modality or intensity.

Our results are in accordance with studies previously published by other [4–6].

References

[1] R. Cheeseman, et al., Fluorescein and Latent Blood Detection, AAFS 50th Anniversary Meeting, 2/98.

[2] W.G. Eckert, S.H. James, Interpretation of bloodstain evidence at crime scenes, CRC Press.

[3] N. Hochmeister, B. Budowle, et al., Validation Studies of an immunochromatographic 1-step test for the forensic identification of human blood, J. Forensic Sci. 44 (1999) 597–602.

[4] A.M. Gross, et al., The effect of luminol on presumptive tests and DNA analysis using the polymerase chain reaction, J. Forensic Sci. 44 (1999) 837–840.

[5] C. Frégeau, et al., Fingerprint enhancement revisited and the effects of blood enhancement chemicals on subsequent profiler plus fluorescent STR DNA analysis of fresh and aged bloody fingerprints, J. Forensic Sci. 45 (2000) 354–380.

[6] B. Budowle, et al., The presumptive reagent fluorescein for detection of dilute bloodstains and subsequent STR typing of recovered DNA, J. Forensic Sci. 45 (2000) 1090–1092.

International Congress Series 1261 (2004) 634–636

www.ics-elsevier.com

The risk of missing one allele with very low DNA quantities using PCR

R. Kobayashi[a,b], K. Satoh[b,c], K. Takahashi[b,c], Y. Itoh[b,*]

[a] Department of Microbiology, Tokyo Medical University, Tokyo, Japan
[b] Department of Forensic Medicine, Juntendo University School of Medicine, 2-1-1 Hongo Bungkyo 113-8421, Tokyo, Japan
[c] Medico-Legal Section, Criminal Investigation Laboratory, Metropolitan Police Department, Tokyo, Japan

Received 1 September 2003; received in revised form 10 September 2003; accepted 11 September 2003

Abstract. TH01 typing was performed by semi-nested PCR using a very low concentration of DNA (TH01 type = 7–11) as a template. With 10 pg of template DNA, the probabilities of obtaining both of two alleles, only allele 7, only allele 11, or no PCR product, were 23.1%, 15.4%, 38.5% or 23.1%, respectively. Our findings suggest that these differences were found because the initial proportions of alleles 7 and 11 in the PCR tube were not equal. However, the allele distribution of TH01 types 7 and 11 using single cells considered to contain equal amount of the two alleles was similar to that obtained using a very low concentration of DNA. These results indicate that correct genotypes could not be obtained by using equal amount of both alleles, when the concentration of DNA was very low. To obtain a correct genotype, it was necessary to use 100 pg of DNA as the template for PCR amplification. © 2003 Elsevier B.V. All rights reserved.

Keywords: Microsatellite; TH01; PCR; DNA

1. Introduction

In molecular studies using forensic samples, the amount of DNA available for genetic typing can be very low. Under these circumstances, it is possible for one allele of a heterozygous individual not to be detected, leading to the incorrect genotyping of this individual as a homozygote. In this study, we clarified the amount of template DNA required for detecting both of two alleles by semi-nested PCR and demonstrated that the cause of invalid genotyping results is not always pipetting errors or PCR samples containing in equal amounts of the alleles per PCR when using single cells for genetic typing.

* Corresponding author. Tel./fax: +81-3-5802-1050.
E-mail address: yitoh@med.juntendo.ac.jp (Y. Itoh).

doi:10.1016/S0531-5131(03)01521-8

2. Materials and methods

2.1. Cell sources

Mononuclear cells were isolated from tonsils extracted from a patient (TH01 type = 7–11) with chronic tonsillitis using Ficoll Hypaque density-gradient separation. DNA was extracted from the tonsillar cells using the DNeasy Tissue Kit (QIAGEN, CA).

2.2. PCR amplification

TH01[AATG]$_n$ PCR primers were as follows (5′ → 3′); TH01F, att caa agg gta tct ggg ctc tgg; TH01R, gtg ggc tga aaa gct ccc gat tat [1]. TH01Ff, cca ttg gcc tgt tcc tcc ctt att, was also synthesized for semi-nested PCR [2]. Using single cells as a template, PCR amplification was performed as described by Zhang [3]. First- and second-round 30 amplifications consisted of a 45-s denaturation step at 94 °C, a 30-s annealing step at 60 °C, and a 30-s extension step at 72 °C. The PCR products were resolved on a 4% agarose gel in 1 × TAE.

3. Results and discussions

Four TH01 typing experiments were performed using a set of 10-fold serially diluted DNA by semi-nested PCR (Fig. 1). At lower concentrations of DNA (below 10 pg), the experiments failed to amplify both alleles (Table 1). At 10 pg of DNA as a template, the probabilities of obtaining both alleles, only allele 7, only allele 11, or no PCR product, were 23.1%, 15.4%, 38.5% or 23.1%, respectively (Fig. 2). This is believed to be because the initial proportions of allele DNA in the PCR tube are not equal [4]. To avoid random sampling of template DNA, whole cells were used for TH01 typing. However, the same variations of the amplified alleles could be observed when using single cells (Fig. 3). The results using single cells showed that the number of tubes with both alleles, only allele 7, only allele 11 or no PCR product, were 8 (36.4% of positive tubes), 7 (31.8%), 7 (31.8%), and 154, respectively.

These results indicate that correct genotypes could not be obtained at very low concentration, even if equal amounts of both allele DNAs were used for PCR amplification. When the amount of template DNA used per PCR reaction is below 10 pg, as is the usual practice, the risk of missing one allele is almost always present. To obtain the correct genotype, it is necessary to use 100 pg of DNA as a template. When the quantity of

Table 1
Results of four TH01 typing experiments at a heterozygous locus (TH01 type = 7–11) for five different concentrations of template DNA

Exp. no.	Amount of DNA				
	10 ng	1 ng	100 pg	10 pg	1 pg
1	7/11	7/11	7/11	not detected	not detected
2	7/11	7/11	7/11	11	not detected
3	7/11	7/11	7/11	not detected	7
4	7/11	7/11	7/11	7	7

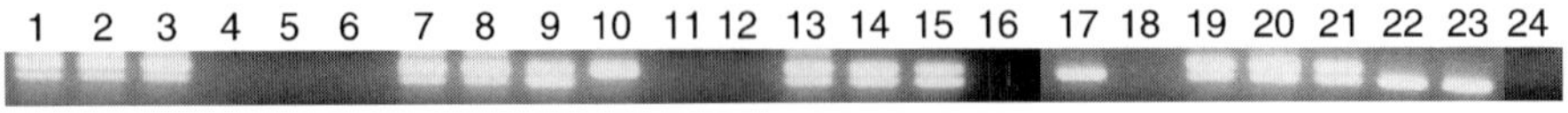

Fig. 1. Allele distribution among four experiments by semi-nested PCR. Lanes 1, 7, 13, 19 = 10 ng of template DNA; lanes 2, 8, 14, 20 = 1 ng; lanes 3, 9, 15, 21 = 100 pg; lanes 4, 10, 16, 22 = 10 pg; lanes 5, 11, 17, 23 = 1 pg; lanes 6, 12, 18, 24 = buffer control.

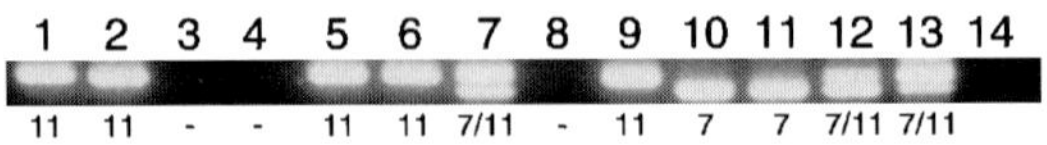

Fig. 2. Allele distribution of TH01 types 7 and 11 among 13 PCRs using 10 pg of template DNA by semi-nested PCR. Lane 14 = buffer control.

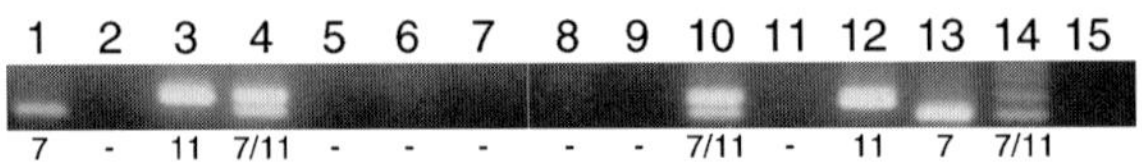

Fig. 3. Electrophoretic pattern of semi-nested PCR products using single cells as a DNA template. Lane 15 = buffer control.

extracted DNA is unknown and this quantity could be high enough to give a PCR product, but insufficient for a reliable genotyping, it is very difficult to determine genotypes correctly.

References

[1] A. Edwards, A. Civitello, H.A. Hammond, C.T. Caskey, DNA typing and genetic mapping with trimeric and tetrameric tandem repeats, Am. J. Hum. Genet. 49 (1991) 746–756.

[2] R. Kobayashi, Y. Itoh, Microsatellite instability in mononuclear cells from non-tumorigenic human tonsils and its use in forensic evaluation, Prog. Forens. Genet. 9 (2003) 685–688.

[3] L. Zhang, X. Cui, K. Schmitt, R. Hubert, W. Navidi, N. Arnheim, Whole genome amplification from a single cell: implications for genetic analysis, Proc. Natl. Acad. Sci. U. S. A. 89 (1992) 5847–5851.

[4] P. Taberlet, S. Griffin, B. Goossens, S. Questiau, V. Manceau, N. Escaravage, L.P. Waits, J. Bouvet, Reliable genotyping of samples with very low DNA quantities using PCR, Nucleic Acids Res. 24 (1996) 3189–3194.

Author index

Keyword index